Law and Custom in Korea

This book sets forth the evolution of Korea's law and legal system from the Chosŏn dynasty through the colonial and postcolonial modern periods. This is the first book in English that comprehensively studies Korean legal history in comparison with European legal history, with particular emphasis on customary law. Korea's passage to Romano-German civil law under Japanese rule marked a drastic departure from its indigenous legal tradition. The transplantation of modern civil law in Korea was facilitated by Japanese colonial jurists who themselves created a Korean customary law; this constructed customary law served as an intermediary regime between tradition and the demands of modern law. The transformation of Korean law by the brisk forces of Westernization points to new interpretations of colonial history, and it presents an intriguing case for investigating the spread of law on the global level. In-depth discussions of French customary law and Japanese legal history in this book provide a solid conceptual framework suitable for comparing European and East Asian legal traditions.

Marie Seong-Hak Kim was born in Seoul, Korea, and was educated at Ewha Womans University (BA and MA), the University of Minnesota (PhD), and the University of Minnesota Law School (JD). Originally trained as a sixteenth-century French historian, Professor Kim teaches and writes on both European and East Asian legal history, concentrating on France, Korea, and Japan. Her book, *Michel de L'Hôpital: The Vision of a Reformist Chancellor during the French Religious Wars*, was published in 1997. Her articles have appeared in journals such as *Law and History Review*, *The American Journal of Comparative Law*, *The Journal of Asian Studies*, *The Journal of Japanese Studies*, *Tijdschrift voor rechtsgeschiedenis*, *Tōyō Bunka Kenkyū*, *Sixteenth Century Journal*, and *French History*. Her major awards and grants include the National Endowment for the Humanities Research Fellowship, Fulbright Senior Scholar Grant, the Academy of Korean Studies Research Grants, and the Japan Foundation Research Fellowship. She served as a visiting professor at the Institut d'Asie Orientale, Ecole Normale Supérieure de Lyon, France, and was a Fellow at the International Institute for Asian Studies in Leiden, the Netherlands. As a Fulbright Visiting Professor of Law, she taught at Handong Global University in Pohang, Korea. From 2011 to 2012, Professor Kim was a Fellow at the Collegium de Lyon (Institut d'Etudes Avancées) in France. She currently teaches at St. Cloud State University. She is an attorney at law and a member of the Minnesota Bar.

Law and Custom in Korea

Comparative Legal History

MARIE SEONG-HAK KIM
St. Cloud State University

CAMBRIDGE
UNIVERSITY PRESS

CAMBRIDGE
UNIVERSITY PRESS

University Printing House, Cambridge CB2 8BS, United Kingdom

Cambridge University Press is part of the University of Cambridge.

It furthers the University's mission by disseminating knowledge in the pursuit of education, learning and research at the highest international levels of excellence.

www.cambridge.org
Information on this title: www.cambridge.org/9781107006973

First published 2012

A catalogue record for this publication is available from the British Library

Library of Congress Cataloguing in Publication data
Kim, Marie Seong-Hak.
Law and custom in Korea : comparative legal history / Marie Seong-Hak Kim.
p. cm.
Includes bibliographical references and index.
ISBN 978-1-107-00697-3 (hardback)
1. Customary law – Korea. 2. Civil law – Korea. 3. Legislative histories – Korea.
4. Customary law – Europe. I. Title.
KPA2340.K56 2012
340.509519–dc23 2012011316

ISBN 978-1-107-00697-3 Hardback

For Christopher, John-Paul,
and Joel

Contents

Illustrations

Tables

Acknowledgments

The detour from early modern France to colonial Korea, a sort of intellectual self-reinvention, has been a journey long and lonely but ultimately rewarding. Having been trained in European history, I had to assure myself that my undertaking of East Asian legal history was not a whimsical or erratic venture. By the time the Fulbright Senior Scholar Grant allowed me to spend a year in Korea in 2004, the country where I was born and raised but had left two decades before, I was certain that Korean history was indeed something I had wanted to study all along. Throughout the writing of this book, I was accompanied by the memories of my parents, Chung Eung-Kyu (1922–2006) and the Honorable Kim Yoon-Haeng (1920–1990). My father received his legal education during the late years of Japanese colonial rule and subsequently served in the Korean judiciary for more than three decades, the last seven years as a Supreme Court Justice (1973–1980). His career was but one example that convinced me that colonial legal history was an integral part of the Korean past and must be understood as such. I am sure my parents would have been pleased to see this book.

James D. Tracy, my doctoral advisor at the University of Minnesota, has taught me that evolving intellectual endeavors across different fields of interest are not only justified but desirable. He read and corrected the drafts of this book, as he did for my other writings innumerable times over the past years. His encouragement is the single most important force that has sustained my professional career. I thank, with all my heart, Jim and his wife Sue, who are my children's godparents, for their unfaltering support. A major inspiration for this book came from Jérôme Bourgon of the Centre National de la Recherche Scientifique and the Ecole Normale Supérieure de Lyon (Institut d'Asie Orientale). I benefited from his unsurpassed knowledge and keen insights in Chinese legal history. In particular, he has shown me that the distance between French history and East Asian history is not insurmountable, and that it is indeed a worthy project to study them together from a genuinely comparative perspective.

This book was supported by grants, fellowships, and research assistance from various institutions and organizations, including the National Endowment for the Humanities, the Fulbright Commission, the Academy of Korean Studies, the Japan Foundation, the Association for Asian Studies, the International Institute for Asian Studies, the Tōyō Bunka Kenkyujō at Gakushuin University, Harvard Yenching Library, and St. Cloud State University. Its final revision was undertaken during my tenure as a resident Fellow of the Collegium de Lyon (Institut d'Etudes Avancées) at the Ecole Normale Supérieure de Lyon. To all the above, and many others, I remain deeply grateful.

Introduction

This book sets forth the evolution of law in Korea from the Chosŏn dynasty through the colonial and postcolonial periods. Its overriding theme is the role of custom in the reception of modern private law in Korean history. Law and custom are issues that bear crucially on the dichotomy of tradition and modernity, a perennial question for scholars of East Asia. It is a topic of particular poignancy for Korea because of the country's colonial past. Following more than 500 years of indigenous rule under the Chosŏn dynasty (1392–1910), Korea became Japan's protectorate in 1905 and remained a Japanese colony from 1910 to 1945. Korea's passage from a legal system belonging to the Chinese legal tradition to the Romano-German civil law system took place mostly under Japanese rule.

The main thesis of this book is that the reception of European civil law in Korea was facilitated by the colonial authorities who conjured up a Korean customary law. The idea of custom as a source of law was nonexistent in traditional East Asia within the imperial Chinese legal sphere, which had predominantly penal state law systems. The concept of customary law was introduced to Japan in the wake of legal modernization in the second half of the nineteenth century. Japan subsequently brought the conceptual framework of customary law to colonial Korea. Through the customary law system constructed by the colonial regime, Korea's traditional law was reconciled with the imposed Japanese legal order. Colonial customary law served as an intermediary regime between tradition and the demands of modern civil law, as new and old laws were negotiated through colonial jurisprudence.

The transformation of Korean law by the brisk forces of Westernization under colonialism presents an intriguing case for investigating the spread of civil law in modern history. Korea's modern legal development was inexorably tied to that of Japan. In Korean scholarship, the view that legal changes that took place under Japanese influence were essentially geared to promote colonial interest has proved largely unyielding. Reluctant to challenge the validity of the prevailing nationalist framework, many historians have shied away from discussing the significance of legal reforms initiated by the Japanese in colonial Korea.

Customary law has of late sparked much discussion among Korean legal historians, stemming largely from the effort to discern elements in indigenous law that withstood foreign influence and continued into Korea's modern law. Korean historiography has often been tinged with a wistful longing for a lost world and infused with national sentiments aiming to underscore the unique nobility in native Korean law, not tainted by Japanese – that is, Western – law. It has been argued that Korea had its own system of civil law and procedures that grew out of customary practices for settling disputes between individuals. In an attempt to reclaim their legal tradition, which was denied by an alien power in the name of modern law, Korean historians have turned to the notion of popular custom, a sort of a spontaneous legal coherence. There are conscious attempts to place an emphasis on custom in the Chosŏn dynasty as a possible means of proving its autonomous legal identity. Some have focused on the suppression and distortion of the Korean legal tradition and culture by the colonial authorities.

Idealization of custom as true national law, a symbol of indigenous cultural values and tradition, is far from unique to Korean scholarship. It was a dominant trend in European historiography in the nineteenth century. The tenets of the German Historical School – that law was the product of the history of the people and that popular practices were the living matter of law – had an immense impact on modern legal historiography. In the wake of national codification in the nineteenth and twentieth centuries, a number of countries enshrined custom as a source of law. The first Korean Civil Code after independence was enacted in 1958 and came into effect in 1960. It declared customary law to be an official source of law next to statutes. Legal modernization conferred on the notion of customary law a sort of historical legitimacy.

The irony for Korea is that invoking the authority of customary law in its traditional legal order had, in fact, a colonial origin. What Korean legal historians refer to as Korean customary law was a historical construct on the part of the Japanese jurists who were given the task of formulating a modern legal order in the colony. This means that the effort to expunge colonialism ended up relying on the colonial framework of law. What has been seen as the intentional distortion of Korean customs by the Japanese judges was in fact a familiar process in history of regulating customs by jurisprudential action. In the meantime, general indifference on the part of scholars to discussing colonial modernity has left unresolved the problem of explaining the transition from Korea's dynastic law to its modern law based on the civil law tradition. Colonial historiography tended to view indigenous Korean law as inferior and underdeveloped, and the significance of the effort to rescue Korean law from the unjust reputation cannot be exaggerated. But understanding the true nature of traditional Korean law may be impeded if such efforts are grounded on the faulty assumption that one can only demonstrate the maturity of Korea's legal tradition by finding in it the features of Western law.

Some historians have tried to find in "living law" in Chosŏn Korea the elements of modern law such as contractual liberty and private rights; they have also disputed the view that traditional Korean law codes were of predominantly penal nature. Yet these assertions pose a problem because they seem to be grounded less in evidence than in a desire to show the advanced state of Korean traditional law by demonstrating that Korea had a tradition of civil law comparable to Euro-American legal traditions. It is important to discuss the development of Korean law without succumbing to the temptations either to show that Korean law followed a trajectory similar to the evolution of European law or to show that Korean law and custom were inherently unique and thereby incommensurable.

It has been argued that legal scholars support the notion of incommensurability of different legal traditions because "incommensurability provides a means of defence – a kind of philosophical Great Wall – against what have been described as 'monistic theories.'"[1] Embracing the incommensurability of legal traditions spares one from the risk of ill-conceived value judgments. But legitimate efforts to avert the rigid viewpoint of a linear development of law may expose historians to a different kind of danger, namely provincialism in the writing of legal history. This book aims to examine the development of Korean law and custom from comparative perspective, mindful of the need to avoid these pitfalls.

Discussion of customary law must start with a definition of terminology. What is custom? What is law? How does custom differ from customs? When do customs become customary law? Generations of scholars – jurists, historians, philosophers, sociologists, and anthropologists – have debated these questions, but there has been little agreement. Essentially the issues can be restated as what qualifies as "legal" to be included in law, and whether state law represents the quintessence of law. Modern debates over the concept of law revolve around two contrasting theories.[2] Legal anthropologists and sociologists tend to argue that all sorts of social control, including social habits and customs, are law. According to them, all forms of normative orders not attached to the state are nevertheless law. It is a theory that harkens back to the maxim, "where there is society there is law" (*ubi societas ibi ius*), or "no society is without law." In contrast, the second theory limits law to state law. In this formula, in the legal positivist tradition, law is narrowly defined as rules and standards recognized by actors with governmental authority and attendant enforcement power.

It is instructive to note that the first theory with its expansive concept of law was prompted by colonization. Colonial powers presented law as the mark of a civilized society and the "civilizing mission" provided a powerful justification for the colonial imposition of legal regimes on the colonized.

[1] H. Patrick Glenn, "Are Legal Traditions Incommensurable?" *The American Journal of Comparative Law* 49 (1991), 137.

[2] See Brian Z. Tamanaha, "The Folly of the 'Social Scientific' Concept of Legal Pluralism," *Journal of Law and Society* 20, no. 2 (1993): 192–217; Brian Z. Tamanaha, "A Non-Essentialist Version of Legal Pluralism," *Journal of Law and Society* 27 (2000): 296–321.

In reaction to this ethnocentric legal centrism, some scholars – mostly legal anthropologists – asserted that indigenous societies without a state still had law, consisting of various native customs and institutions. Recalling that this idea of legal pluralism was a product of colonial circumstances suggests, then, how problematic it would be to apply this loose concept of law to the Korean case. Unlike most European colonies, Korea had a highly advanced and comprehensive codified legal system and a thriving statecraft culture at the time of the arrival of the colonizers. Its state codes were replete with elaborate penal proscriptions and administrative regulations. Legal norms included in the codes of the Chosŏn dynasty were "laws" of Korea and these laws were "rule-bound." Chosŏn Korea embodied the standard state law model. If one starts talking about non-state law and includes all aspects of social life in the realm of law, one may be effectively negating the existence of the whole legal system of traditional Korea.

In the Western legal tradition, law was primarily a system of civil law rules enforced through adjudication. In East Asia, in contrast, legal systems consisted of penal and administrative law, and the notion of private law as judicially enforceable norms governing relations among individuals was absent. In a project concerned with explaining how private law came into existence in East Asia, which is the focus of this book, the overly inclusive concept of law is of limited utility. The broad concepts of law and custom regard customs as the universal origin of law, supposedly emerging spontaneously in social existence. Customs are seen as living law or self-produced legal order. This view embraces the belief that the legitimacy of law can only emanate from the agreement of the people, in the form of social convention. But law as a spontaneous expression of popular will obviously had no place in traditional Korea. Law was the work of the administrative and bureaucratic state, created and imposed by the king to govern the realm. Custom in the legal meaning of the term did not exist in the Chosŏn dynasty. In Korean history, resorting to the narrow definition of law seems unavoidable.

In this book, a basic distinction is drawn between customs (popular practices, habits, or social facts) and custom (a common usage that has acquired the force or validity of law). This divide emphasizes the juridical nature of custom. When custom is written down and recognized as a source of law, one can call it customary law, but in reality the difference between custom and customary law is insignificant. The postulation of custom (or customary law) as a judicial artifact, complete with judicial decisions and doctrinal activities by professional jurists, is essential in laying out a precise criterion for private law or civil law. Custom supposes a certain degree of legal constraint. Practices and usages are distinct from law because there are no legal sanctions for a failure to follow them. Customary rules as a form of private ordering, enforced informally by means of social disapproval, do not have the attributes of law. Living law, de facto law, or practical law is not law because it lacks legal authority. The loose construction of law and custom results in a situation in which law loses any distinctive meaning.

In the traditional view, custom as the embodiment of indigenous cultural values and tradition was often pitted against the influence of alien law. Heightened attention to custom – the movement to record customs for instance – usually took place in the backdrop of stimulus, or perceived threat, from nonindigenous law. But it is worth recalling the dictum of Roscoe Pound that the "[h]istory of a system of law is largely a history of borrowings of legal materials from other legal systems and of assimilation of materials from outside of the law."[3] Here, the concept of "legal transplantation" as a major vehicle of legal change can serve as a useful theoretical framework for explaining the development of custom and civil law.[4] According to Alan Watson, legal transplantation constitutes a process in which lawmaking elites are engaged throughout history, reshaping existing legal order with rules and concepts originating in other legal systems. He asserts that "borrowing from a different jurisdiction has been the principal way in which law has developed."[5] Among the most controversial in Watson's thesis is the claim that there is little correlation between society and legal change.[6] He argued that "legal rules are not peculiarly devised for the particular society in which they now operate."[7] This assertion seems to contradict not only the time-honored observation of Montesquieu that geographical and sociological factors influenced legal changes but also Friedrich Karl von Savigny's *volksgeist* theory that law was properly "custom," the "spirit of the people."

Watson's view stressing the autonomy of law has been subject to round criticisms. Otto Kahn-Freund stated that legal institutions were deeply embedded in a nation's life.[8] Lawrence Friedman has argued that law is a mirror of society and that law changes in response to the internal demands of the people.[9]

[3] Roscoe Pound, *The Formative Era of American Law* (Boston: Little, Brown, 1938), 94. The reception of common law in America began at a time of "political hostility to things English after the American Revolution." Roscoe Pound, "The Development of American Law and Its Deviation from English Law," *Law Quarterly Review* 67 (1951), 66.

[4] Alan Watson, *The Evolution of Western Private Law*, exp. ed. (Baltimore and London: The Johns Hopkins University Press, 2000); Alan Watson, *Legal Transplants: An Approach to Comparative Law*, 2nd ed. (Athens: University of Georgia Press, 1993).

[5] Alan Watson, *Society and Legal Change*, 2nd ed. (Philadelphia: Temple University Press, 2001), 98. For discussions of Watson's legal transplant theories, see Michael H. Hoeflich, "Law, Society and Reception: The Vision of Alan Watson," *Michigan Law Review* 85 (1987): 1083–1094. In European legal history few codes "are original in the sense that they have been made fresh for the territory in which they operate without a great dependence on foreign law." Edward M. Wise, "The Transplant of Legal Patterns," *American Journal of Comparative Law* 38 (Supplement) (1990), 5. A scholar argued that it happened "twice only that the customs of European peoples were worked up into intellectual systems of law," that is, through the Roman system and the common law. See S. F. C. Milsom, *Historical Foundation of the Common Law*, 2nd ed. (London: Butterworths, 1981, 1969), 1.

[6] Watson, *Legal Transplants*, 109.

[7] Ibid., 97.

[8] Otto Kahn-Freund, "On Uses and Misuses of Comparative Law," *Modern Law Review* 37 (1972): 1–27.

[9] Lawrence M. Friedman, "Review of *Society and Legal Change* by Alan Watson," *British Journal of Law and Society* 6, no. 1 (1979): 127–129. For a synopsis of the debate surrounding Watson's

Whether there is a direct relationship between people and the law operating in their community and whether the law of any society is a reflection of the common consciousness of the community are questions that evoke the basic difference between the two kinds of customary law discussed earlier. One arises from accepted practices and one is created by the courts; the former is "sociologists' customary law" and the latter "lawyers' customary law."[10] This difference reverts back to the disagreement on what "law" means. If one focuses attention on the state's legal rules, institutions, and systems, the autonomous nature of law and the social utility of legal reception seem hardly disputable. When one turns attention to legal cultures and social traditions, however, the mere demonstration of the existence of a custom may suffice in order to consider it as a source of law, and the importance of legal reception becomes minimized.

Watson has argued that custom became law only when it was officially recognized or accepted by judges, regardless of whether there actually was an existing custom, and that this recognition was signaled by court decisions.[11] From this, he has asserted that custom matters only "for those who believe that there is a very close correlation between the law of a society and the life of the society."[12] For Watson, most Western societies persist in the myth that customary law emerges from past popular behavior because the belief that a judge is just making up a rule deprives the system of customary law of its authority.[13] But in reality, he argued, the development of private law was primarily the work of jurists. Watson's view downplaying the relation between a society and its law should not be exaggerated. The reception of alien law is certainly propelled by social needs. But the point is that these social needs are largely ascertained and acted on by legal elites.

The postulation of legal transplantation in Europe as a process that was largely independent of, or at most indirectly dependent on, society appears to find an equally remarkable articulation in the context of modern East Asian history. The emergence of custom as a source of law was the result of acculturation on the model of the "learned law," as witnessed in medieval Europe with the reception of Roman law. In fact, the development of customary law in history can be seen in terms of legal imperialism that started with the expansion of Roman law in antiquity. It represented the ruler's effort, supported by legal elites, to unify legal sources and centralize the realm. The same process continued with colonization in the early modern period and in the nineteenth and early twentieth centuries. The cases of Korea, China, and Japan can be seen as part of this general pattern that was witnessed throughout the world.

thesis, see William Ewald, "Comparative Jurisprudence (II): The Logic of Legal Transplants," *American Journal of Comparative Law* 43 (1995): 489–510.

[10] Gordon R. Woodman, "How State Courts Create Customary Law in Ghana and Nigeria," in *Indigenous Law and the State*, eds. B.W. Morse and G.R. Woodman (Dordrecht: Foris Publications, 1988), 181–220.

[11] Watson, *Legal Transplants*, 75–78.

[12] Alan Watson, "The Evolution of Law: Continued." *Law & History Review* 5 (1987), 550.

[13] Ibid., 537, 548–549.

In East Asia, the first attempts to codify customary law took place during 1870–1880 in Japan and 1900–1930 in China, when Japanese and Chinese officials, respectively, attempted the redaction of a modern civil code with a view toward creating a modern state. After Korea became Japan's protectorate, Japan started collecting Korea's old laws, rites, and popular usages. The postulation of customary law in Korea's legal past was a colonial legacy. Following annexation, Japan imposed its civil law as the general law of the colony but allowed Korean customs to govern most private relations among Koreans. Custom was thus declared to be the official source of law and a system of customary law was established. Because Chosŏn Korea did not have a body of written private law, except for some provisions scattered in the criminal code, colonial officials needed to rely on Korea's "custom" in regulating legal relations among the natives. Old customs of Korea were thus redefined and became legal rules.

Recent scholarship in European colonial history has shown that much of colonial customary law was a creation at the hands of the colonial power.[14] In European colonies, all indigenous practices and institutions that governed the natives were subsumed under the comprehensive term "custom," which basically referred to anything that was not law of European origin. The less than scrupulous colonial usage of the term custom became even more problematic in the Japanese colonies. In Korea, anything that was distinguished from Japanese law was dubbed "Korean custom," a category that comprised Korean codes, Confucian texts, popular practices, mores, and so on. The indiscriminate usage of the terms "customs," "custom," and "customary law" that seems to befuddle Korean historiography thus had a colonial provenance. The customary law system allowed colonial officials to control the conditions of the recognition of customary rules and modify or improve their contents. It was mainly through the interpretation of Korean customs that Japan attempted to incorporate the native practices and institutions into the Japanese cultural and legal sphere. Korean customary law was elaborated through colonial jurisprudence on the basis of the Japanese Civil Code.

The role of Japanese civil law in colonial jurisprudence was redolent of the role of French civil law in early Meiji Japan, from 1868 to around 1890. The courts adjudicated customary law disputes according to the general principles of law deriving from the French Civil Code. In turn, the role of the French code in Japan was analogous to the role of the *Corpus iuris civilis* in late medieval and early modern Europe. The Code of Justinian served as "written reason" (*la raison écrite*) to systemize and rationalize French law on the model of Roman law which was the common law (*ius commune*) in Europe. Profoundly influenced by the French Civil Code, and later the German codes and legal science, Japanese law in the late nineteenth century rapidly left the family of Sinicized law to enter the family of civil law. The Japanese Civil Code, completed in

[14] See, among others, Eric Hobsbawm and Terence Ranger, eds. *The Invention of Tradition* (Cambridge: Cambridge University Press, 1983).

1898, was used as the source of the embodiment of civilized justice by the colonial jurists in Korea in the first half of the twentieth century.

This study revises dominant views in Korean legal historiography in several important aspects. Asserting the existence of custom in premodern Korea as a spontaneous legal order is the result of a misplaced emphasis, largely propelled by a nationalistic paradigm.[15] It amounts to postulating indigenous law in order to show that it was distinct from the formal legal regimes imported either from China during the dynastic period or from the West under Japanese rule. An essential problem with this view is that it disregards the question of power in the development of law. By treating law as independent of the state power, one risks explaining the evolution of Korean law in dissociation from political circumstances. On the other hand, supposing the presence of customary law in Chosŏn Korea seems to be grounded in the desire to show that Korean traditional law had the genesis of modern notions of civil justice. But this is tantamount to arguing that Korean law deserves consideration only because it was not different from Western law.

It would, of course, be a complete misrepresentation that before the introduction of modern law Korea had no notion of law or sense of justice. Chosŏn Korea had a legal system that worked efficiently, but it operated in a way different from Western legal systems. Korean traditional law functioned on the basis of penal sanctions that were articulated in the state codes under clearly defined categories of crimes and punishments. The legality of the penalties was a major concern of East Asian law. When the goal of the legal system was to provide uniformity and simplicity in the administration of law, certain notions and practices that could have promoted the development of the concepts and principles of "rights" in civil law were subsumed under the framework of prohibitions and punishments.

Once one acknowledges that custom as a source of private law did not exist in Chosŏn Korea, the assertion that its customary law was destroyed by the Japanese colonizers loses much of its relevancy. Attention then duly focuses on the centrality of law in colonial rule. There is no doubt that law often served as a tool for colonial domination. Law was the key instrument for the construction of the colonial state, which attempted to restructure colonial society comprehensively. But the legitimate effort to defend Korean legal tradition does not need to obscure the significance of legal developments during the colonial period. To date, too much emphasis in Korean historiography has been placed on the issue of cultural assimilation on a policy level, without sufficient attention to how traditional customs were systematized and modified by the colonial courts. The process was not a unilateral or wholesale imposition of Japan's civil law and its legal principles in Korea.

[15] Marie Seong-Hak Kim, "Law and Custom under the Chosŏn Dynasty and Colonial Korea: A Comparative Perspective," *Journal of Asian Studies* 66 (2007): 1067–1097; Marie Seong-Hak Kim, "Customary Law and Colonial Jurisprudence in Korea," *American Journal of Comparative Law* 57 (2009): 205–247.

The Japanese jurists, given the task of deciding cases according to customary law, struggled to make sense of the legal order they themselves found confusing and contradictory. Their use of the term "customary law" was often incongruous and uneven. Overall, the fact that the colonizers and the colonized belonged to the same cultural sphere of Sinicized civilization, sharing common writing systems and values, naturally entailed the formulation of a policy distinct from Western colonialism. The important question to be answered, then, is not whether Korean custom was intentionally distorted as part of Japan's imperial policy but how closely the Japanese chose to engage in reconciling the premodern Korean legal tradition with modern civil law principles, and how these choices influenced the way modern Korean law today addresses essential issues in private law relations.

Historians have long debated the relationship between colonial institutional modification and postcolonial appropriation. In establishing a new independent legal system, many countries necessarily had to confront the legacy of colonial law. The colonial legal system in Korea formed the foundation of the new independent legal system. Custom in modern Korean law, acclaimed as an expression of national identity in the Civil Code, was both the product of colonial and postcolonial exigencies. The notion of custom and its jurisprudential framework derived from colonial law, but it was nationalistic legislative will that led to the recognition of custom with binding force, alongside written law. During the past few years, both the Supreme Court and the Constitutional Court of Korea have been caught up in discussion of "tradition" and "custom" as they grappled with the judicial and constitutional ramifications of those terms. Colonial customary law has thus become a subject of not merely historical inquiry but also critical constitutional consideration. A substantial part of colonial customary law decisions is still recognized as law in postcolonial jurisprudence. Either invoking the authority of custom or rejecting the burden of tradition, the courts seem to continue the maximalist conception of the mission of the judicial power to reform society, which can be seen as a legacy of colonial jurisprudence.

The following chapters proceed through the Chosŏn dynasty (Chapters 1 and 2), Japanese rule (Chapters 3 through 7), and modern Korea (Chapter 8). Chapter 1 provides a theoretical discussion of custom and its relation to law in a comparative perspective. Theories of custom in Roman law and the development of customary law in medieval France will be examined. These discussions will help explain why speaking of custom as informal law in Chosŏn obscures characteristics and priorities underlying the Korean legal tradition and culture. Chosŏn Korea's community compact (*hyangyak*), the topic of Chapter 2, resembled custom in Europe in the sense that it concerned intra-communal self-regulation. But it was an instrument that was essentially geared to correct and transform mores and habits of its members through moral and penal prescriptions. The community compact illustrates the way the state dealt with local practices, by enlisting neo-Confucian *yangban* elites who were mostly interested in maintaining social hierarchy. In such a system, there was no development of the conception of legal rights enforced through an adjudicatory process.

The fundamental metamorphosis of Korea's law and legal system took place from around the turn of the twentieth century. Chapters 3 and 4 examine legal changes in protectorate Korea against the backdrop of legal reforms that had just taken place in Japan. Japanese colonial legal policy cannot be adequately addressed without an understanding of Japan's own domestic experience. In 1875 Japan declared custom an official source of law. Subsequently, the jurists in the early Meiji years proceeded to discover customary law that was to be inserted in the civil code. One individual that emerges prominently throughout this book is Ume Kenjirō. A renowned professor of civil law, Ume was a drafter of Japan's civil code. From 1906 to his death in 1910, he served as legal advisor to the Korean empire, then Japan's protectorate. Under the protection of Itō Hirobumi, the first resident general of Korea, Ume oversaw the modernization of the Korean legal system and undertook the writing of Korea's civil code. He embodied a crucial conduit through which modern European civil law and the legal system were introduced to Japan and subsequently to Korea.[16]

The next two chapters discuss colonial law after annexation. Chapter 5 examines the construction of the colonial law system and the customary law order in Korea in comparison with the precedent in colonial Taiwan. The colonial governors claimed and enjoyed extra-constitutional prerogatives, deemed necessary for efficient colonial management. There was ongoing tension and conflict between Tokyo and Seoul which centered on, among others, colonial judicial affairs including the implementation of custom. Under the customary law regime, Japanese judges resorted to equity-oriented judicial reasoning without being restrained by the requirements of legal formalism. The notion of "custom" served as a powerfully effective legal instrument in reconstructing fluid and shifting Korean principles and procedures into a fixed, written set of rules that could still claim continuity with the Korean past. Chapter 6 examines the colonial courts' interpretation of custom through an analysis of appellate decisions. Little attention has hitherto been paid to how the colonial courts implemented modern legal theories and reconciled them with the indigenous laws. Analysis of jurisprudence will give specific examples of how old usages and practices in Korea were institutionalized as customary law.

Each colonial power's vision of the law and the operation of the legal system encapsulates how it conceived its enterprise and mission in colonial legal history. Comparison of the Japanese colonial customary law policy with European patterns in Chapter 7 is expected to shed light on the nature of Japanese colonialism. The last chapter, Chapter 8, discusses the legacy of colonial customary law in contemporary Korea by examining a series of landmark decisions by the Constitutional Court and the Supreme Court.

[16] Marie Seong-Hak Kim, "Ume Kenjirō and the Making of Korean Civil Law, 1906–1910," *The Journal of Japanese Studies* 34, no. 1 (2008): 1–31.

This book focuses on comparative analysis. The strong nationalist orientation in Korean scholarship has not been favorably disposed toward attempts to discuss colonial law in a broad comparative context. But discussing the creation of customary law in colonial Korea in the context of Western legal history does not mean downplaying the political and economic repercussions of destructive Japanese colonial rule or negating the role of law as an instrument of colonialism. Korea's law and legal tradition have been compared with those of China, Japan, and Vietnam, but little attempt has been made to compare them with those outside the sphere of the East Asian cultural heritage. It appears to be a meaningful exercise to depart from the well-trodden and safe path of a comparison defined by common geographic and cultural frames and push the boundaries of comparative legal history.

One may protest that any comparison of Korea's legal past with that of Europe would be meaningless because the characteristics of each legal system would be culture-specific, meaning that such a comparison would contain no useful conceptual framework for understanding each country's historical development. However, it is precisely the paucity of a conceptual framework suitable to both traditions that justifies a comparative approach that focuses on customary law. One can study each society's legal past without subscribing to an exaggerated form of contemporary cultural relativism. When seemingly disparate legal developments are placed side by side and a legal system's ideological assumptions and institutional attributes are compared with those of other legal systems, historians can expect to measure in a constructive way the relative strength and limitations of each tradition. Highlighting similarities and differences between legal traditions does not need to condemn one society as inferior or less civilized. By casting one's gaze beyond national borders, after all, one can take a step toward fostering meaningful communication, in lieu of erecting a "Great Wall" between civilizations.

Finally, it must be noted that this book was conceived as a constructive protest against the current state of historical scholarship in which Korea is often treated as something akin to an afterthought, overshadowed by Japan and China. In 1980, the late American historian William Shaw wrote that the study of Korean legal history "is still awaiting its Maitland."[17] Shaw, one of the few foreign scholars who studied Korean legal history, lamented in particular the near absence of scholarly activities in Korean legal history in the West. The situation that Shaw described has changed little during the last few decades.[18] The literature on Korean legal history in foreign languages – other

[17] William R. Shaw, "Traditional Korean Law and Its Relation to China," in *Essays on China's Legal Tradition*, eds. Jerome Alan Cohen, R. Randle Edwards and Fu-mei Chang Chen (Princeton: Princeton University Press, 1980), 302.

[18] There is paucity in literature in English on traditional Korean law. Shaw's works remain the best studies of Chosŏn legal history in English: see William R. Shaw, *Legal Norms in a Confucian State* (Berkeley: Institute of East Asian Studies, University of California Berkeley Center for Korean Studies, 1981); William R. Shaw, "Social and Intellectual Aspects of Traditional Korean Law, 1392–1910," in *Traditional Korean Legal Attitudes*, eds. Bong Duck Chun, William Shaw,

than Japanese – is minuscule. One of the reasons for the lack of serious interest in Korean legal history in Western scholarship is the general view among historians outside Korea that premodern Korean law was dominated by, and hardly distinct from, Chinese law, while its modernization in the twentieth century was fastidiously modeled after Japanese law.[19] A focus on customary law can provide a key point of reference in correcting this facile rejection of the importance of studying Korean law.

A study of the history of Korean civil law untrammeled by the nationalist paradigm is long overdue.[20] Korean legal history ought to be freed from the baggage of its colonial past. By considering Korean law and custom from a comparative perspective, this book aims to expand the analytical framework used in studying Korean legal history.

and Tai-kwon Choi (Berkeley: Institute of East Asian Studies, University of California Berkeley Center for Korean Studies, 1980), 15–53; Shaw, "Traditional Korean Law and Its Relation to China."

[19] The misconception that the Japanese Civil Code is still in effect in Korea is not uncommon. See, for example, Hans W. Baade, "Transplants of Laws and of Lawyers," in *Justice in Particular: Festschrift in Honour of Professor P. J. Kozyris* (Athens: Ant. N. Sakkoulas Publishers, 2007), 30.

[20] A number of scholars in both Korea and the West have begun to challenge the simplistic view of nationalist historiography, arguing for the need to go beyond the obsession with overcoming the colonial past. See Gi-Wook Shin and Michael Robinson, eds., *Colonial Modernity in Korea* (Cambridge, MA, and London: Harvard University Asia Center, 1999).

1

Comparative Reflections on the Concepts of Law and Custom

One of the thorniest dilemmas in Korean legal history is that the establishment of modern law and a modern legal system coincided with the loss of national independence. Legal modernization took place abruptly, under the aegis of colonial power. This "involuntary legal reception" created a challenging situation for historians to explain the evolution of Korean law on a continuum. The tendency in postcolonial Korean scholarship to downplay the Japanese influence in the modernization process was perhaps understandable. One such effort was to argue that Chosŏn Korea had its own system of civil law in the form of customary law that grew out of popular practices. It is disconcerting, then, that in many existing studies the theoretical discussion of custom and its relation to law is largely deficient.

In Korean scholarship, *kwanhaeng* (practices), *kugwan* (old customs), *kwansŭp* (custom), and *kwansŭppŏp* (customary law) are used interchangeably. It appears that many scholars tended to apply these labels to any premodern popular practices and to claim that customary law formed an important part of the Chosŏn legal system. The aim was to highlight and give prominence to the indigenous legal order. The eminent Korean legal historian Pak Pyŏng-ho argued that Chosŏn Korea was ruled by legal precedents and customary law and that the state codes were compiled on the basis of traditional customary law.[1] This view, widely shared among Korean scholars, contains a danger of conflating the terms "customs" as social norms and "custom" as legal norms.

[1] Pak Pyŏng-ho, *Hanguk pŏpchesa ko* [A Study of the History of Korean Law] (Seoul: Pŏmmunsa, 1974), 419–421; Park Byoung Ho, "Traditional Korean Society and Law," *Korean Journal of Comparative Law* 5 (1977), 4. Park also wrote that "when a law took the form of a new legislation, its essential elements were those which had taken root in the social system, namely in traditional custom." Park Pyong-Ho, "Characteristics in Traditional Korean Law." *Korea Journal* (1976), 5. Recent studies largely repeat Pak's views: see, for example, Chŏng Kŭng-sik, "Chosŏn sidae ŭi kwŏllyŏk pullip kwa pŏpch'i chuŭi: kŭ siron chŏk koch'al [Separation of Power and Rule of Law under the Chosŏn Dynasty: A Preliminary Examination]," *Seoul Taehakkyo pŏphak* 42, no. 4 (2001), 43 and 47 (stating that codifications incorporated customary law and precedents).

If "precedents" existed in premodern Korea, they were administrative precedents, not judicial precedents. What was incorporated into statutes dealing with civil matters was not custom but usages that had become routine administrative practices. The indiscriminate use of the terms custom and customary law cannot be simply overlooked as an unfortunate muddling in terminology, because postulating customary law during the Chosŏn period amounts to arguing that Korean society sustained a legal order of private law for settling disputes between individuals, distinct and apart from the state penal law order.

Postulation of customary law in the Korean legal tradition rests largely on the nationalistic paradigm that views custom as a manifestation of collective national memory. But it can also be seen as part of the historiographical agenda rippling in East Asian law. Recent work in Chinese and Japanese legal history has greatly contributed to correcting traditional portrayals of law in East Asia. A number of studies have scrutinized the conception that, in East Asian countries before their modernization in the late nineteenth and the twentieth centuries, law remained static and legal process was underdeveloped. For instance, a common belief that most people in East Asia sought to avoid involvement with the courts has been largely replaced by findings that they were in fact much more litigious and procedural-minded than had been believed. Further, the realization that formal and informal legality such as mediation or compromise were not diametrically opposed but instead complemented each other has led scholars to argue that law had a substantial and dynamic presence in East Asian history.

While any comparative legal historian should feel encouraged by this development in recent scholarship, a question remains whether scholars, in their effort to avoid viewing East Asian law with Western models in mind, have nonetheless continued using the very Western categories from which they tried to distance themselves. The traditional view has been that the Chinese empire had no notion of a separate "civil law."[2] But recent attempts to revise the view of a China that remained in an earlier stage of European legal development have spurred studies looking for civil practices and cases that might prove that Chinese law included material recognition of private rights, a principal concept of Western legal traditions. Even if "civil law" was absent from the Qing Code, some historians have argued, it was present in local judicial procedures and in "custom," the true source of private law in East Asia before modernization.[3]

[2] Derk Bodde and Clarence Morris, *Law in Imperial China: Exemplified by 190 Ch'ing Dynasty Cases* (Philadelphia: University of Pennsylvania Press, 1973, 1967), 3–4; Geoffrey MacCormack, *The Spirit of Traditional Chinese Law* (Athens: University of Georgia Press, 1996).

[3] See, among others, Philip C. C. Huang, *Civil Justice in China: Representation and Practice in the Qing* (Stanford: Stanford University Press, 1996); Philip C.C. Huang, *Code, Custom, and Legal Practice in China* (Stanford: Stanford University Press, 2001); Kathryn Bernhardt and Philip C. C. Huang, eds. *Civil Law in Qing and Republican China* (Stanford: Stanford University Press, 1994). The works by Japanese historians such as Shiga Shūzō contradict Huang's study. *Shindai Chūgoku no hō to saiban* [Law and Adjudication in Qing China] (Tokyo: Sōbunsha, 1984). For the ensuing debate, see Karasawa Yasuhiko, Philip C. C. Huang, Shiga Shūzō, and Terada

This kind of argument accepts the concept of customary law as a precedent of modern civil laws and thus continues the classical theory that private law in traditional China resided in customs.

Of late, however, it has been argued that custom and civil law are Western categories that did not exist in Qing China. This assertion is important because it calls to attention the critical need for rigorous conceptual precision and warns of potential interpretive pitfalls residing in the discussion of civil law in East Asia. According to the French legal historian Jérôme Bourgon, China did not have rules abstracted from private relationships that the magistrates were to apply outside the state codes. Bourgon argues that the notion of customary law spread from Europe to Japan and from Japan to China and Korea, springing up in each country only when the redaction of a Western-style civil code was envisaged. Custom was created as a preparation for the codification of modern civil law at the time of each country's mutation into a modern nation-state (or colony of a modern state). Bourgon claims that collecting customs and considering them as a source of law were essentially bureaucratic efforts to devise a legal system equivalent to Western legal systems.[4]

These discussions in East Asian historiography about custom and civil law have only just started to figure prominently in Korean legal historiography. Whether recognizing the existence of customary law in premodern Korea amounts to the presupposition of analogy with European legal history presents an important issue in studying Korea's legal past. Although many scholars have tried to highlight the historical nature of Chosŏn dynasty law, scant attention has been paid to the danger of the methodological faux pas of relying on imported Western – Japanese – concepts and references.

This chapter discusses the concepts of custom and law, drawing from comparisons with European history. This discussion is followed by an examination of the key aspects of law and the legal system under the Chosŏn dynasty. The main aim is to show how the belief in current scholarship in the existence of customary law in Chosŏn Korea risks misrepresentation of traditional Korean law and its relationship with the state. What made law "civil" in the European experience was its reliance on practices among private parties called "custom," collected and recorded at the royal initiative and interpreted and enforced by the courts. Custom was less a sociological than a judicial artifact. In Europe, the articulation of customary law was fundamentally influenced by the renaissance of Roman law in late medieval Europe. Lacking both the process of the

Hiroaki, "Kōki teisei Chūoku ni okeru hō, shakai, bunka [Law, Society, and Culture in Late Imperial China]," *Chūgoku-shakai to bunka* 13 (1998):193–281.

[4] Jérôme Bourgon, "La Coutume et le droit en Chine à la fin de l'empire," *Annales HSS* 54 (1999): 1073–1107; Jérôme Bourgon, "Le Droit coutumier comme phénomène d'acculturation bureaucratique au Japon et en Chine," in *La Coutume et la norme en Chine et au Japon* (Saint-Denis: Presses universitaires de Vincennes, 2001), 125–142; Jérôme Bourgon, "De quelques tendances récentes de la sinologie juridique américaine," *T'oung Pao* 84 (1998): 380–414; Jérôme Bourgon, "Uncivil Dialogue: Law and Custom Did Not Merge into Civil Law under the Qing," *Late Imperial China* 23 (2002): 50–90.

judicialization of custom and the impetus from a "learned law," Chosŏn Korea did not see the rise of private law separate from the state's penal law system.

Concepts of Custom in European and East Asian Legal Traditions

Historians of European law have long debated on the origin of the obligatory force of customary law. In the Roman times, the term *consuetudo* (meaning customs, habit, or usage) was used quasi-synonymously with *mos* (meaning will, inclination, or mores) to refer to the norms of ordinary behaviors, outside the formalist law of the city of Rome.[5] Throughout the classical period, jurisprudence did not recognize custom as a source of law, although some jurists allowed custom to be considered in the interpretation of an ambiguous law.[6]

It has commonly been held that the emergence of customary law in late medieval Europe was the result of the crystallization of preexisting usages of feudal origin transmitted orally. But this traditional idea is now largely debunked. Recently historians of medieval law have called for the revision of the view of custom as a spontaneous manifestation cropping up in one place or another in accordance with local needs. According to these scholars, the notion of custom as "law" was foreign to feudal society.[7] During the medieval period before the twelfth century, *consuetudo* meant fiscal exactions by feudal lords, which were considered by the population to be "arbitrary," "undue," and "bad."[8] The rise of customary law in the thirteenth century was prompted by the revival of the teaching of Roman law at the universities in northern Italy in the twelfth century and its spread to the north.

Discerning the conditions of the validity of custom and its obligatory force in legal construction was one of the most significant achievements of reemerging legal science in late medieval Europe.[9] The thirteenth century saw the first redactions of customary law. Once custom was written down, legal scholars refined it on the basis of the *Corpus iuris civilis*, Justinian's codification of Roman law in the sixth century, and Europe experienced a remarkable rebirth

[5] Robert Jacob, "La Coutume, les mœurs et le rite. Regards croisés sur les catégories occidentales de la norme non écrite," in *La Coutume et la norme en Chine et au Japon*, ed. Jérôme Bourgon (Saint-Denis: Presses universitaires de Vincennes, 2001), 146.

[6] David Ibbetson, "Custom in Medieval law," in *The Nature of Customary Law: Legal, Historical and Philosophical Perspectives*, eds. Amanda Perreau-Saussine and James Bernard Murphy (Cambridge: Cambridge University Press, 2007), 152.

[7] Jacques Krynen, "The Absolute Monarchy and the French Unification of Private Rights," in *Privileges and Rights of Citizenship: Law and the Juridical Construction of Civil Society*, eds. Julius Kirshner and Laurent Layali (Berkeley: University of California at Berkeley, The Robbins Religions and Civil Law Collection, 2002), 27–55; Jacques Krynen, "Entre science juridique et dirigisme: le glas medièval de la coutume," *Droits et pouvoirs* 7 (2000): 170–187; Robert Jacob, "Les Coutumiers du XIIIe siècle ont-ils connu la coutume?" in *La Coutume au village dans l'Europe médiévale et moderne*, eds. Mireille Mousnier and Jacques Poumarède (Toulouse: Presses universitaires du Mirail, 2001), 103–119.

[8] Jean-Louis Halpérin, *Profils des mondialisations du droit* (Paris: Dalloz, 2009), 87.

[9] Krynen, "Entre science juridique et dirigisme," 175.

of jurisprudence. Roman law was the basic juridical standard in recognizing the legal normativity of custom. Referring to Roman texts, the scholars developed the classic theory of custom. There were two elements necessary for custom to obtain the force of law: first, the repetition by people of similar acts, anchored in time immemorial; and, second, *opinio necessitatis*, or popular consent that transformed a habit into an imperative norm. For the Italian jurist Bartolus (1313 or 1314–1357), long use was the *causa remota* of enforceable customs, with the tacit consent of the people their *causa proxima*.[10]

The formalization of custom as law was the work of the judges and royal agents inspired by the Roman model. The ever-increasing jurisdictions of royal courts were critical for the development of customary law. The twelfth and thirteenth centuries each saw the establishment of royal courts in England and France, which quickly encroached upon seigneurial and ecclesiastical jurisdictions. European jurists from early on tended to cling to the distinction – often difficult – between usages, of which the prescriptive character did not have obligatory juridical force, and custom, which was recognized by tribunals or mentioned in law texts. The French legal scholar Philippe de Beaumanoir, the author of the famous *Coutumes de Beauvaisis* in 1283, wrote: "The difference between custom and usage is that, while all customs are to be observed, there are usages such that if anyone wished to deny them and carry his claim to judgment they would become invalid."[11] The Roman jurist Ulpian stated: "when it appears that somebody is relying upon a custom ..., the very first issue which ought to be explored, according to my opinion, is whether the custom has ever been upheld in contentious proceedings."[12] For the Italian jurist Baldus (1327–1400), "the *communis opinio doctorum* – the rules and interpretations on which all or most of the learned lawyers agree – should be enforced as if they were custom."[13]

Custom was inseparable from the proof in justice. In a trial, it had to be decided by what custom the party was to be tried. The party had to establish his custom before the seigneurial court or royal court by proving that it had existed uninterrupted for a long time and that there was a general consent among people that they were bound to observe it. The courts needed some mechanism to inform the judges of the custom of a particular place. In 1270, French king Louis IX formalized the preexisting practice of discovery by introducing the *enquête par turbe* as a judicial process.[14] This local inquest involved

[10] Laurent Mayali, "La Coutume dans la doctrine romaniste," in *La Coutume*, ed. J. Gilissen (Brussels: De Boeck Université, 1990), vol. 2 (*Recueils de la Société Jean Bodin pour l'histoire comparative des institutions*, vol. 52), 21.

[11] Philippe de Beaumanoir, *Coutumes de Beauvaisis* (Paris: Alphonse Picard et fils, 1899–1900); *The Coutumes de Beauvaisis of Philippe de Beaumanoir*, trans. F. R. P. Akehurst (Philadelphia: University of Pennsylvania Press, 1992), no. 684.

[12] *The Digest of Justinian*, trans. and ed. Alan Watson (Philadelphia: University of Pennsylvania Press, 1985), 1.3.34.

[13] Cited from Ibbetson, "Custom in Medieval law," 161.

[14] Mayali, "La Coutume dans la doctrine romaniste," 18–19; L. Waelkens, "L'Origine de l'enquête par turbe," *Tijdschrift voor rechtsgeschiedenis* 53 (1985): 337–346.

calling on local persons, typically numbering ten, possessing special knowledge of the customary practices to express their opinion as to the existence of the custom at issue. Their reply was to be put in writing and sealed. After the inquiry was made, the judge considered the custom's obligatory character and decided to adopt or reject it on a case-by-case basis. Once judgment was rendered, the decision itself manifested the custom. Judicial decisions became a form of proof.[15]

It was the medieval canonists who subjected the authority of customary law (*jus consuetudinis*) to strict ethical criteria. In the second half of the twelfth century, canon law scholars argued that custom must not contradict the authority of the Truth – the Holy Scripture – and must conform to reason.[16] Custom was equated with *usus rationabilis*. The civilists did not consider that inconformity of custom to reason would lead to its invalidation, but the canonists placed custom under explicit moral control.[17] In this context, long usage and the acceptance by the people were far from sufficient to presume custom's normative value. In the *Summa Theologica*, Thomas Aquinas stated that a *lex* against *ratio* is not properly law but "a perversion of law," expression of a tyrannical will; likewise, custom that was not reasonable was not valid.[18]

The right of the king to abolish "bad custom" (*malae consuetudines*) had been exercised in France without challenge from as early as the eleventh century.[19] The king delegated his power to the Parlements, the sovereign courts, and jurisprudence took up the task of classifying customary rules as "odious" or "favorable."[20] Combating bad customs was the subject of judicial interpretation. If the custom was not reasonable, justice required that it be quashed; if it was inadequate or too rigorous, equity required that it be modified.[21] The decisions of the courts, the *stilus curiae* of the Parlements, did not need to be proved. In the theory of the rules of judicial law, the settled course of decision on certain points, engendered by the *usus fori*, became law. The judge confirmed the regularity of a local-specific practice and validated its legitimacy by a judicial decision. This was how customary law emerged in Europe. It was a body of new rules created by the judges. In European history, custom referred

[15] Judicial decisions were not the only form of proof of custom, but it was indisputable that they were important proof of custom. Édouard Lambert, *La Fonction du droit civil comparé* (Paris: V. Girard & E. Brière, 1903).

[16] Krynen, "Entre science juridique et dirigisme," 176.

[17] Ibid.

[18] Ibid., 178.

[19] François Olivier-Martin, "Le Roi de France et les mauvaises coutumes au Moyen Age," *Zeitschrift der Savigny-Stiftung fur Rechtsgeschichte. Germanistische Abtheilung* 58 (1938): 108–137.

[20] Robert Jacob, "La Coutume, les mœurs et le rite. Regards croisés sur les catégories occidentales de la norme non écrite," in *La Coutume et la norme en Chine et au Japon*, ed. Jérôme Bourgon (Saint-Denis: Presses universitaires de Vincennes, 2001), 151.

[21] François Olivier-Martin, *Les Lois du roi* (Paris: Librairie générale de droit et de jurisprudence, 1997, 1988), 48, 97; John P. Dawson, "Remedies of the French Chancery before 1789," in *Festschrift ür Ernst Rabel*, vol. 1 : *Rechtsvergleichung und internationales Privatrecht*, eds. H. Dölle, M. Rheinstein and K. Zweigert (Tübingen: Mohr, 1954), 99–140.

to the normative rules of behavior and institutions that were given legal recognition by courts and were not only followed as a matter of practice but also enforced as a matter of law. Popular practices, habits, or behaviors, selected and modified by professional jurists, were reworked and integrated into civil law through the intermediary of customary law.

The various definitions of custom proposed in modern scholarship can be largely summed up in a formulation by John Gilissen, who defined custom as "an ensemble of usages of legal order, which has acquired obligatory force in a given socio-political group, by the repetition of public and peaceful acts in a relatively long time."[22] The validity of *opinio necessitatis*, that custom "must be considered obligatory by a great majority of the members of the group," depended less on the assent of the community than on judicial validation and acclamation. Otherwise, scholars have pointed out, *opinio juris* would be altogether too uncertain; custom could not acquire the necessary generality without giving rise to a number of disputes and having been approved by jurisprudence.[23]

The French jurist François Gény (1861–1959) was one of the most forceful advocates of customary law at the end of the nineteenth century. Gény argued that usages did not constitute legal custom, even when they reflected the psychological element of will, if they were without *opinio juris* which was "truly specific" of genuine custom.[24] Many acts, such as "the habits of daily life, what we call the mores of the people or of a certain class of people, the economic usages of commerce, agriculture, industry, etc...., the rules of civil behavior, the conventions of the world, such as the mode, or even moral or religious practices," remained "outside the positive legal order."[25] Customary law was far from having a universal character, as it was necessarily limited only to the juridical community where it originated and the sentiments of which it reveals.[26] To become legal custom, the usage had to amount to the exercise of a right by those who practiced it.

In other words, custom became customary law only when it was recognized in a formal adjudication and enforced by the courts.[27] Custom can be used by a judge to support his judgment, but it becomes law only when it is so used.[28] This process of judicialization of custom was undertaken by new elites, educated in the law faculty at medieval universities and recruited to serve for the

[22] John Gilissen, *La Coutume*, in *Typologie des sources du Moyen Age occidental*, ed. L. Genicot, vol. 41 (Turnhout: Brepols, 1982), 20 and 27.

[23] Lambert, *La Fonction du droit civil comparé*, 799.

[24] François Gény, *Méthode d'interprétation et sources en droit privé positif* (Paris: Librairie générale de droit & de jurisprudence, 1932), 320 (no. 110).

[25] Ibid.

[26] Ibid., 323.

[27] See Jean-Marie Carbasse, "Contribution à l'étude du processus coutumier: la coutume de droit privé jusqu'à la Révolution," *Droits* 3 (1986): 25–37.

[28] Yoshiyuki Noda, *Introduction to Japanese Law*, trans. Anthony H. Angelo (Tokyo: University of Tokyo Press, 1976), 218.

emerging state.[29] The French kings achieved control over the relations between private individuals through the systematic instruments of royal courts that had the power to find and enforce local custom. As Robert Jacob pointed out, one cannot disregard the question of power in the development of law.[30] By treating custom as autonomous from the state power, one risks explaining the evolution of law in dissociation from political circumstances.

In 1454, King Charles VII of France ordered that the *coutumes* of all customary law regions be written down, in order to make the law certain and eliminate recurring problems of proof. The ordinance of Montil-lez-Tours observed that by reducing customs to writing "lawsuits would be much shorter and the parties relieved of expenses and costs, and the judges would be able to pass better judgments and with greater certainty." The king ordered that "the customary lawyers, practitioners and people of each of the said provinces in our kingdom" come to an agreement about their customary rules and codify them.[31] Custom in France subsequently underwent systematization and rationalization through the selective process of redaction and homologation.

The recording of local customs marked an integral part of the ambitious legislative agenda of the king, aimed at promoting the legal unity of the kingdom.[32] Custom was selected and redacted by royal commissioners dispatched from the capital and was promulgated by regional charters sanctioned by the crown. The customary law campaign, which reached its peak in the second half of the sixteenth century, was enthusiastically supported by legal professionals who had to practice customary law at the royal courts.[33] Through the effective cooperation of courts and theoretical writers, French customary law was rapidly withdrawn from direct popular control and became enmeshed in all the complications of an elaborate legal technique.[34] The ideal of a common customary law emerged to serve as the basis of a uniform law in the country. The

[29] Peter Stein, "The Civil Law Doctrine of Custom and the Growth of Case Law," in *Scintillae Iuris: Studi in memoria di Gino Gorla* (Milan: Giuffre, 1994), vol. 1, 371.

[30] Jacob, "Les Coutumiers du XIIIe siècle," 105.

[31] Article 125. François Isambert, ed., *Recueil général des anciennes lois françaises depuis l'an 420 jusqu'à la révolution de 1789* (Paris: Belin-Leprieur, 1829), vol. 9, 252.

[32] Marie Seong-Hak Kim, "Civil Law and Civil War: Michel de L'Hôpital and the Spirit of Legal Reforms in Sixteenth-Century France," *Law and History Review* 28, no. 3 (2010): 791–826.

[33] For the reformation of French customs in the sixteenth century, see René Filhol, *Le Premier président Christofle de Thou et la réformation des coutumes* (Paris: Librairie du Recueil Sirey, 1937); Donald R. Kelley, "'Second Nature': The Idea of Custom in European Law, Society, and Culture," *The Transmission of Culture in Early Modern Europe*, eds. Anthony Grafton and Ann Blair (Philadelphia: University of Pennsylvania Press, 1990), 150–157; Marie Seong-Hak Kim, "Christophe de Thou et la réformation des coutumes: l'esprit de réforme juridique au XVIe siècle," *Tijdschrift voor rechtsgeschiedenis* 72 (2004): 91–102; Marie Seong-Hak Kim, "Custom, Community, and the Crown: Lawyers and the Reordering of French Customary Law," in *Between the Middle Ages and Modernity: Individual and Community in the Early Modern World*, eds. Charles H. Parker and Jerry H. Bentley (Lanham, MD: Rowman & Littlefield, 2007), 169–186.

[34] John P. Dawson, "The Codification of the French Customs," *Michigan Law Review* 38 (1940): 765–800.

codification of French civil law in 1804 was an accumulation and culmination of this development.

This brief examination of European history of customary law brings to the fore the problem of postulating customary law in the Chosŏn dynasty. Defined as legal rules, custom is different from what is said to have regulated the everyday lives of the people in premodern Korea. In Europe, judges at the royal courts who were educated in Roman law and canon law recognized and reconstructed local norms as customary law by sorting them according to Roman law vocabularies and concepts. No judicial mechanism to effect such judicial reworking of custom existed in Korea or elsewhere in East Asia. The Chosŏn dynasty had a well-established administrative bureaucracy, but no judicial interpretation took place outside centralized government activity. The decision over the legal status of a usage – whether or not to recognize it as law – was not within the power of the magistrates, whose judicial activity was simply part of comprehensive administrative function based on written formal rules. The magistrates were not specially trained in law; the same officials decided judicial cases and collected taxes.

The centralized nature of the Korean political and institutional tradition assumed uniform rule which was embodied in the state codes. The goal of the legal code was to construct an infallible system, encompassing all possible cases and all circumstances of violation.[35] All crimes needed to be provided for explicitly in the statutes and judges were expected to apply the rules strictly. This emphasis on a comprehensive system left little room for the magistrates to decide cases by anything other than the state codes. Given the significance of the imposing presence of state codes, as discussed in the following pages, and the absence of even a single redaction of customary laws, assertion of the existence of "custom" faces serious hurdles.

Law and Local Customs in Chosŏn Korea, 1392–1910

Comprehensiveness of the State Codes

It is beyond dispute that Korea, along with other East Asian countries, was particularly known for its reverence of written sources of law. The compilation and revision of the codes was given high priority in the Chosŏn dynasty. A native administrative and penal code, the *Kyŏngje yukchŏn* (Six-Division Code for Administration), was promulgated in 1397. It became the basis for the major legislative accomplishment of the early Chosŏn dynasty, the *Kyŏngguk taejŏn* (Great Code for Administering the Country).[36] This code, completed

[35] Shaw, "Traditional Korean Law and its Relation to China," 302.

[36] *Kyŏngguk taejŏn* (Seoul: Seoul Taehakkyo Kyujanggak, 1997). For Korean state codes, see, among others, Pak, *Hanguk pŏpchesa ko*; Cho Chi-man, *Chosŏn sidae ŭi hyŏngsa pŏp – Tae Myŏng ryul kwa kukchŏn* [Penal Law during the Chosŏn Period – The Great Ming Code and the National Law Code] (Seoul: Kyŏngin Munhwasa, 2009); Kim Chae-mun, *Hanguk chŏnt'ong ch'aekwŏn pŏp, kajok pŏp, sosong pŏp* [Obligations, Family Law, and Civil Procedure in

in 1471, remained the central law throughout the dynasty, and was revised, enlarged, and supplemented several times as *Sok taejŏn* (Supplementary Grand Code, 1746), *Taejŏn t'ongp'yŏn* (Great Code for Ruling the State, 1785), and *Taejŏn hoet'ong* (Grand Code for Ruling the State, 1865).

These codes faithfully followed the structure and, to a varying degree, the content of the penal code of the Chinese Ming dynasty (1368–1644). The first article in the penal section of the *Kyŏngguk taejŏn* explicitly stated that the *Ta Ming lü* (Great Ming Code) would be the basic law of the dynasty.[37] The spread of Chinese law to Korea thus took the form of a comprehensive, not piecemeal, reception of the Chinese code. Historians have pointed out, however, that Korean statutes regularly took precedence over Chinese provisions in cases of conflict of laws. The *Sok taejŏn* provided that the *Ta Ming lü*, as stipulated in the *Kyŏngguk taejŏn*, would remain the principle but the articles in the *Kyŏngguk taejŏn* and the *Sok taejŏn* must be enforced, when applicable, before the Chinese provisions.[38] The Chosŏn codes evolved considerably over the dynasty's five-hundred-year rule, but the overwhelming importance of Chinese law in the administration of traditional Korean justice was unquestionable.

The state code was organized according to six categories: *Ijŏn* (personnel), *Hojŏn* (finance), *Yejŏn* (rites), *Pyŏngjŏn* (the military), *Hyŏngjŏn* (punishments), and *Kongjŏn* (public works). The fact that the code's organization followed the administrative structure, which consisted of the six ministries, indicates its bureaucratic nature. The law provisions were basically composed of the definitions of prohibited acts and the punishments spelled out for such acts. The justice system was concerned with adjusting – or tuning – the degrees (*ryul* in Korean; *lü* in Chinese) of punishment to crimes listed in the code. The Chosŏn code was a criminal code that included scattered provisions on civil matters. Areas of private relations among individuals, such as marriage, succession, property, contracts, or sales, were governed by the same provisions as penal law provisions.[39] In the *Taejŏn hoet'ong*, for example, statutes governing inheritance were listed under the heading "private slaves" (*sach'ŏn*) in *Hyŏngjŏn* and under the heading "land" in *Hojŏn*. Adoption and marriage were regulated in *Yejŏn*, and family registry was governed by *Ijŏn*. The *Hojŏn* section further included litigation over

Traditional Korea] (Seoul: Tongguk Taehakkyo Ch'ulp'anbu, 2007). For English, see Shaw, *Legal Norms in a Confucian State*.

37 *Hyŏngjŏn, in Kyŏngguk taejŏn*, stipulated: "Yongyul: yong Tae Myŏng Yul (Use the Great Ming Code)."

38 Sim Chae-u, "Chosŏn malgi hyŏngsa pŏp ch'egye wa *Tae Myŏng ryul* ŭi wisang [The Structure of Penal Law and the Significance of *the Great Ming Code* in the Late Chosŏn Dynasty]," *Yŏksa wa hyŏnsil* 65 (2007), 127 note 12. It is safe to say that Korean law's supremacy was firmly established from the middle of the eighteenth century. Shaw, "Traditional Korean Law: A New Look," *Korea Journal* 13 (September 1973), 41.

39 Cho Yun-sŏn, *Chosŏn hugi sosong yŏngu* [A Study on Litigation in Late Sixteenth-Century Chosŏn] (Seoul: Kukhak Charyowŏn, 2002), 7–8.

land and houses, the collection of private debts, and statutes of limitations for various matters. These laws were mainly expressed as proscriptions or commands specifying the scale of penalties and violations were punished as crimes. The sections dealing with family matters and property included prohibitions with penalties similar to the purely penal sections of the code. Violators of laws concerning ownership of slaves or land were punished by beating and exile.[40]

The history of law and custom cannot be understood in disjunction from political development. Custom is particular to the European legal tradition because it was inseparable from the feudal fragmentation of political power.[41] During the early Middle Ages, the fragmentation of power resulted in a mosaic of jurisdictions and thus localization of custom. The definition of custom necessarily involved territorial limitations and local particularity. Custom was distinguished from civil and canon law because it was the rules of particular places. Medieval European states, lacking a unified legal system, had to control local usages by conferring regularity on them. In East Asia, administrative centralization preceded similar attempts in Europe by eight or nine centuries. Whereas royal courts in Europe competed with seigneurial courts over jurisdictional claims, Chinese provinces were ruled by functionaries controlled by the central government under a body of codified rules, uniform throughout the empire. In the eighth century, the Tang dynasty (618–907) launched a systematic codification of criminal laws and diverse rules, usages, and formulas of administration.

Having achieved administrative centralization and codification of law early on, and enjoying the plenitude of legislative power, neither the Chinese empires nor the Korean kingdoms had any need to confer on private usages the status of local custom independent and insulated from the codes. Korea, along with Japan before the onset of decentralizing tendencies in the late twelfth century, was heavily influenced by the Tang legal codes, a process analogous to the "reception" of Roman law in the European countries in the late Middle Ages. Korea did not witness the rise of local law independent from the state law. Unlike in Europe, the important source of tension in Korea was not between central law and local law but between central law and no law.[42]

The situation in France exemplifies how increasing professionalization of judicial process was effectively seized by the centralizing state. The recording of local customs marked an integral part of the ambitious legislative movements of the crown who set out to promote the legal unity of the kingdom. Local communities often resorted to the notion of equitable custom as a means to attack "unreasonable" seigneurial rights of the traditional landed aristocracy. When they contested feudal custom, they contrasted the "particular interests"

[40] Ibid., 104.

[41] For a succinct presentation of the meaning of custom in European history, see Bourgon, "La Coutume et le droit en Chine," 1088–1091.

[42] Shaw, "Traditional Korean Law and Its Relation to China," 309.

of the feudal class against the "public good," which they identified with the interests of the king and the "poor people."[43] The result was an extension of the sphere of public interest, represented by the king, at the expense of particular interests. There was resistance to this process but, against royal legislation and customary codification, the "old law" had already been seriously weakened as a viable alternative. Tackling seigneurial justice was attempted by the state through enlisting the support of legal professionals. None of these patterns are applicable in the East Asian context. With no competing jurisdictions, the state did not have an incentive to enhance judicial effectiveness.[44] With no seigneurial courts operating in the realm of customs in their histories, the governments in East Asia did not need to promote the development of a legal profession or the legitimation of state or imperial courts.

The role of the state in private conflicts reveals a fundamental difference between Europe and East Asia. In medieval France, the crown was, above all, a judge, the "debtor of justice." The popular image of King Saint Louis meting out justice under an oak tree sums up the mythical notion of royal justice. As a vicar of God on earth, the king was responsible for resolving disputes in an impartial and equitable way. From the notion of royal justice (*roi justicier*) emerged the judicial corps. It is difficult to point to a similar process in Korea, China, Japan, and that part of Vietnam belonging to the sphere of Chinese civilization. In the Sinicized world, the state was responsible for maintaining social order but not for dispensing justice in private relations. Certainly a ruler in East Asia, or anywhere for that matter, was concerned with ensuring propriety, fairness, and justice – in the basic and broad sense of the terms – to prevail among the subjects. But rendering justice as the most fundamental duty of the king was largely absent. Judicial courts in Europe were instruments of royal authority like in East Asia, but they still claimed that royal power was held in check by the "justice" that the law courts embodied.[45] East Asia did not have a similar notion.[46]

Chosŏn Korea had state institutions that were in charge of resolving disputes. But these institutions functioned as part of state administrative bureaucracy instead of separate entities that were responsible for administering justice in the name of the king. The idea of the state rendering judgment in private disputes according to legal principles, outside the state code and hence

[43] Martine Grinberg, *Ecrire les coutumes: les droits seigneuriaux en France, XVIe-XVIIIe siècle* (Paris: Presses universitaires de France, 2006); Marie Seong-Hak Kim, "Custom, Community, and the Crown," 178.

[44] According to Macauley, this lack of "institutional dynamic" led to the absence of lawyers and resulted in much less effective legal constructions in China. Melissa Ann Macauley, *Social Power and Legal Culture: Litigation Masters in Late Imperial China* (Stanford, CA: Stanford University Press, 1998), 9, 248.

[45] According to the sixteenth-century French writer Claude de Seyssel, the three "bridles" that checked royal power were religion, justice, and police (ordinances). Claude de Seyssel, *The Monarchy of France*, trans. Donald R. Kelley (New Haven: Yale University Press, 1981).

[46] The Board of Punishment was a ministry of order, not of justice. Jacob, "La Coutume, les mœurs et le rite," 151.

devoid of the elements of prohibition and punishment, was alien to East Asian legal tradition. Ulpian stated: "public law is that which respects the establishment of the Roman commonwealth, private law that which respects individuals' interests."[47] Private law refers to an ensemble of rule ascertained by legal scholars and applied by a judge to disputes between individuals according to established procedures. Defined as such, private law did not exist in East Asia. In Korea, as in China, laws foremost existed not as a means of resolving disputes between individuals but as an instrument of administrative power and public order. The evolution of Western legal tradition was basically the development of law concerned with resolving private disputes. Such a development was lacking in premodern East Asia, where laws did not address the populace at large but the state officials who needed them to perform their duties in administration.

Law-making in Korea involved piecemeal accumulation of royal edicts called *sugyo*.[48] These edicts were collected and codified as *Sugyo chimnok* (Collected Edicts) in 1698. A supplement, *Sinbo sugyo chimnok*, was issued in 1711. Royal edicts were periodically incorporated into the state codes. Because the state codes were indisputably penal in nature, some historians highlighted these royal edicts as examples of civil law. *Sugyo* supposedly included examples of customary practices that were given formal legal sanction, so the "people's will" was likely reflected in royal edicts.[49] Certainly *Sugyo* in Chosŏn law presents an important subject in Korean legal history. Its nature and function, and whether and how custom was acknowledged and inserted in the royal laws such as *Sugyo* need to be studied. When the state authorities considered local practices, it may well have been their intent not only to rectify them but also to rely on them to settle private disputes. But it seems certain anyhow that the magistrates did not imagine that law could proceed from popular usages. In order to postulate the presence of customary law, it is necessary to prove the commitment by state authority to confer a binding force on local practices. The assertion that the Chosŏn government codified rules from existing customary law that emanated from social reality requires qualification.

Chosŏn "Custom" that Was Not

It seems to be a fair assessment that the term custom has been used in Korean legal historiography with indifference to the difficulties its usages imply and, further, in dissociation from the historical nature of Korean law and its legal system. Two indigenous practices commonly listed by historians as the examples of "customary law" are uxorilocal (or matrilocal) marriage and the equal distribution of inheritance between all male and female heirs. Uxorilocal

[47] *The Digest of Justinian*, 1.1.1.

[48] Shaw, *Legal Norms in a Confucian State*, 32. See Chŏng Kŭng-sik, Cho Chi-man, and Kim Taehong, *Chosŏn hugi sugyo charyo chipsŏng* [Collection of *Sugyo* in Late Chosŏn Dynasty], 2 vols. (Seoul: Hanguk Pŏpche Yonguwŏn, 2009–2010).

[49] Chŏng Kŭng-sik, "Chosŏn sidae ŭi kwŏllyŏk pullip," 43–47.

marriage, known as *ch'ŏsŏhon* or *solsŏhon*, refers to a practice in which the wedding ceremony was held in the bride's house and the newlywed couple set up a household in the wife's parents' house. The couple stayed there until their children were born, usually a few years, before going to live with the husband's family.[50] It was a practice that had prevailed since the Koryŏ dynasty (918–1392), reflecting social equality in gender. The legal implication of this marriage practice concerned the inheritance system. In the Koryŏ dynasty and the early Chosŏn dynasty, daughters were on an equal footing with sons with regard to their right to inherit property. *Kyŏngguk taejŏn* stipulated the equal distribution of inheritance among all heirs, male and female.[51] The division of property took place through inter vivos gifts and postmortem inheritance. The main objects of distribution were slaves and land.[52] Normally slaves were given to children at the time of marriage. The *sach'ŏn* section in the code provided that "slaves not previously given by parents are divided regardless of the children's being alive or dead."[53] Freedom to make a testament was recognized in *Kyŏngguk taejŏn* but equal division among sons and daughters was firmly guaranteed by the provisions of the code.[54]

It has been well established that the institution of family in Korea underwent a significant change during the Chosŏn period because of the influence of the neo-Confucian philosophy that entered Korea in the late fourteenth century.[55] From the seventeenth century, the dominance of orthodox neo-Confucian ideology, which emphasized ancestor worship, led to the Confucianization of Korean lineage culture and organization, resulting in a dramatic transformation of native traditions along the lines of imported Confucian traditions. Ancestor worship became a major agent of change in the family system. The Confucian doctrine of ancestor ceremonies, which favored the eldest son who was to perform the rituals, gradually replaced equal inheritance with unequal divisions of property and made the eldest son the principal heir. Ritual recognition of the

[50] Pak, *Hanguk pŏpchesa ko*, 323–332.

[51] Kim Chae-mun, *Hanguk chŏnt'ong ch'aekwŏn pŏp*, 209–244; Kim Il-mi, "Chosŏn hugi chaesan sangsok kwansŭp: Ilche ha ku kwansŭp chosa pogosŏ rŭl chungshim ŭro [Inheritance Practice in the Late Chosŏn Dynasty: With a Focus on the Old Customs Survey Reports]," *Idae sawŏn* 11 (1973): 33–52.

[52] The Chosŏn society was a slave society. Slavery was legally abolished in 1894.

[53] See Mun Suk-cha, *Chosŏn sidae chaesan sangsok kwa kajok* [Property Succession and Family in the Chosŏn Period] (Seoul: Kyŏngin Munhwasa, 2004), 1–4; Chŏng Kŭng-sik, "Simyuk segi chaesan sangsok ŭi han illye: 1579 nyŏn Kwŏn ji ch'o Chŏng ssi hŏyŏ mungi ŭi punsŏk [A Case of Sixteenth-Century Property Succession: Analysis of *hŏyŏ mun'gi* of 1579 by Madam Chŏng, the Wife of Kwon Ji]," *Seoul Taehakkyo pŏphak* 47, no. 2 (2006), 268–302.

[54] Kim Min-jŏng, "*Kyŏngguk taejŏn* sangsok ippŏp chuŭi e kwanhan yŏngu: yuŏn sangsok kwa pŏpchŏng sangsok ŭl chungsim ŭro [A Study of Legislative Principles of Succession in *Kyŏngguk taejŏn*: With Particular Attention to Testamentary Succession and Intestate Succession]" (Master's thesis, Ewha Womans University, 2006), 28–37.

[55] Martina Deuchler, *The Confucian Transformation of Korea: A Study of Society and Ideology* (Cambridge, MA: Council on East Asian Studies, Harvard University, 1992); Mark Peterson, *Korean Adoption and Inheritance. Case Studies in the Creation of a Classic Confucian Society* (Ithaca, NY: East Asian Program, Cornell University, 1996).

eldest son's special status brought about economic primogeniture. In the early nineteenth century, Chŏng Yag-yong (1762–1836), a leading scholar of the "practical learning" (*sirhak*) school, blamed the partible inheritance of slaves – which he called an example of "bad law" – for the decline of prominent noble families in current economic difficulties.[56] Chŏng's concern about the negative impact of the partible property distribution rules on the maintenance of illustrious families led him so far as to advise the magistrates that they should at times depart from the strict application of law provisions and instead decide cases according to reason. In the cases involving less than prominent families, Chŏng added, the rule of equal distribution as provided in the *Kyŏngguk taejŏn* could be followed without problem.[57]

There is a certain truth in the observation that Koreans were far more orthodox in their interpretation of Confucian precepts than the Chinese. By the seventeenth century, the Korean family system had attained its full patrilineal structure, adapting to the new Confucian order. The stipulation in the Confucian classics that ancestors enjoy a sacrifice only when it is offered by an agnatic descendant led to a number of significant changes in Korean practices in marriage, adoption, and inheritance.

The Confucian ritual texts required that the wedding take place in the groom's house, and the government tried to replace uxorilocal marriage with virilocal marriage.[58] The length of the couple's sojourn with the wife's parents was shortened significantly over time as the characteristics of virilocal marriage became more evident. But, according to Deuchler, no native ceremonial rite in Chosŏn resisted Confucianization more persistently than the wedding rites.[59] For all its unique and entrenched nature, nevertheless, uxorilocal marriage was not "custom," or set of binding rules to which the recognition and force of law were accorded; it was instead a pattern of behavior and habits. The state simply treated the practice as something that needed to be corrected.

Likewise, the division of family property in equal shares was not a customary law; it was a codified law. Once custom is given formal legal sanction and becomes part of the official code, it is no longer custom. Additionally, there is no proof that the law of equal succession had been redacted under the influence of custom. If there was an inheritance "custom" in the Chosŏn dynasty, it was the practice of excluding women and disadvantaging younger sons. Equilateral inheritance, grounded on the uxorilocal marriage practice, was under attack from Confucian ritual practice by the seventeenth century.

56 Chŏng Yag-yong, *Yŏkchu Mongmin Simsŏ* [Annotated and Translated *Mongmin Simsŏ*], ed. and trans. Tasan Yŏnguhoe (Seoul: Ch'angjak kwa Pip'yongsa, 1984), vol. 4, *Ch'ŏngsong* section, Part II, in *Hyŏngjŏn*.

57 Ibid.

58 Early on, Chŏng To-jŏn (1337?-1398), the powerful statesman and neo-Confucian scholar, began to view uxorilocal marriage as a problem.

59 Deuchler, *The Confucian Transformation*, 244; Martina Deuchler, "The Tradition: Women during the Yi Dynasty," in *Virtues in Conflict: Tradition and Korean Women Today*, ed. Sandra Mattielli (Seoul: Samhwa Publishing Co. for the Royal Asiatic Society, Korea Branch, 1977), 15–17.

Transition to primogeniture was based on a popular consensus, first predominantly among the elite segment but spreading to the rest of society as Confucian values and norms were filtered down to the lower classes. Even this transformation of inheritance practice did not amount to the establishment of custom (*contra legem*), however, because there was no judicial approval of the practice.

The Confucian succession system favoring the eldest son apparently escaped the proscriptions by the government. Why the Chosŏn government did not attempt to modify the principle of equal distribution in its law codes has been the subject of debate.[60] The state's general indifference to the regulation of inheritance may be a factor. More fundamentally, it may have been because the state did not have the means to regulate and control private property.[61] Whatever the reason, the government left disputes arising from divergent inheritance practices to the decisions of local magistrates or ad-hoc consultations of the courtiers. Because of the prevalent belief among the people that primogeniture was the norm, there was little litigation initiated by daughters or younger sons. In rare cases in which the younger sons claimed their share, the magistrates dismissed the suits, declaring that unequal distribution was an "extralegal matter," outside the areas of the state's involvement.[62] The practice of preferential division, no matter how widespread from the seventeenth century, did not obtain the obligatory sanction backed by the state. Indeed it is worth recalling that the notion of "property succession" as a legal act requiring the state's approval did not exist in Korea before the colonial period. It was a concept introduced by the Japanese jurists.[63] In Chosŏn, only the practice of dividing the property of the deceased existed, with no involvement of the state. There was no probate or paperwork required.[64]

It becomes clear then that what is routinely referred to as "custom" (*kwansŭp*) in Korean scholarship is either elusive social habits and patterns of behavior that were present during the dynastic periods before the onset of the neo-Confucian influence or traditional laws that existed before the Japanese occupation. These indigenous practices and laws were different from binding local rules that were independent from, and susceptible to oppose, state law. Certain local rules were codified by the central government over time – through *Sugyo* for instance – but these usages were turned into legislation without taking the form of custom, that is, rules observed by people at the local level and discerned and approved through court decisions. Local customs did not

60 Pae Sang-hun, "Chosŏn hugi punhal sangsok kwanhaeng ŭi chisok e taehan sogo [A Short Study on the Continuing Practices of Partible Succession in Late Chosŏn]," *Hanguk minjok munhwa* 34 (2009), 204.

61 Mun Suk-cha, *Chosŏn sidae chaesan sangsok*, 12.

62 Chŏng Kŭng-sik, "Singminji ki sangsok kwansŭp pŏp," 295.

63 See Chapter 6.

64 When heirs inherited slaves, they only had to report the new ownership and obtain the state's certification (the *sach'ŏn* section in *Hyŏngjŏn*, in *Kyŏngguk taejŏn*). See Kim Chae-mun, *Hanguk chŏnt'ong ch'aekwŏn pŏp*, 245–252.

include a concept of legal rights as developed in Western civil law in which a citizen was presumably entitled to the enforcement of obligations.

The Chosŏn state was concerned with maintaining social harmony and order, but less so with refereeing in private relations. Resolving disputes over private interests lay within the realm of Confucian informal normativity, unless provided in the state code to deal with egregious cases, the code itself being a compendium of measures devised to fulfill a moral agenda. Good or bad customs were invariably measured against centrally imposed norms of a moral nature, and correcting them meant to bring them in line with the mainstream practices of state Confucianism.[65] The royal bureaucracy repeatedly voiced the concern to rectify "mores and habits" (*p'ungsok*; *fengsu* in Chinese). In France, judges reworked feudal customs into customary law by abolishing and modifying iniquitous and unreasonable customs and extracting rules that reflected the public good. Combating bad customs was the subject of judicial interpretation in courts through contest between individuals asserting rights, at least after the reception of Roman law procedures. In contrast, local customs in Korea were taken into account by the authorities in order to administer populations, fundamentally bureaucratic in methods. At times, the magistrates considered local practices, but they were not bound by them when they made decisions. Once decisions were rendered in consideration of local usages, the parties did not have recourse for their enforcement. There was no pretense on the part of state officials of respect for local custom as law.

Judicial Administration

Under the Chosŏn legal system, there were three central judicial institutions, Sahŏnbu (Censorate), Hyŏngjo (Ministry of Punishments), and Hansŏngbu (the capital's authorities), together called Sampŏpsa (three grand judicial offices).[66] In the provinces, the governor of each province, and the magistrates under him, were in charge of judicial affairs along with general administrative duties. Ŭigŭmbu was a special court in the capital with jurisdiction over the royal family and the *yangban* class. The *yangban* (aristocracy) were literally the members of the "two orders" (civil and military officials) in the state bureaucracy.[67] Their alleged wrongdoing – violating the Confucian status order – was adjudicated without possibility of appeal. For criminal cases involving the non-*yangban* class, an appeals system was in operation, allowing decisions to be reviewed by the governor, next by officials at Hyŏngjo, Hansŏngbu, or Sahŏnbu, and finally by the king. Hansŏngbu, with jurisdiction over disputes regarding land, forest, and graveyard ownership, and Changyewŏn, which adjudicated disputes

[65] Shaw, "Traditional Korean Law and Its Relation to China," 305; Shaw, "Traditional Korean Law: A New Look," 42.

[66] For the judicial system in Chosŏn, see Kim Chae-mun, *Hanguk chŏnt'ong ch'aekwŏn pŏp*, 329–330, 429–431.

[67] Ki-Baik Lee, *A New History of Korea*, trans. Edward W. Wagner and Edward J. Shultz (Seoul: Ilchogak, 1984), 172–175.

of slave ownership, were the two institutions in charge of civil matters in Seoul. But jurisdictional divisions, defined by subject matter, were not strictly observed, and litigants preferred bringing suits to Hyŏngjo because it could impose more severe penal punishment.[68] Some government officials suggested that this practice be prohibited.[69] But the king was reluctant to dismiss on procedural grounds suits brought to the Hyŏngjo because it felt morally incapable of turning a deaf ear to the subjects pleading against injustice and inequity.[70]

In short, there was a state mechanism in Chosŏn by which disputes were resolved. But it was different from the civil law system. In order to speak of a civil law system, there must be law and procedure, dictated by private interests and implemented by trained legal practitioners. Although "civil suits" (*sasong*) as distinguished from "criminal suits" (*oksong*) existed in Chosŏn, there was no established procedure different from the one used in penal cases. Even for *sasong*, the magistrates applied law provisions that entailed punishments. The presiding officials were not jurists and their decisions were reviewed in the same way as their administrative acts were reviewed.

A crucial factor that distinguished the development of law in Chosŏn Korea from Europe was the absence of legal professionals. Without legal scholars or lawyers, there was no juristic or jurisprudential foundation to develop binding rules from customs to be enforced by the state.[71] French customary law owed its theoretical development to legal practitioners imbued with legal humanism. In the sixteenth century, the activities of doctrinal writers, many of whom were practitioners of private law, were in symbiotic relations with the jurisprudence of the courts, the scholars progressively compiling and systematizing customs that the judges enforced. The establishment of royal courts staffed by professional jurists and the systematic manner in which they intervened in the process of resolving disputes among individuals promoted the development of private law. In Korea, in contrast, there were no legally trained judges, lawyers, scholars, or notaries. The study of law – *yurhak* – existed but it was regarded as a branch of mere technical learning, inferior to Confucian scriptural learning. *Yurhak* was not studied at the National Confucian Academy (Sŏnggyungwan) but was taught and examined as one of the miscellaneous examinations (*chapkwa*). Those who passed these examinations assisted in

[68] Cho Yun-sŏn, *Chosŏn hugi sosong yŏngu*, 81–85.

[69] *Sŭngjŏngwŏn ilgi* [The Daily Records of Royal Secretariat of the Chosŏn Dynasty], ed. Kuksa P'yŏnch'an Wiwŏnhoe (http://sjw.history.go.kr), the reign of King Hyŏnjong, December 12, 1665 (year 6).

[70] Cho Yun-sŏn, *Chosŏn hugi sosong yŏngu*, 86.

[71] No development of civil law was possible, amounting to a situation akin to the "age without jurists" in European legal history in the early Middle Ages. See Manlio Bellomo, *The Common Legal Past of Europe 1000–1800*, trans. Lydia G. Cochrane (Washington D.C.: The Catholic University of America Press, 1995), Ch. 2. Law can exist without jurisprudence, but law without jurisprudence is uncertain. Unless there are jurists to interpret the law, the rights of persons cannot be secure. Ken Pennington, "Law, Feudal," *Dictionary of the Middle Ages: Supplement 1* (New York: Charles Scribner's Sons-Thompson-Gale, 2004), 320–323.

FIGURE 1.1. **Trial scene during the Chosŏn dynasty (1392–1910).** The magistrate is seated on the left; the two parties are sitting on the ground. From *The Second Annual Report on the Reforms and Progress in Korea, 1908–9* (publication of the Residency General of Korea, 1909).

trials but were not expected to undertake jurisprudential activities that could turn the magistrates' decisions into legal precedents.

Pak Il-wŏn, a Chosŏn scholar and official who compiled the cases decided at the Hyŏngjo into *Ch'ugwanji* in 1781, deplored the tendency of the magistrates to view the acquisition of legal knowledge as unnecessary and even demeaning. He wrote:

> The literati only like to talk about the literary classics and regard studying law as a shameful activity. They throw law books in the attic. When a candidate takes the civil service examination or an official takes a test for promotion, they read the *Kyŏngguk taejŏn* but it is only a half-hearted effort to evade responsibilities. It is superficial, with no real outcome. Then, overnight, they become magistrates and find themselves having to adjudicate cases involving imprisonment and convicts. They have no idea which law provision applies to which crime, and they simply rely on law clerks to decide sentences. The law clerks often abuse their power and play tricks: they pick and choose law provisions, depending on whether they want to deal with the parties leniently or harshly, and the sentences go up or down. All the magistrates do is to sit in the office and place their signatures on the judgments. How can one say that this country takes law seriously?[72]

[72] *Ch'ugwanji*, cited from Kim Chae-mun, *Hanguk chŏnt'ong ch'aekwŏn pŏp*, 426–427.

In East Asia, legal specialists were not numerous enough in number, nor influential enough in government, to exercise a consistent, rationalizing influence in the judicial decision-making process.[73] There were litigation experts, called *oejibu*, people who prepared the necessary documents for suits and trials – the functional equivalents of Western attorneys – in the early years of the Chosŏn dynasty.[74] But their activities were proscribed in the last quarter of the fifteenth century, coinciding with the maturation of Confucian philosophy in Korea, because it was thought that they incited disputes and promoted discord. They were blamed for instigating litigations, thereby harming justice.[75] They were called "gangs who reside in Seoul seeking profits" and their abuses, profiting from human disputes, were strenuously denounced. The suppression of litigation helpers continued until 1905.[76] The deeply-ingrained Confucian ideology led to the assumption that litigation was immoral; private legal service could not possibly be morally legitimate.[77] Law existed not to protect individuals' rights but to exact punishment on transgressors of established norms, laying out proper behavior. Just as in China, a person brought before the court was considered, more or less, guilty until proven otherwise and he or she had no right to be assisted in proceedings.[78]

As with any society, there were incessant disputes over private interests in Chosŏn Korea. Evidence shows that Koreans were eager to have their grievances heard in court and filed a flood of suits and appeals over landownership, slave ownership, inheritance, and disputes over gravesite plots.[79] This finding provides a useful corrective to the commonly accepted view that most people sought to avoid involvement with the courts and the legal process at all costs and that there was an excessive emphasis on local arbitration and informal settlement.[80] Petitioners with all manner of complaints could be found at all venues, from the county magistrate's office to various special appeal facilities such as the petition drum outside the royal palace in the capital. William Shaw stated that Koreans in the seventeenth and eighteenth centuries "loved

[73] Shaw, "Traditional Korean Law and Its Relation to China," 317.

[74] Cho Yun-sŏn, *Chosŏn hugi sosong yŏngu*, 279–287. For their Chinese counterparts, see Macauley, *Social Power and Legal Culture*, 112.

[75] Shaw, "Traditional Korean Law," 50; Pak, *Hanguk pŏpchesa ko*, 316.

[76] In China, literati were prohibited from engaging in legal activities as early as 1382, when the Ming emperor Taizu promulgated the Horizontal Tablet. In 1771, a substitute was added to the code to punish licentiates "if they were found to be posing as a plaintiff or a witness in a lawsuit and falsely accusing another person in court." Macauley, *Social Power and Legal Culture*, 112.

[77] Huang, *Civil Justice in China*, 220.

[78] Sim Chae-u, *Chosŏn hugi kukka kwŏllyŏk kwa pŏmjoe t'ongje* [State Power and the Control of Crime in Late Chosŏn] (Seoul: T'aehaksa, 2009). For China, see Bodde and Morris, *Law in Imperial China*, 23–28.

[79] Chŏn Kyŏng-mok, "Sansong ŭl t'onghae pon Chosŏn hugi sabŏp chedo unyong silt'ae wa kŭ t'ŭkching [The Operation and the Characteristics of the Legal System of Late Chosŏn Seen through the Adjudication of the Ownership of Mountains]," *Pŏpsahak yŏngu* 18 (1997): 5–31.

[80] Pak Pyong-ho, *Hanguk pŏpchesa ko*, 235.

to litigate."[81] The magistrate's offices were overloaded with petitioners who wanted to have their cases heard. The district magistrates were not able to accomplish much else.

Some scholars equated this widespread popular litigation culture (*minsok hosong*) with a high legal consciousness.[82] It seems there was relatively easy access to law courts. According to the eighteenth-century Confucian scholar and magistrate An Chŏng-bok (1712–1791), the state could understand the situations of the people only when the doors to the government offices remained wide open.[83] Chŏng Yag-yong stated that going to the law courts should be made as easy as going to one's parents' house.[84] But the finding that there were abundant lawsuits regarding private disputes does not mean that Korea had civil law and an established civil justice system. Private disputes made up a considerable portion of the caseloads, but they were muddled with judgment of moral responsibility and imposition of criminal penalties. Litigiousness is not the same as the assertion of rights. In a strictly status-oriented society, lawsuits were likely the last recourse for ordinary people. Indeed, the fact that the justice system of the Chosŏn dynasty operated with the purpose of resolving grievances of the people, not according to clear and definite set of substantive rules but still giving satisfaction to the people's expectation that the state would adjudicate "fairly," may explain in part how the dynasty's rule lasted for more than 500 years.

The state's lack of interest in meddling in private relations is striking. The government maintained a system in which the state certified property transactions. *Iban* was an official document issued by the state, certifying sale, inheritance, adoption, and other transactions. After purchasing slaves, one obtained a state certificate confirming the transaction.[85] But the state was mainly concerned with eliminating problems that might impede tax collection or lead to litigations.[86] Many disputes involved the practice of multiple ownership of the same land because of so-called topsoil ownership, which occurred when a tenant made significant improvements and obtained ownership of the land under permanent tenancy. The practice proliferated and ownership was often not clear. The state regularly intervened in disputes between the landlord and the tenant when tax liability was at issue.[87] On the other hand, in cases between a

[81] Shaw, "Social and Intellectual Aspects," 42.

[82] Im Sang-hyŏk, "Chosŏn chŏngi minsa sosong kwa sosong iron ŭi chŏngae [Civil Litigation in the Early Chosŏn Dynasty and the Development of Litigation Theories]" (PhD diss., Seoul National University, 2000), 4, 168.

[83] *Imgwan chŏngyo*, cited from Kim, Chae-mun, *Hanguk chŏnt'ong ch'aekwŏn pŏp*, 332.

[84] Chŏng Yag-yong, *Yŏkchu Mongmin simsŏ*, vol. 4 (*Ch'ŏngsong* section, Part I, in *Hyŏngjŏn*).

[85] Obtaining *iban* consisted of five steps: application, submission of documents of proofs, interview of the applicant, interview of witnesses, and issuance of the certificate. It was rare that an *iban* application was rejected. See Chŏng Kŭng-sik, "Simyuk segi iban tu kŏn [Two Cases of *iban* in the Sixteenth Century]," *Seoul Taehakkyo pŏphak* 47, no. 3 (2006): 464–498.

[86] The situation was largely the same in China. See Melissa Macauley, "A World Made Simple: Law and Property in the Ottoman and Qing Empires," *Journal of Early Modern History* 5 (2001): 331–352.

[87] Cho Yun-sŏn, *Chosŏn hugi sosong yŏngu*, 144–152.

landlord and a tenant that involved disputes over rent, the state tended to leave such matters to be resolved by the parties.[88]

Private parties in the Chosŏn dynasty engaged in sales and purchases and concluded contracts. But the existence of contracts itself does not prove that the magistrates decided cases according to legal norms. The state code did not regulate contracts. Contracts certainly provided important proofs for the magistrates who had to rule in disputes between parties. But proofs answer questions of fact whereas civil justice still requires legal norms; the judge needs laws according to which he constructs the contractual language to resolve questions of law before each party's rights and liabilities can be determined.[89] In traditional Korea, the state code did not provide substantive rules to be enforced by the court. Contracts existed; contract law did not.

Judicial Procedures

Recently some Korean scholars called attention to the development of procedural law in the Chosŏn dynasty. Critical of the traditional view that Korean society promoted compromise and settlement through concessions with no regard to rights, they pointed to the existence of procedural rules in various codes and compilations of handbooks for magistrates. Examples of procedural rules included in the *Kyŏngguk taejŏn* were many.[90] The *Sach'ŏn* section in the *Hyŏngjŏn* included elaborate rules: if a party prevailed twice in three trials, the decision was final and the case would not be not heard again (*samdo tŭksin*); a personal appearance at court was required within fifty days after the filing of a suit in order to avoid default judgment (*ch'inch'ak pŏp*); there were also regulations over the change of venue and conflict of interest (*sangp'i*). The *Chŏnt'aek* section in *Hojŏn* provided that suits over land and residence had to be filed within five years following the rise of the disputes; slave ownership disputes had to be filed within three years.

The *Sok taejŏn*, promulgated in 1746, provided statute of limitations of sixty years for reclaiming fugitive slaves. If one filed a suit past the time limit, he was punished for willingly filing an unreasonable suit (*piri hosong*) and the magistrate (*suryŏng*) who knowingly allowed the filing was punished. Assertion of ownership against squatters was not bound by the statute of limitation, although later, in *Sok taejŏn*, the occupier's right was strengthened. In *Taejŏn t'ongp'yŏn*, the duties of the owner for timely assertion of ownership were further specified.[91] The state added new chapters (*Ch'ongni and Mungi*) in the code *Sok taejŏn*, in which were gathered procedural rules that had been scattered

[88] Ibid., 147–148.

[89] Jérôme Bourgon, "Ditan de tu'an: shilun Qingdai falü wenhua zhong de 'xiguan' yu 'qiyue' [Figures in the Carpet: "Customs" and "Contracts" in Qing Legal Culture]," in *Ming Qing falü lianzuo zhong de quanli he wenhua*, eds. Qiu Pengsheng and Chen Xiyuan (Taipei: Lianjing Chuban Gongsi, 2009), 238–246.

[90] Kim Chae-mun, *Hanguk chŏnt'ong ch'aekwŏn pŏp*, 267–278 and 364–370; Cho Yun-sŏn, *Chosŏn hugi sosong yŏngu*, 37; Im, "Chosŏn chŏngi minsa sosong," 92–97.

[91] Cho Yun-sŏn, *Chosŏn hugi sosong yŏngu*, 97.

in different places in the codes. The sixteenth century saw the appearance of handbooks of procedure written by private authors, including *Sasong yuch'wi* (Classification of Legal Proceedings) written by Kim Paek-kan in 1585.[92] Its revised editions in *Kyŏlsong yuch'wi* (Classification of Adjudications) (1649) and *Kyŏlsong yuch'wi po* (Supplement to the Classification of Adjudications) (1707) included additional rules involving suits. Together they revealed a sophisticated level of procedural regulations.

It may be problematic, however, to postulate a system of civil law in premodern Korea with an exclusive focus on procedure. The statute of limitations was not regularly observed and the finality of decisions often ignored.[93] The claimant could continue to file suits until satisfied with the decision. A common method of reopening the case was to bring the same case to a new magistrate who replaced the official that had rendered the original decision.[94] The terms of local bureaucrats were generally short, ranging from one or two years for governors and three to five years for magistrates. Frequent replacement of local magistrates was considered necessary because, apart from the fact the officials preferred posts in the capital, regular transfers supposedly reduced the abuse of power on the local level. The goal of promoting integrity in judicial affairs was attempted less through structural and institutional mechanisms limiting the authority of the officials than through the personnel system limiting the length of their tenure. In any case, the principle of *res judicata* did not exist. Despite the provision in the code providing for tripartite review, there was no method to prevent the existing decision from being overturned by the newly appointed magistrate in the locality.

The representatives of central power only reluctantly intervened in private litigations; when they did they decided the cases without referring to any preconstituted norms. Legal decisions in civil matters were based not on substantive rules to be enforced but on the particularities or circumstances of the case.[95] The administration of law took place by taking people and situations into account in an individual fashion. The Chosŏn government's unwillingness to interfere with private disputes was grounded foremost in the belief that litigation was immoral. The main objective of adjudication was to straighten moral attitudes, and the merit of the individual parties' claims was regarded

[92] See Chŏng Kŭng-sik and Im Sang-hyŏk, eds. *Simyuk segi chipsŏng* [A Compilation of Sixteenth-Century Handbooks for Civil Procedure] (Seoul: Pŏpche Yŏnguwŏn, 1999). For *Sasong yuch'wi*, see Kim Chae-mun, *Hanguk chŏnt'ong ch'aekwŏn pŏp*, 325–400.

[93] Chŏn, "Sansong," 21–26.

[94] There were concerns regarding the proper resolution of penal cases because of the frequent replacement of magistrates, but it was argued that in Korea, with a territory much smaller than China, the problems would be reduced as long as "the order at the court is clearly maintained." *Chosŏn wangjo sillok* [The Annals of the Chosŏn Dynasty], ed. Kuksa P'yŏnch'an Wiwŏnhoe (http://sillok.history.go.kr), *Chungjong sillok*, May 20, 1519 (year 14). There was widespread optimism that central power could effectively regulate the local administration.

[95] Bourgon, "Uncivil Dialogue," 60 ("Legal cases were decided on the basis of the understanding of the circumstances (*qingli*) as the one and only rule").

as less important than the need to propagate virtuous conduct and punish the undisciplined. Procedural laws were geared to "stop suits" (*tansong*) through quick disposition, with the ultimate goal of achieving an ideal society without litigation and restoring original perfection. Tansong dogam, an institution for summary resolutions of suits, was established in the fifteenth century, at a time when cases filed over slave ownership disputes had climbed to an unprecedented level.[96] Filing legal complaints was not prohibited, but it was to be deterred and discouraged as much as possible. Creating harmony in society with no legal wrangling was intended to clear a stream at its source, whereas disposing of disputes would merely have improved the flow temporarily.[97]

Most civil complaints were appeals for a decision of the judge to charge the opponents with a criminal offense. Litigation commonly started with a complaint that the other party had violated his or her moral obligations, as exemplified in Confucian texts, and therefore deserved punishment.[98] When a landowner filed a suit against a party who had set up a gravesite in his land without permission, the owner almost invariably requested that the defendant be punished first for his immoral behavior for trespassing – and creating the dispute – before demanding that the grave be removed.[99] The main concerns of the litigants were to show that they were decent people, had been unjustly harmed, and, above all, were morally superior to their opponents. They flocked to the court to prove that they were "right," not by resorting to established legal principles but by relying on the individual judge's sense of justice and moral indignation. The enforcement of obligations largely remained within the discretion of the magistrate. The absence of legal professionals meant that a trial was not a contest based on legal reasoning but a series of moral appeals to adjudicators. Many cases filed at the state institutions dealt with land sales, tenancy disputes, inheritance disputes, or marriage affairs, but they rarely approximated civil law cases because they were not assertions of private rights; rather they were supplications to the state officials to hear the sufferings of the plaintiffs and the unfairness of the situations. Recognizing that commoners were quite willing to engage in formal litigation does not prove that there was a consciousness of legal rights and obligations.

The legal culture in which enforcing a right was viewed as going against moral principles – potentially against the existing hierarchy – did not provide an environment favorable for the development of private rights. This situation applied to both penal and civil law cases. It is well known that Korean law codes, while adopting the Chinese penal law, included special rules that dealt with crimes allegedly disrupting social hierarchy – for example, crimes against kin and social superiors – more harshly than Chinese rules.[100] Disputes

[96] *Chosŏn wangjo sillok*, *Sŏngjong sillok*, January 12, 1481 (year 12).

[97] *Sŭngjŏngwŏn ilgi*, the reign of King Sukjong, August 19, 1677 (year 3).

[98] Pak, *Hanguk pŏpchesa ko*, 251.

[99] Chŏn, "Sansong," 30–31.

[100] Cho Chi-man, "*Kyŏngguk taejŏn Hyŏngjŏn* kwa *Tae Myŏng ryul*: silch'e pŏp kyujŏng ŭl chungsim ŭro [*Kyŏngguk taejŏn Hyŏngjŏn* and *Tae Myŏng ryul* – Focusing on Substantive Law]," *Pŏpsahak yŏngu* 34 (2006), 20–26.

among family members were viewed with particular aversion, and wrangling between the legitimate and illegitimate branches of a family was decided a priori in the legitimate branch's favor.[101] In theory, slaves could file suits against masters, but the magistrates reviewed such claims only after duly punishing the slaves for violating the established social order by challenging their masters.[102] An Chŏng-bok argued that litigations among family members over property should be resolved by arbitration, not by the regular adjudication process.[103] Chŏng Yag-yong stressed that legal disputes within family should be dealt with strictly in order to discourage them.[104]

The state and the ruling elite's adoption of a strict application of Confucian morality and rites may have been one of the most conspicuous characteristics of Korean legal culture. Under the paramount Confucian influence, rites were inseparable from social norms, and correct observance of rituals was a preeminent concern for the governing elite. Proper ritual behavior (*ye*) was regarded as a moral imperative, and laws and regulations had to play an important role to deter the common people from straying away from it.[105]

In Europe, rites were thought of in terms of liturgy and dogma and the responsibility for ensuring ritual uniformity was entrusted to the church. Ecclesiastical courts existed in separation from state courts. Of course, this does not mean that there was a separation of religion and politics. Europe witnessed recurring religious wars in which the Christian monarchs assumed it as their duty to ensure religious unity within their kingdoms by eradicating heretics. The kings often sanctioned persecutions and massacres to compel ritual uniformity and to impose doctrinal agreement, for example, over the "meaning" of the Eucharist. Nevertheless, a fundamental mark of Christian Europe lay in the Augustinian dualism, the City of God and the City of man remaining two distinct entities. The long conflict between the popes and the emperors which interspersed European history would have been unthinkable in Korea and elsewhere in East Asia. In Chosŏn, rites were detached from religious dogma and their proper observance remained squarely within the responsibility of the state.[106] The reason that statute laws were particularly constraining was because they supposedly implemented ritual rules.

In Chosŏn Korea, as a whole, the absence of an institutional framework to resolve private disputes according to fixed legal principles and concepts

[101] Cho Yun-sŏn, *Chosŏn hugi sosong yŏngu*, 156–157.

[102] Ibid., 219–220.

[103] An Ch'ŏng-bok, *Imgwan chŏngyo* (1738), cited from Kim Chae-mun, *Hanguk chŏnt'ong ch'aekwŏn pŏp*, 331; see also Cho Yun-sŏn, *Chosŏn hugi sosong yŏngu*, 254.

[104] Chŏng Yag-yong, *Yŏkchu Mongmin Simsŏ*, vol. 4 (*Ch'ŏngsong* section in *Hyŏngjŏn*).

[105] Martina Deuchler, "Neo-Confucianism in the Early Joseon Dynasty: Some Reflections on the Role of *Ye*," in *Korean Philosophy: Its Tradition and Modern Transformation*, ed. Korean national Commission for UNESCO (Elizabeth, NJ: Hollym, 2004), 50. See also Martina Deuchler, *The Confucian Transformation of Korea: A Study of Society and Ideology* (Cambridge, MA: Council on East Asian Studies, Harvard University, 1992).

[106] Jacob, "La Coutume, les moeurs et le rite," 152–154.

hindered people's assertion of their rights through formal adjudicative methods. Without institutional machinery to delineate the boundaries of individual rights, Korean customs did not develop into private law.

The Myth of Custom

The tendency of historians of Korean law to ascertain the existence of a spontaneous private law order in premodern society can be seen against the backdrop of a broader historiographical trend. Whether or not custom – or more specifically *opinio necessitatis* – is the universal origin of law is a debate that has long consumed generations of legal historians. The idea of custom as the spirit of law (*volksgeist*) was first proposed and vigorously defended by Savigny (1779–1861) in the nineteenth century. Savigny wanted to create a German code that would reflect the *ius commune*, Roman law as implemented in German historical situations. His teachings transformed the notion of custom into a theoretical and methodological question germane to modern codifications and elaborations of civil law. The German Historical School held that legislation was a statement of preexisting law, embodied in popular customs. This view was a direct rejection of the idea that custom drew its legal force from approval by the legislator.[107] The nineteenth-century Exegetical School unequivocally linked custom to the authority of the state. Scholars of this school, like modern positivists, refused to recognize a source of law other than legislation; custom had legal force only when it was explicitly allowed in the law.[108] According to Gény, the Historical School's supposition of a romantic and mysterious *opinio juris* was as much a fiction as the Exegetical School's hypothesis of tacit approval by the legislator.[109]

Of late, modern historians have downplayed the spontaneous nature of customary law, which they called the "myth" of custom. According to Robert Jacob and Jacques Krynen, medieval European customary law was not a direct exposition of popular usages that somehow matured into law over time. It was instead a result of long and careful doctrinal efforts by jurists and legal practitioners, combined with the initiative of the sovereign which was determined to rationalize the state's legal system. Krynen has argued that the king in late medieval and early modern France was not simply confirming preexisting customs but in fact creating a new law. The king had the mission to preserve "good custom." Custom thus became subject to the force of sovereign commandment, remaining under

[107] In Germany, this debate was known as the debate between the Romanists and the Germanists. Peter Stein, *Roman Law in European History* (Cambridge: Cambridge University Press, 1999), 116–123.

[108] This was called the "recognition theory" (*Gestattungstheorie*). Against this theory, scholars belonging to the Historical School argued that the *opinio juris* of custom existed prior to recognition or implementation by any institutions. Known as the "conviction theory" (Überzeugungstheorie), this latter view emphasizes the nature of customary law as an explicit and spontaneous expression of the spirit of the people.

[109] Gény, *Méthode d'interprétation*, vol. 1, 347.

the constant threat of being denounced as corrupt. Krynen concludes: "the royal policy of censuring and regulating customs unfolded in the full context of legislative power."[110] Customary law in Europe was "above all an instrument forged for the needs of regulation imposed on the society by the state law."[111]

Many theorists in early modern Europe took pains to attribute to the king a plenitude of legislative power. They attributed the legal force of custom to the will of the crown, on the basis of the principle "*princeps legibus solutus est*" (the prince is not bound by the law).[112] The French political thinker Jean Bodin (1530–1596) argued that the power of custom was not at all like that of law, because "custom has no force but by sufferance, and so long as it pleases the sovereign prince," who in turn possessed the sole authority to convert a custom into law "by putting thereupon his own confirmation." Thus, "all the force of laws and customs lies in the power of him that has the sovereignty in a commonwealth."[113] A similar opinion was presented by the English political philosopher Thomas Hobbes (1588–1679): "long use" of custom does not confer the authority of law; only the will of the sovereign does.[114] These statements then render suspect the idea of fortuitous customary law. Just as it is problematic to speak about spontaneous customary law in Europe, so it is misleading to speak about customary law in premodern Asia.

A look at another historiographical trend may shed further light. A group of historians in the late nineteenth and twentieth centuries emphasized the existence of liberal and democratic elements of customary law before the rise of the administrative state that embarked on regulating private legal relations and activities. It was part of the historicist reaction against the rigid dogmatic legal positivism and the purely grammatical mode of the juristic practice of the School of Exegesis. François Olivier-Martin, the great historian of French customary law, tried to rehabilitate custom as original and pure expressions of French law and insisted on presenting a customary law which the French monarchy fully respected.[115] Emphasizing the distinction between the sphere of

110 Krynen, "Entre science juridique et dirigisme," 181.

111 Jacob, "La Coutume, les moeurs et le rite," 151.

112 *The Digest of Justinian*, 1.3.31; William F. Church, *Constitutional Thought in Sixteenth-Century France* (New York: Octagon Books, 1969, 1941), 101; Olivier-Martin, *Les Lois du roi*, 93.

113 Jean Bodin, *Les Six livres de la république* (Paris, 1577), book I, ch. XI, 302.

114 Hobbes wrote: "When long use obtaineth the authority of a Law, it is not the Length of Time that maketh the Authority, but the Will of the Sovereign signified by his silence, (for Silence is sometimes an argument of Consent) and it is no longer Law, then the Sovereign shall be silent therein. And therefore if the Sovereign shall have a question of Right grounded, not upon his present Will, but upon the Lawes formerly made, the Length of Time shal bring no prejudice to his Right: but the question shal be judged by Equity. For many unjust Actions, and unjust Sentences, go uncontrolled a longer time than any man can remember. And our Lawyers account no Customes Law, but such as reasonable, and that evill Customes are to be abolished: But the Judgement of what is reasonable, and of what is to be abolished, belongth to him that maketh the Law, which is the Sovereign Assembly, or Monarch." Thomas Hobbes, *Leviathan*, ed. Richard Tuck (Cambridge: Cambridge University Press, 1991, 1660), 184–185 (Part II, Chapter 26).

115 See Krynen, "The Absolute Monarchy," 29.

private law and the sphere of public law in old France, he argued that the king did not in principle interfere with custom and instead respected the rights of his subjects to govern their legal relations by their own laws. Evidence is abundant, to be sure, that the French monarchy intervened in both the compilation and the implementation of custom. Nevertheless, claimed Olivier-Martin, the compilation of customs did not aim to "modify the nature of customary law in any way."[116]

Just as Olivier-Martin stressed liberties in old France supported by the liberal-minded kings, Korean scholars have tried to present a view of the benevolent kings in dynastic Korea. The French historians' idealization on the liberal nature of the ancient régime monarchy was prompted by certain disillusion with the modern state's expansive reach and its attempts to control minute aspects of private legal relations. The Korean historians, on their part, seemed to be interested in distinguishing the alleged consensual nature of traditional Korean law from the authoritarian nature of colonial law under the firm grip of the colonial governor during Japanese rule. Reluctant to give credit to the colonizers for establishing and unifying the contractual private law regime, these scholars have been inclined to find the traces of democratic institutions in the nation's legal past. They thus conjured up a customary law of popular origin that supposedly coexisted with – and formed the foundation of – the comprehensive state law codes of the Chosŏn dynasty. The romanticized view of custom as living law in Chosŏn Korea combined with the recognition of the centralized power of the king to create a view of law that existed outside the state code and was apparently tolerated by a munificent monarchy. In this portrayal, the kings, restrained by Confucian morality, supposedly allowed the people to be governed by their own law. But the view of Korean kings respecting the legal autonomy of the people cannot be sustained in the historical reality of Chosŏn Korea.

When Korean historians argue that premodern Korea was governed by custom that was a true source of private law, they are inadvertently relying on a notion that was a colonial-era Japanese invention. The tendency in scholarship to emphasize living law and "informal justice" in Korean legal tradition seems to be prompted by a voluntarist bent to downplay the extent of transformation of indigenous law as a result of the influence of alien law. But it amounts to agreeing with the colonizer that in Korea there was nothing in governing private social relations that deserved to be called law. In reality, the comprehensiveness of the Chosŏn legal system, with its elaborate codes, successfully operated to meet social and administrative needs. The resolution of civil disputes took place in the framework of the state codes.

Law functioned in Chosŏn Korea not in the same way as in the West. It follows from this acknowledgment that discussing the importance of the introduction of Western civil law need not sway our understanding of traditional Korean law.

[116] Olivier-Martin, *Les Lois du roi*, 76.

2

Law and Legal Culture under the Chosŏn Dynasty

The Chosŏn dynasty embodied a quintessential state law model. Outside the state codes and royal edicts, there was no body of preestablished rules observed with regularity as legal norms. The state held a monopoly of the production and enforcement of law. The codes, fundamentally penal in nature, were shaped by the Confucian ideology of law that placed preponderant emphasis on ethical responsibilities and moral obligations. The main goals of the legal system were strengthening central royal authority and facilitating administration which operated on the principle of paternalistic edification, correcting behaviors and practices. Laws abstracted from private relations were not of central concern. This represented a crucial difference from the legal systems in Europe where law basically meant private law.

Because the state was not interested in intervening in private relationship, disputes among individuals, when they arose, tended to be relegated to local leaders. In the provinces, the *yangban*, the aristocratic elites, often functioned as quasi-judicial administrators. Korean society was singular in the commanding position of the aristocracy. When *yangban* lineage heads and their mighty clans held the role of mediators in informal justice, it had the effect of local social control. An institutionalized form of the local elites' domination of village life was the community compact, known as *hyangyak*. From the sixteenth century, prominent Confucian scholar-officials formulated community compacts, a sort of village covenants regulating local residents' relationships. Implemented with the main goal of promoting social improvement through moral regeneration, community compacts consisted of members of the elite *yangban* class, but their effect reached the entire village community. It provided village elders, acting as officers and overseers of the compacts, an instrument for fulfilling the task of mediating and reconciling statutory law with social practice in the countryside.

The local *yangban*'s strong position in Chosŏn villages seems to set the Korean case apart from imperial China. In China, incumbent officials and bureaucrats enjoyed privileges by virtue of the posts they held; the perks and influence were limited to individuals. In Korea, in contrast, privileges were granted to prefigured aristocratic clans and geographical groups, extending throughout their family members.[1] The authority of the bureaucrats and magistrates, who were themselves from the *yangban* class, often did not supersede the dominant power of the local aristocracy within their jurisdiction. It has been a subject of debate whether the implementation of *hyangyak* signified that the state conferred, by formal or informal delegation, the role of social control on the local aristocracy, or whether the development of compacts represented a sort of assertion of local autonomy and ambitions by the *yangban* elites. Whatever the case, the facts that the central government did not try to stop the mechanisms for the private exercise of penal power by *yangban* and that rules contained in the community compacts were routinely enforced by magistrates seem to evidence the symbiotic relationship between provincial elites and the state. With its emphasis on coercive rectification of customs, manners, rites, and practices, the ideas behind compacts aligned with the state neo-Confucian ideology.

The term *hyangyak* literally means "village agreements," but agreement or private contract was an elusive notion in premodern East Asian legal culture.[2] *Hyangyak* reflected the strong consideration of ethics on the one hand and coercive rectification of morality on the other – the two elements that were simultaneously pervasive in Chosŏn law. It functioned as a local-level justice system contributing to the maintenance of order in the countryside and to the consolidation of the privileges of the *yangban* class. This chapter examines the development of *hyangyak* as a point of reference from which one can ascertain Korean legal culture and gauge the relationship between the state and society under the Chosŏn dynasty.

The emergence of *hyangyak* coincided with an efflorescence of reformist zeal to propagate the state Confucian values in the villages. In a broader sense, the spread of *hyangyak* can be seen as a phenomenon, often witnessed in history, in which reform-minded intellectuals looked to a foreign prototype to articulate and adapt its conceptions for the purpose of bringing desired changes in their society. Some interesting analogy can be made between the making of *hyangyak* and the redaction and reformation of custom in France that was underway almost contemporaneously. The legal humanists in sixteenth-century France, most of whom were legal practitioners serving as judges or *avocats* in the law courts, clamored for the rationalization and systematization of provincial customs, and the crown spearheaded the campaign of the reformation and formal publication of customary law texts in most regions in France governed by local custom. While the French, when they wanted to update and reform law, turned to Roman law, the Korean literati resorted to Confucian norms and

[1] Sim Hŭi-gi, "18 segi ŭi hyŏngsa sabŏp chedo kaehyŏk [The Reform of the Penal Law System in the Eighteenth Century]," *Hanguk munhwa* 20 (1997): 205–244.

[2] Terada Hiroaki, "The Nature of Social Agreements (*yue*) in the Legal Order of Ming and Qing China" (Part 1), *The International Journal of Asian Studies* 2 (2005), 320–323.

precepts inspired by Chinese models to engender and accommodate changes in their country.

Hyangyak may have been the closest the Koreans came to the formation of local rules of social control. Essentially an instrument of the moralization of customs, nevertheless, it was different from the rules governing legal relations among private individuals in the European model. Korean Confucian scholars and the French legal humanists both called for a more rational social order. Both drew from principles and concepts from outside in order to correct and modify local practices deemed to be iniquitous and unreasonable. But their reformist agendas diverged because their worldviews and intellectual outlooks were different. Korean compacts were expressions of the heavy-handed Confucian precepts that underlay the established social order, with its metaphysical trimming of ethical values. The ideals of stringent moral rejuvenation guided by the forces from above that served as the central impetus for improving human relations represent a distinct vision of society and the polity in Chosŏn Korea.[3]

Overall, emphasis on moral uniformity and concern for the mutual needs of the local community, rather than individual or property rights, prevented, or at least delayed, the development of a law that was suited to meeting the changing conditions of the modern world. In the last decades of the nineteenth century, the Chosŏn dynasty undertook reforms to modernize its law and legal system but they bore little outcome. Korea's unsuccessful attempt for voluntary legal transplantation can be better explained when it is placed against the backdrop of traditional law and legal culture.

The Community Compact

The Korean *hyangyak* was modeled after the Chinese archetype. The Song-dynasty philosopher Zhu Xi (1130–1200) devised a community compact (*xiangyue*), firmly grounded in neo-Confucian moralism. Zhu Xi's compact was based on a text presumably written by Lü Dajun in 1076, called the Lü Family Community Compact. Zhu Xi's emendation contained rules – exhortations – geared for the harmonious interaction of a small village group. The basic principles of the compact were "mutual encouragement of virtuous deeds and duties," "mutual correction of wrongful conducts," "reciprocity according

[3] There are many studies on *hyangyak* in Korean language. For discussion of *hyangyak* in English, see Martina Deuchler, "The Practice of Confucianism: Ritual and Order in Chosŏn Dynasty Korea," in *Rethinking Confucianism: Past and Present in China, Japan, Korea, and Vietnam*, eds. Benjamin A. Elman, John B. Duncan, and Herman Ooms (Los Angeles: UCLA Asian Pacific Monograph Series, 2002), 291–334; James B. Palais, *Confucian Statecraft and Korean Institutions: Yu Hyŏngwŏn and the Late Chosŏn Dynasty* (Seattle: University of Washington Press, 1996), 705–761; Sakai Tadao, "Yi Yulgok and the Community Compact," in *The Rise of Neo-Confucianism in Korea*, eds. William Theodore De Bary and JaHyun Kim Haboush (New York: Columbia University Press, 1985), 328–348.

to the rules of decorum and customs," and "mutual aid in case of illness and disaster."[4] Formulated in terms of moral injunctions, Zhu Xi's compact was popularized in the mid-Ming period by Wang Yangming (1472–1529) who drew up his own village compact in southern Jiangxi. Partly influenced by Wang, neo-Confucian scholar-officials in Korea called for the institution of community compacts to "civilize the village folk and perfect the customs (*hwamin sŏngsok*)." Resorting to mutually-binding agreements was grounded in the neo-Confucian precept that moral regeneration through mutual exhortation was an essential means for resolving social ills and ruptures.

Kim An-guk (1478–1543), governor of the Kyŏngsang province in southeastern Korea, is regarded as the first official to propose a village code to be implemented in the region under his administration. In 1517 Kim translated Zhu Xi's revised version of the Lü Compact into the Korean vernacular and persuaded King Chungjong (reign 1506–1544) to publish the text (titled *Yŏ ssi hyangyak ŏnhae*).[5] The concept of the community compact spread in Korea along with Kim's translation. Earlier community associations for mutual surveillance and aid, called *tonggye* or *tongyak*, were reorganized and refashioned under the ideals of Confucianism to create *hyangyak*. Rationalized in terms of state ideology, the *hyangyak* rules exuded tremendous legitimating power.[6]

The idea of educating the populace through self-governing communities did not impress many local magistrates however, and villagers were only half-hearted in carrying out the new regulations.[7] Some court officials pointed out that the *hyangyak* organization's assumption of the power to reward or penalize behaviors encroached on the prerogatives of local magistrates and that, in particular, harsh punishment meted out by the *hyangyak* officials hardened people's hearts.[8] Following the Chinese model, the Korean compact required maintaining two ledgers, one for recording virtuous conducts and the other for recording bad deeds. In Zhu Xi's *xiangyue*, those whose behaviors were recorded in the demerit ledger were subject to the admonishment and censure by the compact members and leaders. If still recalcitrant, the offending members were allowed to withdraw from the compact. In Korea, the *hyangyak* associations exercised more compulsive power to control the members by imposing punishment on those who broke the rules.

Apart from possible institutional jealousy and inertia, there were certain political overtones in the rocky progress of the early *hyangyak* movement. The idea of a village covenant had been eagerly embraced by the so-called young scholars in the late fifteenth century. Cho Kwang-jo (1482–1519), the young brilliant reformer belonging to this group, was one of the leading spokesmen

[4] Yu Hong-ryŏl, "Chosŏn hyangyak ŭi sŏngnip [The Establishment of *Hyangyak* in Chosŏn]," *Chindan hakpo* 9 (1938), 107–111.

[5] *Chosŏn wangjo sillok*, *Chungjong sillok*, March 15, 1517 (year 12).

[6] Chŏng Chin-yŏng, *Chosŏn sidae hyangch'on sahoesa* [History of Rural Society in the Chosŏn Period] (Seoul: Hangilsa, 1998), 221.

[7] Palais, *Confucian Statecraft*, 712–713.

[8] *Chosŏn wangjo sillok*, *Chungjong sillok*, January 4, 1520 (year 15).

for the community compact.[9] But the early compact movements were fatally intertwined with the political factional strife that brought about frequent political turmoil in the sixteenth century.[10] In a full-scale reaction against the reformist scholars, Cho and Kim An-guk were disgraced and the former was executed in 1519. Although the king did not ban the community compact, it nonetheless practically disappeared.[11]

During the 1540s and 1550s, arguments for implementing the *hyangyak* began in the royal court. In 1546 Chu Se-bung (1495–1554), a renowned scholar-official, asserted that *hyangyak* were desirable in the countryside where the king's moralizing influence did not reach but less necessary at the court where the state's "rites and laws (*yepŏp*)" were properly observed.[12] A few years later an official wrote a memorial to the king arguing that the spread of "*hyangyak* law" (*hyangyakpŏp*) would not threaten the state.[13] Here, one can see that the effects of *hyangyak* were equated to the functions of law, that is, ensuring order in society by guiding the common people who did not understand the true meaning of *ye* (*li* in Chinese, meaning rites) and therefore were unable to follow moral principles. *Hyangyak* were advocated as a means to instill moral precepts among the people, especially in the countryside where the state's power to maintain public order was weakened. The courtiers argued that "if the *hyangyak* succeeded in changing customs the state would not need to rely on criminal law to teach people."[14] They hoped that "*hyangyak* would reduce litigations and inspire morality."[15] It is clear that the Korean elites were keenly focused on the practical advantages that derived from village agreements.

Upon the accession of King Sŏnjo (reign 1567–1608) to the throne, debates regarding the community compact resumed. The idea received the support of a number of prominent Confucian philosophers and scholar-officials who took up the cause of moral education through village covenants. The meaning of the renewal of a community compact in the second half of the sixteenth

[9] The reformist group, representing rural neo-Confucian moralist scholars known as *Sarimp'a*, was increasingly in conflict with the established bureaucrats known as *Hungu p'a*. Yi T'ae-jin, "Sarimp'a ŭi hyangyak pogŭp undong [The Sarim Faction's Movement to Spread Hyangyak]," in *Hanguk sahoesa yŏngu* [A Social History of Korea] (Seoul: Chisik Sanŏpsa, 1986), 274–288. Edward Wagner has interpreted this conflict as a contest between the king and young officials in the Censorate over the limits of legitimate remonstrance and the locus of political authority in the Korean political system. Edward Willett Wagner, *The Literati Purges: Political Conflict in Early Yi Korea* (Cambridge: East Asia Research Center and Harvard University Press, 1974), 33–50.

[10] Palais, *Confucian Statecraft*, 713.

[11] Various entries in *Chosŏn wangjo sillok*, *Chungjong sillok*, January-March 1520 (year 15); Tabana Tameo, *Chōsen kyōyaku kyōkashi no kenkyū* [A Study of the History of the Edification of *Hyangyak* in Chosŏn] (Tokyo: Chōhōsha, 1972), 55–57; Palais, *Confucian Statecraft*, 714.

[12] *Chosŏn wangjo sillok*, *Myŏngjong sillok*, August 10, 1546 (year 1).

[13] Ibid., October 23, 1553 (year 8).

[14] *Chosŏn wangjo sillok*, *Chungjong sillok*, September 5, 1518 (year 13).

[15] Ibid., April 5, 1519 (year 14).

century can be gleaned through the works of Yi Hwang (T'oegye) (1501–1570) and Yi I (Yulgok) (1536–1584), two towering figures of the Korean neo-Confucianism in the Chosŏn dynasty. T'oegye told the king that the implementation of *hyangyak* in previous decades, although commendable, had failed because "young people rushed it."[16] T'oegye compiled a draft of the "Articles of the Community Compact" (*hyangnip yakcho*) in 1556 for his home district of Yean in Kyŏngsang province.[17] In his preamble, T'oegye indicated that, after the drafting of the compact by a select number of upright people, the contents were to be presented to the village people who would be asked to give their opinion. Only then would the definitive version of the compact be promulgated.

T'oegye's compact articles revealed a certain departure from Zhu Xi's version, as they did not include the four principles of the Lü Family Community Compact. Most of T'oegye's articles were instead drawn from Ming or Korean statutes and the provisions of earlier local associations of the elite who held office rank (*Yuhyangso*).[18] As such, there was a strong emphasis on moral commands and penalties for misconduct.

T'oegye's draft enumerated "violations of rites and mores that do harm to local customs," and distinguished them into three categories.[19] Violations that would be punished in the highest degree included disrupting the peace and the structure of the family order, such as disobeying parents or quarreling with brothers, interfering with official business and meddling in village affairs, abusing the power by using public functions to pursue private gain, insulting village elders, and seducing, threatening, or defiling virtuous widows. Violations to be punished in the second degree included actions such as abandoning lawful wives, relying on coercion to intimidate the weak, uniting with vagabonds to commit perverse and violent acts, fabricating evidence and fictitious stories to slander others and incriminate them in disregard of plain principles, and failing to respect village ordinances. Those to be punished in the lowest degree included arriving late for public meetings, sitting in a disorderly manner, and violating decorum by being noisy and argumentative at meetings. Finally, evil village functionaries and their underlings causing harm among the people, those

[16] *Chosŏn wangjo sillok*, *Sŏnjo sillok*, September 21, 1568 (year 1).

[17] Yi Hwang, *Chŭngbo T'oegye chŏnsŏ* [Expanded Complete Works of T'oegye], 2 vols. (Seoul: Sŏnggyungwan Taehakkyŏ Taedong Munhwa Yŏnguwŏn, 1958), book 42.

[18] Palais, *Confucian Statecraft*, 716. The regulations of *Yuhyangso* (*hyanggyu*) contained moral aspirations and penalties for misconduct similar to those contained in the law codes. The Japanese historian Tabana Tameo did not regard *hyangnip yakcho* as *hyangyak* on the grounds that it was modeled more on existing rules and regulations of local organizations than on the Lü Family Community Compact of Song China. Tabana, *Chōsen kyōyaku*, 194–197. See also Tagawa Kōzō, "Richō no kyōkyu ni tsuite [*Hyangyak* under the Yi Dynasty] (Part I)," *Chōsen gakuho* 76 (1975): 35–72. According to Sakai Tadao, the Lü Family Community Compact had been devised on the basis of the tradition of village ordinances, and the differences between village covenants and ordinances were not material. Sakai, "Yi Yulgok and the Community Compact," 325.

[19] A full list is provided in Sakai, "Yi Yulgok and the Community Compact," 324–325.

who hoarded produce for the purpose of manipulating prices, and commoners disrespectful to the gentry were to be reported immediately to the magistrate for punishment. It is not clear whether T'oegye's compact was actually put into practice.[20] In any case, it was respected for the rest of the Chosŏn dynasty as a standard for future advocates of the community compact system.

In 1571 Yi Yulgok, then magistrate of Ch'ŏngju in Ch'ungch'ŏng province, drafted a community compact for Sŏwŏn County under his jurisdiction.[21] He retired to Haeju in Hwanghae province and composed his Haeju Community Compact in 1576. This compact was different from the Sŏwŏn compact as it was to be carried out in conjunction with the communal granary system, a fund for emergency relief, an issue that had a crucial bearing on the livelihood of the peasantry. The Covenant of the Community Granary Compact was attached to the Haeju compact.[22]

In the preamble of the Sŏwŏn County Community Compact, Yulgok lamented that "morality has declined, the Way has become obscure, and the people have lost their sense of direction, while decorum and customs have deteriorated at all levels." He wrote:

> I am determined to help transform the morality of the people.... I have drawn up a new compact ... [which] includes almost all the elements that encourage good deeds and discourage evil acts. I believe that unless the magistrate exerts his utmost effort in his duties, he cannot demand anything from the director of the community compact, and that unless the director is a man of probity, he cannot exhort the village members to do good deeds. Whether the village members turn to good or to evil will depend upon the compact director, and whether the director is moved to urge his people to behave properly will depend upon the magistrate. I therefore should seek good advice and work more diligently so that the director and his staff will follow my wishes, will abide by the regulation, and will exhort the village members.[23]

This statement sums up the core element of community compacts, namely the emphasis on the elite's moral leadership in local communities.

Similar compacts were devised by other local elites throughout the seventeenth century. The *hyangyak* was an organization initiated and implemented by the local gentlemen class, the *yangban*. As the ruling class, the *yangban*

[20] Ibid., 323; Palais, *Confucian Statecraft*, 716.

[21] Yi I, *Yulgok chŏnsŏ* [Complete Works of Yulgok] (Seoul: Sŏnggyungwan Taehakkyŏ Taedong Munhwa Yŏnguwŏn, 1958), book 33 *purok* [appendix], *yŏnbo* [chronology]. For the background of Yulgok's compact, see Deuchler, "The Practice of Confucianism," 297–298; Palais, *Confucian Statecraft*, 717–718.

[22] This was in line with the situation in China where, between the sixteenth and eighteenth centuries, the community compact and community granary were carried out in an integrated manner. Selected articles of the Haeju Communal Granary Compact are translated in Peter H. Lee and William Theodore T. De Bary, eds. *Sourcebook of Korean Civilization*, vol. 2 (New York: Columbia University Press, 1997–2000), 146–157.

[23] *Yulgok chŏnsŏ*, book 16 (Miscellaneous Writings); the text is translated in *Sourcebook of Korean Civilization*, vol. 2, 145–146.

were expected to exhibit a clear sense of moral duty for affairs transcending their own social orbit. The expansive notion of social responsibility appears to be an element that distinguishes Korean neo-Confucianism from its Chinese counterpart, and the nature of community compact seems to corroborate the point. Zhu Xi's compact was primarily a voluntary agreement among the gentry, envisaged as an ethical enterprise confined to the elite alone, excluding the common people. Yet by the Ming period, the effect of community compacts had reached local residents far beyond the registered members. Recent studies have shown that the mid-Ming compacts represented not simply voluntary mutual agreements of participants but coercive regulations extending over the villagers.[24] Even compared with the Ming models, however, the Korean compacts were far more comprehensive in their target subjects, ensuring the participation of commoners as well as *yangban*. The official membership of Yulgok's compacts consisted only of the members of the elite as in the Chinese models, but the compacts were designed to engage the non-elite more actively. Regular meetings, which all residents including commoners and slaves were required to attend, were used as public occasions to commend and reward good conduct and admonish bad conduct of the entire membership of the community.

In the Korean adaptation of the Chinese prototypes, the "liberal features" found in Zhu Xi's community compact were considerably less conspicuous.[25] The seriousness with which scholars and community leaders interpreted their responsibility of promoting and supervising the transformation of commoners is vividly exhibited in the Korean compact's prohibitory character. Compact members were required to provide aid in conducting funerals, lend labor to cultivate the land of anyone who was too sick to work, and instruct men under the age of thirty who had not been educated in civil and military matters.[26] Failure to fulfill these requirements resulted in punishments. The use of coercive power, not just for moral rejuvenation but the conformity to moral norms and tight control of general conduct, was one of the most remarkable characteristics of Korean community compacts.[27] As the late American historian James Palais stated, "the line between instruction and indoctrination was paper thin in the Confucian tradition."[28]

Punishments were prescribed for stealing property, wrongfully diverting water from irrigation channels, or taking over someone else's land for cultivation. Tardiness in paying taxes, bribery, short-changing the village granary, and even

[24] Terada, "The Nature of Social Agreements (*yue*)," 320–323.

[25] For the emphasis on the liberal aspect of *xiangyue*, see William Theodore De Bary, "The Community Compact," in *Asian Values and Human Rights: A Confucian Communitarian Perspective* (Cambridge, MA: Harvard University Press, 1998), 58–89; William T. Rowe, *Saving the World: Chen Hongmou and Elite Consciousness in Eighteenth-Century China* (Stanford: Stanford University Press, 2001).

[26] Palais, *Confucian Statecraft*, 722.

[27] Deuchler, "The Practice of Confucianism," 294, 326.

[28] Palais, *Confucian Statecraft*, 706.

laziness or lack of attention to one's work were all criminal actions warranting various degrees of penalty specified in the compact text. Refusing to grant a loan to someone in need or damaging a borrowed object would be recorded as a misdemeanor. If villagers failed to read the assigned texts, they would be punished. The Japanese historian Tabana Tameo lamented Yulgok's obsession with exposing all possible examples of human immorality and corruption.[29] The fact that Yulgok's compact involved the participation of the lower class may explain why he viewed it as necessary to list numerous examples of errors, corruption, and immorality. Anyone who failed to conform to rules for proper observance of rites and good customs was subject to discipline.

The organization of the Korean *hyangyak* was firmly based on existing social hierarchy. The social divisions and class distinctions underlying the basic social structure in the Chosŏn state – *yangban*, freeborn commoner (*yangin* or *sangmin*), and slave – was clearly reflected in the compact regulations and practice. The remarkable continuity of the leading *yangban* lineages in Korean history has been well studied. Edward Wagner defined the *yangban* of the Chosŏn dynasty more as a status elite, associated with inherited prestige and ongoing entitlement, than as an elite rank acquired by virtue of office or degree-holding.[30] Sustaining a hereditary ruling class was a crucial issue in Chosŏn. It can be argued that the Korean *hyangyak* served the purpose of perpetuating the existing social stratification by invoking the standard norms of Confucian behavior.

The non-elite rarely had any input into the provisions of the covenants that governed them. Yulgok's compact was administered by the director, chief officers, and regular officers who were chosen from among the elites.[31] They meted out discipline according to the ledgers of good and bad deeds. The heads of the subdivisions had the authority to punish anyone on the spot for a misdemeanor that called for less than forty strokes. The gradation of punishment in Yulgok's rules was based on the social status of both perpetrator and victim.[32] The sitting arrangement in bi-monthly compact meetings was strictly determined in accordance with one's stratum.[33] From her study of the compact meetings, Martina Deuchler argued that *hyangyak* ritually underscored the distinctions of elite and non-elite and thus represented the reality of social stratification

[29] Tabana, *Chōsen kyōyaku*, 345–348.

[30] Edward W. Wagner, "Social Stratification in Seventeenth-Century Korea: Some Observations from a 1663 Seoul Census Register," *Occasional Papers on Korea* 1 (April 1974): 36–54.

[31] Articles of organization of the Haeju Community Compact provided that officers should be men of scholarship and that the officer of the month should be able to command the services of slaves and servants. These offices thus excluded non-elites. Lee and de Bary, eds., *Sourcebook of Korean Civilization*, vol. 2, 146–149; Sakai, "Yi Yulgok and the Community Compact," 328.

[32] Palais, *Confucian Statecraft*, 729. Palais concluded that "Yulgok was definitely a defender of the status quo in social relations, particularly discrimination in favor of *yangban*, slaveholders, and landlords and against slaves, particularly in his detailed prescriptions for penalties for transgressions of the law and the rules of the compact based on age and status." Ibid., 728.

[33] Deuchler, "The Practice of Confucianism," 297–299.

justified in a well-ordered moral system.[34] Yulgok's *hyangyak* took seriously the elites' duty for exemplary behavior. Malfeasance in office, such as committing evil acts on the pretext of official business or demanding more than was due in repayment of loans and interest, were subject to penal sanction.[35]

Korean neo-Confucian literati found in Zhu Xi's social philosophy the ideological framework for their reform projects, but they revised it to make it suitable for Korean situations. Some historians have seen the Korean *hyangyak*'s adaptation of the Chinese model as evidence that Chosŏn Koreans did not always blindly copy the Chinese legal and cultural traditions. According to Deuchler, Korean compacts were "a creative recourse to Chinese antiquity."[36]

The significance of *hyangyak* began to decline in the eighteenth century. It is likely that socioeconomic changes in the countryside diminished its effectiveness as a mechanism for social control. Scholars have shown that the eighteenth century witnessed the growing attempt by the government to rationalize and systematize the legal system by eradicating private punishment and resolving disputes through law rather than exhortation.[37] Such efforts may have had repercussions on the local *hyangyak* order and its reliance on the social hierarchy. When the state tried to convert the compacts into machinery for implementing economic or military policies, the local elites largely withdrew their support. By the end of the century, the community compact in its original form had largely disappeared, and subsequently continued only on a smaller basis, confined to the immediate lineage of a *yangban* family and nearby commoners.[38]

In China, community compacts had metamorphosed into imperially mandated "village lectures," with the gradual loss of the dynamism of the earlier neo-Confucian idealism. As the local gentry in the Qing was made to assist with propagating the edict of the Kangxi emperor and the imperial ideology, lamented William Theodore de Bary, a "moral uplift campaign" became an instrument of official indoctrination and a routine bureaucratic function, performed more by prefects, magistrates, or their deputies and less by independent or quasi-autonomous local gentry.[39] As pointed out earlier, the extent of idealism in Korean *hyangyak*, although surely present, was more moderate than in the Chinese equivalent. At any rate, in both countries, the community compact as a system of social control was gradually submerged into a bureaucratic state order.

[34] Ibid., 306–312. For the Chinese community pact ritual, see Joseph P. McDermott, "Emperor, Elites, and Commoners: The Community Pact Ritual of the Late Ming," in *State and Court Ritual in China*, ed. Joseph P. McDermott (Cambridge: Cambridge University Press, 1999), 299–351.

[35] Palais, *Confucian Statecraft*, 727–728.

[36] Deuchler, *The Confucian Transformation*, 20–27; 111–118. See also Shaw, *Legal Norms in a Confucian State*, 5.

[37] See Sim Hŭi-gi, "18 segi ŭi hyŏngsa sabŏp chedo kaehyŏk"; Sim Chae-u, *Chosŏn hugi kukka kwŏllyŏk*.

[38] Deuchler, "The Practice of Confucianism," 325.

[39] De Bary, "The Community Compact," 70.

By the early twentieth century, the compact had evolved into quasi-covenant private associations called *kye* among the individuals for the purpose of pulling capital and lending it to members. Cooperative societies known as *chohap* also belonged to this category. These institutions' right of self-regulation is acknowledged under private contract laws in modern Korean law.[40]

Law versus Standard of Behavior

In Korea, private law matters lay in the field of *ŭi* (*i* in Chinese), meaning justice, righteousness, or equity. Methods for settling disputes between private individuals did not develop outside the realm of the Confucian informal normativity. The goal of adjudication was to find out who was responsible for violating *ŭi*, punish the culprit, and restore harmony in society. This was in direct contrast to the tradition in Europe. According to H. Patrick Glenn, customs' metamorphosis into legal custom reflected one of the key characteristics in Western thought. The transformation was the result of growing "presentism" as a way of thinking about time.[41] Custom had been mere information from the past. Reduced to writing – "captured" – in the *coutumiers* from the late Middle Ages, custom now became the present, enabling individuals to react to the teaching of the past. The "reconstruction" of custom consisted in its "reformulation as a form of ongoing plebiscite, in which the essential is found in present decision, rather than in anything which may be internal to the custom itself." The sense of presentism or contingent time in Western society was largely a product of religious impulses. In this context, custom came to derive its legitimacy not from the correctness or validity of its content but from the implicit consent by individuals who reacted to it *in the present*.[42] One can speak about the existence of "law" when it satisfies certain elements, namely, "recognition, change and adjudication."[43] These are what separate law from other prescriptive rules or practices, such as religion, morals, or even political systems. This "rule of change" turned law in European history into "something essentially dynamic."[44]

The concept of custom as a contemporary legal representation did not exist in Chosŏn Korea or elsewhere in East Asia. The timelessness of Confucian teaching endowed the present and the individual with few special privileges. The absence of the centrality of the individual instead led the immutable principles of morality, extracted from the Confucian texts, to be regarded as sufficient to regulate private relations. One of the most important devices by which

[40] Article 706 of Korean Civil Code (*Minpŏp*).

[41] H. Patrick Glenn, "The Capture, Reconstruction and Marginalization of 'Custom'," *American Journal of Comparative Law* 45 (1997), 617–618.

[42] Ibid., 618.

[43] Jean-Louis Halpérin, "The Concept of Law: A Western Transplant?" *Theoretical Inquiries in Law* 10 (2009), 336.

[44] Ibid.

law was formally legitimized was the concept that it embodied certain principles not susceptible to change.[45]

In Korea, bringing deviant customs into line with immutable norms and punishing behaviors that transgress the centrally imposed boundaries was the main purpose of the state law and the ruling elites who promulgated and perpetuated it. These objectives of law were closely appropriated in local *hyangyak* rules.[46] The overriding issue for the community compact regulations was their transformatory value, ritually perpetuating the social reality. Providing rules that would resolve interpersonal disputes arising in human relations in an objective manner was of secondary concern. Terada Hiroaki argued that the *xiangyue* in China devised not a specific form of a law but "conditions" under which a standard of behavior was shared by the villagers.[47] This characterization equally holds true in the Korean situation.

The intellectual maturity of Korean neo-Confucianism convinced the scholar-officials of the probity and propriety of their program. The neo-Confucian gentry's firm grip on the acceptable criterion of behavior and the paradigm of social order remained unchallenged. The Korean scholars, confident in their achievement of Confucian philosophy and the ideological correctness of their initiative, had no moral qualms in resorting to coercive commands in propagating moral behaviors. As Palais aptly stated, the Korean *hyangyak* was an example of "the tradition of muscular Confucianism that backed up the rhetoric of persuasion by the threat of force and supported the status quo in discriminatory social relations."[48]

Custom, Society and the State

A classic study of *hyangyak* argued in the 1930s that the *hyangyak* became the core of Korea's social law and the vehicle of a degree of local autonomy for its villages.[49] An emphasis on the progressive nature of indigenous norms and institutions was an important part of historical writing during Japanese rule that strived to ascertain a national history of Korea. Some saw in *hyangyak* an assertion of local power as part of the ongoing struggle between the central bureaucracy and regional elites during the Chosŏn dynasty.[50] But attributing

[45] Shaw, "Traditional Korean Law and Its Relation to China," 313.

[46] Deuchler, "The Practice of Confucianism," 305.

[47] Terada, "The Nature of Social Agreements," 314.

[48] Palais, *Confucian Statecraft*, 717. Palais was not impressed by the Korean *hyangyak*, which "had not been much of a success in the Chosŏn dynasty." Ibid., 732. Historians have pointed out that *hyangyak*, firmly grounded in the theory of moral uplifting, lacked any program for practical application for society. Tabana, *Chōsen kyōyaku*, 554.

[49] Yu Hong-ryŏl, "Chosŏn hyangyak," 138.

[50] See, among others, Yi T'ae-jin, *Hanguk sahoesa yŏngu*. It is interesting to observe a certain connection between the historiographical trend that viewed *hyangyak* as a force of local autonomy against state centrism and the political climate of contemporary Korea. The emphasis on the independent streak of the community compacts and the local elites largely coincided with the proliferation of political discourses in the late 1980s and 1990s that called for the implementation of self-governing local system. Local autonomy, however, may no longer be *la parole du jour* in contemporary Korean politics.

local liberty to community compacts seems removed from historical truth. The interests of the state and the local elites in Chosŏn were more in symbiotic relationship than in conflict.[51] A more balanced view is that, as stated by Key Yang and Gregory Henderson, in the wake of compact movement "new codes of penalties and punishment were written, new rules of conduct and ritual formulated and, most interesting of all, Korean local administration, long informal and inchoate, was for the first time given a legal basis."[52]

It is important to note that the central government or the local magistrate did not formally delegate local administrative power to the *hyangyak* officials. The *hyangyak*'s assumption of judicial power to regulate private relations did not constitute an exception to the official theory that every case had to come to the attention of the central government. Instead, it seems that some *yangban* elites were granted a tacit approval to wield limited control power as the royal government found the quasi-judicial functions provided by the *hyangyak* helpful in remedying disputes short of lawsuits. In this sense, *hyangyak* played a role in helping systematize local administration. The Korean *hyangyak* denoted a realm in which social control and respect for harmony were internalized without apparent contradictions. *Hyangyak* can be viewed as the sites of negotiation between society and the state, individual and community, and regional and central forces. Local *yangban*, by enforcing Confucian norms on the villagers through *hyangyak*, performed quasi-judicial and administrative functions in the countryside in conjunction with state power.

This consideration suggests an important question about the relationship between the state and the local community in premodern Korea. The interests of the central state and the provincial elites in Chosŏn were largely in unison in relying on the propagation of the state neo-Confucian values to regulate relations in the villages and also to maintain existing social hierarchy. This is not to say that there was no conflict between state authorities and regional elites. As the Korean neo-Confucian scholars achieved their remarkable ideological sophistication from the late fifteenth century, some reaction against the center-dominated development seemed inevitable. Local scholar-elites increasingly boasted that they were the truthful custodians of Confucianism. Some viewed the provisions on family rituals in the state law codes as incorrect or unsatisfactory and concluded that the formal codes were inadequate to fulfill the function of civilizing popular customs. The *hyangyak* provided a ground in which the neo-Confucian scholars could create their ideal society based on their "correct" interpretation of Confucianism. It was an attempt to bring the non-elite – the commoners and the slaves – into the elite's cultural realm. The

[51] Chŏng Tuhi and Edward J. Shultz, eds., *Hanguksa e issŏsŏ chibang kwa chungang, POSCO International Symposium on Korean History* (Seoul: Humanities Research Institute, Sŏgang University Center for Korean Studies, 2003); Ch'oe Sŏn-hye, *Chosŏn chŏngi chibang sajok kwa kukka* [The Local Literati and the State in Early Chosŏn] (Seoul: Kyŭngin Munhwasa, 2007).

[52] Key P. Yang and Gregory Henderson, "An Outline History of Korean Confucianism, Part II: The Schools of Yi Confucianism," *The Journal of Asian Studies* 18 (1959), 263–264.

gentry wanted to create an ordered world built on their interpretations of the universally valid moral principles of Confucianism.

As such, local elites posed a potential challenge to the center over who was more faithful to the Confucian teaching. But this was a competition that took place within the boundaries of the reigning ideology. In Korea, the statist values had been fully internalized by Confucian officials and this may have been the reason why the state regarded the community compacts with benign indifference. The arrangement of allowing the *yangban* a semi-independent judicial authority through *hyangyak* was possible because the intensely Confucianized *yangban* was no serious threat to the state's dominant value system. The *hyangyak* can be seen as an intermediary realm between public and private, an instrument through which the local aristocracy pursued their particular interests while maintaining public order.

Historians of China have emphasized the significance of the ongoing struggle between the center and the periphery in the imperial period, in particular the conflict between the Manchus and the Han Chinese in the provinces during the Qing dynasty. In Korea, the demarcation between the center and the periphery was less salient. The relationship between the royal court and the local power in Chosŏn Korea was less one of conflict and competition than one of cooperation and coexistence.[53] Because the Korean monarchs could not overwhelm the powerful hereditary *yangban* families, the king chose instead to cooperate with them and enlist their support in administration. The center thus endorsed and supported *yangban*'s control of the countryside and the periphery remained loyal to the center. By posing as a crucial balancing force between the capital and the provinces, the community compacts contributed to the extraordinary stability of the state.

According to William Shaw, the legal codes in Korea aided in the diffusion of Confucian ethical concepts, but at the same time the use of a written, uniform and widely diffused law and legal system had the effect of weakening the potential of Confucianism for independent, varied development.[54] Law in Chosŏn Korea significantly reinforced the power of the central government because the authority of law was based on confidence in the moral propriety of the penalty in the codes. This centralizing effect of the state codes, not neo-Confucianism per se, led to rigidity of Confucianism as an intellectual system. Shaw argued that the most important source of tension in Chosŏn government was "between the combination of law and morality together embodied in the codes, and local interests; and between the civil morality of the state and the personal moral insight of Confucian scholars and high officials alike."[55] The comprehensiveness of the Chosŏn legal system was a strong factor in

[53] Yi Sŏng-mu, "Chosŏn sidae hyangch'on chibae seryŏk ŭi ch'ui [The Development of the Local Powers in Dominance in the Chosŏn Period]," *Chosŏn yangban sahoe yŏngu* [A Study of *Yangban* in the Chosŏn Dynasty] (Seoul: Ilchogak, 1995), 210.

[54] Shaw, "Traditional Korean Law and Its Relation to China," 313–317.

[55] Ibid., 309.

challenging regional and religious elites which had been active during the late Koryŏ period. The codes were seen as the embodiment of the natural order.

Yulgok appears to have understood this subtle power dynamic well. He emphasized the need for cooperation with local magistrates for the effective operation of the community compacts. His Haeju *hyangyak* demanded that utmost obedience and respect be given to the local magistrate. The attendance requirement at the frequent inauguration and farewell ceremonies for the magistrates was enforced more strictly than the regular spring-autumn meetings of the community compact.[56] It was Yulgok's belief that officials ought to play a primary role in transforming the people's ways in the countryside. Early on, Yulgok opposed the nationwide implementation of *hyangyak* and instead favored its implementation on a local level. The viability and durability of the Korean community compacts largely depended on private and local initiative and commitment, but in close – although unofficial – cooperation with the local magistrates. The contemporary neo-Confucian scholars were mindful of the importance of local governance. They increasingly believed that their self-worth depended on educating and civilizing the people in rural communities, just as much, if not more than, on serving in the central government. Yulgok may well have thought that the civilizing force of the *hyangyak* would eventually bring about the reform of the state bureaucracy.

The existence of quasi-legal machinery at the local elites' disposal in controlling village life powerfully sustained the existing social order. The *hyangyak* exhorted the members to pay taxes, obey the law, and remain loyal to the state. The creation of an additional level of organization in the form of community regulations beneath the local administrator or district magistrate allowed the ruler in the capital to enlist the prominent members of the villages in keeping officials in check. As Deuchler has cogently stated, the "village codes as an embodiment of *ye* became one of the most effective means to control the moral and, by extension, the political atmosphere of localities outside the capital."[57] The binary of public and private was at best ambiguous and fuzzy in institutions, rituals, and rhetoric. After all, *ye* was an encompassing concept that glossed over both private and public legal spheres.

When the Confucian scholars called for a reform of customs through village codes, they naturally followed the framework of the state code of a predominantly penal nature. Among *hyangyak*'s ideals of mutual encouragement, correction, reciprocity, and cooperation, disproportionate emphasis was placed on mutual correction of wrongful conducts. In this light, touting *hyangyak* as an informal law "promoting a good harmony between Confucian custom and legal regulation," in which "social dynamics worked quite peacefully and harmoniously" contributes little to the accurate understanding of Korean legal

56 *Yulgok Chŏnsŏ*, book 16, 3; see Han Sang-kwŏn, "16–17 segi hyangyak ŭi kujo wa sŏngkyŏk [The Structure and Character of *Hyangyak* in the Sixteenth and Seventeenth Centuries]," *Chindan hakpo* 58 (1984), 36–37.

57 Deuchler, "Neo-Confucianism," 52.

past.[58] Equating community compacts to informal law standing next to state law only adds confusion. Some historians lamented that students of Korean law hardly acknowledged the existence of autonomous, unofficial, folk "law."[59] But not all social control can be viewed as law.

Rule of Law and the Role of Law

The fact that *hyangyak* represented a realm in which coercive social control and respect for harmony were internalized without apparent contradictions may be instructive in explaining important characteristics of Korean legal tradition. Historians have been engaged in a continuing debate on Korean legal culture. For more than the last forty years, the prevailing view of traditional Korean law was more or less shaped by the so-called Hahm thesis. Pyong-Choon Hahm, a former professor of political science and later a high-ranking government official, was the first scholar who published on Korean legal history in English, and therefore his description and characterization of Korean law dominated the outside view of the country's traditional law. He argued in the 1970s and 1980s that Koreans lived in an "affective" and dispute-averse culture, mainly due to the unique influence of Confucianism in the legal past.[60] His portrayal of traditional Korean law, marked by a relative lack of rights consciousness, a heavy emphasis on informal settlement, and the negative perception of lawsuits, has come under severe criticisms lately. Many scholars have criticized him for exaggerating the indolent nature of Korean legal culture. In particular, they refuted Hahm's claim that Koreans were disinclined to assert their rights in an adversary adjudicative setting. Pointing to the staggering number of lawsuits in Chosŏn and the state's struggle to control them, they claimed that the traditional Korean justice system was as vigorous as the Western models.[61]

This debate on Korean legal culture seems parallel to the broader historiographical trend that rejected the conventional wisdom that East Asian legal culture was non-litigious, averse to legal proceedings. For instance, the

[58] Chongko Choi, "Law and Custom in Korean Society: A Historical and Jurisprudential Approach," *Seoul Taehakkyo pŏphak* 47 (2006), 229–232.

[59] Dieter Eikemeier, "Law, Contract, and Covenant: Aspects of a Korean Mutual Insurance Venture," in *Anthropology of Law in the Netherlands*, eds. Keebet von Benda-Beckmann and Fons Strijbosch (Dordrecht: Foris Publications, 1986), 260–287.

[60] Pyong-Choon Hahm, *The Korean Political Tradition and Law: Essays in Korean Law and Legal History*, 2nd ed. (Seoul: Royal Asiatic Society Korea Branch, 1971) (first published in 1967); Pyong-Choon Hahm, *Korean Jurisprudence, Politics and Culture* (Seoul: Yonsei University Press, 1986).

[61] Kun Yang, "Law and Society Studies in Korea: Beyond the Hahm Theses," *Law and Society Review* 23 (1989): 891–901; Im Sang-hyŏk, "Sosong kip'i ŭi munhwa chŏnt'ong e taehan chaego wa Hangŭk sahoe [A Reconsideration of the Tradition of Anti-Litigation Culture and Korean Society]," *Pŏp kwa sahoe* 24 (2003): 145–160; Chulwoo Lee, "Talking about Korean Legal Culture: A Critical Review of the Discursive Production of Legal Culture in Korea," *Korea Journal* (Autumn 1998): 45–76.

once influential view of Kawashima Takeyoshi that the Japanese were reluctant to engage in litigation has been powerfully revised by John O. Haley.[62] Similarly, as seen in the previous chapter, scholars such as William Shaw have shown that the Chosŏn dynasty was congested with legal proceedings. From this, recent studies have questioned the view that Koreans lacked a strong notion of rights and tended to avoid courts. This development has significantly deepened our understanding of traditional Korean law and legal culture. But one cannot but point out certain hollowness in the debate on the "Hahm Thesis," especially in the arguments of Hahm's detractors. Those who disagreed with the opinion that Korea was "alegal" (Hahm's term) tried to dispute the view that traditional law codes were penal laws and to contend further that Korea had a tradition of civil law.[63] But these opinions are at best overdrawn. The non-existence of legal custom or private law in Chosŏn does not make Korean law incomplete. Korean law was complete in a way different from European law. Korea and East Asia had law formalized by the state, but its notion was not the same as the Western notion of law. These different concepts of law require a cautious approach to traditional Korean law and its legal system.

There has been a trend to trace the contemporary notion of the rule of law in the Confucian culture in Korea. It has been argued that the Confucian emphasis on order and procedure approximates it to the rejection of arbitrary rule.[64] In this view, the conventional belief that Confucianism was opposed to the rule of law is mistaken because it misconstrues the way "law" was used in the Chosŏn dynasty.[65] The Confucian concept of *li* (*ye*), ritual propriety, functioned in premodern East Asia as a public political norm that effectively restrained and disciplined political rulers whose "political legitimacy depended on correctly regulating their conduct according to *li*."[66] According to this opin-

[62] John Owen Haley, "The Myth of the Reluctant Litigant and the Role of the Judiciary in Japan," *Journal of Japanese Studies* 4 (1978): 359–390; John Owen Haley, *Authority without Power: Law and the Japanese Paradox* (Oxford: Oxford University Press, 1991); Takeyoshi Kawashima, "Dispute Resolution in Contemporary Japan," in *Law and Japan: The Legal Order in a Changing Society*, ed. Arthur Taylor von Mehren (Cambridge, MA: Harvard University Press, 1963), 41–72.

[63] Im Sang-hyŏk, "Chosŏn chŏngi minsa sosong," 35–36; Pak Pyŏng-ho, *Hanguk pŏpchesa ko*, 235.

[64] Daniel B. Bell and Chaibong Hahm, "Introduction: The Contemporary Relevance of Confucianism," in *Confucianism for the Modern World*, eds. Daniel A. Bell and Chaibong Hahm (Cambridge: Cambridge University Press, 2003), 2.

[65] Chaihark Hahm, "Law, Culture and the Politics of Confucianism," *Columbia Journal of Asian Law* 16, no. 2 (2003), 259, note 20. See also Chaihark Hahm, "Negotiating Confucian Civility through Constitutional Discourse," in *The Politics of Affective Relations: East Asia and Beyond*, eds. Chaihark Hahm and Daniel A. Bell (Lanham: Lexington Books, 2004), 277–308; Chaihark Hahm, "Ritual and Constitutionalism: Disputing the Ruler's Legitimacy in a Confucian Polity," *The American Journal of Comparative Law* 57, no. 1 (2009): 135–203.

[66] Chaihark Hahm, "Constitutionalism, Confucian Civil Virtue, and Ritual Propriety," in *Confucianism for the Modern World*, eds. Daniel A. Bell and Chaibong Hahm, 45.

ion, the Confucian aversion toward punishment and litigation is compatible with the theory of rule of law.

These are views definitely insightful. It is certainly important to point out that there were instances of bureaucratic resistance to the royal will. But one may ask: can rule of ethics (*tŏkch'i chuŭi*) coexist with rule of law (*pŏpch'i chuŭi*)?[67] A rudimentary definition of rule of law is that the state is subject to law, namely, judgment by a tribunal enforcing law. Rule of law requires the existence of political institutions and theoretical foundations that impose restraints on the state. In Korea, the king was above the restraint of law. The principle of "*yeju pŏpchong*" means that *ye* is the main and law is the supplementary. Even if the limits imposed by *ye* in the form of religious or natural law, or human rights in modern parlance, existed, it would be difficult to view them as a kind of "bridle" on the ruler, embodied in the form of institutionalized machinery.

There is no question, on the other hand, that the role of law in traditional Korea was clear and unequivocal. The state officials in Chosŏn Korea were committed to the supremacy of law and the moral propriety of the penalty prescribed in the code. One official stated: "Since the statute covers the matter, there can be no grounds for judgment by analogy which would enable the penalty to be raised. In our use of the law, we cannot simply disregard a statute and increase the penalty provided by law."[68] It has been argued that rule of law was achieved in Chosŏn through "the codification of laws" which brought about "lasting stability and continuity."[69] This statement itself needs a qualified reading but it still captures an important aspect of Korean law. Korea had a legal system formalized by the central government that ensured regularity and specificity of law and punishment, thereby contributing to social stability and cogency.

The forces of modernization unleashed in the nineteenth and early twentieth centuries and the tides of legal transplantation across the world seemed to wipe out hurriedly the divergences between legal systems and traditions. Yet legal modernization did not render irrelevant differences that had existed earlier. Many of the elements of the Korean legal tradition observed in the Chosŏn period have survived into modern law. The notion of civil morality dominated virtually all daily-life activities of the Korean people. The experience of redrawing local customs and practices was largely dominated by the dictates of collective moral responsibility and harmony. As seen in *hyangyak*, the domination of village life by *yangban* was not conducive to the affirmation of the communal spirit of the local village or provincial liberties, and were instead incorporated into the official value system stressing the virtues of social stability and permanency.

Law and morality were enmeshed in Korean society. Wrongdoers were expected to repent and apologize. Those who remained unrepentant tended

[67] See James Palais, "Chosŏn wangjo ŭi kwallyo chŏk kunju che [The Bureaucratic Monarchical System in the Chosŏn Dynasty]," in *Tongyang samguk ŭi wangkwŏn kwa kwallyo che*, ed. Chosŏn sidae sahak hoe (Seoul: Kukhak Charyowŏn, 1999).

[68] A case of 1674 in *Sinbo sugyo chimnok*, cited in Shaw, "Traditional Korean Law and Its Relation to China," 309.

[69] Chŏng, "Chosŏn sidae ŭi kwŏllyŏk pullip," 47.

to be punished more severely. It is not difficult to find in modern law the vestiges of the traditional dispute resolution measures that relied on coercive harmony building, shrouded with the imperatives of moral regeneration. Confucian civil morality influenced the inclination in the modern justice system to stress reasonable outcomes rather than the strict application of legal principles. In modern Korea, the sense of shame and honor fares significantly in the legal arena. An offence is often transmuted into a moral offence, with its social impact shared by the surrounding community. The public's reception of the outcome of criminal trials and the resolution of civil litigations tends to be swayed by whether or not the guilty or responsible party was truly sorry. The tendency of public opinion to muddle civil and criminal cases still continues.

The fundamental transformation of Korean law began to take place during the late nineteenth century. Before Korea fell under Japanese rule, there were serious autonomous efforts for legal reform. Why did Korea's reform endeavor remain largely ineffective, whereas Japan's modernization attempts scored, by all accounts, remarkable success? The modernization of the Japanese legal system will be examined Chapter 3, but a brief comparison here may be in order. The Japanese legal past differed from both imperial China and Chosŏn Korea. The prolonged feudal era with a fragmented political structure meant the absence of comprehensive legislation, a situation that endured until the Meiji Restoration. The Meiji government was determined to break from the feeble and chaotic past legal order decisively, abruptly, and comprehensively. In contrast, the high level of political centralization and legal uniformity in Chosŏn was such that it resisted and blocked much-needed changes; the weight of Korea's entrenched legal system dragged down burgeoning reform initiatives. The resulting debilitating inertia deprived Korea of the kind of nimbleness and flexibility with which Japan pursued its legal reforms.

Korea's Autonomous Attempts for Legal Reform

Chosŏn Korea opened its doors to the outside world as a result of Japan's gunboat diplomacy. The First Korea-Japan Treaty was signed in 1876, followed by a series of treaties with Western powers. Korea launched an overhaul of the government and the legal system in 1894, known as the Kabo Reform. In 1897, the beginning of the Taehan Cheguk (Great Korean Empire) was declared, and further changes, known as the Kwangmu Reform, were introduced.[70] These

[70] For Korea's legal reforms in the 1880s and 1890s, see Kim Pyŏng-hwa, *Hanguk sabŏpsa* [A History of the Judiciary in Korea] (Chungse p'yŏn) (Seoul: Ilchogak, 1979), 3–19; Pŏpwŏn Haengjŏngch'ŏ, ed., *Pŏpwŏnsa* [History of Courts] (Seoul: Pŏpwŏn Haengjŏngch'ŏ, 1995); Chŏn Pong-dŏk, *Hanguk kŭndae pŏp sasangsa* [A History of Modern Legal Thought in Korea] (Seoul: Pagyŏngsa, 1981); Chŏn Pong-dŏk, "Hanguk kŭndae sabŏp chedosa [A History of the Judicial System of Modern Korea]," *Taehan Pyŏnhyŏp hoebo*, vols. 1–3 (1970–1973); Chŏn Pong-dŏk, "Ilche ŭi sabŏpkwŏn kangt'al kwajŏng ŭi yŏngu [A Study of the Forcible Takeover of Judicial Power by Imperial Japan]," *Aesan hakpo* 2 (1982), 182–183; Sin U-ch'ŏl, "Kŭndae sabŏp chedo sŏngnip sa pigyo yŏngu: Hanguk e issŏsŏ 'sabŏp tongnip' wŏlli ŭi t'aedong suyong kwa

reforms were as much propelled by external political exigencies as internal momentum for nation building. The enactment of a uniform corpus of civil law and the establishment of modern courts were essential in order to revise the unequal treaties and abrogate extraterritoriality by which consular jurisdiction had been granted to foreign powers. Overall, however, the scope of the judicial reforms was limited and its effect minimal. One of the reasons was that the attempted changes reaffirmed, not limited, the traditional royal control of the courts. The notion of independent judicial power was a novelty in the Chosŏn dynasty. The deeply-engrained beliefs that courts were part of the administration and that judicial institutions were instruments of royal authority were rarely challenged even in the late nineteenth century.

The concepts of the separation of powers and judicial independence were introduced to Korea through the observers the government dispatched abroad.[71] The newspapers and intellectuals in the 1880s and 1890s widely discussed the concepts of separation of power and constitutionalism. But there was little voice openly demanding an independent judiciary to exist outside the king's prerogatives.[72] Tongnip hyŏphoe, which actively called for a citizen assembly, was largely silent on judicial independence.[73] Reforms initiated by the government seemed to depart little from the traditional legal system. The Hongbŏm Fourteen Articles issued in 1894 in the wake of the Kabo Reform stipulated the separation of royal family affairs and national affairs (Article 4), the separation of civil law and criminal law, and the prohibition of abusive penalties (Article 13), but no establishment of independent courts.[74]

chŏngae [A Comparative Historical Study of the Establishment of Modern Judicial Systems: The Beginning and Development of the Principle of Judicial Independence in Korea]," *Seoul Taehakkyo pŏphak* 49 (2008): 256–285. For the changes in legal consciousness in Korea during this period as reflected in newspapers, see Kim Chae-mun, *Hanguk chŏnt'ong ch'aekwŏn pŏp*, 412–424.

71 The reports of 1881 by Pak Chŏng-yang and Ŏm Se-yŏng, who had been sent to Japan, stated that "judicial affairs are decided exclusively by the courts" in which the administrators could not interfere. See Hŏ Tong-hyŏn, ed. *Chosa sich'altan kwangye charyojip* [Sources on the Investigation and Observation Commission] (Seoul: Kukhak Charyowŏn, 2000), vol. 12, 175–176, 386, 467; Sin U-ch'ŏl, "Kŭndae sabŏp chedo sŏngnip sa pigyo yŏngu: uri pŏpwŏn chojik pŏpche ŭi ch'ogi hyŏngsŏng [A Comparative Historical Study of the Establishment of Modern Judicial Systems: The Early Organization of Our Court Structure]," *Pŏpcho* 612 (September 2007), 87–88.

72 Sin, "Kŭndae sabŏp chedo" (2008), 266, citing articles in *Hansŏng Sunbo*, December 9, 1893; January 30, 1894; February 7, 1894; February 17, 1894; and August 31, 1894. See also Sin U-ch'ŏl, "Kŭndae sabŏp chedo" (2007), 89–91.

73 The only exception was the memorial authored by Pak Yŏng-hyo in 1888, in which he emphasized the need for adjudication by the professional judge. See Sin, "Kundae sabŏp chedo," (2007), 93–94; Sin, "Kundae sabŏp chedo," (2008), 266. The text of Pak's memorial is found in Chŏn, *Hanguk kŭndae pŏp sasangsa*, (1981), 159–161; Kim Kap-ch'ŏn, "Pak Yŏng-hyo ŭi kŏnbaeksŏ: Naejŏng kaehyŏk e taehan 1888 nyŏn ui sansomun [Pak Yŏng-hyo's Petition: The Memorial of 1888 Regarding Internal Reform]," *Hanguk chŏngch'i yŏngu* 2 (June 1990), 259–260.

74 The Fourteen Articles were based on the Twenty Articles presented by the Japanese Consul Inoue Kaoru (*Naejŏng kaehyŏk yomok*) of 1894. The latter included an article demanding "the independence of judges for judicial impartiality, that is, the separation of judges from the

Korea's first Court Organization Law (Law Number 1) was promulgated in 1895. The high court, Kodŭng Chaep'anso, was established, under which circuit courts on the appellate level and district courts, Hansŏng Court, and Open Port Courts on the trial level were established, in addition to special courts. The court organization law was closely based on the Japanese Court Organization Law of 1890 which had been devised according to the draft by the German jurist Otto Rudolf.[75] Compared with the Japanese law, the Korean law conferred far more extensive power on the justice minister.[76] The posts of judges and prosecutors continued to be occupied by administrators who were answerable to the minister. The court organization law was revised on May 30, 1899, in the aftermath of the Kwangmu Reform. The high court was renamed Pyŏngniwŏn and was given expanded jurisdiction, but it continued to remain under the control of the emperor and the justice minister. The new system was seen as the revival of the old Chosŏn judicial structure, the new high court being equated with Hyŏngjo, the Ministry of Punishments. Local courts were attached to the administration and local administrators continued to serve as judges (Articles 59–61).[77]

In October 1899, the Ministry of Justice forbade the Hansŏng Chaep'anso from rendering decisions without the ministry's prior approval. The procedural regulations were revised so that the ministry would have a review power over the cases decided by even the Pyŏngniwŏn. The chief judge of the Pyŏngniwŏn complained to the emperor about rampant irregular judicial selection practices, apparently condoned by the justice ministry, but he was forced to resign from his post. Historians explain that the altercations between the Pyŏngniwŏn and the justice ministry during this time were caused more by the personal enmity between the heads of the two institutions than by genuine jurisdictional disputes.[78] In July 1900, the graduates of the Judicial Training School (Pŏpkwan yangsŏngso, established in 1895) protested that they had to wait five to six years

administrators" (Article 10), but it was left out from the Hongbŏm Articles. Sin, "Kundae sabŏp chedo" (2007), 96–97.

75 See Saigo Saibansho Shimu Sōmukoku ed. *Saibansho hyakunen shi* [The Centennial History of Courts] (Tokyo: Saigo saibansho shimu sōmukoku, 1990). For the text of the Japanese Court Organization Law (1890), see Nakano Bunko at http://www.geocities.jp/nakanolib/hou/hm23-6.htm.

76 The text is in *Hanmal kŭndae pŏmnyŏng charyo chip* [A Collection of Modern Laws and Regulations in Late Traditional Korea], ed. Song Pyŏng-gi, Pak Yŏng-ok, and Pak Han-sŏl (Seoul: Kukhoe Tosŏgwan, 1970–1972), vol. 1, 491. The justice minister had the power to decide the locations of the courts (Article 2), the assignment of personnel (Article 3), the jurisdictions (Article 4), the establishment of branch courts (Article 7), the status of district court judges (Article 9), the personnel matters of the judges and prosecutors (Articles 14, 21, 24, 27–28), and the establishment and supervision of special courts (Article 26). The minister held control over the appointment of judges (Article 56). Local magistrates were allowed to continue to serve as district court judges and prosecutors (Article 56).

77 Chŏn, "Ilche ŭi sabŏpkwŏn kangt'al"; Kim Pyŏng-hwa, *Hanguk sabŏpsa* (Chungse p'yŏn), 53.

78 Sin, "Kŭndae sabŏp chedo" (2008), 276; To Myŏn-hoe, "1894–1905 nyŏn gan hyŏngsa chaep'an chedo yŏngu [A Study of the Criminal Adjudication System between 1894 and 1895]" (PhD diss., Seoul National University, 1998), 234.

to be appointed to judgeship and were often discriminated against when they lacked political ties. But in August, the justice minister's power to review judicial decisions was reconfirmed and the nascent ideal of judicial independence was frustrated.[79] The reforms of the judicial system accomplished through the Kabo reform were mostly undone during this period.

Some comparisons with the contemporary Chinese and Japanese situations may be instructive. Efforts for judicial reform in China at the turn of the century coincided with the struggle by the Qing government to resist the rising pressure from Chinese bureaucrats. Afraid of their control of judicial power slipping away into the hands of local Chinese officials, the Manchu governing elites viewed the overhaul of the judicial system as crucial. Chinese judges seemed to put forward more professional and formidable challenges to the government demanding judicial independence than their Korean counterparts. Korea lacked a charismatic personality like Shen Jiaben (1840–1913) who led a well-focused opposition to the Qing government.

In Meiji Japan, the government acknowledged early on the importance of the separation of powers in a modern judicial system. Judicial authority was guaranteed in the decree of the Great Council of State (Dajōkan), issued in 1875, which ended the old rule that the court sent difficult cases to a higher government authority.[80] Article 5 of the decree stipulated that the instructions given by administrative authorities for concrete cases were not binding for the tribunal, except when they concerned special declarations and notifications. The principle that only the courts were competent to interpret the law of the country laid the foundation of the modern judicial system. The Meiji Constitution (1889) provided the right to demand a trial (Article 24), established judicial power of the courts (Article 57), and guaranteed judicial tenure (Article 58).[81]

In Korea, the emperor seemed to have little incentive to consider similar changes. The view that "judicial power was part of royal prerogatives" remained unchallenged.[82] The separation of powers thus became a serious issue only when it was required by outside powers as a precondition for the abolition of extraterritoriality. Between 1899 and 1905, there were as many as thirty-one new judicial ministers and twenty-eight new chief judges. Their tenure was often less than three months.[83] In this situation, efforts for judicial modernization were inevitably limited in scope, unable to take on fundamental structural and institutional changes.

[79] To, "1894–1905 nyŏn gan hyŏngsa chaep'an," 233–236, 239–241, 252–254.

[80] See Chapter 3.

[81] Although the Meiji Constitution did not mention "judicial independence" of the judges, the only branch of government that exercised authority "in the name of the Emperor" was the judiciary. See Haley, *Authority without Power*. The constitution of 1946 (Article 76) stipulated that judicial independence was guaranteed.

[82] The statement of the contemporary intellectual Yu Ch'i-hyŏng. Yu Ch'i-hyŏng, *Hŏnpŏp* [Constitutional Law] (Seoul: Asia Munhwasa, 1981, 1908), 76.

[83] Sin, "Kŭndae sabŏp chedo" (2008), 276.

Despite the overall tepid progress of judicial reform, however, the rapid flow of Western legal concepts into Korea during this period seemed unstoppable. There was an interesting incident that evinced the impact of the introduction of civil law principles.[84] In July 1896, a Confucian local scholar named Chŏng Sŏng-u presented a memorial to Emperor Kojong. In his strongly-worded appeal, he denounced Sŏ Chae-p'il, the president of the *Tongnip sinmun*, the Minister of Interior Pak Chŏng-yang, the Minister of Military Yi Yun-yŏng and other prominent officials. Claiming that they pursued their private interests by colluding with foreign powers, Chŏng demanded their punishment. Normally such a case would have been treated as a political matter or a criminal law issue. To everyone's surprise, however, Sŏ and the other targeted individuals responded by filing a suit for defamation. In Korean traditional law, there were no provisions for damages for defamation. The court took a creative step by applying by analogy a provision in the *Hyŏngpŏp taejŏn*, a criminal code, that stated that the assailant in a serious assault case must pay for the victim's care until the latter's recovery from injury. The court thus ordered Chŏng to pay reparation to those whom he maligned. This case is likely the first incident in which civil law recovery was inferred from existing penal law provisions. One must add that Chŏng was convicted, apart from the civil suit, for presenting an untruthful memorial to the crown and was sentenced to three years of imprisonment.[85]

Civil justice thus began to take root in Korea, but the government's efforts to implement a modern legal system were largely ill-focused and poorly executed. Before the reform efforts could yield any real results, Korea became Japan's protectorate. It is important to note that Korea underwent legal reforms under Japan, a country that was overrun by modernity during the very same time when it was trying to impose its modernity on Korea. Both in Japan and Korea, and also in China, attempts to create a modern legal system were prompted initially by external pressures. The goal of the abolition of extraterritoriality was a powerful motivation for legal modernization. In Japan, to be sure, internal momentum for nation building played as great as, if not greater than, outside pressure. There is a sense that the whole extraterritoriality issue was willfully exaggerated by the Japanese elites who, mindful of military, economic, and political gains that would accompany the introduction of Western law and institutions, saw a way to assuage the possible opposition to their legal reform. It is beyond dispute that the Meiji elites were convinced of the superiority of Western legal and political institutions. In their official stance, nonetheless, they continued to formulate the extraterritoriality question as the principal factor in the push for Western law. In both Japan and China, the self-imposed

[84] This case is cited from Mun Chun-yŏng, "Hanguk ŭi hyŏngsa sabŏp kwa minsa punchaeng hyŏng koso sakŏn: ku Han mal kwa ilche sidae ŭi kyŏnghŏm [Korea's Criminal Justice and Civil Disputes: An Experience in Late Traditional Korea and the Japanese Colonial Period]," *Pusan Taehakkyo pŏphak yŏngu* 48, no. 1 (2007): 1401–1437.

[85] Ibid., 1408–1409.

trek to legal modernization was pursued with a sense of urgency because legal reform, more accurately the transplantation of Western law, was perceived as having a direct relation to national independence. Neither country fell victim to colonization but their legal modernization was dictated by the threat of Western imperialism.[86]

The making of civil law in Japan and China still constituted a voluntary reception of European law. It took the form of conscious and deliberate effort by legal elites to translate, imitate, and adopt the civil codes from France and Germany. In fact, their march to modern civil law was not a "long march" because the reformers tried to duplicate a legal development – that had taken hundreds of years in Europe – within a couple of decades or less. Traditional laws and legal institutions were quickly abandoned and local practices and usages were classified and interpreted in terms of Western legal categories. The process amounted to a "self-colonization" by the newly imported civil laws. When their legal traditions were sufficiently civilized to warrant the abolition of extraterritoriality, Japan and China – the latter to a lesser degree of success – joined the international community as full-fledged sovereign nations. Within a few years, Japan, this time as a colonizer, undertook a deliberate legal transplantation of Japanized Western law in its colonies in Taiwan and Korea.

Colonial legal campaign in Korea was grounded on Japan's own experience of legal reform. In order to understand legal modernization in Korea, it is necessary to examine the process in Japan, to which the next chapter turns.

[86] Asano Toyomi, *Teikoku Nihon no shokuminchi hōsei* [The Colonial Legal Structure of Imperial Japan] (Nagoya: Nagoya Daigaku Shuppankai, 2008).

3

Custom and Legal Reception: The Japanese Precedent

The Japanese precedent of legal modernization foreshadowed the path of legal modernization in Korea. Japanese legal policy, in both the metropole and the colonies, was an unapologetically bureaucratic instrument of nation building. It allowed Japan to pursue a remarkably effective process of centralization, tightly coordinated by the ruling elites. The imported notion of customary law proved to be a critical element in receiving foreign law into Japan. The Japanese did not initially perceive customs as the material of law, empowered by popular wishes; the creation of law as a popular process was a foreign idea, as it was elsewhere in East Asia. But the concept of custom appealed to the Meiji elites, who were eager to replace the Tokugawa legal order with Western law and the legal system but also needed, at least officially, to maintain and preserve indigenous law and legal tradition. Japan declared custom to be a source of law in 1875. Once defined as a legal source, custom became crucial machinery in reconciling tradition with modernity. The interpretation of custom by the courts consisted of adjusting existing laws and local usages to the imported European law, and reframing the former in terms of the latter's principles and vocabularies. In this way jurisprudence of customary law helped acclimate the traditional legal order without a detrimental rupture. The redaction of the civil code aimed at inserting the elements of old law into a Western legal framework so that the new code was acceptable to the Japanese people.

What occurred in Japan in the late nineteenth century was not very different from what had happened in Europe in the medieval and early modern periods. A key common instrument in the process of legal reception in history, transcending time and space, was customary law. In late medieval France, in the wake of the reception of Roman law, jurists reduced customs into writing and systematized them, resorting to the received civil law principles as written reason. Newly redacted and reformed customary law eased the transition of French law to a new legal order that fully incorporated the "civilized" and "learned" Roman law. A similar development took place several hundred years later in Japan. When the Japanese subscribed to the imported notion of customary law, however, they departed from European legal philosophy in some important aspects. The German school's representation of custom as the spirit of the people entailed a historicist critique of the intervention by an all-powerful state. The evocation of custom in nineteenth-century European historiography was of a liberal nature, defending the legal autonomy of the populace. In contrast, the Japanese idea of custom had little concern for the expression of popular will. Legal centralism, the idea that the state grants law its force, was an enduring feature in the East Asian legal tradition.

An analogy can be made between Meiji Japan and the French Third Republic. Eugen Weber has argued that the modernization of rural France in the late nineteenth century marked a distinct phase of internal colonization. It was a self-colonization process led by the state, replacing traditional, regional, and feudal elements with modern, central, urban, and national elements.[1] This process of turning "peasants into French" seemed similar to the reform effort launched in Meiji Japan whose nation-building process, it has been argued, "resembled colonial expansion in that it replaced local cultural and political institutions with central hegemonic institutions."[2]

Japanese legal modernization has been regarded as a successful example of a voluntary large-scale reception of foreign law. Deliberate legal reception is less frequent than the imposition of new law via colonization. In history, the efficiency of the transplant process was most conspicuous during the times of colonialism, as the colonial powers brought to the colonies their own laws or enacted laws inspired by them. Other than Japan, the case of Turkey is a notable example of legal reception in non-colonial situations. The Turkish Civil Code of 1926 represented a swift passage from one legal family to another by the wholesale adoption of foreign law, specifically the Swiss law. The codification in Turkey was a sort of "social engineering through law," envisioning the eventual change of the country's legal culture.[3] In both the Turkish and Japanese codifications, law was perceived more as a force that would initiate social change than as one that reflected social change. The process of legal modernization in these countries was not an organic growth but a case of carefully-coordinated legal reception. Japan later brought its model of legal reform to colonial Korea.

In order to understand Korean colonial law, it is essential to examine the development of law in Japan. Much of private legal relationship among

[1] The incorporation of the Midi, the regions from Provence to the Pyrenees known as Languedoc, into "modern France" created as much challenge as the crusade against the heretical Albigensians in the thirteenth century. Eugen Weber, *Peasants into Frenchmen: The Modernization of Rural France, 1870–1914* (Stanford: Stanford University Press, 1976).

[2] Mark E. Caprio, *Japanese Assimilation Policies in Colonial Korea 1910–1945* (Seattle: University of Washington Press, 2009), 54.

[3] Esin Örücü, "The Impact of European Law on the Ottoman Empire and Turkey," in *European Expansion and Law: The Encounter of European and Indigenous Law in 19th- and 20th-Century Africa and Asia*, eds. W. J. Mommsen and J. A. de Moor (Oxford: Berg, 1992), 39–58. The Swiss Code and the Law of Obligations were received en bloc, including the areas of family law and succession.

Koreans was redefined and reconfigured through the operation of customary law order that was faithfully based on the Japanese experience. This chapter examines the Japanese reception of Western law and the notion of custom as a precursor to legal transplantation in Korea.

The Introduction of the Legal Theory of Custom in East Asia

Dajōkan Decree Number 103 and Custom as a Source of Law

The early Meiji years witnessed a dizzying array of the competing forces of modernization and tradition. The reform of the legal system was grounded on the principles enunciated in the famous "Meiji Charter Oath." The Oath, issued by the emperor in April 1868, set forth the fundamental directions of the Japanese state following the imperial restoration. Of particular importance was the fourth article of the charter which declared: "Such ancient customs as are unworthy shall be abolished and things shall be adjusted in accordance with the eternal principles of justice."[4] The need for suppressing evil customs of the past was deeply engrained in the Meiji reformist mentality. Along with the professed goal of overcoming the feudal past, the early Meiji period also witnessed a movement to return to antiquity, a trend replete with its political and ideological implications. The Great Council of State, Dajōkan, was established in 1868, restoring the ancient Daijōkan that was the central organ of government in the eighth century.[5] Reactions from conservative factions against the reformist forces, seemingly subservient to Western influences, took the form of exaggerated respect for tradition, which some may have welcomed as a moral palliative for Japan's inferiority in industrial and economic achievements.[6]

The reform of the judicial system began with the establishment of the Ministry of Justice, Shihōshō, on August 24, 1871. The ordinance of the justice ministry, issued on September 9, 1872, declared a separation of civil and criminal matters in adjudication, a significant departure from the traditional practices of confounding civil and criminal instances. The gist of the reform was rejecting the entrenched idea that the administration of justice was an "authoritarian act of mercy."[7] The pressing need for a modern code was mounting. Justice Minister Etō Shimpei (1834–1874), a person with little patience, tried

4 Kenzo Takayanagi, "Occidental Legal Ideas in Japan: Their Reception and Influence," *Pacific Affairs* 3, no. 8 (1930), 741–742.

5 See Ono Shusei, "Comparative Law and the Civil Code of Japan" (Part I), *Hitotsubashi Journal of Law and Politics* 24 (1996), 36, note 43, citing Wada Hidematsu, *Kanshoku yōkai* (Tokyo: Meiji Shoin, 1925), originally published in 1902.

6 Eric Seizelet, "European Law and Tradition in Japan during the Meiji Era, 1868–1912," in *European Expansion and Law: The Encounter of European and Indigenous Law in 18th- and 20th-Century Africa and Asia*, eds. W. J. Mommsen and J. A. de Moor (Oxford: Berg, 1992), 80. See also Richard H. Minear, *Japanese Tradition and Western Law: Emperor, State, and Law in the Thought of Hozumi Yatsuka* (Cambridge, MA: Harvard University Press, 1970); Robert Charles Epp, "Threat to Tradition: The Reaction to Japan's 1890 Civil Code" (PhD diss., Harvard University, 1964).

7 Wilhelm Röhl, *History of Law in Japan since 1868* (Leiden: Brill, 2005), 659.

to create a Japanese code by quickly translating the French Civil Code into the Japanese language.[8] Mitsukuri Rinshō (1846–1897) began translating the Code Napoleon in 1869. The failure of Etō's hasty codification effort seemed to corroborate the argument of those who believed that Japan's own tradition and culture must serve as the foundation of legislation. Etō resigned in October 1873. His successor, Ōki Takatō (1832–1899), was convinced that the new civil code should be based on traditional customs.[9]

The year 1875 marked a turning point for the modernization of the Meiji judicial system. The Great Court of Cassation, Daishinin, was instituted on April 14, 1875. Two months later, on June 8, the Dajōkan issued Fukoku [Decree] Number 103, the Rules for the Conduct of Judicial Affairs (*Saiban jimu kokoroe*). This promulgation set the criteria for the administration of justice.[10] The most important was Article 3 which stipulated: "In civil trials, those matters for which there is no written law are governed by custom, and those matters for which there is no custom shall be adjudicated by inference from reason." The sources of civil law were thus explicitly declared and the hierarchy among them established.[11]

The importance of the 1875 proclamation deserves full attention.[12] The Civil Code of China completed in 1930 (currently in force in Taiwan), the Civil Code of Manchukuo of 1937, and the Civil Code of Korea written in 1958 include exactly the same language as that of Article 3 of the Japanese decree that declared custom and reason to be official sources of law.[13] This language is strikingly similar to a provision in the Swiss Civil Code of 1907 on the sources of law. The much celebrated Article 1 of the Swiss code provided: "In the absence of an applicable statute, the judge must decide according to customary law and, in the absence of custom, according to the rules which he would enact were he a legislator. He must follow the solutions recognized by doctrine and jurisprudence" (Article 1, Sections 2 and 3). Most textbooks in

[8] Fukushima Masao, "Meiji shonen ni okeru seiō hō no keiju to Nihon no hō oyobi hōgaku [The Reception of Western Law and Japanese Law and Legal Science in the Early Meiji Period]," in *Nihonhō to Ajia, Niida Noboru hakushi tsuitō ronpunshū* [Japanese Law and Asia: In Memory of Dr. Niida Noboru], vol. 3 (Tokyo: Keisō Shobō, 1970), 172–177; Robert Epp, "The Challenge from Tradition: Attempts to Compile a Civil Code in Japan, 1866–78," *Monumenta Nipponica* 22, nos. 1 and 2 (1967): 15–48.

[9] Fukushima, "Meiji shonen ni okeru seiō hō," 177–183.

[10] The Dajōkan was then the legislature, so the Dajōkan proclamation meant a law.

[11] For the complete text of the decree, see Appendix B. Its English translation has been taken from Ishii Ryosuke, *Japanese Legislation in the Meiji Era*, trans. William J. Chambliss (Tokyo: Pan-Pacific Press, 1958), 307–308; also in Röhl, *History of Law*, 665.

[12] See Ōkawa Sumio. "Meiji hachi nen Dajōkan fukoku dai 103 gō saiban jimu kokoroe no seiritsu to Inoue Kaoru [The Proclamation of Dajōkan Decree Number 103 of Meiji Year 8 regarding the Conduct of Judicial Affairs and Inoue Kaoru]," *Ritsumeikan hōgaku* 205–206 (1989): 506–526 (Part 1); 227 (1993): 1–17 (Part. 2); 234 (1994): 174–207 (Part 3).

[13] The wording of Article 1 is identical in both the civil codes of Taiwan and Korea: "In civil cases, if there is no applicable written law, the case shall be decided according to custom. If there is no such custom, the case shall be decided according to reason of law."

Korea explain that Article 1 of the Korean Civil Code was adopted from the Swiss code. It is true that the Swiss law, pronouncing with precision the nature and the hierarchy of sources of law, inspired the legislators around the world and became the prototype of many national codes. But there is little doubt that the language in the Chinese and Korean laws was lifted from the Dajōkan proclamation instead of the Swiss code. Considering the role and influence of Japanese jurists in the framing of the Chinese and Manchu codes (including the draft codes), and the Korean colonial past under Japanese rule, the affinity between these codes and the 1875 decree is not surprising. Whereas the Swiss code required the judges to follow scholarly doctrine and practice, the Japanese law and the East Asian codes were silent on such and also overlooked the legal force of precedents. Article 4 of the Japanese decree forbade the judges to pronounce for the future by way of a general regulation, thereby denying judicial decision as a source of law. At any rate, it is remarkable that the Japanese decree preceded the Swiss law by more than thirty years.

The Japanese Civil Code was promulgated in 1896 (Books I through III) and in 1898 (Books IV and V). It did not contain a provision listing the sources of law, unlike other East Asian codes it later inspired. It is up to debate precisely why the Japanese code did not include an article like Article 3 of the Dajōkan decree and thus failed to declare custom to be an official source of law. But one can conjecture that the reason was similar to the considerations that had surrounded the making of the French Civil Code. The French code of 1804 did not have a provision dedicated to the source of law. The French revolutionaries rejected customary law because it was in their view equated with the feudal order. Officially, custom lost legal force except as provided for in the civil code.[14] The main consideration for the drafters of the Code Napoleon, and for the entire generation of jurists imbued with the revolutionary ideology since 1789, was to blot out the remnants of the *ancien régime*. Customary law had no place in the revolutionary framework of uniform law. With its preponderant emphasis on legislative supremacy and the universal ideals of natural law principles, the French code eschewed a specific reference to custom as a legal source.

The first draft of the German Civil Code of 1888 served as a model for the Japanese Civil Code. The draft code stated in Article 1: "in the absence of law, the judge follows provisions of similar matters; in the absence of such provisions, the judge follows the principles born out of the spirit of provisions." But this article was deleted in the final version, despite strong opposition from Savigny and his followers. The civil code of 1900 made no mention of customary law, mainly because of the consideration that custom was vague and

[14] Law of March 21, 1804, that brought the Civil Code into effect, stated that all preexisting laws, including Roman law, ordinances, custom, statutes, and regulations, lost their force of law. See Gény, *Méthode*, vol. 1, 331 (no. 112); Jean Bart, *Histoire du droit privé: de la chute de l'Empire romain au XIXe siècle* (Paris: Montchrestien, 1998), 439.

varied in different parts of Germany. A similar concern was raised during the redaction of the Swiss Civil Code. But Eugen Huber, the redactor of the code, persuasively asserted that custom could be applied only in the case of a gap in the code and therefore could not possibly contravene any provisions in the text. His argument prevailed and the provision in question was inserted in the code that took effect in 1912.[15]

Hozumi Nobushige (1856–1926) was an eminent Japanese jurist and one of the drafters of the civil code along with Tomii Masaakira (1858–1935) and Ume Kenjirō (1860–1910). Hozumi praised Article 3 of the Dajōkan decree: "this provision, truly deserving to be called a masterpiece of modern legislation, may be regarded as the ultimate achievement in legislative evolution; it was the forerunner to Article 1 of the Swiss Civil Code which commanded the admiration of the world a half century later."[16] Sugiyama Naojirō (1878–1966), the prominent comparative law scholar in the early twentieth century, argued that the 1875 law was the precursor of the Swiss Civil Code and other codes that derived from the Swiss law. Whereas the Swiss code had no safety mechanism to prevent subjective decisions by judges, he asserted, the Japanese law "is comprehensive as well as coherent because free research is combined with the prohibition of the denial of justice and at the same time it provides a guarantee against the abuse of free research by precise prohibition." In this sense, it is "superior to the *lex imperfecta* of Article 1, Section 3 of the Swiss code."[17] It is impossible to prove a direct relationship between the 1875 decree and the Swiss code. What is perhaps more important is to examine the origin of Article 3, especially from where the idea of custom and reason as sources of law derived. Scholarly opinions about the decree are largely divided over whether Article 3 was inspired by Japanese traditional law or by foreign law.

For Hozumi, the heart of Article 3 lay in traditional sources. He cited the provision in *Shinritsu kōryō* (Outline of the New Criminal Law) of 1871, which stated: "even if there are no applicable provisions in the code, those who commit something that does not conform to reason are subject to thirty lashes."[18]

[15] Ivy Williams, *The Sources of Law in the Swiss Civil Code* (Humphrey Milford: Oxford University Press, 1923), 38. In practice, to ignore custom altogether was impossible because custom meant Swiss cantonal laws.

[16] Hozumi Nobushige, *Hōritsu shinka ron* [A Theory of the Evolution of Law], vol. 1 (Tokyo: Iwanami Shoten, 1924), 228.

[17] Sugiyama Naojirō, "La Loi du 8 juin 1875 sur l'administration de la justice et les sources du droit privé," in *Recueil d'études sur les sources du droit en l'honneur de François Gény*, vol. 2 (Paris: Librairie du Recueil Sirey, 1934), 453–454; also Sugiyama Naojirō, "L'Evolution générale du droit japonais moderne (1869–1919)" in *Les Transformations du droit dans les principaux pays depuis cinquante ans (1869–1919): Livre du cinquantenaire de la Société de législation comparé*, vol. 2 (Paris: Librairie générale de droit et de jurisprudence, 1923), 219–248. Swiss Civil Code delegated legislative power to the judiciary, but Swiss judges, while following the provision, had to pretend to follow statutes in order to deflect criticisms of their decisions. Sugiyama, "L'Evolution générale," 223.

[18] Hozumi, *Hōritsu shinka ron*, vol. 1, 224 and 228–229.

Shinritsu kōryō, replaced by the Criminal Code enacted in 1880, was the first code designed for nationwide application; it was based on traditional Chinese and *bakufu* law without Western influence.[19] According to Hozumi, the idea of "conforming to reason" in this law became the foundation of the 1875 decree, which officially declared reason to be a source of law. Sugiyama agreed that Article 3 was inspired by traditional law, although he acknowledged that its interpretation – the meaning of the "inference from reason" – evolved under the influence of natural law of the European origin, specifically the French Civil Code.[20] Noda Yoshiyuki, a student of Sugiyama's and himself an authority in comparative law, was more skeptical.[21] For Noda, the author or at least instigator of the language of Article 3 was the French jurist Gustave Boissonade de Fontarabie (1825–1910).

Boissonade, professor at the faculty of law in Paris, came to Japan in 1873 at the invitation of the Japanese government to serve as a legal advisor.[22] He, along with the drafting committees, prepared the criminal code (1880) and the civil code (1890), known as the Old Civil Code (*Kyū minpō*).[23] There exists a letter written by Boissonade in June 1875, a few days before the promulgation of the 1875 decree. It was a reply to the questions posed by the Justice Ministry. Boissonade wrote that, in French law, when there was no custom "reason – natural law – applies" and that "in France, Article 4 of the code orders judges to supplement the insufficiency of the written law with natural reason [*équité naturelle*]."[24] From this evidence, Noda concluded that the origin of Article 3 was French legal thought and that "it is impossible to speculate that the provision of the modern hierarchy of legal sources of statutes, customary law, and reason (*jōri*) came from traditional legal thought."[25]

The influence of French law in early Meiji years was considerable. Aside from the element of reason in traditional law, which will be discussed in the following pages, the Dajōkan decree seemed mostly modeled after the general

[19] See Röhl, *History of Law*, 24–25 and 171.

[20] Sugiyama, "La Loi du 8 juin 1875," 447.

[21] Noda Yoshiyuki, "Meiji hachi nen ni okeru Furansu hō no kenkyū [A Study of French law in Meiji Year 8]," *Nichi Butsu hōgaku* 1 (1961), 3–59; Noda, "Meiji hachi nen Dajōkan fukoku dai hyaku san go dai san jō no jōri ni tsuite no zatsukan [Reflections on Reason in Article 3 of Dajōkan Decree Number 108 in Meiji Year 8]," *Hōgaku kyōkai hyaku shūnen kinen ronbun shū* (Tokyo: Yūhigaku, 1983), vol. 1, 244–280.

[22] Boissonade played a pivotal role in the reception of Western law in Japan. See Ikeda Masako Kobayashi, "French Legal Advisor in Meiji Japan (1873–1895): Gustave Emile Boissonade de Fontarabie" (PhD diss., University of Hawaii, 1996); Ōkubo Yasuo, *Nihon kindai hō no chichi Bowasonado* (Tokyo: Iwanami Shoten, 1977); Hoshino Tōru, *Meiji minpō hensan shi kenkyū* [A History of the Codification of Meiji Civil Law] (Tokyo: Daiyamondosha, 1943); Hoshino Tōru, *Minpōten ronsō shi* [A History of the Civil Code Debate] (Tokyo: Nihon Hyōronsha, 1944).

[23] See the civil code debate in the following pages.

[24] Noda, "Meiji hachi nen Dajōkan fukoku," 247–250, citing *Boasonado tōmonroku*, ed. Hōsei University, 1978. See also Ōkubo, *Nihon kindai hō no chichi Bowasonado*, 70; Oyama Kenichi, "Kanshuhō riron no denrai [The Introduction of the Theory of Customary Law] (Part I)," *Kantō Gakuen Daigaku hōgaku kiyō* 1 (1991), 85.

[25] Noda, "Meiji hachi nen ni okeru Furansu hō," 10.

provisions of the French Civil Code.[26] Still there were differences. Article 4 of the French code stated: "The judge who refuses to judge under the pretext of the silence, obscurity, or insufficiency of the statute may be prosecuted as guilty of denial of justice." Article 5 stipulated: "Judges are forbidden to pronounce by way of general and regulatory disposition upon the causes which are submitted to them." But the same code did not provide rules as to how to supplement the inadequacy of positive law.[27] Thus the French laws prohibiting denial of justice only implicitly acknowledged reason as a source of law, unlike the Japanese provision that explicitly attributed to custom and reason a subsidiary role vis-à-vis positive law.

Other European national codes, such as the Austrian Civil Code of 1811 (Das allgemeine Burgerliche Gesetzbuch) and the Dutch Civil Code of 1838 (Burgerlijk Wetboek) stipulated that positive law be supplemented by natural law, yet they fell short of the Dajōkan decree that declared unambiguously the force of custom and reason.[28] In preparation for the creation of the mixed courts in 1876, Egypt proceeded to the writing of the codes. Article 7 of the draft code provided for the situation when written laws did not exist: "when law is nonexistent or inadequate or not clear, cases are decided by the true meaning and principles of natural law." This draft was translated into Japanese in 1874, and some historians have speculated that the drafters of the Dajōkan decree used it as a model.[29] At any rate, it seems clear that the nature of the

[26] Kenzo Takayanagi, "A Century of Innovation: The Development of Japanese Law, 1869–1961," in *Law in Japan*, ed. Arthur von Mehren (Cambridge, MA: Harvard University Press, 1963), 25.

[27] There are close similarities between Articles 1 and 3 of the 1875 law and Article 4 of the French Civil Code, and also between Article 4 of the 1875 law and Article 5 of the French Civil Code. For comparisons between the Dajōkan decree and the French Civil Code articles, see Ōkawa, "Meiji hachi nen Dajōkan fukoku dai 103 gō" (Part 2), 3–6; Sugiyama Naojirō, "Meiji 8-nen fukoku dai 103 gō saiban jimu kokoroe to shihō hōgen [The Proclamation of Decree Number 103 of Meiji Year 8 regarding the Conduct of Judicial Affairs and the Sources of Private Law]," *Hōgen to kaishaku* [Sources of Law and Interpretations] (Tokyo: Yūhigaku, 1957), 8–9.

[28] The Austrian code declared the obligation of civil adjudication to supplement positive law "according to the principles of natural law" (Article 7). Absent statutes or customary law, interpretation based on analogy was allowed, but analogy was limited as much as possible and emphasis was placed on the principles of natural law. The Dutch code included the following provisions: custom has legal force to the extent that law allows its application (Article 3); intrinsic merit or equity of law is not to be contested (Article 11). The Italian Law of the Application of Law of 1865 stated: the judge decides according to analogy and, if doubts remain, according to general principles of law (Article 3, Section 2). The Spanish Civil Code of 1889 prohibited the refusal of adjudication: in case of the absence of law, the judge follows custom of land and principles of law (Article 6, Sections 1 and 2). These examples are cited from Ōkawa, "Meiji hachi nen Dajōkan fukoku dai 103 gō" (Part 3), 174–207; Sugiyama, "Meiji 8-nen fukoku dai 103 gō," 42–52.

[29] Ōkawa, "Meiji hachi nen" (Part 3), 181. The Egyptian code that took effect in 1876 provided: "in case of the silence of law, insufficiency or obscurity of law, the judge conforms to the principles of natural law and to the rules of equity" (Article 11), cited from Sugiyama, "Meiji 8-nen fukoku dai 103 gō," 50.

1875 law should be seen in the broader context of the codifications in the nineteenth century.

Concepts of "Custom" and "Reason"

Studies have shown that the Dajōkan decree draft initially used the term "*shūkanhō*" (customary law) but that it was later changed to "*shūkan*" (custom). It was likely in order to distinguish custom from written statutes (*seibunhō*).[30] The choice of terminology was probably not accidental, although it is not clear whether the drafters of the decree were fully cognizant of the lexicological and juridical meanings of the terms. The difference between *shūkanhō* and *shūkan* was that the former was regarded as written government laws and the latter unwritten government rules. Customary law meant "old law." Understood as such, the language of Article 3 recognizing *shūkan* as a source of law was not revolutionary. Certain confusion seemed inevitable, however, because suppressing evil customs of the past was the underlying principle of legal reform in Japan.

From the outset, questions arose over what *shūkan* meant. A few days after the decree's promulgation, the justice ministry issued a reply to the inquiries from courts in Osaka, Nagasaki, and Fukushima regarding the meaning of "custom." The ministry defined "custom" as "whatever has been enforced by the prefectural offices and law courts."[31] Here "custom" corresponded with the government rules that remained unwritten. When the Shiga Prefecture inquired in October 1875 if it was necessary to apply an unreasonable custom, the justice ministry issued a directive stating that "there are no rules which allow reason, arrived at by deduction in the absence of custom, to overrule custom."[32] The Shiga Prefecture's use of the term custom referred to the customs practiced among the people, but the ministry's notion of custom remained the good old laws of the *bakufu* government. Certainly it was distant from the meaning of custom as popular practices that qualified as a source of private rights. A month later the government officials declared emphatically that "custom (*shūkan*) is not the customs and manners observed by private individuals."[33]

The drafters of Decree Number 103 thus understood "custom" to mean the traditional legal order and decisions of the Tokugawa government, not popular customs. Seen as old laws of the government, "custom" included "reason," so it would be impossible to set aside custom by the application of reason. There was no need to be concerned about whether custom might be "wrongful." This was why, according to Maki Kenji, the hierarchy of legal sources provided in the decree placed custom before reason. No abrogation of custom by reason was possible. In this sense, the Meiji government's interpretation of *shūkan* in

[30] Ōkawa, "Meiji hachi nen" (Part 3), 196.

[31] Ishii, *Japanese Legislation*, 50; Röhl, *History of Law*, 123.

[32] Ishii, *Japanese Legislation*, 52; Maki Kenji, "Meiji hachi nen minji saiban no gensoku [The Principles of Civil Adjudication in Meiji Year 8]," *Hōgaku kenkyū* 17, no. 2 (1927), 361.

[33] Maki, "Meiji hachi nen," 359.

1875 did not depart from the traditional legal framework in premodern East Asia. As seen in the preceding chapters, customs among the people were understood in Korea invariably as the subject of the government actions to correct and modify. The state constantly tried to teach the people and change their practices. The Japanese historian Ōkawa Sumio has suggested that the change of the decree's language from "*shūkanhō*" to "*shūkan*" was a compromise with the emergence of the new word "*kanshū*," a term favored by influential Meiji figures. The new lexicon seemed to have the connotation of legitimate and regular practices. According to Ōkawa, Inoue Kaoru (1836–1915), Japan's vice minister of finance at the time, called the traditional patriarchal family order as *kanshū* and stated that the Confucian status hierarchy order was the nature's order, *jōri* (meaning "reason"). Inoue's *kanshū* theory threw its weight behind the term by equating *kanshū* with *jōri*.

The Meiji jurists were notorious for using the terms custom (*kanshū*), practices (*kankō*), habits (*shūkan*), and ancient usages (*kyūkan*) interchangeably without distinguishing among them.[34] There is an interesting explanation as to how the word *kanshū* with legal meaning (*guanxi* in Chinese; *kwansŭp* in Korean) came into existence in the East Asian legal glossary. The Japanese were known for neology, for example, regrouping the Chinese characters and thereby giving old Chinese terms new meanings. This was the case with the term "custom" – a lexical hijacking, according to Jérôme Bourgon, committed by the Japanese for the needs of legal modernization.[35] *Shūkan* (*xiguan* in Chinese; *sŭpkwan* in Korean) denoted a habit or practice; the new term, *kanshū* – the same characters in reverse order – designated custom, with additional legal notions. The legal glossary composed by the Japanese in order to translate the Western terms that had no equivalents in Sino-Japanese civilization still remains the basis of modern legal nomenclature in East Asia.[36] All this amply attests to the daunting tasks, and confusion, the Meiji jurists faced in these years.

When scholars argued that Article 3 of the 1875 decree was a continuation of the legal theory from the Tokugawa period, they pointed to the relationship between *shūkan* and *jōri*.[37] The term *jōri* was taken as synonymous with *dōri*, which served as a supplementary source in the old codes and rules in primordial Japan as a gap-filling device.[38] Adjudication according to reason was an integral part of the East Asian legal tradition.[39] It was textually preserved in

[34] Eric Seizelet, "*Contra legem ou Para legem*? La Coutume de l'union matrimoniale de fait en droit civil japonais avant 1945," in *La Coutume et la norme en Chine et au Japon*, ed. Jérôme Bourgon (Saint-Denis: Presses universitaires de Vincennes, 2001), 109.

[35] Bourgon, "La Coutume et le droit," 1091–1092; Bourgon, "Le Droit coutumier," 126–128.

[36] Bourgon, "La Coutume et le droit," 1091–1092.

[37] Maki Kenji argued that the meaning of "*jōri*" in 1875 could not refer to natural law, and that it instead derived from the traditional notion of *dōri*.

[38] An example is *Ritsuryō Kyakushiki*. Takayanagi, "A Century of Innovation," 25.

[39] Sugiyama, "Meiji 8-nen," 15; Röhl, *History of Law*, 731. For *jōri*, see also Dan Fenno Henderson, *Conciliation and Japanese Law, Tokugawa and Modern* (Seattle: University of

the Chinese penal code since the Tang dynasty and was incorporated into the Japanese codes.[40] *Dōri*, meaning the common ethics or moral principles prevalent among the ruling warrior class, was different from the notion of natural law in Europe as the fount of rights.[41] The concept of natural law as an independent source of law, as in Aristotle's sense of reason, was absent in premodern East Asia.[42] The meaning of *jōri* in the early Meiji years was closer to the idea that was inherent in positive law, especially penal law. But the drafters of Article 3 of the Dajōkan decree were ready to apply the same principle in civil matters.[43] It was necessary to fill the vacuum in regulating private legal relations. Before long, as the concept of "reason" as natural law began to spread in Japan, a new notion of custom emerged.

In a famous edict of 1872, the government criminalized long-term indentured service.[44] The official decree, the Emancipation Order for Licensed Prostitutes, forbade indentured prostitution as a "violation of human reason." This law had the effect of voiding all indenture contracts as unreasonable and unethical. The Ministry of Justice instructed the courts to dismiss claims for damages that arose from such contracts. This meant that old popular customs were subject to the standard of reason in adjudication and that those which were determined to be contrary to reason were to be invalidated by the court. In March 1875, a Saitama court inquired of the justice ministry about the validity of an I.O.U. in which children were entered as security. Should the court enforce the loan contract that had been concluded on the condition that, in default, the debtor's children perform indentured services?[45] In reply, the justice ministry stated that such a contract was "unreasonable" and therefore invalid in the meaning of the decree of 1872.

Washington Press, 1965), vol. 2, 210 and 225; Carl Steenstrup, *A History of Law in Japan until 1868* (Leiden: Brill, 1991), 84; John Owen Haley, "The Adjudicatory Jurisdiction of Japanese Courts in Transnational Litigation," in *Law and Justice in a Multistate World: Essays in Honor of Arthur T. von Mehren*, eds. James A. R. Nafziger and Symeon Symeonides (Ardsley, NY: Transnational Publishers, 2002), 708–709; Haley, *Authority without Power*.

[40] Most recently the penal code of *Kaitei Ritsurei* of 1873, following the same rule in the penal code of *Shinritsu Kōryō* of 1870.

[41] Maki, "Meiji hachi nen," 358.

[42] Sugiyama, "Meiji 8-nen," 25.

[43] Sugiyama, "La Loi du 8 juin 1875," 447.

[44] Dajōkan Decree Number 295 (1872): "Article 1. Whereas the sale of persons for a life time or for a fixed term of service, during which they are exploited according to the will of the employer, has been prohibited from time immemorial as a breach of human ethics and as wrongful conduct, there has existed in the past the practice of taking employees into the home of the master under the pretext of apprenticeship. In reality this is tantamount to purchase of the individual; and hereafter such outrageous practices are strictly forbidden." The translation is from Ishii, *Japanese Legislation*, 51. See Maki, "Meiji hachi nen," 357; J. Mark Ramseyer, "Indentured Prostitution in Imperial Japan: Credible Commitments in the Commercial Sex Industry," *The Journal of Law, Economics, & Organization* 7 (1991), 97.

[45] The court reasoned that the contract appeared to be an almost unlimited term of indenture because, even if the fixed term of service expired on termination of the liability, the amount and rate of wages during the period of services was nowhere stipulated.

Following this interpretation, a contract which violated good morals as defined by the state was denied legal effect. This development indicated that in private law the government began measuring popular practices with the yardstick of "reasonableness" of natural law to determine whether to grant legal force to such practices. Now that reasonableness was required of private legal relations based on popular customs and customs that violated reason were denied legal validity, the justice ministry's interpretation of the meaning of *shūkan* in Article 3 changed dramatically by 1879. Custom (*shūkan*) as a source of law in the Dajōkan decree of 1875 was now redefined so as to include popular customs filtered through juridical lens. In a decree directed to the Shizuoka court in January 1879, the ministry defined custom as "those usages not contrary to reason, which are recognized in civil law as popular practices and precedents heretofore in use in the dealings between the government and the people."[46]

The evolution of the meaning of "custom" represented an important transition in Japanese civil law. Previously, Japanese law lacked a clear distinction between criminal and civil law. In early Meiji Japan there was no tradition of popular custom capable of becoming an official source of judicial decision. Old Japanese laws did not entertain popular practices as law. This is why in 1875 custom was still understood as something akin to administrative decisions and rules, and emphatically not popular practices. The fact that rules of private relations would be enforced through something other than administrative action by the state was a novelty to the Meiji reformers."[47] The meaning of "reason" at the time of the 1875 decree's enactment did not constitute the essential condition for determining the validity of custom.[48] But by 1879, the notion of custom as law governing private dealings ascertained and recognized by the court took root in Japanese law, closely circumscribed by the consideration of reason. Not being "wrongful" became the basic condition of validity for the custom. It was this element that was subsequently enunciated in terms of "public order" and "good morals," the terms imported from the West. By rejecting wrongful customs, the courts were seen as essentially upholding the principle of the Charter Oath that vowed the abolition of evil customs and directed old practices to be adjusted "in accordance with the eternal principles of justice."

Once they declared custom and reason as sources of law, the Japanese undertook a vast survey of custom. On January 7, 1875, Justice Minister Ōki ordered that all justice ministry courts dispatch officials to investigate local customs and laws and report the results of their inquiry to Tokyo by March 1875. A Bureau for the Investigation of Local Customs (Chihō kanrei torishirabe kyoku) was established in 1876 in the Department of Civil Law (Minpōka) under the Ministry of Justice.[49] The result was the compilation of two collections

[46] Maki, "Meiji hachi nen," 351; Ishii, *Japanese Legislation*, 51; Röhl, *History of Law*, 123.

[47] Röhl, *History of Law*, 173.

[48] Ishii, *Japanese Legislation*, 53.

[49] Röhl, *History of Law*, 174.

of customary law, *Minji kanrei ruishō* (The Classified Collection of Customs in Civil Matters) in 1877 and *Zenkoku minji kanrei ruishō* (The Nationwide Classified Collection of Customs in Civil Matters) in 1880.[50] Japanese jurists educated in Western legal science were highly skeptical about the normative force of collected customs and their utility for civil law. Undertaken by the notables of the old feudal regime, the surveys largely consisted of usages and local practices seen through the eyes of the heads of samurai clans who naturally tended to confuse civil custom with their privileges.[51] Thus scholars viewed the reports simply as compilations of the vestiges of the feudal system, not of popular usages that had achieved the validity of law.

The 1875 Dajōkan proclamation was not repealed after the codification of civil law in 1898. In fact, it remains a valid law today.[52] The decree, however, may have been conceived only as a temporary measure. The Japanese scholar Ishida Minori argued that the 1875 law, like other laws promulgated in the early Meiji years, was expected to function only until the full comprehensive codification of civil law.[53] According to Ishida, the legislative intent of Article 3 was different from that of Article 1 of the Swiss code.[54] The Swiss provision clearly intended to allow the judge freedom to interpret law. In contrast, argued Ishida, the Japanese lawmakers were mainly concerned with devising a mechanism that could dispose of the legal suits that were clogging the judicial system, exacerbated by the absence of applicable statutes and the shortage of trained judicial professionals. The exigency to meet the demands of rapidly changing society was pressing and overwhelming, and the Meiji government actively promoted arbitration and summary resolution. Trials by reason and custom were expected to promote conciliatory, arbitration-based adjudication, appealing to traditional legal sentiments. In this sense, the effects of the recognition of custom and reason as sources of law were rather inadvertent, far exceeding the initial expectation of the drafters. Ishida thus warned against giving too much credit to the advanced nature of Article 3; it hardly embodied the natural law theory that the defects of positive law needed to be corrected by custom and reason.

The full extent of the legislative intent of the 1875 decree may be difficult to know. What is certain is that the Dajōkan decree promoted, incidentally or not,

[50] *Minji kanrei ruishū*, ed. Tezuka Yutaka (Tokyo: Keio Gijuku Daigaku Hōgaku Kenkyūkai, 1969, 1877); *Zenkoku minji kanrei ruishū*, ed. Hōmushō Shihō Hōsei Chōsabu (Tokyo: Shōji Hōmu Kenkyūkai, 1989, 1880).

[51] Collected materials were bits of "mores and usages…, constituting neither laws nor obligations," in other words, "information without legal content." Bourgon, "Le Droit coutumier," 130.

[52] Article 9 of the Civil Code Implementation Law of 1898 left out the law of 1875 from the list of abolished laws and thus implicitly preserved it. Tomii Masaakira, one of the drafters of the Japanese Civil Code, confirmed in 1922 that Law Number 103 was still valid after the promulgation of the civil code. See Ōkawa, "Meiji hachi nen Dajōkan fukoku dai 103 gō" (Part 1), 508.

[53] Ono, "Comparative Law" (Part 2), 35.

[54] Ishida Minori, "Suisu minpō ichi jō no hōgen ideorogi [The Ideology of the Source of Law in Article 1 of the Swiss Civil Code]" (Part 5), *Hōgaku kyōkai zasshi* 89 (1972): 615–635.

the rapid reception of foreign law. Where there was no written law, "custom" and "reason" as sources of law opened the door for active judicial interpretation, allowing considerable latitude to the judges. In the name of reason and justice, Meiji judges applied general principles drawn from the French code; in the name of legal custom, they evaluated old customs and practices and selectively enforced what they regarded as reasonable. The significance of Article 3 in the development of Meiji law should not be underestimated.

Custom as the Basis of the Civil Code

Arguments can be made that Japan's feudal past under warrior rule developed institutions, structures, and practices that were similar to those in Europe, and that this situation rendered it easier for Meiji reformers to implement a Western law system. But Japanese law evolved without the kind of conceptual framework available in Western Europe since the reception of Roman law. In the Kamakura period (1185–1333), following the onset of military rule, civil and criminal cases were distinguished but this distinction was more of a procedural rather than substantive nature.[55] The law of the Shogunate government was not directly applicable in the jurisdictions of feudal princes (*daimyo*).[56] During the Tokugawa regime, laws were not allowed to be published or printed.[57] Village communities lived under a form of private ordering akin to custom but it lacked attributes of law. It is an understatement that these customs remained confusing and archaic. During the Meiji years, the maze of different laws and customs confronted judges with significant challenges, but at the same time it created considerable jurisprudential opportunities.

In implementing "custom" in post-1875, the content of which was far from clear, it was natural that the judges both resorted to their subjective judgment of what was just and reasonable and also followed the general principles of law. According to Sugiyama, in the absence of the formal source of law, Decree Number 103 set forth "the power of the judge to conduct free research based on reason and equity or the nature of things."[58] Judicial opinion in early Meiji years repeated formulas such as "It is obvious according to the general principles of law…"; "According to the nature of things…"; or "Equity requires that…"[59]

[55] Henderson, *Conciliation and Japanese Law*, 101; Röhl, *History of Law in Japan*, 168. See Jeffrey P. Mass, *The Kamakura Bakufu: A Study in Documents* (Stanford: Stanford University Press, 1976); Steenstrup, *A History of Law in Japan*; Haley, *Authority without Power*.

[56] Ono, "Comparative Law (Part II)," 34.

[57] Hozumi stated: "Previous to the Restoration of 1866, there was no idea that publication was essential to law." *The New Japanese Civil Code, as Material for the Study of Comparative Jurisprudence* (Tokyo: Maruzen Kabushiki-Kaisha, 1912), 19–20.

[58] Sugiyama, "La Loi du 8 juin 1875," 447.

[59] Noda Yoshiyuki, *Introduction to Japanese Law*, trans. Anthony H. Angelo (Tokyo: University of Tokyo Press, 1976), 44, note 4. According to Noda, it is impossible to provide definitive evidence in the judicial decisions in the early Meiji period, but, judging from the Daishinin cases report around the year 1877, it is possible to conjecture that when these cases mentioned "… is the legal principle of nature," or "… is reason," their contents likely came from the French code. Still, it is difficult to prove it because the decisions did not cite sources. Noda, "Meiji hachi nen," 59.

The Daishinin decision of July 17, 1879, stated: "regarding damages arising from the violation of the contract by a party, ... it is the nature's legal reason that that party bears the obligation to pay the damage."[60] In most cases, judges relied on the "general principles" formulated in the French code that directed them in construing customs in accordance with those principles of law.[61] Inoue Masaichi, justice of the Daishinin, stated that "the French code translated by Mitsukuri shed light dissipating the darkness," and that "commentaries on the French Civil Code were like a treasure trove for the judges. It was a precious source of *jōri*."[62] In this way, Japanese jurists assimilated the laws in the French code to "reason and equity" as foreseen in Article 3 of the Dajōkan decree.

Conflation of reason and custom has a long history in Europe. It has been seen in preceding chapters how late medieval judges employed the notion of reason to select good customs as opposed to bad customs. All customs that were judged contrary to the truth, reason, law, legislation, or even public utility could be declared to be *mala consuetudo* and denounced as corrupt.[63] The invocation of reason, good morals, and equity provided a broad realm of maneuver for royal judges. Scholars of European legal history have shown that lawyers had the habit of confusing reason and custom. In early modern Europe, proving custom through the traditional procedure of interviewing local witness became increasingly difficult, creating an "evidentiary crisis of custom."[64] As lawyers struggled to fill the gaps in the customary system of proof, they needed some new means of "proving" custom and the solution was to use lawyers as witnesses to custom, thus blending customary and natural law into a peculiar concoction.[65] Not only did the royal courts represent the royal prerogative of appreciating the reasonable character of customs, they also had the power of defining or rejecting ancient usages under the cover of respecting procedural rules and modes of proof. All this generated new rules.[66]

In late medieval France, the reception of Roman law as written reason (*ratio scripta*) allowed the jurists to receive selectively civil law principles that they viewed as not destructive to French customs. Roman law's authority was precisely that it was just.[67] Jurists, in the absence of legislation, appealed to general

[60] For example, *Daishinin minji hanketsuroku*, 1879, 222–234 (the quote is on 225).

[61] For the Meiji courts' reliance on the French code as "reason," see Fukaya Itaru, "Meiji denki no Hiroshima saibansho ni okeru jōri saiban to Furansu minpō" [Adjudication by Reason by the Court of Hiroshima in Early Meiji Years and French Civil Law], *Seinan Gakuin Daigaku hōgaku ronshu* 37 (2004): 1–54; Fukaya, "Meiji denki no Kumamoto saibansho ni okeru jōri saiban to Furansu minpō [Adjudication by Reason by the Court of Kumamoto in Early Meiji Years and French Civil Law]," *Seinan Gakuin Daigaku hōgaku ronshu* 38 (2006): 59–160.

[62] Cited from Noda, "Meiji hachi nen," 58; see also Noda, *Introduction to Japanese Law*, 44.

[63] Krynen, "Entre science juridique et dirigisme," 177.

[64] James Q. Whitman, "Why did the Revolutionary Lawyers Confuse Custom and Reason?" *University of Chicago Law Review* 58 (1991), 1332.

[65] Ibid., 1331.

[66] Krynen, "Entre science juridique et dirigisme," 183.

[67] Watson, "The Evolution of Law," 556; Filhol, *Le Premier président*, 67.

law in the form of Roman law or Canon law which had, in theory, universal application to all litigants. The purportedly custom-bound courts were compelled, and were willing, to apply a learned law quite alien to the litigants before them. Likewise, Meiji judges drew the principles of universal law from French law. They engaged in judicial reasoning, relying on the principles of equity and justice, and applied the rules that they deemed most reasonable. In France, customs became law through the declarations by the royal courts, carefully managed by the state and crucially supported by legal elites. Customary law eased the transition of indigenous law to a new legal order that incorporated the imported Roman law. Meiji Japan saw the repetition of largely the same process.

Boissonade wrote in 1883 that "the judges of Japan who, since the Restoration of the Imperial Government, have already applied the principles of the French Civil Code as '*ratio scripta*' would find them in their national law."[68] The judges, unable to rely on laws or fixed and certain customs, were obliged to decide the lawsuits according to the principles of natural law:

> In Japan today, where new civil and commercial laws are not yet completed, the judges constantly find themselves confronted with the difficulties because of the silence or insufficiency of ancient laws and customs. Still they are obligated to resolve new questions that arise. Therefore one cannot contest their power to decide the cases according to equity and natural reason. It is at the same time their duty.[69]

The recognition of custom and reason as sources of law served as a conduit for receiving Western law, which was viewed as the embodiment of civilized justice. It facilitated the transplantation of Western law. Japanese law underwent a profound metamorphosis but this did not involve an abrupt rupture from the past. The reason was, in part, that the concepts of custom and *jōri* provided the instruments that filled and bridged the gap between the traditional and the new legal orders. Before the codification of civil law, when express legal provisions were few in number, custom and reason served as apparatus in which traditional law and old usages, including the ancient codes and administrative practices, were filtered through the general principles of law. Bourgon has argued that judicial custom in nineteenth- and twentieth-century East Asia was

[68] Gustave Boissonade, *Projet de code civil de l'Empire du Japon* (Tokyo, 1882–1889), vol. 2 (1883), Introduction, vii.

[69] Ibid., vol. 5, 24–25. Boissonade also stated: "In France, the obscurities [of law] are, at least in part, clarified by numerous works of eminent jurists and by learned jurisprudence of the courts; the lacunae are also filled more or less by the light shed by Roman law and ancient French customary law." But in Japan, where such sources are lacking, "the new legislation should be self-sufficient, preventing any doubts, and it should resolve the controversies that still subsist in France." Ibid., vol. 1, 5. With a new code, the judges would, before relying on "equity and pure reason," resort to the "general principles of positive law." Ibid., vol. 5, 25. See also Boissonade, *Les Anciennes coutumes du Japon et le Nouveau Code Civil, à l'occasion d'une double publication de M. John Henry Wigmore. Memoire présenté à l'Institut de France* (Tokyo, 1894).

mainly outlines of a translation of civil law principles into a local language.[70] "Unreasonable" customs – that is, those elements of the legal past that were viewed as less than desirable – were declared void by the courts in European history. The early Meiji years exemplified the similar development.

It has been a common view that the spread of Western law to East Asia took place mostly through legislation. In Japan, the codification of civil law marked a drastic departure from its legal tradition, introducing new norms and implementing reforms. It is important to observe, however, that judicial decision-making was an equally decisive and effective instrument of legal transplantation. In early Meiji years, transplantation through jurisprudence played a crucial role in preparing the ground, so to speak, for the codification. Sugiyama argued that the period from 1868 to 1888 was "the age of free interpretation," in which the Japanese adopted Western law through jurisprudential and doctrinal routes, well before the formal campaign of legislation began.[71] It was a fertile ground for judicial lawmaking. Hozumi Nobushige stated that Western jurisprudence entered Japan "not only indirectly through the *University* and other law colleges, but also directly through the *Bench* and the *Bar*."[72] The codification of civil law followed this jurisprudential transplantation.[73]

It seemed inevitable that there was a growing reaction against the influence of foreign legal theories, in particular the universal and abstract principles of rights enshrined in the French Civil Code. Opposition to Western law was dramatically expressed in the so-called civil code debate (*hōten ronsō*). The controversy revolved around the fate of the civil code that had been drafted by Boissonade. Boissonade submitted a completed code to the Japanese government in 1890. The code was scheduled to take effect in 1892, but it immediately met strong resistance from those who claimed it was a mere compilation of Western laws, having little connection to Japanese tradition and indigenous customs. They demanded its promulgation be postponed.

One of the most prominent scholars who argued for the immediate enforcement of the Boissonade code was Ume Kenjirō. Professor of civil law at Tokyo Imperial University, Ume was the pride of modern Meiji Japan's

[70] Bourgon, "Le Droit coutumier," 133.

[71] Sugiyama, "L'Evolution générale," 232. It is interesting to note that Japanese jurists understandably took pride in their successful legal modernization but at the same time were self-conscious of the substance of such transformation. Sugiyama wondered whether one might ask if the rapid progress of the transformation of the Japanese civilization was a phenomenon fundamentally superficial or something ephemeral that would "disappear after brief shining like a comet." In such moments of self-doubt, the significance of Law Number 103, especially Article 3, and its modern implications could not have been more assuring.

[72] Hozumi, *The New Japanese Civil Code*, 40 (emphasis in the original).

[73] Sugiyama regretted that, with the push for the codification of civil law, Japanese were compelled to "sacrifice the progress of their law through jurisprudential interpretation" and "were rushed to codify laws without much time to study our traditional customs." Sugiyama, "La Loi du 8 juin 1875," 448.

intellectual achievement. The depth of his juristic ideas and the breadth of his activities, almost unrivalled among contemporaries, prompted the observation that "there was no one like Ume, before or after him."[74] His legal thought, gleaned from his role in the Japanese codification of civil law, sheds significant light on the influence of the civil law tradition on the intellectual innovations in Meiji Japan, and also legal changes in Japanese colonies. It was this Ume who would later find himself in Seoul as a legal advisor to the Korean empire.[75] The following discussion examines the making of the Japanese Civil Code from the vantage point of Ume's activities and legal thought.

The Making of the Japanese Civil Code and Ume Kenjirō

Ume Kenjirō

Ume was born on June 7, 1860, in Matsue, in what would become Shimane Prefecture, as the second son of a doctor in service of a local lord. He graduated from Tokyo Foreign Language University's French Department.[76] Despite childhood poverty due to the fall of the samurai class that directly affected his family, Ume received the finest education available in the early Meiji period. In 1880 he entered the Justice Department Law School, which later became part of Tokyo Imperial University Law School. In December 1885 Ume received a government scholarship and left for France to study at the University of Lyon. He received a doctorate in law in July 1889 with a dissertation entitled "De la transaction en droit romain et dans l'ancien droit français."[77] "Transaction" is a Roman law principle of settling a suit or controversy between litigating

[74] Asano, *Teikoku Nihon*, 90.

[75] See Chapter 4.

[76] Much work has been done on Ume in Japanese, but the only study of Ume in Western language is Kim, "Ume Kenjirō and the Making of Korean Civil Law." Ume's papers are housed in the Hōsei University Library. Some documents regarding the codification of the civil law are available online: http://www.hosei.ac.jp/general/lib/rare/Top.html. For a comprehensive list of Ume's papers, see Ume Monjo Kenkyūkai, ed. *Ume Kenjirō monjo mokuroku: Hōsei Daigaku toshokan shozō* [The Catalogue of the Ume Kenjirō Papers: Hōsei University Library Collection] (Tokyo: Hōsei Daigaku Boasonādo Kinen Gendaihō Kenkyūjo, 2000). Most of Ume's extant writings are compiled into a 5-volume CD set, *Ume Kenjirō chosaku zenshū shibidan* [The CD Collection of the Complete Works of Ume Kenjirō], ed. Oka Takashi (Tokyo: Maruzen, 2000). The annotated list of Ume's writings is provided in Oka Takashi and Edo Keiko, "Ume Kenjirō chosho oyobi ronpun mokuroku: sono shoji gaku teki kenkyū [The Catalogue of the Books and Articles Written by Ume Kenjirō: A Bibliographical Study]," *Hōgaku shirin* 82, nos. 3 & 4 (combined) (1985), 137–214. The full-length biography of Ume, written nearly a hundred years ago, is Higashikawa Tokuji, *Hakushi Ume Kenjirō: denki Ume Kenjirō* [Dr. Ume Kenjirō: Biography of Ume Kenjirō] (Tokyo: Ōzorasha, 1997, 1917). See the articles in the special issue, "Minpō 100 nen to Ume Kenjirō [The Centennial of the Civil Code and Ume Kenjirō]," in *Hōritsu jihō* 70, no. 7 (1998); Ume Kenjirō Hakushi Kenshō Kinenshi Henshū Iinkai, ed. *Waga minpō no chichi Ume Kenjirō hakushi kenshōhi konryū no kiroku* [A Testimonial on the Occasion of the Construction of the Monument of Dr. Ume Kenjirō, Father of Our Civil Code] (Matsue, 1992).

[77] Oumé Kendjiro [Ume Kenjirō], *De la transaction en droit romain et dans l'ancien droit français* (Paris: L. Larose et Forcel, 1889).

parties without referring it to arbitration or trial.[78] Ume's thesis represented the current juristic trend to turn to the potential of Roman law to deal with modern problems. His thesis received the highest honor and was published the same year in Paris, paid for by the city government of Lyon.[79]

Ume's sojourn in Europe, capped by a year of study in Berlin, critically formed his legal thought. The last quarter of the nineteenth century in France witnessed the decline of the School of Exegesis that had dominated legal science for many decades since the promulgation of the civil code in 1804. Scholars belonging to this school held to a formalist conception of law and judicial practice, emphasizing literal interpretation of the codes, and treated other sources of law – custom, scholarship, case law, or natural law – with only secondary importance. French jurists gradually opposed the blind acceptance of positive laws, however, and advocated the shift in legal philosophy from a speculative and mechanical approach to rational and functional jurisprudence. French legal scholars also faulted the tendency of the Historical School to reject permanent and immutable rules founded on reason. Raymond Saleilles (1855–1912) deplored that contemporary jurists were inclined, following certain tendencies of Savigny, to rid judicial opinion of any appearance of the judges' concern with the universal concepts of reason, equity, or justice.[80]

Ume was fully immersed in this new direction of French legal consciousness. He eagerly embraced the natural law theory, and later he also acknowledged the influence of German Pandectists such as Bernhard Windscheid (1817–1892) and Rudolf von Jhering (1818–1892).[81] The various trends of the contemporary European legal philosophy are fully on display in his writings.

The Japanese Civil Code Debate

Ume returned to Japan in August 1890 and was appointed to the faculty of law at Tokyo Imperial University. He was soon embroiled in the fierce debate over the fate of the Boissonade civil code. It was a clash of scholarly views over how to preserve Japanese tradition in civil law. Hozumi Nobushige recalled that the debate between those who argued for the immediate adoption of the Boissonade code and those who demanded its postponement was "in reality, a contest between the Historical School and the School of Natural Law, resembling in many respects the famous controversy between Savigny and Thibaut" in the beginning of the nineteenth century.[82] The debate between Savigny and A. F. J. Thibaut began when Savigny objected to the proposal made by Thibaut

[78] Stein, *Roman Law in European History*, 120; Tamura Akio, "Wakai no kakutei kō [The Effect of the Settlement by Compromise]," *Shimadai hōgaku* 35, no. 4 (1992): 35–81; Tamura Akio, "Ima, naze Ume Kenjirō ka: Ume Kenjirō to wakairon [Why Ume Kenjirō Now: Ume Kenjirō and the Theory of Compromise]," *Hōgaku semina* 435 (1991): 76–78.

[79] Higashikawa, *Hakushi Ume Kenjirō*, 11.

[80] Raymond Saleilles, "Ecole historique et droit naturel d'après quelques ouvrages récents," *Revue trimestrielle de droit civil* (1902): 80–112.

[81] Ume, "Hōritsu no kaishaku [Interpretation of Law]," *Taiyō* 9, no. 2 (1903): 56–62.

[82] Hozumi, *The New Japanese Civil Code*, 16.

to create a common civil code for all German states on the model of the unified French code.[83]

Hozumi's observation, while perceptive, risks oversimplification, because ideological boundaries between the "postponement faction" and the "immediate adoption faction" were not so clear-cut as in the German debate. In Japan, the juristic clash roughly represented a rivalry between the English law scholars and the French law scholars. The emphasis on Japanese custom and tradition also provided key ammunition for the partisans of German legal science who were in opposition to the French model of codification. But those belonging to the French law faction did not entirely support legislation as the key promoter of legal development; they fully recognized the insufficiency of legislation and the importance of jurisprudence.

The Boissonade code, like the French Civil Code, followed the format of the *Institutes* of the *Corpus Iuris Civilis*, divided into three sections: the Persons, the Things, and the Actions.[84] The section that became the core target of criticisms was the laws of succession, covered in the Book III under the title "Acquisition of property." The gist of opposition was that Boissonade ignored Japanese tradition. Historians have pointed out that the postponement faction, although it clamored for preserving customs in the code, made relatively few arguments of substance regarding the legal concept of custom during the debate. It was the French law faction that made doctrinal expositions of theoretical significance about custom.[85] The scholars of French law pointed out early in the debate that there was a distinction between mere customs that varied according to region and customary law created by judicial precedents. They reminded the postponement faction that many of Japan's old customs did not have legal effects because they had not been given normative recognition by courts through adjudication. They emphasized that it was only after the Meiji reforms that the courts began to create customary law.

John Henry Wigmore (1863–1943), the American jurist who was teaching at Keio University at the time, supported the immediate adoption of the Boissonade code. He compared the provisions of the Boissonade code with the laws he had collected of the Tokugawa period and concluded that the new code was not incompatible with indigenous customs.[86] In 1892, a series

[83] Stein, *Roman Law in European History*, 116–117.

[84] For the comparison of the structure of the French code and the Boissonade code, see Ono, "Comparative law" (Part 1), 42–43.

[85] Fukushima Masao, "Kyū-minpō to kankō no mondai [The Questions of Old Civil Code and Custom]," *Matsuyama shōdai ronshu* 17, no. 6 (1966), 296.

[86] Wigmore's collection of laws of the Tokugawa Shogunate was edited and translated into English as *Materials for the Study of Private Law in Old Japan*, 4 vols. (Tokyo: Asiatic Society of Japan, 1892). On Wigmore, see Annelise Riles, "Wignore's Treasure Box: Comparative Law in the Era of Information," *Harvard International Law Journal* 40 (1999): 221–283; Iwatani Jūrō, "Wigumoa ate Boasonado shokan 14 tsū no kaidai teki kenkyū: minpōten ronsō to futari no gaikoku hōritsuka [A Bibliograpahical Introduction to the Fourteen Letters Written by Boissonade to Wigmore: The Civil Code Debate and the Two Foreign Jurists]," *Hōgaku kenkyū* (Keio Gijuku Daigaku Hōgaku Kenkyūkai) 73, no. 11 (2000): 154–204.

of articles appeared in *Japan Weekly Mail* under the title "New Codes and Old Customs of Japan."[87] Published anonymously, these articles supported the Boissonade code. The author pointed out that there had been no development of legal science before the Meiji years. There was no official recognition of private rights and no legal commentaries existed on private law matters. The author complained that contemporary scholars paid scant attention to the concept of civil custom.[88] In conclusion, the author declared that the Boissonade code respected Japan's old customs and that it should be implemented without delay.

Ume was one of the most articulate and prominent suppoters of the Boissonade code. He pointed out that customs were in flux in Meiji Japan and were not yet examined by the courts that had only recently been established. The courts needed time to interpret and stabilize customs, which would then be transformed into customary law through judicial precedents. In Japan's new society, old customs were no longer functional.[89] Ume reminisced on the jurisprudential confusion following the promulgation of the Dajōkan decree of 1875:

> In the early Meiji years when it became possible to have access to trials, Article 3 [of Decree Number 103] provided that when there is no written law decision is made by custom, and when there is no custom, by reason. Those who were educated in yesterday's Japan tended to decide problems on the basis of yesterday's ideals of reason, those who studied English law regarded the principles of English law as reason, those who studied French law regarded the principles of French law as reason, and those who studied German law regarded the principles of German law as reason. All these problems created a very strange situation, and people's rights and obligations became unclear. Therefore, in order to conduct trials consistently and clarify people's rights and obligations, even an imperfect code with defects was better than no code. I believed that the benefit of having a code was clear.[90]

87 The articles were published in five segments: October 29; November 19, November 26, December 10, and December 17, 1892.

88 Article of October 29, 1892, *Japan Weekly Mail*, 531. Wigmore pointed out this problem in *Materials for the Study*, vol. I, 5. Wigmore may well have been the author of these articles.

89 Ume Kenjirō, "Hōten ni kansuru jukkai [Reflections on the Civil Code]," *Meihō shisō* 17 (1893), 2; "Minpō jisshi iken [An Opinion on the Adoption of the Civil Code]," *Meihō shisō* 3 (1892). The latter text is printed in Hoshino, *Meiji minpō hensan shi kenkyū*, 524–531. Ume stated: "It is no longer possible to resolve legal matters by old customs. Even if we consider old customs, it is in reality impossible to decide legal questions in adjudication by them because there was a great variety of old customs among feudal estates.... Since the Meiji reforms, old customs in civil and commercial matters gave way to the customs of Western countries. But new customs were yet not established and, because judges were compelled to decide cases according to their own judgment, there was little consistency and people's rights were not firmly established. Therefore it was necessary to write law codes as quickly as possible." Ume Kenjirō, *Minpō genri* [The Principles of Civil Law] (Tokyo: Wafutsu Hōritsu Gakkō, 1899), 17–18. For Ume's theory of the interpretation of law, see Uchida Shunichirō, "Meiji minpō no kaishaku to Ume hakushi no kaishaku riron [The Interpretation of Meiji Civil Law and Dr. Ume's Theories of Interpretation]," *Matsuyama shōdai ronshu* 17, no. 6 (1966): 35–61.

90 Ume Kenjirō, "Itō kō to rippō jigyō [Prince Itō and Legislative Activities]," *Kokka gakkai zasshi* 24, no. 7 (1910), 47–48.

The absence of learned doctrinal elaboration and jurisprudential activity in traditional Japan prevented the rise of customary law as distinguished from popular practices and usages. Mere old customs devoid of legal normative values could not serve as the basis of trials. Absent customary law, argued Ume, it was necessary to write a code as soon as possible.

The scholar who was the most vocal among the postponement faction was Hozumi Yatsuka (1860–1912), a professor of constitutional law at Tokyo Imperial University and younger brother of Hozumi Nobushige. Hozumi argued that the civil code was anti-Japanese and anti-tradition. He claimed that the code was based on Christian and individualistic premises and that protecting people's rights would weaken the family system.[91] Hozumi contended that once the Boissonade civil code came into effect loyalty to the emperor and filial piety would be in jeopardy. Ume mused over Hozumi's contention that Christianity taught disrespect to parents: "I am not a Christian, nor do I wish to advocate Christian views, but as scholars we must get things straight. Christianity teaches filial piety, respect to parents."[92] For Ume, it was nothing less than slander to claim that the Boissonade code would destroy Japanese tradition. Japan's customs were not able to keep up with social changes taking place since the Meiji Restoration and, Ume flatly pointed out, Japan urgently needed a civil code to protect individuals' rights.[93]

In 1892, the Diet decided in favor of postponing the promulgation of the civil code drafted by Boissonade. In April 1893, Hozumi Nobushige, Tomii Masaakira, and Ume were appointed to the Code Investigation Commission in charge of the codification of new civil law and commercial law.[94] The fate of the Boissonade code confirmed that the new code had to conform to the wishes of Japanese traditionalists. It would have to be a reflection of Japanese tradition as well as a construct of reason. The code drafting committee proceeded under the slogan of respecting Japanese old customs, as it wished to avoid being accused of not having taken proper account of Japanese customs. Guidelines for the revision of the code stressed the need to heed "the effect of customary law and actual customs."[95] Appearing before the Diet, Ume declared that traditional Japanese institutions and practices were carefully taken into account in writing the new code. The drafters "worked with the spirit not to

[91] Hozumi published an article titled "The Enactment of the Civil Code Sounds the Death-Knell of Our Traditional Virtues: Loyalty and Filial Piety." See Minear, *Japanese Tradition and Western Law*. Note Hozumi and Ume were born in the same year. Both died relatively young, Ume preceding Hozumi by two years.

[92] Ume, "Minpō jisshi iken."

[93] For the question of customs during the Japanese civil law codification process, see Fukushima, "Kyū-minpō to kankō no mondai," 295–322.

[94] See Ume's letter to Itō, April 17, 1893, in Itō Hirobumi Kankei Monjo Kenkyūkai, ed. *Itō Hirobumi kankei monjo* [Papers Related to Itō Hirobumi] (Tokyo: Hanawa Shobo, 1973–1981), vol. 3, 175–176.

[95] Hoshino Tōru, "San hakushi to minpō seitei [Three Doctors and the Enactment of the Civil Law]," *Hōgaku shirin* 49, no. 1 (1950), 52.

FIGURE 3.1. **Ume Kenjirō, May 1909.** Ume (1860–1910) was one of the drafters of the Japanese Civil Code and a legal advisor to the Korean government between 1906 and 1910. Collection of the Editorial Committee on History of Hosei University. Reprinted with permission.

destroy customs." [96] Yet Ume also stated that "one needs to follow our traditional customs as long as they conform to the progress of the society."[97]

The organization of the new civil code followed the *Pandekten* system. The first three books – General Principles, Properties, and Obligations – were enacted and took effect in 1896. They were followed two years later by the promulgation of the books on Family and Successions. The complete code that took effect on July 16, 1898, was in many ways a compromise between the conservative and progressive agenda. While the first three books were largely based on the principles in continental European laws, family and succession matters included a number of customs then in existence in Japan.

[96] Ume's statement on October 28, 1895, cited from Hoshino, "San hakushi," 53.

[97] "Principles of the revision of the civil code," in "Drafts of law in memory of Dr. Ume," a collection at Tokyo Imperial University, cited in Higashikawa, *Hakushi Ume Kenjirō*, 173. See also Hoshino, "San hakushi," 52.

Ume held a flexible attitude toward custom. He recognized the importance of custom as he acknowledged the imperfection of the statutes. Because the Japanese Civil Code was written in haste, he pointed out, there were not a few defects; in many cases it was necessary to make up for these deficiencies with judicial interpretation. Following the completion of the code, much of Ume's attention was devoted to the question of the interpretation of law. He argued that in Japan there was an excessive emphasis on the formal language of the laws and that laws were implemented often with complete disregard to the needs of the times. Ume wrote:

> Because laws are made by humans, they necessarily reflect the imperfection of the human nature and cannot avoid being more or less inadequate. In other words, it is not within human power to write law provisions that foresee every single state of affairs that arise in society each day. For this reason, even laws that are seemingly perfect often contain provisions that cannot respond to real situations. In practice, it is necessary to adjust the provisions through interpretation so that they are applicable to real situations. Therefore the court must consider it as its duty to interpret laws in accordance with real situations.... The judges must adjudicate in response to contemporary needs without being restrained by the language of the law texts.[98]

One needs to look at the entirety of the law to determine its meaning, stressed Ume. If the words in the law are clearly against common sense or if the results of their literal application would be against the purpose of the law, one needs to construe them in a flexible manner.[99]

From 1902, Ume published a number of commentaries on the court decisions. They were published as *Saikin hanrei hihyō* (Commentaries on Recent Judicial Decisions) in 1906, followed by a supplement in 1909. According to him, "law is in principle a dead thing," and hence it was the responsibility of the scholars and practitioners to seek its reasonable interpretation.[100] "Once questions are submitted to the court, it is the court that has to resolve them, but if defects are found in the court decisions, it is the duty of scholars to critique them and make their works available so that judges can consult them in their efforts to achieve the best possible results in adjudication."[101] As someone who participated in the codification of the civil code, he hoped to provide a model for fulfilling scholarly obligations and responsibilities, wrote Ume.[102]

[98] Ume, "Hōritsu no kaishaku," 57.

[99] Ibid., 61.

[100] Ume Kenjirō, *Saikin hanrei hihyō* [Commentaries on Recent Judicial Decisions] (Tokyo: Hōsei Daigaku, 1906), 3–4 (preface). For an analysis of *Saikin hanrei hihyō*, see Katayama Naoya, "'Saikin hanrei hihyō' wo yomu [Reading *Saikin hanrei hihyō*]," '*Hōritsu jihō* 70, no. 7 (1998): 23–28; Uchida, "Meiji minpō," 53–57.

[101] Ume Kenjirō, *Saikin hanrei hihyō zoku hen* [Commentaries on Recent Court Decisions Supplement] (Tokyo: Hōsei Daigaku, 1909), 2 (preface). A combined volume of *Saikin hanrei hihyō* and *Saikin hanrei hihyō zoku hen* was published in 1909.

[102] Ume, *Saikin hanrei hihyō zoku hen*, 2–3; Uchida, "Meiji minpō," 53.

Ume sharply criticized the court opinions which he thought were far removed from the spirit of the laws. He wrote: "The legislator is not god and sometimes uses the words [in the law provisions] that are not suitable. Therefore, when the meaning of the law is unclear, one must always follow reason, resorting to common sense, and try to find out what the legislator intended to say."[103] Ume stressed that the language of the law should be read in its ordinary meaning. Words are, after all, no more than a tool to express human thoughts.[104] "It is the duty of those who construe the law to render reasonable interpretations according to common sense. It is lamentable that recently our judges focus merely on the tails of the law language and render interpretations that effectively kill the law."[105] Ume argued that the court is not fulfilling its duty properly if it dismisses a case because of minute defects in pleading. Normally the party is not a legal scholar, he pointed out, so it is natural that the words he uses in the pleading sometimes have legal flaws.

In 1907, Ume criticized a decision by the Daishinin that invalidated a contract due to defective language. Ume was indignant: "the parties do not always completely understand the law. In the interpretation of the contract, it is important to investigate the intent of the parties, without being bogged down by the words."[106] Instead of following a literal and grammatical meaning of the law provisions, the judge must consider utility in the law's interpretation. After all, the purpose of interpreting laws as the norms that control the trial is to decide each party's rights and obligations and resolve disputes in a most effective manner. "One must interpret laws in a way to bring desirable results to society and economy."[107] An ideal civil law in Japan, Ume stressed, would be the one that serves as a means for the country's rapid economic development and social transformation.[108]

Ume's criticism of a blind acceptance of positive law significantly affected the theoretical and practical bases of modern Japanese jurisprudence and legal philosophy. His emphasis on the utility of law and the cooperation between doctrine and jurisprudence revealed a clear influence of the contemporary European legal philosophy. Perhaps the jurist whose legal thought exhibited most affinity to that of Ume was the French jurist François Gény. In Europe, the extreme position of the School of Exegesis, upholding the supremacy of

[103] Ume, *Saikin hanrei hihyō*, 55.

[104] Ibid., 199.

[105] Ibid., 329.

[106] Ume, *Saikin hanrei hihyō zoku hen*, 70–71, cited from Uchida, "Meiji minpō," 56.

[107] Ume, "Hōritsu no kaishaku," 61–62.

[108] Ume's pragmatic approach to law was widely acknowledged. Tomii testified: "Always practical, [Ume] very much disliked empty theoretical arguments.... He had strong belief that law was a study of the reality, and even in academic discussion, he always emphasized reality." Ume's legislative works reflected his no-nonsense attitude, Tomii continued, as "writing law provisions for easy understanding was Ume's greatest strength." Speech of November 27, 1910, at the conference held in memory of Ume, sponsored by Hōsei University. Cited from Higashikawa, *Hakushi Ume Kenjirō*, 217.

legislation, was in retreat by the end of the nineteenth century. The newly emerging school of legal thought, the so-called Free Law School, acknowledged the inadequacy of statutes and sought an objective-oriented approach to judicial judgment. Gény proposed a theory of rational and functional jurisprudence.

Ume wrote: "recently in French legal science, a theory has been presented that, in cases other than those which are directly controlled by a specific law text, one must interpret the law in a way that it can be applied to real cases according to the needs of the times. The scholar who most vocally defends this theory is François Gény, professor of the Faculty of Law at the University of Dijon." Gény wrote a tome of some six hundred pages, reported Ume, and "the French scholars eagerly accept his theory."[109] Ume said that "I am not one of those who are completely converted to this trend in French legal science." Despite this demurral, Ume's legal interpretations as distilled from his legal commentaries and his view of custom contained remarkable resemblance to those of Gény.[110]

Gény's Doctrine on Custom and Jurisprudence

The first edition of Gény's *Méthode d'interprétation et sources en droit privé positif* was published in 1899. Gény distinguished between factual usage and custom, the latter being imperative norms of a juridical nature. He was critical of the German Historical School on the grounds that it attempted a purely subjective conception of customary law for no specific gains; such an abstract and idealistic concept not only lacked utility but also risked "denaturizing" the custom's "objective reality."[111] But, because of the necessity to coordinate competing interests in society and maintain legal stability, it was essential to recognize sources of law other than statutes. The inevitable lacunae and obsolescence of statutes over time justified the function of custom as a key source of law.

As examined in Chapter 1, Gény argued in favor of granting jurisprudence the force of customary law, which should be viewed as a formal source of law that supplemented statutes.[112] The gaps in legislation could be filled by custom.[113] "Although custom seems to have only a narrow role in our social organization," Gény stated, "it still retains its indispensable productive force and, supported by authorities or tradition, which are only its rudimentary

[109] Ume, "Hōritsu no kaishaku," 57–58.

[110] Some scholars viewed that Ume opposed Gény's scientific approach to legal interpretation. See Nakamura Tetsu, "Ume Kenjirō no senken [Ume Kenjirō's Prescience]," *Hōritsu gaku no yoake to Hōsei Daigaku* [The Dawn of Legal Science and Hōsei University], ed. Hōsei Daigaku Daigakushi Shiryō Linkai (Tokyo: Hōsei Daigaku, 1992), 347. But similarities in juridical thought between Ume and Gény are hard to dispute.

[111] Gény, *Méthode*, vol. 1, 347 (no. 116).

[112] Ibid., vol. 1, 406–417 (no. 129).

[113] "Sometimes the written law will be filled in and specified by custom." Ibid., vol. 2, 222 (no. 183).

elements, it still reserves an important place in our civilization."[114] In the absence of any formal directives, nevertheless, and in the face of numerous questions that cannot be neatly resolved by either law or custom,

> the jurisconsult will have no other resource than to scrutinize directly the nature of things, and to question the social elements himself, from which he must fix the rule. In this vast complexity of necessary data, he must make numerous classifications and distinguish the objects of investigation, depending on how enlightening and certain they are. As the legislator himself would do, he must determine their true nature and the laws that harmonize them, keeping his eyes fixed on the ideal of justice or social utility that must be satisfied above all.[115]

Gény's theory of jurisprudence, inviting judges to seek guidance from all sources and to take social realities and needs into consideration, found a sympathetic ear in Ume and other Japanese jurists. His idea that when no appropriate formal norm is available the judge must seek guidance from doctrine, custom, and decisional laws as persuasive authorities largely coincided with that of Ume. In interpreting law, one must consider utility. Justice and social utility dictate that a judge use all legitimate resources when he decides, and the judge must be free to search for a rule on which to base his decision.[116] Like Gény, Ume believed in the symbiotic relationship between jurisprudence and custom. Through doctrinal and jurisprudential activities, customs would be discovered, noted, and translated into legal formulae. Judicial decisions promoted popular convictions in certain customs which then created customary law. Ume's theory of the interpretation of law suggests that judges should take a liberal stance without being constrained by the words of the positive law and construe the law depending on the concrete states of affairs to which the law applied.

Ume argued that law was not a mere product of the natural development of history. Society evolves and its law develops accordingly, but law is controlled by a kind of vision that dominates a specific time period.[117] According to him, this vision is called ideal law or natural law and it serves as the standard for the making and revising of positive laws.[118] In reaction to legal positivism, Ume stated in 1903: "positive law is what imperfect human beings create; it therefore cannot avoid deficiency. Such deficiency is to be corrected by general principles of law and by customary law, and when there is no customary law by natural law."[119] The introduction into Japan of the notion of reason as

[114] Ibid.

[115] Ibid., 223.

[116] See Saleilles, "Ecole historique."

[117] Ume Kenjirō, *Minpō sōsoku* [The General Provisions of the Civil Code] (Tokyo: Hōsei Daigaku, 1914), 4–8.

[118] Ibid., 89–90. See Kanayama Naoki, "Sōchi to shite no hōten to hōgaku: Ume Kenjirō to iu shinwa [The Civil Code and Legal Science as an Apparatus: A Legend Called Ume Kenjirō]," *Hōritsu jihō* 70, no.7 (1998): 6–11.

[119] Ume, *Minpō genri*, 12.

natural law is attributed to Boissonade. Boissonade viewed positive law as the realization of natural law in particular forms. In Japan, he taught that natural law was "the code of legislator himself."[120] Ume was influenced by Boissonade whose lectures he likely attended at the Justice Ministry Law School.[121]

Ume unequivocally declared: "I forever believe that the natural law school's theory is correct."[122] Reason meant the logic of things; being contrary to reason meant "something is wrongful or ought not to be." Legislation, custom, or other rules set forth in advance were only imperfect approximations of this rationality. The rationality of legislation cannot be guaranteed for good in changing social conditions. The legislator can give only the general normative outline and, emphasized Ume, this is why the prudence of the solution given by the judge in applying a legislative framework to concrete cases becomes critical.

During the Japanese civil code debate, Ume was not in disagreement with the postponement faction's argument that customs that operated in the people's lives should be incorporated into Japanese civil and commercial laws. However, he was critical of the contention that a faithful acceptance of old customs into the codes was required, regardless of how antiquated and unreasonable they might be, simply because they had existed for a long time. He opposed the idea that the legislator's role should be limited to the restatement of preexisting customs. For Ume, customary law in Europe had developed through juristic debate by legal scholars and practitioners, not through unquestioned adherence to tradition.

Ume's opposition to the blind respect for old customs was grounded in his belief in individual freedom. He was against the traditional customs that he believed were incompatible with the norms of private property rights and the freedom of contract. His stance was clearly expressed in his antagonism to one of the most peculiar customs in Japan, the "house" (*ie*) system.[123] The house system is a conspicuous example of the old feudal institutions that thrust their way into the civil code of 1898. Under the institution of the "house," a family was built not around the conjugal unit of husband and wife but around a vertical line of ancestor and descendant. Each member of the house was

[120] Gustave Boissonade, "Leçon d'ouverture d'un cours de droit naturel," *Revue de législation ancienne et moderne française et étrangère* (Paris: Thorin, 1874), 517, cited from Jean-Louis Sourioux, "La Pensée juridique de G. Boissonade: aspects de droit civil," *Revue internationale de droit comparé* (1991), 362. The 1991 issue of *Revue internationale de droit comparé* (1991) includes a special section devoted to Boissonade, "Boissonade et la réception du droit français au Japan," 327–424.

[121] Boissonade lectured at the Justice Ministry Law School's accelerated program and Ume was a student in the regular program. The two programs were often combined to listen to lectures. Nojima Mikio, "Boasonado to Ume Kenjirō hakushi [Boissonade and Dr. Ume Kenjirō]," *Hōgaku semina* 3, no. 435 (1991): 78–79.

[122] Ume, *Minpō genri*, 2.

[123] For Ume's negative opinion of the house system, see Uno Fumie, "Meiji minpō kisō iin no 'ie' to koshuken rikai [The Meiji Civil Code Drafting Committee Members' Understanding of 'Ie' and the Household Headship]," *Hōsei kenkyū* (Kyushu Daigaku Hōsei Gakkai) 74, no. 3 (2007): 523–591.

subject to the control of the head of the house to whom he or she was bound by obedience and filial piety. The house system had its historical roots in ancestor worship. Many of its accompanying features, such as adoption, were based on the necessity of maintaining a line of successors who would continue the worship of the ancestors of the house. The house formation flexed its muscle because the preservation of the patriarchal family system was considered necessary in order to buttress the newly constructed emperor-centered political order.[124] The system was ostensibly modeled on tradition and thereby justified as customary practice, but scholars have shown that it had in fact been limited to warrior households.

Boissonade did not hide his hostility to the house system and the law of primogeniture, which he viewed as relics of feudalism.[125] The house institution was included in the civil code of 1898 only with utmost reluctance and reservation on the part of the drafters. In the new law, still, succession to the headship of a house was treated as the principal feature, with the acquisition of the property of the house being a consequence of this succession.

Once the codification of the civil code was over, Ume felt obligated to profess his views in frank terms, closely reflecting his juristic ideas. Evidence shows that in the early 1900s Ume was still reeling from the polemical controversy that surrounded the codification debate, during which the universal validity of natural law was denounced on the grounds of traditional morality. He was particularly concerned about the return of feudal ideology perpetuating unequal rights and duties. Historians have generally agreed that the Japanese society witnessed a rising tide of nationalistic reaction between 1880 and 1890. The reemergence of Confucian ideology was highly noticeable during this period.[126] In the first few years after the turn of the century, Ume began to express his opposition to feudal customs in a remarkably forthright manner. His main target was the institution of the "house" preserved in the new code.

Ume criticized the artificiality of the *ie* system, primarily based on the notion of duty instead of right, stifling natural family relations. He saw it as pure anachronism, subordinating the individuality of the family members to the collective good of the house. Ume noted that in Europe family rights or parental rights were shifting to a new concept of family on the basis of spousal relationship, and stated that "there is nothing to be concerned about" this seemingly

[124] See Haley, *Authority without Power*.

[125] Boissonade, *Les Anciennes coutumes du Japon et le Nouveau Code Civil*, 199–200. Boissonade had expressed the same opinion as early as 1875. See Ōkubo Yasuo, "La Querelle sur la premier code civil japonais et l'ajournement de sa mise en vigueur: refus du législateur étranger?" *Revue internationale de droit comparé* (1991), 393, note 13. See also Ōkubo Yasuo, "Gustave Boissonade, père français du droit japonais moderne (1825–1910)," *Revue historique de droit français et étranger* 59 (1981): 29–54.

[126] Carol Gluck, *Japan's Modern Myths: Ideology in the Late Meiji Period* (Princeton: Princeton University Press, 1985); Donald H. Shively, "The Japanization of the Middle Meiji," in *Tradition and Modernization in Japanese Culture,* eds. Donald H. Shively and Carmen Blacker (Princeton: Princeton University Press, 1971).

abrupt development, which he viewed as unavoidable.[127] In January 1900, Ume contributed an article on the future of Japanese law in the new century. He confidently predicted the disappearance of the house system, along with the *inkyo* (relinquishment inter vivos of the household headship and other rights to the successor) and adoption systems in the near future: "although it is not clear whether it will be in fifteen years or twenty years, at a certain point the *ie* system will be abolished."[128] Ume's prescience was not amiss; the house system was abolished, but not before 1947.

Sources of Law in the Japanese and the French Civil Codes

The case of the house system evidences that legislators in the Meiji years were under considerable pressure to recognize the importance of customs that supposedly embodied Japanese tradition. The idea that family relations and succession should conform to customs was paramount. The choice of adopting the German Pandectist model, with the last two of the five books reserved for family law and succession, bespoke the emphasis the Japanese placed on these areas. Yet the fact that the drafters of the code declined to declare custom to be a source of law reveals that they were mindful of the uppermost exigency of achieving the unification of law under imperial authority. Excessive deference to custom implied the preservation of diverse regional identities that impeded legal uniformity. There were competing demands of the time: on the one hand, there was consensus that evil customs needed to be quashed; on the other hand, in the midst of ignominy of unequal treaties and extraterritoriality, customs seemed to matter as an expression of national tradition and the manifestation of Japanese society and culture. The Meiji legislators had no choice but to give utmost heed to tradition.

The force of custom as a supplementary source of law was preserved in the *Hōrei*. The *Hōrei*, the Law on the General Rules of the Application of Laws (Law Number 10), was issued on June 21, 1898, a few weeks before the civil code.[129] It contained rules relating to the general application of law and private international law. Its Article 2 read: "Customs which are not contrary to public order or to good morals shall have the force of law to the extent that

[127] Ume Kenjirō, "Kajoku sei no shōrai wo ronsu [Discussing the future of the Family System]," *Hōgaku shirin* 3 (1902), 33–34. See Nakamura Tetsuya, "Minpō dai ni hen shinzoku an [The Proposal to Insert Family Law into Book Two of Civil Law]," *Hōritsu jihō* 70, no. 7 (1998), 34.

[128] Ume Kenjirō, "Nijū seiki no hōritsu [Law of the Twentieth Century]," *Yomiuri shinbun*, January 5, 1900. Ume expressed the similar prediction in "Kajoku sei no shōrai o ronsu," 34; and *Minpō yōgi* [A Digest of Civil Law], vol. 4 (Shinzoku hen) (Tokyo: Shiritsu Hōsei Daigaku, Yūhigaku Shobō, 1916, 1899), 13. Ume was in favor of equal distribution succession. See Hirano Yoshitarō, *Nihon shihon shugi shakai to hōritsu* [Japanese Capitalist Society and Law] (Tokyo: Rironsha, 1955), 98.

[129] For English translation of the text of *Hōrei*, see Oda Hiroshi, ed. *Basic Japanese Laws* (Oxford: Clarendon Press, 1997).

they are authorized by a statute or a statutory instrument, or concern matters not otherwise prescribed by a statute or a statutory instrument."[130] This provision thus pronounced that custom was a subsidiary source of law that a judge could apply when state law was silent. Article 1 of the Commercial Code declared the precedence of commercial custom to the provisions of the civil code. Custom in commercial matters was allowed to override the texts of the civil law. In this way, the Japanese law reserved room for incorporating deep-seated Japanese custom into the state law regime. Still, Article 2 of the *Hōrei* denied the legal force of custom that was against public order, or the moral sense of the times. Only customary rules that were suitable to the modern sense of justice – cultured through judicial practice – would be recognized as law.

Here one notes that the relationship between statutes and custom as provided in the 1875 decree was sharply refined and clarified during the intervening decades. The validity of custom as law was made contingent on its not being against public order or good morals. The principle that the content of a juristic act should not be contrary to either public order or good morals dated from Roman law, and was stipulated in French and German law.[131] It is commonly accepted that *ordre public* denotes, on the one hand, the order necessary for the commonwealth, that is, a definite system indispensable for the administrative activity, and, on the other hand, the common moral sense of the general public. Together, they set forth the requirement of social appropriateness for juristic acts and hence the compulsory regulation of private law. This legislative arrangement, crucially reinforcing the role of jurisprudence, appears to have been one of the most important elements of civil law. The development in Japanese law was in line with what transpired in other countries in the nineteenth and the early twentieth centuries.

Some comparisons between the treatment of custom in the Japanese Civil Code and the French Civil Code may be illuminating. The Meiji laws were crucially influenced by French law, in particular through the medium of Boissonade. The influence of French law and legal science in Japan began to dwindle toward the last decade of the nineteenth century as German law gained ground. In 1887, the Justice Ministry Law School was transferred to Imperial University and the German law section was created in the College of Law.[132] French law suffered a definite blow after the postponement of the

[130] The *Hōrei* was revised in 2006 through Law Number 78. Article 2 became Article 3, with no change in language. The phrase "ōyake no chitsujō" is often translated as "public order and good morals." It originates from the French *ordre public* and German *öffentliche ordnung*.

[131] See, for example, the French Civil Code: "Individuals cannot by their agreements derogate from the force of laws made for the preservation of public order and good morals" (Article 6); "The cause is illegal, when it is prohibited by law, when it is contrary to good morals or public order" (Article 1133).

[132] For the increasing German influence in Japan, see Kenneth B. Pyle, "The Technology of Japanese Nationalism: The Local Improvement Movement," *The Journal of Asian Studies* 33 (1973): 51–65; Kenneth B. Pyle, "Advantages of Followership: German Economics and Japanese Bureaucrats," *The Journal of Japanese Studies* 1 (1974): 127–164.

Boissonade code. After the turn of the twentieth century, Japanese legal science was dominated by German academic legal doctrines. Still, the influence of the French Civil Code on Japanese law, especially in the early Meji years, should not be underestimated.[133]

It is interesting to compare, in particular, how France and Japan conceived the relations between statutes and customary law in terms of each country's historical past. As noted earlier, when the French rejected custom as a source of law, they were renouncing not so much the content of custom as the prerevolutionary judicial system. The redactors of the civil code were concerned less with the principle that custom was a source of law than with the power of the judges to make customary law. The French revolutionaries were determined to limit the judge's power to make law by finding the existence of a custom.[134] In prerevolutionary France, the Parlements, the sovereign law courts, had extraordinary power to resist royal efforts to centralize the state. In the last years of the monarchy, the judges had earned such notoriety for their reactionary disposition that the revolutionaries of 1789 were determined to defeat judicial power altogether. The "revolutionary tradition" of French law consisted in large part of restraining the unbridled judiciary.[135] The French dismantled the reactionary law courts and their entrenched power in the provinces, and along with them rejected custom as a source of law.

French customary law was, however, carefully incorporated into the civil code. The code, a construct of reason, was a culmination of the doctrinal and jurisprudential development of customary law that had taken place during the old regime. In the aftermath of the massive campaigns to record and reform local customs in the late fifteenth and the sixteenth centuries, the deliberate and coherent efforts by professional jurists to create a common customary law in France became the foundation of the civil code of 1804.[136]

The relationship between judicial decisions and custom in the French code continued to raise difficult questions. Article 5 of the *Code civil* forbade judges to rule on cases in a manner intended to be binding in future cases. Decisions of high courts are treated not as binding rules governing situations with similar facts but merely as sources of pronouncement of higher authority, regardless of facts in the case. Thus Article 5 disallowed the general legal force for court

[133] The commentaries written by Ume on the civil code kept the influence of French law alive in the first decade of the twentieth century. After his death in 1910, however, the interpretation in the French style was largely forgotten. See Ono, "Comparative Law" (Part 2), 47. For the view that the Meiji legal science was marked by the influence of a mélange of legal thoughts, far from being shaped exclusively by conservative German social science, see Erik Grimmer-Solem, "German Social Science, Meiji Conservatism, and the Peculiarities of Japanese History," *Journal of World History* 16 (2005): 187–222.

[134] Robert A. Pascal, "The Sources of Civil Order according to the Louisiana Civil Code," *Tulane Law Review* 54 (1980): 916–941.

[135] [Marie] Seong-Hak Kim, "'Gouvernement des Juges' ou 'Juges du Gouvernement'?: The Revolutionary Traditions and Judicial Independence in France," *Korean Journal of International and Comparative Law* 26 (1998): 1–42.

[136] Kim, "Christophe de Thou et la réformation des coutumes." See Chapter 1.

decisions. While resorting to prior judicial decision as a source of law was prohibited, however, scholars argued that Article 4 of the code supported the validity of the doctrine of *jurisprudence constante*. This article prohibited a judge from refusing to decide a case on the grounds of the silence, obscurity, or insufficiency of the written law.[137] The French Civil Code thus reduced the role of the judges to resolving private disputes, applying preexisting legislative norms without liberty to interpret them. Article 1351 of the civil code states the principle of the "decided matter" (*chose jugée*):

> The binding authority of a judgment applies only to that which was the object of the judgment. The thing requested must be the same; the request must be based on the same cause, be between the same parties and formed by them and against them in the same quality.

This article is cited as the basis of the rejection of an Anglo-American doctrine of *stare decisis*.[138] The limitation on the application of precedents creates a problem for the judge, however, when the applicable statute seems unclear, when there appears to be a conflict between two or more applicable rules, or when there seem to be no applicable rules. Regardless, judges who refuse to render a decision because of the absence of applicable rules can be prosecuted as guilty of denying justice.

The judges are told not to interpret laws but they are subject to punishment for refusing to decide a case. The judge, obeying Article 4, is hence required to fill in the gaps left by incomplete statutory materials. If justification for the judgment is not found in the law, it must be found in the judge.[139] Before rendering a judgment, the judge determines the meaning of a legislative text by choosing among many possible meanings. This interpretation or choice of the applicable norm inevitably results from the will of the judge himself. Such power of decision confirms that the French judge creates law despite the mandate of the revolutionary ideals. Within the framework laid down by revolutionary and Napoleonic legislation, judges have managed to preserve a creative role. In fact, the law-making role of French judges, within the distinct legal confines imposed on the judiciary, appears to represent a reasoned, yet inevitable, compromise, concocted to safeguard the integrity of the judicial process and preserve the revolutionary ideals of republican France.

Judges in search of equity often have had to create whole areas of the law with little guidance. Article 12 of the Civil Procedure Code states that judges may

[137] The *Titre préliminaire* of the French Code consist of six articles: Articles 4 and 5 are provisions of the application of law and Articles 1, 2, 3, and 6 are provisions about the effects of law.

[138] Jacques Ghestin, *Traité de droit civil* (Paris: Librairie générale de droit et de jurisprudence, 1977), vol. I, 434–440. According to Damaska, the rejection of precedents is representative of features of the hierarchical ideal, in which the underlying belief is that society is "governed by a few unalterable principles from which clear rules can be deduced so that the law can be made surveyable." Mirhan R. Damaska, *The Faces of Justice and State Authority: A Comparative Approach to the Legal Process* (New Haven: Yale University Press, 1986), 34.

[139] Michel Troper, "Fonction juridictionnelle ou pouvoir judiciaire?" *Pouvoirs* 16 (1981), 10.

decide cases "in accordance with the rules which are applicable." This can be taken as an explicit reference to and recognition of the existence of case law rules. Therefore, although barred from having the force of precedents as in common law decisions, French judicial decisions, constituting *jurisprudence constante*, have considerable authority in that most judges have repeatedly decided the same way in the same fact situations.[140] Decisions of higher courts also operate as precedents controlling lower courts to a far greater degree than acknowledged in judicial opinions. In other words, while Articles 5 and 1351 of the French Civil Code place limits on the ability of judges to create general rules, Article 4 makes it inevitable that judges refer to precedents and case law. Jean-Etienne-Marie Portalis (1746–1807), the leading draftsman of the civil code, foresaw this problem when he stated: "In the absence of a precise text on a matter, a former usage, constant and well-established, an uninterrupted series of similar decisions, an opinion or a received maxim takes the place of the statute."[141]

Gény persuasively argued for the important role of judicial decisions in generating custom. According to him, the development of general law through *jurisprudence constante* fell under the rubric of customary law. He stated:

> Jurisprudence is, in our modern times, the only truly fertile, and in any case the most frequent, occasion to form legal custom, especially general custom. In fact, once established, on a certain point, jurisprudence, with its uncontestable authority, at least in fact, and also because of the continuity and consistency of our extra-judicial practice, frequently determines the practices in harmony with its tendencies.... When the practices suggested [by jurisprudence] have taken roots through long usages, we have all the elements of a true legal custom ... of which the jurisprudence represents the point of departure and the essential determinant.[142]

Under Article 5 of the French code, judicial decisions were not a formal source of law, but Article 4, by forbidding a judge to refuse to decide where the text is insufficient, compelled him to turn to other sources of law. Thus the crucial relationship between jurisprudence and custom could not be exaggerated.[143]

140 Concerning the growing significance of case law as a source of law, see Mitchel de S.-O.-L'E Lasser, *Judicial Deliberations: A Comparative Analysis of Judicial Transparency and Legitimacy* (Oxford: Oxford University Press, 2004).

141 Cited in Boris Starck, *Droit civil: Obligations*, 2nd ed. (Paris: Librairies techniques, 1972), 49.

142 Gény, *Méthode*, vol. 2, 50–51 (no. 149). But he cautioned: "it is important to note that jurisprudence does not here constitute a source of independent law, nor even a custom *sui generis*. In these hypotheses, it functions only as a force of propulsion of the custom, but a propeller which is so indispensable, and of such inevitable effects in our social and political condition, that a transposition of ideas and even a simplification of the formula would suffice to bring to it all the credit for the creation of which it is in effect the capital instrument." Ibid. For Gény's view of jurisprudence, see Lasser, *Judicial Deliberations*, 170–174.

143 Gény's view that Article 5 limited, rather than eliminated, jurisprudence as a source of law, was further elaborated by others. Edouard Lambert argued that Article 5 prohibited only decisions that create legal norms (law-making decisions) and that recognizing legal force of decisions did not violate Article 5. See Lambert, *La Fonction du droit civil comparé*, book 1; Henri Capitant, *Introduction à l'étude du droit civil: notions générales* (Paris: A. Pedone, 1927), 50–54 (nos. 20–22) (the judicial decision creates custom).

The examination of the interpretation of sources of law in French law has important relevance to Japanese law. Ume seemed to be essentially in agreement with Gény's opinion of the role of jurisprudence to "fill [the legislation] with the light of equity."[144] It amounts to a credible claim for the acceptance of judicially-found custom and equity as supplementary sources of law.[145] Some political implications should be pointed out, too. Both the French and the Japanese laws were concerned about legal uniformity and the centralization of the state, and custom represented regionalism. The civil code was an attack on local autonomy. While the French allowed jurisprudential law only implicitly through Article 4, using negative language, the Japanese recognized the legal force of custom through the positive language of Article 3 of the Dajōkan Decree Number 103. Even after the codification of the Japanese civil law, the imperfection of written law was widely admitted by scholars. Scholars like Ume did not want to restrict the court's role to literal implementation of law provisions.

Unlike the French, the Japanese had no reason to deny the courts power to create customary law. They actively entrusted the judges with the power to discern good customs from bad customs and implement the former as law suitable in a modern liberal state. This was a continuation of the long East Asian tradition of the state's duty to "correct" popular customs. There was general consensus among the judges with modern legal training that the customary law they were establishing needed to conform to general principles of law and more crucially needed to promote the tide of modernization. It was in these circumstances that the provision in the *Hōrei* provided that custom was to be followed when state law was silent. The formulation of the hierarchy of legal norms in Japanese law bore powerful imprints of European laws but also revealed a distinctive force of acculturation at work.

Japanese judges, like their French counterparts, were under constraints because they were supposed to "apply" norms, and not to "create" them. The general doctrinal tendency was to deny the legal force of custom that had not been incorporated into the civil code. But custom provided significant freedom for the judges. The efficacy of resorting to custom in adapting imported

[144] "When, after the purge of this assembly and the organization of an official communication, the draft of the previously rejected preliminary title returned to the legislature, everyone was in agreement in condemning irreversibly the revolutionary utopia, acknowledging the existence of gaps and obscurities in the legislation, and recognizing the interpreter's power to fill them with the light of equity. The judge was even to be under an obligation and a strict duty to do this, according to the provision of Article 4 of the Civil Code, which was definitely enacted and obviously inspired by all these ideas." Gény, *Méthode*, vol. 1, 102 (no. 48). But even Gény acknowledged that the influence of the Revolutionary tradition carried such weight that his opinion was not shared by the majority of scholars. See Yvon Loussouarn, "The Relative Importance of Legislation, Custom, Doctrine, and Precedent in French Law," *Louisiana Law Review* 18 (1958): 235–270; William Thomas Tete, "The Code, Custom and the Courts: Notes toward a Louisiana Theory of Precedent," *Tulane Law Review* 48 (1973): 1–24.

[145] For example, Article 593 and Article 590, Section 2 allow the usage of provinces; Article 1135 provides equity and custom, and law; and Article 565 provides principles of natural equity.

laws was fully demonstrated in jurisprudence. Judgments often considered customary rules, albeit incompatible with the code provisions, in order to give a reasonable solution to the parties.[146] The interaction between the judges and custom was one of the key doctrinal issues that were debated in Europe at the turn of the century. Japanese law seemed to represent an ideal test case of the rational and functional jurisprudence that originated in Europe.

A number of Japanese jurists stressed the originality of their legal thought, some claiming even the superiority of Japanese legal science to French legal science. For them, Article 3 of the 1875 decree, by contemplating the relationship between the authority of the statutes and judicial autonomy, foreshadowed Gény's theory of sources of private law and his call for the scientific method of free legal research. Be that as it may, the important point is that the legal development in East Asia in the late nineteenth and the early twentieth centuries should be seen as something of a continuation of the legal development in European history many centuries earlier. The link between Western European legal history and East Asian legal history may have been closer than has been commonly acknowledged.

Finally, what does the development of Japanese law and legal science have to do with Korean law? Meiji legal science that called for a broad definition of customary law was faithfully imported to colonial Korea. The Second Korea-Japan Treaty, signed on November 17, 1905, rendered Korea Japan's protectorate. Japan had been involved in the modernization of the Korean judicial system from since 1894, but it was after Korea became a Japanese protectorate, and then a colony, that full-scale reform attempts were launched. Japan applied its hierarchy of sources of law in its colonies in Korea and Taiwan. Ume's presence in Korea from 1906 personified the process of the spread of modern civil law from Europe to Japan and then to Korea. Just as flexible interpretations of custom and *jōri* facilitated the introduction of Western private law concepts into Japan, colonial jurisprudence of customary law facilitated a relatively smooth reception of Japanese law in Korea. The process witnessed a merger of modern and traditional laws, engendering a sort of common law. Chapter 4 examines how Korea's traditional legal system and the indigenous social and legal arrangements underwent transformation under Japanese influence.

[146] Noda, *Introduction to Japanese Law*, 224. The courts' treatment of *naien*, common law marriage, exemplifies this situation. See Seizelet, "Contra legem ou para legem?"; S. Anan, "Mariage extra legem et notion de droit au Japon," *Mélanges Paul Roubier* (Paris: Dalloz and Sirey, 1961), vol. 1, 1–6.

4

Legal Reforms in Protectorate Korea, 1905–1910

"It is the tragedy of modern Korean legal history," lamented a prominent Korean scholar, "that every step of the 'reforms' and 'modernization' was accompanied by a progressive loss of national independence."[1] The fact that the establishment of modern law and a modern legal system in Korea was imposed by the Japanese, he argued, created a tremendous amount of ill will among the Korean population against the Westernized legal system, identified with much-resented Japanese rule, and it adversely affected post-independence legal development in Korea. This insightful observation, made more than forty years ago, may have lost some of its relevance today as Western legal values and institutions have pervaded modern industrialized Korea. Its diagnosis of one of the thorniest dilemmas in Korean legal history remains nonetheless as pertinent as ever.

Hostility in Korea toward colonial law and legal regime is grounded in large part in the fact that the colonial military government imposed Japan's laws and other repressive measures on Korea as a means to facilitate colonial control. Yet significant attempts by Japan to implement modern legal reform had started before Korea became its formal colony in 1910. Itō Hirobumi (1841–1909), the first resident general between 1906 and 1909, instigated a series of changes to modernize Korea's law and legal system, claiming that legal reform was the key to his Korean policy. Itō remains one of the most intriguing figures in Korean-Japanese relations. Uncertainty surrounding his real intentions in Korea, that is, how much credence should be given to his repeated declarations on Korean independence, has continued to vex historians.

It is generally agreed that Itō did not believe, at least before 1909, in the need for immediate annexation. Moriyama Shigenori has argued that Itō, like other Japanese politicians, "viewed annexation as *an ultimate goal*, but it was after all a future problem" for him, and that Itō instead regarded as a more

[1] Pyong-Choon Hahm, "Korea's Initial Encounter with the Western Law, 1866–1910 A.D.," in *Korean Jurisprudence, Politics and Culture* (Seoul: Yonsei University Press, 1986), 136 (first published in *Korean Observer*, vol. 1, no. 2, January 1969).

pressing task the consolidation of Japan's influence over Korea free from other countries' intervention.[2] Part of the confusion surrounding Itō's Korean policy arises from the fact that he, a consummate politician, carefully guarded his sentiment and deliberately kept his goals enigmatic. Moriyama is reluctant to assent to the view that the resident general's "nurturing self-rule policy," including efforts to modernize the Korean judiciary and promote the development of the Korean economy and industry, was merely dissimulation of the wily statesman to hide his true intent to colonize Korea. The recent work by Asano Toyomi has also argued that Itō envisioned creating the legal systems in Taiwan and Korea with the full guarantee of judicial independence.[3] Both Moriyama and Asano claim that Itō's legal policy in Korea, building a modern court system and creating new codes, presupposed the existence of an independent Korea and proceeded under the assumption of Korean autonomy. They thus try to strike a balance between the view rationalizing Itō's position in Korea as one of sensible realism and the view disregarding Itō's Korean policy as hypocrisy disguised under legalism in a bid to take over Korea.[4]

Legal reform under the protectorate can shed important light on the evolution of Japan's imperial policy in Korea. Itō's legislative efforts to establish a modern legal system were avowedly prompted by the need to hasten the abolition of extraterritoriality. Under him, the Japanese mounted a considerable effort to abrogate unequal treaties and extraterritorial privilege granted to foreign powers. Itō was particularly driven by the desire to create a private law system and to write Korean codes of civil law and civil procedure. Itō's legal campaign in Korea was grounded on his profound analysis of the Japanese experience of legal modernization that it had undergone only a few decades earlier. The fact that he was reluctant to give in to the call for quick annexation and the demand by most contemporary Japanese scholars and politicians for imposition on Korea of the Japanese Civil Code indicates that his legislative goal in Korea may have been something more than absorbing Korea's laws and legal system into the Japanese colonial imperial system.

[2] Moriyama Shigenori, *Kindai Nikkan kankeishi kenkyū: Chōsen shokuminchika to kokusai kankei* [A History of Modern Japanese-Korean Relations: The Colonization of Korea and International Relations] (Tokyo: Tōkyō Daigaku Shuppankai, 1987), 201; see also Moriyama Shigenori, *Nikkan heigō* [The Annexation of Japan and Korea] (Tokyo: Yoshikawa Kōbunkan, 1992) (emphasis in the original).

[3] Asano, *Teikoku Nihon.*

[4] Classic studies argued that the annexation in 1910 marked the defeat of the Meiji liberals and the failure of Itō's realist policy. Hilary Conroy contended that Itō was opposed to colonization and that he was intent on building Korea into an independent and reliable ally by hastening reforms in Korea. See Hilary Conroy, *The Japanese Seizure of Korea: 1868–1910: A Study of Realism and Idealism in International Relations* (Philadelphia: University of Pennsylvania Press, 1960); Peter Duus, *The Abacus and the Sword: The Japanese Penetration of Korea, 1895–1910* (Berkeley: University of California Press, 1995). Dong Wonmo, "Japanese Colonial Policy and Politics in Korea, 1904–1945: A Study in Assimilation" (PhD diss., Georgetown University, 1965), criticizes Conroy and argues instead that Itō was consistently in favor of annexation.

Itō's politics can be seen as an ultimate example of *realpolitik*. If successful codification and the abrogation of extraterritoriality in Japan secured Japan as a sovereign nation state recognized by the Western powers, the revision of unequal extraterritoriality treaties in its colonies marked a crucial threshold for Japan to cross before it could be accepted as an equal of the imperial powers in the international legal order. Establishing judicial independence was a prerequisite for the abolition of extraterritoriality.[5] Itō's commitment to the ideal of judicial independence in Korea emerges as an important issue in this context.

Instead of speculating on Itō's intentions, this chapter attempts to examine the legal developments in protectorate Korea through the activities of a jurist who was entrusted with overseeing legal reforms in Korea. In 1906 Itō invited Ume Kenjirō to become legal advisor to the Korean empire to lead the formation of a modern legal system. Ume's work in Korea during the next four years centered on building a modern court system and creating new codes.[6] Ume was, by far, the most pivotal figure in the modernization of Korean law. His legislative reform in Korea is remarkable not only because it provides a critical vantage point from which one can assess the nature and scope of Japan's legal undertaking in Korea but because, more broadly, it illuminates different facets of ideological conceptualizations of imperial Japan as a modern state at the turn of the century.

The question of how Japan should frame legal relations with its overseas territory had a significant bearing on the perception of its national identity. Legal reform in Korea pursued by Itō and Ume was a continuation of their earlier collaboration in Taiwan. Almost immediately after the writing of the Japanese Civil Code was over, Ume was recruited in December 1897 by Itō to serve as the Minister of Legislative Affairs in his new government, known

5 Asano, *Teikoku Nihon*, 1. Francis C. Jones, *Extraterritoriality in Japan and the Diplomatic Relations Resulting in Its Abolition, 1853–1899* (New York: AMS Press, 1970, 1931).

6 For Ume in Japan, see Chapter 3. For Ume in English, see Kim, "Ume Kenjirō and the Making of Korean Civil Law"; Marie Seong-Hak Kim, "Law and Reform, Colonial Style: Japanese Judicial Policy in Korea," in *Mélanges offerts à Marc Orange et Alexandre Guillemoz*, ed. Institut d'Etudes coréennes (Cahiers d'Etudes coréennes, No. 8), Paris: Collège de France (2010), 311–321. The following works in Japanese deal with Ume's activities in Korea: Yi Yŏng-mi [I Yonmi], *Kankoku shihō seido to Ume Kenjirō* [The Korean Legal System and Ume Kenjirō] (Tokyo: Hōsei Daigaku Shuppankyoku, 2005), translated into Korean as *Hanguk sabŏp chedo wa Ume Kenjiro*, trans. Kim Hye-jŏng (Seoul: Ilchogak, 2011); Oka Takashi, "Meiji minpō to Ume Kenjirō [The Meiji Civil Code and Ume Kenjirō]," *Hōgaku shirin* 88, no. 4 (1991), 3–47; Naitō Masanaka, "Kankoku ni okeru Ume Kenjirō no rippō jigyō [Ume Kenjirō's Legislative Activities in Korea]," *Shimadai hōgaku* 25, no.3 (1991), 1–26; Chŏng Chong-hyu, "Ume Kenjirō to Kankoku kindai rippō jigyō [Ume Kenjirō's Modern Korean Legislative Activities]," *Hōritsu jihō* 70, no. 7 (1998), 57–61. One of the best analyses, although only a few pages long, of Ume's legal thought in relation to Korean annexation is Ōkawa Sumio, "Gaikoku jin no shiken to Ume Kenjirō [Civil Rights of Foreigners and Ume Kenjirō]," *Ritsumeikan Hōgaku* 253 (1997): 26–48 (Part 1), and 255 (1997): 105–40 (Part 2). Ume has received only cursory treatment by Korean historians, who generally viewed Ume's activities in Korea as part of Japan's imperial policy, facilitating Japanese economic advances and political control of the peninsula.

as Itō's third cabinet. Ume was charged with overseeing the establishment of the legal system of Taiwan so as to hasten the abolition of extraterritoriality on the island. Nine years later, in 1906, they were brought together again in an enterprise to build a modern legal system in Korea. Their collaboration in Taiwan and Korea, a meeting of one of the most powerful statesmen and one of the most brilliant legal minds of Meiji Japan, deserves attention. Hozumi Nobushige remarked that "Dr. Ume is Itō's Tribonian."[7]

Ume's determination to create a modern civil code for Korea, against all political odds, suggests his belief that the Japanese Civil Code he had helped write fell short of his juridical ideals. It indicates that he viewed the writing of a Korean civil code as a crucial opportunity to bring to fulfillment his liberal legal ideals without being restrained by the kind of virulent objections from conservative forces that Japan had experienced. The Korean codification efforts by Ume represent an important ideological nexus between Japan and Korea that allows a parallel approach to legal modernization in the two countries.

Ume's saga in Korea, cut short by annexation and his own death on August 25, 1910, three days after the annexation treaty was signed, presents a powerful case that the Japanese-initiated legal reforms need to be considered from a perspective detached from the nationalist paradigm. In addition, his legal thought provides a rare point of reference in discussing the spread of law from Europe to Japan to Korea and Taiwan in a comparative perspective. They can serve as vignettes through which one can consider the role of Japan in the transplantation of Western law and the legal system to East Asia. What Ume achieved, and also failed to achieve, in Korea can shed light on both theoretical construction and practical implementation of Japanese colonial legal policy.

This chapter discusses the unfolding of Japan's legal policy in Korea from 1905 to the eve of Korea's annexation in 1910, focusing on the reformist campaign led by Ume. One scholar wrote that the Japanese legal reforms were prompted by the realization that "if they were to gain full legitimacy in Korea as an enlightened exploiter, they should establish new legal codes in their protectorate," and that Ume's legislative effort in Korea was nothing more than an example of Japan's "performative display" of legalism.[8] Ume, and Itō, certainly believed in Japan's "civilizing mission." But this is different from saying that they were merely interested, in some disingenuous way, in demonstrating Japan's beneficence to other imperial powers. The view that they undertook modernizing Korean law with ulterior motives appears to be overly convoluted and is often in conflict with empirical evidence.

It has been pointed out that a major problem in the historiography of Japanese colonialism is that it relies overwhelmingly on Japanese colonial sources and that historical writings of the Korean colonial period tended to

[7] Higashikawa, *Hakushi Ume Kenjirō*, 259. Tribonian served Emperor Justinian in the codification of Roman law into the *Corpus iuris civilis* in the sixth century.

[8] Alexis Dudden, *Japan's Colonization of Korea: Discourse and Power* (Honolulu: University of Hawaii Press, 2005), 100 and 102.

come precariously close to reproducing versions of Japanese colonial discourse.[9] One should be duly wary of the self-justifying colonial claims of modernization. But rejecting colonial rhetoric need not obscure the significance of the legal developments during this period. Colonial discourses, such as diffusive celebrations of legal reforms in Korea in annual reports published in English, were just what they were meant to be: colonial propaganda.[10] The nature and reach of legal modernization in Korea requires a detached approach, swayed by neither condonation nor condemnation of colonialism.

Precedents of Reform: The Building of a Colonial Legal System in Taiwan

Many issues that the Japanese government had to deal with at the time of Korea's annexation in 1910 had been visited when Taiwan became Japan's first overseas colony in 1895. The course of creating a colonial structure in Korea proceeded with a sense of deja-vu, although there were some important differences. Examination of the Taiwanese precedent can help understand Japan's Korea policy and the broad implications for the colonial legal order.[11]

The annexation of Taiwan raised weighty constitutional questions for Japan. The core issue was whether Taiwan should be regarded as an integral part of Japan, to which the Meiji Constitution fully extended, or as a separate colony outside the constitutional reach, in which colonial subjects would have limited rights and duties. The colony's constitutional status was translated into the question whether the colonial government should have the authority to legislate colonial laws. Under Article 5 of the constitution, the Imperial Diet had the exclusive power to make law: "The emperor exercises legislative power with the consent of the Imperial Diet." The constitutionality of the colonial governor's legislative power was an issue that was to determine the basic directions of Japanese colonial policy.

A group of politicians and scholars argued that the Meiji constitution was not applicable to overseas territories that had not been part of Japan at the time of the constitution's promulgation in 1889. The colonial government should be able to make its own laws and develop its own legal institutions, free from

[9] Andre Schmid, "Colonialism and the 'Korea Problem' in the Historiography of Modern Japan: A Review Article," *The Journal of Asian Studies* 59 (2000), 952.

[10] Residency General of Korea, *Annual Report on Reforms and Progress in Korea* (Seoul, 1907–1911); Government General of Korea, *Annual Report on Reforms and Progress in Chōsen (Korea)* (Seoul, 1911–1922).

[11] For legal reform in colonial Taiwan, see Tay-Sheng Wang, *Legal Reform in Taiwan under Japanese Colonial Rule, 1895–1945: The Reception of Western Law* (Seattle: University of Washington Press, 2000); Edward I-te Chen, "The Attempt to Integrate the Empire: Legal Perspectives," in *The Japanese Colonial Empire, 1895–1945*, eds. Ramon H. Myers and Mark R. Peattie (Princeton, NJ: Princeton University Press, 1984), 240–274; Ebashi Takashi, "Shokuminchi ni okeru kenpō no tekiyō: Meiji ritken taisei no hito sokumen [The Application of Constitutional Law in the Colonies: An Aspect of the Meiji Constitutional System]," *Hōgaku shirin* 82 (1985): 3–36.

constitutional constraints. Others claimed that the constitution was applicable to all Japanese territories regardless of the timing of their inclusion into Japan, and that legislation by the colonial government would be unconstitutional without authorization from the Imperial Diet.[12] Following heated debates in the Diet and in the intellectual circle, a compromise was struck in early 1896 in the so-called Title 63 (Law Number 63).[13] This law, "Law concerning Laws and Regulations to be Enforced in Taiwan," was devised on the understanding that the constitution extended to Taiwan but that not every provision of the constitution was enforceable.[14] Provisions that limited the power of the emperor, including Article 5, did not govern the territories outside Japan and were therefore inapplicable to the colonies.[15] The consequence of this interpretation was that the laws enacted by the Imperial Diet and the cabinet's executive orders did not automatically extend to the colonies. The principle that only the legislature could make laws was ostensibly maintained, but it was construed that the Imperial Diet delegated to the colonial administration in Taiwan the power to issue executive ordinances with the force of law. Accordingly, Article 1 of Law Number 63 provided that "the governor general of Taiwan may issue ordinances that have the same effect as the laws under his jurisdiction."

Law Number 63 laid the fundamental schemes of structuring future territories in Japan's nascent colonial empire. The division of legislative power was now firmly in place, and the governor general of Taiwan received broad lawmaking power to issue executive orders, called *ritsurei*, subject to the

[12] The difference between the two positions rested on textual construction of the constitution. The constitutional scholar Hozumi Yatsuka argued that "there are no provisions in our constitution that limit its application" and that "in order to prevent the constitution from taking effect in newly acquired territories one would need to amend the constitution to add such language." Hozumi Yatsuka, *Kenpō teiyō* [A Summary of Constitutional Law] (Tokyo: Yūhigaku, 1935), 177–185. Hozumi vehemently opposed the division of legislative power, which he viewed as a "suicide." He contended that the constitutional arrangement under Law Number 63, delegating law-making power to the colonial governor, was a "law that is not law," plainly unconstitutional. Hozumi Yatsuka, "Taiwan sōtoku no meirei ken ni taishite [Concerning the Ordinance Power of the Colonial Governor of Taiwan]," *Hōgaku gakkai zasshi* 23 (2) (1905), in *Hozumi Yatsuka hakushi ronbunshū*, ed. Hozumi Shigetaka (Tokyo: Yūhikaku, 1943), 669. For Hozumi's position during the Japanese Civil Code debate, see Chapter 3.

[13] Issued on March 29, 1896. The text in English translation is in Wang, *Legal Reform in Taiwan*, 192–193. See also Chen, "The Attempt to Integrate the Empire," 248; Asano, *Teikoku Nihon*, 28.

[14] Asano, *Teikoku Nihon*, 28.

[15] It was construed that the effect of certain constitutional articles was limited to defined territorial areas. "Territorial laws" among the constitutional provisions included the provision of the Diet's legislative power (Article 5), the emperor's emergency order power (Article 8), and imperial power to issue ordinances (Article 9). They were applicable to Japan only, not overseas territories. Whether to extend these provisions to the colonies was up to the emperor. Yamazaki Tansho, *Gaichi tōchi kikō no kenkyū* [A Study of the Structure of Governing the Overseas Territories] (Tokyo: Takayama Shoin, 1943), 368–370; Oguma Eiji, *'Nihonjin' no kyōkai': Okinawa, Ainu, Taiwan, Chōsen shokuminchi shihai kara fukki undō made* [The Boundaries of the Japanese: From the Colonial Domination of Okinawa, Ainu, Taiwan and Korea to the Return Movement] (Tokyo: Shinyōsha, 1998), 110.

emperor's approval through the minister of the colonial affairs. In reality, the colony constituted a legally separate territory. This system made it possible, at least initially, for the governor general of Taiwan, and later his counterpart in Korea, to rule the colonies with little interference from the legislature or the cabinet.

The colonial judicial order in Taiwan was created on this constitutional construction. The French advisor to the Ministry of Justice, Michel Revon (1867–1943), recommended that the Japanese government follow the French example in Algeria.[16] In the French system of *rattachement*, Algeria was regarded as an integral part of metropolitan France, endowed with the equal legal status with the French departments.[17] Revon proposed the extension of the metropolitan judicial system to Taiwan and argued that it was necessary to "devise a structure with numerous levels of judges, implementing Japan's court organization law, and establish inferior courts under Tokyo's Daishinin and the Ministry of Justice."[18] On the other hand, the British advisor William Montague Kirkwood supported the creation of a separate judicial hierarchy in Taiwan as an autonomous entity.[19] Kirkwood suggested that the organization and jurisdiction of the courts in Taiwan be determined by colonial laws. In the end, the laws governing the judiciary were construed as territorial laws, and the organization of

[16] Ebashi, "Shokuminchi ni okeru kenpō no tekiyō," 9–10. Revon's name has been consistently misspelled as "Lubon" in literature in English language. Revon was the first professor to hold the chair of "Japanese history and civilization" established in 1920 in the faculty of literature at the University of Paris. He taught French law at Tokyo Imperial University from 1893. See the abstract of Yoshiko Imaizumi's presentation at CRJ/EHESS (France), "Michel Revon: A Forgotten Japanologist and His Study of Shintoïsme," available at http://crjehess.wordpress.com/2010/01/11/michel-revon-a-forgotten-japanologist-and-his-study-of-shintoisme/. See also a book review by Nöel Péri of Revon's book, *Anthologie de la littérature japonaise des origines au XXe siècle* (Paris: Delagrave, 1910), in *Bulletin de l'Ecole française d'Extrême-Orient* 11 (1911), 226–231.

[17] The French constitution fully applied to Algeria, which was allowed to elect its representatives to the Senate and to the Chamber of Deputies in Paris. In contrast, Britain viewed most of her overseas possessions as colonies, granting broad powers to colonial governors. The Parliament made no effort to repeal, amend, or enact colonial laws.

[18] Oguma, '*Nihonjin' no kyōkai*, 85, 113, 128; Chen, "The Attempt to Integrate the Empire," 249; Caprio, *Japanese Assimilation Policies*, 71–72; Mun Chun-yŏng, "Cheguk Ilbon ŭi singminji hyŏng sabŏp chedo ŭi hyŏngsŏng gwa hwaksan: Taeman ŭi sabŏp chedo rŭl dullŏ ssan chŏngch'i ippŏp kwajŏng ŭl chungsim ŭro [The Establishment and Spread of the Colonial Criminal Legal System of Imperial Japan: With Particular Attention to the Political Process of Legislation Surrounding the Taiwanese Judicial System]," *Pŏpsahak yŏngu* 30 (2004): 189–231. The most outspoken supporter of integration was Hara Takashi, Vice-Minister of Foreign Affairs at the time of the annexation and a member of the sub-cabinet level Taiwan Affairs Bureau. Haruyama Meitetsu and Wakabayashi Masahiro, *Nihon shokuminchi shugi no seiji teki tenkai, 1895–1934: sono tōchi taisei to Taiwan no minzoku undō* [The Political Development of Japanese Colonialism, 1895–1934: Its system of Domination and Taiwan's Nationalist Movement] (Tokyo: Ajia Seikei Gakkai, 1980), 23.

[19] Kirkwood's opinion submitted to the cabinet in August 1895 in *Gōtō Shimpei Monjo* 7–34 (Microfilm reel 25), cited in Mun, "Cheguk Ilbon ŭi singminji hyŏng sabŏp chedo," 194–197; Caprio, *Japanese Assimilation Policies*, 71–73.

the courts was left to the governor general of Taiwan to decide by *ritsurei*. The Ordinance of the Government General Courts in Taiwan was issued on May 1, 1896. The colonial courts were established under the direct control of the colonial governor. Since the courts in Japan and Taiwan constituted two separate systems, no appeals were allowed from the colonial courts to the Daishinin, Japan's highest court.

Itō's Judicial Policy in Taiwan

The legal structure of Taiwan reemerged as a critical issue in early 1898 when the revision of the unequal treaties in Taiwan was debated. Negotiations for the revision of treaties in Japan had begun in July 1894, and the deadline for establishing a modern legal system as a condition for abolishing extraterritoriality had been set for July 1898.[20] In March 1898, the drafting of the civil code was completed, awaiting ratification by the Diet. As the deadline for treaty revision approached, a strategic reconsideration of the Taiwan policy was necessary. Itō was in favor of the full implementation of the revised treaties in Taiwan and the extension of the constitution to Taiwanese.[21]

Ume, then minister of legislative affairs in the Itō cabinet, penned a classified report, "Opinion regarding Taiwan," in which he scrutinized Law Number 63 that had in practical sense placed the Taiwanese outside the protection of the Japanese constitution.[22] Ume argued that inhabitants in Taiwan, legally part of Japan, should enjoy the rights and liberties guaranteed in the constitution. He referred to the examples of the English and French colonial empires.[23] According to Ume, there was a difference between the spirit of French law, which aimed at "improving society on the basis of the constitution embodying the principles of liberty, equality and fraternity," and the spirit of English law, which aimed to be a truthful reflection of the society.[24] France extended its constitution to overseas territories. Since "the English constitution is mainly customary law," it was inapplicable to the colonies that had different customs. Japan, a country with a written constitution like France, should extend its supreme law to the indigenous population, argued Ume. The geographical proximity between Japan and Taiwan also set their relationship apart from the relationship between England and India.

Ume rejected as irrelevant the examples of the Dutch Constitution of 1815 and the Spanish Constitution of 1876, both of which restricted the constitution's coverage to their respective territories in Europe.[25] Ume said: "there is general agreement that the constitution extends throughout the imperial

[20] Asano, *Teikoku Nihon*, 8.

[21] Oguma, *'Nihonjin' no kyōkai*, 126; Asano, *Teikoku Nihon*, 28.

[22] Ume's classified report, titled "Taiwan ni kansuru hiken," is analyzed in Ōkawa, "Gaikoku jin no shaken" (Part 2), 125, and Oguma, *'Nihonjin' no kyōkai*, 126–128.

[23] For the discussion that took place between Kirkwood and Ume in March 1898, see Asano, *Teikoku Nihon*, 88; Oguma, *'Nihonjin' no kyōkai*, 126; Mun Chun-yŏng, "Cheguk Ilbon."

[24] Cited in Oguma, *'Nihonjin' no kyōkai*, 126, Note 24.

[25] Chen, "The Attempt to Integrate," 249.

territory, unless there are provisions otherwise."[26] According to Asano, Ume was the only person who linked treaty revision in the colonies to the guarantee of constitutional rights.[27] Ume was unequivocal in arguing that the fundamental principles of law should be common throughout the empire. Kirkwood suggested the possibility of electing the natives to serve in the colony's legislature, but Ume favored the prospect that the Taiwanese send their representatives to the Diet. He also stated that "in the future the Taiwanese people should be made to fulfill military service." In terms of the two major rights and duties of suffrage and military duties, Ume advocated a complete incorporation of the Taiwanese into the Japanese.

Historians have shown that Itō and Ume opposed granting the lawmaking power to the colonial governor as it would abrogate the principle of legislation by the Diet.[28] In their view, it was preferable that the Diet create Taiwan's laws and apply them to every inhabitant, native or foreign, without discrimination. Ume favored an arrangement in which all political and legal institutions of the colony were tightly tied with those of Japan. His ideal was legal integration under the uniform jurisdiction of the Meiji Constitution and laws. The governor general's legislative power through *ritsurei* should be limited to cases involving Taiwanese and the Qing people. Ume envisioned the eventual creation of a code that would govern both Japanese and the Taiwanese. In the meantime, however, Taiwan needed civil law that ought to be established in consideration of Taiwanese and Chinese customs and particular situations. "In principle our codes should be implemented in Taiwan," but in reality applying Japan's laws directly would cause difficulties because of different legal foundations. Awaiting the writing of Taiwan's codes, "the natives should be governed for some time by old customs. In matters regarding real estate, old customs should be applied throughout Taiwan, or at least in most of Taiwan, until the land cadastre is completed." Any conflict arising between customs and Japan's laws in family and succession relations should be resolved "in accordance with the international principles of private laws." Criminal law and civil and criminal procedures would need certain special provisions.[29]

Itō's cabinet pushed for the enactment of a "Law for the implementation of the codes in Taiwan." According to this proposed law, civil and criminal codes would be imposed on Taiwan, while "legal or illegal activities among the Taiwanese and the Qing people, except when non-Taiwanese and non-Qing people were involved, would be governed by provisions to be established by *ritsurei*." But this plan was abandoned when the Itō cabinet fell in June 1898.[30] The Regulation regarding Civil, Commercial, and Criminal Matters (*ritsurei* Number 8) was issued on July 20, 1898. It embodied the principle of

[26] Oguma, *'Nihonjin' no kyōkai*, 126–127.
[27] Asano, *Teikoku Nihon*, 90.
[28] Oguma, *'Nihonjin' no kyōkai*; Asano, *Teikoku Nihon*.
[29] Ume, "Taiwan ni kansuru hiken," cited from Oguma, *'Nihonjin' no kyōkai*, 126–128.
[30] Asano, *Teikoku Nihon*, 92–94.

personality law. Article 1 decreed that civil, commercial, and criminal matters in Taiwan conform to the Japanese codes. But it stipulated: "matters mentioned below shall specially conform to present practice: (i) civil and commercial matters involving only Taiwanese or Chinese; (ii) Criminal matters relating to Taiwanese or Chinese."[31] Under these provisions, civil and commercial matters involving Japanese were governed by the Japanese laws but those involving Taiwanese or Chinese only were to be governed by Taiwan's old customs unless there were laws providing otherwise.

Itō and Ume were of the opinion that, even though broad power had been given to the government general under Law Number 63, judicial power should remain outside the colonial administrators' authority. In June 1898, the Itō cabinet sent a bulletin to the government general of Taiwan, stating that the colonial courts should be created by the legislature under the constitution and outside the colonial governor's administrative power, but it became moot when the cabinet fell the same month.[32] The revised court regulations of 1898 established the two-level courts, appellate and district courts, under the supervision of the governor general. A bill in the Diet proposing Daishinin's appellate jurisdiction over Taiwanese courts was voted down. The House of Representatives was in favor of promoting a unified interpretation of law throughout the empire by the Daishinin's review power, but the Peers opposed on the grounds that allowing appeals to Japan's highest court would be inconsistent with the policy to entrust the rule of the colony to the government general.[33]

The vision of Itō and Ume of creating a constitutional legal system in Taiwan failed to materialize. They believed it was an essential step for incorporating the colonies into the Japanese empire.[34] Instead, the Japanese imperial order was formulated in such a way that Taiwan became a quasi-independent legal territory governed by the colonial governor. The island was placed in practice outside the constitutional coverage and the Diet's control. The establishment of an autonomous colonial judicial system, independent from the Japanese judiciary, was justified on the grounds of Taiwan's unique situation. Similar arguments were to be presented later by the colonial officials in Korea. As will be seen Chapter 5, the colonial governor in Korea exercised full legislative and judicial power until the end of colonial rule. It is possible to speculate that Itō and Ume would have favored, after the annexation of Korea, the extension in Korea of the Japanese Court Organization Law that provided for judicial independence. At any rate, their position in Taiwanese matters foreshadowed the direction of their legal reforms in Korea.

When Ume was enlisted by Itō in 1906 to build Korea's legal system, Ume must have perceived an opportunity to try, once again, to put into practice his

31 The text of this regulation is translated into English in Wang, *Legal Reform in Taiwan*, 195. For its discussion, see *ibid.*, 49; Asano, *Teikoku Nihon*, 96–97.

32 Oguma, *'Nihonjin' no kyōkai*, 131; Asano, *Teikoku Nihon*, 103–104.

33 Mun, "Cheguk Ilbon," 210–212; Asano, *Teikoku Nihon*, 319.

34 Chen, "The Attempt to Integrate," 251.

juridical beliefs. There is reason to believe that Ume in 1906, then 46 years old, saw Itō's invitation to join him in Korea as a turning point in his career. Since 1903 Ume had served as the president of Hōsei University, successor of Wafutsu Law School, in addition to his professorship at Tokyo Imperial University. Previously he was also the director general in the Ministry of Education in 1900. As a scholar Ume was in his prime and, having completed the writing of the civil code, he was looking for an opportunity, or another challenge, to enlarge his sphere of activity. By the latter half of the 1890s, Japan had entered the period of German law's predominance and the influence of French law declined sharply. As French law lost its appeal, the opportunity for those belonging to the French school to exert influence in legislative matters dwindled.[35] The codification of the new civil law marked a fundamental redirection of Japanese legal studies, as the committee took up revising Boissonade's civil code, with its French orientation, in the new light of the German Civil Code. As a jurist, Ume seems to have taken it as his mission to introduce to Korea the modern private law firmly based on the liberal individualism that he had embraced during his studies in France. After the less than satisfactory experience in Taiwan, Korea may have appeared to him as a place where he could implement, under the powerful and sympathetic patronage of Itō, Western legal concepts and civilized jurisprudence without being deterred by resistance from political and social conservatives.

It was in this situation that Itō recommended Ume to the Korean cabinet to assist with the legal modernization projects. Itō emphasized that Ume was "an authority in law second to none, either in Japan or in the West" and that "Dr. Ume's works are used as textbooks in France." Ume was different, said Itō, from typical foreigners who were loitering in Korea looking for jobs; Ume graciously agreed to share his expertise with Koreans in legislative activities.[36] It has often been erroneously believed that Ume was dispatched by the Japanese justice ministry to work at the residency general.[37] But Ume himself said: "I came to Korea not as a counsel to the residency general but at the request of Mr. Itō. Officially I was a counsel to the Korean government."[38] During his four-year effort to reform Korea's legal system, Ume continued to reside in Japan but returned to Korea regularly during the university breaks in summer and winter.

Ume seemed to take tremendous pride in Itō's trust in him. His testimonial in May 1910 to Itō, who had died the previous year, affirms their relationship: "since Meiji 25 [1892] I provided my meager help to the late prince's legislation work.... I enjoyed his trust all this time, often beyond my

[35] Oka, "Meiji minpō to Ume Kenjirō," 22. For the increasing influence of German studies in Japan, see Chapter 3.

[36] Kim Chŏng-myŏng, ed. *Nikkan gaikō shiryō shūsei* [The Collection of Documents involving the Diplomatic Relations of Japan-Korea] (Tokyo: Gannando, 1962–67), vol. 6, part 1, 220–221.

[37] Dudden, *Japan's Colonization of Korea*, 112.

[38] *Hōritsu shinbun*, no. 386 (October 30, 1906). The fact that Ume was not a full-time advisor indicates that he was little involved in the politics of the residency general, and that his legislative activities took place largely outside Japan's political dealings with the peninsula.

worthiness."[39] Above all, Ume was proud of his collaboration with Itō in Korean legislation: "the late prince reportedly said that the most successful part of his enterprise in Korea was [the reform of] judicial power, and I fully agree."[40]

Ume Kenjirō and Reforms of Korean Law and the Legal System

Ume in Seoul

Ume arrived in Seoul on July 2, 1906. His first task was to investigate the Korean land ownership system and customs. Itō had repeatedly emphasized that the protection of land ownership was the most crucial element in private law, requiring immediate attention in Korea. Shortly after Ume's arrival, the Real Property Law Investigation Commission was established in the Korean cabinet with Ume as its head, and the commission began gathering Korean land regulations and usages, researching old Korean law codes and conducting field surveys of these local customs. The investigation, focused on studying Korean concepts of land ownership and land use rights, was to provide material for the new civil code.

While awaiting the results of comprehensive research, however, Itō wanted to implement quickly regulations to prevent fraudulent transactions and proposed to the Korean cabinet measures requiring certification of transactions of real property.[41] Itō argued that, while Korea needed an extensive overhaul of property law, for which Ume was conducting a customs survey, a speedy, albeit temporary, measure was necessary.[42] The legal status of real property owned by foreigners was a question that required urgent attention. Korea limited foreigners' land ownership rights to areas within ten *li* outside the settlements.[43] Gradually, however, land possession by foreigners, in particular Japanese, spread into the Korean hinterland disregarding the treaty

[39] Ume, "Itō kō to rippō jigyō," 32 (962).

[40] Ibid., 45 (974).

[41] *Nikkan gaikō shiryō shūsei*, vol. 6, part I, 299. Ume's activities in Korea are well documented in Yi Yŏng-mi, *Kankoku shihō seido to Ume Kenjirō*. For the Japanese economic policy during the resident general period, see Chŏng Chong-hyu, *Kankoku minpōten no hikaku hō teki kenkyū* [A Comparative Legal Study of the Korean Civil Code] (Tokyo: Sobunsha, 1989); Chulwoo Lee, "Modernity, Legality, and Power in Korea Under Japanese Rule," in *Colonial Modernity in Korea*, 21–51; Chŏng Kŭng-sik, "Ilbon ŭi kwansŭp chosa wa kŭ ŭiŭi [The Significance of Customs Investigation by Japan]," in *Hanguk kŭndae pŏp sa ko* [A Study of Modern Korean Legal History] (Seoul: Pagyŏngsa, 2002), 205–257; Ch'oe Wŏn-kyu, "Taehan cheguk kwa Ilche ŭi t'oji kwŏn pŏp chejŏng kwajŏng kwa kŭ chihyang [The Establishment and Development of Real Property Law under the Taehan Empire and the Japanese Colonial Period]," *Tongbang hakchi* 94 (1996), 111–168; Yi Sang-uk, "Hanguk sangsok pŏp ŭi sŏngmunhwa kwajŏng [The Process of the Codification of Succession Law in Korea]" (PhD diss., Kyŏngbuk National University, 1986).

[42] *Nikkan gaikō shiryō shūsei*, vol. 6, part I, 299.

[43] Chŏn Pong-dŏk, "Sabŏp chedosa [A History of the Judicial System]" (Part 9), *Pyŏnhosabo* 21 (1976), 51; Duus, *The Abacus and the Sword*, 367.

limit. As the number of Japanese residents and their investment in Korea increased rapidly since the turn of the century, the absence of laws defining clear land ownership rights presented serious problems for the protectorate government.

In September and October, Ume drafted a series of laws in collaboration with the Korean Justice Ministry.[44] The new laws, including the Land and Building Certification Regulations, required official certification and authentification for transaction contracts in order to prevent forged ownership documents.[45] The residency general orders that followed imposed the substantially same regulations on Japanese residents.[46] Most significant, these laws legally confirmed the foreigner's right to own land in Korea.[47] It has been contended that the measures, especially the one allowing foreigners to own land, were drafted on the pretext of facilitating land transactions and preventing fraud and forgery, and that they marked in fact a systematic effort to protect Japanese speculators.[48] By sanctioning the unrestricted sale of land, according to Ume's critics, the new laws removed any remaining legal impediments to Japanese land ownership in Korea and opened the door for the economic advances of Japanese imperialism by accelerating the Japanese land grab in Korea.

44 These laws were closely modeled after Japanese laws, such as The Land Pledge and Mortgage Regulations (January 1873), the Regulations for the Mortgage, Pledge, Sale, and Transfer of Buildings (September 1875), and the Regulations for the Sale and Transfer of Land (November 1880). The acquisition, loss, or change of a real right in property could be set up against a third person only if such right had been registered according to the Registration law. Ishii, *Japanese Legislation*, 616.

45 The new laws required certification, not registration, of land ownership. Without the registration of titles, the land transaction document served as the only proof of ownership. Koreans were accustomed to the saying that when the house is on fire you should run out with two things: the home sales document (*chip munsŏ*) to prove your home ownership and the genealogy register (*chokpo*) to prove your clan pedigree.

46 The process of the making of the land laws is described in detail in Yi Yŏng-mi, *Kankoku shihō seido*, 67–86; Chŏng Chong-hyu, *Kankoku minpōten no hikakuhō teki kenkyū*, 28–43.

47 See Ume, "Kankoku no gappō ron to rippō jigyō" [The Theory of Korean Annexation and the Legislation Project] (Speech of May 24, 1910), *Kokusai hō zasshi* 8, no. 9 (1910), 34–35 (739–740).

48 Chŏng, *Kankoku minpōten*, 43; Kang Ch'ang-sŏk, *Chosŏn T'onggambu yŏngu* [A Study of the Residency General of Korea] (Seoul: Seoul Kukhak Charyowŏn, 1995). Edwin Gragert disputed the contention that the Japanese, by introducing the modern land ownership system, were waging "a colonial conspiracy" to deprive Koreans of their land and showed that Japanese land acquisition at the time of annexation was not more than 3–4 percent of all arable land. Edwin Gragert, *Landownership under Colonial Rule: Korea's Japanese Experience, 1900–1935* (Honolulu: University of Hawaii Press, 1994), 148. In recent years, economic history of Korea under Japanese colonialism has been given a close scrutiny by both Korean and foreign scholars. A group of Korean economic historians question the claim that the Japanese overtook as much as 40 percent of Korean land through its cadastral survey during 1912–1918. Kim Hong-sik, *et al.*, *Chosŏn t'oji chosa saŏp ŭi yŏngu* [A Study of the Cadastral Survey in Korea] (Seoul: Minŭmsa, 1997), 13–51. The paths followed by these scholars may point in some general directions for writing a more diverse history of colonial legal history in Korea.

While these criticisms have some validity, it is important to remember that legalizing foreigner's land ownership rights was not something that Ume newly concocted for Korea. His approach to Korean land law reforms was largely consistent with the position he had taken in Japan. Ume's views in favor of foreigners' enjoyment and exercise of private rights in Japan have been analyzed in depth by Ōkawa Sumio.[49] Ume strongly opposed attempts to limit private rights of foreigners in Japan. In 1898, a proposal was presented at the Imperial Diet to change the draft language of the General Principles section of the civil code (Chapter 1, Article 2), from "foreigners shall enjoy private rights except in those cases where such enjoyment is prohibited by applicable laws" to "foreigners shall enjoy principal rights within the extent specially allowed by applicable laws." Ume forcefully argued against the change, contending that the equal enjoyment of rights by foreigners should be the general rule and limitations and prohibitions the exceptions. The proposal was eventually defeated.[50]

In order to achieve the goal of abolishing extraterritoriality, Ume asserted in Japan and repeated in Korea, it was necessary to impose the same rights and duties on foreigners. It would be better to create laws common to both Koreans and Japanese and bring Japanese residents in Korea under them. He stated:

> The land system should be unified because having two separate land registers would cause great inconvenience. The land system needs to be made common to Japanese and Koreans as well as foreigners. It would be desirable to regulate the system by Korean law to be implemented when the civil law is established.[51]

Ume reasoned that the prohibition of foreign ownership, often condoned at the local level for many years, no longer had any practical justification and that it made more sense to legalize it and increase tax revenues from foreign-owned real property. In Japan, Dajōkan Decree Number 18 of 1873 had prohibited foreign landownership, but the rule was modified in 1910 and the nationals of a foreign country were allowed to own land as long as that country allowed the same right to the Japanese.[52] Full landownership rights were granted to foreigners in 1925.[53]

The real property laws Ume devised for Korea were essentially based on the notion of nineteenth-century individualism, with its principles of absolute ownership and freedom of contract. The new laws would provide unencumbered rights and obligations uniformly to every individual, regardless of

[49] See Ōkawa, "Gaikoku jin no shiken to Ume Kenjirō."

[50] Higashikawa's *Hakushi Ume Kenjirō* contains, in 153–164, a text supposedly authored by Ume opposing the revision of Article 2 (Article 3, Section 2 in the current civil law). See also Hoshino, *Meiji minpō hensan shi kenkyū*, 196; Hoshino, "San hakushi to minpō seitei," 53–54.

[51] Ume, "Kankoku no hōritsu seido ni tsuite [On the Korean Legal System]" (Part 2), *Tokyo keizai zasshi* 60, no. 1514 (1909), 10 (796).

[52] Asano, *Teikoku Nihon*, 662 and note 34.

[53] Ibid., 15.

nationality or status, and promote a liberal market society. Ume's belief in the individual's exclusive ownership right was central to his legislative efforts in both Japan and Korea. Some historians claimed, however, that Ume's entire legislative activities constituted preparations for the Japanese exploitation of the Korean people and that his call for a common land law for Koreans and Japanese was proof of such a scheme. Certainly it would be difficult to argue that Ume pushed for legislation that contradicted Japan's interest. But these laws were grounded on Ume's consistent position that universal tenets of equal rights should not be confined within the bounds of any state. Throughout the 1890s and the first decades of the twentieth century, Ume devoted a number of articles, textbook pages, lectures, and speeches to the question of foreigners' rights, expounding on his belief in universal natural rights theory.[54]

Incidentally, it is little known that Ume objected to the Korean law requiring the family head's permission and seal for land transfers by family members. As seen in Chapter 3, Ume was strongly opposed to "bad customs" of a feudal nature in Japan. Asked by Itō to review the Korean Justice Ministry's legislation, Ume tried to delete the provision that limited in this way independent exercise of property rights by individuals.[55] Ume's attempt, although unsuccessful, was a clear indication of his respect for the property and the person of individual family members.

Ume's legislative campaign revealed his keen understanding of the plights of the Korean people and his resolve to improve it by creating a modern legal order. On many occasions, Ume discussed the harm caused by the absence of property regulations that left the Korean people vulnerable to exploitation by shrewd Japanese speculators. Korean land customs did not conform to the modern principles of real property rights and, as suits against Japanese were handled by Japanese consular courts, Koreans had practically no protection under the law.[56]

Ume was in particular concerned about the situation in which many Koreans were left helpless in defending their property rights against Japanese usurers. He noticed that, in Korea, land ownership transfer occurred more frequently as a result of foreclosure than through sale. The Korean notion of *chŏndang* included the concepts of a pledge involving the transfer of movable property to the creditor as well as a mortgage with no transfer of real property.[57] When the debtor failed to meet the specified period for the performance of the debt,

[54] Ume, "Gaikoku jin no kenri [Rights of Foreigners]," *Hōgaku gakkai zasshi* 11, no. 1 (1893): 37–39 (Part 1); no. 3: 220–227 (Part 2); no. 9: 746–751 (Part 3, Incomplete); Ume, "Gaikoku jin no toji shoyūken [The Land Ownership Right of Foreigners]," *Hōgaku shirin* 4 (1900): 18–37.

[55] *Nikkan gaikō shiryō shūsei*, vol. 6, part I, 348. Yi Yŏng-mi, *Kankoku shihō seido*, 167; Ch'oe Wŏn-gyu, "Taehan cheguk kwa Ilche ŭi t'oji kwŏn pŏp," 125–126.

[56] Ume, "Kankoku no hōritsu seido" (Part 1), 8 (702).

[57] Ume, "Kankoku no chŏndang [Korea's *chŏndang*]," *Hōgaku kyōkai zasshi* 26, no. 10 (1908), 780.

the security property was forfeited to the creditor, regardless of the difference between the value of the property and the amount of the debt. The creditor had neither the obligation to do an accounting to the debtor nor the right to demand the amount short of the original loan. Ume strongly argued for the need to reform this "cruel and nasty custom."[58] Most serious harm was caused by Japanese usurers who foreclosed land by taking advantage of the security custom. He described how Japanese loan sharks exploited Koreans by lending money at exorbitant interest rates secured by land:

> Before the establishment of the residency general ... Japanese money lenders came to Korea hoping to make a fortune. They lend money by mortgaging land and, when the debtor cannot pay the money back within the stipulated time, take over the land according to the custom that land is simply forfeited to the creditor.... It even happens that, when the debtor comes to pay the money back, the creditor hides so as not to receive the money, and as soon as the loan becomes delinquent he suddenly shows up to take over the land.[59]

This kind of unjust land forfeiture tactic used by impudent Japanese usurers, criticized Ume, caused enormous suffering among Koreans.

The Regulations for the Pledge and Mortgage Execution of Land and Buildings proclaimed in September 1906 were a close reflection of Ume's view of the mortgage regulations Korea needed. The security instrument had to be affixed with the endorsing seal of the town head; without the seal, the pledge or mortgage instrument could not be used as evidence of a loan. The laws provided that, absent an explicit forfeiture contract, land under pledge or mortgage was to be brought to public auction. The auction proceeds, after satisfying the loan, were returned to the mortgagor. The separate usury regulations, also proclaimed in the same month, limited the maximum annual interest rate to forty percent; without a special contract, it was limited to twenty percent. This interest limitation measure aimed to protect hapless Korean debtors. In Japan, Ume had opposed regulating usurious loans, arguing that it would place undue burden on the flow of capital. This position was consistent with his fundamental advocacy of freedom of contract. When he witnessed the harm inflicted by Japanese creditors in Korea, however, he was willing to compromise his legal belief. Ume's juristic flexibility is exhibited in his effort to prevent unjust consequences and diminish the suffering of Korean farmers.

Ume's speech given in October 1907 at the Kokka Gakkai (National Studies Association) meeting in Tokyo is remarkable in that it revealed his sentiment in extremely candid terms. He began by praising the superiority of Korean civilization:

[58] Ume, "Fudōsan ni kansuru Kankoku kanshūhō ippan [General concepts of the Korean Customary Law of Real Property]," *Hōsō kizi* 18, no. 6 (1908), 9–10.

[59] Ibid.; Ume, "Kankoku no hōritsu seido" (Part 1), 7 (701).

> Korea became a civilized country before our country did. About a thousand years ago, its civilization was more advanced than ours, and we are indebted to Korea in many respects. We have progressed rapidly during the last thousand years, but at the beginning we either directly borrowed civilization from China or Korea, or received Chinese civilization through Korea. There are many areas in which our civilization entirely imitated that of Korea.[60]

Despite its auspicious beginning, however, Korea began to decline during the Chosŏn period. It is revealing that Ume acknowledged that "although it is a little embarrassing for us to say this," Korea's decline was "specifically caused by Hideyoshi's invasion of Chosŏn." Following the 1592 aggression, the Korean peninsula was entirely destroyed and its industry mercilessly plundered by the Japanese. For example, "many master potters were forcibly brought to Japan as war prisoners. This is how Japan's ceramics industry became as advanced as it is today while that of Korea, its origin, was left in ruin."[61] That Koreans blame Hideyoshi for their current misery "is not unreasonable." Korea's misfortune was compounded by a long succession of tyrannical rulers and corrupt officials. As the popular Korean saying went, Korea's despotic government was more dreadful than the peninsula's famous tigers.[62]

According to Ume, Korea is a "difficult" country because, while Korean people lack a sense of enlightened nationalism, they still strongly cling to the notion of the fatherland. "There are some Japanese," he pointed out, "who misinterpret this and say that, since Koreans do not care about their country, if we simply go there and conquer the peninsula, Koreans will happily obey us as long as we enhance the happiness of at least a few people there. This is completely wrong; whoever says this does not know the Korean people."[63] In Korea "there is widespread animosity against the Japanese people. This is something you immediately realize once you set foot in Korea. Korean people think the Japanese simply cause harm to them and are their enemies." If the Japanese would take one step back and view the situation from the Korean perspective, mused Ume, this kind of hostility would not be difficult to understand. Furthermore, during the previous several decades, a number of Japanese ruffians had come to Korea and inflicted much harm and misery on the Korean people. They committed despicable acts such as taking over

[60] Ume, "Kankoku no hanashi [A Talk on Korea]," *Kokka gakkai zasshi* 21, no. 12 (1907), 2 (1438). See Yi Yŏng-mi, *Kankoku Shihō Seido*, 62–64.

[61] Ume, "Kankoku no hanashi," 3 (1439). Ume's admiration of Korean civilization and acknowledgement of the disastrous effect of the Japanese invasion strike the same chord as those of Yanaihara Tadao some thirty years later. Susan C. Townsend, "Yanaihara Tadao and the Irish Question: a Comparative Analysis of the Irish and Korean Questions, 1919–36," *Irish Historical Studies* 30 (1996), 195–205; Susan C. Townsend, *Yanaihara Tadao and Japanese Colonial Policy: Redeeming Empire* (Richmond: Curzon, 2000).

[62] "Kankoku no hanashi," 6 (1442) and 4 (1440).

[63] Ibid., 26–27 (1462–1463).

Korean land through irregular usurious loans and dishonest dealings in commerce. So "Japanese have become the worst enemy among the foreigners in Korea."[64]

These statements by Ume amount to an expression of his doubts about Japan's imperial ambition in Korea. He warned against the complacent and misguided belief among some Japanese that Koreans would welcome annexation. To the contrary, Koreans strongly resented the Japanese and would vehemently protest Japanese territorial aggression. In particular, Koreans are certainly mindful of the law under which they would be governed, and this is why independent Korean laws must be codified, he argued. For Ume, the codification of Korean civil law was not a mere stepping stone toward the full-blown application of Japanese civil law. Ume consistently worked under the assumption that Korea would eventually regain its full independence and viewed his task as developing a legal code that could stand up to the scrutiny of the international community. He declared that he came to Korea to create law codes that could be "on par with the law codes of civilized countries," adequate to bring about the "abolition of extraterritoriality."[65]

Behind this laudable goal, however, lay a contradiction Ume failed to see, or at least was hesitant to admit. Japan's policy, as promoted by Itō, was to protect Korea's independence and promote the Korean people's interest while also maintaining a firm political grip under the protectorate arrangement. Ume appears to have genuinely believed that Itō's intervention in the administration of Korea was necessary to resuscitate Korea's strength after a long period of misrule and put it back on the track of progress. Itō the statesman, a perennial pragmatist, was primarily concerned with keeping Korea as a reliable, and pliable, ally. He felt that annexation would have a negative political and financial impact on Japan, but he was ready to adjust, if necessary, his course of action to suit Japan's interest. Ume the comparative jurist, on the other hand, focused on the absurdity of imposing Japan's law on Korea that had a starkly different historical and cultural background. He remained convinced that Korea needed an independent civil code. The incongruity that Japan was helping Korea survive and prosper by dictating its national policy was apparently less obvious to Ume than to modern observers. A true partisan of universal natural law, Ume seemed to believe that the interests of the two countries need not be in conflict.

The Creation of a Modern Judicial System

Japan's efforts to establish modern property rights in Korea were closely linked to the reform of judicial administration. Both Itō and the Korean cabinet members agreed that reform was needed to separate judicial and administrative

[64] Ibid., 28 (1464).

[65] Ume, "Kankoku no hōritsu seido ni tsuite" (Part 1), *Tokyō keizai zasshi*, vol. 60, no. 1512 (1909), 8 (702).

affairs and ensure judicial independence.[66] Between 1906 and 1909, the protectorate government's judicial policy went through several phases. As Itō formulated the issue, there were two options: unify Korea's judiciary with Japan's judicial power, or maintain Korea's judicial authority and reform it under Japan's protection. Itō initially opted for the latter, pursuing gradual improvement of Korea's judicial system.

Since provincial magistrates lacked legal training, Itō decided to invite Japanese legal professionals to assist with Korean officials. In January 1907, Japanese advisors, chosen from incumbent judges and prosecutors, were assigned to Korean courts throughout the country. It led to a major flow of Japanese jurists to Korea. Itō told them: "even if decisions are rendered in the name of provincial magistrates, judicial business is in fact in your hands."[67] They were cautioned, though, to avoid transgressing the authority of Korean judges.[68] If Korean officials refused to receive the advisors' recommendations, Itō stated, it might be necessary to threaten them that Japan would take over Korean judicial power. But, he quickly added, "it is only a threat; if it becomes a reality, it will cause big trouble for everyone."[69] This statement is important because it shows that, although he conferred substantial practical authority on the advisors, Itō did not plan yet to take over judicial affairs of Korea.[70] Once the Japanese jurists started their duties, they complained that local governors were not willing to accept their advice.[71] The most crucial problem was prevalent confusion between judicial and administrative affairs. They observed that as much as eighty percent of the work of local officials, *kunsu*, involved adjudication.[72]

[66] At the twelfth meeting held on November 16, 1906, the Korean cabinet member Pak Che-sun concurred on the need to separate judicial business from administration. Kim Chŏng-myŏng, *Nikkan gaikō shiryō shūsei*, vol. 6, part I, 393–394.

[67] Itō's speech to Japanese legal professionals, January 5, 1907, appears in Yūhō Kyokai, ed. *Chōsen ni okeru shihō seido kindai ka no sokuseki* [The Course of the Modernization of the Korean Legal System], in *Chōsen kindai shiryō kenkyū*, vol. 6 (Tokyo: Kuresu Press, 2001, 1966), 9–16 (the quote is on 10). This book is the transcript of a roundtable discussion held in Tokyo in 1940, in which a number of Japanese legal professionals who had served in the colonial government participated. For a Korean translation, see Nam Ki-jŏng, trans. *Ilche ŭi Hanguk sabŏppu ch'imnyak sirhwa* [The Real Story of the Invasion of the Korean Judiciary by Imperial Japan] (Seoul: Yukpŏpsa, 1978). See also Edward J. Baker, "The Role of Legal Reforms in the Japanese Annexation and Rule of Korea, 1905–1919," in David R. McCann, John Middleton, and Edward J. Shultz, eds., *Studies on Korea in Transition* (Honolulu: Center for Korean Studies, University of Hawaii, 1979), 17–42.

[68] Yi Yŏng-mi, *Kankoku shihō seido*, 234.

[69] Yūhō Kyokai, *Chōsen ni okeru shihō seido*, 21.

[70] "If [Korea] does not allow the advisors' intervention in trial matters, we can hold the cabinet responsible. It does not guarantee success but we do not have an alternative." Yūhō Kyokai, *Chōsen ni okeru shihō seido*, 22.

[71] See complaints voiced by the Japanese advisors regarding difficulties of working with Korean officials." Yūhō Kyokai, *Chōsen ni okeru shihō seido*, 17–22; Nam, *Ilche ŭi Hanguk sabŏppu* ch'imnyak sirhwa, 33. For the legal advisors, see Yi Yŏng-mi, *Kankoku shihō seido*, 9–35.

[72] Yūhō Kyokai, *Chōsen ni okeru shihō seido*, 18.

Itō's legal policy in Korea centered on the paramount objective of abolishing extraterritoriality. In a meeting with the Korean cabinet in 1907, Itō pointed out that, under the treaty relations, foreigners remained completely outside Korean jurisdiction. Even when Koreans were defendants in civil suits, the lack of a modern trial system caused those cases to evolve into diplomatic questions, seriously disadvantaging the Korean parties.[73] As foreigners spread inland, they enjoyed various rights without fulfilling duties. In order to bring foreigners under Korean laws, Itō stressed, it was necessary to write modern codes and establish independent and competent courts. Absent legal reforms, "it is no use being angry about [extraterritoriality] because it is strictly in accordance with the treaty."[74] Korea needed to build a legal system which would stand on the same footing with the legal systems of civilized nations. It was the standard of international acceptability. Separation of judicial and administrative powers was essential for judicial reforms.

A critical turning point in judicial modernization in Korea was reached with the signing of the Third Korea-Japan Agreement on July 24, 1907. This treaty, known as the Ŭlmi Seven Treaty, was prompted by the so-called Hague secret emissary affair.[75] The Korean Emperor, Kojong, dispatched confidential emissaries to the Second Peace Conference at The Hague in June 1907 in order to declare to the international community the invalidity of the Second Korea-Japan Treaty of 1905 that rendered Korea Japan's protectorate. But the delegates were not allowed to enter the conference on the grounds that Korea was not an independent nation.[76] Itō was enraged by this secret mission and forced Kojong to abdicate. The Third Korean-Japanese Treaty soon followed.[77]

The treaty stipulated that the promulgation of laws by the Korean government and important administrative dispositions henceforth be approved by the resident general (Article 2). The treaty specifically required that judicial affairs be separated from ordinary administrative affairs (Article 3), and that Japanese judges and prosecutors be appointed to the Korean courts (Article 5).[78] This agreement prescribed for the first time in Korea the separation of the judiciary from the administration, ending adjudication by administrators. To ensure its implementation, Japanese bureaucrats were appointed in each ministry in the Korean cabinet as deputy ministers. In September 1907 Kuratomi Yuzaburō (1853–1948) took office as deputy minister of justice.

[73] *Nikkan gaikō shiryō shūsei*, vol. 6, part II, 512 (June 4, 1907).

[74] Itō's statement at the meeting with provincial governors, ibid., vol. 6, part I, 928.

[75] For the events surrounding the agreement, see C. I. Eugene Kim and Kim Han-Kyo, *Korea and the Politics of Imperialism 1876–1910* (Berkeley: University of California Press, 1967), 141–149.

[76] Carter J. Eckert, Ki-baik Lee, Young Ick Lew, Michael Robinson, and Edward W. Wagner, *Korea Old and New: A History* (Seoul: Ilchokak and Korea Institute, Harvard University, 1990), 245.

[77] Asano, *Teikoku Nihon*, 154–161.

[78] Kim, ed. *Nikkan gaikō shiryō shūsei*, vol. 6, part II, 634–638.

The reform of the Korean legal system raised widespread criticism in Japan, mainly because of the costs incurred by the Japanese government. Itō's proposal of writing a Korean civil code was opposed on the grounds that a separate legal system would result in excessive independence in Korea. Many Japanese scholars expressed concerns that the lack of uniformity in civil law between Korea and Japan would cause confusion in economic transactions and create difficulties for investors. An article in *Hōritsu Shinbun* in 1907 lambasted Itō's judicial policy:

> Resident General Itō characteristically stresses formality and procedural regularity in all matters. Since he came to Korea, he has written and implemented many laws through which he tried to regulate the Korean people and protect their rights and interests. All this is good, and so is his intention.... But if adhering to complicated procedures increases burden on the [Japanese] state, the resident general must pay attention to the matter and lay blame upon himself.[79]

Another article in *Hōritsu shinbun* in 1907 asked why Korea needed to have a supreme court:

> Resident General Itō wants to establish, as a way of reforming Korea, a tripartite hearing system and a supreme court just like in civilized countries.... But there is sufficient proof that it is too early to establish a tripartite hearing system in Korea, due to the low level of civilization of the Korean public.... The resident general is wise and experienced; why does he not realize this?[80]

For Ume, the architect of Korea's judicial structure, the outcry against Itō's legal policy was groundless and shortsighted. After Itō's death, Ume denounced in the strongest terms those who claimed that "establishing a tripartite system in a country like Korea is wrong, implementing a collegiate bench judgment is wrong, and the late prince Itō focused on formalities in making laws ignoring practical benefits."[81] Itō believed, recalled Ume, that "judicial independence was the most urgent matter." Some people misunderstood Itō's intention, he continued, and said "there is no need to stipulate the matters of judicial power in the [Third Korean-Japanese] treaty because judicial matters are after all part of politics and naturally will be governed under the resident general's guidance." But the fact that Itō demanded inclusion of the specific provision of judicial independence in the treaty corroborated, according to Ume, his vision to reform the Korean courts without delegating judicial power to Japan. Ume stated that Itō's policy was "based on the belief that a civilized rule can be implemented by improving the judicial system of Korea, by promoting the people's rights, and by making the courts truly independent institutions by separating the judiciary from the executive."[82]

79 "Shihō jō yori kantaru Nikkan shin kyōyaku [The Japan-Korea New Agreement as Seen from a Judicial Perspective]," *Hōritsu Shinbun*, vol. 442 (August 10, 1907), 6.

80 "Kankoku hatashite Daishinin wo okuno hitsuyō ariya [Is There Really a Need to Establish a *Daishinin* in Korea?]," *Hōritsu Shinbun*, vol. 463 (November 25, 1907), 2.

81 Ume, "Itō kō to rippō jigyō," 44–45 (974–975).

82 Ume, "Kankoku no hōritsu seido ni tsuite" (Part 2), 793. See also Ume, "Kankoku no hanashi," 12 (1454).

On December 23, 1907, the Court Organization Law (Law Number 8) was proclaimed, followed by Court Organization Law Implementation Law (Law Number 9) and the Court Establishment Law (Law Number 10), all drafted by Ume.[83] Four levels of courts were created, headed by a supreme court in Seoul, Taesimwŏn (The Great Court of Cassation; Daishinin in Japanese), and a tripartite hearing system was established. Three appeals court (Seoul, Pyŏngyang, and Taegu), eight district court (Seoul, Kongju, Hamhŭng, Pyŏngyang, Haeju, Taegu, Chinju, and Kwangju), and 113 (112 established) county courts were set up. Each court had separate civil and criminal divisions. This structure was based on the model of the Japanese system, which itself had been modeled after the German court system.[84] This is how Korea came to have a judicial organization similar to that of Germany. The judicial structure formulated at this time was retained by the government general and continued throughout the Japanese colonial period. It remains fundamentally intact in the modern Korean judicial system.

The opening of the courts took place on August 1, 1908, except for several county courts.[85] This marked the beginning of the independent judiciary in Korea. A number of Japanese jurists were recruited to fill the posts of judges and prosecutors.[86] Watanabe Nobu, the Tokyo District Court chief judge, was appointed chief justice of Taesimwŏn, and Kokubu Sangai, the Osaka District Court chief prosecutor, was named chief prosecutor. The appointment roaster during the four-month period from February to June 1908 reveals that thirty-six judges, nine prosecutors, and seventy-one law clerks were Koreans; and eighty judges, twenty-seven prosecutors, and

[83] *Hanmal kŭndae pŏmnyŏng charyo chip*, vol. 6, 160–169. The Court Organization Law of 1907 and the accompanying laws and rules, including the Law of Civil and Criminal Procedure issued in 1908, were translated into English and published in 1909. See "English Translation of the Korean Law of the Constitution of the Courts of Justice, The Rules for the Operation of the Law of the Constitution of the Courts of Justice, and The Korean Law of Civil and Criminal Procedure, with Supplementary Rules and Orders." The texts are printed in *Pŏpsahak yŏngu* 22 (2000): 231–274 (Part 1); 23 (2001): 165–204 (Part 2). For the background of the writing of these laws and the judicial system under the residency general, see Kim Pyŏng-hwa, *Hanguk sabŏpsa* (Chungse p'yŏn), 94–95; Pŏpwŏn Haengjŏngch'ŏ, *Pŏpwŏnsa*, 16–61.

[84] The Korean law omitted several provisions in the Japanese law that were crucial for judicial independence. For example, the latter's provisions such as legal qualifications for appointment of judges and prosecutors (Articles 57–66), permanent tenure and the guarantee of status for judges (Article 73), and limits on the power of the Judicial Minister to interfere with judicial administration (Article 143) were not explicitly stipulated in the Korean law. Sin, "Kŭndae sabŏp chedo sŏngnip sa pigyo yŏngu: Hanguk e issŏsŏ 'sabŏp tongnip' wŏlli," 279.

[85] Kim Pyŏng-hwa, *Hanguk sabŏpsa* (Chungse p'yŏn), 99. The problem of recruiting qualified judges caused the delay of the opening of some lower courts. Also procuring court buildings and prisons posed difficulties.

[86] See Yoshikawa Ayako, "Ilche sigi ihon sosong kwa Ilbon in p'ansa: 1910 nyŏn dae rŭl chungsim ŭro [Divorce Litigation and Japanese Judges during Japanese Rule: Focusing on the 1910s]," *Pŏpsahak yŏngu* 44 (2011): 171–209.

FIGURE 4.1. **First modern courts, circa 1910.** All four levels of Korea's first modern courts that opened doors in 1908 were housed in this building in Kongpyŏngdong in Seoul. The colonial Chosŏn High Court moved to Sŏsomundong in 1911 and the lower courts followed in 1920. Reproduced with permission from *Sajin ŭro ponŭn kŭndae Hanguk*, vol. 1 (Seoul: Seomoondang, 1996), page 30.

eighty-four law clerks were Japanese.[87] Many of them had already been working at Korean courts as legal advisors. In theory, the Japanese judges applied Korean laws, but, in the absence of a Korean civil code, they naturally resorted to Japanese civil law. A Japanese judge at the Pyŏngyang district court testified: "we followed [Korean] civil procedure rules, but in substantive law, we generally resorted to Japanese civil law. There were some difficult cases, but most cases, involving monetary debts, land disputes, or gravesite disputes, were relatively easy to resolve and we were able to render judgments based on our knowledge of Japanese civil law, perhaps with the exception of family law cases."[88]

Itō and Judicial Independence

Judicial reform pursued by Itō in Korea has traditionally been seen as a tool for advancing Japan's imperial ambition. But recently some historians have

[87] Chŏn, "Ilche ŭi sabŏpkwŏn kangt'al," 182–183. The large number of Japanese judicial officials employed in Korean courts apparently created concerns in legal circles in Japan about the depletion of Japanese legal talents.

[88] Nam, *Ilche ŭi Hanguk sabŏppu ch'imnyak sirhwa*, 49.

attempted to reexamine this view. According to them, Itō formulated his ideal of reform foremost in terms of judicial independence, which he viewed as a precondition for the independence of a state free from foreign interference.[89]

The equation of judicial independence with national independence, predicated on the abolition of extraterritoriality, was a critical issue in Japan. In the wake of the "Ōtsu incident," there was a widespread understanding that the independence of judicial power was a key issue in international politics. In 1891, Russian crown prince, later Tsar Nicolai II, was attacked by a Japanese ruffian in the Japanese city of Ōtsu. The Japanese government and the court came under heavy pressure from the Russian government to execute the culprit although the penalty prescribed in Japanese law for attempted murder was life imprisonment. It was argued that the provision in the criminal code, providing an exception for crimes against the emperor and the crown prince (Article 116), should be extended to this case. The judge presiding over the case eventually resisted the political pressure and sentenced the convicted to life imprisonment. This judgment is celebrated as a landmark case for judicial independence in Japan.[90]

There exists a little known opinion written by Ume regarding the Ōtsu incident. Mutsu Munemitsu, Minister of Agricultural and Commerce, ordered Ume, then barely thirty years old and an attaché at the ministry, to write a legal memorandum on the case.[91] Ume cogently argued against the execution of the convicted, because the status of the victim – whether a foreigner or a national, and whether a commoner or a royal family member – had no bearing on the nature of the crime. If Japan "dared to distort law" and tried to "earn other countries' favor by allowing an illegal trial," he wrote, Japan could not hope to be regarded as an independent country. This opinion illustrates Ume's conviction in judicial independence. One can conjecture that the position held by Itō and Ume regarding judicial independence in Korea was not much removed from their stance on the same issue in Japan.

Itō reflected on judicial independence in Korea in an address to Japanese jurists who had just been appointed judges and prosecutors in Korean courts:

> I declared judicial independence the most immediate goal of the reform of Korean politics.... In my opinion, it is the most important matter among the hundreds of reform measures and nothing will have any meaning without it.

89 Moriyama Shigenori, "Hogo seiji ka ni okeru shihō seido kaikaku no rinen to genjitsu [Ideals and the Reality of Judicial Reforms in Protectorate Korea]," in Asano Toyomi and Matsuda Toshihiko, eds. *Shokuminchi teikoku Nihon no hōteki kōzō* (Tokyo: Shinzansha, 2004), 277–317.

90 See, among others, Sakai Akira, "'Shihō ken no tokuritsu' to Kojima Iken: Ōtsu shiken o tsuishin ni shite [The Independence of Judicial Power and Kojima Iken: With Particular Attention to the Ōtsu Affair]," *Kyushu Ryukoku Tanki Daigaku kiyō* 53 (2007): 27–41.

91 The Mutsu Munemitsu Papers deposited at the National Diet Library in Japan contains the document written by Ume. The text of Ume's opinion is published with analysis in Yasuoka Akio, "Ōtsu jiken ni kansuru Ume Kenjirō ikensho [The Opinion Paper by Ume Kenjirō regarding the Ōtsu Affair]," *Hōgaku shirin* 94, no. 3 (1996): 141–147.

> Of course projects of improving and advancing education, planting trees and maintaining mountains are important. In order to correct the problems unique in Korean situations, however, one must consider judicial independence to be the most pressing business. Koreans in general do not understand the significance of adjudication and its relations to politics. To exaggerate a bit, it can be said that they do not have a concept of trial. But I am determined, no matter what they think and no matter whether they like it or not, to establish judicial independence.[92]

For Itō, the lack of a systematic judicial system weakened the foundation of Korea as a modern independent country. So far, other Japanese had called for judicial reform in Korea but no one addressed it in terms of national survival. Moriyama argued that Itō was the first who linked judicial independence in Korea to the independence of the country.[93] Asano argued that Itō wanted to achieve his goal of the abolition of extraterritoriality by building a judicial system that the foreign powers could trust and thereby acquire approval in the international community. Judicial independence meant independence from extraterritoriality, the independence of the nation.[94] Constructing a national court system was central to the country's survival and territorial sovereignty.

Itō's commitment to judicial independence appears beyond dispute. Of course, one cannot overlook that there was an inherent contradiction in Itō's vision of judicial independence, because he believed that Korea could not achieve judicial independence without protection from Japan.

Reform of Procedural Laws

Modernization of procedural rules was an important issue for judicial reform in Korea. Extraterritoriality was justified on account of procedural irregularities and injustices existing in the administration of justice. The dismal situations of the Korean judicial system at this time were attested by Ume, who stated: "one can safely say that courts do not exist.... A trial is not what you can imagine to be a trial."[95] A serious problem was the lack of distinction between criminal and civil matters.[96] It was common that civil parties were put in custody, even

92 Cited from Mun Chun-yŏng, "Hanguk kŏmch'al chedo ŭi yŏksajŏk hyŏngsŏng e kwanhan yongu [A History of the Establishment of the Prosecution System in Korea]" (PhD diss., Seoul National University, 2004), 102, note 48. See also Itō's statement to the Korean cabinet, the 43th meeting, June 24, 1908, in Kim Chŏng-myŏng, ed., *Nikkan gaikō shiryō shūsei*, vol. 6, part II, 947–948.

93 Before the Sino-Japanese War in 1894, Fukuzawa Yukichi called for the promulgation of laws and the reform of Korea's political and legal structures, but he did not envision that judicial independence was necessary in Korea. Moriyama, "Hogo seiji ka Kankoku," 282, 287.

94 Asano, *Teikoku Nihon*, 240.

95 Ume, "Kankoku no hōritsu seido ni tsuite" (Part 2), *Tokyo keizai zasshi* 60, no. 1514, 793; Ume, "Kankoku no hanashi," 12 (1454).

96 At the twelfth meeting held on November 16, 1906, Itō emphasized the need to separate civil law from penal law. Kim Chong-myong, ed., *Nikkan gaikō shiryō shūsei*, vol. 6, part II, 393–394. The Korean cabinet and Itō discussed the draft of "Law of the Revision of the Judicial System" on June 25, 1907. Ibid., 551.

before the start of the trial, and they were often tortured.[97] The losing party was placed in prison to force him to pay civil debt.

Throughout 1907 and 1908, a flurry of laws and regulations were issued to reform procedures.[98] The law promulgated on June 27, 1907, "Matters regarding Civil and Criminal Procedures," limited the judicial power of administrative officials to civil cases and criminal cases in the first instance involving sentences other than corporal punishment (Article 1). Detention of the parties to a civil case in custody was prohibited, and the magistrate's power to order search and seizure of the parties' property was curtailed (Article 6). Another law, "Matters regarding Interrogations," prohibited the use of torture in both civil and penal matters.[99] The right to file appeals was guaranteed.[100]

Evidence shows that Ume was working on civil procedure in October 1907, even before he completed the court organization law in December.[101] Ume returned to Korea in February 1908 and submitted the completed draft to the residency general in April.[102] Consisting of 577 articles, the proposed civil procedure was shorter than the Japanese equivalent (755 articles) proclaimed in 1890. Ume acknowledged that his draft was based on Japanese civil procedure, although he took care not to copy rules that were overly formalistic: "In order to ensure fair trials, I decided that it was necessary to simplify procedures. Other than these differences, however, I thought I could resort to Japanese civil procedure law. A number of Japanese judges are working at the courts in Korea and, although Japan's civil procedural laws are not perfect, they are trained in applying them."[103] Ume stated: "In Korea, substantive law must be based on Korean customs, but procedural law can be borrowed from Japanese law."[104] He said: "since our country and Korea must become like one country, it is better not to have different systems."[105] This last statement has been seen by some as evidencing Ume's support of Japan's annexation of Korea. But what would

[97] The Japanese legal advisors sharply criticized these practices. Nam, *Ilche ŭi Hanguk sabŏppu ch'imnyak sirhwa*, 57–58.

[98] See Son Kyŏng-ch'an, "Kaehwa gi kundaejŏk minsa sosong pŏpkyu toip e kwanhan yŏngu [A Study of the Reception of Modern Civil Procedural Laws during Late Choson's "Enlightenment" Period]" (MA thesis, Seoul National University, 2002).

[99] *Hanmal kŭndae pŏmnyŏng charyo jip*, vol. 5, 545–546. See Mun, "Hanguk kŏmch'al chedo," 103. The law of "Statute of Limitations for Civil Trials" (Law Number 20), published on July 23, 1908, provided that filing a lawsuit for obligations was allowed up to 10 years from the rise of the cause; actions for property disputes had to be filed within 20 years (Article 3). This law provides the rules that are similar to the rules in the current Korean Civil Code (Article 162). *Hanmal kŭndae pŏmnyŏng charyo chip*, vol. 7, 94–95.

[100] The Justice Ministry Order Number 4, "Regulations to Process Appeals." *Hanmal kŭndae pŏmnyŏng charyo chip*, vol. 5, 378–380.

[101] "Kankuko shihō seido [The Legal System of Korea]," *Hōritsu shinbun*, vol. 455 (October 15, 1907), 26.

[102] Higashikawa, *Hakushi Ume Kenjirō*, 29, 184.

[103] Ume, "Kankuko no hōritsu seido ni tsuite" (Part 2), 795–796.

[104] Kawasaki Bunzō, "Chōsen ni okeru Ume hakushi [Dr. Ume in Korea]," *Hōgaku shirin* 49, no.1 (1950), 99.

[105] Ume, "Kankuko no hōritsu seido ni tsuite" (Part 2), 795–796.

be the use of a separate civil procedure if he were expecting Japan's colonization of Korea anyway? Would it not be more reasonable to read his statement in connection with his remark that he wanted to avoid "sudden application of a civil procedure based on a different 'ideology' that could create much confusion"?[106] There is little doubt that Ume believed in the transplantation of Japanese law in Korea. He did not question that Japanese law should be the model of Korean law he was writing. But the view that this position of Ume proves his support of annexation lacks persuasion. Ume boasted that his draft code was based on more advanced doctrinal principles than the Japanese code that closely followed the German system.[107] He believed that it was an improvement of the Japanese model.[108]

Ume's draft of civil procedure soon fell victim, however, to new turns in Japan's policy. The growing prospect of entrusting Korean judicial power to Japan diminished the need for an independent Korean code. Its planned proclamation on July 1 was postponed without explanation. Upon Ume's return to Korea in July, the draft was discussed in the Code Investigation Bureau, only to be put on hold by the time he went back to Japan in late August.[109] Ume later confirmed that while "the draft had already been completed, entrustment of judicial power required some modifications of the code."[110] Ume's codification scheme had clearly been based on the assumption of the continuing existence of a sovereign Korea, but it was inevitable that his entire legislative enterprise was to be influenced by the rapidly evolving political situation.

With Ume's draft shelved indefinitely, Regulations of Civil and Criminal Procedure (Law Number 13) were proclaimed on July 13, 1908.[111] Combining both civil and criminal procedural rules in 177 articles, these regulations were markedly simpler compared with Ume's version. They provided basic rules regarding court jurisdiction, arraignment prescription, and the police. Changes from the existing rules included the provisions that the prevailing creditor could request that the debtor be placed in custody for a limited time period, if the former paid the expenses of custody (Articles 138–142). The court had to free the debtor when he paid the debt (Article 141). These articles allowing post-trial custody were characterized as an enforcement measure, different from pre-trial custody, so they were viewed as an improvement from earlier practices.[112] On

[106] Ibid.

[107] "Ume hakushi to kataru," *Hōritsu shinbun*, vol. 546 (January 20, 1909).

[108] Ume's handwritten drafts are preserved in the Hōsei University Library, *Ume Kenjirō monjo*, part 3 ("Kankoku rippō jigyō tannin tōji ni okeru kian shorui"), A5a/33–37, and a printed Korean version is in the Waseda University Library. The Korean text was published in Chŏng Chong-hyu, "Hanguk minsa sosong pŏp an [A Draft of Korean Civil Procedure]," *Pŏpsahak yŏngu* 10 (1989): 231–336.

[109] Chŏng, *Kankoku minpōten*, 39; Higashikawa, *Hakushi Ume Kenjirō*, 30.

[110] "Ume hakushi dampen [A Little Talk with Dr. Ume]," *Hōritsu Shinbun*, vol. 619 (January 25, 1910), 20.

[111] *Hanmal kŭndae pŏmnyŏng charyo jip*, vol. 7, 25–45.

[112] Ibid., vol. 5, 308–309.

FIGURE 4.2. **Courtroom scene from the Japanese protectorate period (1905–1910).** The Korean defendants face the judges in Western suits. From *The Second Annual Report on the Reforms and Progress in Korea, 1908–9* (publication of the Residency General of Korea, 1909).

July 23, the *Hyongpŏp taejŏn* was revised, deleting contradictory provisions on procedural rules. Kuratomi, the deputy justice minister, was commissioned to compile Korean criminal law and criminal procedure.

Contemporary newspapers applauded the progress in the reforms of judicial administration. *Maeil Sinmun* declared "it is wrong for the police to arrest a person in the dispute between private parties."[113] *Tongnip Sinmun* wrote: "it is good that the police does not adjudicate or send the defendant to the Justice Ministry."[114] Korean jurists evaluated the reform measures favorably. A legal commentator emphasized the distinction between criminal and civil matters and welcomed civil law taking root in Korea:

> Criminal law regulates the relationship between the state and people, and civil law regulates relationship between individuals. Criminal law is public law governing crime and punishment, and civil law is private law governing rights and obligations between private individuals.... In civil law, the judge can adjudicate, even when there are no law provisions, according to reason and customs.... In our country, we have traditionally applied *Taejŏn hoet'ong* and the Myŏng Code

[113] The June 7, 1898 issue. Cited in Son Kyŏng-ch'an, "Kaehwa gi kŭndaejŏk minsa sosong pŏpkyu toip," 90.

[114] The August 22, 1896 issue.

> rules, but because of the absence of detailed provisions the individuals' disputes were decided according to custom. Now we anticipate the promulgation of civil law in a few years and naturally the diminishment of reliance on custom.[115]

Another scholar wrote:

> Our country has not focused on developing law that serves as the foundation of establishing, operating, and governing the state. The people have not known it well. So we have not established a country of rule of law.... We must remember that a citizen, regardless of a status high or low, old or young, or noble or base, cannot avoid, as long as one lives in the country, his legal responsibility on the grounds of the ignorance of law. This is a famous adage since the Roman times (*nul n'est présumé ignorer la loi*) [Everyone is presumed to know the law].[116]

Legal Education and the Attorney System

This period also saw the beginning of professional legal training. The first modern legal education started in March 1895 with the establishment of the Judge Training School.[117] The Korean attorney system was established in November 1905 through a series of laws including the Attorney Act, Regulations of Bar Exams, and the Regulations of Attorney Registration.[118] The Attorney Act, comprising thirty-five articles, was modeled after the Japanese Attorney Act proclaimed in 1893. Soon Japanese attorneys began to arrive in Korea en masse. As the prestige of the legal profession rose in line with the establishment of the modern legal system, more advocates arrived, looking for a lucrative alternative to working in Japan. Officially their activities were regarded as illegal. Article 200 of *Hyŏngpŏp taejŏn* proscribing foreign attorneys ("those who hire foreigners to handle affairs regarding our country's law such as filing suits are subject to fifteen years of imprisonment") was technically still in force. Soon, however, as Japanese judges were appointed to Korean courts starting 1907, legal practice by Japanese attorneys, as "assistants of the party," received a tacit approval.[119]

115 Yun Hyo-jŏng, "Hyŏngpŏp kwa minpŏp ŭi kubyŏl [Distinction between Criminal Law and Civil Law]," *Taehan chaganghoe wŏlbo* 11 (May 25, 1907), 49–52.

116 Sŏk Chin-hyŏng, "Pŏmnyul ŭi p'ilyo [The Necessity of Law]," *Taehan hyŏphoe hoebo* 2 (May 25, 1908), 27–28, and 29.

117 Yang Sŭng-du, "Pŏpkwan Yangsŏngso e kwanhan sogo [A Short Study of the Judge Training School]," *Serim Hangukhak nonch'ong* 1 (1977): 485–506; Pak Pyŏng-ho, "Hanguk pŏphak kyoyuk ŭi kiwŏn: Pŏpkwan Yangsŏngso chedo wa Kyŏngsŏng Chedae [The Origin of the Education of Judges in Korea: The Judge Training School System and Kyŏngsŏng Imperial University]," *Kosigye* (April 1995): 86–99. For the birth of legal education in Korea, see Seoul Taehakkyo Pŏpkwa Taehak Tongch'anghoe, ed. *Seoul Taehakkyo Pŏpkwa Taehak paengnyŏnsa, 1895–1995* [The Centennial History of the Law School of the Seoul National University] (Seoul, 2004).

118 Chŏng Chong-hyu, "Hanmal ŭi sŏgupŏp kyesu [The Reception of Western Law in the Late Chosŏn Period]," *Chŏnnam Taehakkyo nonmumchip (Pŏp, haengjŏnghak p'yŏn)* 32 (1987), 126–136. See Taehan Pyŏnhosa Hyŏphoe. ed. *Hanguk pyŏnhosa sa* [A History of Attorneys at Law in Korea] (Seoul, 1979).

119 "Chōsen ni okeru bengoshi seido [The Attorney System in Chosŏn]," *Chōsen ihō* (June 1917), 174.

Japan was well aware that improvements in judicial administration alone would not bring about the abrogation of extraterritoriality. Consular jurisdiction continued to exist as long as Korea lacked modern laws. Codifying modern laws in Korea was an urgent task for the protectorate government.

Investigation of Customs and the Making of a Korean Civil Code

In December 1907, the Code Investigation Bureau was created in the Korean cabinet with the mandate to draft civil law, criminal law, civil procedure, criminal procedure, and supplementary laws. Ume held the title of advisor, and Deputy Justice Minister Kuratomi was appointed chairman. The bureau conducted studies of Korean codes, ritual texts, and Chinese laws that had substantial impacts on Korea, and it undertook field surveys to collect Korean practices and customs governing private relations. The investigation was structured to gather answers to the 206 questions written by Ume. Ume himself traveled throughout the country, directing the campaign.[120]

Various administrative texts containing articles from the codes (*Kyŏngguk taejŏn*, *Sok taejŏn*, *Taejŏn hoet'ong*, *Ta Ming lü*, *Ta Ming lü commentaries*, and *Ta Qing lü*), Confucian texts (*Chuja karye*, *Yegi taejŏn*, and *Sarye p'yŏllam*), and new laws proclaimed since the Kabo Reforms of 1894 were compiled. The survey also collected private documents and legal forms, such as sales contracts, land deeds, mortgage transactions, receipts, or tenancy contracts. A large part of the survey concerned ethnological subjects, such as marriage ceremonies and mourning and funeral rites. The materials were organized according to the Japanese Civil Code categories, following the *Pandekten* system, of "Civil Matters" and "Commercial Matters," with the former subdivided under "General Principles," "Properties," "Obligations," "Family," and "Successions." The results of the survey, redacted in Japanese, were first published in 1910. It remains today the only comprehensive collection of Korean customs, rites, and practices.[121]

The survey of customs followed the precedents in Japan and colonial Taiwan. As noted in Chapter 3, Japan launched campaigns to collect customs in 1875 and the results were published first in 1877 and then in 1880.[122] Shortly after the annexation of Taiwan in 1895, the Japanese began collecting Taiwanese laws and practices. Gōtō Shimpei, Civil Administrator (*Minsei chokan*) of the government general of Taiwan from 1898, established the Taiwanese Old Customs Investigation Bureau in 1901 and invited Okamatsu Santarō, the English law

120 See the recollection of Kawasaki Bunzō, Ume's assistant, in "Chōsen ni okeru Ume hakushi," 98–100.

121 Chōsen Sōtokufu, ed. *Kanshū chōsa hōkokusho* [Report on the Investigation of Customs] (Seoul: Chōsen Sōtokufu, 1910, rev. ed. 1913; Tokyo: Ryukei Shosha, 1995). A Korean translation is based on the 1912 edition: *Kaeyŏk p'an kwansŭp chosa pogosŏ* [Revised Translation of the Report on the Investigation of Customs], trans. Chŏng Kŭng-sik (Seoul: Hanguk Pŏpche Yŏnguwŏn, 2000). See Chōsen Sōtokufu Chūsūin, ed. *Chōsen kyūkan seido chōsa jigyō gaiyō* [A Summary of the Investigation Project of the Korean Old Customs System] (Seoul: Chōsen Sōtokufu Chūsūin, 1938), 18.

122 *Minji kanrei ruishū*, 1877, and *Zenkoku minji kanrei ruishū*, 1880. See Chapter 3.

specialist at Kyoto University, to investigate and collect customs and traditions of the island's many ethnic groups.[123] Survey reports were compiled in 1902.[124] Together with subsequent reports, they were published as *Private Law of Taiwan* (*Taiwan shihō*) in 1910 and 1911.[125] Okamatsu strongly argued for a civil code specially enacted for Taiwan that would include Taiwanese customs. Between 1909 and 1914, several drafts of civil codes for Taiwan were prepared. The Taiwanese project was eventually abandoned, however, as the principle of assimilation came to dominate colonial policy.[126]

Ume's survey of Korean customs was fundamentally of the same nature as Okamatsu's. Ume emphasized the investigation and recording of Korean customs so he could gain thorough insight into Korean society. It is likely that Ume, a French civil law specialist, was mindful of the fact that the absence of learned doctrinal elaboration and jurisprudential activity had prevented the rise of customary law in Korea. He was well aware that Korean usages were not legal rules that could be directly converted to modern civil codification. The main objective of the survey was to gather indigenous content to insert selectively into the Western legal framework to facilitate the adoption of Western laws in Korea. Ume had no illusion about the nature of the investigation enterprise that he led in Korea; his goal was to create a code with indigenous contents using the Japanese concepts and categories. As in Japan, Ume was critical of blindly adhering to traditions. Unjust or inequitable usages needed to be modified, updated, or discarded. Refined customs were to be standardized and reordered to produce common principles, which would then be reduced into the code provisions and incorporated into a legal framework embodying the universal principles of individual rights.

Ume's operation signaled in Korea the beginning of the transplantation of modern civil law and doctrinal formulation of custom as a matter of law. In Korea, absent functional private law, a written code was urgently needed to establish the modern legal order. What Ume tried to do amounted to an effort to accomplish, within a matter of a few years, what legal development in Europe had achieved over several hundred years, extracting rules from local usages that could be incorporated into the proposed civil code. Ume thus took it upon himself to perform single-handedly jurisprudential and doctrinal work that had been undertaken by judges and legal scholars in France during several centuries since the late Middle Ages, a process that culminated in the promulgation of the Napoleonic Code in 1804.

Ume's Korean campaign was very much a continuum of his activities in Japan. He was determined to ferret out unreasonable usages and customs

123 Bourgon, "Le Droit coutumier," 131–133; Wang, *Legal Reform in Taiwan*, 142.

124 Okamatsu Santarō, *Provisional Report on Investigations of Laws and Customs in the Island of Formosa* (Taipei: Ch'eng Wen Publishing Company, 1971, 1902).

125 Taiwan Sōtokufu Rinji Taiwan Kyūkan Chōsakai, *Taiwan shihō* [Private Law of Taiwan] (Taihoku: Taiwan Sotokufu Rinji Taiwan Kyūkan Chōsakai, 1910–1911).

126 Wang, *Legal Reform in Taiwan*, 144. See Chapter 5.

through the provisions of the code. He flatly remarked: "In order to revise bad customs [in Korea], it is necessary to establish a civil code similar to those of civilized countries. Bad old customs must be reformed."[127] During the code debate in Japan, individualism was viewed as a menace to Japan's "national polity," and it became the ideological scapegoat for Japanese nationalists. In drafting a Korean civil code, Ume hoped to put into practice his ideals of natural law principles, unencumbered by the kind of wrangling over the theories of Japanese tradition or national identity. His emphasis on investigating old Korean customs and practices was prompted by the need to create a civil law that blended tradition with the demands of modernity, by preserving good indigenous customs and at the same time correcting and improving those that hampered legal relations by drawing from irreducible principles of natural law.

Ume believed that the investigation of genuine Korean customs through field inquiry was essential in the writing of the Korean law. From his experience in Japan, Ume had reason to place particular emphasis on Korean customs, so as not to repeat Boissonade's mistake. After all, what contributed to the unfortunate fate of Boissonade's code was the strong feeling among the Japanese that their code was drafted by a foreigner. Mindful of his own position in Korea, Ume tried to avoid the same criticism. But many contemporaries still criticized his survey of Korean customs. The Japanese jurist Asami Rintarō claimed that "making questionnaires and asking for answers from Koreans, who are even worse than the Chinese in lacking scientific thinking, only led to nothing other than contradictory results."[128] For Ume's detractors, his entire legislative campaign in Korea was excessively cumbersome or simply unnecessary. Would it not be more desirable, they argued, to impose the advanced Japanese civil law on Korea so Korean people could quickly benefit from it?

It is ironic that, despite the fact that Ume himself consistently opposed the direct imposition of Japanese law on Korea, his own findings were construed as justification for those who argued for the extension of Japanese law.[129] An important aim of the customs survey was to investigate whether notions of rights equivalent to those in the Meiji civil law existed in Korean customs.

[127] Ume, "Kankoku no hōritsu seido" (Part 2)," 10.

[128] Asami Rintatō, *Chōsen hōsei shi kō* [Legal History of Chosŏn] (Tokyo: Ganshodo Shoten, 1922), 380. Asami (1869–1943), a former member of the Real Property Law Investigation Commission and later Chosŏn High Court judge, called Ume's customs survey efforts "misdirected" and its methodology flawed. He questioned the reliability of field surveys: "the content of replies to survey questions was often contradictory and unreasonable; much seemed to come from piecemeal knowledge, law codes, or Zhu Xi's ritual textbook," and in many occasions "it got mixed up between customs and laws." Asami Rintatō, "Chōsen hōkei no rekishi teki kenkyū [A Historical Study of the Legal System in Chosŏn]," *Hōgaku kyōkai zasshi* 39, no. 8 (1921), 35, 62.

[129] Chŏng, *Kankoku minpōten*, 89–92.

From his survey of Korean land customs, Ume concluded that "land ownership rights were certainly recognized" in Korea. He wrote:

> of course the concept of ownership rights are different in different countries. For example, there is a big difference between the Roman legal concept and the German legal concept. Although it is not clear whether Korean land ownership rights coincide precisely with those in our country, there is no doubt that the right to acquire ownership has been recognized in Korea for several hundred years.[130]

This conclusion was not welcomed by those jurists in Japan who asserted the primitiveness of the Korean land tenure system. They subsequently turned Ume's findings around to support the imposition of Japanese law in Korea. Asami Rintarō claimed that the civil customs studied by Ume "appear to be something copied from the civil and commercial provisions in the current Japanese law, and it seems to amount to the confirmation that Chosŏn had customs equivalent to our civil law."[131] Not missing a beat, Asami went on to say that he was happy to see these findings because they confirmed that Japanese laws could be directly extended to Korea.

For others, Ume's land ownership reform was fundamentally deficient because he mistakenly believed in the existence of unencumbered land ownership rights in Korea. Ume was accused of being one of those "individualistic mechanical jurists who are unaware of land system other than Roman law's sole ownership right," and his advocacy of measures confirming modern land ownership rights of landlords was blamed for causing the expulsion of Korean farmers from land.[132] Ume was blamed that, by confirming the existence of land ownership rights in the Chosŏn dynasty, he unwittingly "supported the theory of those who assert the existence of land ownership rights for the purpose of attracting Japanese capital to Korea."[133]

The effort to create independent Korean codes on the basis of a conscientious study of old laws and practices encountered sustained criticism. From nearly the beginning of his Korean enterprise, Ume was subject to attacks by those who favored the quick imposition of Japan's civil law on Korea. No sooner had he arrived in Korea than an anonymous article in a Japanese newspaper blasted his investigation: "Professor Ume is allegedly studying Korea's laws but is making the mistake of valuing old papers as Korea's customary law documents, when in fact they are nothing other than waste paper."[134] The article continued: "Korea's traditional law codes have rarely been observed.

[130] Ume, "Fudōsan," 7–8.

[131] Asami, "Chōsen hōkei no rekishi teki kenkyū," 33.

[132] Itani Zenichi, *Chōsen keizaishi* [An Economic History of Chosŏn] (Tokyo: Daitōkaku, 1928), 72. Tokyo Imperial University's Kondō Yasuo wrote that Ume's "modern land ownership concept based on Roman law ... freed land and people in Korea to the flow of capitalism. Sale and transfer of land became simple and clearly confirmed, and it gave freedom to elite landowners to displace farmers." Cited from Naitō, "Kankoku ni okeru Ume Kenjirō," 4.

[133] Itani, *Chōsen keizaishi*, 72.

[134] *Tokyo keizai zasshi* 1346 (July 21, 1906), 107.

Therefore, instead of committing the folly of getting entangled with these codes, we should proceed to imposing forcefully our civilized and equitable civil law [on Korea]." The reform of Korean land ownership laws was resisted by Japanese residents in Korea.[135] In fact, broad opposition from the Japanese in Korea to the residency general's effort to abolish extraterritoriality posed serious obstacles, threatening to derail any reform agenda.[136]

The Evolution of Japanese Politics and Legal Policy in Korea

The changes that took place in 1908 had significant impact on the direction of Japanese legislative policy in Korea. In that year, there were early signs of a shift in Itō's legal policy. From the beginning, the entire fate of Ume's work in Korea hinged on Itō. Ume's codification efforts had a chance to survive only as long as Itō remained faithful to the idea of keeping Korea independent. In 1906, Itō stated:

> If Japan had wanted to annex Korea, it could have easily achieved it. But, instead of spending huge sums of money to annex Korea and control it ourselves, our country judged it wiser to preserve our own security by leading Korea to prosperity and having the Korean people take complete charge of their own defense in alliance with us.[137]

The genuine goal of Itō's so-called nurturing self-rule, modernizing the Korean judiciary and promoting the development of Korean economy and industry, has been scrutinized in colonial historiography. But it is difficult to deny that a substantial amount of effort was made, and money spent, for Itō's reform policy during his tenure. It was indeed in reaction to Itō's costly legal reform that critics in Japan began to lambaste his Korean policy as a detriment to national interest and prestige. Itō was too powerful and canny a figure to bow before such political pressure, but it is certainly possible that it caused him to grow increasingly weary and skeptical about the wisdom of his reform policies.[138]

In the summer of 1908, Itō seemed ambivalent. He was sending out conflicting messages. At a meeting with Korean cabinet members in June, Itō stated that he was rushing judicial reforms because they were essential for the abolition of extraterritoriality. It was his hope that, once the codes were completed, "Japan will abolish its consular jurisdiction of its own accord and have other countries follow its example."[139] How serious was Itō about abolishing Japan's privileges in Korea? Were the Japanese not beneficiaries of extraterritoriality in Korea? It is certainly possible to question the sincerity of Itō's commitment to renegotiating unequal treaties with Korea. Yet, his repeated statements that Japan would be the first country to abrogate extraterritoriality

135 Asano, *Teikoku Nihon*, 166–180.

136 Ibid., 243–247.

137 *Nikkan gaikō shiryō shusei*, vol. 6, part I, 267 (July 12, 1906).

138 Duus, *The Abacus and the Sword*, 235.

139 *Nikkan gaikō shiryō shusei*, vol. 6, part I, 947–948 (June 24, 1908).

on Korea's successful legal reform should be taken, absent contrary evidence, at face value. As mentioned in Chapter 3, the extraterritoriality argument in Japan may have been promoted in part as a means to placate opposition to adopting Western law. In Korea, on the other hand, Itō's idea of abolishing extraterritoriality contingent on legal reform met persistent resistance from the Japanese residents who perceived his policy as a threat to their interest. After all, what is remarkable is that neither Itō nor Ume appeared to have reason to promote law reform to end extraterritoriality in Korea, other than the fact that they were motivated primarily by a sense that Japan could help Korea achieve gains from legal modernization and, in doing so, likely keep Korea dependent on the Japanese initiative.

A newspaper article reported in November 1908 that the improvement of the Korean judicial system following Japanese judges' employment and the progress in Ume's codification projects led Japan and the United States to begin talks of abolishing consular courts, and it stated that abolition depended on the completion of codification.[140] In fact, however, a new development dimmed the prospect of an independent Korean code. In May 1908, Japan and the United States had negotiated a treaty in which the U.S. government offered to withdraw its consular jurisdiction over intellectual property matters in Korea when the Japanese government implemented in the peninsula an intellectual property law equivalent to the one in force in Japan.[141] The treaty was aimed at preventing the violation of U.S. citizens' patents, trademarks, or copyrights by Japanese citizens residing in Korea. The question facing the Japanese government was whether to write a new Korean patent law to be issued by the Korean government or simply to extend Japanese law to the peninsula, having its legal effect acknowledged by the Korean government. By June, Itō decided to go with the latter option and demanded that the Korean government implement the Japanese intellectual property law as law in Korea. This development presented a new solution to the Japanese goal of revising unequal treaties in Korea; extraterritoriality could be abolished by bypassing the entire process of writing codes. Why wait for the codification of Korean laws when quick imposition of Japanese law would achieve the same objective?

According to Asano, Itō took the momentous step in June 1908 to reject the personality law system in Korea. Itō now adopted a policy of territoriality law, according to which Koreans, Japanese, and foreigners were placed under Japanese law.[142] So far he had recognized the legal force of Korean law. The residency general's position was to create two different structures of law, placing

[140] "Kankuko to chigai hō ken [Korea and Extraterritoriality]," *Hōritsu shinbun*, vol. 536 (November 30, 1908), 21.

[141] Ogawahara Hiroyuki, "Tōkan Itō Hirobumi no Kankoku hōchi kokka kōsō no katei [The Development of Resident General Ito Hirobumi's Ideal of Creating a State of Rule of Law in Korea]," in *Nichō kankeishi ronshū: Kan Tokusan sensei koki taishoku kinen* [A Collection of Articles on the History of Japan-Korean Relations]: (Tokyo: Shinkansha, 2003), 162–187.

[142] Asano, *Teikoku Nihon*, 189.

the Japanese and foreigners under Japanese law and Koreans under Korean law. But now Itō pursued the extension of Japanese law. Whether this change was temporary with the expectation that Ume's code of Korean civil law, once completed, would replace Japanese law is not clear, but likely. In any case, the intellectual property law administration and the related matters in the judicial system were now comprehensively controlled by Japan. Asano argued that in August 1908 Itō already contemplated the entrustment of Korean judicial affairs to Japan.[143]

The demand for a new strategy to end extraterritoriality was supported by Kuratomi, the chair of the Code Investigation Bureau. Kuratomi argued in a memo, likely written sometime between May 1908 and July 1909, that:

> We can use the example of the American-Japanese treaty ... that led to the effect of subjecting foreigners to Japanese courts. If we establish Japanese courts and take over judicial affairs in Korea, it becomes possible to bring foreigners under Japanese jurisdiction and to obtain the same result as the abolition of extraterritoriality.[144]

Kuratomi thus recommended that Japanese residents in Korea be tried not by consular courts but by permanent Japanese courts staffed by Japanese judges who adjudicate according to Japanese laws. Soon foreigners would be brought under Japanese jurisdiction. He thus in effect suggested the complete takeover of Korean judicial affairs by Japan. The fact that Kuratomi was the official head of the Code Investigation Bureau did not deter him from claiming the supposed futility of new Korean codes. It is interesting to note that Kuratomi and Ume, the two key individuals in Japan's legal venture in Korea, seemed to represent fundamental theoretical and ideological disagreement over Japan's legal policy. Kuratomi was a career bureaucrat, Ume an academic. Kuratomi called for Japan's swift takeover of Korea's judiciary, the imposition of Japanese law, and, by implication, annexation. Ume responded to Kuratomi's memo by authoring "My humble opinion regarding the improvement of the judicial system in Korea" and also "My opinion regarding the implementation of the judicial affairs entrustment agreement," in which he discussed and questioned Kuratomi's suggestions to create residency general courts.[145] Ume had largely steered away from political discussions in Korea, but in these papers he dissected Kuratomi's proposal to establish Japanese courts in Korea in his typically analytical fashion, raising questions about technical matters such as

[143] Ibid., 184, 230.

[144] "Kankoku ni okete saiban jimu ni kansuru ken," *Kuratomi Yuzaburō Monjo*, vol. 30, no. 19, The National Diet Library (Japan), Bureau of Constitutional Documents. I used the papers' microfilm versions at the Kyoto University Library of the Graduate School of Letters. The Kuratomi Papers have recently been subject to extensive examination by Japanese historians in relation to colonial Korean studies. See Nagai Kazu, "Tōkanbu no shihō seido kaikaku to so no tenkan o meguru kenkyū [A Study of the Reform of the Judicial System by the Residency General and Its Evolution]," 3 parts (Web Publication Version), in *http://www.bun.kyoto-u.ac.jp/~knagai/kuratomi/judiciaryreform1.html.*

[145] *Ume Kenjirō monjo*, part 3, A5a/25, no. 19; no. 18.

the expenses involved and the legality of procedures. It was not theoretical arguments regarding procedural regularity but politics, however, that mattered at the time.

The large body of Japanese scholarship on Itō in Korea seems to agree that his conversion to annexation was complete by April 10, 1909, when he met with Premier Katsura Tarō and Foreign Minister Komura Jūtarō.[146] To their surprise, Itō readily consented to the annexation proposal. Itō had been increasingly disillusioned about the efficacy of his self-rule policy. He expressed deep disappointment about the low quality of Japanese judicial officials employed in the Korean government. According to Moriyama, the biggest reason for Itō's volte-face was the realization that his more than three years of protectorate rule failed to earn Koreans' hearts and minds and instead resistance intensified in massive *ŭibyŏng* (righteous army) uprisings all over the country. Faced with mounting opposition and criticism from Japan to his policy, Itō decided he could no longer fulfill his repeated promise of Korean independence. But presiding over the process of annexation as the resident general would be too embarrassing for him because it would amount to an open acknowledgment of defeat. Itō's solution was simple: let someone else bear the responsibility of annexation; he would rather not be associated with it.[147] Itō was formally relieved of his post in Korea on June 14, 1909 and was appointed head of the Privy Council.

The Establishment of Japanese Courts in Korea

Itō's departure from Korea marked a dramatic change in Japan's legal policy in Korea. It shifted from one calling for the improvement of Korean judicial affairs as preparation for abolition of extraterritoriality to one advocating a direct control of the Korean judiciary by Japan. This change was prompted by Itō's realization that judicial reform could not be achieved overnight and that further neglect of the extraterritoriality problem would result in failures of Japanese policy. The sense of urgency rationalized the takeover of the entire Korean judicial affairs by Japan. On July 6, the Japanese cabinet passed a resolution confirming the annexation of Korea. On July 12, a "Memorandum concerning the Administration of Justice and Prisons in Korea" was signed.[148] Korean judicial courts and prisons were formally "entrusted" to Japan and the Korean Justice Ministry was dissolved. Korean courts were replaced by the residency

[146] It has been pointed out that there existed differences in approach between factions in Japanese government, the so-called civilian faction opposing annexation (Itō and Inoue Kaoru) and the military faction aggressively pushing for annexation (Katsura Tarō, Yamagata Aritomo, and Terauchi Masatake). Kang Tong-jin, *Nihon no Chōsen shihai seisaku shi kenkyū: senkyūhyaku nijūnen dai o chūshin to shite* [A History of the Japanese Policy to Control Korea: With Particular Attention to the 1920s] (Tokyo: Tokyo Daigaku Shuppankai, 1977), 131–132. see Yamabe Kentarō, *Nikkan heigō shōshi* [A Brief History of the Annexation of Japan and Korea] (Tokyo: Iwanami Shoten, 1966).

[147] Moriyama, *Nikkan heigō*, 173–175; *Kindai Nikkan kankeishi kenkyū*, 225.

[148] The text is in Kim, ed. *Nikkan gaiko shiryo shusei*, vol. 6, part III, 1256–1260.

general courts in October.[149] The name of the highest court was changed from Taesimwŏn to Kodŭng Pŏpwŏn (Kōtō Hōin in Japanese), apparently to distinguish Korea's highest court from that of Japan also called Daishinin.

The entrustment of the judiciary created a number of complicated situations. The July Memorandum provided for "the application in principle of Japanese law in trials," and that "Japanese courts in Korea shall apply Korean law to Korean people, unless there are special provisions in the agreement or law" (Article 3).[150] Previously, the court structure and personnel had been imported from Japan but the courts were Korean courts. They applied Korean law and had jurisdiction over the population, although the Japanese were tried by Japanese consular courts according to the extraterritoriality principle. Now the newly established residency general courts, which opened on November 1, 1909, were Japanese courts applying Japanese law, and the judges were personnel of the Japanese institutions working under the Japanese judicial system. Ume explained in his speech at the Tōkyō Keizaigaku Gakkai (Tokyo Economic Studies Association) in September 1909:

> Until now it was Korean law that governed lawsuits between Koreans parties and also those in which Japanese citizens were plaintiffs. The Korean code was supposed to control all cases involving foreigners once consular jurisdiction came to an end. But now, the courts will apply Japanese law to the Japanese, and Korean law to Koreans. Except for the special provisions in the agreement and other laws, Korean law will not be applicable to the Japanese. Therefore, the new Korean civil code is entirely for Koreans.[151]

This framework outlined by Ume – application of Japanese civil law to cases in which one or both parties were Japanese or foreigners and application of Korean civil law or old customs to cases involving Koreans only – postulated the coexistence of Japanese civil law and Korean civil law. Korean law would not be applicable when at least one party was non-Korean.

Ume further stated regarding the establishment of Japanese courts:

> Through this agreement, Korean judicial power was transferred to our country and its courts became Japanese courts that conducted trials over Koreans.... This is clearly one of our successful achievements. Although there is an increased burden on our treasury, I think it is an extremely advantageous measure for the protection of Korea.[152]

[149] Imperial Order, No. 236, October 18, 1909. The Korean Residency General Court Regulation issued on October 31 (No. 238) was drafted by Ume. See Ume Kenjirō, "Kankoku no hōritsu seido ni tsuite" (Part 2), 794; Ume, "Kankoku no hanashi," 12 (1454). See also Yūhō Kyokai, *Chōsen ni okeru shihō seido*, 65; Kawasaki, "Chōsen ni okeru Ume hakushi," 99.

[150] *Nikkan gaikō shiryō shusei*, vol. 6, 256–260; Ichikawa Masaaki, ed., *Kankoku heigō shiryō* [Documents regarding the Annexation of Korea] (Tokyo: Hara Shobō, 1978, 1965), vol. 3, 256–264.

[151] Ume, "Kankoku no hōritsu seido" (Part 2), 10 (796).

[152] Ibid., 17 (793). Naitō says Ume was bragging about the achievement of establishing Japanese courts in Korea. "Kankoku ni okeru Ume Kenjirō," 16.

This statement has been seen, not unreasonably, as Ume's support for the Japanese takeover of the Korean judiciary. But perhaps a more nuanced interpretation is possible. The abolition of the Korean judiciary not only scrapped his work to establish modern Korean courts but rendered his codification virtually pointless. The writing of Korean laws had progressed during the previous three years on the assumption that Korea would stand on its own, and the prospect of continued independence now all but evaporated. In this situation, he understandably tried to salvage his work of writing Korean codes. Perhaps sensing a crisis for his codification campaign's future, Ume told a newspaper a few days after the Japanese takeover of the Korean judiciary that he expected to see the completion of the civil code by the end of the following year.[153] In the aforementioned speech in 1909, his first public statement after the proclamation of the establishment of the Japanese courts in Korea, Ume needed to explain to his audience why independent codes were still necessary when Korean courts no longer existed.

Ume stated:

> It is necessary to write a civil code, because civil law exists in all countries including Korea. It simply has not been written down and one must now turn it into codified law. Traditional customs, if they are bad ones, must be changed. Abolition of consular jurisdiction requires a code similar to that of a civilized country. Commercial law should be incorporated into civil law. I have been drafting the code and since last year have been investigating customs. I should be able to complete the investigation before the end of the year.[154]

The new civil code he was drafting would be independent from Japan's Civil Code but not equal in its authority. Ume reluctantly accepted the Japanese government's decision and drafted the residency general court organization law as the next best alternative.[155] His endorsement of the new courts should be seen in this light.

The Japanese courts in Korea were created under the residency general instead of Japan's Ministry of Justice. Deputy Law Minister Kuratomi was appointed minister of the residency general law department that controlled the administration of the new courts. The qualifications of the judges became the same as those in Japan, as governed by Japan's Court Organization Law, although exceptions were provided for those Korean and Japanese judges already in employment under the previous court system. In November 1909, there were 192 Japanese judges and 87 Korean judges; 57 prosecutors were Japanese, while only 7 prosecutors were Korean.[156] Korean judges were allowed to preside in civil cases only when both the plaintiff and defendant were Korean and in criminal cases only when the defendant was Korean.

153 "Ume hakushi no dan," *Hōritsu shinbun*, vol. 582 (July 20, 1909).

154 Ume, "Kankoku no hōritsu seido" (Part 2), 10 (796).

155 Asano, *Teikoku Nihon*, 266.

156 Yi Sŭng-il, *Chosŏn ch'ongdokpu pŏpche chŏngch'aek: Ilche ŭi singmin t'ongch'i wa Chosŏn minsaryŏng* [A Study on the Legal Policy of the Chosŏn Government General: The Colonial Rule by Imperial Japan and *Chosŏn Minsaryŏng*] (Seoul: Yŏksa Pip'yŏngsa, 2008), 65.

The anomaly of Japanese courts being in charge of judicial affairs in Korea had serious ramifications. The 1909 Memorandum stated "Japanese courts in Korea shall employ qualified Japanese and Koreans as judges." Some Japanese objected to appointing Korean nationals to the judgeship in the new "Japanese" courts. They argued that Article 19 of the Japanese Constitution, which provided "Japanese subjects may, according to qualifications determined in laws or ordinances, be appointed to civil or military or any other public offices equally," excluded non-Japanese from holding public offices including judgeship. Ume rejected this "silly" argument. He wrote: "If we interpret this provision as saying that foreigners do not have such rights, we must conclude that in the past many violations occurred. For example, many foreigners have been hired in university professorship which constitutes a public office."[157]

Another challenge was raised on the basis of Article 24 of the constitution which read: "No Japanese subject shall be deprived of his right to be tried by the judges determined by law." The Residency General Court Organization Regulations of October 31, 1909, were imperial ordinances (*chokurei*), not Diet-enacted statutes (*hōritsu*). Since these courts were not established by laws, the argument went, their judges were not judges appointed by law under Article 57 of the constitution ("The organization of the Courts of Law shall be determined by law"), and subjecting imperial citizens to these courts was a violation of their constitutional right. Ume tried to allay the concerns of the Japanese citizens by pointing out that "in practical terms litigation among the Japanese residents in Korea is adjudicated by Japanese judges," not by Korean judges.[158]

Evidence suggests, however, that there were serious concerns about potential constitutional issues. As the author of the court organization regulations, Ume had objected to the formation of the residency general courts through a legal instrument other than legislation passed by the Diet. Ume proposed that the new courts be established as an act of the Diet, with a provision that special laws regarding judicial administration be issued by imperial ordinance.[159] He argued that "in order to avoid controversy involving fundamental constitutional

[157] Ume Kenjirō, "Kankoku kongo no shihō [The Administration of Justice in Korea in the Future]," *Keizai jihō* 42 (October 20, 1909), reprinted in Kŭm Pyŏng-dong, *Shiryō zasshi ni miru kindai Nihon no Chōsen ninshiki: Kankoku heigōki zengo* [Modern Japan's Perception of Chosŏn as Seen from Documents and Magazines: Surrounding the Period of the Annexation of Chosŏn] (Tokyo: Ryokuin shobō, 1999), vol. 3, 216–217.

[158] Ibid; see also Ume, "Kankoku no hōritsu seido ni tsuite" (Part 2), 10 (796).

[159] Ume Kenjirō, "Kankoku ni okeru saiban seido kaitei ni kansuru hiken [My Humble Opinion regarding the Implementation of the Judicial Affairs Entrustment Agreement]," likely written between August and September 1909, in Ume Monjo Kenkyūkai, ed. *Ume Kenjirō monjo mokuroku, Hōsei Daigaku toshokan shozō* [The Catalogue of the Ume Kenjirō Papers, Hōsei University Library Collection], part 3, A5a/25, no. 18. For a transcription and Korean translation of this document, see Mun Chun-yŏng, "T'onggambu chaep'anso sŏlch'i e kwanhan charyo: Kuratomi Yuzaburō wa Ume Kenjirō ŭi ŭigyŏnsŏ [Documents regarding the Establishment of the Residency General Courts: The Opinion Papers of Kuratomi Yuzaburō and Ume Kenjirō]," *Pŏpsahak yŏngu* 36 (2007), 331–366. Ume expressed a similar opinion: "Since courts are now

issues, and also to follow our government's principles, it is necessary to observe the formality of Diet-enacted law. This will avoid raising suspicion in the Imperial Diet that the government is trying to circumvent the legislature and it will also prevent the situation where the government and the legislature differ in their opinions regarding constitutional interpretations."[160]

As seen previously, Ume had argued that the courts in colonial Taiwan needed to be created by the legislature as ordinary courts under Articles 57 and 58 of the Constitution. As ordinary courts, their organization and judicial tenure were to be regulated by law outside the colonial governor's administrative power.[161] He called for the application of Japanese law in Taiwan so that the Imperial Diet would take the responsibility of guaranteeing the public and private rights of the Taiwanese.[162] Likewise, Ume's ideal in Korea was to create courts under the Imperial Diet's law. He asserted that the residency courts must be governed by the Japanese constitution. Ume's position centered on the principle of judicial independence, which he believed should be extended to all Japanese courts overseas. But his arguments were overridden by politicians, and the residency general court organization was implemented as an executive order instead of a law, setting a precedent for the colonial courts following annexation.

Ironically, Japan had so far insisted on ensuring the separation of the judiciary from the administration in Korea. Now the Japanese courts that replaced Korean courts openly disregarded that principle. It was a step backward from the extension of the constitutional system that had been advocated by Itō. Itō and Ume, caught between the opponents in Korea and Japan, were both accused of dissimulation.[163]

A Liberal Jurist's Uphill Battle

The creation of an independent Korean civil code came under increasing criticism, pitched now in more explicit ethnic and cultural tones. In September 1909, an anonymous author argued in *Kokusai hō zasshi*:

> Korea is an old country in the Orient, and traditionally its people's social existence has been governed by customs and traditional laws. Suppressed by their own government's despotic and tyrannical rule, the Korean people do not have a civilized notion of the fundamental rights of person and property. Korea has long been an agricultural country with no commercial and technological development, and Koreans do not have any concept of commercial legal rights that developed in the West. Therefore it is possible to say that it is completely absurd to attempt to codify laws of family, property, and commercial matters based on

Japan's courts, the court organization to be promulgated is of course Japan's law, and must be promulgated along with the Imperial Diet's cooperation in the form of law, or can be promulgated as an emergency imperial order." Ume, "Kankoku kongo no shihō."

160 Ume, "Kankoku ni okeru saiban seido kaitei."

161 See Chapter 5.

162 Asano, *Teikoku Nihon*, 261.

163 The vision of Itō and Ume seemed completely defeated. Ibid., 263–265, 282–284.

the principles of private law in the European legal tradition and to try to govern Korean people in the same way as governing civilized people.[164]

Ume had so far held a rather passive position in the political discussion, maintaining a critical distance from the annexation question. He preferred not to let his legislative campaign be part of the political controversy. The polemical debate now on the rise, however, threatened to negate the entire cause of his work over the last several years and thus compelled him to confront the future of Korean law after annexation. Ume gave a speech in reply to the aforementioned article. It was published the following May in the same journal under the title "The Korean Annexation Theory and the Legislative Campaign":

> In my opinion, imposing Japan's civil and commercial laws directly in Korea is impossible even after annexation. First, customs of family law and succession law diverge greatly among countries, and especially Korean customs are remarkably different from those of Japan. Therefore, it is beyond doubt that a special law needs to be established for the Korean people.... Even in Taiwan, despite the fact that it became part of our territory, we have spent an enormous amount of money over many years to investigate its customs and now we hear that the drafting of Taiwanese civil law has started. I believe it is natural that we need a special code in post-annexation Korea.[165]

For Ume, the prospect of Korean annexation should have had no impact whatsoever on the need for a Korean civil code. Investigations of Korean customs convinced him that Koreans had legal traditions and practices different from those of the Japanese. For instance, permanent tenancy, a sort of emphyteusis, was far more widespread in Korea than in Japan.[166] This practice was so deeply entrenched in Korea that Ume concluded that an attempt to change it, as had been done in the new civil code in Japan, was bound to create tremendous problems. The ownership of land and buildings were often separate. The owner of the land was required to acknowledge the transaction when the building was sold and could not oppose the transfer of ownership.[167] These were but a few examples of divergent property customs, yet they were sufficient to justify independent civil and commercial laws for Korea. It was then out of the question, in Ume's opinion, to impose Japanese family and succession laws on Koreans who had a fundamentally different kinship structure and customs. Ume sounded rather resigned when he professed that he had no interest in politics: "I do not have any desire to express my opinion regarding political matters, whether there will be annexation or

[164] *Kokusai hō zasshi* 8, no. 1 (September 25, 1909), 5.

[165] "Kankoku no gappō ron to rippō jigyō," 34 (740).

[166] *Kaeyŏk p'an kwansŭp chosa pogosŏ*, 187–196 (No. 35). The tenant obtained from the landlord the right to cultivate waste land and hold it permanently, provided he paid a fixed sum as rent. This right was not affected even when the land was sold and could be bequeathed or sublet without the landlord's consent. See Chapter 6.

[167] Ume, "Fudōsan," 8–9.

when."[168] At least, however, he resolutely refused to let his legal convictions be swayed by politics.

Itō's exit from Korea in June 1909 marked a critical juncture for Ume's campaign. Deprived of their main supporter, Ume's attempts at codification seemed devoid of any realistic prospect for survival. Although there is no concrete evidence, it is possible to conjecture that Ume was disappointed by Itō's retreat from his earlier commitment to the independence of the Korean judiciary. One clue allows a glimpse of the conflict between the resident general's legislative agenda and Ume's perceived objectives for his campaign in Korea. In September 1909 Ume rather frankly acknowledged that the landownership laws he had helped draft in 1906 failed to reflect Korean land customs.[169] He said that subsequent research on the Korean situation led him to realize that Korean land customs significantly diverged from modern property concepts and that the laws issued under the residency general had underestimated complex tenancy relations and common rights in Korean farm villages. Ume hinted that he had been rushed by Itō into drafting the land certification system before he had a chance to grasp the complete nature of the Korean land system. Although he complied with Itō's wish to create measures that would ensure the safety of land transactions by the Japanese, Ume would rather have waited for the completion of the government-sponsored survey of Korean land customs before drafting any laws.

Ume's critics viewed these statements, not without justification, as his attempt to avoid being blamed for overturning Korea's land system.[170] More significant, however, one can see here that Ume was cautiously distancing himself from at least a certain part of the resident general's Korean legal policy. It would be a mistake to argue that Ume harbored ill feelings toward his patron or failed to remain loyal to his legacy. Yet Ume wanted to stress the fact that he came to Korea not to write politically motivated, haphazard regulations "to meet temporary needs," such as administrative laws related to the governing of Korea, but to establish the five codes of "civil law, commercial law, criminal law, civil procedure, and criminal procedure."[171] What he preferred was not a certification system but a full registration system recording the titles and contracts of sales. The new land laws should have been preceded by an extensive land survey. His claim that he was not in favor of halfway measures in Korea evinces that he perceived his job as creating permanent modern legal codes in Korea commensurate with any "civilized codes" in the world.

168 Ume's son reminisced that his father was firmly opposed to annexation. Ume Toku, "Chichi o kataru [Talking about My Father]," in Takaru Shigeru, ed., *Kitte ni natta Nihon bunkajin* [The Japanese Cultural Elites Who Appeared in Postal Stamps] (Tokyo: Hifumishobo, 1953), 156.

169 Yi Ha-yŏng, Korean justice minister, complained to Itō: "people think I am a thief who sold out Korean land to foreigners.... When the Japanese farmers come to villages, they cut off waterways that had been in communal use for ages and prevent Koreans from using water resources." *Nikkan gaikō shiryō shūsei*, vol. 6, part I, 447 (April 9, 1907).

170 See Naitō, "Kankoku ni okeru Ume Kenjirō no rippō jigyō," 15.

171 Ume, "Kankoku no gappō ron to rippō jigyō," 34 (739).

Itō's assassination by a Korean patriot, An Chung-kŭn, in November 1909 dealt a decisive blow to Ume's effort to save his work. An assembly was held on May 19, 1910, at Tokyo Imperial University, dedicated to the memory of Itō. In his testimonial, Ume wanted to set the record straight for Itō's legacy and his own Korean campaign. He emphasized that it was *after* Itō's resignation as residency general that the decision was made to entrust the Korean judicial affairs to Japan:

> After the late prince resigned from the office of resident general and the current resident general succeeded to the office, as you are all aware, an agreement was signed to entrust [Korea's] judicial power to Japan. Its results were as follows. Until then, Japanese were appointed to the Korean courts, and when they conducted trials, they did so as Korean courts' judges. The laws they applied were of course Korean laws. But by last year's agreement, it is now Japan's courts, Japan's judges, that conducted trials according to Japan's laws.[172]

One cannot fail to notice here a tinge of disapproval and disillusion, although he halfheartedly added that "this is a sort of progress."[173] Ume had tirelessly worked to write Korean laws. In order to end consular jurisdiction, "it was necessary to establish well-equipped codes" actively in imitation of "law codes of civilized countries."[174] He had pushed toward this goal all these years, but now his work was on the verge of collapse. Yet Ume mustered a sense of lofty confidence in his mission. The Korean civil code was still necessary. Therefore, he declared, he would continue his efforts for codification in order to fulfill the goals of the late prince.

With the final annexation decision passed by the Japanese cabinet in June 1910, the fate of Ume's Korean code was now sealed. Ume went back to Seoul in July. It is not clear what he was doing in that city of impending doom. He contracted typhoid and, after suffering more than two weeks of high fever, died in Seoul on August 25, 1910. He was fifty years old. Ume's body was brought to Japan on August 29, the same day the annexation of Korea was proclaimed. In Korea, the codification projects he had led came to an abrupt halt. The Code Investigation Bureau was abolished the following month.[175]

Itō, Ume, and Modern Korean Law: Appraisal

How should Japan's legal policy during the protectorate be appraised? The gist of Itō's policy lay in keeping Korea solidly under Japan's sole tutelage. His main concern was to guarantee the security of Japan by not allowing Korea to be dominated by a third power, and, for that purpose, preserving Korea's

[172] Ume, "Itō kō to rippō jigyō," 46 (976).
[173] Ibid.
[174] Ume, "Kankoku no hōritsu seido" (Part 2), 10 (796).
[175] The collection of Korean usages continued during the colonial period, but it now represented a bureaucratic campaign to gather administrative information or material in Korean law and tradition which could be useful in creating a new colonial order.

independence was essential. Itō stated: "allowing a different country to penetrate to Korea, which is separated [from Japan] only by a sea, will amount to endangering the independence of Japan."[176] The reform of Korea's judicial system was prompted by the need to abrogate extraterritoriality and repel foreign intervention. Still, historians have argued that Itō's call for judicial independence through the abolition of extraterritoriality should be given due consideration, regardless of the outcome of annexation.[177] Or, the other way around, Itō's view of annexation was premised on judicial independence.[178] Along with Ume, Itō appears to have envisioned a judicial system that was fully under the Japanese constitutional coverage. It is possible to conjecture that Itō would have envisioned, post annexation, a high court in Korea independent from the colonial governor.

This line of assessment of Itō may strike one as overly favorable. After all, Itō wanted to keep Korea securely in Japan's grip and he cannot be insulated from the consequences of annexation that followed his tenure. Itō's vision of Korean sovereignty may have been an illusion at best, if not dissimulation. Nevertheless, Itō's efforts to separate the judiciary from the administration marked an important page in Korea's transformation into a modern state. His emphasis on judicial independence and his push for Japan's advances in Korea need not be mutually exclusive. Itō seemed genuinely committed to the codification of Korean law; law would temporarily be implemented by Japanese courts but eventually Korean courts would be in charge.[179]

Ume seemed convinced that Itō's policy to ameliorate Korea's courts and judicial system would have rendered it unnecessary for Japan to take over Korea. Here, one witnesses the core dilemma in Ume's enterprise. His foremost goal had been to abolish extraterritoriality by means of a modern code, to be drafted following the Western model. Once it became certain that Korea would become Japan's colony, however, his argument for an independent Korean code seemed moot, as the imposition of Japanese law was naturally expected to follow.

In an article published posthumously on "The Legal System in Korea after Annexation," Ume wrote:

> If we consider the Korean situation in theoretical terms, Korea becomes part of Japan, and applying Japan's legal system to Korea becomes a natural result. Starting first with constitutional law, civil law and criminal law all will be imposed on Korea. However, the question whether it is possible to apply them directly would require study of the examples of a variety of legal systems.[180]

[176] Itō Hirobumi, *Zoku Itō Hirobumi hiroku* (1930, reprinted ed. Tokyo: Hara Shobō, 1982), 230, also 221.

[177] Moriyama, "Hogo seijika ni okeru shihō seido kaikaku."

[178] Asano, *Teikoku Nihon*, 639.

[179] Ibid., 634.

[180] Ume, "Heigō ato no Kankoku hōsei [The Korean Legal System after Annexation]," *Keiji hō hyorin* 2, no. 9 (1910), 53.

He still resisted the indiscriminate imposition of Japan's law in Korea, but he could not deny that the direct application of Japanese law in the colony was fully justified. After 1909, as he was compelled to rationalize his codification campaign in the post-annexation scenario, his argument became precariously untenable. As long as Ume perceived Japan's civil law as the law of a civilized country, and as long as he was unable to argue against the very issue of annexation, he could not forcefully refute the imposition of Japanese law in Korea, whether in part or in entirety.

A Tale of Two Assimilations

As one of the most prominent technocrat jurists of the time, Ume was an advocate of the extension of fundamental rights prescribed in the Japanese constitution throughout the empire. Oguma Eiji has pointed out that Ume was among the few Meiji intellectuals who discussed colonial assimilation in the pure constitutional meaning of electoral rights of the native population.[181] Ume supported legal assimilation in terms of the spread of enlightened principles of private property and equal rights, distinct from cultural assimilation. His reform in Korea was characterized by elements of nineteenth-century liberal individualism in the Pandectist legal tradition and natural law theory. At the same time, he was mindful of the importance of indigenous cultural practices and popular customs for regulating private relations in a colony. Ume contended that people in Korea and Taiwan should be governed by modern laws drawn up in the model of the codes of civilized countries, but he also warned against the wholesale enforcement of Japan's laws in the peninsula and in the island. Ume's legal arguments represent an important perspective in the intellectual debate over the nature of Japan's colonial empire, in continuity with the liberal tradition of Fukuzawa Yukichi (1835–1901) and, later, Yoshino Sakuzō (1878–1933) and Yanaihara Tadao (1893–1961).

Ume's colonial theory, mainly discussed in the context of Taiwan, entailed creation of a legislative assembly based on European democratic institutions, in which the colonized people would have electoral rights and be governed by native laws. While there were many arguments about incorporating the Taiwanese into Japanese citizenship, Ume was the first person who raised the question of the political rights of the Taiwanese.[182] Hozumi Yatsuka also regarded the Taiwanese as Japanese, but his Japanization meant assimilation – all becoming imperial subjects owing loyalty to the emperor – accompanied by discrimination in rights. In contrast, Ume was little interested in cultural assimilation or promotion of imperial loyalty. Gōtō Shimpei, Taiwan's Minister for Civil Affairs, was one of the most articulate colonial strategists.

[181] Oguma, *'Nihonjin' no kyōkai*, 131, see also 129, 177, 250. For a recent discussion of Japanese assimilation policies, see Caprio, *Japanese Assimilation Policies*.
[182] Oguma, *'Nihonjin' no kyōkai*, 127.

According to Asano, both Gōtō and Ume opposed the system of law based on persons under which natives were governed by customs while foreigners and Japanese were governed by metropolitan Japanese law. Gōtō stated that the territoriality principle, not the personality principle, was the international norm.[183]

There were important differences in the two individuals' thoughts, however. The key divergence lay in their conception of the rights to be enjoyed by the natives. Ume envisioned that these rights included fundamental individual rights in the sense of natural rights. Gōtō's ideas seemed more circumscribed. His so-called politics of biology was based on skepticism about the feasibility of assimilating the Taiwanese into Japanese society.[184] For Gōtō, a civilized system or civilized laws were not suitable to the Taiwanese.

While Ume wanted to create a judicial system in Taiwan, and later in Korea, independent of the administration, Gōtō called for the governor general's complete control of the judiciary. Gōtō argued that, if Japan's Court Organization Law was applied in Taiwan, the fundamental principle of Taiwan's "separate jurisdiction" system would be destroyed. Under his scheme, the Taiwanese courts would remain under the full authority of the colonial administration. Gōtō argued: "If we wish to see our rule in Taiwan succeed, the central government should refrain from interfering in the Taiwan Administration, entrust the full authority to the governor-general, and let the Taiwan Administration handle its business in its own way."[185] This was precisely what Ume wanted to prevent by all means. Ume, powerfully supported by Itō, tried to create a judiciary that was independent from the administration and that promoted rule of law.[186]

Both Ume and Gōtō agreed on the importance of native customs and they tried to reform the judicial system on the grounds of Taiwan's unique situation. But Gōtō's idea of codifying old customs was simply a step toward creating the autonomy of the colonial legal structure through a separate legislative process. Gōtō opposed the extension of the Japanese legal system, favoring "self-government" in Taiwan.[187] The governor general of Taiwan resisted the incorporation of Taiwan into the Japanese constitutional order. Gōtō was a quintessential colonial administrator who wanted a completely separate

[183] Asano Toyomi, "Nihon teikoku no tōchi genri 'naichi enchō shugi' to teikoku hōsei no kōzō teki tenkai [The 'Inland Extension Ideology' as a Principle of Japanese Imperial Rule and the Evolution of the Structure of the Imperial Legal System]," *Shakai kagaku kenkyū* 21 (2001): 207–284, trans. Ch'oe Sŏk-hwan, "Ilbon cheguk t'ongch'i wŏlli 'naeji yŏnjang chui' wa cheguk pŏpche ŭi kujojŏk chŏngae," *Pŏpsahak yŏngu* 33 (2006), " 212–213; Asano, *Teikoku Nihon*, 114.

[184] Edward I-te Chen, "Gōtō Shimpei, Japan's Colonial Administrator in Taiwan: A Critical Reexamination," *American Asian Review* 13 (1995): 53.

[185] "Taiwan tōji kyukyu an [Emergency Remedies for the Taiwan Administration], a statement prepared by Gōtō in January 1898. Cited from Chen, "Gōtō Shimpei," 49.

[186] Asano, *Teikoku Nihon*, 266.

[187] Ibid., 111–119.

"kingdom of Taiwan ruled by the governor general of Taiwan."[188] He took as his model the British approach: the British did not try to change the lifestyle of the Hongkong Chinese by applying British laws but were able to win over their allegiance by improving their living conditions through science and technology. Gōtō emphasized that what was most important was changing the environment; people then would change.

But historians have argued that Gōtō's support of the British system was "only tactical" and his real aim was to obtain maximum freedom from the meddling of the Tokyo officials, a freedom which he perceived was crucial in the governance of the new colony."[189] The reality of the government general's policy was far from the English model advocated by Kirkwood.[190] While insisting on emulating British practices, Gōtō did not support other British ideas such as creating a colonial council in Taiwan that would allow the indigenous participation in the colonial administration and eventually make the island a self-governing entity. He was squarely opposed to governing the Taiwanese "by following the constitutional code brought overnight from … Japan."[191]

Ume's role in Japan's civil code controversy often led him to be misrepresented as favoring the destruction of local traditions and customs. But Ume's colonial theory of assimilation did not call for substituting the customs of the mother country for those of the native people. He opposed the sweeping imposition of Japan's law in Korea and instead argued for the establishment of an independent code that would incorporate the indigenous customs and practices of the Korean people. Ume advocated colonial codes in terms of private international law which would allow, for example, the natives' customs for family relations. Each colony would remain under the constitution which guaranteed the rights of the subjects. This is likely what he envisioned for Korea when he reluctantly accepted the reality of annexation. When he said that the Taiwanese were Japanese, he meant that the Taiwanese enjoyed the rights of the Japanese people.[192] When he argued that Koreans should be like the Japanese, he meant that Koreans should be guaranteed the same level of protection for life and property as the Japanese people.

There was, however, plenty of skepticism about the feasibility of this ideal of legal assimilation. The problem for Ume was his delicate differentiation

[188] Oguma, *'Nihonjin' no kyōkai*, 137.

[189] Chen, "Gōtō Shimpei," 49–50.

[190] Oguma, *'Nihonjin' no kyōkai*, 137.

[191] Baron S. Gōtō, "Our Colonization Policy in Formosa" (in English) in Gōtō *Shimpei Monjo*, National Diet Library microfilm, nos. 23, 3–4. Cited from Chen, "Gōtō Shimpei," 48. The governor general of Taiwan strongly resisted the incorporation of Taiwan into the Japanese constitutional order. The colonial officials wanted a completely separate "kingdom of Taiwan ruled by the governor general of Taiwan." Oguma, *'Nihonjin' no kyōkai*, 137.

[192] Oguma, *'Nihonjin' no kyōkai*, 129.

between the extension of the constitution and the general principles of law to overseas territories – with which he agreed "in principle" – and his contemporaneous support for separate law codes for the non-Japanese population residing under Japan's sphere of influence. In the eyes of most Japanese people, the distinction seemed to be overly technical and to pose an intrinsic contradiction.[193] Short of outright rejection of annexation of Korea, his eloquent defense of the independent Korean code sounded contrived and rather hollow. As he tried to harmonize the imperial system with the fundamental principles of law, he could not avoid the criticism that his colonial theory was no more than a constitutional fiction.

It would be unfair, of course, to blame Ume for failing to oppose annexation or even accuse him of being contradictory. His goal in Korea was to help construct a modern legal state endowed with equitable codes that would stand against challenges in the international community. Ume, an enlightened democrat, seemed to believe, much in line with the turn-of-the-century French liberal colonial argument, that imperialism did not need to conflict with liberal democracy. Ume shared Itō's belief that Korea could benefit from working with Japan in its goal to maintain independence. He was convinced that, at the beginning of the twentieth century, Korean could avail itself of Japan's intervention as a sort of stimulus to renew its strength. Indeed, his misfortune lay in his belief that he could promote both Japanese and Korean interests in the true fashion of a universal natural law theorist. Unfortunately, it was this idealism of Ume, trying to defy the logic of the time that Japan was Korea's foe, not friend, that was thrust against the stricture and dictates of imperial legal reform and, it can be further suggested, against the bureaucratic in-fighting within the Japanese government.

There is a coda to Ume's saga in Korea. Immediately after Ume's death, the results of the four-year survey of Korean laws and customs were edited by his student, Oda Kanjirō. *The Report on the Investigation of Customs* was published in December 1910 under the direction of Kuratomi, in the capacity of the former head of the Code Investigation Bureau and the chief of the Justice Department in the newly established Chosŏn government general. Kuratomi dedicated the volume to Governor General Terauchi Masatake, who unleashed the forceful imposition of Japanese law and militarism on the Korean people. The volume thus bears the name of Kuratomi, and not that of Ume, who literally met his death while he was laboring on it. Such was the crux of a Meiji liberal reformer's sorrow and tribulations in protectorate Korea.

Japan's annexation of Korea led to a fundamental reconfiguration of its legal policy. The project of writing a Korean civil code was abandoned. One of the primary objectives for codifying Korean civil law had been to abolish extraterritoriality. Since this goal was presumptively achieved by annexation,

[193] Ōkawa, "Gaikoku jin no shaken" (Part 2), 122–123.

there was no longer a need for independent Korean law.[194] The goal of unifying the Japanese colonial empire did not condone the prospect of writing a separate legal code in the colony. Chapter 5 will examine the establishment of the colonial legal system and the construction of the customary law order in Korea.

[194] "Declaration regarding the Annexation of Korea," September 2, 1910 (vol. 5), in *Chōsen Sōtokufu Kanpō* [Official Gazette of the Government General of Chosŏn]. Actual negotiations with the foreign powers regarding the concession areas started in February 1913, resulting in the agreement of April 14, 1914, that abolished foreign settlements. See Yi Hyŏn-chong, "Happyŏng hu chaehan kakkup kŏryuji ch'ŏlp'ye go [A Study on the Abolition of Foreign Settlements in Korea after Annexation]," *Chindan hakpo* 32 (1969): 39–71.

5

Colonial Law and the Legal System, 1910–1945

This chapter examines the establishment of colonial courts and the construction of the customary law system under Japanese rule. The building of the judicial system was a question closely related to larger constitutional issues. One of the important characteristics of Japanese colonialism is that, while Japan promoted the homogenization of colonial legal institutions with those in Japan, it created multiple legal territories within the empire and each colony constituted a separate legal jurisdiction. The traditional view that the policy of the Japanese government never wavered from the French model of assimilation has been roundly challenged. While the metropolitan government professed the legal incorporation policy, colonial governors claimed and enjoyed remarkable autonomy, deemed necessary for efficient colonial management.

It is important to note that colonial courts in Korea duplicated Japanese courts in their structure, organization, and procedures but they were not part of the Japanese judicial hierarchy. The colonial legal system was run not by legislative enactment but by the colonial governor's executive order; the courts were subordinated to the governor general, who exercised executive, legislative, and judicial powers concurrently. The fact that colonial courts were under the control of the governor was widely criticized in Japan as a violation of the constitutional principle of judicial independence. The colonial administrators naturally resisted the extension of the Japan's Court Organization Law to Korea.

The government general of Korea devoted special attention to demonstrating efficient administration of justice, so that it could claim that the legal system in Korea was managed most effectively by comprehensive rule under the colonial governor. The result was an almost exaggerated emphasis on judicial probity. The colonial government repeatedly stressed the importance of integrity and efficiency in the judicial process and administration. The emphasis on tackling judicial corruption and misconduct was prompted in large part by the need to legitimatize colonial governance in the eyes of Tokyo, but it promoted legality in Korea. The courts in general successfully fulfilled their judicial duties without open interference from the colonial governor. The common view that colonial courts were mere administrative instruments under the military government calls for reconsideration.

A major criticism of colonial legal policy is that Japan, in pursuit of assimilation policy, forcibly modified Korea's laws and customs. The reality of the colonial customary law order seemed a bit more complicated, however. The Japanese followed the general imperial trend in recognizing the legal force of native "custom" to govern most private legal relations among the colonized subjects. The Chosŏn Ordinance on Civil Matters of 1912 imposed Japanese law as general law in the colony but declared that certain matters – notably capacity, family, and succession relations – among Koreans be governed by Korean customary rules. The colonial government insisted on recognizing old Korean customs as a source of law and it behaved almost as a supporter of Korean customs against the movement for the full imposition of Japan's civil law. Of course it was not because the government general was an enlightened protector of the Korean tradition but because it wanted to preserve its autonomy; the administrators were interested in protecting not so much the Korean culture as their own sphere of interest. Maintaining customary law was justified on the grounds that it promoted effective colonial rule. This consideration makes it necessary to appraise the evolution of customary law policy against the backdrop of political conflicts and negotiations between Seoul and Tokyo.

The customary law system, in which each colony was governed by its own custom and law, was crucially related to the legal structure of the Japanese empire. In 1918, the Japanese government enacted the Coordination Law (*Kyōtsūhō*), a law designed to resolve the conflict of laws between *naichi* (literally "inland," meaning Japan proper) and *gaichi* (literally "outlands," meaning overseas territories) and also among the different territories and to develop a uniform system of cross-border jurisdiction in the colonial empire. The *Kyōtsūhō* system, by preserving the customary law order in the colonies, perpetuated the personality law system based on extraterritoriality that had existed in both Taiwan and Korea before the expansion of the Japanese empire. By providing a higher level of legal order linking different territories, the Coordination Law helped consolidate the imperial legal system.[1] Discussion of the effects and limitations of the creation of a common legal order can shed important light on the understanding of Japanese imperialism.

Japanese legal policy in Korea was by no means static or stagnant during the forty years of protectorate and colonial rule. Scholars have begun to pay attention to the changing relationship between the colonial government in Seoul and the Japanese cabinet and legislature in Tokyo. Without losing sight of the fact that colonial law and the legal system were established and operated for the interest of the colonizer, this chapter aims to place Japanese legal policy in the broader context of colonial modernity and legality.

[1] Asano, *Teikoku Nihon*, 297.

The Constitutional Status of the Colony

The annexation of Korea was concluded through a treaty signed on August 22, 1910. A week later, on August 29, the treaty was officially proclaimed and Korea became a colony of Japan. The rules governing the basic framework for the colonial administration were announced the same day in a series of emergency imperial orders in accordance with Articles 8 and 70 in the Constitution, without waiting for the approval of the Diet. Earlier, the Foreign Ministry had proposed that the organization of the colonial government be carried out through imperial prerogative outside the purview of the legislature.[2] Since Japan had declared in theory the extension of the Japanese constitution to Taiwan in Law Number 63, the officials had to steer the Korean annexation clear of any blatant violation of the constitutional principles. Terauchi Masatake, who took office as the last resident general on May 30, 1910, warned that the extension of the constitutional provisions to Korea would be detrimental to colonial rule. He argued that Japan's approach to Korea should be different from that to Taiwan.[3] The cabinet agreed in June 1910 that "for the time being" the effect of constitution would be put on hold in Korea.[4]

The creation of the colonial system in Korea closely followed the experience in Taiwan, with certain variances. The Chosŏn government general, in which the governor general ruled the colony on behalf of the emperor, was established.[5] Under the Imperial Ordinance regarding Laws and Regulations to be Enforced in Korea, the governor was given the power to issue ordinances, called *seirei* (meaning cabinet orders), to "regulate matters requiring the enactment of

[2] Yi Sŭng-il, *Chosŏn Ch'ongdokpu pŏpche chŏngch'aek*, 89–96.

[3] "Hi: Heigō go kanhantō no tōchi to teikoku kenpō to no kankei [The Relationship between the Post-Annexation Governing of the Korean Peninsula and the Imperial Constitutional Law]," *Terauchi Masatake Monjo*, cited in Yi, *Chosŏn Ch'ongdokpu pŏpche chŏngch'aek*, 90. Mindful of Taiwan's precedent, Prime Minister Katsura Tarō replied that "it can be interpreted that once Korea's annexation is completed imperial law would naturally be applicable to the new territory. In reality, however, with the understanding that the application of each provision of the constitution to the new territory is not desirable, we have decided to create exceptions within the scope of the constitution." Katsura's communication to Terauchi, July 12, 1910, cited from Hirano Takeshi, "Nihon tōchi ka no Chōsen no hō teki chii [The Legal Status of Chosŏn under Japanese Rule]," *Handai hōgaku* 83 (1972): 49–50. See Komatsu Midori, *Chōsen heigō no rimen* [Behind the Scenes of the Annexation of Chosŏn] (Tokyo: Chūgai Shinronsha, 1920), 94–96.

[4] A document titled "Directions for the Administration of Korea" was approved in the cabinet on June 3, 1910. Hirano, "Nihon tōchi ka," 37.

[5] Imperial Ordinance Number 319. For the establishment of the colonial system in Korea, see Chen, "The Attempt to Integrate the Empire," 254–266; Hirano, "Nihon tōchi ka," 42–56; Ebashi, "Shokuminchi ni okeru kenpō no tekiyō," 3–36; Kim Ch'ang-rok, "Ilbon chekuk chŭi ŭi hŏnpŏp sahang kwa singminji Chosŏn [Constitutional Aspects of Japanese Imperialism and Colonial Chosŏn]," *Pŏpsahak yŏngu* 14 (1993): 137–174; Kim Ch'ang-rok, "Cheryŏng e gwanhan yŏngu [A Study of *cheryŏng*]," *Pŏpsahak yŏngu* 26 (2002): 109–171; Kim Ch'ang-rok, "Singminji p'ijibaegi pŏpche ŭi kich'o [The Foundation of the Legal System under Colonial Rule]," *Pŏpche yŏngu* 8 (1995): 50–78.

a law" (Article 1).[6] The *seirei* had the same effect in Korea as Japanese statutes (*hōritsu*) enacted by the Diet. Japanese law did not automatically take effect in Korea; its extension to Korea, in entirety or in part, had to be authorized by imperial ordinance (*chokurei*) (Article 4).[7] The only limitation on the governor general's legislative power was that *seirei* could not violate existing laws or imperial ordinances (Article 5).

The governor general reported to the emperor, not the cabinet ministers. The Regulation of the Organization of the Government General of Korea was issued in September to determine the functions and organization of colonial institutions. It specifically stated that the governor general was directly accountable to the emperor.[8] This language was dropped when the regulation was revised in 1919, but the new regulation still did not provide that the governor general was subordinate to the prime minister. It was not until 1942 that the colonial government was brought under the control of the cabinet.[9]

Law Number 30

The emergency imperial orders were submitted, as constitutionally required, to the Diet on January 24, 1911. Unlike in Taiwan, no serious constitutional debates followed. The sense of fait accompli was pervasive. Both the cabinet and the Diet had practically been in agreement that Korea would be governed, like Taiwan, by executive orders issued by the governor general. The "Law regarding Laws and Regulations to be Enforced in Korea" (Law Number 30) was promulgated on March 25, 1911. It had virtually the same content as the imperial order that established the *seirei* power but now its enactment satisfied the constitutional formality that legislative power was delegated by the Diet. Law Number 30 remained in force, never revised, until the end of Japanese rule as the foundation of the colonial legal order.[10]

Japanese laws, other than those enacted with the specific purpose of enforcement in the colony, took effect in Korea through incorporation by reference, that is, being made applicable by allusion in the executive orders of the governor general.[11] The Chosŏn Ordinance on Civil Matters (*Chōsen Minjirei*)

[6] Imperial Ordinance Number 324.

[7] Yamazaki, *Gaichi tōchi kikō*, 306; Kim Un-t'ae, *Ilbon cheguk chŭi ŭi Hanguk t'ongch'i* [Japanese Imperial Domination of Korea] (Seoul: Pagyŏngsa, 1998), 166–173.

[8] Imperial Ordinance Number 354.

[9] Chen, "The Attempt to Integrate the Empire," 264.

[10] Kiyomiya Shirō, *Gaichi hō josetsu* [Introduction to Overseas Territory Law] (Tokyo: Yūhikaku, 1944), 87–117. The text of Law Number 30 is in Appendix B.

[11] Kim Ch'ang-rok, "Singminji p'ijibaegi," 69–70. During thirty-five years of colonial rule, 676 *seirei* were proclaimed (of which about 270 were new regulations, not revisions of previous regulations) and about 130 Japanese laws were imposed. In contrast, during fifty years of colonial rule in Taiwan, 533 *ritsurei* were issued (of which 272 were new regulations) and 370 Japanese laws were enforced. Kim, "Cheryŏng e gwanhan yŏngu," 127. The number of *hōritsu* or *chokurei* issued specifically for the purpose of implementation in Korea was low. Yamada Saburō, "Shokuminchi hō to naichi hō no kankei ni tsuite [On the Relationship between Colonial Law and *Naichi* Law]," *Hōgaku kyōkai zasshi* 30, no. 8 (1912), 97–98. See also Niida Noboru and Masao Fukushima, eds., *Nihon hō to Ajia* [Japanese Law and Asia] (Tokyo: Keisō Shobō, 1970), 322–323.

and the Chosŏn Ordinance on Criminal Matters (*Chōsen Keijirei*), issued both as *seirei* in March 1912, imposed on Korea principal laws of Japan, including the civil code, civil procedure, criminal code, criminal procedure, and commercial law. It was not the legislative prerogative of the Diet but the government general's *seirei* power that made Japanese laws valid in the colony. This system allowed enormous legislative flexibility for the governor general: he could enforce Japanese laws in Korea without going to the trouble of promulgating new laws when there were already pertinent laws in Japan; at the same time he could choose selectively which laws to adopt and modify them whenever he saw fit. In Korea, *seirei* was the principle, *hōritsu* was the exception.[12] By recognizing the colonial governor's delegated law-making power, Japan created an autonomous legal zone and placed Korea effectively outside the jurisdiction of the Japanese legislature.

There were several important differences in the colonial structures in Korea and Taiwan. Comparisons of Law Number 63 in Taiwan and Law Number 30 in Korea illustrate divergence in the Japanese approaches to the two colonies. Law Number 63 included the stipulation that its mandate be renewed by the Diet every three years. Law Number 63 was replaced by Law Number 31 ("Law regarding Ordinances to be Enforced in Taiwan") in 1907, which now required reauthorization every five years. Each renewal of these laws was preceded by constitutional debates in the Diet as to whether the law should be terminated and Taiwan be placed under Japanese laws. Law Number 30 for Korea did not have such a duration limit, giving the government general permanent legislative power without being subject to periodic interference from the Imperial Diet.[13]

In 1921, in the wake of the rise of party politics in Japan, Law Number 31 of Taiwan was replaced by Law Number 3. The new law was a perpetual law that did not require reauthorization. It declared that the governor general's *ritsurei* power was subordinate to the Diet's legislative power. The extension of the Diet's enactment to Taiwan became the governing principle: "Those portions of statutes that are to be applied to Taiwan shall be provided by ordinance" (Article 1). The governor general's legislative power was limited to the cases when "there are no laws to apply or when it is difficult to apply existing laws" (Article 2). In other words, the governor general could resort to *ritsurei* and make laws only when there was no applicable Japanese law or when local conditions did not warrant the application of Japanese law. Japan's parliamentary law was now the law in principle in Taiwan and the colonial governor's law-making power was significantly diminished. This was clearly different from the situation in Korea where, under the arrangements in Law Number 30,

[12] The question arose: when Japanese laws that had been extended to Korea through *seirei* were later revised by the legislature, would the new laws automatically take effect in the colony? The colonial government answered in the positive but added the condition "except for when there are provisions otherwise." *Seirei* Number 11 of June 22, 1911.

[13] Oguma, *'Nihonjin' no kyōkai*, 148; Chen, "The Attempt to Integrate the Empire."

delegated legislative power of the colonial governor remained undiminished and the Diet laws continued to lack legal force on their own.[14]

These differences point to the disparate power dynamic between Tokyo-Taiwan and Tokyo-Seoul. While the governor general of Taiwan accepted the overall supervision of the prime minister as well as the control of the army and navy ministers in Tokyo, the governor general of Korea enjoyed extensive independence. The civilian statesmen in the central government found it far more difficult to bring under their supervision the successive colonial governors of Korea, most of whom were career military generals.[15] Effectively outside the Diet's oversight, and armed with the *seirei* power, the governor generals' authority was allegedly greater than that of the prime minister.[16]

The Creation of Colonial Courts

The basic structure of the court system that had been laid down during the protectorate period continued after annexation. The Chosŏn Government General Court Organization Regulation (*Chōsen Sōtokufu Saibanshorei*) was issued as an executive order in October 1910.[17] The fact that the judicial system in Korea was created not through a Diet-enacted statute (*hōritsu*) but through the government general's order (*seirei*) had significant ramifications. It gave rise to the question whether the colonial courts were "ordinary courts" under Article 57 of the Constitution or "special courts" under Article 60.[18] Article 57 of the Constitution provided: "The Judicature shall be exercised by the Courts of Law

[14] Asano, *Teikoku Nihon*, 313–316. For the colonial legal and administrative systems in Korea and comparisons with those in Taiwan, see Edward I-te Chen, "Japanese Colonialism in Korea and Formosa: A Comparison of the Systems of Political Control," *Harvard Journal of Asiatic Studies* 30 (1970): 126–158.

[15] Hagiwara Hikozō, *Nihon tōjika ni okeru Chōsen no hōsei* [The Legal System in Chosŏn under Japanese Rule] (Tokyo: Yūhō Kyōkai, 1969), 11–13.

[16] The fact that Terauchi concurrently held the position of the Minister of War in Tokyo explains in part why the governor general of Korea could not be subject to other cabinet member's supervision. Korea was placed outside the jurisdiction of Japanese law; the Diet had no control over the colonial administration of Korea, other than the budget matters. Yamazaki, *Gaichi tōchi kikō*, 90. Concerning the structure and personnel of the colonial government, see "Chōsen Sōtokufu no hōtei ni tsuite [On the Legal System of the Government General of Chosŏn]" (lecture of Hagiwara Hikozō held at Yūhō Kyokai on November 21, 1962, Yūhō Bunko, the collection of Tōyō Bunka Kenkyūjo, Gakushuin Daigaku), "Mikōkai shiryō: Chōsen Sōtokufu kankeisha rokuon kiroku (3) [Undisclosed Documents: Audio Recording of the Personnel of the Chosŏn Government General]," *Tōyō bunka kenkyū* 4 (2002), 189–232, and the accompanying introduction, Okamoto Makiko, "Chōsen Sōtokufu: soshiki to hito [The Government General of Korea: Its Organization and Personnel]," *Tōyō bunka kenkyū* (Gakushuin Daigaku) 4 (2002): 141–188.

[17] *Seirei* Number 5. Kim, *Hanguk sabŏpsa* (Kŭnse p'yŏn); Kim Sang-su, "Chosŏn Kodŭng Pŏpwŏn kwa hyŏndae Hanguk pŏp: Chosŏn Kodŭng Pŏpwŏn ŭi saengsŏng ŭl chungsim ŭro [The Chosŏn Kodŭng Pŏpwŏn and Modern Korean Law: With Particular Attention to the Establishment of the Chosŏn Kodŭng Pŏpwŏn]," *Pŏp kwa sahoe* 23 (2002): 91–109.

[18] Yamazaki, *Gaichi tōchi kikō*, 369.

according to law in the name of the Emperor. The organization of the Courts of Law shall be determined by law." Article 60 read: "All matters that fall within the competency of a special court shall be specially provided for by law." Since colonial courts were not established by law, an objection was raised to their jurisdiction. The substance of the challenge was the same as the one that arose in 1909 when residency general courts were established.[19] The argument went that, since the judges of the colonial courts were not constitutionally-mandated judges, subjecting imperial citizens to their judgments was a violation of the citizens' constitutional right.

The constitutional scholar Sasaki Sōichi (1878–1965) justified the colonial judicial organization. According to him, the government general courts were not established by a Diet-enacted law but the governor general's authority to issue the ordinances creating the courts came from an imperial ordinance, which effectively authorized him to regulate matters that were otherwise regulated by law. Therefore, he argued, the court organization regulation in Korea was equivalent to law and the government general court judges were, by extension, judges established by law.[20] From this theory followed the conclusion that imperial citizens' constitutional rights were not abridged when they were subject to the jurisdiction of the colonial judges.

Colonial officials insisted that colonial courts were fully constitutionally-mandated courts, but they also stressed that the courts in Korea were not part of the Japanese judicial hierarchy. Technically, the laws enforced by the judges were not Japanese law enacted by the Imperial Diet but executive orders of the colonial governor.[21] Japan's Court Organization Law (1890) was not extended to Korea. The colonial courts had no vertical links with the Daishinin, Japan's highest court, or the Justice Ministry. No appeals could be made to Daishinin and the judges were not bound by the legal interpretations of the Daishinin.[22] Of course the colonial High Court closely followed the rulings of the Daishinin, but theoretically independent jurisprudence developed in the colony. Taiwan's colonial judicial system, independent from the Japanese judiciary, had been justified on the grounds of the island's unique situation. Similar arguments were presented in Korea as the colonial officials opposed the call for unifying the Japanese and Korean courts.

Judicial Independence in the Colonial Context

The governor general's control of the courts met criticism almost from the beginning. In September 1910, barely a week after annexation, *Hōritsu*

[19] See Chapter 4.

[20] Sasaki Sōichi, *Nihon kenpō ron* [A Theoretical Study of Japanese Constitutional Law] (Tokyo: Kanesashi Hōryūdō, 1932). See Kim Ch'ang-rok, "Ilbon cheguk chuŭi ŭi hŏnpŏp sasang," 149–154.

[21] Matsuoka Shūtarō, "Gaichihō [Overseas Territory Law]," in *Gyōseihō* [Administrative Law], vol. 4 (Tokyo: Nihon Hyōronsha, 1936–1940), 47.

[22] For the jurisdictional relationship between the overseas territories and the *naichi*, see Tanaka Ryūichi, *Manchūkoku to Nihon no teikoku shihai* [Manchukuo and Japanese Imperial Rule] (Tokyo: Yūshisha, 2007), 235–245. More generally, see Asano, *Teikoku Nihon.*

Shinbun, the influential legal newspaper published in Tokyo, reported on the "citizen's suspicion" about the governor general's *seirei* power which, unlike the *ritsurei* power of the governor general of Taiwan, was not subject to a periodic reauthorization by the Diet. The newspaper called for the unification of judicial systems of the colony and the metropole and demanded that colonial courts be placed outside the governor general's authority.[23] This evidences that, from early on, there was a strong opposition to the colonial governor's so-called comprehensive administration. The Court Organization Regulation of 1910 did not have a provision equivalent to Article 143 of the Japanese Court Organization Law that declared that the supervisory power of the Justice Minister could not "influence or limit the judge's adjudicatory power."

There is an interesting incident regarding the issue of judicial unification. In January 1912, Miyawaki Umekichi, a judge of the Government General Keijō County Court, was reprimanded by the Judicial Disciplinary Committee. The reason for the disciplinary action was that he had "contributed an article titled the 'Reform of the judicial system in Chosŏn' to *Hōritsu Shinbun*" in Tokyo two months earlier, "in violation of professional responsibility" of judges.[24] A few days later Miyawaki resigned from his post.[25] This episode involving a low-level judge apparently caused little repercussion in legal circles, but it has an important bearing on understanding the nature and the workings of judicial administration in colonial Korea. Miyawaki got into trouble because he had boldly criticized the government general's judicial policy.[26] In particular, he called for the incorporation of the colonial courts into Japan's judicial structure, a rather untactful move considering the delicate nature of the issue. Demanding the unification of judicial systems of Japan and Korea was nothing new, but raising the question in Tokyo's prominent legal newspaper was a different matter; the government general officials were not amused.

The unfortunate fate of Judge Miyawaki can be seen as a snapshot of the brewing tension between Tokyo and Seoul. The colonial government practically formed a state within a state. While the ultimate task of the governor general was to integrate the colony into the Japanese empire, he wanted to carve out an autonomous area of influence for himself by maintaining a legal system which supposedly the colonial officials, not the politicians in Tokyo, knew best. The judicial unification issue was a reflection of the power dynamic in the empire. The implementation of Japan's Court Organization Law in Korea was advocated in some quarters in the name of judicial independence, but demanding the protection of judicial tenure and appeals right to Daishinin was an indirect way of criticizing the governor general's grip of the colonial judiciary.

[23] *Hōritsu Shinbun*, September 5, 1910.

[24] *Chōsen Sōtokufu kanpō*, January 18, 1912 (v. 415).

[25] *Chōsen Sōtokufu kanpō*, February 1, 1912 (v. 426).

[26] Miyawaki Umekichi, "Chōsen shihō seido no kaikaku [Reform of the Legal System of Chosŏn]," *Hōritsu Shinbun*, November 10, 1911, 5–6. See Kim, "Law and Reform, Colonial Style."

TABLE 5.1. *Number of Judicial Posts (as prescribed in the Imperial Ordinance of 1920)*

	Judges			Prosecutors	
High Court (KōtōHōin)	Chief Judge Senior Judge Judge	1 1 6	High Court Prosecutor's Office	Chief Prosecutor Prosecutor	1 2
Appeals Courts (Fukushim Hōin)	Chief Judge Senior Judge Judge	3 6 23	Appeals Court Prosecutor's Office	Chief Prosecutor Prosecutor	3 6
District Courts (Chihō Hōin) & Branch Courts	Chief Judge Senior Judge Judge	8 9 142	District & Branch Court Prosecutor's Office	Chief Prosecutor Prosecutor	8 52

Source: Pŏpwŏn Haengjŏngch'ŏ [Office of Court Administration], ed., *Pŏpwŏnsa* (Seoul: Pŏpwŏn Haengjŏngch'ŏ, 1995), 90.

In order to rebut the charge that its control of the courts compromised the constitutional principle of the separation of powers, the government general devoted special attention to judicial administration. The officials claimed that efficient and equitable administration of justice could be best guaranteed by the comprehensive control under the colonial governor. The quest for autonomy then entailed a singular situation in which colonial administrators portrayed themselves as the advocates of judicial independence in Korea.

A major restructuring of the colonial courts took place in 1912. The court organization regulation of October 1910 was revised thirteen times during Japanese rule, but the judicial structure and organization as delineated in 1912 remained with little change until 1945. The colonial courts were comprised of Kōtō Hōin, the highest court; three appeals courts (Fukushim Hōin) in Seoul, Pyŏngyang and Taegu; and eight district courts (Chihō Hōin) in Seoul, Kongju, Hamhŭng, Pyŏngyang, Haeju, Taegu, Chinju, and Kwangju. County courts that had existed during the protectorate were abolished in 1912 and instead branch offices were set up under district courts. There were talks of abolishing the High Court and reframe the court system into two levels like that in Taiwan, but Korea maintained the tripartite court system until the end of Japanese rule.[27] Table 5.1 indicates the number of judges and prosecutors of the courts in 1920.

In order to enter the judicial profession, one had to pass the competitive judicial examination, open to both Japanese and Koreans. A special recruitment system was in place for Koreans: those who studied law for more than three years at designated law schools could be appointed to judgeship on passing a special civil service exam.[28] In 1920, the government general allowed

[27] Kokubu Sangai's article published in October 1910 in the journal *Chōsen*, "Heigō to shihō seido to no kankei [The Relationship between Annexation and the Judicial System]," reprinted in Kŭm, *Shiryō zasshi ni miru kindai Nihon no Chōsen ninshiki*, vol. 4, 263.

[28] *Seirei* Number 7, October 1, 1910. Pŏpwŏn Haengjŏngch'ŏ [Office of Court Administration], *Hanguk pŏpkwansa* [History of Judges of Korea] (Seoul: Pŏpwŏn Haengjŏngch'ŏ, 1976), 51.

Koreans who had served in certain law-related posts, such as law clerks or court interpreters, for more than five years to be appointed to the judgeship in district court branch offices after having passed an examination.[29] Despite these efforts, the number of Korean judges and prosecutors in colonial courts seriously lagged behind that of the Japanese judges and prosecutors, on average not more than a quarter of the judicial population.

Table 5.2 lists the numbers of judges, prosecutors, and civil service staff employed in the government general courts between 1910 and 1944.[30] The small number of judicial professionals, compared with the country's population, was typical of the Japanese and Korean legal systems that continued into the modern times. As shown in the table, the extremely low proportion of Korean prosecutors in the colonial judicial system is striking. This situation persisted throughout Japanese rule. Obviously the colonial authorities were not at ease with entrusting Koreans with criminal prosecution. As with the residency general courts during the protectorate, serious restrictions were placed on the authority of Korean judges: in civil cases they were allowed to preside only when both the plaintiff and the defendant were Korean; in criminal cases only when the defendant was Korean.[31] This rule was not abandoned until 1920.[32] In 1925, the Korean newspaper *Tong-A Ilbo* reported that there were widespread grievances among Korean legal professionals that they suffered discrimination. For instance, Korean judges were not appointed the presiding judge in the collegiate bench; the three-member bench had to include at least one Japanese judge, who could veto the panel's decision. Korean lawyers were furious, wrote the newspaper.[33]

Judicial administration was handled by the Department of Judicial Affairs (Shihōbu, renamed Hōmukyoku in 1919).[34] Both judges and prosecutors were appointed by the governor general. The basic selection and promotion criteria of

[29] *Chōsen Sōtokufu kanpō*, July 29, 1920 (vol. 2391) (*Seirei* Number 11); August 13, 1920 (vol. 2403) (*Furei* Number 108); *Hanguk pŏpkwansa*, 54.

[30] "Chōsen Sōtokufu tōkei nenpyō (1912–1942)," cited from Mun, "Hanguk kŏmch'al chedo," 123–124. Hata Ikuhiko, *Sen zenki Nihon kanryō sei no seido: seido, soshiki, jinji* [The Wartime Bureaucratic System: System, Organization, Personnel Management] (Tokyo: Tokyo Daigaku Shuppankai, 1981), 392–395. For the recruitment of Korean judges, see Pak Ŭn-gyŏng, *Ilche ha Chosŏn in kwallyo yŏngu* [A Study of Korean Officials under Japanese Imperial Rule] (Seoul: Hangminsa, 1999), 125–128.

[31] The Court Organization Regulation (1910), Article 25. Cited from Kim, *Hanguk sabŏpsa* (Kŭnse p'yŏn), 45.

[32] Kim, *Hanguk sabŏpsa* (Kŭnse p'yŏn), 33.

[33] "Chosŏn in Ilbon in taeu ch'abyŏl kwa chŏlp'ye kyŏrŭi an ... Chosŏn Pyŏnhosa Hyŏphoe pungi [Discriminatory Treatment between the Koreans and the Japanese and Suggestions for Its Abolition ... The Chosŏn Lawyers' Association Is Furious]," *Tong-A Ilbo*, July 4, 1925, 2, in "Hanguk kŭn hyŏndae sa sinmun charyo" [Materials of Korean Modern and Contemporary Newspapers], Kuksa P'yŏnch'an Wiwŏnhoe [National Institute of Korean History] (http://db.history.go.kr/).

[34] Chōsen Sōtokufu, *Chōsen no shihō seido* [The Judicial System of Chosŏn] (Seoul: Chōsen Sōtokufu Hōmukoku Hōmuka, 1935), 2–3.

TABLE 5.2. *Population and Judicial Personnel, 1910–1944*

( ) = Koreans

Year	Population	Judges	Prosecutors	Civil Service[a]
1910	13,313,017	254 (71)	60 (6)	437
1911	14,055,869	249 (62)	60 (4)	421
1912	14,827,101	199 (38)	57 (3)	391
1913	15,458,863	190 (25)	58 (5)	396
1914	15,929,962	191 (32)	58 (5)	408
1915	16,278,389	194 (32)	61 (7)	419
1916	16,648,129	193 (33)	62 (9)	483
1917	16,968,997	194 (34)	62 (9)	533
1918	17,057,032	195 (35)	69 (10)	604
1919	17,149,909	186 (34)	70 (10)	644
1920	17,288,989	191 (40)	71 (11)	647
1921	17,452,918	193 (37)	76 (10)	663
1922	17,626,761	191 (38)	79 (10)	676
1923	17,884,963	203 (37)	83 (10)	741
1924	18,068,116	183 (33)	75 (9)	674
1925	19,015,526	183 (33)	75 (9)	684
1926	19,103,900	183 (33)	77 (9)	687
1927	19,137,698	186 (31)	82 (9)	698
1928	19,189,699	186 (33)	87 (9)	703
1929	19,331,061	190 (33)	87 (9)	708
1930	20,256,563	196 (38)	86 (7)	714
1931	20,262,958	198 (39)	87 (7)	683
1932	20,599,876	192 (40)	85 (7)	704
1933	20,791,321	190 (40)	84 (7)	710
1934	21,125,827	193 (41)	86 (7)	716
1935	21,891,180	192 (38)	88 (7)	733
1936	22,047,836	204 (39)	93 (7)	809
1937	22,355,485	224 (45)	107 (11)	823
1938	22,633,751	225	109	836
1939	22,800,647	228	111	861
1940	23,709,057	232	127	907
1941	24,704,000	242	130	953
1942	26,361,000	246	135	941
1943	26,662,000	268	145	971
1944	25,918,000	254	139	–

[a] Includes judicial clerks and court interpreters.

Source: Pŏpwŏn Haengjŏngch'ŏ [Office of Court Administration], ed., *Pŏpwŏnsa* (Seoul: Pŏpwŏn Haengjŏngch'ŏ, 1995), 90–91.

the colonial judges were the same as those provided in Japan's Court Organization Law. Once stationed in Korea, a Japanese judge usually spent his career there. This was in line with the general pattern that personnel transfers between the Japanese metropolitan bureaucracy and the colonial bureaucracy were rare.[35] Kitō Heiichi, the last chief justice of the colonial High Court before Korea's independence, spent his entire career in Korea. After passing the judicial examination, he was assigned to the entry-level judgeship at the Keijō County Court in 1910. Having climbed the ladder in the promotion system, he was appointed the head of the High Court in January 1943. Upon the liberation of Korea in August 1945, he returned to Japan, allegedly carrying a single briefcase. Kitō subsequently practiced law as a private attorney until his death in 1954.[36]

The major incentive for Japanese judges to pursue their careers in Korea seemed to be monetary. The same pay scale applied to both colonial and metropolitan judges but Japanese judges assigned to the colonial courts enjoyed higher remuneration as they were paid additional amounts in the form of housing subsidies and other expenses. During the early colonial years, they were paid, on average, extra sums ranging from forty to fifty percent of their base salary.[37] Toward the end of colonial rule, though, Japanese judges in Korea complained that their compensations trailed behind those of judges in Japan.[38] They certainly were paid more than their Korean colleagues because they were entitled to overseas relocation expenses and other perks. The former Chief Justice Yokota Gōrō of the High Court acknowledged in 1936 that this uneven remuneration system was problematic. For instance, a Korean judge from a northern province could be transferred to a southern province but he did not receive relocation subsidies. Short of demanding the abolition of the preferential treatment of the Japanese judges, Yokota called for an increase in judicial compensation across the board in order to maintain the quality of the judicial personnel in the colony.[39]

Protection of Judicial Tenure

The most serious difference that set colonial judges apart from their counterparts in Japan concerned job protection. The colonial judges did not enjoy

[35] Lewis H. Gann, "Western and Japanese Colonialism: Some Preliminary Comparisons," in *The Japanese Colonial Empire, 1895–1945*, eds. Ramon H. Myers and Mark R. Peattie (Princeton, NJ: Princeton University Press, 1984), 497–525.

[36] Kim Sang-su, "Chosŏn Kodŭng Pŏpwŏn p'ansa ka pon Chosŏn ŭi ch'injok sangsok e kwanhan kwansŭp [The Family and Succession Custom of Chosŏn as Observed by a Judge of the Chosŏn Kodŭng Pŏpwŏn]," *Sŏgang pŏphak* 10, no. 1 (2008): 25–46; Kim Sang-su, "Kankoku hō no rekishi: Saigo no Chōsen kōtō hōinshō no koto [Korean Law and History: A Matter of the Last Chief Justice of the Chosŏn Kodŭng Pŏpwŏn]," *Kokusai shōji hōmu* 29, no. 8 (2001), 1020–1021.

[37] Okamoto, "Chōsen Sōtokufu: Sosiki to hito," 161. All Japanese officials in colonies, including Taiwan and Karafuto received additional stipends for being stationed away from home. For the appointment and remuneration system of colonial officials, see ibid., 156–164.

[38] Nam, *Ilche ŭi Hanguk sabŏppu ch'imnyak sirhwa*, 204–205. See An Yong-sik, O Yŏn-suk, O Sŭng-ŭn, and Song Hae-gyŏng, "Chosŏn Ch'ongdokpu ha Ilbon in kwallyo yŏngu [A Study of Japanese Officials under the Government General of Korea]," *Tongbang hakchi* 137 (2007), 209–210.

[39] Yokota Gōrō, "Shihōkan no zōin to yūgū wo nozomu [Desiring the Increase in the Number of Judicial Officials and the Improvement of Their Conditions]," in *Chōsen tōchi no kaiko to hihan* [Reflections and Criticisms on the Governing of Chosŏn], ed. Chōsen Shinbunsha (Tokyo: Ryūkei Shosha, 1995, 1936), 237–239.

the constitutional protection of judicial tenure as provided in the Japanese Court Organization Law.[40] The revised Court Organization Regulation and the Regulation for Judicial Discipline in May 1911 provided measures of protection. A colonial judge could not be dismissed against his will unless he had been sentenced to penal servitude or subjected to disciplinary actions.[41] When a judge was incapable of performing duties because of mental or physical incompetency, dismissal required the approval of a panel composed of the High Court justices.[42] Discipline of judges was determined by a judicial disciplinary committee composed of the chief justice of the High Court and four other members appointed by the governor general. Unlike their counterparts in the Japanese courts, however, colonial judges did not have the right to appeal the decisions of the disciplinary committee. Under the Japanese Court Organization Law, judges were shielded from arbitrary transfer, suspension, or pay reduction, but such protections were not extended to the judges in Korea. The governor general's power to suspend judges was rescinded in 1921. But the lack of comparable job security continued to be an issue in the colonial courts.

Korea did not witness a high-profile controversy regarding judicial tenure like the Takano Takenori case in Taiwan. Takano was the chief justice of the High Court in Taiwan but was forcibly removed in October 1897 in the aftermath of political controversies. Takano claimed that he was protected under Article 58 of the Constitution, but his removal was confirmed on the grounds that Taiwanese courts were not ordinary courts and therefore outside the said constitutional provision.[43] Understandably, the lack of the constitutional guarantee of judicial tenure was widely resented by judges in Taiwan and Korea. It seemed natural that colonial judges called for the extension of Japan's Court Organization Law and the incorporation of colonial courts within the Japanese judicial hierarchy.

In March 1914, the Japanese Bar Association issued "A proposal to unify judicial institutions and civil and criminal laws in Japan, Chosŏn, and Taiwan." The Justice Ministry was in favor of the proposal because it would allow the ministry to control the judicial management throughout the empire, but the cabinet feared its possible repercussions on colonial administration. In 1916, bills were submitted, unsuccessfully, to the Diet to extend Japan's Court Organization Law and Attorney Law to Taiwan.[44] The legal personnel in Korea repeatedly made similar demands but had no success.[45]

[40] Article 58 of the Meiji Constitution provided: "The judges shall be appointed from among those who possess proper qualifications according to law. No judge shall be deprived of his position unless by way of criminal sentence or disciplinary punishment. Rules for disciplinary punishment shall be determined by law."

[41] Yamazaki, *Gaichi tōchi kikō*, 379–382.

[42] Kim, *Hanguk sabŏpsa* (Kŭnse p'yon), 32,

[43] Wang, *Legal Reform in Taiwan*, 68; Asano, *Teikoku Nihon*, 64–65.

[44] Mun, "Cheguk Ilbon," 224–226.

[45] Nam, *Ilche ŭi Hanguk sabŏppu ch'imnyak sirhwa*, 204.

Kokubu Sangai

During the first decade of the colonial rule, Kokubu Sangai (1863–1962), the Director of the Law Department, presented the most articulate arguments on behalf of the government general against judicial unification.[46] A former Osaka District Court chief prosecutor, Kokubu came to Korea in 1908 and served as the chief prosecutor of the residency general court and later the government general court. In 1913, he succeeded Kuratomi Yuzaburō to become the colonial government's top judicial official, the position he held concurrently until his retirement in 1920. A pivotal figure during the formative years of the colonial courts, Kokubu advocated the colonial judicial structure. In 1915, he forcefully argued against the subjection of the colonial judicial system to Japan's judicial hierarchy. Kokubu acknowledged that allowing appeals to Daishinin would promote consistency in legal interpretations throughout the empire. But he argued that "laws must be unified first, and only then one could plan to unify judicial systems. Discussing the unification of legal systems when laws are not yet unified is like putting the cart before the horse."[47]

Kokubu claimed that the colonial courts were constitutionally-mandated courts: "The courts in Korea exercise judicial power in the name of the emperor in accordance with Article 57 of the constitution.... The fact that the courts were established by *seirei*, which has the same force as statutes, means that they satisfy the requirement of Article 57, Section 2, that the organization of courts be established by law." According to him:

> Article 1 of the Court Organization Regulation stipulates that "Chosŏn government general courts are directly attached to the government general." Some people misinterpret it in such a way that judicial power in Korea is subordinate to the governor general. If judicial power were subordinate to the colonial governor and judicial power under his control, it would clearly be a violation of the constitution. But the language "directly attached to the government general" means that it is under the direct supervision of the governor general. It is in the same spirit as the Court Organization Law [of Japan] which says in Article 135: "The Judicial Minister supervises courts and the prosecutor's office." Likewise, Article 1 of the Regulation simply refers to supervision in judicial administration and has nothing to do with the question of judicial independence. It is consistent with the Court Organization Law in the *naichi*, and there is no room for any doubt.[48]

In short, the fact that the courts were placed under the authority of the governor general did not mean that judicial independence was amiss in Korea. For Kokubu, the colonial governor was the guarantor of judicial independence.[49]

[46] For a brief biography, see Nomura Masao, "Kokubu Sangai," *Hōsō hūun roku* (Tokyo: Asahi Shinbunsha, 1966), 18–30.

[47] Kokubu Sangai, "Shihō seido tōitsu ron ni tsuite [On the Theory of the Unification of Judicial Systems]," *Chōsen kōron* 3 & 4 (April 1915), reprinted in Kŭm, ed. *Shiryō zasshi ni miru kindai Nihon no Chōsen ninshiki*, vol. 5, 478–480.

[48] Ibid., 480.

[49] In fact, judicial independence under the colonial governor was not an assertion as preposterous as it may sound today, especially to American ears. Article 64 of the French constitution

The colonial judicial system was constitutional, Kokubu pointed out, because under the constitution all three powers emanated from the emperor and the authority of the governor general was granted by the emperor.[50] The colonial governor, as the deputy of the emperor, was the fount of judicial power in Korea. Losing control over the courts would diminish the legitimacy of the colonial government. The warning not to harm the prestige of the colonial governor who "personally represents the emperor" carried serious weight. In 1931, some members of the Upper House of the Parliament viewed the intervention of the cabinet or the legislature in colonial affairs as improper, because "he who knows best the people's will in the colony is doubtless the governor general."[51]

The revolving issue was whether to implement the Japanese Court Organization Law in Korea. A classified memorandum submitted to Governor General Saito Makoto in 1919 methodically analyzed the advantages and disadvantages of unifying the Japanese and Korean courts.[52] The advantages included: it could dispel distrust of the colonial judiciary caused by the belief that it lacked judicial independence and the guarantee of judicial tenure; next, it could create favorable impressions among Koreans who were sensitive to any separate treatment or discrimination; in addition, it would promote the unification of laws and their interpretations which would help to deal with the problems of conflict of laws between the *naichi* and overseas territories. On the other hand, a serious disadvantage was that the supervision of judicial affairs would be transferred to the Judicial Ministry, creating disarray in colonial judicial administration. It would negatively affect the governor general's ability to control colonial affairs because he would lose power to supervise prosecutors

provides: "The President of the Republic shall be the guarantor of the independence of the Judicial Authority" (Le Président de la République est garant de l'indépendence de l'autorité judiciaire).

50 Kokubu, "Shihō seido tōitsu ron ni tsuite." See Mitani Taichirō, *Seiji seido to shite no baishinsei: kindai Nihon no shihōken to seiji* [The Jury System as a Political System: The Judicial Power and Politics of Modern Japan] (Tokyo: Tokyo Daigaku Shuppankai, 2001), 51–56.

51 Okamoto Makiko, "Sōtoku seiji to seitō seiji: nidai seitōki no sōtoku jinji to sōtokufu kansei yosan [The Politics of Colonial Governors and the Party Politics: The Personnel of Colonial Governors and the Colonial Government's Operating Budget during the Two-Party Period]," *Chōsen shi kenkyūkai ronbunshū* 38 (2000), 47.

52 Chōsen Sōtokufu Hōmukoku, "Hi: Saibanshō kōsōhō wo Chōsen ni shikō suru kahi [Classified: The Question of Implementing the Court Organization Law in Chosŏn]," in *Saito Makoto Monjo: Chōsen Sōtoku jidai kankei shiryō* (Seoul : Koryŏ Sŏrim, 1999), vol. 5, 89–100. The document included neither the author's name nor the date, but it was likely written by Kokubu because it repeated closely the arguments presented by him earlier. Also handwritten additions and corrections made to the transcribed original copy make it certain that the author is Kokubu. See Tanaka Ryūichi, "Teikoku Nihon no shihō rensa [The Linkage in the Administration of Justice in Imperial Japan]," *Chōsen shi kenkyūkai ronbunshū* 38 (2000), 66. The fact that Kokubu in 1936, then in retirement, provided largely the same arguments further supports his authorship of the document. See Kokubu Sangai, "Chōsen shihō seido no kakuritsu [The Establishment of the Judicial System in Chosŏn]," in *Chōsen tōchi no kaiko to hihan*, ed. Chōsen Shinbunsha (Tokyo: Ryūkei Shosha, 1995, 1936), 46.

who, in turn, would be unable to work closely with the police. The author of the memorandum argued that it was essential to have a judiciary that "understands the Korean situation," and that "the governor general must be assured of power to oversee judicial, legislative, and administrative matters in order to rule Korea effectively. Taking judicial power away from the governor general will confound the basic structure of colonial rule."

It is beyond doubt that the colonial government's foremost concern was to maintain a tight control of the colonial populace. When the government general demanded autonomy in judicial matters and opposed the unification of the courts, it found itself compelled to pay more than lip service to the independence of the courts. The colonial governor's desire to inspire respect for the courts under his supervision prompted efforts to promote efficient and equitable judicial administration. It is interesting to note that the colonial government framed the whole issue in terms of building public trust in the colonial courts. On many occasions, Governor General Terauchi exhorted judicial officials to work to gain trust among people. Efficiency in judicial administration was essential, he stressed, because delays in civil and criminal matters were directly related to people's welfare.[53] These statements were, to a large degree, the colonial government's legitimizing discourse of its power and autonomy. Nevertheless, its professed deference for judicial independence – decisional independence if not institutional independence – and its push for judicial probity contributed to promoting legality in colonial Korea.

Evidence suggests that the government general was keen on stamping out corruption and improving judicial accountability.[54] In one case in 1926, the chief judge of Kongju District Court Takeo Ichirō was disciplined for failing to supervise court employees properly. Takeo served as the chief judge from 1924 and during his tenure a Kim, a low-level clerk at that court, committed a series of frauds by using the judges' seals without authorization and forging receipts. Another low-level employee, a certain Chu, was found to have committed similar acts. The disciplinary committee determined, on the findings of the chief prosecutor of the High Court, that Takeo failed to exercise due diligence in supervising his subordinate personnel and thus "violated his professional duties." In a separate case, Judge Sakata Ichirō at the Ch'ŏngju branch of Sinŭiju District Court and Judge Sukie Jirō at the Hoeryŏng branch of Ch'ŏngjin District Court were censured as they "failed to know" that a clerk named Egashira Saburō was involved in various misconduct. The committee

[53] Speech to the judicial personnel on June 26, 1915. *Chōsen Sōtokufu kanpō*, June 29, 1915 (vol. 871). Colonial officials stated in 1922: "it is necessary to improve the judiciary's status and authority so that Koreans as well as the Japanese can trust the judiciary. It is a very important question in ruling Chosŏn." "Chōsen sōtokufu saibanshōrei kaitei an [A Proposal to Reform the Court Organization Regulation of the Government General of Chosŏn]," November 23, 1922, cited from Mun, "Hanguk kŏmch'al chedo," 133.

[54] *Chōsen Sōtokufu kanpō*, April 30, 1926 (vol. 4107). See Kim Pyŏng-hwa, *Hanguk sabŏpsa* (Kŭnse p'yŏn), 123–124.

found that the two judges "failed to supervise properly the court employees and thus failed to fulfill professional duties."

In 1918, on the tenth anniversary of the establishment of modern Korean courts, Chief Justice Watanabe Nobu reminisced on Korea's judicial reform and stated that "there has been no pressure on the exercise of judicial power" under Itō or Terauchi.[55] This favorable appraisal of the independence of the courts was affirmed by judicial officials toward the end of the colonial period.[56] These self-assessments may have to be taken with a grain of salt; the commitment to judicial independence was preconditioned on achieving effective colonial control. But at least it is necessary to reconsider the simplistic view that the colonial courts were a mere instrument of lawless colonial oppression.

Hara Takashi (1856–1921), Japan's prime minister from 1918 to 1921, tried to bring the colonial governors of Korea and Taiwan under the control of the Japanese cabinet and the parliamentary system. In the aftermath of the March First Movement in 1919, a massive protest by Koreans demanding independence, the Hara cabinet attempted to subject colonial judicial institutions to the Ministry of Justice and unify judicial systems of Japan and Korea, as part of a comprehensive plan to revise the structure of the colonial government.[57] But the Privy Council put the brakes on his plan. It reasoned that placing under the prime minister's supervision the colonial governor of Korea, "who has the important responsibility of controlling the special territory comprising several tens of millions of people," would harm the governor's prestige. The council members cautioned that Korea was different from Taiwan in the manner in which it became Japan's territory and that there was a huge gap between the two colonies in their history as well as the people's sentiments. The two colonial governments needed to be treated differently, it was argued. The prime minister's supervision over the governor general of Taiwan could be justified but the governor general of Korea was a different matter.[58]

The judicial unification issue that resonated in the colonial scene was also laden with ramifications of bureaucratic and political infighting in the metropole. The parliamentary groups viewed the colonial order as an irregular expedient that needed an overhaul. The ascendancy of parliamentary politics in the 1920s initially seemed to promise weakening of the governor general's power.[59] Before long, however, the eruption of scandals involving the members of the Diet boosted the argument that Korea should be shielded from politics in the metropole. Newspapers argued that the governor general of Korea "must

[55] *Kyŏngsŏng Ilbo*, May 18, 1918, cited in Mun, "Hanguk kŏmch'al chedo," 129.

[56] Nam, *Ilche ŭi Hanguk sabŏppu ch'imnyak sirhwa*, 211 and 213–215.

[57] Oguma, *'Nihonjin' no kyōkai*, 265.

[58] Okamoto, "Sōtoku seiji to seitō seiji," 33.

[59] Haruyama Meitetsu and Wakabayashi Masahiro, *Nihon shokumin shugi no seijiteki tenkai*, 1–75; Mun, "Hanguk kŏmch'al chedo," 130, note 27. See also Okamoto, "Sōtoku seiji to seitō seiji," 31.

absolutely repel private interests abound in party politics" and that he "must maintain his authority against the interference from the cabinet."[60] The Korean newspaper *Chosŏn Ilbo* wrote: "it is necessary to keep Korea from becoming victim to the party politics [in Japan] vying for interests over Korea."[61] The governor general's autonomous policy was seen as desirable because it would prevent Korea from being tied with rash imperial policy undertakers. This view became especially vociferous during the premiership of Tanaka Giichi (1863–1929) whose expansion policy toward Manchuria and Mongolia in the late 1920s aroused concern in the colony.

These situations contributed to the colonial governor's increased grip on colonial politics. In the 1920s, political situations in the *naichi* and the colony could not be more different. In Japan, parliamentary party politics was in full swing, with its policy directions constantly vacillating with unpredictable results; in Korea, the premise that the fundamental direction as laid down in the Meiji emperor's rescript were immutable rendered the existing colonial legal structure practically unchangeable and unassailable. The governor general's power, emanating directly from the emperor, was deemed to be beyond political debate and reproach.

Kuratomi Yuzaburō

Kuratomi Yuzaburō was a senior statesmen in Tokyo whose opinion regarding colonial legal policy in Korea carried significant weight. Kuratomi's involvement in Korea dated from the protectorate period. A career prosecutor, Kuratomi came to Korea in 1907 to become the first deputy minister of law, the highest ranking Japanese law official employed at the Korean government under the residency general.[62] He was subsequently appointed the first law minister in the government general. As the predecessor of Kokubu, Kuratomi was, without exaggeration, a figure most responsible for the inception of the colonial judicial system.

From early on, Kuratomi supported the unification of Korea's law and legal system with those of Japan. During the protectorate, as seen in Chapter 4, Kuratomi was skeptical of Ume Kenjirō's campaign to create an independent civil code for Korea and argued instead that the most efficient way to reform Korea's law and courts was the imposition of the Japanese system.[63] Evidence suggests that, after annexation, Kuratomi's position in Korean judicial policy did not always agree with Tarauchi's. Kuratomi was widely respected by the colonial judicial personnel for standing up against Terauchi's attempt to reduce the size of the judiciary and abolish the appellate courts, turning the tripartite system into a two-level system as in Taiwan.[64] Kuratomi resigned his post in

[60] *Asahi Shinbun*, December 1, 1927, cited from Okamoto, "Sōtoku seiji to seitō seiji," 34–35.
[61] Okamoto, "Sōtoku seiji to seitō seiji," 35.
[62] See Chapter 4.
[63] "Kankoku ni okete saiban jimu ni kansuru ken," in *Kuratomi Yuzaburō Monjo*.
[64] Nam, *Ilche ŭi Hanguk sabŏppu ch'imnyak sirhwa*, 164. See "Kankoku ni okeru shihō oyobi kankoku no seido," August 2, 1910. *Kuratomi Yuzaburō Monjo*, vol. 30, no. 17, the National

1913 and went back to Japan to become the chairman of the Privy Council. Once back in Japan, Kuratomi became a vocal advocate for the extension of the Court Organization Law to Korea, which he argued was essential for guaranteeing the tenure of colonial judges. The main architect of the colonial judicial system, he boasted that the courts commanded trust from Koreans; he warned that this hard-earned trust would be jeopardized if the government general failed to guarantee judicial independence.[65]

Historians agree that Japanese legal policy underwent considerable changes after 1919. Japan opened the colonial governorship in Korea and Taiwan to non-military officials.[66] The new governor general in Korea, Saito Makoto, was a navy admiral, not part of the powerful army faction.[67] The demand for the unification of the judicial systems seemed to gain a new momentum. Under Saito, high-ranking judges of the colonial courts submitted an opinion demanding the implementation of the Court Organization Law in Korea.[68] While he was opposed to placing the courts under the colonial governor, Kuratomi was equally critical of the fact that colonial legal policy was influenced by the parliamentary politics in Japan. He did not hide his distaste for raucous wrangling in the Diet. When corruption scandals broke out in 1929 implicating Governor General Yamanashi Hanzō (1864–1944; governor general of Korea 1927–1929), Kuratomi lamented that the colonial governors were too cozily attached to the parliamentary interest groups. He stated: "when the governor general is swayed by the party politics, it is inevitable that trust in the judiciary declines."[69]

In 1940, Kuratomi was unequivocal when he stated that "the supervisory power of prosecutorial affairs should belong to the prosecutor general and the minister of justice [in Japan]. The governor general's abuse of power, overstepping his authority, is incompatible with this principle."[70] His opinion directly opposed those of the colonial administrators, for whom the exigency of colonial management required flexibility in judicial affairs. It is interesting to see that both the advocates and critics of the governor general's control of the courts

Diet Library (Japan), Bureau of Constitutional Documents. See Mun, "Hanguk kŏmch'al chedo," 121, note 5.

65 In the journal entry of September 19, 1920, Kuratomi expressed concern about the government general's attempt to interfere with the judiciary by encroaching on judicial tenure. See Nagai, "Tōkanbu no shihō seido kaikaku."

66 Imperial Ordinance Number 386.

67 In Taiwan, the first civilian governor Den Kenjirō took the office in 1919. In Korea, the governorship continued to be filled by military generals until the end of the colonial rule.

68 Nam, *Ilche ŭi Hanguk sabŏppu ch'imnyak sirhwa*, 209.

69 Okamoto, "Sōtoku seiji to seitō seiji," 38. Kuratomi also wrote in his journal that "when a new colonial governor is appointed following the cabinet change, inevitably the independence of the judiciary in Korea is placed in suspicion" (entry of August 26, 1929). See Okamoto, ibid.; Mun, "Hanguk kŏmch'al chedo," 131, note 32.

70 Kuratomi, "Chōsen no shihō seido ni kansuru shaken [A Personal Opinion regarding the Judicial System of Chosŏn]," July 30, 1940, *Kuratomi Yuzaburō Monjo*, vol. 30, No. 22. For the translation in Korea, see Nam, *Ilche ŭi Hanguk sabŏppu ch'imnyak sirhwa*, 215–219.

invoked the ideal of judicial integrity. Kuratomi's position can be contrasted, for example, with that of Kokubu, his successor in the law department, who defended in the strongest terms the governor's independence from Tokyo.

In 1936, Kokubu, then in retirement, contended that the application of Japan's Court Organization Law in Korea was undesirable for the following reasons. First, the budget allocated to the government general for the administration of the courts and prisons would be taken away and incorporated into the budget of the justice ministry, causing a drain of the financial resources for the colonial government. More serious was that the judicial unification would cause the colonial government to lose its control over the prosecutors and the police forces who were responsible for maintaining public order.[71] Kokubu warned: "If the [Court Organization] Law is implemented, the relation between the prosecutors and the governor general of Korea will be severed as the prosecutors will be placed under the minister of justice. The governor general will lose the power to command them."[72] The unification of judicial systems in Japan and Korea might be the ultimate goal but, he argued, it should not obstruct the power of the government general and "jeopardize the preservation of public order." He concluded: "the time is not ripe for the implementation of the Court Organization Law in Korea. Until we reform the current administrative system of Korea and improve it to the same level as that of Japan, we cannot expect to see the law's extension to Korea."

In 1940, a roundtable talk was held in Tokyo, attended by retired Japanese judicial officials who had served in Korea. Kokubu presided over the meeting. The transcript of this meeting is an important source for colonial history, providing a number of insights about the working of the colonial judicial system.[73] Yamaguchi Sadamasa, who served as the Keijō Appeals Court judge and later the head of the law bureau under Kokubu, articulated reasons why the application of the Japanese Court Organization Law in Korea was necessary. First, salaries and benefits for judges serving in Korea trailed behind their counterparts in Japan, creating difficulties in recruiting qualified Japanese jurists to Korea; equal remuneration of judges in Korea and Japan would help promote personnel exchange and the unification of the judicial systems. Second, judicial tenure was not guaranteed in Korea because the courts remained under the governor general's control. Third, since the Chosŏn High Court rendered the final judgments, with no appeals to the Daishinin, interpretation of law lacked uniformity between Japan and Korea.[74] In reply, Kokubu acknowledged that the prestige and status of the judiciary in Korea declined since the time when Itō was the resident general.[75]

[71] Kokuhu, "Chōsen shihō seido no kakuritsu," 46.

[72] Ibid.

[73] Nam, *Ilche ŭi Hanguk sabŏppu ch'imnyak sirhwa*, 208.

[74] Ibid., 203–207.

[75] Ibid., 213.

Ever a loyal colonial administrator, he still repeated the argument he had made some twenty years earlier: the application of Court Organization Law would destroy the governor general's control and it would jeopardize colonial domination.[76]

Here it must be pointed out that the debate over judicial unification essentially reflected bureaucratic infighting and that the discussion of judicial independence represented a critically limited outlook. Kuratomi's concept of judicial independence was colored by colonial ideology. His demand for implementing Japan's Court Organization Law in Korea was largely prompted by the desire to keep the judiciary away from the control of the colonial governor. It was in line with his earlier position in favor of the comprehensive imposition of Japan's laws in protectorate Korea. His support for judicial unification envisioned strengthening the protection of judicial tenure and improving the prestige of the judiciary. But it is questionable that he was genuinely concerned about judicial independence for the benefit of the colonial population. Indeed, his advocacy of the unification of the courts seemed to be detached from the consideration to extend constitutional protection to Koreans.[77] In short, Kuratomi's conception of judicial independence may have operated within the bounds of colonialism.

The continuing demands for the unification of the judicial systems indicate that there was no unanimous support for the governor general's legislative and judicial power. Under Governor General Saito, high-ranking judges of the colonial courts submitted an opinion demanding the implementation of the Court Organization Law.[78] In 1933, the Korean Bar Association adopted a resolution demanding the same. In 1935 and again in 1940, Japan's Imperial Bar Association proposed the establishment of a unified judicial structure throughout Taiwan, Korea, and Japan.[79] Lawyers argued that the inactive bar in Korea could be stimulated by the unification with the bar in Japan. In 1938, chief justice of the Taegu Appeals Court stated: "the activities of the Korean Bar are rather calm compared with Japan, or to put it bluntly, very weak.... We wish for more active movements for the development of Korea's judicial system."[80]

[76] Kokubu reiterated his earlier argument: "I think it is unreasonable from the perspective of power distribution to place the prosecutors outside the supervision of the governor general. It is necessary to give the governor general some power. It is a very difficult question how to balance the jurisdictional relationship between the governor general, the law minister and the chief prosecutor." Ibid., 208.

[77] Okamoto,"Sōtoku seiji to seitō seiji." Kuratomi wrote in his diary that educating Koreans would promote resistance to Japan (entry of May 7, 1929). See Nagai, "Tōkanbu no shihō seido kaikaku." Nagai has argued that judicial independence called for by Kuratomi was different from judicial independence advocated by Itō in 1906–1909.

[78] Nam, *Ilche ŭi Hanguk sabŏppu ch'imnyak sirhwa*, 209.

[79] Ibid., 204.

[80] *Hōsei shinbun* vol. 383 (April 20, 1938), cited in Mun, "Hanguk kŏmch'al chedo," 126, note 18.

The basic contours of the colonial system and legal policy were shaped by continuing conflicts – both ideological and institutional – and negotiations between the metropole and local administrators. The approach of the colonial government to legal matters, zealously guarding against interference from Tokyo, is best exemplified in its customary law policy. In the midst of attempts to reform colonial administration, customary law featured as one of the key sources of the tension between imperial and colonial officials.

The Colonial Customary Law Order

In February 1911, Governor General Terauchi Masatake appeared before the Imperial Diet and outlined the shift in the legal policy from the protectorate to the colonial period. He stated: "now that Korea was entrusted [to Japan] through annexation, creating independent law was no longer necessary. Based on this consideration, I suspended Mr. Ume's legislation campaign."[81] Terauchi went on to declare that the ultimate goal of colonial policy was assimilation (*dōka*) of the Korean people into the Japanese society. The long historical and cultural ties between the two peoples underscored the logic of such a policy. Yet Korea, previously "an independent country with several thousand years of history and a population over ten million," had "a different tradition and its practices and customs are all very different from those of Japan. There are elements of Korean customs that cannot be understood from the sentiments of the imperial citizens." Therefore, Terauchi cautioned, "it is not desirable to impose Japanese law immediately in Korea" and instead it would be necessary to allow Korean customs to govern legal relations among the Koreans.

Evidence suggests that the colonial government initially wanted an extensive application of customs. In November 1910, it drew up a draft ordinance that broadly stated that Korean customs would apply to disputes among Koreans.[82] Using the language similar to that in the Taiwanese Civil Ordinance (*Minjirei*) issued on August 28, 1908, the draft provided that civil matters were governed by Japanese civil law, commercial law, and other supplementary laws, but that "civil matters among Koreans follow the existing rules." Here the "existing rules" referred to the rules under the arrangement in 1909 when the Japanese took over the Korean judiciary, according to which legal relations between Koreans were governed by Korean laws and customs. But the plan was abandoned, likely rejected by the politicians in Tokyo. The cabinet did not want a system that would apply Korean laws and customs in such an open-ended way and instead preferred a system with a much narrower scope.

[81] Speech at the 27th Imperial Diet (February 1, 1911), cited from Oguma, *'Nihonjin' no kyōkai*, 149; the same speech was cited in the deliberations of the committee on the enactment of the *Kyōtsūhō* (Coordination Law) at the 44th Imperial Diet in 1918. See Yi Sŭng-il, *Chosŏn Ch'ongdokpu pŏpche chŏngch'aek*, 101–102.

[82] Yi Sŭng-il, *Chosŏn Ch'ongdokpu pŏpche chŏngch'aek*, 104–107.

The Chosŏn Ordinance on Civil Matters

On March 18, 1912, the colonial government issued the Ordinance on Civil Matters (*Chōsen Minjirei* or *Chosŏn Minsaryŏng*; hereinafter referred to as the Civil Ordinance), to take effect on April 1. This was the regulation that created the basic civil legal order during the colonial era. Under the decree, Japan's Civil Code became the governing law in the colony. Article 1 of the *Minjirei* provided that "Unless otherwise provided in this ordinance or other laws or regulations, civil matters shall be governed by the following laws," and listed civil law, civil procedure, commercial law, and other Japanese laws, altogether numbering twenty-three laws.[83] It was declared, however, that a significant part of private law matters among Koreans be regulated by Korean customary rules. Under Articles 10 through 12, matters of capacity, family and succession, and real property rights were decreed to be governed by Korean customs instead of Japanese laws. The provisions are as follows:

> Article 10: Civil matters involving Koreans only are governed by Korean custom, even if a specific custom is different from law, as long as the law is not related to public order.
>
> Article 11: The provisions on capacity, family, and succession in the laws listed in Article 1 do not apply to Koreans. The said matters involving Koreans are decided according to Korean custom.
>
> Article 12: The kinds and effects of real property rights are governed by custom, except for the property rights stipulated in Article 1.

As a result of these articles, the first three books of the Japanese Civil Code – General principles, Properties, and Obligations – were imposed in Korea, but not the last two books on Family and Succession. All contract and commercial issues were subject to Japanese law.

Comparisons between the Taiwanese Civil, Commercial, and Criminal Ordinance (1908) and the Korean Civil Ordinance reveal important differences. The Taiwanese rule provided that civil, commercial, and criminal matters must conform to the Japanese codes and other statutes but "matters mentioned below shall specially conform to present practice: (1) Civil and commercial matters involving Taiwanese or Chinese only; (2) Criminal matters relating to Taiwanese or Chinese."[84] According to this language, all civil and commercial matters among the natives were governed by custom. In Korea, in contrast, the scope of the application of customs was narrower because of Article 10. Under Article 11, capacity, family, and succession matters among Koreans were governed by custom but other civil matters were governed by custom only if the custom did not violate laws of public policy. In other words, application of Korean customs in matters other than capacity, family, and succession areas triggered the same requirements as those in Articles 90 through 92 of the Japanese Civil Code.[85] The

[83] For the text of the Ordinance, see Appendix B.

[84] Wang, *Legal Reforms in Taiwan*, 49–50. The text of the ordinance is printed in ibid., 195.

[85] See Chapter 6.

Japanese were intent on limiting the operation of Korean customs; this indicates that cultural and social affinities between Koreans and Japanese as the undercurrents of law were perceived greater than between Taiwanese and Japanese.

Another difference can be found in the question of who were governed by custom. Application of Taiwan's old customs was limited to matters among the Taiwanese or the Chinese only ("*nomi no aida*"). If one party was non-Taiwanese or non-Chinese, the Japanese Civil Code applied. In Korea, Article 11 provided that Korean family and succession customs apply to Koreans. If one party was Korean and the other was Japanese, for example in marriage or adoption, both Korean custom and the Japanese law applied, creating the issue of conflict of laws.[86]

Why did the Japanese hold off a wholesale imposition of Japanese laws in Korea? The main reason appears that the Japanese were mindful that radical changes would risk a total or partial failure of the new colonial legal order. Compliance with laws depended on the subjects being persuaded that the new laws were broadly acceptable to them. In Japan, the old civil code drafted by Boissonade had been rejected in 1892 on the grounds that it failed to reflect Japanese tradition and customs. One can speculate that Japan's officially professed respect for tradition deterred in part the policymakers from imposing Japanese civil law in matters directly related to Korean identity. The prevailing trends of Japanese legal science, especially the influence from the German Historical School, also seem to have played a role.

Under the new ordinance, the civil code, civil procedure, commercial law, and others took effect in Korea through the medium of the governor general's *seirei* power. As stated earlier, this cumbersome system affirmed the autonomous authority of the colonial governor. The recognition of custom as a source of law crucially upheld the claim of independent colonial administration. The political nature of customary law is manifest from the statements of colonial officials. Hara Masakane, the director of the law department, stated in 1921: "custom is a kind of legal system which has very delicate operations and significant values." The intent of Article 11 of the Civil Ordinance was "not to respect old customs and follow them as unchangeable, fixed rules" but to use them as an instrument to "make changes according to the progress and development of society."[87] The advantages of customary law in attempting the assimilation of Koreans were obvious.

The judicial process concerning custom was complicated. When cases were brought to the court under Articles 10 through 12 of the Civil Ordinance, the judges had to find the custom, ascertain its content, and decide whether to apply or reject it on a case-by-case basis. Chosŏn Korea did not have an official collection of custom, and the best available reference material for the

[86] Asano, *Teikoku Nihon*, 327, note 109. This question is discussed in detail later.

[87] Hara Masakane, "Minjirei kaitei shushi [The Key Points of the Revision of the *Minjirei*]," *Chōsen* 82 (December 1921), 55–56.

judges was the customs survey reports that had been compiled by Ume a few years earlier. There were a few cases between 1908 and 1910 in which the courts summoned "experts" to inquire about custom, but all available evidence shows this practice did not survive into the colonial period.[88] When the judges were in doubt about the legal relations in old customs, they sent inquiries to the executive authorities of the colonial government. The law director and the civil administrator in the government general issued administrative notices and bulletins (*t'ongch'ŏp*) and also sent out replies (*hoedap*) to inquiries from the courts or local administrative agencies as to the specific content of customs.[89] Both replies and notices constituted the colonial government's official position. They were normally followed by the courts, although occasionally the Kōtō Hōin, the High Court, distinguished its decisions from the governmental advice.

The courts were required to report to the governor general any disputes regarding family and succession matters.[90] There were systematic efforts to coordinate institutional reviews of customs. Special commissions were established "in order to review the customs and decide whether or not to adopt them."[91] In 1918, the Review Committee for Old Customs was established, composed of several judges and officials of the government general, to review the customs and to recommend their applicability as law.[92] A semi-independent association of jurists, *Chōsen Shihō Kyōkai*, was established in 1921. Its members included judges, prosecutors, and officials of the law bureau, and its chairman was the chief judge of the High Court. Its office was located in the High Court. The association discussed and reviewed customs and published the results in its journal *Chōsen shihō kyōkai zasshi*. The journal, published monthly between 1922 and 1945, functioned as both the official bulletin of the government general's legal policy and a research journal for jurists in Japan and Korea, playing a critical role in the shaping of colonial jurisprudence and doctrine.[93]

88 Mun Chun-yŏng, "Hanmal ŭi minsa punjaeng kwa singminji sabŏp kwŏllok: kwansŭp e kwanhan chaep'an rye rŭl chungsim ŭro [Civil Disputes and Colonial Judicial Power in Late Chosŏn: Focusing on Litigation concerning Custom]," *Pusan Taehakkyo pŏphak yŏngu* 52, no. 4 (2011), 243.

89 Chōsen Sōtokufu Chūsūin, ed., *Minji kanshū kaitō ishū* [The Compilation of Replies regarding Civil Custom] (Seoul, 1933).

90 See the notices from the Law Department, *Shihō kyōkai zasshi* 2, no. 8 (1923): 24–25; *Shihō kyōkai zasshi* 6, no. 7 (1927), 23.

91 Chōsen Sōtokufu Chūsūin, ed. *Chōsen kyūkan seido chōsa jigyō gaiyō*, 74.

92 The Review Committee for Old Customs was replaced by the Investigation Committee for the Old Customs and Their System in 1921. The latter's resolutions were compiled in Chōsen Sōtokufu Chūsūin, ed., *Minji kanshū kaitō ishū*, Appendix.

93 Chŏng Kŭng-sik and Ch'ang-min, eds. *Singminji gi sabŏp kwallyŏn charyo: Chosŏn Sabŏp Hyŏphoe chapchi ŭi punsŏk* [Materials Related to the Administration of Justice during the Colonial Period: Analysis of the Journal of the Jurist Association] (Seoul: Hanguk Pŏpche Yŏnguwŏn, 2004).

The Household Record Association, established with the goal of creating an official family registration system, also reviewed the content and the scope of customs in family and succession matters and issued resolutions. In addition, the Chosŏn High Court Judgment Investigation Committee studied court decisions based on custom and sought to reconcile discrepancies. In this way, the civil custom of Korea was defined and manufactured by Japanese jurists. There was not much of a sense that custom constituted the will of the people. The requirement for custom of *opinio necessitatis* – the conviction among the local population that a certain practice is binding – was supplied not by popular consent but by institutional procedures through the resolutions of the government-appointed judicial commissions.[94]

The need to abstract the substance of custom from various usages and to formulate it in modern legal terminology posed serious problems. Most legal terms had already been concocted by Japanese jurists using Chinese characters, which could be used in Korea. Still, there were Korean practices that had no equivalents in Japan, for example, ritual succession. Contradictory replies and resolutions were frequent, creating difficulty and confusion for the judges. Understandably, lawyers and judges called for a more stable basis of law, a written body of customary rules, on which they could base their arguments and decisions. In October 1917, the government general solicited some leading jurists' opinions regarding the implementation of custom. The judges overwhelmingly favored the codification of Korean customary law on personal capacity, family, and succession matters.[95] The idea of writing a systematic customary law text seems to have been given serious consideration by the colonial officials. But the authorities in Tokyo objected to it because it conflicted with the Japanese policy of unifying the legal systems of Japan and Korea.

The Politics of Customary Law

The evolution of the customary law policy should be viewed in terms of negotiations over different presumptions and interests between the colonial and metropolitan officials. The government general and the Japanese cabinet seemed to have a different priority. Colonial administrators considered it imprudent to interfere immediately with the private law of the native population. According to them, it was necessary to respect customs and traditions of the Korean society, preserving them as much as possible and implementing changes, when necessary, gradually. They argued that Korean customs needed to be steadily brought into line with Japanese law, without being totally abolished. The officials identified efficient colonial management with a successful customary law regime; they perceived customary law, with its fluid nature, as a tool with which they could mold Korean society toward a desired goal. The metropolitan government on the other hand was less concerned with the local

[94] See Chapter 1.

[95] Chōsen Sōtokufu Chūsūin, Shihōkan kaigi shimon jikō tōshinsho [Report of the Advisory Opinions for the Jurist Conference] (1917), cited from Yi Sŭng-il, *Chosŏn Ch'ongdokpu ŭi pŏpche chŏngch'aek*, 158.

situations, keen instead on achieving the integration of the colonial legal system into the Japanese system.

The customary law order was doused with political considerations. For the colonial government, wary of Tokyo's encroachment in colonial matters, the importance of a legal system based on Korean custom was substantial. Recognition of Korean customs as a source of law supported its claim of autonomous legislative and administrative authorities necessary for implementing customs. The situation was reminiscent of European colonies in Africa, where the unfamiliarity of indigenous custom was often presented by colonial administrators as a justification for their autonomous rule.[96] The "peculiarity" of Korean society was the colonial government's raison d'être. Emphasis on the uniqueness of Korean customs bolstered the argument that local officials, not policymakers in Tokyo, should decide the legal matters in the colony. The government general believed that the unifications of laws should take place through the gradual process of customary codification and also through jurisprudence, both taking place under its firm control. In this light, it would have been surprising if the colonial officials had not exaggerated the importance of Korean customs.

Various statements of the colonial officials evince the government general's reluctance toward the drastic imposition of Japanese laws. Kokubu, the director of the Law Department, argued in 1915:

> Korea is different from Japan in customs, mores, people's emotion, and many other aspects, and imposing the same law as the *naichi* is out of the question. In particular, Korea is at a juncture of changes in every aspect and is ever in need of new systems. If we abolish the system of delegated legislation all of sudden and subject Korea to the control of the *naichi* legislature, one risks losing crucial momentum and the delicate balance that has so far been maintained in colonial affairs will be destroyed, causing much inconvenience. In short, the movement to unify laws is untimely, and so is the movement to unify legal systems.[97]

Governor General Hasegawa Yoshimichi (1850–1924; governor general of Korea 1916–1919) stated: "[Koreans] have thousands of years of history and traditional national characteristics. Even if we were similar people using the same language, achieving assimilation overnight by imposing new law would be impossible. Therefore, we pursue assimilation as the main governing principle but it is a principle of gradualism, not destruction."[98]

The goal of colonial legal policy was integration. Integration, as advocated by the colonial administrators, was different from unification in that it purported to create a legal order which could bring together laws of different

[96] See Brett L. Shadle, "'Changing Traditions to Meet Current Altering Conditions': Customary Law, African Courts and the Rejection of Codification in Kenya, 1930–60," *Journal of African History* 40 (1999): 411–431. See Chapter 7.

[97] Kokubu, "Shihō seido tōitsu ron ni tsuite," 478–480.

[98] *Saito Makoto Monjo: Chōsen Sōtoku jidai kankei shiryō* (Seoul: Koryŏ Sŏrim, 1999), vol. 1, 331–335; see Yi Sŭng-il, *Chosŏn Ch'ongdokpu ŭi pŏpche chŏngch'aek*, 203.

origins instead of imposing a uniform law. The government general was understandably concerned that abrupt changes in law would create serious opposition from the Korean people. For instance, there was discussion from the early 1920s to revise the *Minjirei* to introduce the Japanese law of allowing adoption of a son-in-law. The legalization of the adoption of a son-in-law, patently against the Korean practice, was a potentially explosive issue. Eventually, the government general postponed the measure as it concluded that "rejecting old customs and implementing a new system [of adoption] would surely damage [Korean] sentiment."[99] Yet the ultimate goal of integration stood unchanged. The chief justice of the High Court, Yokota Gorō, who had also been Kokubu's successor as the law director, stated in 1923: "It is necessary to respect special customs of Korea; it is also necessary to pay attention to the changes of customs in order to promote unification with the Japanese laws."[100] In 1924, Matsudera Takeo, who succeeded Yokota as the highest law official in the colonial government, argued: "It is wrong to adhere to customs simply because they are old customs. It is necessary to observe and systematize them in order to make sure that they conform to the present situations before deciding whether or not to adopt them."[101]

Revisions of the Civil Ordinance

The scope of Korean custom to govern family and succession matters under Article 11 of the Civil Ordinance gradually diminished over time. In Taiwan, its Civil Ordinance was revised so that from January 1, 1923, Japanese civil law came to apply in principle to the Taiwanese.[102] In practice, only a few family and succession provisions in the Japanese Civil Code were imposed on the Taiwanese, but the change still constituted a fundamental modification of the customary law order.[103] In Korea, piecemeal revisions of Article 11 of the Civil Ordinance were introduced, each revision expanding the areas to be governed by Japanese civil law provisions instead of custom. The application of Japanese civil law was still limited to enumerated areas and the main language of Article 11 in the Civil Ordinance that "matters [regarding family and succession matters] involving Koreans are decided according to [Korean] custom" did not change until 1945. But continuous additions to the exceptions to this rule significantly reduced the operation of Korean custom.

Hyŏngpŏp taejŏn, the last Korean code issued in 1905, included certain regulations on family relations. For example, Article 62 regulated family relation degrees; Articles 572 through 574 prohibited marriage between those of the same surname and place of origin; and Articles 578 through 581 stipulated that a wife cannot demand divorce. These civil matter provisions were

[99] *Maeil Sinbo*, May 22, 1921.
[100] *Shihō kyōkai zasshi* 2, no. 5 (1923), 37.
[101] Ibid., 25.
[102] Ordinance Number 406 of 1922. See Wang, *Legal Reform in Taiwan*, 55; 145–146.
[103] Imperial Ordinances Numbers 406 and 407. See Asano, *Teikoku Nihon*, 92–92; Wang, *Legal Reform in Taiwan*, 55.

officially deleted from *Hyŏngpŏp taejŏn* in 1908, but were still recognized as Korean custom in the meaning of Article 11 of the Civil Ordinance.[104] The revisions of the Civil Ordinance changed this situation.

Revisions of Article 11 reflected the colonial officials' appraisal of the changes in Korean society and, above all, the supposed level of tolerance – the level of anticipated resistance – by the Korean populace toward Japanese laws. The first revision, issued on November 14, 1921 (*Seirei* Number 14), adopted the Japanese Civil Code provisions on parental rights, guardianship, assistantship, and clan association established for the legally incompetent person; these matters were no longer governed by Korean custom.[105] It was soon followed by another revision on December 7, 1922 (*Seirei* Number 3), to take effect in July 1923. This revision coincided with the promulgation of the Regulation of the Chosŏn Family Registration (*Chosŏn Hojŏngnyŏng*) in December 1922.[106] The Regulation of the Chosŏn Family Registration (*Seirei* Number 154) required that Koreans be registered in the Korean family registry. The system of family registration, recording birth, death, marriage, adoption, division and revival of a family, has become the most fundamental family and individual record of identity. The 1922 revision of the Civil Ordinance mandated that the civil code provisions apply to minimum ages for marriage, divorce by trial, acknowledgment, approval of succession, and division of property. Registration was required for the establishment of a collateral family, the closing and the reestablishment of a discontinued family, divorce by consent, adoption, and dissolution of adoptive relationship by agreement.[107] Needless to say, these changes expanded the state's regulation of population. Divorce by consent and divorce by trial that had not existed in Korean law began to be allowed by court decisions.

On November 10, 1939, the last revision of the Chosŏn Civil Ordinance before 1945 took place as *Seirei* Number 19. Article 11 was revised to allow non-agnatic adoption. The traditional prohibition of adoption between different surnames was abolished and the adoption of a son-in-law was allowed. The prohibition of marriage between the persons of the same surname and place of origin was also nullified. These changes of customs that were fundamental to Korean society reflected a shift in the Japanese government's policy direction toward the unification of Korean and Japanese laws and, further, cultural assimilation.[108] The same day, the Decree Limiting the Selection and Change of Family Name was issued, introducing the Japanese-style house system. The

104 See Yi Pyŏng-su, "Chosŏn minsaryŏng e kwanhayŏ: che sibilcho ŭi kwansŭp ŭl chungsim ŭro" [A Study of the Chosŏn Civil Ordinance: With Particular Attention to Custom in Article 11]," *Pŏpsahak yŏngu* 4 (1977): 649–676.

105 For the texts of these revisions, see Appendix B.

106 Nomura Chōtarō, *Chōsen koseki rei gikai* [Interpretation of the Regulation of Chosŏn Household Registration] (Tokyo: Ganshōdō Shoten, 1925), 12.

107 Chŏng Kwang-hyŏn, *Hanguk kajok pŏp yŏngu* [A Study of Korean Family Law] (Seoul: Seoul Taehakkyo Ch'ulp'anbu, 1967), 22.

108 For the text of the provision, see Appendix B.

adoption of the Japanized form of Korean surnames was encouraged. The Regulation of Chosŏn Family Registration was revised in December. These changes modified the very heart of Korean family institutions, to be reshaped thenceforth by Japanese civil law.

After the adoption of a son-in-law was legalized, Iwashima Hajime, the head of the civil section in the Law Department, asserted that "the system of the son-in-law adoption was established to meet natural human need" and that it was "not any formalistic attempt to unify the Korean system with the Japanese system."[109] It was a statement made to assuage Korean resistance to the new system, which was a dramatic departure from Korea's custom. But one can also get a glimpse of the colonial officials' resistance to the unification of the Japanese and Korean legal systems. The government general had political reason wanting to take a gradual approach to legal unity. The traditional view that the Japanese legal policy in Korea was pursued in full harmony between the Tokyo government and the colonial administration, with a monolithic goal of forced unification of Korean and Japanese laws and cultures, needs reconsideration.

Conflict of Laws in the Colonial Empire: The Coordination Law System

The customary law regime shows that the formulation of the legal structure of the Japanese colonial empire was a result of complex political and constitutional compromises. Despite the avowed ideal of integration, Japan, Korea, Taiwan, and other territories each formed a separate jurisdiction governed by different laws and customs, the legal effect of which extended only within that jurisdiction. The principle of delegated legislative power, dating from Law Number 63 of 1896, resulted in the creation of the separate legal jurisdictions in the empire, in which each colony and Japan proper formed an independent legal territory (*hōchiiki*), commensurate to a quasi-sovereign entity. As seen previously, the acts of the Diet could be implemented in Korea only through the imperial or the colonial governor's decrees. The goal of assimilation seemed compromised by the dictates of colonial management. The need for a law to coordinate legal matters among different regions in the empire emerged as an urgent issue, especially after the annexation of Korea.[110] What was needed was a body of interregional law of conflict, or quasi-private international law, that would govern legal relations between persons subject to different legal regimes within the Japanese imperial system.[111]

[109] Iwashima Hajime, "Chōsen minjirei ni okeru hi ni tsuite [On the Adoption of a Son-in-Law in the Chosŏn *Minjirei*]" (Part 1), *Koseki* 1, no. 1 (1941), 18, cited inYi Sŭng-il, *Chosŏn Ch'ongdokpu ŭi pŏpche chŏngch'aek*, 308–309.

[110] For a recent in-depth treatment of the legal structure of the Japanese colonial empire, especially the conflict of laws, see Asano, *Teikoku Nihon*, 347–364. See also Matsuoka, "Gaichihō," 12; Yamada Saburō, "Kyōtsūhō an ni tsuite [On the Bill of Kyōtsūhō]," *Hōgaku kyōkai zasshi* 36 (1918), no. 4 (Part 1): 66–69, and no. 6 (Part 2): 82–84; Sanekata Masao, *Kyōtsūhō* (Tokyo: Nihon Hyōronsha, 1939), 14–15; Yi Sŭng-il, *Chosŏn Ch'ongdokpu ŭi pŏpche chŏngch'aek*, 152–155.

[111] For conflict of law in European colonies, see A. Arthur Schiller, "Conflict of Laws in Indonesia," *The Far Eastern Quarterly* 2, no. 1 (1942): 31–47.

Territorial Law versus Personal Law

In the early colonial years, the Japanese refrained from using the term "colony" (*shokuminchi*). They simply used the term *chiiki* (territories), as distinguished from *naichi*, and each territory was identified by its own name – Chosŏn or Taiwan.[112] It was not until the end of the 1920s, coinciding with the establishment of the Ministry of Colonial Affairs in 1929, the term *gaichi* began to be used, as a counterpart to *naichi*.[113] The dominant opinion among scholars was that law in the colonies, where the ethnic Japanese coexisted with the natives, should be different from the *naichi* law based on the territoriality principle.[114]

The *gaichi* were distinguished from the *naichi* in two aspects. First, the *naichi* referred to areas in which law enacted through the regular legislative process applied; *gaichi* referred to the areas governed by delegated legislative authority. *Gaichi* was a territory into which the *naichi* should "extend" in principle, but in fact it reflected Japan's policy acknowledging the existence of separate legal jurisdictions (*hōiki*) within its empire.[115] Secondly, the *naichi* was governed by territorial law, whereas each colony was governed by a system which was territorial in principle but to which rules of personal status were added. Koreans, the Taiwanese, and the Japanese were all imperial subjects, but they were each governed by their own local civil status regulations. The colonized were distinguished from the Japanese according to the family status registry (*hojŏk; koseki* in Japanese) on the basis of which customs were applied to the natives. Prior to annexation, Chosŏn Korea maintained the civil status registry. The first modern census act was issued in 1909. After annexation, the colonial government imposed the *Chosŏn Minjŏngnyŏng* (Chosŏn Civil Status Regulation) in 1915, requiring ethnic Koreans to be entered in the colonial civil status register. It was replaced with the Family status register in 1922.[116] Japanese people by birth were enrolled in the Japanese civil status register, according to the Law on Nationality of 1899. On the basis of civil status, Koreans were governed by custom in the matters enumerated in Articles 10 through 12 of the Civil Ordinance.

In the Japanese colonial empire, the colonized people were imperial subjects but they were under separate treatment. Yamada Saburō (1869–1965),

[112] Matsuoka stated that the Japanese used the term "territories," because the Korean people did not like being called "*shokuminchi*." Matsuoka Shutarō, *Chōsen gyōseihō teiyō* [A Summary of the Administrative Law of Chosŏn] (Seoul: Tōto Shoseki Keijō Shiten, 1944), 5; Matsuoka, "Gaichihō," 6–7.

[113] Hirano, "Nihon tōchi ka no Chōsen no hōteki chii," 57; Kiyomiya, *Gaichihō josetsu*, 16.

[114] Asano, *Teikoku Nihon*, 296.

[115] Yamazaki, *Gaichi tōchi kikō*, 1.

[116] For the household registration system, see Yi Sŭng-il, "Chosŏn hojŏngnyŏng chejŏng e kwanhan yŏngu [A Study of the Establishment of the Chosŏn Hojŏngnyŏng]," *Pŏpsahak yŏngu* 32 (2005): 37–68; Yi Sŭng-il, "Ilche sigi Chosŏn in ŭi Ilbon kungmin hwa yŏngu: hojŏk chedo rŭl chumsim ŭro [A Study on Turning Koreans into Japanese Nationals during the Japanese Imperial Period: With Particular Attention to the Establishment of the Household Registration System]," *Hangukhak nŏnjip* 34 (2000): 67–115.

professor of international private law at Tokyo Imperial University and later the president of Keijō Imperial University in Seoul from 1931 to 1936, opined in July 1910 that Koreans would obtain the Japanese nationality by annexation but it did not mean that Koreans and Japanese were of the same status; it only meant that Koreans were Japanese nationals in the relations with the foreign nations.[117] The Civil Ordinance system applied the Japanese Civil Code as territorial law but inserted the personality law principle, securing the separation between the Japanese and colonial subjects. According to Asano Toyomi, the customary law order in the Japanese empire was a continuation of the earlier consular jurisdiction system. The revision of unequal treaties in Taiwan and Korea, argued Asano, led them closer to the nation-state international order but the resulting system solidly encapsulated them within the imperial order. Within each Japanese colonial territory, the *naichijin*, the *gaichijin*, and the foreigner coexisted under personality law.[118] At the same time, legal relations between the *naichi* and each overseas territory, as well as the relations between the overseas territories, were governed by separate territorial laws. In this double framework, Japanese residents in the *naichi* and in the overseas territories had different rights and duties. For instance, the election law was not extended outside the *naichi* and the Japanese residents in the colonies were not granted political franchise.[119]

In European colonies, conflict of laws involved the determination of what body of legal rules applied in interracial and interlocal laws. The Japanese colonies faced slightly different issues because the conflict of law problems arose on the imperial level by the existence of separate legal jurisdictions which could not be addressed by either private international law or national law. Inherent contradictions and exasperating complexity abounded. There was no legal mechanism to determine the rights or obligations arising from transactions between individuals in different territories. Most laws that the colonial courts applied were not legislative enactments but executive orders issued by the colonial governors. Since these ordinances took effect in Korea not as statutes (*hōritsu*) but as cabinet orders (*seirei*), juristic acts performed in Korea under the Japanese civil law had no legal force in Japan, not to mention any territories outside Korea. The legal effect of Japanese laws that were incorporated by reference in the decrees was limited to Korea, regardless of the fact that their contents were the same in other overseas territories.

The judicial structure in each colony was independent from the judiciary of Japan or the judiciaries in other territories. The decisions rendered on the basis of the Japanese Civil Code provisions were not recognized in jurisdictions outside the original jurisdiction that rendered the decision.[120] The effects of the

[117] Yamada Saburō, "1910 nen 7 gatsu 15 nichi: heigō ato ni kansuru Kankoku jin no kokuseki mondai [July 15, 1910: The Question of the Nationality of Koreans Following Annexation]," *Terauchi Masatake Monjo*, cited in Yi Sŭng-il, *Chosŏn Ch'ongdokpu pŏpche chŏngch'aek*, 94.

[118] Asano, *Teikoku Nihon*, 21.

[119] See Matsuoka, "Gaichihō."

[120] Ibid., 47.

judicial decisions ended at the borders of each colony.[121] There was no legal basis for reciprocal recognition of judicial rulings throughout the empire. The courts in Korea, created through the colonial governor's executive order, had no ties with the courts in Japan. As noted previously, no appeals of the colonial cases were allowed to the Daishinin, and Korean courts were not bound by the legal interpretations of the Daishinin. This system inevitably impeded consistency in the interpretations of laws within the empire. Suzuki Sōgen, chief judge at the appellate court in Taiwan, claimed in 1905 that, since the constitution was in effect in Taiwan, the colonial governor's *ritsurei* and court decisions had legal effect throughout the empire. But his argument was little heeded.[122]

The situation was even more complicated when consular courts were involved. Japan's consular courts were part of the *naichi* judicial system. According to Law Number 70 of 1899, Law regarding the Affairs of the Consulate, appeals from consular courts were heard at the Nagasaki District Court and Nagasaki Appeals Court. But it was often preferred to send the appeals to nearby colonial courts instead of Nagasaki because of the economy of time and money. Starting in 1922, consular cases in Manchuria were sent to Kanto shū (Kwantung peninsula) colonial courts, Gando cases to the residency general courts and later government general courts in Korea, and cases from southern China to the colonial courts in Taiwan.[123] But colonial courts' appellate jurisdiction over consular courts raised a problem because consular courts were governed by the *naichi* law whereas colonial courts were governed by the executive orders of colonial governors.

There had been efforts to facilitate cooperation between different jurisdictions and create a coherent legal network throughout the expanding empire. In March 1908, the Diet discussed a bill that would grant a judgment

[121] A crime committed in one jurisdiction could not be punished in another jurisdiction, despite the fact that the Japanese criminal law was in force in all the territories. When a criminal fled one jurisdiction to another, the second jurisdiction had no authority to arrest him. A territory could not accord the judgment of a court in another territory the legal force to which it was entitled. When someone who had a prior record commited a crime in other jurisdiction, for example, it was impossible to punish him for repeated offenses. Tanaka, "Teikoku Nihon no shihō rensa."

[122] Suzuki Sōgen, "Naichi oyobi Taiwan aida ni okeru hōritsu ritsurei no kōryoku ni tsuite [On the Effects of Laws and *Ritsurei* between *Naichi* and Taiwan]," *Hōgaku kyōkai zasshi* 23, no. 4 (1905): 533–534.

[123] The prosecution and the trial of An Chung-kŭn, the Korean patriot who assassinated Itō Hirobumi in the railway station in Harbin in November 1909, exemplify the jurisdictional maze in the Japanese colonial empire. An was arrested by the Russian officials in Eastern Qing Railway Annexed territory, which was the Russian administrative area within the Chinese territory. In pursuance of the Korea-Chinese Treaty signed in 1899, Korea enjoyed extraterritoriality in China. But the Korea-Japan Treaty signed in 1905 provided that Japan's diplomatic representatives and consuls protected the Korean people and their interest against foreign countries. Thus An was transferred to the Japanese consulate in Harbin that had jurisdiction over the area where his arrest took place. Subsequently, in accordance with the "Law Concerning Consular Adjudication in Manchuria," An's trial was held at the Kanto shū court and he was executed in Lushun. See Tanaka, "Teikoku Nihon no shihō rensa," 73.

rendered in a territory the same effect throughout the empire, but the bill was abandoned. The following year, another bill was proposed to allow appeals from the appellate courts in Taiwan to Daishinin and to confer the same effects on decisions by Japanese and Taiwanese courts, but it also failed.[124] In 1911, the Law on Coordination of Judicial Administration (Law Number 52) was enacted to promote communications between the colonies regarding warrants and crime investigation, in particular cooperation between consular courts and ordinary courts in both the *naichi* and the *gaichi*. But these arrangements aimed only at promoting coordination of judicial administration; still a Japanese court did not have jurisdiction over a crime or a legal act in another jurisdiction. The courts in each jurisdiction remained completely separated.

Serious difficulties arose from the enforcement of native customs in the colonies. For instance, the judgments of colonial courts concerning legal capacity, such as incorporation or incompetency, were not recognized in Japan because they were decided based on custom. In Korea, the legal capacity issue was governed by custom under Article 11 of the Civil Ordinance, until the revision of the ordinance in 1921 placed it under the control of the Japanese Civil Code.[125] Before 1921, a Korean company incorporated in the peninsula was not regarded as a legal entity in Japan and it was impossible to move the headquarters or merge with the companies outside Korea. A foreign corporation was recognized in Japan just like a Japanese corporation, but corporations formed in the colonies were neither foreign nor Japanese companies.[126]

The most serious problems involved family law issues. The Japanese and the Koreans had a distinct civil status and transfer between the categories of civil status was strictly forbidden. As contacts between Koreans and Japanese increased, questions arising from marriage, divorce, acknowledgment, and adoption between different population groups posed myriad problems. It was far from clear, for example, under which law the marriage or divorce proceedings of a Japanese female who married a Korean male in Japan would be heard.[127] Other complicated problems ensued. When a Korean female entered the *naichi* house through marriage, her Korean record was allowed to be expunged. When a Korean male entered the Japanese house through adoption or adoption of a son-in-law, however, his family record in Korea was not allowed to be removed.

[124] Mun, "Cheguk Ilbon ŭi singminji hyŏng sabŏp chedo," 224–226.

[125] Kokubu Sangai, "Kyōtsūhō ni tsuite [On Kyōtsūhō]," *Chōsen ihō* (June 1918), 9–10.

[126] Yamada Saburō, " Kyōtsūhō an ni tsuite," 68–70; Yi Sŭng-il, *Chosŏn Ch'ongdokpu ŭi pŏpche chŏngch'aek*, 145.

[127] Unlike the common perception, the government general did not prohibit or discourage marriage between Koreans and Japanese. On the contrary, intermarriage was perceived by colonial officials as a means to promote assimilation between the people. Kokubu, "Sōtoku shisei no hōshin." Saito Makoto openly encouraged intermarriage. See Yi Sŭng-il, *Chosŏn Ch'ongdokpu ŭi pŏpche chŏngch'aek*, 163–165. Early on, the colonial government ordered that marriage between a Korean male and a Japanese female be processed like marriage among Koreans.

This incongruent policy was intended to disallow Korean males to become Japanese citizens.[128] On the other hand, the Japanese wife of a Korean male was enrolled on the Korean husband's family record. The problem was that her existing record on the Japanese registry continued to exist. The government general had no control over the Japanese household registry law so there was no means to avoid her being listed on both registries, holding two civil statuses. It was perfectly legal for a Japanese female who married a Korean in Korea to return to Japan and marry another, since her marriage in Korea, governed by Korean custom, had no legal effect in Japan. When a child born out of wedlock from a Japanese mother was acknowledged by the Korean father, the child entered the Korean household and was registered as the latter's secondary son, but he or she was regarded as an illegitimate child in Japan.[129] It was an understatement that a law was needed to resolve these and other irregular situations.

On April 17, 1918, the Coordination Law (Law Number 39) was enacted with the aim to strike a balance between the management of separate legal jurisdictions and the coordination between them. The law, *Kyōtsūhō*, took effect on June 1, 1918 (except Article 3 which took effect in July 1, 1921), and established a common legal order covering legal territories, modifying the existing separate jurisdiction system that confined the authority of the courts within the boundaries of the territories.[130]

Article 1 defined the "territory" (*chiiki*) to be covered in this law to the *naichi*, Chosŏn, Taiwan, Kantōshū, and Nanyō (South Sea islands). The subsequent articles dealt with civil matters (Articles 2 through 12) and criminal matters (Articles 13 through 19). The provisions can be divided into two kinds: those dealing with the conflict of laws, namely the choice of law; and those dealing with the coordination of laws, namely the reciprocity of law. Article 2 provided that, when a territory decided to apply laws and regulations of other territories, those laws and regulations would apply in each territory. It also stipulated that the provisions of Japanese law regarding conflict of law, as provided in the Law on the General Rules of the Application of Law (*Hōrei*), would apply in the territories with necessary changes and that, in this case, laws and regulations applicable in the region to which either party belonged would be regarded as sovereign laws of the region. These provisions made it possible that the effect of legal acts performed under the provisions of the Diet-enacted laws extended to other territories across the boundaries of the colonies.[131]

Article 11 of *Kyōtsūhō* provided that "decisions in litigation or non-litigation matters in a territory would have the same legal effects in other territories." Through this provision, the courts in Japan, Taiwan, Korea, the Kwangtung

[128] Yi Sŭng-il, *Chosŏn Ch'ongdokpu ŭi pŏpche chŏngch'aek*, 149–150.

[129] Kokubu, "Kyōtsūhō ni tsuite," 9–10; Yi Sŭng-il, *Chosŏn Ch'ongdokpu ŭi pŏpche chŏngch'aek*, 151.

[130] Issued as Law Number 39 on April 17, 1918. For the text of selected provisions of the law, see Appendix B.

[131] Article 4 stipulated that a legal corporation established in a territory be recognized in other territories.

peninsula, and Nanyō were required to confer on the judgment of courts in other territories the same effect that the judgment would have in the original jurisdiction. In criminal matters, the common application of Japan's criminal laws across different jurisdictions now made it possible to punish in a third territory the crime committed in a territory (Article 13).[132] The criminal law provisions of the Coordination Law were prompted in particular by the need for the Japanese authorities to prosecute efficiently Korean nationalist movement cases, especially in the Gando region.[133] Since Japan enjoyed extraterritoriality in China, cases subject to consular jurisdiction in China could now be prosecuted and punished under Japanese law by colonial courts. The decisions of the colonial courts in Korea following the promulgation of the Coordination Law demonstrated how these provisions were interpreted in Korea. Less than a month after the law went into effect, the High Court declared: "a convict with a prior conviction record in the consular court can be punished in Korea under the repeated offense provisions."[134] The court also wrote that, since Japan maintained consular jurisdiction in China, territories in China were treated the same as the *naichi* under the operation of the Kyōtsūhō.[135]

Article 3 of the Coordination Law recognized the legal effect of marriages and adoptions between peoples from different territories throughout the empire. It provided:

> A person who enters a family in a region under the law of the region shall withdraw from a family in another region. A person who may not withdraw from a family in a region under the law of the region may not enter a family in another region.

A Japanese citizen who joined a Korean household through marriage or adoption was now allowed to register in the Korean family register and to have his or her record removed from the Japanese civil status register. In other words, a person could now move across jurisdictional boundaries, unless prohibited by law or ordinance.[136]

The significance of the Coordination Law was considerable. The law provided a solution for the interregional conflict of law problems arising from the existence of multiple jurisdictions. Still, complex legal problems

[132] Article 14: In criminal matters, when a territory provides application of another territory's laws, each territory applies another territory's laws – application of criminal laws across different jurisdictions.

[133] Tanaka, "Teikoku Nihon," 72–75.

[134] Judgment of June 29, 1918. *Chōsen Kōtō Hōin hanrei yōshi ruishū* [Summary Reports of the Decisions of Chōsen Kōtō Hōin] (Seoul: Shihō Kyōkai, 1937), 1072.

[135] Judgment of August 26, 1920, *Chōsen Kōtō Hōin hanrei yōshi ruishū*, 1073.

[136] The government general of Korea had already been preparing the revision of *Chōsen Minjirei* when the Coordination Law was promulgated in 1918. The Investigative Commission for the Revision of Korean Civil Ordinance and Civil Record Regulation was established in January 1918. The main objective of the commission, composed of current or former judges, was to prepare for the systematization of official family registration system by revising the existing civil record system. Yi Sŭng-il, *Chosŏn Ch'ongdokpu ŭi pŏpche chŏngch'aek*, 160.

originating from the existence of the customary law order abounded. Korean custom recognized in the Civil Ordinance came to take effect under the scope of the conflict of laws provided in the *Hōrei*. *Hōrei* (Law Number 10) was a Japanese law promulgated on July 16, 1898, the last date set for notifying the Western powers of the completion of the treaty revision preparations.[137] The law was an enactment providing the principles of private international law – that is, rules of procedures in legal communications between Japan and foreign countries. This law was enforced in Korea by Imperial Ordinance Number 21 on March 28, 1911. The Coordination Law (Article 2, Section 2) stipulated that a legal act was governed by the *Hōrei*; under the *Hōrei* the law of the place where the legal act took place controlled. For example, an act relating to personal status that took place in Korea between a Korean and a Japanese (or foreigner) was governed by Korean custom. This was different from cases in Taiwan where the restriction of the "among the Taiwanese or the Chinese only" provision in Taiwan's Civil Ordinance triggered the application of Japanese civil law.[138]

The complex interplay of all these different laws – the conflict of laws – is witnessed in several postwar cases decided by the Japanese Supreme Court. These cases illustrate how the customary law order in the Japanese colonial empire operated in practice. The two cases examined here dealt with the effect of the *Hōrei* and the Coordination Law on Korean custom.[139] The first case, decided in 1998, involved a child who was born out of wedlock in 1948 to a Japanese mother and was acknowledged by the Korean father. The issue was whether the child subsequently lost Japanese citizenship on the signing of the Peace Treaty of 1950 because she had been entered in the Korean family register. At the time of the Peace Treaty, those who had been entered in Korean family registers under the Regulation of Korean Family Registration (1922) were regarded as having acquired Korean nationality and hence lost Japanese nationality. The pertinent issue here was how Korean custom came to govern the child's entry in Korean family register.

In 1948, Japanese laws including the Civil Ordinance were still in force in Korea. They continued to have legal force until they were replaced by the first Korean Civil Code that was promulgated in 1958 and enforced in 1960.[140] Under the Coordination Law, when an act was conducted between people who belonged to regions where different laws were in operation, the law applicable to the act needed to be determined in accordance with the *Hōrei*. In the present case, Korean custom was applicable to the Korean father under the *Hōrei*. Articles 1 and 11 of the Civil Ordinance provided that the Japanese Civil Code (Article 827, Section 2) governed the act of acknowledgment. Once

[137] See Chapter 3.

[138] Asano, *Teikoku Nihon*, 327 and note 109.

[139] Judgment of March 12, 1998, 1994 (Gyo-Tsu) Number 109, Minshu vol. 52, no. 2, at 342. See an analysis in Kawakami Hiroshi, "Saigo Saibansho hanrei minji kankei [Decisions of the Supreme Court of Cases Related to Civil Matters]," *Hōsō jihō* 53 (5) (2001): 1351–1387.

[140] See Chapter 8.

acknowledgment took place, however, the effect of the acknowledgment came under Korean custom. A child born to a Korean father and a native Japanese mother became a secondary child of the father through his acknowledgment. According to Korean custom, such a child still entered the Korean father's family.

Here, the court distinguished between the "act" of acknowledgment and the "effect" of acknowledgment. The civil code governed the act of acknowledgment, but the effect of that acknowledgment was governed by a law in force in Korea, because Korea was the region to which the acknowledging person (the father) belonged. From this construction of law, the Supreme Court of Japan found that the child entered the Korean household. She obtained Korean nationality and lost Japanese citizenship through the effectuation of the Peace Treaty.

This case can be contrasted with the second case decided in 2004, in which the Japanese Supreme Court seemingly reached an opposite conclusion.[141] Here, as in the 1998 case, a child was born out of wedlock to a native Japanese mother and a Korean father, and was acknowledged by the father. The difference from the previous case was that the acknowledgment took place on September 8, 1950, after the enforcement of the new Nationality Law on July 1, 1950, which replaced the old Nationality of 1899. Article 23 of the old Nationality Law had provided: "A Japanese child shall lose Japanese nationality when he has acquired foreign nationality due to acknowledgment." But the new Nationality Law had no provision pronouncing an act relating to the person's status, such as acknowledgment, as a cause of the loss of Japanese nationality.

The Court found that the effect of Article 3 of the Coordination Law did not apply to this case because the Coordination Law operated only in the context of the old Nationality Law. Here, unlike the first case, acknowledgment took place after the new Nationality Law of 1950 and therefore was not controlled by the Coordination Law. In accordance with the new Nationality Law, the Court reasoned, the child did not lose Japanese nationality by the acknowledgment, which was the father's unilateral declaration of intent. Therefore the child fell under the category of "a person who may not withdraw from a family in a region under the law of the region" set forth in Article 3, Section 2 of the Coordination Law and did not fall under the category of a person who was to enter a Korean family register. The Court concluded that the child therefore did not lose Japanese nationality despite the effectuation of the Peace Treaty.

These cases highlight the complexity abounding in legal constructions in the Japanese colonial empire. The *Kyōtsūhō* provided a basic instrument on the basis of which customary law orders were coordinated. It comprehensively redefined the empire's legal space by linking legal territories. Previously, the

[141] Judgment of July 8, 2004, 2000 (Gyo-Hi) no. 149, Minshu vol. 58, no. 5.

legal realms in the *naichi* and *gaichi* were disjointed, occupying two separate legal realms: the *naichi* was a territory in which Japanese civil and criminal laws rejected the personality principle; the *gaichi* was a territory in which the same principle was fully implemented. By lowering the boundaries of the personality jurisdictions in each colonial territory, the Coordination Law aimed to reconcile the two kinds of legal space. It amounted to a crucial step toward adopting the principle of a territorial nation-state as recognized in the international legal order while adjusting it to fit in the imperial legal order.[142] By freeing the empire's legal system from the structural obstacles based on separate jurisdictions, the Coordination Law promoted legal integration and orderly administration of the empire.

There were, however, certain limits in the Coordination Law's readjustment of the imperial legal order. Although it recognized the common effects of judicial decisions from various territories, it did not consolidate their judicial structures. The basic framework of separate jurisdictions remained intact. When a consular case was appealed to a colonial court, further appeals to the *naichi*'s Daishinin were impossible because colonial courts were not part of the judicial hierarchy in Japan. The Coordination Law was not aimed at unifying laws among the colonies; it simply extended the effect of the existing laws and orders by confirming legal reciprocity between different legal territories (jurisdictions). It did not change the internal legal order in the colonies and had no effect on the legal force of *seirei* or *ritsurei*. Addressing only civil and criminal laws, the Coordination law did not cover administrative law that either excluded the *gaichi* territorially, as in the law of political franchise, or excluded the *gaichijin* personally, as in the conscription law.

In principle, Japanese officials envisioned full integration of the empire. They emphasized the racial and cultural affinity between the Japanese and the Koreans. But assimilation as an imperial ideology was compromised from the outset by the creation of separate territories.[143] Japan viewed the coordination law as a temporary measure and emphasized the ultimate need for a full unification of legal jurisdictions. It was maintained that each territory formed a jurisdiction under Japan's territorial control, imperial power, and the constitution.[144] But the creation of the Coordination Law meant a de facto confirmation of the existence of independent jurisdictions. The colonial legal systems were based on custom; custom existed as law, transcending public and private law boundaries. In contrast, the metropolitan legal systems were based on the modern system where there was a division between public and private laws.

142 See Asano, *Teikoku Nihon*.

143 The Japanese policy has been characterized in terms of "differential incorporation" and "double-edged authenticity." Cheng-Yi Huang, "Enacting the 'Incomprehensible China': Modern European Jurisprudence and the Japanese Reconstruction of Qing Political Law," *Law & Society Inquiry* 33 (2008), 963 and 971.

144 Yamazaki, *Gaichi tōchi kikō*.

The government general of Korea welcomed the reciprocity law. According to Yamada, Governor Terauchi took the initiative in suggesting the need for a common law to the cabinet as early as 1911.[145] Kokubu Sangai testified that he pushed for the establishment of the law because he felt much inconvenience without it.[146] For colonial administrators and Japanese policymakers alike, the arrangement provided by the Coordination Law may have provided an acceptable solution – a compromise – in which the exigencies of colonial management on both the local and imperial levels could be met for the time being.

Taiwan, Japan, and Korea remained separate jurisdictions until the end of the colonial empire. The *naichi* extension policy that the Japanese government actively pursued after World War I was hemmed in by this fundamental handicap. The official policy of professed incorporation and integration of the colonies to Japan, but in practice a unified legal order in the empire was still a distant premise. Full legal assimilation and the extension of the Japanese legal system to the colony required the complete application of the constitution, a prospect neither most intellectuals nor politicians in Tokyo, not to mention colonial officials in Seoul, were ready to embrace.

While the pursuit of unification through legislation was deflected by various political forces and motives, legal integration proceeded through doctrinal elaboration and jurisprudential activities. Colonial officials called for the gradual introduction of modern legal principles in Korea. Jurisprudential reconciliation of Korean custom and provisions in the civil code was crucial in preparing the ground for the full imposition of the Japanese civil law on Koreans. Instead of being totally obliterated, Korean customs were thus steadily brought into line with Japanese ideas of law, justice, and procedure. The colonial government supported active jurisprudential activities in customary law.[147]

The colonial government was intent on preserving its sphere of influence when it emphasized the uniqueness of Korean customs. By doing so, it inadvertently supported the transformation of customs into civil law. The colonial authorities continued to apply Korean customs to legal relations between Koreans as long as they were not, in the estimation of the judges and officials who supervised judicial administration, against public order and good morals. In the colonial situations, public order also meant the concept of colonial public order – a flexible order to suit administrative needs – which was expected to align itself on the metropolitan model. But the construction of customary law also allowed colonial judges to modify traditional customs and practices so as to bring them into line with their ideals of justice and equity and the principles of modern law and institutions.

In most nationalist literature, the colonial court has been invariably depicted as if it were a faithful piece of a machine churning out decisions for the benefit of the colonial government. But courts were more than a mere rubber stamp

[145] Yamada, "Kyōtsūhō an ni tsuite" (Part 2), 82 (566).

[146] Nam, *Ilche ŭi Hanguk sabŏppu ch'imnyak sirhwa*, 178–179.

[147] See "Chōsen shisei yōkō," June 1919, in *Saito Makoto Monjo*, vol. 1.

of the colonial government, cooperating with the imperial agenda by blindly validating its policy direction through judicial decisions. It is difficult to prove empirically that the court decided civil cases solely according to the directives from the government general. Penal cases may have been more closely tied with the elements of colonial domination, but colonial criminal justice is beyond the scope of this study. As Pyong-choon Hahm pointed out, it would be unfair, and inaccurate, to characterize colonial justice as merely oppressive or ruthless. As a whole, one may agree with the statement that "the Japanese judges in Korea were honest and conscientious in the performance of their judicial duties."[148] A careful examination of the court decisions and juristic writings is essential in understanding the nature of the making and remaking of Korean law in the colonial period. Highly sophisticated jurisprudential activities took place during the colonial period. It is to this topic that Chapter 6 turns.

[148] Pyong-Choon Hahm, "Korea's Initial Encounter with the Western Law 1910–1948 A.D.," in *Korean Jurisprudence, Politics and Culture* (Seoul: Yonsei University Press, 1986), 141.

6

Colonial Jurisprudence and the Construction of Korean Customary Law

In colonial Korea, custom became the basic source of law for private relations among Koreans. Colonial court judges were given the mission to decide most civil law matters according to custom. But their commitment to applying customary rules for objective and equitable adjudication was subject to practical and theoretical limits. Article 10 of the Chosŏn Civil Ordinance – custom prevailed over any law not related to public policy – recognized an extremely broad scope of custom to govern juristic acts but this provision did not explain what constituted "custom." The language of Article 11 that Korean custom governed in matters of family and succession of the Koreans left unanswered the question of what Korean family and succession custom was. In the absence of official redactions of custom, the judges found themselves operating in a void, lacking any written guidance that would inform them of the legal acceptability of a particular custom claimed by the parties.

The judges, the majority of whom had no personal familiarity with Korean customs and who now had to select and recognize custom with legal force, were inclined to equate custom with the general principles of law. Where there was no definition of custom, the judges were practically free to choose or reject old Korean law provisions and popular practices depending on whether they were consistent with their notions of justice and equity. Conflation of the law of reason and custom was nothing new; as examined in Chapter 3, it was a common jurisprudential practice in Japan. The colonial judges were in a situation similar to that in pre-codification Japan. Where there were no concretely formulated rules in the form of written custom or legislation, the early Meiji judges turned to "reason." Naturally colonial jurisprudence took its cue from the Japanese jurisprudence of customary law. Just as the judicial reasoning of customary law in the early Meiji era was based on the general principles of rights enshrined in the French Civil Code, Korean customary jurisprudence was grounded in written reason derived from the Japanese Civil Code.

Entrusted with determining rights and obligations of the parties on the basis of uncertain usages and practices, the colonial judges were compelled to devise flexible interpretive principles in order to make the customary law system workable. The colonial judges were in general receptive to the instrumentalist approach of the judges in Japan who were reluctant to limit the court's role to literal implementation of law. They maintained a similar approach to the interpretation of custom. This chapter discusses how old Korean customs were reworked into customary law in colonial jurisprudence by examining the decisions of the Chōsen Kōtō Hōin (Chosŏn Kodŭng Pŏpwŏn), the highest court in the colony. In both Japan and colonial Korea, the modernization of civil law took place as much by transplantation through legislation as transplantation by way of judicial decision-making using the medium of customary law. The significance of colonial customary jurisprudence appears to be more profound and widespread than has been acknowledged.

The Interpretation of Custom

Custom in Japanese Law

The language of Article 10 in the civil ordinance was a curious amalgam of the provisions from the Japanese *Hōrei* and the civil code, both enforced in 1898. The following are the texts of these provisions:

> Article 2 of *Hōrei*: Customs which are not contrary to public order or to good morals shall have the force of law to the extent that they are authorized by a statute or a statutory instrument or concern matters not otherwise prescribed by a statute or a statutory instrument.
>
> Article 92 of the Japanese Civil Code: In cases where there is any custom which is inconsistent with a provision in any law or regulation not related to public policy, if it is found that any party to a juristic act has the intention to abide by such custom, such custom shall prevail.
>
> Article 10 of the Chosŏn Civil Ordinance: Civil matters involving Koreans only are governed by Korean custom, even if a specific custom is different from law, as long as the law is not related to public order.

According to Article 2 of the *Hōrei*, custom that was not contrary to public order or morality had the force of law, provided that it was not excluded by legislation and that it dealt with matters that had not been provided for by statute or regulation. Custom was a subsidiary source of law that the judge could apply but only in the absence of legislation. While the *Hōrei* stipulated that legislation took precedence over custom, the civil code seemed to provide a conflicting rule. The only provision in the Japanese Civil Code that directly mentions the legal force of custom is Article 92, which provided that custom has the same legal effect as statutes over juristic acts. But Article 92 went beyond recognizing the legal force of custom: legislation which did not deal with matters of public policy – non-imperative law – could be avoided by the parties and replaced by customary rules with a contrary meaning. Articles 90 through 92 seemed to provide an all-inclusive principle to invalidate custom against the compulsory provisions and the moral of the public in general.[1]

The question involves a distinction between compulsory or mandatory law (*ius cogens*) and non-compulsory or default law (*ius dispositivum*). The former (*kyōkō kitei*) are laws the application of which cannot be evaded by means of a different expression of intention by the parties, whereas the latter (*nini kitei* or *hi kyōkō kitei*) are those whose application can be evaded by the parties by means of a special expression of intention. Differently put, the latter, optional provisions, may govern either where no arrangement has been made by the parties in regard to a given legal relation, or where, even if an arrangement has been made, that arrangement is incomplete or defective.[2] This distinction embodies the principle of the freedom of contract.

Japanese jurists have long struggled to reconcile the two provisions in the *Hōrei* and the civil code. Whereas the *Hōrei* provision excluded custom where there existed applicable legislation, Article 92 declared that custom prevailed over the law which was not related to public order when the party intended to abide by such custom. The general view was that custom in Article 92 of the civil code was "custom in fact," whereas custom in Article 2 of the *Hōrei* was "customary law." Customary law must be followed irrespective of the intention of the parties. In other words, customary law is binding on the parties regardless of the expression of intent to abide by it or even without the parties' knowledge of its existence, whereas custom in fact becomes applicable only if the parties intended to follow it or it can at least be presumed that they intended to follow it. Naturally the question arose as to how nonobligatory custom under Article 92 could have greater force as a source of law, trumping legislation, than binding custom under Article 2. The *Hōrei* did not explain whether "a statute or a statutory instrument" included laws related to public policy only or referred to non-public policy laws as well. But it was generally believed that "statutes" in the *Hōrei* were laws related to public policy only, excluding non-imperative laws.[3]

The relationship between provisions of law and custom was an issue of fierce debate from the time of the codification of civil law. In order for the parties to avoid the application of the default law, the expression of intention (*ishi hyōshi*) is necessary. The civil code did not define the expression of intention to follow custom, nor did it stipulate that such an expression take any specific form.[4] Legislative history indicates that Article 92 had not been included

[1] Article 90: "A juristic act with any purpose which is against public order or good customs is null and void"; Article 91: "If any party to a juristic act manifests any intention which is inconsistent with a provision in any laws and regulations not related to public order, such intention shall prevail."

[2] J. E. De Becker, *The Principles and Practice of the Civil Code of Japan*, vol. 1 (Yokohama: Kelly & Walsh, 1921), x, 66–67.

[3] Chŏng Chong-hyu, "Kwansŭppŏp kwa sasil in kwansŭp [Customary Law and Custom in Fact], in *Hanguk minpŏp iron ŭi palchŏn: Muam Yi Yŏng-jun paksa whagap kinyŏm nonmunjip* (Seoul: Pagyŏngsa, 1999), 15.

[4] Röhl, *History of Law in Japan*, 196.

in the original draft proposed by the framers but was inserted at a later time as a compromise when a broader scope of the applicability of custom was demanded.[5] Apparently, even the drafters of the code were not of the same opinion over the question of how to interpret intentions where there was a doubt in regard to the meaning of an expression of intention. Tomii Masaakira argued that custom in fact could override non-imperative law only when there was a clear declaration of the parties' intent to follow the custom. Ume Kenjirō and Hozumi Nobushige, on the other hand, contended that, in order for the parties to avoid the application of default rules, the expression of intention to follow custom was necessary but that it could be either by an explicit or formal expression of intention or by an implied expression of intention.

Ume expounded his view as follows:

> There is disagreement among scholars regarding the nature of custom. In my opinion, when the state recognizes custom as a legal norm, then it becomes *customary law* and exerts legal force in the same way as written provisions of legislation. If not, custom becomes a mere custom in fact, with limited effect in law. I believe, following the general principles in the *Hōrei*, that custom has legal force over the matters that are not governed by civil law or other law. When there are provisions in civil law or other laws, if such laws are not related to public policy, custom that is against them does not have force as customary law but can still be enforced if the parties so intended.[6]

Ume apparently wanted to grant the courts broad power to decide whether to attribute legal force to custom. Under Article 92, the finding of the parties' intent to abide by custom was necessary for the custom to take effect. But a court should be capable of deciding whether custom took precedence over non-imperative law without requiring the express declaration of intent. When there was no clear intent, the court was to determine the intent as a factual question.

Ume's position seems to have dominated the contemporary scholarly opinions in Japan. This was a view that would see full exposition by the French jurist Gény. According to Gény, it was reasonable to presume that, when there is no special circumstance that says that the party rejected custom, the party intended implicitly to follow custom.[7] The general doctrinal agreement in Japan has been that the intention of the parties to follow custom is presumed in the absence of evidence to the contrary. Article 92 is construed in such a way

[5] For the background behind the making of Article 92, see Hoshino Eiichi, "Hensan katei kara mita minpō shūi: minpō 92 jō – hōrei 2 jō ron, minpō 97 jō -526 jō -521 jō ron [Gleanings from the Civil Code Seen from Its Compilation: Discussions of Article 92 of the Civil Code and Article 2 of *Hōrei*, and Articles 97, 526, and 521 of the Civil Code]," *in Minpō ronshū*, vol. 1, 151–224 (1970); Chŏng Chong-hyu, "Kwansŭppŏp kwa sasil in kwansŭp."

[6] Ume Kenjirō, *Minpō kōgi* [Lectures on the Civil Code] (Tokyo: Dōbunkan, Meihōdō, 1901), 50–51 (original emphasis). Ume stated: "when there is custom, the parties do not need to express explicitly their intent to follow the custom. But the court must find enough evidence to determine that the parties intended to follow the custom." Ibid.

[7] Gény, *Méthode*, vol. 1 401–406 (no. 128).

that, where there is a custom different from the provisions of laws not relating to public order and where the parties have not made an expression of intention departing from such custom, the parties are legally assumed to have acted according to such custom. The substance of the juristic act is determined in view of the custom which differed from the provisions of laws.[8]

Both the *Hōrei* and the Japanese Civil Code were fully in effect in colonial Korea. This led jurists to question the purpose of Article 10 of the Chosŏn Civil Ordinance that was seemingly of a redundant nature. The continued existence of Article 10 throughout Japanese rule suggests that its main utility lay in the fact that colonial judicial authorities were spared the question whether customs they implemented lacked legal normativity. Article 10 of the Civil Ordinance was substantially similar to Article 92 of the Japanese Civil Code, except for the fact that it lacked the language concerning the intent of the parties. The language of intent was omitted in Article 10, it has been argued, because "Korean custom" included not only "custom in fact" but also "customary law." The absence of the distinction between customary law and customs allowed the requirement in the *Hōrei* – customs not be contrary to public order or good morals in order to have legal force – to apply to Korean customs in the civil ordinance.

In the early 1910s, when the colonial courts in Korea started implementing Korean custom, the prevailing view in Japan was that custom had the same legal effect as legislation and that legislation which did not deal with matters of public policy could be avoided by the parties and replaced by customary rules with a contrary meaning. Imperative law overrode custom but custom could have a value superior to that of supplementary, non-imperative, law.[9] Japanese courts interpreted the absence of contrary intent as presumptive evidence of the parties' intent to be governed by custom. The Daishinin, the Supreme Court, ruled that "where there is custom that is applicable under law, the parties who would reasonably act according to the custom are presumed to have intended to abide by the custom unless there is intent to the contrary."[10] It also stated that "where custom exists regarding certain transactions, the parties are presumed to have acted according to custom unless there is a contrary intent."[11] Thus the court could apply custom *contra legem*, even when the parties' intent was not explicitly stated. These decisions were characteristic of the instrumental approach of Japanese courts in the tradition of the so-called free scientific

[8] De Becker, *The Principles and Practice of the Civil Code of Japan*, vol. 1, 66–67; Hoshino, "Hensan katei kara mita minpō shūi," 164–165.

[9] Noda, *Introduction to Japanese Law*, 219; Hoshino, "Hensan katei kara mita minpō shūi," 165–171.

[10] Judgment of October 27, 1914, in *Daishinin minji hanketsuroku*, cited from Yoshida Heijirō, "Chōsen ni okeru kanshū to minji hōki to no kankei" [The Relationship between Korean Custom and Civil Law Provisions], *Shihō kyōkai zasshi* 2, no. 4 (1923), 7 (47). Yoshida's article is analyzed in Chŏng Chong-hyu, "Kwansŭppŏp kwa sasil in kwansŭp."

[11] Judgment of October 16, 1912, in *Daishinin minji hanketsuroku*, cited from Yoshida, "Chōsen ni okeru kanshū," 7 (47).

research movement in Europe. The broad scope of the applicability of custom recognized by the Japanese court was closely watched by colonial jurists in Korea.[12]

Interpretation of the Chosŏn Ordinance on Civil Matters

The insertion of Article 10 into the Chosŏn Civil Ordinance evidences that the Japanese were mindful of the need to demonstrate their respect for Korean custom. This article seemed to leave private legal transactions between Koreans to be covered comprehensively by Korean custom. The Chosŏn Kodŭng Pŏpwŏn, the highest colonial court, confirmed this interpretation when it wrote in 1925:

> Article 10 of the Ordinance on Civil Matters has provided that legal relations among Koreans be governed by custom, even if such custom is different from law, as long as that law is not related to public order. It thereby intended to respect custom that had been observed in Korean legal relations. Thus, when there is custom covering certain legal relations and such custom is different from the statute that otherwise would govern the same matters under Article 1 [of the civil ordinance], the ordinance has intended to allow the custom to control as a matter of law, as long as it is not against the law dealing with matters of public policy, and to treat the said custom as customary law.[13]

Yoshida Heijirō, chief judge of the Keijō (today's Seoul) Appeals Court, analyzed in detail the meanings of custom in Article 92 in the Japanese Civil Code and Article 10 in the Chosŏn Civil Ordinance. In an article that appeared in *Shihō kyōkai zasshi* in 1923, he attempted a doctrinal reconciliation of the two provisions on the basis of the current juristic trend in Japan. According to Yoshida, "custom" in Article 92 was regarded as custom in fact, as opposed to custom in law. It was the parties' intent that gave legal effect to custom under this article. On the other hand, argued Yoshida, the civil ordinance did not distinguish between custom in fact and custom in law. Custom in Article 10 was treated as customary law, with its legal normativity recognized regardless of the parties' intent. In other words, Korean custom, once its existence was recognized by the courts, had legal force to override written statute not related to public order, without requiring further roof of intent.

Unlike Article 92, Article 10 was silent of the parties' intent. But Yoshida argued that there was no material difference in the court's power to implement custom under Article 92 and under Article 10 because

[12] Even in modern times, scholars have pointed out that the court, of its own power, can investigate and apply law regardless of statutory law or customary law. See Tanabe Kohji, "The Process of Litigation: An Experiment with the Adversary System," in *Law in Japan: The Legal Order in a Changing Society*, ed. Arthur Taylor von Mehren (Cambridge, MA: Harvard University Press, 1963), 85–90.

[13] Judgment of October 9, 1925, reported in *Chōsen Kōtō Hōin hanketsuroku* [Law Reports of Chosōn High Court] (Seoul: Kōtō Hōin Shokika, 1908–1943), vol. 12, 360. For Korean translation of *Hanketsuroku*, see *Kugyŏk Kodung Pŏpwŏn P'angyŏllok* (Seoul: Pŏpwŏn Haengchŏngch'ŏ, 2004–2011). As of 2011, vols. 1–14 have been translated.

> when the existence of custom relevant to a juristic act can be confirmed, it is inferred that the parties had the intention to abide by such custom. In the absence of the contrary intention, such custom becomes, before law, the standard to determine the establishment and the effect of the juristic act. In transactions between Koreans, it is natural to presuppose that, absent any special circumstances, the parties intended to abide by custom. So any difference between Article 92 and Article 10 exists only in concept and not in actual application.[14]

The jurisprudence of the Chosŏn High Court closely followed the jurisprudence of the Japanese Supreme Court. The colonial court ruled in 1917 that it was presumed that the party acted with the intent to follow local custom when there was no proof of contrary intent.[15] In 1921, it further found that "in order to determine the parties' intent to abide by custom, an explicit expression of intent is not required; such intent can be inferred from the circumstances."[16]

According to Yoshida, the only difference between Article 92 and Article 10 could be found in regard to a provision in the Japanese Code of Civil Procedure concerning the proof of custom. Article 219 of the civil procedure provided: "Local customs, usages of trade and regulations, and the law in force in foreign states must be proved. The court may of its own motion procure the necessary information, regardless of whether the above are proved by the parties." In general, the court has power to investigate law, whether statutory or customary law, or take judicial cognizance, and the litigants do not have the duty to prove it. Yet under Article 219, the parties have the burden to prove local customs and commercial customs. The important point is that the parties must raise the applicability of local and commercial custom under Article 92 of the civil code in order to retain the right to appeal in case the court fails to apply that custom.

The duty to raise the issue of custom and prove its existence at the court did not exist in colonial law because all Korean custom was construed as general customary law, not just local custom in fact. Korean custom was therefore seen to lie outside the boundaries of Article 219 of the civil procedure. In litigation, argued Yoshida, the parties did not have the responsibility to prove the existence of the custom through either expert testimony or witness interrogations and they could raise the issue for the first time on appeal. If the court failed to apply custom, the litigant could challenge the court's decision on appeal, no matter whether he had pleaded it and produced the evidence of the alleged custom. Yoshida wrote:

> regardless of the litigant's assertion and proof, the decision of the court is unlawful if the court fails to apply existing customary law, so the litigant can claim customary law on appeal and ask the reversal of the decision. Therefore one must admit that customary law is treated differently from a mere custom in fact in procedure.[17]

[14] Yoshida, "Chōsen ni okeru kanshū," 7–8 (47–48).
[15] Judgment of June 5, 1917, *Hanketsuroku*, vol. 4, 864 (*Kugyŏk*, 357).
[16] Judgment of December 23, 1921, *Hanketsuroku*, vol. 8, 574–581 (the quote is in 580–581).
[17] Yoshida, "Chōsen ni okeru kanshū," 10 (50).

In colonial Korea, the courts had to apply Article 92 to the Japanese and Article 10 to Koreans. Yoshida argued that enforcing two different standards of proof in a small country like Korea caused unnecessary confusion. He called for the revision of Article 10 so that the same trial procedure as under Article 219 of the civil procedure would apply to all the transactions taking place in Korea and to all the parties regardless of their national origins.[18] According to Yoshida, Article 10 of the civil ordinance, exempting the parties from pleading and producing evidence of custom, had been put in place to protect Korean custom. Such a consideration was no longer valid, he argued, because the established jurisprudence of Korean customary law rendered it unnecessary to provide protection.

The seeming breadth of Article 10 of the Chosŏn Civil Ordinance that custom prevailed over any law not related to public policy is striking. Historians have debated whether the language of this provision should be interpreted in such a way as to mean that Korean custom prevails in all civil matters, taking precedence over nonmandatory statutory provisions. But this interpretation is problematic because it would mean that the provisions of Books 1 through 3 of the Japanese Civil Code did not apply to Koreans. The colonial courts certainly applied the General Principles and contract provisions in the civil code to Koreans. Also, it is difficult to believe that Article 10 excluded the operation of Article 91 of the civil code among Koreans and that custom applied to Koreans regardless of the intent of the party.[19] Therefore, it would be more reasonable to believe that the expansive language of Article 10 only meant that, in applying custom in the context of Article 91 of the Japanese Civil Code, custom to be applied is Korean custom, not Japanese custom.[20]

Judge Yoshida's position reflected the effort to reduce the scope of the applicability of Korean custom in matters that would otherwise be covered by the provisions in the first three books of the Japanese Civil Code. The general jurisprudential trend was to keep Article 10's sphere of operation as narrow as that of Article 92. Sometimes the Chosŏn High Court declared that whatever Korean custom had existed was abolished when the civil ordinance came into effect on April 1, 1912. Other times the court chose to state that custom still existed but was inapplicable because it was against the civil code provision that the court viewed as imperative law involving public order. This way, the language of Article 10 was construed in a limited course. Often, however, the court's position was not consistent, as the following cases exemplify.

In 1914, the court acknowledged that Korean custom did not allow the assignment of designated obligation without the consent of the debtor. But,

[18] Ibid., 11 (51).

[19] Article 91 provides that the party's expressed intent governs over the provisions not related to public order.

[20] See Pak Ch'an-ju, ""Pulmunpŏp ŭi pŏpwŏnsŏng e taehan saeroun ihae," *Pŏpchŏ* 612 (September 2007), 69, note 57.

noted the court, this custom was abolished when the civil ordinance came into effect in April 1912 and imposed Japanese obligation law in Korea.[21] Under Article 467 of the Japanese Civil Code, the creditor had freedom to assign obligation on the condition that the assignor gave a notice to the debtor of the assignment or the debtor acknowledged the assignment. For the assignee to collect, the debtor's consent was not required. In 1917, the court ruled that the Korean custom of allowing the party to void a contract had been "abolished" with the enforcement of the civil ordinance in 1912.[22] The court acknowledged that a few years earlier it had recognized the existence of a Korean custom that a party could repudiate a contract when the other party failed to perform after receiving the demand to do so. In the 1917 case, however, the court noted that the contract had been signed in 1915, after the civil ordinance came into effect. Therefore, according to the court, the Japanese Civil Code, not Korean custom, governed the present case and the civil code did not allow the repudiation of contract when notice was given without a specific time limit.

In 1937, in another case dealing with assignment, the court did not deny the existence of custom that allowed repudiation of a contract but still rejected the custom's legal effect because it conflicted with the Japanese law that was an imperative law.[23] Here it is interesting to note that the court now regarded the assignment provision in question as a mandatory law. In the 1917 case, the court did not think it was necessary to decide whether the law was an imperative law that would automatically trump custom. As one can gather from these decisions, the overall effect of the court's reasoning was to confirm that Korean custom was inapplicable in contract and obligation matters.

The ultimate objective of full application of Japanese law in Korea was not questioned throughout the colonial period, and the jurisprudence of customary law underwent a gradual evolution toward that goal. As seen earlier, even matters in family and succession customs moved in that direction as the civil ordinance was revised in 1921, followed by a series of further revisions.[24]

A quick look at the contents of the *Shihō kyōkai zasshi* suggests the growing influence of Japanese doctrinal work and jurisprudence on the colony's law. Initially the journal served as a main medium for official legal bulletins of the government general and for the publication of the Shihō kyōkai's findings

[21] Judgment of March 3, 1914, *Hanketsuroku*, vol. 2, 390 (*Kugyŏk*, 294).

[22] Judgment of October 23, 1917, *Hanketsuroku*, vol. 4, 868 (*Kugyŏk*, 650). See Yi Chun-hyŏn, "Ilche kangjŏm ch'ogi Chosŏn Kodŭng Pŏpwŏn e ŭihan pudongsan ijung maemae, ijung chŏndang ŭi pŏpchŏk ch'ŏri: *Chosŏn Kodŭng Pŏpwŏn p'an'gyŏllok* che 1–6 kwŏn ŭi punsŏk" [Judicial Interpretation of Double Sale and Double *Chŏndang* of Real Property by the Chosŏn Kodŭng Pŏpwŏn in the Early Japanese Colonial Period: Analysis of the *Chosŏn Kodŭng Pŏpwŏn Reports*, vols. 1–6]." *Pŏpsahak yŏngu* 28 (2003): 79–108.

[23] Judgment of June 8, 1937, *Hanketsuroku*, vol. 24, 245.

[24] See Chapter 5.

of Korean custom. From Volume 7 (1928), the resolutions of the Japanese Bar Association and the notices of the Justice Ministry began to appear in the journal in large numbers.[25] This can be seen as evidence that the colonial jurists' initiatives in discovering Korean custom became less critical and instead the jurists focused on reforming custom in line with Japanese law and jurisprudence.

Reconfiguring Korean Customs into Customary Law

Proof of Custom

The colonial authorities sustained the loosely defined customary law regime in Korea. "Custom" was so malleably defined that even no immemorialness was required. The Chosŏn High Court stated in 1923: "Custom requires a practice of immemorial observance. But immemorial observance of a usage does not require observance for several decades. A practice can be regarded as immemorial custom even if it is a practice that has been in existence for one or two years."[26] The validity of custom as a legal norm depended almost exclusively on the determination of the judge.

The court's position regarding the proof of custom was not always coherent. Whether the parties have duty to prove custom or the court can take judicial cognizance of custom (*jura novit curia*) on its own authority is a question that has long been debated by scholars. If the burden of proof is placed on the litigant who invokes a custom, the scope of the application of custom substantially diminishes because it is obviously difficult to prove the existence of custom. In Korea, as noted previously, the court acknowledged the party's duty to prove local custom but it did not regularly require it. At the same time, the court denied that it had a duty to investigate the existence of custom. In a case in 1915, the appellant argued that the lower court failed to determine what Korea's custom was regarding the minimum age for legal capacity to act. The court rejected the appeal: the lower court was not obligated to decide whether the party was legally capable when it was not manifest whether Chosŏn had such custom. Where the parties did not plead the issue, the existence or absence of the custom was not within the scope of judicial investigation.[27] The court cited the report of the customs survey which stated that Korea did not have customs of legal capacity.[28] So each case involving legal capacity had to be determined as a question of fact.[29]

[25] See Chŏng Kŭng-sik and Chang Ch'ang-min, eds. *Singminji gi sabŏp kwallyŏn charyo.*

[26] Judgment of February 27, 1923, *Hanketsuroku*, vol. 10, 51–52.

[27] Judgment of November 2, 1915, *Hanketsuroku*, vol. 3, 318 (*Kugyŏk*, 234).

[28] *Kaeyŏk p'an kwansŭp chosa pogosŏ*, 89 and 99–100 (No. 2).

[29] This view was maintained in a number of cases. See Judgments of May 2, 1913, *Hanketsuroku*, vol. 2, 193–195 (*Kugyŏk*, 147–149), and December 26, 1916, *Hanketsuroku*, vol. 3, 1018–1031 (*Kugyŏk*, 747–759).

Of course it was a different matter when there was a clear-cut custom which had to be recognized as customary law. In 1918, the court declared that it had the duty to apply "obvious" local custom even if neither party proved its existence. It stated:

> When local custom is at issue, the party normally has obligation to prove its existence and the court has no duty to conduct its own investigation. But if it is manifest that such custom exists, the court must apply it even if neither party has proved its existence. It violates law if the court fails to do so.[30]

In other words, when there was local custom, the existence of which was indisputable, the judge's failure to apply it was grounds for reversal. Previously the court had said that it needed to determine whether there was binding custom. The court now claimed that it was its duty to apply "self-evident" local custom, even though it was not required of the party either to show what custom was or even to call it to the judge's attention. The court did not explain what would make local custom manifest and evident enough to become binding for the judge; it was apparently up to the court to decide case by case, depending on whether it was desirable to enforce the custom at issue.

The court was unequivocal that it could take judicial notice of law and dispense with the need for formal evidence or pleadings regarding what custom was. The court pronounced in 1925 its power to define and interpret custom under the articles in the civil ordinance:

> When local custom is concerned, the parties must prove the existence of such custom. But the court can investigate [custom] and take a judicial notice under its authority regardless of the proffered proof. The court does not need to wait for the parties to present the relevant proof. When the court has knowledge of the existence or the content of custom, the court must render a judgment on the basis of that knowledge. The court should be bound neither by the parties' proof nor by the lack of dispute among the parties [regarding the custom's content].[31]

Throughout the colonial period, the courts enjoyed wide discretion regarding what to treat as notorious, that is, the content of custom not in dispute, hence not requiring proof. The judges made no distinction between customs judicially noticed as a matter of fact and those judicially noticed as a matter of law. In practice, the method of establishing the existence of a custom was exclusively by judicial cognizance. The proof of custom was subsumed under the court's authority to declare its existence. Ch'oe Pyŏng-chu, the Korean judge at P'yŏngyang District Court and one of the few Korean jurists who contributed articles to *Shihō kyōkai zasshi*, confirmed in the journal in 1938 that doctrinal writers were in agreement that "custom" in Article 11 of the

[30] Judgment of March 8, 1918, *Hanketsuroku*, vol. 5, 173 (*Kugyŏk*, 118).
[31] Judgment of October 9, 1925, *Hanketsuroku*, vol. 12, 360–361.

Chosŏn Civil Ordinance amounted to customary law, not mere custom in fact.[32] If "custom" in the articles of the civil ordinance had been construed as "custom in fact," he explained, its existence would have become a factual, not a legal, question and the court would have been compelled to distinguish between local customs. Instead, the courts rendered judgments disregarding local differences. In consequence, the creation of a common customary law could advance quickly.

The implementation of custom was insulated from the requirement of proof, subject only to the judge's determination. Since the court did not need to wait for the parties to plead and prove applicable custom, the judges were free to draw from reason. Here some reference to European legal history may be helpful. The late medieval and early modern French courts were instrumental in reforming "hard, iniquitous and unreasonable" custom. Difficulties involved in proving custom were done away with through the official recording of local *coutumiers*. When the written codes of customs were made available, homologated under the authority of the crown, the judges were no longer constrained by the requirement of particular proof.[33] Popular customs underwent transformation in the hands of legal professionals into supposedly reasonable and equitable law. In Korea, a similar process was undertaken by the colonial courts. Trained in Roman law jurisprudence, both French and Japanese judges (and a few Korean judges sitting at the colonial courts), several hundred years apart, saw it as their mission to reform irrational practices from the traditional legal order. In both situations, the courts oversaw the metamorphosis of popular, empirical, and collective practices to learned judicial rules.

Colonial jurists acknowledged that the concrete content of "custom" remained unclear. Justice Kitō Heiichi at the Chosŏn High Court stated that certain expansive interpretations were inevitable in order to implement Korean custom in terms of Japanese law.[34] The situation seemed similar to that in Taiwan, where some substantive contents of old Taiwanese practices were flatly modified to conform to Japanese civil law. A Japanese judge in Taiwan stated that a judge should not merely discover local customs but should be mindful of "improving" Taiwanese customs when he applied them in making decisions, so that custom might not be contrary to public order or good morals.[35] In colonial jurisprudence, the conceptual distinction between custom

[32] Ch'oe Pyŏng-chu, "Minjirei jūichi cho no kanshū to sōson ken oyobi isan no sōzoku ken [Custom in Article 11 of the Civil Ordinance and the Succession Rights of the Eldest Grandson and the Widow]," *Shihō kyōkai zasshi* 17, no. 1 (1938), 21.

[33] See Chapter 1.

[34] Preface by Kitō Heiichi in Nagumo Kōkichi, *Genkō Chōsen shinzoku sōzoku hōruishū* [The Collection of Current Family and Succession Laws of Korea] (Seoul: Ōsakayagō Shoten, 1935), 1–2.

[35] Wang, *Legal Reform in Taiwan*, 143.

that had the validity of law and old customs with no legal force was largely ignored. The Japanese treated indigenous customs as if they were a self-sufficient system, equipped with a body of rules that were waiting to be applied. In reality, these customs, never reduced to writing, lacked legal normativity. It took jurisprudential activities of colonial courts for customary law to arise. What emerged was a comprehensive artificial creation by the courts. In this course, customary law in Korea was gradually assimilated with the civil law of Japan.

As seen in the previous pages, all custom in Korea was treated as common custom and the court rarely recognized local variations. In a few cases involving local custom, the court treated the question as a matter of evidence to be judged by lower courts. Two decisions, issued in 1914 and 1915, illustrate how the high court dealt with a supposed local custom. Both cases involved the legality of the interest rate of a loan.[36] In the first case, the appellant challenged the lower court's finding that charging three percent monthly interest was the custom of Chŏlla namdo, a southern province. He claimed that such custom did not exist and, alternatively, even if such custom existed it was superseded by the Interest Regulation Law promulgated in 1906, of which Article 2 limited the maximum interest rate to twenty percent per year. The high court dismissed the appeal, rejecting both arguments. It wrote that "this court has recognized the existence of the custom of charging interest. Such custom is valid, even after the promulgation of the Interest Regulation Law, as long as it did not exceed the maximum limit of interest rate agreed by the parties."[37] Article 1 of the Interest Regulation Law set the maximum interest rate at forty percent in case there was a special contract. The court found that the lower court did not err in inferring the parties' agreement on a higher interest rate from the fact that the appellant had earlier paid three percent monthly interest to the appellee. The appellant was therefore stopped from claiming the invalidity of the agreement terms.

It is remarkable that the question of the proof of the custom was not raised at all in this brief decision – the court's reasoning was contained in one short paragraph. The alleged custom, as noted by the court, was a local custom existing in Muan Kun, Chŏlla namdo, but the court treated it as equivalent to "Chosŏn's custom." It simply took judicial notice of the existence of the custom in question and enforced it by saying that it had previously been recognized by the court as the "custom of Chosŏn."

In the second case, the court again reached the judgment based on both Korea's custom and a modern legal theory. The 1915 case involved a custom in

[36] Judgment of December 22, 1914, *Hanketsuroku*, vol. 2, 533 (*Kugyŏk*, 400–401); judgment of December 24, 1915, *Hanketsuroku*, vol. 3, 374–375 (*Kugyŏk*, 277–278). See Chŏn U-hyŏn, "Ilche kangjŏm ch'ogi p'allye e nat'anan sang haengwi (kaekchuŏp) sang koridae ŭi yŏksa chŏk p'yŏngka [Historical Assessment of Usury in Commercial Transaction (Loan-Sharking Business) as Seen in Judicial Cases during the Early Japanese Colonial Period]," *Pŏpsahak yŏngu* 35 (2007): 109–145.

[37] Judgment of December 22, 1914, *Hanketsuroku*, vol. 2, 533 (*Kugyŏk*, 400–401).

both P'yŏngan pukto and P'yŏngan namdo of charging three percent monthly interest for a loan. As in the earlier case, the appellant challenged the existence of such a custom. He argued in particular that the party claiming the existence of the custom had the burden of proof since the alleged custom was a custom in fact and furthermore particular to a specific region. He thus contended that the lower court failed to require the opponent to proffer the requisite proof.

The high court rejected the appellant's argument that proof of custom was necessary. It said that "this court has ruled in earlier decisions that in Chosŏn there is custom to charge interest in transactions between merchants. We have also recognized that there is custom in P'yŏngan namdo and P'yŏngan pukto of charging three percent interest. It is beyond question that the court has the power to admit the existence of custom even when the parties failed to present the proof." The court reasoned:

> In adjudication of civil and commercial transactions, the court can apply custom when there is no statutory law. The application of custom can be allowed even if there is a statutory law. But if a statutory law exists and that law prohibits the legal effect of custom, the court cannot apply custom, disregarding the statutory law. In the instant case, the statutory law in effect at the time of the transaction was the Interest Regulation Law issued in Kwangmu Year 10 as Law Number 5. Article 2 of the said law provided that maximum annual interest rate was twenty percent of the principal, where there was no special agreement between the parties. The appellant argues that this statute is an imperative law dealing with public order, and that custom that is against such law does not have legal force. Thus he claims that the lower court wrongly allowed charging an interest rate higher than was allowed in law, despite the fact that there was no special agreement between the parties. He claims that the lower court plainly disregarded the law.
>
> We find, however, that the custom of charging three percent monthly interest is lawful under Article 1 of the Interest Regulation Law that allowed a higher maximum rate when there was a special agreement. When it is established that the parties have done an accounting according to custom, the parties' intent to abide by the custom can be established. The parties' intent to do so can be inferred from the beginning of the transaction and it produces the same effect as having made a special contract. In the present case, the lower court found that the parties did an accounting according to the above custom. Its decision in favor of the appellee did not violate law. The appellant's argument has no merit.[38]

Here, the court at first seemed to treat the alleged custom – or trade practice – as local custom by considering the parties' intent to abide by it. In fact, however, the finding of such intent was regarded as material only for establishing the existence of a special contract to agree to an interest rate higher than legally allowed. Thus, the case was really disposed of by the statutory rule, not by custom. As in the 1914 case, there was little pretense of considering the local nature of custom. The party simply alleged the existence of specific custom without any effort toward corroboration, and the court, in an equally summary

[38] Judgment of December 24, 1915, *Hanketsuroku*, vol. 3, 374–375 (*Kugyŏk*, 277–278).

manner, dismissed the party's claim of customary authority. The court opinion did not engage in any discussion of the proof of custom.

These opinions touched on a number of interesting interpretive issues. First, the court argued that it had the power – and sometimes the duty – to apply custom even when the parties did not plead it or failed to prove its existence. Second, the court confirmed that it could apply custom even when there was a statutory law contrary to that custom, as long as the law did not specifically prohibit the application of such custom. Whether the law in question was imperative or non-imperative was up to the court's determination. Third, the court argued that the existence of the parties' intent was also for the court to decide and inferable from the relevant facts. Together these arguments amounted to a forceful affirmation of the Chosŏn High Court's broad power to control private relations among Koreans under the civil ordinance.

The colonial judges pronounced on customary rules as if they had been common knowledge for years. Custom was simply treated as an immutable principle with few particular, concrete elements. Whereas the determination of custom by definition would require inductive reasoning, colonial discourse about custom was deductive, a discourse of self-evident norms. The essence of custom, unique to the specific locality, was summarily discounted. Since custom was the governing rule, there was no need for citing other authority or evidence. "Custom" was invariably stated in the form of an abstract principle and the plain declaration of custom itself commanded legal significance.

Judicial Opinion

Judicial opinions rendered by the Chosŏn High Court reveal that the court tended to speak in broad language, favoring often sweeping generalizations. The majority of the reported appellate decisions in customary law followed a general pattern. The introductory part begins with the summary of the holding, based on the finding whether or not certain custom is "Chosŏn's custom." The case is placed in the procedural context (for example, "this court decides as follows the case at bar that is an appeal from the Keijō Appeals Court"), followed by the summary of the disposition ("the petition is dismissed," or "the case is remanded to the court below"), and the assignment of the court cost.

The main part of the opinion consists of the court's reasoning. First, it provides a brief summary of relevant facts and the appellant's arguments alleging an applicable custom ("material allegations of the petition are as follows"). Next, the court considers the arguments presented, rejecting or confirming the validity of the party's arguments and the custom invoked. The holding is in many cases drawn from "custom" alone. The court typically states "we have declared this Chosŏn's custom" or "it is not Chosŏn's custom." In the last paragraph of the opinion, a short sentence states the conclusion that "the appellant's arguments have no valid grounds" or that "the lower court rested its judgment on valid grounds." Finally, the court renders its disposition ("on these grounds, we decide as the above and dismiss the petition") and cites the relevant civil procedure article.

The broad language employed by the high court indicates that the court needed to draw general rules from specific Korean usages and to standardize the judicial decision-making process. The main goal of the judges was to effect a reasonable restructuring of social practices through judicial abstraction so that these practices did not contradict the governing legal principles of state law. It is often assumed that judges in the civil law tradition are inclined to use abstract and general language, limiting judicial opinion to citing applicable statutes. Colonial judges followed a similar judicial style, yet without acknowledging that custom lacked the formal authority of the statutes. It is also possible that the court avoided giving detailed reasons in order to demonstrate the correctness and legitimacy of their decisions because the judges wanted to maintain the fiction of a customary law regime, sustained by the theory that they simply discovered and applied preexisting custom that had long regulated social relations in Chosŏn Korea.

The Chosŏn High Court effectively engaged in creating law based on precedents. The colonial customary law regime amounted to a common law system in Korea. The lower courts were strongly urged to follow the highest court's decisions, although there was no recognition of the principle of *stare decisis*.[39] Precedents were simply posited as supplemental arguments. Faithful to the widespread traditions in the civil law system, the courts did not openly rely on precedents because they were reluctant to admit that customary law was declared by judicial decision. In colonial Korea, it was doubly important to avoid the appearance that Japanese judges were making up rules to control the private relations of the Korean people. The courts had to take public opinion into account, and the judges were mindful of the reception of their decisions by the colonial population. Even under a colonial regime, they had to seek some degree of public legitimacy, and their implementation of "customary law" rationalized their decisions. In continental Europe, a court-made rule could not become a rule of law unless the court applied a preexisting rule of customary law.[40] In Korea, the colonial courts "declared" customary law and thus essentially circumvented the civil law doctrine that court decisions are not law.

Colonial jurisprudence on customary law bridged the gap between the concepts of Western law and well-formed social practices. The high court needed to redefine and reinterpret traditional Korean practices so they could be reconciled with modern civil law principles. The judicial reworking of customs proceeded with the goal of making a modern state in a radically different ideological and intellectual context. For this purpose, the judges rejected or reconstructed a number of customs that they deemed irrational or impractical in terms of the social and economic realities of the new colonial Korea.

[39] Chōsen Sōtokufu, *Chōsen no shihō seido*, 29.

[40] D. K. Lipstein, "The Doctrine of Precedent in Continental Law with Special Reference to French and German Law," *Journal of Comparative Legislative & International Law* 28 (1946), 34; Lambert, *La fonction du droit civil comparé*, 144.

Theoretically, Korea's custom was the source of law, but such custom was viewed as something different from a body of enforceable legal norms. Colonial jurists tended to equate a variety of social practices with legal custom and treated them as one and the same thing. In short, the judges decided cases citing the authority of Korean customs, not because they were laws but because they served as a framework in which the blunt clash between traditional legal order and the new modern legal order could be assuaged. The impact of modern Japanese legal concepts and principles needed to be mitigated by conjuring up elements that could still claim continuity with the Korean past. In this sense, the customary law regime provided a crucial instrument for economic and social modernization.

The Chosŏn High Court Judgment Investigation Committee, consisting of all the high court judges, confirmed the objectives of colonial court jurisprudence as follows:

> First, when the court interprets law, law provisions should be the place to start from, but the court should attend to the law's spirit and avoid being restrained by detailed language of the law text; second, legal reasoning is important but the court should maintain a balance between upholding social norms such as morality and enforcing economic regulations on the other, and take caution not to fall into the trap of pursuing mere formalistic research; third, the court should maintain a perfect balance between criminal and civil cases; fourth, the court should respect Korean customs but should also notice how customs have changed and promote unity with Japan's laws.[41]

As seen in Chapter 5, colonial customary jurisprudence tended to be shaped by the consensus reached among the high court judges in coordination with the policy directions of the Law Department in the government general. Nevertheless, colonial judges were not mere automatons blindly implementing the colonial government's policy. Evidence shows that there were genuine efforts by the courts and among jurists to reconcile Korean customs with the Western legal concepts and principles.

The flexible role played by judges in the process of reinterpreting and modifying custom is well exemplified in court opinion. Under the civil ordinance, a significant part of private law cases were decided by judicial validation or rejection of custom. A reading of the decisions rendered by the Chosŏn High Court illustrates how the customary law system functioned in Korea.

Analysis of Customary Law Cases

During the first years after Japanese judges started deciding cases according to Korean custom in 1909, the courts tended to take a passive stance, applying what they believed were traditional customs. This soon changed as the courts moved away from the ad hoc approach and took a more systematic approach, trying to implement Korean customs in light of the Japanese code or at least to

[41] Chōsen Sōtokufu, ed. *Chōsen no shihō seido*, 31.

develop a more coherent structure of customary law. Efforts to reform Korean customs through jurisprudence progressed earnestly in the 1910s.

The first task of the colonial judges was to decide whether custom was or was not in existence to apply to the case before them. When the court denied the existence of applicable Korean custom, cases were often quickly disposed of through factual determination. In a case of ownership dispute in 1917, the appellant disputed the appellee's ownership of land which the latter's grandfather had purchased and used as burial plots for his parents. The appellant argued that Korean custom had it that the land or mountain used for gravesites for family members belonged to the clan and that members of the clan, such as himself, had joint ownership of that land. The high court rejected that such custom existed in Korea: the ownership of property, including burial plots, either belonged to an individual or to a clan, which was a factual question. When the court refused to accept the existence of a Korean custom that rendered burial plots into the clan's property, only a question of fact remained to be decided.[42]

There was general consensus among the judges with modern legal training that the customary law they were establishing needed to conform to modern legal theory as well as sound reasoning. If a dispute over custom touched on a matter that was governed by the Japanese Civil Code, the court took a firm position. In such cases, the court did not hesitate to abrogate or modify traditional practices so they could agree with Japanese law. The following cases involving the issue of a wife's legal capacity to own and bequeath property exemplify the court's efforts to reconcile Korean custom with Japanese civil law.

Legal Capacity of the Wife

Article 807 of the Japanese Civil Code provided that "the wife's property that she had owned before marriage or that she acquired under her name during marriage belongs to her. When ownership is not clear, it is presumed to belong to the husband or the wife who is the household head." The decision of February 28, 1912, of the Chosŏn High Court involved the issue of whether the wife could bequeath land that had been obtained with her own money but was registered under the husband's name.[43] The appellant argued that "it is well recognized that the wife does not have legal capacity regarding property rights .... It is not lawful that the wife makes a bequest of property acquired during the husband's lifetime." The court rejected the appellant's argument. It wrote:

> There is neither law nor custom in Korea that prohibits the wife from purchasing land with her money and bequeathing it to her son. The appeals court found, on the basis of evidence, that the property in dispute had been obtained by the wife

[42] Judgment of June 22, 1917, *Hanketsuroku*, vol. 4, 589 (*Kugyŏk*, 442).

[43] Judgment of February 28, 1912, *Hanketsuroku*, vol. 1, 441 (*Kugyŏk*, 315). For a discussion of this case and the related cases concerning the wife's property rights, see Kim Wŏn-t'ae, "Ilche kangjŏm ch'ogi ch'ŏ ŭi t'ŭkyu chaesan e kwanhan kwansŭppŏp: Chosŏn Kodŭng Pŏpwŏn p'an'gyŏl ŭi punsŏk ŭl chungsim ŭro [Customary Law of the Wife's Special Property in the Early Japanese Colonial Period: Analysis of the Chosŏn Kodŭng Pŏpwŏn Decisions]," *Pŏpsahak yŏngu* 31 (2005): 197–236.

> with her own money while she lived with the husband and that she gave it to the appellee. Its ruling is not against law.[44]

In another case decided in 1913, a party invoked the custom of joint ownership with survivorship, arguing "It is Chosŏn's custom that a cohabiting spouse enjoys usufruct and eventually succeeds the husband's property.... The lower court ruled in violation of Article 11 of the civil ordinance by not applying Chosŏn's custom." The high court dismissed the appellant's claim. It said: "We cannot accept the supposed existence of customs that the wife has the survivorship right over the husband's property and that she receives it automatically even when there are legitimate or secondary sons."[45] The court placed the burden of proof on the wife claiming joint ownership.

In 1916, an appellant argued:

> The [appeals] court misinterpreted Chosŏn's custom by saying that it is unusual in Korea for the wife to have title to her property. It is incontrovertible that the wife, or the concubine as in this case, who accumulated property through her own business, is entitled to the property. There is hardly any practice that the property goes to the husband. It is against the law that the original ruling interpreted Chosŏn's custom in a contrary manner.

The high court ruled: "We cannot say that the lower court's ruling contradicted Chosŏn's custom when it decided that it was unusual in Korean custom for women to own their own property."[46] The court explained that it could not recognize that, between 1898 and 1902, the period that concerned the facts of this case, the property owned by the wife or the concubine while living with the husband did not belong to the husband, in the absence of the proof to the contrary. The court's reasoning was based on the fact that there was no clear evidence that the property claimed by the appellant had indeed been earned by her.

In the following year, in a case with a seemingly similar fact situation, the appellant argued that it was Korea's custom that the property which the concubine accumulated by running her own business belonged to her. The court wrote:

> In Korea, the property whose ownership is not clear is presumed to belong to the husband. But it is merely a presumption when ownership is unclear. It does not defeat the legitimate ownership of property by the wife or the concubine. Therefore, for example, real property bought with the money earned by the wife or the concubine by conducting commercial business belongs to the wife or the concubine. In our earlier decision that found that during 1898–1902 real property ownership by the wife was extraordinary does not negate the rightful ownership of property by the wife or the concubine (see the decision of October 3, 1916).[47]

The court thus stressed that its reasoning was consistent.

These cases, and their related decisions, were formulated in terms of Korea's customs but what dictated their dispositions was not so much the

[44] Judgment of February 28, 1912, *Hanketsuroku*, vol. 1, 441 (*Kugyŏk*, 315).
[45] Judgment of May 23, 1913, *Hanketsuroku*, vol. 2, 221–222 (*Kugyŏk*, 169–172).
[46] Judgment of October 3, 1916, *Hanketsuroku*, vol. 3, 746 (*Kugyŏk*, 537–549).
[47] Judgment of February. 16, 1917, *Hanketsuroku*, vol. 4, 102 (*Kugyŏk*, 78).

presupposed customs as evidence and property law concepts. The judges rarely departed from the principles in Japan's civil code.[48] When the alleged custom was consistent with the provision in the Japanese Civil Code, the court was ready to affirm the existence of such custom; when the alleged custom differed from Japan's civil law, the court either denied the existence of the custom or, in the few cases where it upheld the custom, limited the scope of its ruling.

It was inevitable that there often existed a gap between the laws applied by the court and actual practices in Korea, and the courts' attempt to smooth the gap by reworking supposed customary rules was not always without friction. There is a certain truth in the argument that premodern Korean customs were disregarded by Japanese judges whose priority was not in preserving old practices but in implanting modern legal theory. Yet, rather than marginalizing traditional popular practices by strictly enforcing abstract legal principles in the name of modern law, the colonial courts attempted reasonable restructuring of the practices through modification and reinterpretation to turn them into binding normative rules under the precept of customary law. In general, when they did not know what the governing rules might be, the judges could only do what lawyers were trained to do, that is, to apply general principles to the particular parties before them. In this way custom was blended with natural law to create a sort of common customary law.

Public Order and Good Morals

There are a number of opinions in which the Chosŏn High Court expressly emphasized the importance of reason (*jōri*) and public order in adjudication. The pervasiveness of policy considerations was unmistakable when the court justified its decision by saying that "it is crucially necessary and also it agrees with *jōri*."[49] Article 90 of the Japanese Civil Code provided: "A juristic act with any purpose which is against public order or good customs is null and void." The colonial court maintained that custom applied as long as it was not against social order and good morals.[50] The test of public order afforded the court extensive discretion in selecting customary rules for enforcement. Citing public order, for example, the court refused to apply the custom acknowledging gambling debts.[51] It also disregarded a rather common practice that held siblings or family members jointly responsible for debt. The judges flatly stated that "we do not recognize such a custom."[52] In these and other cases, the main concern of the justices was to balance the interests of the parties and bring out equitable

[48] Judgment of March 14, 1916, *Hanketsuroku*, vol. 3, 439 (*Kugyŏk*, 322) (even if the wife needs to obtain the husband's permission in performing a legal act, she does not need to do so in bequeathing her own property); Judgment of January 16, 1917, *Hanketsuroku*, vol. 4, 1 (*Kugyŏk*, 1) (there is no custom in Korea to deny the mother to inherit the property of her son).

[49] Judgment of September 29, 1914, *Hanketsuroku*, vol. 2, 478 (*Kugyŏk*, 361).

[50] Judgment of July 17, 1911, *Hanketsuroku*, vol. 1, 336–340 (*Kugyŏk*, 243–243).

[51] Judgment of June 8, 1909, *Hanketsuroku*, vol. 1, 22–23 (*Kugyŏk*, 16–18).

[52] Judgment of March 7, 1913, *Hanketsuroku*, vol. 2, 147; (*Kugyŏk*, 112).

solutions. The court declared that a legal act performed on the condition of not remarrying was not against public order or good morals because there was no law requiring remarriage.[53] It ruled that, when a tenancy contract failed to specify the duration, neither the landlord nor the tenant could unilaterally end the contract during the growing season.[54]

Some cases involved a complicated reasoning process regarding the public order issue. The case of 1917 was one such example.[55] It illustrates how the principle of public order limited the operation of custom. The appellant sought the payment on a promissory note. The facts were seriously disputed. According to the appellee, he consulted the appellant with the intention to bribe an official whose favor he sought in order to get elected to a local commission. Relying on the appellant's words that he tendered on the appellee's behalf 200 *wŏn* to the said official, the appellee wrote an I.O.U. to the appellant for that amount. Later, however, he claimed that the appellant in reality did not give the cash to the official and that he therefore was not obligated to honor the I.O.U. The appellant disputed the appellee's assertion and instead claimed that the I.O.U. was written for a cash loan. Apart from the fact disputes, the appellee presented an interesting argument drawing from the public order clause in Article 90 of the civil code: he did not have an obligation to pay the I.O.U., regardless of whether the appellant indeed tendered the bribe, because seeking to bribe an official was against good morals and any juristic act performed in violation of good morals was invalid. The lower court had found for the appellee on the public order grounds, which now became the central point of the appeal.

The appellant argued that the lower court misinterpreted Article 90 when it accepted the appellee's argument. According to him, Article 90 did not void a juristic act when reasons, motives, or methods for that act were against public order or good morals; the provision voided a legal act only when the substance of that legal act was against public order and good morals. Put differently, Article 90 invalidated a legal act when its nature was illegal and its purpose was to violate laws related to public order, but it did not invalidate legal acts simply because they were remotely connected with a breach of laws related to public order. Here, claimed the appellant, the act of bribing lacked necessary causality for the act of writing an I.O.U. Illegality of the motives or methods of a legal act did not affect the legal force of the contract.

The court rejected the appellant's argument. It agreed with the appellant that Article 90 voided a juristic act not when reasons, motives, or methods for that act were against public order or good morals but when the substance

[53] Judgment of December 25, 1911, *Hanketsuroku*, vol. 1, 415 (*Kugyŏk*, 296).

[54] Judgment of October 19, 1917, *Hanketsuroku*, vol. 4, 864 (*Kugyŏk*, 647). Other cases decided in reference to reason include: judgment of January 23, 1931, *Hanketsuroku*, vol. 18, 4; judgment of July 6, 1917, *Hanketsuroku*, vol. 4, 648 (*Kugyŏk*, 486); judgment of November 24, 1916, *Hanketsuroku*, vol. 3, 856 (*Kugyŏk*, 627); judgment of October 10, 1913, *Hanketsuroku*, vol. 2, 337 (*Kugyŏk*, 260).

[55] Judgment of October 26, 1917, *Hanketsuroku*, vol. 4, 888 (*Kugyŏk*, 664).

of that act was against public order or good morals. The court pointed out, however, that it was necessary to determine the nature of the legal act and to decide whether the elements of motives or methods also constituted the substance of the legal act. When the party expressed his intent to include the motives or the means as part of the contract, and when it could be inferred that the party would not have concluded the contract without the consideration of those motives or means, those elements must be seen as the substance of the contract. Bribing a public official was clearly an illegal act and it was the gist of the contract. There was the requisite sufficient causal link. Therefore, the court concluded, the contract was void under Article 90.

Family and Succession Cases

The decision guidelines for the Chosŏn High Court in the 1930s illustrate the court's expansive perception of its mission to reorder private legal relations among Koreans, in particular to reform traditional family and succession customs. The guidelines stated:

> As the highest court, the court renders decisions to promote unity in the interpretation of law, maintain balance between civil and criminal cases, and harmonize law and social norms. The court controls lower courts' decisions and provides guidelines for adjudication. Without exaggeration the court defines social norms through this process. Korea has diverse family and succession customs, and the court plays a special role in adjusting these customs.[56]

The bulk of customary law cases dealt with family and succession issues under Article 11 of the Chosŏn Civil Ordinance. The matters that demanded the most serious attention from the colonial judges were the customs based on Confucian rituals. Confucian ritual practices, covering the vast area of family relations in Chosŏn Korea, were most explicitly at variance with the legal concept of rights in the Roman law tradition. Japanese judges often deemed them to be irrational and impractical in terms of the social and economic realities of the new colonial Korea. Confronted with the problems of incongruities and conflicts between the Confucian worldview and Japanese law, the colonial judges moved to relax the rigid observance of various Confucian rituals and to abolish their oppressive elements through the reworking of Korean customs. In fact, what many Korean historians claim to be the traditional Korean custom that suffered suppression and distortion at the hands of the colonizers was, rather, neo-Confucian ritual practices. The need to consider the profound influence of the Confucian tradition on Korean society and reconcile its remnants with modern laws created particular challenges for the judges.

Under the Chosŏn dynasty, adoption was practiced to secure the perpetuation of the descent line which would ensure uninterrupted ancestral ceremonies. Under ritual succession, couched in Confucian lineage ideology, the eldest son succeeded the status as the presider of the ceremony. Adoption took place

[56] Chōsen Sōtokufu, ed. *Chōsen no shihō seido*, 29–30.

when the eldest son did not have a male heir, but only a lineal male, usually the child of a younger brother or cousin, was suitable for adoption so as to offer proper sacrifices to ancestors. The resulting prohibition of nonagnatic adoption was responsible for highly complex, convoluted, and perplexing adoption rules. Adoption was practiced either during the lifetime of the person to be succeeded or after his death. The nineteenth-century German jurist Joseph Kohler found posthumous adoption immensely intriguing. As he explained in 1886, when a person had a son who was married but died without a son, the former adopted a child, not for himself but for the soul of his deceased son, and the adopted person became his grandson, not his son.[57]

Adoption was given the status of law in Korean codes as an institution to establish an heir. A thorny issue was whether adoption was allowed when there was a son from the secondary wife. This issue translated into the question whether the latter had the right to perform an ancestor worship ceremony – that is, whether the family line could be succeeded through an illegitimate son. The law permitted establishing a jural-ritual heir only if neither the primary nor the secondary wife had a son.[58] There was widespread practice among elite families, however, of adopting a son even when there was a son from the secondary wife.[59]

The colonial court initially confirmed such a practice as Korean custom without distinguishing between lifetime and posthumous cases. The high court stated in 1913 that the statutory provision prohibiting adoption with the presence of an illegitimate son was not well observed under Chosŏn: "it was general custom in Chosŏn, both among commoners and royal clansmen, that there was no impediment to adopting a son, no matter whether there was a legitimate son or son born of a concubines, without obtaining permission from the Board of Rites."[60] The practice, which became widespread from the seventeenth century, was in fact mostly limited to the higher elite families.[61] But the court was willing to interpret the practice expansively to include lower nobles, military nobles, and commoners. In 1914, the civil administrator of the government general advised the court that in Korean custom the adopted child preceded the secondary son (*sŏja*) in succession.[62] The Chosŏn

[57] Joseph Kohler, "Uber das Recht des Koreaner" [On Korean Law], *Zeitschrift für vergleichende Rechtswissenschaft* 6 (1886), 403.

[58] *Kaeyŏk p'an kwansŭp chosa pogosŏ*, 330, citing *Kyŏngguk taejŏn* (*Yejŏn*, *Iphu cho*) and *Hyŏngpŏp taejŏn*, Article 582.

[59] According to a study, both practices of allowing an illegitimate son to succeed or adopting a son were in existence in late Chosŏn. See Pae Chae-hong, "Chosŏn hugi sŏŏl hŏt'ong kwa sinbun [The Abrogation of Discriminations against *sŏŏl* and Personal Status in Late Chosŏn]" (PhD diss., Kyŏngbuk University, 1994), 229–253.

[60] Judgement of May 20, 1913, *Hanketsuroku*, vol. 2, 200–219 (*Kugyŏk*, 153–169). See the earlier reply from the head of the Investigation Bureau (May 10, 1911) recognizing the validity of adoption with the presence of a secondary son. *Minji kanshū kaitō ishū*, 55–57.

[61] Pae, "Chosŏn hugi sŏŏl hŏt'ong," 253.

[62] *Minji kanshū kaitō ishū*, 179–181, 215–216.

High Court duly rendered a decision in a subsequent case in favor of the child adopted inter vivos.[63]

In 1917, an illegitimate son sued a party who had been established as an heir after the death of the father.[64] The lower court decided that adoption after death, regardless of whether there was a son from the secondary wife, was a Korean custom. The high court reversed this decision, however, distinguishing between inter vivos and postmortem practices.[65] The court declared that the adoption of an heir when there was already a son from the secondary wife was "valid only when the arrangement had been made during the lifetime or in the will" and that the act by the widow or the clan members of adopting an heir for the decedent disregarding the son from the secondary wife could not be recognized as custom. The court added that even "postmortem adoption despite the presence of a secondary son is not an established custom, and remains an individual, and exceptional, practice among the powerful. It does not have effect as customary law."[66] The significance of this decision is that the court distinguished mere practice from customary law. Later, the court reasoned that postmortem adoption should be disallowed because it would create the effect of delaying the beginning of succession, thereby creating confusion and disruptions in society.[67] In more practical terms, the effect of the adoption practice that put secondary sons at a disadvantage was limited. What the court was doing, in fact, was loosening the rigid observance of the lineage system based on Confucian kinship organization. Jurisprudential streamlining of customary law under the impulsion of colonial legal system was fully at work.

The high court confirmed the existence of the practice of fostering a child with a different surname (*suyanja*).[68] *Suyanja*'s legal effect was to be distinguished from adoption for the performance of ancestor ceremonies, which prohibited nonagnatic adoption, but the court's sympathy for nonagnatic adoption, justifiable in terms of human activity, could not be mistaken.

In certain issues, the courts simply applied the Japanese Civil Code, without any discussion of Korean custom. Cases of dissolving adoptive relations were such examples. The customs survey reported that the dissolution of adoption was allowed when the adopted son failed to fulfill filial obligations.[69] When the adopted son did not care for the adoptive father who was ill, the father could dissolve the adoptive relations, the court ruled, because it amounted to

[63] Judgment of January 29, 1915, *Hanketsuroku*, vol. 3, 9 (*Kugyŏk*, 7).

[64] For an analysis of the case, see Sim Hŭi-gi, "Ilche kangjŏm ch'ogi singminji kwansŭp pŏp ŭi hyŏngsŏng" [The Making of Colonial Customary Law in Early Japanese Rule]," *Pŏpsahak yŏngu* 28 (2003), 18–22.

[65] Judgment of November 7, 1917, *Hanketsuroku*, vol. 4, 1018 (*Kugyŏk*, 764).

[66] The Old Custom and System Investigation Committee voted in 1920 against allowing adoption when there was an illegitimate son. See *Minji kanshū kaitō ishū*, appendices, 23–24.

[67] Judgment of February 15, 1927, *Hanketsuroku*, vol. 14, 33–34.

[68] Judgment of May 5, 1922, *Hanketsuroku*, vol. 9, 170.

[69] *Kaeyŏk p'an kwansŭp chosa pogosŏ*, 334–336 (No. 138).

a violation of filial duty.[70] In 1923, however, the court stated that Chosŏn's custom allowing unilateral dissolution of adoption were no longer in effect; it instead enforced dissolution of relationship by agreement, as provided in Japanese law.[71]

The revision of the Chosŏn Civil Ordinance in 1939 rendered adoption to be governed by the Japanese Civil Code. Nomura Chotarō confirmed that jurisprudence construed Korean custom to conform to the civil code provision. Nomura served as the Chosŏn High Court judge from 1923 to 1934 and as the chief judge of Pyŏngyang Appeals Court until his retirement in 1941, after which he worked as an attorney in Korea.[72] He was one of the most eminent authorities on Korean family and succession laws and a frequent contributor to *Shihō kyōkai zasshi.* Following the revision of the civil ordinance in 1939, Nomura wrote:

> The custom was unclear regarding what constituted the elements necessary for demanding dissolution, and there was no rule about the time limit during which dissolution could take place. [The custom] remained very unreasonable. Therefore today's revision was necessary. The courts must from now on follow the provision of the Article 866 of the civil code.[73]

Korean "customs" – more precisely, Confucian ritual practices that were in conflict with Japanese Civil Code provisions – were progressively transformed through law and jurisprudence.

Cases involving spousal relationship customs were examples in which the Chosŏn High Court distanced its decisions early on from traditional practices. The court deemed a number of marriage and divorce customs to be unreasonable and provided for new rules as demanded by civil law principles. In 1912, the court upheld the concubine's right to terminate the relationship unilaterally. The justices were apparently determined to abolish concubinage. The court wrote: "it is Chosŏn's custom that concubinage can be terminated by any party; it does not require judicial approval."[74] In Chosŏn Korea, the wife could not demand divorce, which took place by unilateral declaration by the husband.[75] The customs survey report enumerated the grounds on which the

[70] Judgment of November 28, 1919, *Hanketsuroku*, vol. 6, 588 (*Kugyŏk*, 437).

[71] Judgment of July 13, 1923, *Hanketruku*, vol. 10, 217.

[72] See Hong Yang-hŭi, "Chosŏn ch'ongdokpu p'ansa Nomura Chotarō ŭi Chosŏn sahoe insik," *Kajok pŏp yŏngu* 23, no.1 (2009): 61–86; Kim Sang-su, "Chosŏn Kodŭng Pŏpwŏn p'ansa," 33–35.

[73] Nomura Chōtarō, "Chōsen kajoku seido no suii [The Transition of the Family System of Chosŏn]," *Chōsen* 296 (January 1940), 33.

[74] Judgment of December 13, 1912, *Hanketsuroku*, vol. 2, 84 (*Kugyŏk*, 64–66).

[75] *Kyŏngkuk taejŏn*, Articles 578–581. *Hyŏngpŏp taejŏn*, promulgated in 1905, confirmed that a wife cannot demand divorce. As in Korea, divorce in old Japan was a unilateral act of the husband. Divorce was completed simply by sending a letter to the wife, in which the husband "dismissed" her. The Japanese phrase, "a note of three and a half lines," testifies to the ease with which divorce was obtained by the husband. Traditional divorce custom was abrogated by the civil code. Ume Kenjirō stressed the serious legal consequences of marriage as a contract: "In the

husband could expel the wife.[76] No divorce by mutual agreement existed. In many cases, whether to end marriage was a decision made by the parents of the spouses, not the spouses themselves.[77]

Disregarding traditional pratices, the Chosŏn High Court recognized early on the spouse's right to file for divorce.[78] In 1915, the wife's right to seek judicial divorce was affirmed. The case involved a situation in which the husband abused the wife's mother and assaulted her causing injury. The court stated: "This court has recognized that, even among Koreans, the wife has the right to demand divorce from the husband when there are legitimate reasons for divorce."[79] The court allowed the wife to seek divorce not on the grounds that this practice was Korean custom (it was not); rather, it did so in order to reach an equitable result. It was unmistakable that this decision, which effectively became a judge-made law, was prompted by the court's desire to change what it regarded as an unreasonable custom. The Old Customs and the System Investigation Committee stated in 1921: "Divorce initiated by the wife used to be not allowed. Recently some people filed suit for divorce and the court granted divorce by trial when there was sufficient cause."[80] After the court allowed judicial divorce, divorce filing i ncreased rapidly. The number of divorces was 6.5 times higher during the period of 1917–1921 compared with the period of 1908–1916.[81] It reveals that judicial divorce – and the availability of the system put in place by judicial lawmaking – provided Korean wives with the framework and instrument with which to exert their right of divorce.

Divorce cases indicate that the court's stance was unequivocal when the disputes over custom involved individual liberty and rights protected in the Japanese Civil Code; in such cases the judges had no qualms in simply ignoring the Korean practices which they deemed inequitable. There was a close

new civil code, marriage is more stricty regulated than in the past. Likewise, divorce must not be easily allowed unless there is agreement by both parties, and in particular must not be granted upon a unilateral request by one party." *Minpō yōgi* [Digest of Civil Law], vol. 4 (Shinzoku hen) (Tokyo: Shiritsu Hōsei Daigaku, Yūhigaku Shobō, 1916, 1899), 197–198. See Uchida, "Meiji minpō no kaishaku," 60.

76 *Kaeyŏk p'an kwansŭp chosa pogosŏ*, 323–326 (No. 134); see Fujita Tōzō, *Chōsen shinzokuhō sōzokuhō shu to shite Chōsen Kōtō Hōin hanrei o chūshin to shite no kōsatsu* [The Succession Law of Chosŏn, An Examination in Particular on the Basis of the Decisions of the Chōsen Kōtō Hōin] (Seoul: Ōsaka Yagō Shoten, 1933), 111.

77 *Kaeyŏk p'an kwansŭp chosa pogosŏ*, 312–321 (No. 130).

78 Judgment of December 13, 1911, *Hanketsuroku*, vol. 2, 84.

79 Judgment of July 6, 1915, *Hanketsuroku*, vol. 3, 215 (*Kugyŏk*, 156); the quote is in 223 (*Kugyŏk*, 164). See also the judgment of October 23, 1917, *Hanketsuroku*, vol. 4, 873–879 (*Kugyŏk*, 653–658); judgment of December 23, 1921, *Hanketsuroku*, vol. 8, 597. For divorce litigation, see Yoshikawa, "Ilche sigi ihon sosong."

80 Resolution of the Old Customs and Legal System Investigation Commission, August 6 and 17, 1921, *Minji kanshū kaitō ishū*, appendix, 19–20.

81 The statistics of divorce between 1908 and 1916 in Chōsen Sōtokufu Shihōbu Hōmuka, "Chōsenjin aida no rikon soshō [Divorce Litigation among Koreans]," *Chōsen ihō* (February 1918), 112.

coordination on the judicial and administrative level to promote the reform of customs. When the judges were reluctant to disregard Korean custom openly, the colonial officials used administrative means to abolish certain customary practices. The example was seen in underage marriage, a deeply entrenched custom in Korean society. The customs survey condemned the underage marriage practice as evil custom.[82] The colonial government began to impose administrative sanctions on marriages between minor parties – a male under seventeen years of age and a female under fifteen – as stipulated in the Japanese Civil Code. While marriage itself was outside bureaucratic control because it did not require official recognition under Korean custom, the registration of marriage was subject to the family registration law, allowing the government to intervene. The official bulletin issued on August 7, 1915, instructed local administrative offices not to process applications to record underage marriages on the civil registry. The effect was that the children born out of such marriages were treated as illegitimate children.[83]

Case law in family matters was incorporated into legislation in the form of periodic revisions of the Chosŏn Civil Ordinance. As seen previously, the revision of the civil ordinance issued on December 7, 1922, provided that marriage and divorce be governed no longer by custom but by the Japanese Civil Code. The result was the statutory legalization of divorce by consent and divorce by trial and the prohibition of underage marriage.

The court in general took care to formulate its reasoning in terms of custom but its reference to the term "custom" was not always persuasive or juridically convincing. In 1930, the court declared that a party could ask the court to void marriage concluded by fraud. But the court somewhat puzzlingly stated that this "was Korea's custom that was naturally created following the establishment of the judicial system."[84] Here, there was little question that what the court called custom was in fact a trend or practice, not custom in the legal meaning that the judges had to apply with the force of law.

The Chosŏn High Court's role in reordering Korea's succession relations requires special attention. As seen in previous chapters, a system of property succession did not exist in Chosŏn Korea. Strictly speaking, the only succession that took place was the succession by ritual heir who was the eldest son. The customs survey report of 1910 categorized the Korean succession system into ritual succession, property succession, and household headship succession, but acknowledged that these classifications were not an accurate representation of the Korean system. The report stated:

> The Japanese Civil Code's categories distinguishing between household headship succession and property succession are not suitable for explaining the Korean succession system. Nevertheless, we intend to follow temporarily the existing categories, and explain ritual succession and family headship succession in terms

[82] *Kaeyŏk p'an kwansŭp chosa pogosŏ*, 312 (No. 130).
[83] Yi Sŭng-il, *Chosŏn ch'ongdokpu pŏpche chŏngch'aek*, 186–189.
[84] Judgment of July 18, 1930, *Hanketsuroku*, vol. 17, 151.

> of our house [*ie*] succession and describe property inheritance under our property succession category regardless of whether it takes place simultaneously with ritual succession and family headship succession.[85]

The colonial jurists continued to apply these "provisional" classifications and the concept of property succession, with attendant legal rights, came to take root in Korea.[86] As the Japanese jurists observed in 1923: "Previously the term succession was not used in Chosŏn; it is only a recent development that it came into use in laws and court decisions and also in ordinary usages."[87]

The Chūchūin (Chungch'uwŏn) was the government general's advisory council composed of Korean notables. The Chūchūin's report in 1935 explained the establishment of the concept of property succession in Korea in the following terms:

> In the old times,... property was divided according to the agreement of all heirs and thus no one could monopolize it. There was a concept in Korea that the property before division still belonged to the decedent. No one could make a claim on the property before division.... In recent times, however, no property can exist for a moment without ownership, and the succession of property has come to occur concomitant with the succession of the family headship.[88]

When Japan introduced the house (*ie*) system into Korea and imposed household headship succession through the family registration regulation, it treated the new system as if it were the equivalent to Korea's ritual succession because both involved the succession of status. In reality, the Korean concept of family head was different from the Japanese household head.[89] The family head in Chosŏn referred to the oldest male, designated as such for the purpose of tax or military obligations. It did not refer to any special status within the family and had no relevance to property succession. But the colonial authorities saw in it ready grounds for transplanting the Japanese succession system. As a Korean colonial judge observed, the colonial courts "tried to incorporate the Civil Code's household headship concept into Chosŏn's custom."[90]

The Korean succession custom was now construed in such a way that the entire property of the deceased was bequeathed to the ritual heir, the eldest son,

[85] *Kaeyŏk p'an kwansŭp chosa pogosŏ*, 347 (No. 158).

[86] The resolution of the Old Customs and the System Investigation Committee confirmed this categorization. *Minji kanshū kaitō ishū*, Appendix, 25. See Hong Yang-hŭi, "Singminji sigi ch'injok kwansŭp ŭi ch'angch'ul kwa Ilbon minpŏp [The Creation of Succession Custom during the Colonial Period and the Japanese Civil Code]," *Ch'ŏngsin munhwa yŏngu* 28, no. 3 (2005): 121–145.

[87] *Minji kanshū kaitō ishū*, Appendix, 42–43.

[88] Cited from Chŏng Kwang-hyŏn, *Hanguk kajok pŏp yŏngu*, 202; see Yang Hyunah, "Envisioning Feminist Jurisprudence in Korean Family Law at the Crossroads of Tradition/Modernity" (PhD diss., New School for Social Research, 1998), 57.

[89] The Japanese jurists acknowledged differences between house succession and household head succession. *Minji kanshū kaitō ishū*, 45–46.

[90] Ch'oe Pyŏng-chu. "Minjirei jūichi cho no kanshū," 35.

who then divided the property among the heirs.[91] To share in the distribution, the other heirs had to establish separate households. In principle, males in the household succeeded, although women could become household heads when there were no male members.[92] This is how, historians argue, the Japanese system caused the demise of the equal distribution principle in Korea and Koreans have come to mistake primogeniture for their traditional succession rule.[93]

The Korean ritual succession system was incompatible with the Japanese civil law. Nomura Chōtarō pointed out that although ritual succession was a pivotal feature of the Korean succession system it did not implicate any legal rights: ritual succession was only the standard for deciding who would become the household head.[94] In 1933, the colonial high court set aside ritual succession all together, declaring that it was a mere practice of acquiring an "ethical status" to perform ancestor ceremonies.[95] In this way, the Japanese turned the fluid succession system of Korea into a fixed system that conformed to the civil code provisions.

Court cases concerning individual inheritance disputes were largely resolved with a view to produce just and reasonable results. Evidence shows that the Chosŏn High Court was keen on protecting the property rights of women. In a series of decisions regarding property succession involving women, the court initially hinged its decisions on whether the decedent and the successor were in the same household, in other words, listed in the same family register (*hojŏk*). In 1913, the court rejected the appellant's argument that it was Korea's custom that the descendants of the husband inherited the property of the concubine who died without children. The court noted that the concubine was the household head and that the appellant was not in the same household as the deceased. The court wrote:

> At the death of the former concubine who became the household head, even the descendants of the decedent's husband cannot succeed if they are not in the same household as the deceased. In case there are no natural heirs of the deceased, one can entrust ritual ceremony to a descendant in the maternal line and let that person succeed the property. This is Korea's custom.[96]

[91] Judgment of July 1, 1913, *Hanketsuroku*, vol. 2, 23; *Minji kanshū kaitō ishū*, 141.

[92] Judgment of December 1, 1922, *Hanketsuroku*, vol. 9, 53; *Minji kanshū kaitō ishū*, 136–137.

[93] Pak, *Hanguk pŏpchesa go*, 16; Pak Pyŏng-ho, "Ilche ha ŭi kajok chŏngch'aek kwa kwansŭp pŏp hyŏngsŏng kwajŏng [Family Policy and the Process of Customary Law Formation under Japanese Rule]," *Seoul Taehakkyo pŏphak* 33 (1992) 1–3; Yi Sang-uk, "Ilche ha hoju sangsok kwansŭp pŏp ŭi chŏngnip [The Establishment of the Household Headship System under Japanese Rule]," *Pŏpsahak yŏngu* 9 (1988): 23–61.

[94] Nomura Chōtarō, "Sosen no saishi to genkō no hōritsu [Ancestor Worship Ceremony and Current Law]," *Shihō kyōkai zasshi* 5, no. 4 (1926), 17. Nomura stated: "one cannot understand household headship succession relations without ritual succession. In Korea status succession is based on ritual succession." Nomura Chōtarō, "Chōsen ni okeru shinzoku kanshu no jitsujō to sono hōritsu ue no shuyō mondai [The Reality of Family Succession Custom in Chosŏn and Its Principal Legal Questions]," *Hōritsu jihō* 11, no. 9 (1939), 18.

[95] Judgment of March 3, 1933, *Hanketsuroku*, vol. 29, 154.

[96] Judgment of May 6, 1913, *Hanketsuroku*, vol. 2, 196–99. This opinion is translated into Korean in Chŏng Kwang-hyŏn, *Hanguk kajok pŏp yŏngu*, 285–87. For an analysis, see Yang Hyŏn-a,

This decision represented the court's position that both ritual succession and property succession could take place through the maternal line as long as the deceased and the heir were in the same household.

A case from 1924 concerned the impact of divorce on succession. In this case, the daughter was raised by the mother following divorce. The mother remarried and had her daughter inscribed on her new husband's family record. When the daughter died before marriage, the court upheld the succession of her property by her mother, not natural father, on the grounds that the mother and the daughter were in the same household. The court stated:

> Regardless of whether the deceased was the household head or a member of the family, the successor must be in the same household as the deceased. Those in other households cannot succeed. This is Korea's custom.[97]

The court emphasized that it was Chosŏn's custom that a married daughter who entered to the husband's household lost the right to succeed. In a number of similar cases, the court confirmed the requirement that the decedent and the successor be in the same household.[98]

Several years later, however, the court's position took a different turn. A case was brought to the court in 1933 in which the daughter claimed her right to inherit her mother's property. The daughter, married, was not in the same household as the mother. Finding in her favor, the court simply departed from its earlier decision that required that the deceased and the heir be in the same household. The court wrote: "The deceased's property is succeeded by her heir, regardless of whether the heir belongs to the same household as the decedent. Korea's custom does not make any distinction."[99]

Note that each time the court repeated the formula, "this is Korea's custom." One can see that such a statement was less a reference to actual custom than an appeal to the legitimacy of the rules the court applied. The contents of the "custom" were adaptable depending on the situations, as dictated by particular circumstances. The court was most concerned with rendering equitable decisions. Under the broad rubric of customary law, the judges were essentially free to execute their jurisprudential assumptions.

In 1935, the high court reviewed the statute of limitations on the recovery of succession rights. The court found in 1920 that "Chosŏn does not have a fixed custom" denying the legitimate successor's claim.[100] In case an unqualified

"Singminji sigi Hanguk kajok pŏp ŭi kwansŭp munche (I): sigan ŭisik ŭi silchong ŭl chungsim ŭro [The Question of Custom in Colonial Korean Family Law: With Particular Attention to the Loss of the Concept of Time]," *Sahoe wa yŏksa* 58 (2000): 35–70.

97 Judgment of September 2, 1924, *Hanketsuroku*, vol. 11, 168–172; see a Korean translation of the opinion in Chŏng Kwang-hyŏn, *Hanguk kajok pŏp yŏngu*, 289–292.

98 See judgment of September 22, 1922, *Hanketsuroku*, vol. 9, 370; judgment of December 15, 1925, *Hanketsuroku*, vol. 12, 483.

99 Judgment of December 8, 1933, *Hanketsuroku*, vol. 20, 461–64; see the Korean translation in Chŏng Kwang-hyŏn, *Hanguk kajok pŏp yŏngu*, 293–95.

100 Judgment of June 23, 1920, *Hanketsuroku*, vol. 7, 287.

person had already succeeded, the legitimate successor could exercise his right to reclaim succession without time limit.[101] Fifteen years later, however, the court reversed its own decision, citing the authority of Korean custom. The right of the legitimate successor to reclaim succession "is clearly established as custom in Chosŏn," but

> it is also recognized as Chosŏn's custom that, if the successor or his legal representative fails to exercise his rights to claim recovery of succession to household headship and property within a certain time limit, either from the knowledge of the violation of his rights or from the beginning of succession, such rights expire.[102]

The decision, rationalized by the court's consideration of "custom," was favorably received by jurists that the statute of limitation would ensure the validity of succession transactions. However, Yasuda Kanta, professor of law at Keijō Imperial University, pointedly criticized the court's ruling on the grounds that it had abused the concept of custom.[103] According to him, the rule stipulating a time limit for the legitimate successor's claim was both necessary and desirable; both Korean legal consciousness and the principle of law required it. Nevertheless, he argued, it was wrong for the court to say that "custom" to that effect governed in Korea. In reality, the court's decision was merely responding to the requirements of reason (*jōri*). Yasuda argued:

> In order to call those rules custom, it is necessary to confirm that such practices existed in the past and were repeatedly observed. [But] the practice [of imposing time limitation] is not witnessed in Korea. The present decision states that it is based on the existence of custom but it is not more than a justification intended to satisfy the formality that the decision was reached under Article 11 of the civil ordinance. In reality, the court appropriated the term custom to establish precedents that satisfy the demands of reason.[104]

The court should have justified its decision in terms of reason, Yasuda castigated, rather than taking refuge behind custom.

This case, similar to the adoption case cited earlier in which the court reversed itself upon *finding* a different custom, evinces the mutable and pliant nature of judge-made customary law. The concept of custom provided the legal machinery with which Korean practices could be fashioned and revised to produce desirable outcome.

[101] Judgment of March 12, 1920, *Hanketsuroku*, vol. 7, 88. For the colonial jurisprudence of the recovery of succession rights, see Yun Chin-su, "Sangsok hoebok ch'ŏnggukwŏn ŭi yŏngu: yŏksa chok mit pigyopŏp chŏk koch'al [A Study of the Rights to Demand Succession Recovery: From Historical and Comparative Legal Perspectives]." *Seoul Taehakkyo pŏphak* 41, no. 1 (2000): 172–208.

[102] Judgment of July 30, 1935, *Hanketsuroku*, vol. 22, 302–308 (the quote is in 306–307).

[103] Yasuda Kanta, "Sōzoku kaihuku seikyūken no honsitzu" [The Nature of Succession Recovery Claim], *Shihō kyōkai zasshi* 15, no. 3 (March 1936), 109–140.

[104] Ibid., 126–127.

FIGURE 6.1. **The Chosŏn High Court building shown in a postcard, circa 1935.** Both the colonial high court and, after independence, the Supreme Court of Korea (Taepŏpwŏn) occupied this building in Sŏsomundong in Seoul continuously from 1928 to 1995. Collection of Korea Creative Content Agency (KOCCA). Reproduced with permission.

Customary Property Rights

Article 12 of the Chosŏn Civil Ordinance recognized customary property rights among Koreans. It was a departure from the Japanese Civil Code rule that property rights could be created and enjoyed only through statutory rules.[105] The customs survey report of 1910 listed six kinds of customary real rights in Korea: ownership, tenancy, superficies, the right of common, lien, and pledge.[106] Korean property customs were seemingly similar to those in Japan and these similarities led some jurists to argue that it was not necessary to recognize in law the property custom of Korea. Judge Yoshida Heijirō, who called for the abolition of Article 10 of the civil ordinance, argued for the abolition of Article 12 of the civil ordinance as well. He claimed that there were no unique Korean customs in real rights that could not be covered by the Japanese Civil Code. In Meiji Japan, property customs were comprehensively reworked during the codification of civil law and selected customs were incorporated into the statutes. Article 12 was not abandoned before the end of the colonial period. But in practice its scope was substantially reduced and Korean customs of property rights were rapidly subsumed under the Japanese Civil Code.

105 Article 175 of the Japanese Civil code stipulated: "No type of real property rights can be created other than through regulations in the Civil Code or other laws."

106 *Kaeyŏk p'an kwansŭp chosa pogosŏ*, 137–139 (No. 22).

Establishing a modern type of proprietorship was a pressing concern in both Japan and Korea. The colonial judges were particularly wary of customs that might create confusion in land ownership rights and tax liabilities.[107] The registration and publication system of real property was viewed as a key element of establishing modern property rights. Article 13 of the civil ordinance, the equivalent to Article 177 of the Japanese Civil Code, provided that "registration or certification is required for the acquisition and transfer of real property ownership in order to resist the third party's claim." The Chosŏn Real Property Registration Regulation was issued on March 20, 1912, the same day the civil ordinance was issued. In this situation, it was only natural that the judges tended to interpret property customs narrowly within the limits allowed in various statutes.

A property custom which drew considerable attention from the jurists in both Japan and colonial Korea was superficies. A superficies (*chisangkwŏn* in Korean; *chijōken* in Japanese) is the right to own buildings or trees separately from the ownership of the land on which they stood. How the Meiji laws regulated superficies is illuminating in understanding the superficies in Korea. The Japanese custom of treating buildings and land as separate real properties was a departure from the Roman law principle "*superficies solo cedit* [the surface yields to the ground]," that is, the legal destiny of a building was connected irrevocably to that of the land it was standing on. This was the principle incorporated in French and German law. In Japanese customs, land in pledge did not include the building.[108] Ume Kenjirō, who was responsible for drafting provisions on real rights in the civil code, advocated the unified system of land and the building and a combined registry.[109] All the drafters, including Tomii and Hozumi, were in favor of adding to Article 86 of the civil code the language, "the attachment to land is part of land unless there is a provision otherwise." But their position met opposition that it was against Japan's old custom. Eventually the Japanese Civil Code treated land and the building separately and statutory superficies were recognized. The drafters had to be content with the final version of Article 86 that said "land and things fixed thereto are immovables."[110]

Superficies were categorized in the civil code as a real right rather than an obligation. It constituted a right separate from the land ownership of another person.[111] As such, it could be set up against a third person whereas the right of leasing – which superficies really was – could not. After the civil code took effect, landowners rented out residential land for the most part under contracts of lease rather than superficies. A number of laws were enacted to protect the

[107] Röhl, *History of Law in Japan*, 206.

[108] Hironaka Toshio and Hoshino Eiichi, *Minpōten no hyakunen* [The Hundred Years of the Civil Code] (Tokyo: Yūhigaku, 1998), vol. 2, 645.

[109] Ibid., 647.

[110] Hoshino, *Hōgaku ronshu*, vol. 1, 147; Röhl, *History of Law in Japan*, 219.

[111] Ishii, *Japanese Legislation*, 626; Röhl, *History of Law in Japan*, 219.

lessees: the law of May 1909 made it possible for the lessee and the superficiary to set up against third persons as long as the buildings were registered.

In traditional Korea, there was no clear distinction between real property and movable property. Sale or pledge of the building normally included land unless special notation was made to the effect that the building was sold without land. The customs survey report of 1910 noted that the building was the main property and the land was the supplementary property.[112] As seen in Chapter 4, a series of land ownership laws were drafted by Ume Kenjirō during the protectorate period on the model of the Meiji laws, and the 1906 Land and Building Certification Regulations required that the building and land be separately certified. The customs survey report stated: "there is no custom recognizing the preemption right of the landowner. The lease right can be set up against a third person. Even if the ownership of the land is transferred, the lease holder can demand his right to lease from the new landowner. When the lease is transferred, the transferee succeeds the lease right."[113]

In May 1910, the Pyŏngyang District Court queried the protectorate government whether it was Chosŏn's custom that the landowner could not demand the removal of the house built on his land without permission. The Code Investigation Bureau replied:

> According to Korean custom, one cannot refuse, other than in exceptional cases, the request to lease or purchase uncultivated land for the purpose of construction of the house. Building a house on someone else's land without permission is not allowed and is illegal, but once construction is completed the owner of the land cannot demand its removal. This is what we are told to be Korean custom. The landowner can only demand rent payment. Therefore it seems that the landowner cannot demand the removal of the building. But this custom has become less acceptable during the last several decades. Consequently, nowadays the landowner can refuse the request for lease or purchase of the land, even in the case of uncultivated land, and also force the removal when someone builds a house on his land without permission. He can demand payment for such use."[114]

Here one can see that the existence of the traditional land usages was acknowledged but the officials stressed the change of such customs and were inclined to limit their effect.[115]

How did the colonial courts deal with superficies? The courts originally found that Korean custom regarded land as part of the building.[116] Superficies

[112] *Kaeyŏk p'an kwansŭp chosa pogosŏ*, 120 (No. 10).

[113] Ibid., 186 (No. 34).

[114] *Minji kanshū kaitō ishū*, 24–25 (Reply from the Code Investigation Bureau of June 29, 1910, to the inquiry from Pyŏngyang District Court).

[115] *Kaeyŏk p'an kwansŭp chosa pogosŏ*, 186 (No. 34).

[116] Song Yŏng-min, "T'oji wa kŏnmul ŭl pyŏlgae ŭi mulgŏn ŭro ch'wigŭp hanŭn mimpŏp t'aedo e kwanhan pŏpsahak chŏk il koch'al [An Examination of the Position of the Civil Code that Treats Land and Building as Separate Things, a Legal and Historical Perspective]," *T'oji pŏphak* 19 (2003): 3–23; Kwŏn Chae-mun, "Kwansŭp pŏp sang pŏpchŏng chisangkwŏn ŭi injŏng

survived the transfer of land. But the Chosŏn High Court limited the scope of superficies by strictly implementing the registration requirement. Questions arose when both land and the building initially belonged to the same owner but later came to be owned by different persons as a result of legal act such as auction. Did the building owner have the right to purchase the land on the expiration of the real property lease which included no agreement regarding the rights of land use? In 1916, the high court heard a case on these issues.

The facts of the case were as follows.[117] The plaintiff obtained the ownership of a field from auction. The defendant had been maintaining a house on the same land. The plaintiff sued, demanding the demolishment of the house and alternatively damage payments. The defendant stated that the land and the house had originally belonged to a Yun and that in auction the land was sold to the plaintiff and the building to a Pae, from whom the defendant purchased the house. The defendant argued that the plaintiff was aware of the existence of the house when he purchased the land and that this fact amounted to the plaintiff's tacit approval of the continued existence of the house. The defendant claimed that in traditional Korea there was no custom that the owner of the land had the right to demand the building's removal.

The defendant's argument was accepted in part and rejected in part. The court stated that "when land and the house that had once belonged to a single person came to be owned by two different persons, it is Chosŏn's custom that, unless there was an agreement on the sale of the land to remove the house, the owner of the house obtains superficies and the landowner cannot force the removal of the house." The court found that such custom applied to the cases when the ownership changed through mandatory auction and that "the duration of superficies and the amount of the rent to be charged need to be decided through the agreement between the owner of the land and the owner of the house." In other words, the terms of the agreement were up to the two parties to decide. "Only when such agreement exists," the court stated, "one can request the court to render a decision. This is Chosŏn's custom."

Here the court formulated the issue as a contract question. If the auction took place with the agreement that the purchaser of the house would remove the house, the party who bought the house from the original purchaser would have no right to maintain the house. On the other hand, absent such an agreement, "it is presumed that the parties intended to maintain the building as it was." The court concluded that the lower court, Taegu Appeals Court, made the error of not determining whether the auction took place

kunkŏ wa p'ilyosŏng e kwanhan pip'anjŏk koch'al [A Critical Examination of the Foundation and Necessity for Recognizing Superficies in Customary Law]," *Pŏpsahak yŏngu* 37 (2008): 99–127; Kang Sin-ung, "kwansup pŏp sang pŏpjŏng ch'isangkwŏn e kwanhan yŏngu [A Study of Superficies in Customary Law]," *Pŏphak yŏngu* 31 (2008): 97–118. The modern Korean civil law treats land and buildings separately, maintaining separate registries (The Real Property Registration Law, Article 14).

[117] Judgment of September 29, 1916, *Hanketsuroku*, vol. 3, 722 (*Kugyŏk*, 531). This case is discussed in Song, "T'oji wa kŏnmul," 11.

under the agreement that the house be removed. Regardless of the finding, however, a superficiary could resist the third party claim only when he had completed the registration requirements. In the case before the court, the defendant failed to satisfy these conditions, stated the court. In other words, while it confirmed that the separate treatment of land and building was Chosŏn's custom and that superficies was customary law, the court strictly enforced the statutory requirements that the acquisition and transfer of property rights be registered. It was a ruling that seriously limited the exercise of customary rights.

In another case in 1930, the court reaffirmed that superficies needed registration. The purchaser of the building obtained a superficies right but failed to register his right. So the party could not resist the successor of the landowner "even after his right was confirmed by the court against the purchaser of the land."[118] These decisions revealed that the court, while recognizing the Korean customary right of superficies, neatly formulated it to conform to the provisions in the Japanese Civil Code. In order to prevent the situation in which the landowner could not stop the unauthorized building of a house on his land or demand its removal, the justices limited the effect of custom by resorting to the official registration requirement. The fundamental concern of the court was to clarify property ownership.[119]

In traditional Korea and Japan, there existed a kind of tenancy which was distinct from ordinary fixed-term tenancy. This was called emphyteusis (*yŏng sojak kwŏn* in Korea; *ei kosaku ken* in Japanese). The tenant, emphyteuta, held his land permanently unless the owner purchased the right from the tenant.[120] The tenant's right was not affected by the change in ownership of the land. This right could be bequeathed, assigned, or leased without the consent of the owner, and it could set up against a new landlord when the land was sold to another.[121] The colonial officials observed that one obtained a

[118] Judgment of May 30, 1930, *Hanketsuroku*, vol. 17, 126.

[119] For the Japanese court decisions on superficies, see Taniguchi Tomohei, "La Loi et la coutume au Japon," in *Etude juridique offertes à Léon Julliot de la Morandière* (Paris: Librairie Dalloz, 1964), 574, citing the judgment of February 10, 1917. The Daishinin repudiated a custom that had allowed the owner of land to terminate unilaterally the simple superficies in order to increase real estate rent. In Korea, the colonial judicial construction of legal superficies was sustained by the postcolonial courts. The Korean Supreme Court stated in 1968: "legal superficies was a system recognized due to the need for the economy of the nation." Judgment of August 30, 1968 (68 ta 1029).

[120] *Kaeyŏk p'an kwansŭp chosa pogosŏ*, 187–194 (No. 35). For property rights during the colonial period, see Yi Ch'ŏl-u, "T'oji chosa saup kwa t'oji soyu pŏpche ui pyŏnch'ŏn [The Land Cadastre and the Evolution of the Land Ownership System in Law]," in *Hanguk pŏpsahak nonch'ong* (Seoul: Pagyŏngsa, 1991), 349–370.

[121] For permanent tenancy in Japan, see Ishii, *Japanese Legislation*, 627. In the agricultural reform of June 1873, the Meiji government recognized the possessor of fief as the owner of immovable property but granted the right to cultivate the soil to the cultivator. This way, ancient real estate ownership was replaced by a modern type of proprietorship but the right to cultivate was preserved on the condition of payment for tenancy. In order to distinguish the tenant from the landowner so that the latter could be issued a land title, the government ordered in 1875 that

permanent tenancy right when he improved uncultivated land with the consent of the owner; this right was recognized as a customary property right.[122] The customs investigation report found that permanent tenancy was much more widespread in Korea than in Japan.[123] In Japan, the need to distinguish the tenant from the landowner led to a provision in the new civil code that limited the duration of an emphyteusis to not fewer than twenty years but not more than fifty years.[124] The colonial court in Korea followed suit and construed emphyseusis as lease rights. It ruled in 1915: "In accordance with the civil ordinance, permanent tenancy is limited to fifty years as in the Japanese Civil Code."[125]

Another customary property right concerned the practice of *chŏnse*. *Chŏnse* was a unique Korean custom in which the tenant obtained the right to use the house in return for the deposit of key money to the landlord. The colonial judge Yoshida argued that a *chŏnse* contract created not a property right but an obligation only.[126] The colonial court treated the custom of *chŏnse* as a credit as part of an obligation – like leasing – instead of a real property right. The *chŏnse* contract was equated to a consumer loan in which the house served as the security.[127] In this way, the colonial court interpreted the *chŏnse* custom in terms of the Japanese civil law concept.

The Daishinin's Jurisprudence of Korean Customary Law

The examination of colonial jurisprudence reveals that the term "customary law" as used in the courts was rather incongruous and often malleable. Perhaps it is not surprising that the treatment of Korean custom by the colonial high court was more elastic and its interpretation more voluntarist than the interpretation of the same custom by the Japanese Daishinin. Because of the personality law system of customary law that the colonial empire maintained, the courts in Japan often had to adjudicate cases involving Korean residents according to Korean custom. Their construction of Korean custom was relatively conservative. There is an interesting decision rendered by the Daishinin in 1941 that sheds light on the Japanese courts' position regarding the relationship between Japanese law and Korean custom. It is instructive to note that, while the colonial courts were generally eager to promote jurisprudential

the title "emphyteuta" be abolished for anyone who had enjoyed this status for twenty years; tenancy could not be contracted for more than twenty years at a time.

122 *Minji kanshū kaitō ishū*, 184–5 (August 1914) and 201.

123 *Kaeyŏk p'an kwansŭp chosa pogosŏ*, 187–196 (No. 35).

124 Ishii, *Japanese Legislation*, 627; Röhl, *History of Law in Japan*, 216. Ume Kenjirō came to the conclusion that a similar change in Korea would result in serious problems. See Chapter 4.

125 Judgement of July 2, 1915, *Hanketsuroku*, vol. 3, 205 (*Kugyŏk*, 148).

126 Yoshida, "Chōsen ni okeru kanshū," 14–15 (54–55).

127 Decision of June 22, 1943, *Hanketsuroku*, vol. 30, 33. See Yun Tae-sŏng. "Ilche ŭi Hanguk kwansŭp chosa saŏp kwa chŏnse kwansŭp pŏp [The Project of the Investigation of Korean Custom under Japanese Rule and the Custom of *Chŏnse*]," in *Hanguk pŏpsahak nonch'ong* (Seoul: Pagyŏngsa, 1991), 331–347.

unification of Korea and Japan, the Daishinin seemed to take a more reserved approach.

The case involved the custom of disqualifying the presumed household headship successor.[128] The substantive and procedural laws that were at stake included not only the Chosŏn Civil Ordinance and the Japanese Civil Code but also the Coordination Law as well as the *Hōrei*. Both the appellant and the appellee were Korean. As the eldest son of the appellant, who was the household head, the appellee was the legal presumptive household successor. The appellee, when he was nine years old, ran away from the parental home. The father looked for the son for twenty-plus years and eventually discovered that he was running a photo shop in Tokyo. The father came to Tokyo and pleaded with the son to go back to his rural hometown with him, but the son refused. He instead frequently demanded money from the father and, when the father refused, hit him and yelled at him. On one particular occasion, when the father refused to give him money, the son grabbed the father's neck and shook him, shouting "you father, fool, never come back to Tokyo." The father suffered injury that required two weeks of recovery time.

The father filed a suit at the Tokyo District Court. The Japanese court had jurisdiction over the case under Article 2 of the Coordination Law that allowed the Japanese court to hear cases involving colonial customs. The appellant (the father) sought the removal of the appellee from the status of the legally presumptive family headship successor. He argued that the son's behavior amounted to abuse and infliction of serious harm, constituting sufficient grounds for the disqualification of a successor under the Japanese Civil Code (Article 975, Section 1). But the court of first instance ruled that the case needed to be determined according to Korean custom instead of Japanese law, because Article 26 of the *Hōrei* provided that "succession shall be governed by the national law of the decedent." Under Article 11 of the Chosŏn Civil Ordinance, succession matters among Koreans were governed by Korean custom.

The trial court noted that in Korea the eldest son of the family head was called the legal family head successor, whose status was equivalent to that of the legal presumptive household successor in Japan. But the court determined that there was no custom in Korea to disqualify a legal family head successor. It relied on the official bulletin issued by the Chosŏn government general that there was no such custom in Korea except when the prospective successor became a Buddhist monk. Thus the court dismissed the plaintiff's suit, and the Tokyo Appeals Court affirmed.

On appeal to the Daishinin, the appellant argued that the lower court erroneously interpreted Article 11 of the civil ordinance. According to him, the provision that family and succession matters among Koreans were governed by custom and not by laws enumerated in Article 1 of the civil ordinance – which

[128] Judgment of May 31, 1941, in *Daishinin hanreishū* (Civil Cases Report), vol. 20, no. 12, 756. I consulted the Korean translation of the text in Chŏng Kwang-hyŏn, *Hanguk kajok pŏp yŏngu*, 311–316.

included the Japanese Civil Code – meant that Korean custom governed only when there existed an applicable custom; matters for which there were no applicable custom reverted to Article 1 and hence to the civil code. When the court could not find an applicable custom in matters of family and succession, argued the appellant, it was required to apply the civil code provisions.

Next, the appellant claimed that the lower courts mistakenly relied on the opinion issued by the government general. The government bulletin confirmed that there was no custom disqualifying the legally presumptive family head successor but, the appellant asserted, it did not say that there was custom that prohibited the disqualification of the legally presumptive family head successor. In other words, according to the appellant, the said bulletin stated in negative language that custom did not exist regarding the exclusion of the legal presumptive successor, but it did not state in positive language that the custom existed that disallowed the exclusion of the legal presumptive successor. The mere fact that custom or precedents did not exist did not mean that the court must absolutely disallow the supplications like this case arising from real needs. The lower courts failed to decide whether or not it was prohibited to exclude the successor in Korea, asserted the appellant, and this constituted a failure on the part of the court to execute its duties. In short, the appellant claimed, where there was no custom to follow under Article 11 of the Chosŏn Civil Ordinance and where there was no custom that was divergent from Article 975 of the Japanese Civil Code, a plea to disqualify the presumptive successor must be allowed in accordance with Article 975 of the civil code.

The appellant raised another interesting issue. Even if family and succession matters among Koreans were subject to custom instead of civil law, he argued, custom under the civil ordinance must not be against public order or good morals. If the court were to dismiss a reasonable request to remove the legal presumptive successor simply because there was no custom that expressly authorized it, the result would amount to a judicial declaration of the existence of a custom in Korea that prohibited the exclusion of the legal presumptive successor. Such a custom, even if it existed, should not be granted legal force because, according to the appellant, it would be against public order or good morals. If no legal presumptive successor could ever be removed regardless of immoral conducts, contended the appellant, it would be tantamount to condoning terrible behaviors that went against filial piety. It would be a violation of good customs and beautiful habits which were the backbone of the ancient Eastern filial duty. This would bring about a serious result in Korea where propriety between parents and children was even more strictly observed than in Japan. Finally, the appellant argued that the lower courts' decisions, relying solely on Korean custom and rejecting the application of the Japanese Civil Code, would jeopardize the unity of jurisprudence in Japan and Korea, thereby impeding the effort to build a new comprehensive legal order in East Asia.

The highest court was not persuaded by this panoply of animated arguments. Its opinion seemed rather tepid compared with a barrage of impassioned pleas from the appellant. The court found that the intent of Article 11 of the Chosŏn Civil Ordinance was such that family and succession matters involving Koreans – other than the exceptions stipulated – were governed not by the laws listed in Article 1 including the civil code but by custom alone. According to the court, it clearly did not mean that civil law applied whenever there was no applicable custom. The court pointed out:

> In Korea it would be problematic to approve the act of disqualifying the legal presumptive family head successor and thereby deprive him of his succession right, where there is no law or custom that allowed such actions. Absent legal provisions or custom to that effect, it is necessary to decide that disqualification is impermissible.[129]

The court concluded that the lower courts were not in error in finding that there were no procedural provisions in the Regulation of the Chosŏn Family Registration regarding the disqualification of a successor. The court rejected the appellant's argument that the lower courts' decisions amounted to the recognition of a custom that was against public order and beautiful customs. Disallowing the exclusion of a legal presumptive household head successor was different from condoning the abuse of the father or infliction of serious harm on him, expounded the justices.

This decision prompted a flurry of criticisms among the Japanese jurists. The court's position that there was no recourse whenever applicable legal provisions or custom were absent met with sharp disapproval. A commentator, Arakawa Yoshihito, admitted that one should not readily allow the removal of the legally presumptive successor because it would result in depriving him of his succession rights.[130] Nevertheless, argued Arakawa, the absence of custom authorizing the removal of the successor heir should not become sufficient grounds for rejecting such a request. According to him, where there was no applicable custom or law in a civil trial, it would be more desirable for the Daishinin to "adjudicate according to *jōri*."

Arakawa cited the famous precedent of the Chosŏn High Court of 1935 regarding the recovery of succession rights. In this case, the court departed from its earlier decision but was still able to rationalize its new position through a judicious interpretation of "custom." As Arakawa acknowledged, the 1935 case might appear to have no relevance to the present case because the Chosŏn High Court in 1935 positively recognized the presence of custom, whereas the Daishinin in the present case negatively confirmed the absence of custom. But both decisions hinged on the question whether the custom at issue really existed in Korea. When the colonial high court reversed its earlier decisions because of the new finding of custom, it was clear that the precise content of the custom was of secondary importance. Here, Arakawa's point was that the colonial court in 1935 found it reasonable to limit the succession recovery

[129] Ibid.

[130] Arakawa Yoshihito's commentary in *Minshōhō zasshi* 14, no. 6 (1941), 98–105, translated in Chŏng Kwang-hyŏn, *Hanguk kajok pŏp yŏngu*, 317–323.

right regardless of the veritable nature of the custom. Should not the Daishinin have also decided the present case in terms of reasonableness, instead of strait-jacketing itself by trying to prove the presence or absence of the custom?

Arakawa called to attention that the high court in Taiwan had decided in 1932 that "even if there is no system in this island's custom to require time limit for the exercise of succession recovery right ... we cannot but recognize it upon the consideration of reason."[131] In Arakawa's opinion, the Taiwanese court's position was more forthright than the Chosŏn court's but they were basically of the same spirit: "The Chosŏn High Court recognized the existence of custom as demanded by *jōri* and the Taiwan High Court applied *jōri* directly." Legal scholars might debate which court's approach was more desirable in juridical techniques, but the key point was that both decisions established precedents of recognizing certain rights and also limiting them in terms of *jōri*. Of course, continued Arakawa, this does not mean that the present case should also have been decided entirely in terms of *jōri*. But at least it raised a legitimate question about the present ruling that the request for removing an heir must be denied under any circumstances. In Arakawa's view, *jōri* demanded the grant of the appellant's request. He regretted that the appellant did not assert this point more forcefully. At any rate, he concluded, the Daishinin's decision could not be justified.

Arakawa's spirited criticisms seemed to touch on a number of important issues. The Daishinin's reasoning appeared in many respects rather perfunctory and circumspect. Its summary dismissal of the issue of public order and good morals exuded an air of indifference. Perhaps the highest court in Japan wanted to avoid the impression that it was ignoring Korea's custom in favor of Japanese law. In comparison, the justices at the Chosŏn High Court seemed more enterprisingly inclined to rule resorting to reason rather than being bogged down to the content of custom. Finally, there was a legitimate concern that the Daishinin's decision jeopardized the goal of jurisprudential uniformity in Japan and Korea. It is interesting to note that the colonial judges were more eager than their metropolitan counterparts to achieve legal unity in the colonial empire.

Jurisprudence of Customary Law and Colonial Policy

Close scrutiny of the Chosŏn High Court's opinions reveals that the court was engaged in patient and progressive jurisprudential construction, cast in a pattern of creative adaptation, to rework Korean custom in terms of modern concepts of legal rights. The colonial jurists undertook a doctrinal reformulation of both specific popular practices and provisions from the old codes in Korea to reconcile them with the Japanese Civil Code. The colonial customary law regime was set up with the objective of converting selective usages into civil law of strict obedience. The assumption of adjudication in accordance with customary law was

[131] See Yasuda, "Sōzoku kaihuku seikyūken," 126.

faithfully sustained in colonial jurisprudence, but the scope and nature of old customs was closely controlled and restricted by the court, to be applied only as far as they did not overstep the boundaries of modern legal notions. The validity of custom depended to a large extent on the opinion of the judge. The result was a judicial legislation, a customary law without *opinio necessitatis*.

The colonial judges, while functioning within the framework of legal formalism, were in fact engaged in a judicial reasoning process characteristic of instrumentalism. Custom, with its fluid nature, was a means of creating a legal system responsive to the needs of modern colonial society. The colonial judges used a mechanism that approximated case law but without the kind of frame of reference that had been provided for judges in Europe, whether precedents in English common law courts or the interpretation of local *coutumes* in French royal courts. In arriving at decisions, judges were often engaging in a sort of casuistic construction of law. The implementation of Korean law and custom by state judges who naturally ascertained and interpreted native normative rules and principles through the Japanese concepts of legal rights expedited the transformation of the Korean legal order. Old Korean customs were redefined as institutionalized legal rules and formulated in the Japanese legal language. This is how traditional Korean law was approximated to modern civil law.

For some scholars, the courts were abusing the notion of custom in efforts to steer the Korean legal system in a new direction as part of colonial state building. The colonial government repeatedly professed its willingness to respect Korean customs. Colonial judges were legally bound to decide cases according to custom. But in reality they were largely free to define its content. Just as the legal instrument of custom was powerfully useful in molding Japanese practices and procedures in early Meiji years in accordance with Western law, so was the colonial customary law order in transforming Korean customs into law compatible with Japanese law, all the while claiming continuity with the Korean past.

The judges took pains to defend the customary law regime from criticism that it lacked rigorous legal standards. The Korean judge Ch'oe Pyŏng-chu argued that customary law as law containing abstract legal principles was conceptually different from reason or a mere body of sound principles insulated from society's general opinion. The objectives guiding the interpretation of customary law were not identical with reason. In construing custom, liberty of argument should be recognized but it should also depend on scientific method. According to Ch'oe, custom was thus different from the interpreter's sense of justice but, just as with written law, extensive interpretation of customary law should be allowed.[132] The colonial court was careful about invoking reason openly, preferring to remain under cover of custom. It declared "this is Chosŏn's custom" or "there is no such custom in Chosŏn." But such statements were less a reference to custom than appeals to the validity of the rule chosen by the court. The custom declared by the judge as the dispositive rule was usually

[132] Ch'oe, "Minjirei jūichi cho," 20.

stated in the form of an abstract principle, not followed by any citations. It was as if the declaration of "custom" with plain wording had legal significance. Custom as found by the court was simply set forth as a safe, immutable principle with no particular, concrete elements. The discourse of custom is supposedly a discourse of the peculiar and the local notions.[133] Colonial discourse of custom was instead a discourse of the universal.

Propelling the transformation of popular convention and custom into law through jurisprudence was not a Japanese invention. The relationship between court decisions and customary law was an issue that was actively discussed among the European jurists at the beginning of the twentieth century, in particular in colonial contexts.[134] The Dutch jurist Barend Ter Haar (1892–1941) in the Netherlands East Indies encouraged the independent role of the judges in *adat* law decisions and acknowledged the importance of the "decision doctrine" for achieving the transformation of customs into law.[135] Compared with the Dutch jurist's devotion to the indigenous values and tradition, the Japanese colonial judges' commitment to Korean custom may appear pale, but the basic juristic approach was of a similar nature.

Like its European counterparts, Japan created a customary law system consistent with basic legal principles and responsive to the needs of the colonial administration. The creation of customary law as a tool to push colonized societies toward a desired goal was universally shared by colonial powers. In most colonies, the customary law regime constituted a series of transactions between tradition and change on the one hand and between indigenous legal culture and Western legal concepts and theories on the other. There were, however, significant differences in actual policy courses. The Japanese legal reform in Korea was part of the waves of legal transplantation through colonization that swept around the world in the nineteenth and early twentieth centuries, but it represented a unique direction derived from the historical and political conditions that set it apart from the dominant path followed in European colonies. Customary law revealed this characteristic of the Japanese venture most conspicuously. Chapter 7 turns to the comparisons of the Japanese and European colonial customary law policies.

[133] "[T]he discourse of custom is inductive, a discourse of the contingent, the historical." Whitman, "Why Did the Revolutionary Lawyers," 1327.

[134] The similar opinion was expressed in non-colonial contexts as well, for example, by John Chapman Gray in the U.S. and by François Gény. Gény and Edouard Lambert acknowledged that the courts constantly reconstructed new customary law through case decisions outside the codes.

[135] Barend Ter Haar, *Adat Law in Indonesia*, trans. E. Adamson Hoebel and A. Arthur Schiller (New York: Institute of Pacific Relations, 1948); Daniel S. Lev, "The Supreme Court and *Adat* Inheritance Law in Indonesia," in *Legal Evolution and Political Authority in Indonesia, Selected Essays* (The Hague: Kluwer Law International, 2000), 101–102.

7

The Japanese Deviation: Comparison of Colonial Customary Law Policies

Invoking custom as law governing the colonial subjects was not unique to Japanese colonialism; European colonies in Africa and Southeast Asia also saw the establishment of the customary law order. Imperial powers introduced European laws to colonial territories but allowed the continuance of indigenous practices and local institutions. The European colonial legal policy envisioned a process in which native laws and usages were turned into customary law and eventually into a civilized civil law on the European model. In this context, custom became an anteriorized colonial category.

Japan carefully imitated European models in both colonial rhetoric and practical management. While the professed goal of civilizing native law underlay both the Japanese and European colonial ventures, their customary law policies diverged from each other in ideology, operation, and consequences. In European colonies, maintaining native practices and institutions was an essential part of colonial management. The implementation of custom was largely left in the hands of traditional authorities in native courts. In contrast, Japanese customary law policy was a judicial acculturation process. The Japanese legal reform consisted of a sweeping substitution of the Korean institutions with new ones duplicated from the Japanese system. There were no multiple legal authorities; there was only one system of courts that had jurisdiction over both Koreans and Japanese. Custom in Japanese colonies was not an implement of legal pluralism but one of legal centralism, an instrument of assimilation. Custom, a term which comprehensively included both old Chosŏn laws and popular usages, was reformulated and applied by the colonial courts according to Japanese metropolitan legal principles and procedure. The standardization of Korean customs and their approximation to modern law through jurisprudence led to the colony's legal transformation. While the Chosŏn Civil Ordinance system created in 1912 a legal order based on the personal law principle, it was different from the European pluralistic colonial justice system because, in colonial Korea, customary law did not exist in separation from the dominant legal system and was instead completely subsumed to it.

Recent scholarship in African and Indonesian history has shown that much of colonial customary law was a creation at the hands of the colonial power and the native elites. The discussions of the "invention of tradition" in Africa and the "myth of *adat*" in Indonesia are such examples. In the case of colonial Korea, the extent of the invention of custom was broader and more thorough, arguably with more lasting effect.

The colonizers' choices regarding what kind of colonial legal structures should be established were dictated by essentially administrative and political reasons. But they were also shaped by historical and cultural factors.[1] An examination of how different colonial powers approached the legal instrument of custom in dealing with indigenous practices and conventions can provide an important reference point in understanding colonialism in the global context. This chapter approaches the theme of the singularity – "deviation" – of Japanese colonialism in Korea by comparing it with European colonial legal policies in Africa and Southeast Asia in the late nineteenth and early twentieth centuries. The term "Japanese deviation" as used here implies that there was certain divergence in the Japanese undertaking of legal imperialism from what unfolded in the European colonies.[2]

Comparisons of European and Japanese legal policies must proceed with caution. The fact that in East Asia the colonizers and the colonized belonged to the same cultural sphere of the Sinicized civilization, not to mention the same race, entailed the formulation of a policy distinct from that in the European colonies. The Japanese settler colonialism in Korea, with far more intrusive direct rule, was clearly different from the contemporary European colonial ventures. Japanese colonialism may be likened to "internal colonialism" in European history, such as the English expansion into Wales, Scotland, and Ireland.[3] A case can also be made that Japanese colonialism was closer to Manchu colonialism in the seventeenth and eighteenth centuries than contemporary European colonialism.[4] To be sure, Japanese colonial policy was shaped by the perception of

1 Martin Chanock, "The Law Market: The Legal Encounter in British East and Central Africa," in *European Expansion and Law: The Encounter of Europe and Indigenous Law in 19th- and 20th-century Africa and Asia*, eds. W. J. Mommsen and J. A. de Moor (Oxford: Berg, 1992), 281.

2 Emphasizing the uniqueness of Japanese colonialism, some studies suggested the concept of "oriental colonialism," that is, Japanese colonialism as an a- or anti-colonialism. See Rwei-ren Wu, "The Formosan Ideology: Oriental Colonialism and the Rise of Taiwanese Nationalism, 1895–1945" (PhD diss., University of Chicago, 2003), 54; Naoyuki Umemori, "Modernization through Colonial Mediations: The Establishment of the Police and Prison System in Meiji Japan" (PhD diss., University of Chicago, 2002).

3 See Michael Hechter, *Internal Colonialism: The Celtic Fringe in British National Development*, 2nd ed. (London: Transaction Publishers, 1999, 1975). Mark Caprio argued that Japanese colonization in East Asia, "peripheral colonization," was an intermediate state between "internal colonization" and "external colonization." See Caprio, *Japanese Assimilation Policies*.

4 For earlier Asian colonialism, see Dorothea Heuschert, "Legal Pluralism in the Qing Empire: Manchu Legislation for the Mongols," *The International History Review* 20, no. 2 (1998): 310–324.

ethnic and cultural disparities between the Japanese and Koreans and racial ideologies abounded. Yet cultural and ethnic determinism is not sufficient to explain fully Japanese colonial law.

As noted in previous chapters, postcolonial discourses have been dominated by the efforts to rediscover "authentic" customary law untainted with the colonial past and to hail it as a symbol of the indigenous cultural and legal identity. But the demand in formerly colonized countries for a modern and unified law draws attention to the effectiveness, or the lack thereof, of colonial judicial administration. By considering the dynamics of custom and its relations to legal transplantation in the nineteenth and twentieth centuries, one may get closer to a more accurate balance sheet of colonial law in Korea.

Legal Pluralism in European Colonies

Legal pluralism is a corollary of European colonialism. The colonial legal order in the early modern and modern European states was characterized by the coexistence of different legal systems in a given territory. The administration of law witnessed the unfolding of complex jurisdictional politics, in which the law of the colonizers and the laws and customs of the colonized were juxtaposed in the pluralistic scheme.[5] The dual legal system remained the norm in European colonial settings in the nineteenth and early twentieth centuries. There was one set of laws and courts for Europeans and one for the natives. M. B. Hooker explained legal pluralism in terms of the existence of two classes of law, the "dominant" and the "servient." The European imperial powers introduced law of European origin as the general law of the colonial territories (the dominant system), while allowing the continuance of indigenous customs and local institutions (the servient system).[6] Yet the uneven relationship between the two – the normative weight of native "custom" being dependent on the norms of European law – highlighted the complex nature of colonial customary law, inviting the criticism that colonial legal pluralism was a "weak" pluralism because it was part of the state-controlled system.[7] The main objective of legal pluralism is to identify an unofficial system of law coexisting with state law in order to dispute "state law monism" and "Western law

[5] M. B. Hooker, *Legal Pluralism: An Introduction to Colonial and Neo-colonial Laws* (Oxford: Clarendon Press, 1975); John Gilissen, *Le Pluralisme juridique: études publiées sous la direction de John Gilissen* (Brussels: Editions de l'Université de Bruxelles, 1972); Lauren A. Benton, *Law and Colonial Cultures: Legal Regimes in World History 1400–1900* (Cambridge: Cambridge University Press, 2002); Sally Engle Merry, "Law and Colonialism," *Law and Society Review* 25, no. 4 (1991): 889–922.

[6] Hooker, *Legal Pluralism*, 4.

[7] J. Griffiths, "What Is Legal Pluralism?" *Journal of Legal Pluralism and Unofficial Law* 24 (1986), 5. The school of legal pluralism, which has dominated colonial historiography for some time, viewed European colonial customary law as a product of legal positivism, as opposed to living law. See Franz and Keebet von Benda-Beckmann, "The Dynamics of Change and Continuity in Plural Legal Orders," *Journal of Legal Pluralism and Unofficial Law* 53/54 (2006), 26.

universalism."[8] Martin Chanock argued that "the concept of legal pluralism, as it has been usually employed in the African context in the sense of the co-existence of relatively discreet systems, could be damaging to attempts to understand the process of legal colonization."[9]

The presumed analogy of customary law to indigenous practices has been widely questioned. The majority of rural populations in Africa were governed by native chiefs enforcing "customary law." From various and often contradictory decisions and representations made in the native courts where the bulk of disputes were heard, colonial officials, aided by lawyers and legal anthropologists, tried to articulate certain rules, which they then labeled "customary law" of the native peoples. But it has been argued that what was enforced in colonial courts was far from a reflection of immemorial traditions in precolonial reality.[10] According to these studies, what imperialist powers in Africa termed "customary law" was often anything but customary; it was at best a bureaucratic artifact created by the imperial powers in an effort to remold indigenous society along the lines of "modern" law and justice. According to Terence Ranger, "What were called customary law, customary land-rights, customary political structure and so on, were in fact *all* invented by colonial codification."[11] Once flexible and unwritten "traditions" of the precolonial period were "written down in court records and exposed to the criteria of the invented customary model, a new and unchanging body of tradition had been created."[12]

In order to make colonial rule work with a limited number of administrators, European powers were compelled to use local sources and forums. By turning tribal chiefs into the heads of native tribunals and official agents of the colonial government, the native court system created a sort of state-sanctioned extension of traditional rule.

[8] Masaji Chiba, "Japan," in *Asian legal Systems: Law, Society and Pluralism in East Asia*, ed. Poh-Ling Tan (Sydney: Butterworths, 1977), 85–87; Masaji Chiba, *Legal Pluralism: Toward a General Theory through Japanese Legal Culture* (Tokyo: Tokai University Press, 1989). For a historical survey and a criticism of the contemporary conception of legal pluralism, see Brian Z. Tamanaha, "Understanding Legal Pluralism: Past to Present, Local to Global," *Sydney Law Review* 30 (2008): 375–411; Tamanaha, "The Folly of the 'Social Scientific' Concept of Legal Pluralism," 192–217; Tamanaha, "A Non-Essentialist Version of Legal Pluralism."

[9] Chanock, "The Law Market," 302.

[10] See Francis G. Snyder, "Colonialism and Legal Form: The Creation of 'Customary Law' in Senegal," *Journal of Legal Pluralism* 19 (1981): 49–90; Martin Chanock, *Law, Custom, and Social Order: The Colonial Experience in Malawi and Zambia* (Cambridge: Cambridge University Press, 1985); Peter Burns, *The Leiden Legacy: Concepts of Law in Indonesia* (Leiden: KITLV Press, 2004). Clifford Geertz quipped: "The mischief done by the word 'custom' in anthropology, where it reduced thought to habit, is perhaps only exceeded by that which it has done in legal history, where it reduced thought to practice." *Local Knowledge: Further Essays in Interpretive Anthropology* (New York: Basic Books, Inc., 1983), 208.

[11] Terence Ranger, "The Invention of Tradition in Colonial Africa," in *The Invention of Tradition*, eds. Eric Hobsbawm and Terence Ranger (Cambridge: Cambridge University Press, 1983), 250 (emphasis in the original).

[12] Ibid., 251.

In general, the transplanted European private laws were applied to the white population only. There were examples of the private law of the European type – in contracts and the property relations – imposed on the natives. But most colonizers did not seriously consider replacing the indigenous legal order with a European one. The strategy of respecting local substantive rules while substituting metropolitan procedural rules for traditional procedures was the gist of the expansion of European law in history, not just in external imperialism but also in internal imperialism. Scholars have argued that since classical times legal imperialism proceeded through the means of separating between procedural and substantive rules and effecting a sort of compromise. James Q. Whitman called it "the grand bargain," through which medieval monarchical power negotiated with local "customary" powers; the royal governments agreed to honor local customary rights but insisted that the proof of custom must take place through royal procedures.[13] A similar method was used in European expansion to the Hispanic New World from the sixteenth century. The native litigants who flocked to the pluralistic colonial courts were, unbeknownst to them, part of a process of creating a hierarchical order of legal pluralism.[14] The same pattern was seen in the European colonies in the nineteenth and twentieth centuries. The application of bifurcated laws administered by separate courts, with a clear line drawn between substantive rules of each group, characterized the European imperial pattern of legal pluralism.

The British Policy

In British Africa, English law was introduced as general law but substantial exceptions were made for the native population. The theory of "indirect rule" was powerfully advocated by Frederick Lugard, governor general of Nigeria from 1914 to 1919, who called for a more systematic use of indigenous institutions.[15] Some scholars argued that the British system of managing the subjugated through local collaborators did not start in Asia and Africa but had originated in the medieval times, in which the use of Norman Irish chiefs and Angevin seneschals could be seen as analogous to the enlisting of local chiefs in the British indirect rule.[16] In the early modern period, the English incorporations of Wales, Scotland, and Ireland were facilitated by the co-optation of local gentry by the English Crown. In the more recent past, local chiefs were recruited and served in Africa as the agents of the colonial government. In Southern Nigeria the Native Court Proclamation of 1900 established native courts. In South Africa the Black Administration Act of 1927 recognized native courts as part of the official court system. Retention of local laws and rule through

13 James Q. Whitman, "Western Legal Imperialism: Thinking about the Deep Historical Roots," *Theoretical Inquiries in Law* 10 (2009), 328.

14 Benton, *Law and Colonial Cultures*, 161–164.

15 Frederick D. Lugard, *The Dual Mandate in British Tropical Africa*, 5th ed. (London: Frank Cass & Co. Ltd, 1965, 1922).

16 Peter Burroughs, "The imperial gospel according to Frederick Madden," *The Journal of Imperial and Commonwealth History* 30, no. 3 (2002), 115.

indigenous institutions was dictated on the British officials because protectorate governments "had neither power nor the resources to overhaul them."[17]

The British colonial administrators had little control over intra-African legal matters. Indigenous law was subject to the repugnancy clause which provided that native law and custom were to be applied only as far as they did not overstep the boundaries of civilized law, that is, not "repugnant to natural justice, equity or good conscience."[18] But intervention in native justice was infrequent and it became even rarer during the inter-war years because such entanglement was feared to undermine the power of chiefs who were important allies.[19] In Kenya, few African disputes came before British officials: in 1942 less than three percent of the civil cases heard by African courts were appealed to European administrators.[20]

British India was initially controlled by indigenous legal authorities but it gradually shifted to a legal order governed by state law that closely reflected English legal sources and procedures.[21] The use of increasingly uniform legal procedures caused the absorption of the indigenous legal system into British law.[22] Yet, even in India, the legal unification attempt usually left most areas of substantive law unaffected. Prasenjit Duara has pointed out that in India "the colonial state deliberately sustained the separation of colonial law from customary law even though customary or community law was itself produced or reified by legal procedure."[23]

In African native courts, considerable freedom was given to native judges as to how to determine and interpret custom and also what procedures to follow. The proliferation of native courts was the result of the "keenness in the Whitehall to avoid full political responsibility and unwelcome expense."[24] For some scholars, it was more than wariness and indifference that pervaded the colonial policy of customary law. In their opinion the native customary legal

[17] Kristin Mann and Richard Roberts, eds., *Law in Colonial Africa* (Portsmouth, NH: Heinemann, 1991), 18.

[18] This general formulation was found in many laws of British colonies, for example Northern Rhodesia, Gold Coast, and Nigeria. Vincent O. Orlu Nmehielle, *The African Human Rights System: Its Laws, Practices, and Institutions* (The Hague: Kluwer Law International, 2001), 26.

[19] Richard Rathbone, "Native Courts, Local Courts, Chieftaincy and the CPP in Ghana in the 1950s," *Journal of African Cultural Studies* 13 (2006), 126.

[20] Brett L. Shadle, "'Changing Traditions to Meet Current Altering Conditions': Customary Law, African Courts and the Rejection of Codification in Kenya, 1930–60," *Journal of African History* 40 (1999), 413–414.

[21] Lauren Benton, "Colonial Law and Cultural Difference: Jurisdictional Politics and the Formation of the Colonial State," *Comparative Studies in Society and History* 41, no. 3 (1999): 563–588.

[22] Jonathan K. Ocko and David Gilmartin, "State, Sovereignty, and the People: A Comparison of the 'Rule of Law' in China and India," *The Journal of Asian Studies* 68 (2009), 66–69. For the effort to codify customary law in India, see Sandra den Otter, "Rewriting the Utilitarian Market: Colonial Law and Custom in Mid-Nineteenth-Century British India," *The European Legacy* 6, no. 2 (2001): 177–188.

[23] Prasenjit Duara, "The Limits of Legal Sovereignty: China and India in Recent History," *The Journal of Asian Studies* 68 (2009), 123.

[24] Burroughs, "The Imperial Gospel," 123.

order, created on the distinction between subject and citizen, was a means of disguising the bluntness of alien domination. The whole point of indirect rule was "to find a chief and build a court around him" and the courts dispensing justice according to customary law were nothing other than instruments of "decentralized despotism."[25]

The French Policy

The patterns of establishing colonial rule were structurally similar in European colonies.[26] The native justice system and the implementation of customary law were part of a larger administrative strategy. It has been pointed out that while the changes in judicial administration in the British colonies represented a relatively consistent evolution of legal positions, changes in the French colonies were more reflective of political policy considerations.[27] In French colonies, the increasing prevalence of pluralistic legal structure coincided with the expansion of the empire. Algeria was joined to France in 1848 in the wake of the thoroughly republican popular democracy of the Second Republic. French policy during the Third Republic was dominated by discussions of integrating Algeria and Indochina into the French body politic. As the burden of colonial administration increased, however, assimilation policy gave way to the colonial ideology of indirect rule. From the end of the nineteenth century, assimilation gradually lost its intellectual appeal in France and Western Europe. Imposing metropolitan laws in the colonies was criticized on the grounds of the infeasibility of applying the French Civil Code to the indigenous people.[28] The ideal of legal assimilation, an adoption of legal institutions by the indigenous, was largely abandoned by the turn of the century.[29]

25 Mahmood Mamdani, *Citizen and Subject: Contemporary Africa and the Legacy of Late Colonialism* (Princeton, NJ: Princeton University Press, 1996), 125.

26 Benton, *Law and Colonial Cultures*, 154.

27 Hooker, *Legal Pluralism*, 203. For British colonial policy of customary law, see, among others, Mamdani, *Citizen and Subject*; Sally Falk Moore, "Treating Law as Knowledge: Telling Colonial Officers What to Say to Africans about Running 'Their Own' Native Courts," *Law & Society Review* 26 (1992): 11–46; Roger Gocking, "British Justice and the Native Tribunals of the Southern Gold Coast Colony," *Journal of African History* 34 (1993): 93–113; Rathbone, "Native Courts, Local Courts," 125–139; Shadle, "'Changing Traditions'," 411–431; and articles in Mann and Roberts, eds., *Law in Colonial Africa*.

28 Raymond F. Betts, *Assimilation and Association in French Colonial Theory 1890–1914* (New York: Columbia University Press, 1961); Martin Deming Lewis, "One Hundred Million Frenchmen: The 'Assimilation' theory in French Colonial Policy," *Comparative Studies in Society and History* (1962): 129–153.

29 The French colonial authorities were often frustrated by its reliance on the native administrative system. In 1914, Governor General William Ponty blurted out, exasperated, "so many intermediaries, so many thieves." But he still confirmed the need for implementing native law: "Transported into a different milieu than that of France, our Civil Code would be an agent of disorder, and an architect of anarchy...; to impose it indirectly, through judicial decisions, would be an artificial and dangerous procedure." Alice L. Conklin, *A Mission to Civilize: The Republican Idea of Empire in France and West Africa, 1895–1930* (Stanford: Stanford University Press, 1997), 116, 129–130.

Significant divergence existed within the French imperial policy. Algeria saw an almost complete destruction of native political and legal institutions, whereas in Tunisia, a protectorate, the system of native courts was maintained. In French West Africa and Equatorial Africa, most population remained under precolonial forms of justice unless they obtained French nationality.[30] In 1903–1904 Governor General Ernst Roume created the first colonial court system in French West Africa. The ordinance on the organization of justice, issued on November 10, 1903, set up two different hierarchies of courts: a hierarchy of French courts applying French law to French citizens, and a hierarchy of native courts applying customary law to native subjects.[31] Subsequent decrees reorganizing the system (1912, 1924, and 1931) reaffirmed the system in which native courts were presided over by village chiefs who were supervised by French administrators. The colonial bureaucrats, who mostly lacked legal training, relied on native assessors and interpreters.[32] A distinction was drawn between those Africans who had a customary status (*statut coutumier*) and those who had a French civil status (*statut civil français*).[33] The vast majority of Africans, as *sujets* belonging to the first category, could not bring their grievances before the metropolitan system of courts. Their disputes were instead decided by the native courts applying customary law.

The principle that continued to guide French policy was that native courts would apply local customs in so far as they were not contrary to the principles of French civilization. Like the British, the French prohibited native customs which were contrary to "public order."[34] "Custom" was gathered and codified in many territories. From 1905, the government general in sub-Saharan Africa enlisted administrators to "clarify, articulate and coordinate methodically the principles of law which they encounter in practices." A codification was partially achieved in 1939 and published as the custom of French West Africa.[35]

[30] Mann and Roberts, eds., *Law in Colonial Africa*, 49.

[31] The text of the decree can be found in G. Deherme, *L'Afrique occidentale française: action politique, action économique, action sociale* (Paris: Librairie Bloud, 1908), 75–82, and in David Robinson, "Ethnography and Customary Law in Senegal," *Cahier d'Etudes africaines* 32, no. 126 (1992), 231. For Governor Ernst Roume's instructions, see F. J. Clozel and Maurice Delafosse, *Haut-Sénégal-Niger (Soudan français)* (Paris: E. Larose, 1912), vol. 1, 18–19. See also Pierre Meunier, *Organisation et fonctionnement de la justice indigène en Afrique occidentale française* (Paris: A. Challamel, 1914); Gary Wilder, *The French Imperial Nation-state: Negritude & Colonial Humanism Between the Two World Wars* (Chicago: University of Chicago Press, 2005), 107–117.

[32] William B. Cohen, *Rulers of Empire: The French Colonial Service in Africa* (Stanford: Hoover Institution Press, 1971).

[33] Hooker, *Legal Pluralism*, 220.

[34] In Belgian Congo it was decreed: "the natives of the Belgian Congo who are not matriculated enjoy the civil rights recognized to them by the legislation of the colony and by their customs, inasfar as these are not contrary to the legislation or to public order." Cited in Filip Reyntjens, "The Development of the Dual Legal System in Former Belgian Central Africa (Zaire-Rwanda-Burundi)," in *European Expansion*, eds. Mommsen and de Moor, 114.

[35] Emmanuelle Saada, "Citoyens et sujets de l'empire français: les usages du droit en situation coloniale," *Genèses: Sciences Sociales et Histoire* 53 (2003), 13.

The view of an irreducible African difference loomed large. Even under the broad coverage of the civil code, "it was not the intention of the French architects of the colonial legal system to require that Africans conform exactly to French metropolitan legal procedure."[36]

In Indochina, the French attempted legal assimilation in Cochin China where it undertook direct rule, but it proved largely unsuccessful.[37] The decree of July 25, 1864, provided for the application of Vietnamese law where the parties to any civil action were Vietnamese.[38] During 1879–1881 the French Third Republic decided, with renewed republican zeal, to bring the legal institutions in the colony in line with those in the metropolitan system. By 1881 French tribunals were organized throughout the province, although the natives were left to be governed by their customs in such matters as marriage, divorce, inheritance, and paternity. But the official destruction of native justice created the widespread belief among the people that the new French-style justice system was far less efficient, convenient, and affordable than the previous dual justice system. The inaccessibility of the new system for the majority of the people led to a gradual loss of confidence in the system, which quickly lapsed into disuse. As a result, the natives were cut off from their traditional justice system without being assimilated to the French system.[39] In areas other than Cochin China, native law and institutions were maintained.[40] The civil codes produced in Tongking (1931) and Annam (1936–1929) continued the application of native law to the local population.[41] This policy formed the foundation of the French colonial administration in Indochina until March 1942 when French rule was taken over by Japan.[42]

[36] Richard Roberts, "Representation, Structure and Agency: Divorce in the French Soudan during the Early Twentieth Century," *Journal of African History* 40 (1999): 389–410.

[37] The Indochina Union was created in 1887, consisting of Cochin China (South), Tongking (North), Annam (Middle), and Cambodia. In Cochin China, the retreat of the local mandarins forced the French to undertake direct rule. Cochin China was a colony and the rest were protectorates. Tongking and Annam were ruled by the emperor of Vietnam and Cambodia by a king. The Union was first under the Navy's colonial department and subsequently under the Colonial Ministry created in March 1894. Dennis J. Duncanson, *Government and Revolution in Vietnam* (Oxford: Oxford University Press, 1968), 86–87. Laos was added to the Union in 1899. See Direction de l'administration de la justice, ed., *La Justice en Indochine, organisation générale, la justice indigène* (Hanoi: Imprimerie d'Extrême-Orient, 1931).

[38] E. A. F. Garrigues, "La Cochinchine: du droit applicable aux indigènes et des jurisdictions le prononçant," in *La Justice en Indochine, organisation générale, la justice indigène*, ed. Direction de l'administration de la justice, 41–81; Hooker, *Legal Pluralism*, 232.

[39] James Barnhart, "Violence and the Civilizing Mission: Native Justice in French Colonial Vietnam, 1858–1914" (PhD diss., University of Chicago, 1999), 464–484, 602.

[40] Minister of Colonies Etienne Clémentel sent instructions to Governor Jean-Baptiste Paul Beau in Indochina in December 1905 that the colony's improvement should be achieved by "the protection, education, and association of the native." Betts, *Assimilation and Association*, 124.

[41] Hooker, *Legal Pluralism*, 232.

[42] Duncanson, *Government and Revolution in Vietnam*, 87.

The Dutch Policy

The Dutch policy in the Netherlands East Indies seemed to be a standard model of legal pluralism. The dual legal system was in place since the Dutch gained control of the interior of Java. In civil matters Indonesians followed *adat* law which varied from area to area.[43] The *adat* law system existed alongside the European statutes based on the Napoleonic Dutch civil and commercial codes. The Government Regulation of 1854 provided that the natives were subjected to their own "religious laws, institutions, and customs" as long as they were "not in conflict with generally recognized principles of equity and justice" (Article 75). There were two separate judicial structures, one for Indonesians and one for Europeans. According to John Ball, "European self-interest and indifference to the indigenous legal order ... contributed most to the evolution of dualism in the colonial legal system."[44]

The Dutch government seriously considered imposing a unified law throughout the colony in the early twentieth century. After the fall of the liberal government in 1901, the new government proposed a radical modification of Article 75 of the Government Regulation of 1854. According to this plan, European law would be applied in native society as the general rule; *adat* law would be the exception, to be used if "the different needs" – family law or intestacy – of the indigenous population required it and if the European law referred expressly to the use of *adat* law. But this proposal was opposed by the intellectuals who argued that legal unification would destroy native culture.

In 1914 a misdemeanors court (*landgerecht*) was created for all residents of the colony, and in 1918 a common criminal code was promulgated. But the draft of a unified code of civil law published in 1923 was abandoned after vehement criticisms by Cornelis van Vollenhoven, the Leiden University law professor.[45] Spirited campaigns led by van Vollenhoven and other Dutch *adat* law scholars persuaded the government to give up the uniform code policy in the late 1920s and to maintain instead the *adat* law policy, *adatrechtpolitiek*, intended to keep local law in local hands.[46] As a whole, the Dutch approach to indigenous law seems to have been based on a more profound intellectual appreciation of the native culture than other European counterparts.

It was during the Japanese occupation of Java that major steps were taken toward the unification of the legal system. Following the invasion in 1942,

[43] See, among others, John Ball, *Indonesian Legal History 1602–1848* (Sydney: Oughtershaw Press, 1982); Ter Harr, *Adat Law in Indonesia*; Lev, *Legal Evolution*.

[44] Ball, *Indonesian Legal History*, 236.

[45] Van Vollenhoven, "Juridisch confectiewerk; eenheidsprivaatrecht voor Indië," *Koloniale Studiën* 9 (1925): 293–318, cited in C. Fasseur, "Colonial Dilemma: Van Vollenhoven and the Struggle Between Adat Law and Western Law in Indonesia," in *European Expansion and Law,* eds. W. J. Mommsen and J. A. de Moor, 237–256. See also J. M. Otto and S. Pompe, "The Legal Oriental Connection," in *Leiden Oriental Connections, 1850–1940*, ed. Willem Otterspeer (Leiden: Brill, 1989), 230–249.

[46] Lev, *Legal Evolution*, 36.

the Japanese military administration swiftly replaced the dual court structure with a single three-instance hierarchy apart from Islamic courts.[47] Although the Japanese proclaimed the continuation of custom as legal sources, as it had done in Taiwan and Korea, the various procedural codes gave way to a single instrument, the Revised Indonesian Regulation for all population groups.

As seen in this brief survey, European imperial powers resorted to a plural system of law and courts. Even at the apogee of colonialism, Europeans and the indigenous people existed under different legal orders. The constitutions of European colonial states in the nineteenth century explicitly stipulated that the colonies were governed by laws separate from metropolitan laws.[48] In general the European powers did not aspire – with possible exceptions for early French colonial policy – to a legal unification within the colony, not to mention a legal unification between the metropole and the colony. Customary law in European colonies was an essential element of the indigenous policy of "tribalization," each group of population being encased by its tradition.[49] "Custom" was elaborated or codified by the administrators, often in collaboration with a fringe of the population which had its interest involved. Local chiefs and elites retained and accumulated considerable legal power. Often it led to abuses of the judicial system in which newly invented and reified customary law was implemented.[50] The operation of indigenous legal systems in the colonial context allowed local people to reshape their experience through the "representation" of custom.[51]

Comparison of Japanese and European Customary Law Policies

What distinguished the Japanese case from the European cases was, above all, that the former's colonial customary law policy was a duplication of the colonizer's own domestic legal modernization agenda. Long before Japan became a colonial power, the Meiji elites civilized their legal tradition by consciously subjecting themselves to the newly imported Western civil law.[52] Japan closely

47 Koichi Kishi and Shigetada Nishijima, *Study of the Japanese Occupation of Indonesia* (Ithaca, NY, 1960); Daniel Lev, *Legal Evolution*, 28, 37–38, 120.

48 The French constitution of 1795 provided that "the colonies of France are an integral part of the Republic, and are subject to the same constitutional law" (First Title, Article 6). After initial revolutionary enthusiasm subsided, however, the constitution of 1799 stated that "the form of government of the French colonies is determined by special laws" (Article 91). The Charter of 1814 (Article 73), the Charter of 1830 (Article 64), and the Constitution of 1848 (Article 109) each repeated that the colonies were to be governed by special laws and regulations. The Belgian constitution of 1831 (revised in 1893) and the Dutch constitution (revised in 1922) provided similar provisions.

49 Saada, "Citoyens et sujets," 13.

50 According to Peter Fitzpatrick, colonialism reworked social relations and gave them back to the natives as their own, and in this process, "history was denied and tradition created instead." Peter Fitzpatrick, "Is It Simple to Be a Marxist in Legal Anthropology?" *Modern Law Review* 48 (1985), 479.

51 Mann and Roberts, eds., *Law in Colonial Africa*, "Introduction," 22.

52 See Cheng-Yi Huang, "Enacting the 'Incomprehensible China'," 964.

appropriated the European colonial "dominant-servient scheme" in reforming its own law. The dominant law was modern civil law that was in the making by the Meiji state on the model of European laws; the servient system was Japanese traditional customs and *bakufu* laws. Both the content and the normative weight of the servient system were closely controlled by the dominant system through jurisprudence. Custom as law facilitated acculturation of Western law in Japan.[53] This process of legal modernization, which can be called "self-colonization," prepared Japan to take up a unique path in "colonizing" and "civilizing" its East Asian neighbors by transplanting modern law through a uniform interventionist approach. The imperial pattern of legal colonization was adopted by the Japanese with a twist.

While the European vision of colonial legal assimilation focused on unifying procedural rules without the standardization of substantive rules of the natives, such a nuanced divide was not feasible in Meiji Japan or in its colonies. Legal modernization was perceived as a comprehensive overhaul of the existing system in both substantive and procedural areas, to take place within a clearly defined framework through centrally-controlled methods. Japanese imperial ventures were marked by a sense of urgency and preference for a blitz-like strategy, geared for rapid results. The European imperialists seemed more committed to preserving local practices. It may have been either due to the liberal outlook of the Europeans who restrained themselves from attempting forcefully to change the native lives or, more likely, due to the colonial states' administrative inability combined with downright indifference. Whatever the reason, they were less motivated to set aside the natives' family or succession practices as long as they did not ruffle European sensibilities.

The notion of "public order" in francophone Africa, the equivalent of the "repugnancy clauses" in British colonies, served as a limitation on the application of local rules. These were patently European concepts. The principle, dating from Roman law, that the content of a juristic act should not be contrary to public order and good morals was stipulated in French and German codes and it was now extended to the colonial arena. Native customs were recognized insofar as they were compatible with the dictates of natural law and morality and, of course, were not in conflict with the demands of colonial administration.[54] The French colonial jurist Henry Solus stated in the 1920s: "[By public order] we understand that the native personal law, even if it is recognized by the colonizer, shall not prevail when it is contrary to a rule considered essential for the success of the task of colonization."[55]

Meiji Japan applied the imported principle of public order to domestic law to effect a sort of voluntary purge of old customs. As noted in the previous

[53] The process was aided by the notion of reason as a source of law. See Chapter 3.

[54] Reyntjens, "The Development of the Dual Legal System," 114, 120.

[55] Henry Solus, *Traité de la condition des indigènes en droit privé: colonies et pays de protectorat (non compris l'Afrique du Nord) et pays sous mandat* (Paris: Recueil Sirey, 1927), 303.

chapters, the Japanese Law on the Application of Laws (*Hōrei*) of 1898 declared that only customs that were not contrary to public order had the force of law.[56] Article 92 of the civil code provided that custom prevailed over the law which was not related to public order when the party intended to abide by such custom. Once the Japanese successfully completed the process of legal self-colonization, they set out to apply the same mechanism in their overseas colonies. The Chosŏn Civil Ordinance of 1912 created in Korea a personality law system similar to those in the European colonies. But it was not an implementation of native customs in the officially-sanctioned pluralistic scheme of justice. Just as in Meiji Japan, "custom" in the civil ordinance was intended to play a role in adopting modern law principles. Implementation of customary law in Korea was a transient process toward the creation of a unified state law. It goes without saying that the "colonial public order" had to be flexible enough to suit the colonial administrative needs.

It is necessary to point out the different dynamics of penal and civil law in European and Japanese colonialism. The main emphasis of the European legal policy rested on introducing the concept of public offense to the natives. A large part of the imperial legal mission was to impose a sense of criminal act as an offense against the public. It was presumed that primitive men made no distinction between "the civil wrong which is compensated by damages to the individual, and the criminal wrong which compensated by fine or forced labour exacted by the community."[57] Colonizers tried to abolish severe and arbitrary customary criminal law; otherwise the authority of the government would be undermined.

The situation was different in Japanese colonies. East Asian countries did not need colonial lessons on the concept of penal law. Korea boasted sophisticated state codes, minutely and systematically regulating every aspect of crimes and punishments. Korea's long tradition of a centralized government and standardized law codes meant that the infrastructure of a bureaucratic state already existed before the arrival of the Japanese. What was deficient was instead the idea of resolving civil cases without resorting to punishments. East Asian countries were deemed uncivilized by the Europeans not because they lacked the notion of public law but because they lacked civil law, the idea that private relations between individuals be governed by established rules separate from penal rules. The abolition of extraterritoriality hinged on the creation of a system in which individuals enjoyed private rights recognized by the state.

Another difference between European and Japanese customary law policies concerned the fact that Europeans had to deal with the religious laws of

[56] See Chapter 3 and Chapter 6.

[57] Chanock, "The Law Market," 282. The broad strategy of the colonial governments was one of "endeavouring to introduce to the African the conception of the public offense ... and punishment ... instead of ... compensation and other forms of arbitral adjustment." Baron Hailey, *Native Administration and Political Development in Tropical Africa 1900–42*, ed. A. Kirk-Greene (Nendeln, 1979), 285, cited in Chanock, "The Law Market," 282.

the natives. The Japanese were able to steer Korean family customs in line with Japanese law with relative efficiency because Korean family legal relations lacked a religious dimension. Confucianism might be viewed as a religion but certainly not in the same sense as the Muslim religion. In many European colonial territories, Muslim populations were allowed to use religious courts to adjudicate cases involving personal status. Family law was largely left to Muslim *qadis*.[58] In Java, for example, European, Muslim, and *adat* legal systems functioned in tandem. Clarifying the jurisdictional boundaries among them was not easy. The colonial judicial officials tended to oppose the concept of religiously inspired private law but their effort to restrict the Muslim legal jurisdiction conflicted with the political consideration of the colonial administrators who favored preserving Muslim law.[59] The Japanese were spared these concerns. Disputes over family and related civil law matters were decided by the state judges. Although the Japanese recognized native customs, disputes among Koreans were comprehensively channeled into Japanese civil law categories and principles. Lacking the elements of religious law, custom was much more manageable to be brought under the coverage of Japanese civil law. The colonized populations were squarely and entirely subject to the state jurisdiction. The secular legal tradition of East Asia potentially facilitated the Japanese goal of legal unification and assimilation, diminishing the tensions between colonial law and traditional law.

In Japanese and European colonies, interpretation of customs took place in a different way. When questions arose about customs, colonial officials in Africa turned for answers to native chiefs and those who were regarded as the repositories of local knowledge and upholders of local authority. These local chiefs recreated custom, often in order to further their own economic or political interests. Chanock has shown that in central Africa chiefs and elders cooperated with colonial administrators to invent customary rules regarding marriage that strengthened the control of senior men over women and junior men.[60] The European authorities largely condoned these practices.[61] In colonial Korea, without native courts, there was no process of questioning local population about customs. When the judges were in doubt of the legal relations in old customs, they sent inquiries to the executive authorities of the colonial government. The discovery of the content of custom took place from the center and in this aspect the production and management of custom differed little from state law. The customary law regime in Korea was recognized by the colonial government as part of the state law system and was used in recasting the colony's law and society comprehensively in line with those of the

[58] Dominique Sarr and Richard Roberts, "The Jurisdiction of Muslim Tribunals in Colonial Senegal, 1857–1932," in Mann and Roberts, eds., *Law in Colonial Africa*, 141.

[59] Ibid., 134.

[60] Chanock, *Law, Custom, and Social Order*, 145–216.

[61] The French colonial officials stated in 1906: "we will under no circumstance alter especially those essential rights that result from the husband's authority over his wife, the father's authority over his children or guardianship." Conklin, *A Mission to Civilize*, 88.

metropole. This "judicial customary law" was often at variance with what was actually followed in precolonial society and, in this sense, a sort of "invention of tradition" took place. But this was attempted with a clear goal of integrating native custom into the general law and the legal system of the colonial state. With much smaller colonial possessions than European colonies, the Japanese did not need to depend on indirect rule. The fact that Japan had already launched the reform of Korean courts under protectorate rule, doing away with Korea's traditional judicial institutions and procedures, rendered the bureaucratization of Korean customs and their integration into the central system relatively coherent and consistent.

The Japanese were little encumbered by legal pluralism. Customary law was enforced according to metropolitan legal procedure, and *the* customary law, rather than pluralistic normative systems, was constructed through streamlined legal rationalization schemes. The result was a highly effective case of colonial legal centralization and modernization. As will be seen in the following discussion, this proved to be the result of both recognition and simultaneously rejection of the notion of cultural and racial affinity between the colonizers and the colonized. The differences between the Japanese and Koreans in social mores, customs, or religions were not viewed serious enough to present obstacles in administering Korean customs alongside Japanese laws. Still, the two peoples needed to remain distinguished. Here lay the complexities of Japanese assimilation policy.

Law, Civilization, and Assimilation

In a speech given shortly after the promulgation of the Chosŏn Civil Ordinance in 1912, Colonial Governor Terauchi declared that the spirit of the new legal system was to govern all population groups, whether Japanese or Korean, by the same substantive and procedural laws. The recognition of the legal force of Korean customs was a temporary exception to the principle that "all rules are applied with no distinction between Koreans, the Japanese, or foreigners."[62] Terauchi reiterated in the following month that in Korea "we reformed the old legal structure that had two separate legal hierarchies for the Japanese and the foreigners on one hand and the Koreans on the other. They used to cause serious inconveniences, but now we have unified both substantive and procedural rules for all the population."[63] The memories of psychological wounds from the extraterritoriality arrangements, through which foreigners in Japan stood outside the reach of Japanese law and courts, still seemed raw. Having gone through, and only recently recovered from, the humiliation of consular jurisdictions imposed by the Western powers, Japan was eager to present itself as a new kind of imperial power that would, in principle, eschew a pluralistic

[62] *Chōsen Sōtokufu kanpō*, March 22, 1912 (extra edition).
[63] *Chōsen Sōtokufu kanpō*, April 8, 1912.

legal order in which the colonized people were subject to different laws and, hence, discrimination.[64]

Of course, Terauchi's statements should be taken with a grain of salt. It is well known that under the colonial penal system serious cases of murder and robbery committed by Koreans were punished according to the provisions of *Hyŏngpŏp taejŏn*, the old Korean code which the Japanese supposedly abhorred for its cruel punishments that included flogging. Korea's traditional punishment methods needed to be retained, argued the colonial governor, because the application of Japan's laws in these areas would "jeopardize the preservation of public order." Still, Terauchi's statements about uniform law were not entirely empty rhetoric. Japanese civil law was extended to all subjects in the colonies. Applying the same laws by the same courts to all population groups departed from the common European colonial feature of distinguishing between procedure and substantive law and also between "citizen" and "indigenous subject."

In the current scholarship of colonialism in Korea, the disastrous colonial legacy of assimilation (*donghwa* or *dōka*) was so devastating that the meaning of the term has been blurred under the weight of emotional baggage. The Japanese colonial practice of urging Korean people to adopt Japanese names was an example of an inherently unjust assimilation policy, bent on erasing the ethnic and national identity of the colonized.[65] But the colonial theory of assimilation in the late nineteenth century was framed mainly in terms of political and legal assimilation, as opposed to the cultural assimilation of the natives. In the contemporary colonial debate in France, assimilationists grounded their theory in the idea that the natives should be subject to French law that exemplified universal rights.[66] In this meaning of assimilation – granting the natives the same legal guarantees as those in the metropolis – the leading intellectuals of the Japanese enlightenment, such as Ume and Fukuzawa Yukichi, were assimilationists. There is little irony about Meiji liberals' support for assimilation.

In the reality of colonial management, legal assimilation had limitations. Legal pluralism required separate designations of the population, which

[64] For a discussion of Japanese imperialism as a "new imperialism," see Prasenjit Duara, "The New Imperialism and the Post-Colonial Developmental State: Manchukuo in Comparative Perspective," *Japan Focus*, posted January 30, 2006 http://japanfocus.org/-Prasenjit-Duara/1715.

[65] See Mizuno Naoki, "Chosŏn singminji chibae wa irŭm ŭi 'ch'aihwa': naejiin kwa hondong toegi swiŭn irŭm ŭi kŭmji rŭl chungsim ŭro [Colonial Rule in Korea and the Differentiation of Names: With Particular Attention to the Prohibition of the Names that Could Be Mistaken as the Names of the Japanese People]," *Sahoe wa yŏksa* 59 (2001): 147–174; Kim Yŏng-dal, "Ch'ang ssi kaemyŏng ŭi chedo [The System of Creating and Changing Names]," in *Ch'ang ssi kaemyŏng*, ed. Ch'ong Un-hyŏn (Seoul: Hangminsa, 1994), 41–70; Caprio, *Japanese Assimilation Policies*.

[66] Arthur Girault, *Principes de colonisation et de législation coloniale* (Paris, 1895). See Lewis, "One Hundred Million Frenchmen," 129–153, for the analysis of the debate over assimilation as a colonial theory at the Congrès Colonial National of 1889–1890. For the influence on colonial theory of the French Revolution's natural law concepts and the Enlightenment thought, see Betts, *Assimilation and Association in French Colonial Theory*, 17–21.

constituted the heart of segregation. The pluralistic legal order institutionalized the invidious distinction between Europeans and natives. Normally status was supposed to determine the kind of norms to apply to a particular individual, but in colonial situations it was from the legal systems already in force that one tried to establish concrete categories among the populations. The distinction between citizen and subject was created to place the indigenous people within their own customary boundaries. Emmanuelle Saada has argued that the basic categories of the French colonial order, "citizen" and "indigenous subject," were the result of legal construction.[67] The distinction became necessary as the colonial administrators needed to maintain the traditional institutions that governed the natives. The colonial state faced a double constraint: the necessity to maintain the French nationals under the sovereignty of the French empire and the simultaneous necessity to govern the indigenous according to their custom. The French would remain French while the indigenous would remain in their indigenousness, and this had to be done while sustaining the sovereignty of the metropolitan state. Customary law was the main pillar of indigenous policy. This dialectic of sovereignty and governmentality underlay the joint construction of the citizen and the native.

When it became difficult to decide which law or custom to apply, and to whom, the colonial state was compelled to classify individuals in terms of race. This is how, starting in the mid-nineteenth century, the concept of nationality came to be dissociated from that of citizenship. The extralegal concept of race began to take root as a basic framework, replacing the existing citizen/native dichotomy.[68] It was less the result of a political scheme of colonial segregation, placed a priori in the metropole, than the practical consequence of the existence of legal systems distinct to the colonies.[69]

In this scheme, explained Saada, race, civilization, and the legal system were closely intertwined. Civil status became a legal translation of racial grouping. Each race corresponded to a state of its civilization and its artifact, namely, the legal system. In other words, a particular legal system is the reflection of the stage of civilization reached by a race. The conclusion from this premise seemed natural: the French Civil Code could not be applied to the natives because of the differences in race and civilization. Race came to be regarded as the main reason why the assimilation policy was not workable – hence the need for legal pluralism. This was a theory that was only tentatively entertained by the Japanese. For them, law did not correlate to race. The Japanese did not accept the notion that the legal system intrinsically reflected culture. Just as they caught up with the European legal development, their colonies could be brought up to the civilized level.[70]

67 Saada, "Citoyens et sujets," 13–15.

68 Emmanuelle Saada, *Les Enfants de la colonie: Les métis de l'Empire français entre sujétion et citoyenneté* (Paris: Editions de la Découverte, 2007).

69 Saada, "Citoyens et sujets," 18.

70 For the so-called rule of colonial difference, see Partha Chatterjee, *The Nation and Its Fragments: Colonial and Postcolonial histories* (Princeton, NJ: Princeton University Press, 1993), 19.

Excluding the natives from the civil and political rights of citizenship was a defining characteristic of all colonial regimes, and Japanese policy in Korea closely fit in this pattern. Distinctive to Japanese policy, then, was that political exclusion took place without openly assigning a separate identity to the colonized populace in legal hierarchy. Whereas European colonial rule rested on the demarcation between "advanced" Europeans and "backward" natives, Japan, faithful to its professed goal of building a pan-ethnic Asian empire, downplayed differentiated legal designation among population groups, resorting instead to an inclusive definition of imperial subjects (*shinmin*). Since there was no need to rely on the traditional legal structure, it was not essential to buttress native custom; there was no compelling need to distinguish citizen from subject in law and thus the effect of the ethnicity-based personality law – customary law – was minimized. The depth of racialization of law was shallower than in European cases.

Scholars have shown that the boundaries of "the Japanese" were flexible and constantly shifting in the early twentieth century. The ethnic minorities – Koreans, Taiwanese, Okinawans, and others – were either accepted as Japanese or excluded as non-Japanese, depending on the perceived national interest of the time. The direction of the discourse on national identity continuously fluctuated.[71] Oguma has argued that the "myth" of the Japanese as a homogeneous people is a relatively recent origin. Before Japan lost World War II and was forced to give up Taiwan and Korea, there was consensus that the Japanese were a "hybrid" people. This inclusive outlook helped the policy of assimilation. Culture or ethnicity was not as principled a category in Japanese colonial domination as in the European context.

The Japanese needed ideological rhetoric to justify their colonial rule and they zeroed in on their mission to bring about legal assimilation. The premise that the new colonial territories should sooner or later become one with Japan was rarely disputed, and it highlighted the significance of the role of the colonizer state to submit the indigenous to its ideal of law so as to create an integrated political and cultural community. The Japanese were free from the quandary that plagued the French, that is, the presence of "subjects" in the republic. The French attempted to rationalize the situation by proposing that those who were worthy and capable, in other words, sufficiently acculturated would obtain citizenship and enjoy the rights under the French law.[72]

[71] Kevin M. Doak, "What Is a Nation and Who Belongs? National Narratives and the Ethnic Imagination in Twentieth-Century Japan," *American Historical Review* 102, no. 2 (1997): 283–309. Oguma argued that the Japanese rarely entertained the notion of racial homogenization before the end of the World War II. Oguma, *'Nihonjin' no kyōkai*, 168; Oguma Eiji, *A Genealogy of 'Japanese' Self-images*, trans. David Askew (Melbourne: Trans Pacific Press, 2002).

[72] Alice L. Conklin, "Colonialism and Human Rights, A Contradiction in Terms? The Case of France and West Africa, 1895–1914," *The American Historical Review* 103, no. 2. (1998): 419–442.

To be sure, Japanese colonial officials frequently pointed to the low "*mindo*" (literally, the degree of the people or nation) among the colonial subjects to justify their oppressive measures. They continued to impose on Koreans the punishment of flogging, arguing that Koreans deserved it because of their inferior civility level. But the meaning of the perceived gap in cultural level seems different from the innate feeling of cultural superiority prevalent in European colonialism that propelled the *mission civilisatrice*. The Japanese did not subscribe to the notion that the legal system was equivalent to the level of civilization deduced from race. An Asian imperial power in domination of other Asian peoples, Japan was unable to divide population groups according to racial lines on the grounds of physiological anthropology.[73] As a recently "civilized" country Japan considered legal modernization in terms of a much shorter time span, something that could be achieved rather quickly if pursued with a concerted state effort. When it imposed the personality law arrangement in Korea, as in the civil ordinance system, the government general stressed that it was a temporary expedient.

The Japanese made it a point to distinguish their colonial enterprise from the European sort. Their relationship with the colonies was "fundamentally different" in nature from those of the European imperial powers which "civilized semi-civilized or inferior people." The European powers

> based their systems on a practical hierarchy of the dominant and the dominated, and they needed to maintain distance between the mother country and the colonies. More fundamentally, there were differences in environment and race and also in practices and customs. It is their fate that political and social assimilation ultimately cannot be achieved. Our relationship with Korea is the opposite. We are geographically close to each other and we have shared similar interests from the ancient time. We use the same writing system and there is no big difference in customs or religion. Therefore we must be united and assimilated.[74]

The government general of Korea declared in largely similar terms in 1914:

> European colonies are far in distance from the metropole, and the natives are different from the colonizers in race and customs. Overcoming this problem is an impossible matter, so the colonies are destined to remain colonies permanently. In contrast, the relation between the *naichi* and Chōsen is different: they are close in

[73] Recent studies on Manchukuo show that official racial classifications were complex and fluid. Mariko Tamanoi, "Knowledge, Power, and Racial Classifications: the "Japanese" in Manchuria," *Journal of Asian Studies* 59, no. 2 (2000): 248–276; Barbara J. Brooks, "Peopling the Japanese Empire: The Koreans in Manchuria and the Rhetoric of Inclusion," in *Japan's Competing Modernities: Issues in Culture and Democracy 1900–1930*, ed. Sharon A. Minichiello (Honolulu: University of Hawaii Press, 1998), 25–44 (Koreans were not always excluded from the category of "Japaneseness").

[74] "Ch'ongdokpu sisŏl yŏksa chosa sŏryu" (1915), *Terauchi Masatake Monjo*, cited from Hong Yang-hŭi, "Singminji sigi ch'injok sangsok kwansŭp pŏp chŏngch'aek [The Colonial Legal Policy regarding Family and Succession Custom]," *Chŏngsin munhwa yŏngu* 29, no. 3 (2006), 290–291.

> geography and are of the same race. Therefore there are no obstacles in pursuing assimilation of the two people.[75]

Substantial cultural sharing and contacts between the two peoples attested to the absurdity of the effort, in the European fashion, to justify colonization by pointing to the innate difference in the civilized level. Most Japanese intellectuals were not oblivious to the cultural superiority of Koreans in premodern history.[76] Colonization of Korea required a new kind of rhetoric. Yamada Saburō emphasized the need to "abolish colonial policy sooner or later and incorporate [Korea] into the Japanese administrative jurisdiction under the constitution and make it part of [Japan]." He concluded: "European colonies are colonies in law in perpetuity, but our colonies are colonies in law only temporarily."[77]

Assimilation en masse

The theme of the civilizing force of law was eagerly professed in both Japanese and European colonies, but there was certain disparity in the realm of cultural sensibilities. For the Europeans, the colonial task of improving native law coexisted with cultural relativism. The ideal of a "civilizing mission" did not mean applying the same law by the same courts to the citizens and natives uniformly. Considerations for individual development underpinned colonial policies. Citizenship was offered to the natives who passed the qualifications for assimilation, that is, who showed "by one's training and way of life a state of civilization implying the ability to enjoy the rights and to fulfill the duties provided for by the written laws."[78] In Europe, the issue of assimilation or the inclusion of the natives was discussed as ideological and aspirational rhetoric. Those who achieved civilized status – passed the assimilation test – were theoretically treated as Europeans. In reality, the fundamental lines drawn along the racial divides were difficult to overcome. Explicit racialization through which native subjects were denied access to the many prerogatives enjoyed by Europeans has been seen as emblematic of a hollow content of the colonial claim of liberalism.

In Japan, the assimilation question had more utilitarian, instrumental, and functional dimensions. Assimilation meant assimilation *en masse*, that is, assimilation of a people or a nation. In this collective scheme, individual matriculation of the subject people was not an issue. Assimilation was perceived fundamentally as a communal and national integration of the colonized populations, regardless of the civilized level of individuals. Civilization meant modernizing the way of life through a monolithic, uniform, inflexible, and unyielding push for oneness. The Japanese "civilizing mission" may have been devoid of the

[75] Chōsen Shōtokufu, "Chōsen tōchi san nen kan no seiseki, 1914 [The Result of the Three Years of Governing Korea, 1914]," 10, cited from Kang Man-Gil, ed. *Ilbon kwa sŏgu ŭi singmin t'ongch'i pigyo* (Seoul: Sŏnin, 2004), 250.

[76] See Ume's comment in Chapter 4.

[77] Yamada, "Shokuminchi hō to naichi hō," 110; Yamada, "Kyōtsūhō an ni tsuite," 70–71.

[78] Reyntjens, "The Development of the Dual Legal System," 117. See also Sarr and Roberts, "The Jurisdiction of Muslim Tribunals," 142.

Enlightenment element of the improvability of an individual. In some European colonies, native litigants in directly governed areas could choose to abandon their customary status and remove themselves from the competence of the native courts.[79] Such individual initiatives were not available in Japanese colonies. The colonized people had to become like the Japanese people, not just figuratively but in every possible aspect, in culture, spirit, and loyalty.

What prompted brutal authoritarianism in the Japanese colonies and justified the exclusion of the subject people from liberal reforms was, then, less racial ideologies than the imperative of holding the empire together. Preserving peace and order in the colonies populated by a massive number of non-Japanese people was an imminent concern. Discrimination was justified not so much by the low level of civility of colonial subjects as their dismal level of loyalty to the Japanese emperor. This was why Koreans were notoriously excluded from political rights. Colonial officials' testimony amply affirms their fear that allowing Koreans to elect members of the Japanese House of Representatives would place in the Diet a large number of persons whose loyalty to Japan was an unknown factor.[80] For the same reason, the conscription law was withheld from the colonies until nearly the end of colonial rule. Koreans were denied the same rights as the Japanese because the Japanese feared that ungrateful Koreans would undermine and eventually destroy colonial domination.[81]

Some Korean intellectuals adhered to the hope that cooperating with the Japanese cultural assimilation policy would help end discrimination, but their illusion was the result of pervasive confusion surrounding assimilation.[82] The Japanese policy emphasized the racial and cultural affinity between the Japanese and its East Asian subjects and the integration of the empire, but it had no pretension of extending constitutional rights to all the subjects. The Japanese vision of national assimilation led them to reject creating a European-type dual legal order. As a result, the colonizers were left deprived of institutionalized

[79] In Belgian Congo, two decrees of May 17, 1952, completed by a Decree of December 8, 1953, allowed the natives to matriculate and abandon their "customary status." The registered natives were removed from the competence of the native courts. Reyntjens, "The Development of the Dual Legal System," 117. For similar situation in Dutch East Indies, see Ter Harr, *Adat Law in Indonesia*, 38.

[80] Miyata Sesuko ed., *Singmin t'ongch'i ŭi hŏsang gwa silsang: Chosŏn ch'ongdokpu koui kwalli ŭi yuksŏng chŭngŏn* [The Falsity and the Reality of Colonial Rule: Live-Voice Testimonies of the Elite Officials of the Government General of Korea], trans. Chŏng Chae-sŏng (Seoul: Hyean, 2002).

[81] In the late 1930s, Japan actively studied the native representation systems in the French and American colonies, but did not implement any serious reform until the last days of its colonial rule. See "Furansu oyobi kitabeigatshūkoku no gaichi daihyō seido (seijichōsa shiryō hō) [The System of Overseas Representation in France and North America], in Mizuno Naoki, ed., *Senjiki shokuminji tōchi shiryō* [Documents of Wartime Colonial Rule], vol. 3 (Tokyo: Kashiwa Shobō, 1998).

[82] Caprio, *Japanee Assimilation Policies*. See Marie Seong-Hak Kim, "Review Article of *Japanese Assimilation Policies in Colonial Korea, 1910–1945*, by Marc Caprio," *Journal of Japanese Studies* 37, no. 2 (2011): 434–439.

justifications for withholding political franchise from colonial citizens. It is not difficult to see that in colonial Korea, where the supposed virtue of assimilation was touted in official discourse *ad nauseum*, discrimination struck painfully egregious. The customary law system was set up on the basis of the personality law principle and the subject population was excluded from legal and political rights by virtue of ethnicity. Yet, Japan implemented the election law of the House of Representatives as territoriality law, and the people residing outside the *naichi* were excluded from the law. Japanese residents in Korea had no suffrage whereas Korean residents in Japan could vote and even get elected to the Diet.[83] This attests to the anxiety among the colonial policymakers about controlling the population in the imperial peripheries. Japanese colonial legal policy was geared foremost to maintaining a workable legal framework in its far-flung empire.

The uniqueness of Japanese colonialism, trumpeted by the imperial policymakers as a justification for their assimilatory mission in Korea, spelled instead a disaster in the eyes of contemporary liberal intellectuals. In 1937, Yanaihara Tadao, a prominent scholar and one of the foremost voices of conscience in prewar Japan, eloquently pointed out a quintessential contradiction in Japanese colonial policy in Korea. Japan required of the colonized people "profound, not superficial, Japanization," even to a psychological level, "so as to promote ideological and emotional integration and feelings of brotherhood toward the Japanese people," but this "assimilatory colonial policy, while demanding economic and social integration of the colonized, refused the assimilation of political rights."[84] Yanaihara deplored that Japan's continued failure to grant suffrage to colonial subjects destined its domination in Korea to become "a despotic rule unprecedented in the world."[85]

The hollowness of Japanese assimilation policy, in which ideological assimilation was demanded without extension of constitutional rights, has been amply documented by historians. Ramon Myers has stated: "the legal-cultural policies pursued by the Japanese for the assimilation of non-Japanese Asians into their empire were always rooted in a profound ambivalence as to how far to go and as to whether their colonial servants could ever really become Japanese citizens."[86] Some scholars decried Japan's assimilation policy as a deceptive facade for its imperial ambitions; others dismissed it as an exaggerated reaction to its own insecurity at a time when the Japanese were unsure of their national

[83] Oguma, *'Nihonjin' no kyōkai*, 362; Hagiwara, *Nihon tōjika ni okeru Chōsen no hōsei*, 11–12.

[84] Yanaihara Tadao, "Gunji teki to dōka teki Nichi-Futsu shokumin seisaku higaku no ichiron [A Comparative Study of Japanese and French Colonial Policy from Military and Assimilative Perspectives]," 305, and "Chōsen tōchi jō no ni san mondai [Two or Three Problems regarding the Governing of Chosŏn]," 324, *Shokumin seisaku kenkyū*, vol. 4 (1937), in *Yanaihara Tadao zenshū* (Tokyo: Iwatami Shoten, 1963).

[85] Yanaihara Tadao, "Chōsen tōchi no hōshin [The Korean Policy]," *Shokumin seisaku kenkyū*, vol. 1 (1926), 739.

[86] Ramon H. Myers, "Post World War II Japanese Historiography of Japan's Formal Colonial Empire," in *The Japanese Colonial Empire, 1895–1945*, eds. Myers and Peattie, 460.

identity.[87] In Oguma Eiji's words, "in order to resolve their anxiety and lack of self-confidence," the Japanese felt that they had to make the colonized peoples "prove their love and dedicated loyalty" through self-sacrifices.[88] Mark Peattie claimed that Japan's "anomaly of modern history" prevented it from shaping a coherent colonial doctrine.[89] The Japanese opted to create separate jurisdictions in the empire but expected the colonies to be integrated with the *naichi* in ideology. Yamamoto Yūzō concluded that Japan's assimilation policy was a policy of "no direction" and at best "a temporary expediency."[90] Even when the Japanese openly pursued the *naichi* extension policy, Haruyama Meitetsu stated, "there was no change in the presumption of the separateness of the colonized subjects regarding the latter's human rights and political freedom."[91] Mark Caprio pointed out that the egregious gap between rhetoric and reality in assimilation policy doomed Japanese colonial rule in Korea.[92]

Colonial rhetoric exacerbated as Japan's war efforts intensified. Examination of the evolution of legal policy and especially the relationship between Tokyo and Seoul over customary law policy can shed light on how this seemingly blind pursuit of colonial policy, marred with contradictions, was sustained until the demise of the colonial empire.

The Evolution of Colonial Legal Policy

Conflicts between the colonial administrators and the metropole politicians over the autonomy of colonial governance were a familiar picture in European imperial politics. Customary law was closely tied to colonial management as it determined the extent to which the metropolitan government could intervene in the colonial judicial matters including the control of the native courts. The similar pattern was witnessed in the Korean colonial scene.

The Politics of Customary Law

Colonial customary law was increasingly caught up in politics. It was intertwined with the question of unifying laws and the legal systems in Korea and

87 Komagome Takeshi, *Shokuminchi teikoku Nihon no bunka tōgō* [The Cultural Unity of the Japanese Colonial Empire] (Tokyo: Iwanami Shoten, 1996), 6–8, 356–378; Oguma, *'Nihonjin' no kyōkai*; Doak, "What is a Nation." For the *naichi* extension policy (*naichi enchōshugi*), see Meitetsu and Wakabayashi, *Nihon shokuminchi shugi no seijiteki tenkai*; Kwŏn T'aeŏk, "Tonghwa chŏngch'aek ron [A Study of Assimilation Policy]," *Yŏksa hakpo* 172 (2001): 335–365 (*naichi* extension policy was in name only because of Japan's refusal to grant suffrage to Koreans).

88 Oguma, *'Nihonjin' no kyōkai*, 630.

89 Mark R. Peattie, "Introduction," in *The Japanese Colonial Empire, 1895–1945*, 6.

90 Yamamoto Yūzō, "Nihon ni okeru shokuminchi tōchi shisō no tenkai [The Evolution of Colonial Domination Ideology in Japan]," Parts 1 and 2, *Ajia keisai* 32 (1991), nos. 1 & 2, 1–2; Yamamoto Yūjō, *Nihon shokuminchi keizaishi kenkyū* [A Study of Japanese Colonial Economic History] (Nagoya: Nagoya Daigaku Shuppankai, 1992).

91 Haruyama and Wakabayashi, *Nihon shokuminchi shugi*, 122.

92 Caprio, *Japanese Assimilation Policies*.

Japan, and more broadly the issue of the independent authority of the colonial governor. The government general in Korea emphasized the uniqueness of Korean custom, presenting it as a key justification for its autonomous power. Revisions of the Chosŏn Civil Ordinance which limited the areas governed by Korean custom and extended the application of Japanese law bore the imprints of serious politicking.[93] The colonial government seriously contemplated codifying Korean family and succession customs and promulgating it through *seirei* as the governing law for the Korean people. A newspaper reported in 1920 that the colonial authorities wanted to replace the civil ordinance with a comprehensive codification of Korean custom and that its eventual goal was to establish "a complete civil law."[94]

In 1937, the government general conducted a survey among the chief judges and prosecutors of the colonial judiciary to gather the jurists' opinions regarding the customary law order.[95] The replies were varied, some in favor of the codification of Korean customs and others against. Hara Masakane, the chief judge of the Taegu Appeals Court, was one of the vocal critics of the colonial government's legal policy that separated the colonial courts from the Japanese judiciary. He argued that the codification of Korean customary law would impede the unification of laws in Korea and Japan. In general, colonial judges supported the unification of the judicial hierarchy in Korea and Japan. Many were in favor of a more comprehensive extension of the Japanese Civil Code although they agreed on the need to provide exceptions for Korean customs. They naturally resisted the colonial governor's extensive control of the courts. Hara's position reflected the growing concerns in Tokyo about the colonial governor's quasi-independent legal policy. A few years later Hara, who became the chief justice of the Chosŏn High Court in 1939, recalled that in the early decades of colonial rule Tokyo "strongly opposed solidifying and codifying customs in separation from the civil code. It was of the opinion that customs should remain customs, and that customs should be modified to conform to the *naichi* law."[96] The Japanese government opposed the codification of customs; if

[93] See Chapter 5. Kokubu Sangai explained in 1919 that legal assimilation meant the extension of the Japanese legal system to the colony. It was the ultimate goal, but it cannot be achieved through forceful imposition of Japanese law and ideology. "It is necessary," he argued, "to respect legal customs in Korea as long as they are not against public order and good morals and not to rush to destroy them. But one must also avoid fossilizing customs. It is necessary to modify them one at a time in accordance with the changes of the times and to assimilate them with the Japanese customs." "Sōtoku shisei no shōrai no hōshin ni kansuru ikensho," May 1919, in *Saitō Makoto Monjo*, vol. 13, 137.

[94] *Maeil sinbo*, May 14, 1920, cited from Yi Sŭng-il, *Chosŏn Ch'ongdokpu pŏpche chŏngch'aek*, 164.

[95] Yi Sŭng-il, *Chosŏn Ch'ongdokpu pŏpche chŏngch'aek*, 269–274. For the colonial judges' criticisms of the government general's legal policy, see Nam Ki-jong, trans. *Ilche ŭi Hanguk sabŏppu ch'imnyak sirhwa*.

[96] Hara Masakane, "Koseki rei seitei toji no kaiko," *Koseki* 3, no. 7 (1943), 5, cited in Yi Sŭng-il, *Chosŏn Ch'ongdokpu pŏpche chŏngch'aek*, 172. Hara was referring to the Japanese cabinet's position surrounding the revision of the Civil Ordinance in 1921. Hara was the chief justice until 1943.

indigenous customs were to be given legal effect, they had to be left as unwritten customs.

In European colonies as well, customary law was at the center of conflict between the metropolitan government and the colonial administrators. Studies have shown that customary law served in diverse ways as a strategy for the colonial officials. In French colonies, colonial administrators tried to preserve custom and codify the *coutumier général* to serve as the rule of native tribunals, whereas colonial judicial magistrates favored legal assimilation.[97] In Kenya, in contrast, the colonial officials opposed the codification of customs; it was in their interest to leave custom as fluid as possible to maximize their control.[98] The situation in Korea seemed to reflect both respects. The government general initially favored the codification of customary law on the consideration that the codified customary law would exist solidly under the colonial governor's prerogative; the colonial governor already enjoyed legislative and judicial power, further reducing intervention from Tokyo. There were concerns, at the same time, that customary law, once codified, would no longer remain in the administrative realm. It reveals the colonial government's ambivalent position in its customary law policy.

The unfolding of Japan's war efforts was the main impetus that pushed the colonial legal order toward a tighter integration into the Japanese empire. In the late 1930s, Japanese policy in Korea shifted markedly toward assimilation and the demand for the unification of Korean and Japanese law acquired new vitality. In 1939 the Ministry of Overseas Affairs in Tokyo summed up the situation in Korea in the following terms:

> From early on, the judiciary has attempted through precedents to render family and succession customs with the family and succession laws in [Japan's] civil law, and the civil ordinance has seen its regular revisions to conform to the civil code. Through many years of the court's efforts, now there is a greater demand among Korean people for the unification of the legal systems.[99]

Following the jurisprudential initiatives that had remolded Korean law and custom after Japanese law, legislative actions were now in order to bring the unification of the laws. The revision of the civil ordinance in 1939 was a clear indication of this thrust toward legal and cultural assimilation.

With Japan's invasion of China in 1937, intensifying war efforts demanded an all-out mobilization of Korean manpower resources. The slogan of the Japanese-Korean integration (*naisen ittai*) was pitched to a new level. The Japanese government had so far chosen not to apply the Japanese nationality

97 Sarr and Roberts, "The Jurisdiction of Muslim Tribunals," 135–137.

98 See Shadle, "'Changing Traditions'."

99 *Kōbun ruishu* [Collection of Official Documents], Ajia Rekeshi Shiryō Sentā [Japan Center for Asian Historical Records], 63rd Compilation, vol. 36 (1939), "Amending ordinance for installation of temporary employees within the Government General of Korea (Personnel increase to administer enforcement of laws and ordinances on family relations, inheritance and other matters)."

law and the family registry (*koseki*) law in Korea. But as Japan needed Korean soldiers, changes in the imperial policy were inevitable. Koreans had been denied political rights on the grounds that they were exempt from military service. With the implementation of the volunteer system among Koreans, there was no justification for excluding Koreans from constitutional rights; the Japanese government could no longer close the eyes to the need to grant them equal legal treatment and dismantle discrimination.[100] In 1941, Governor General Minami Jirō rebuked those who viewed the *naisen* unification as the complete equality between Korean and Japanese people; they thought that the "abolition of separate treatment was a precondition for the realization of the *naisen* unification," but "this is a misunderstanding."[101] Minami's view was, however, flatly repudiated by his successor Koiso Kuniaki. In his inaugural speech as governor general in June 1942, Koiso stated that some Japanese were completely mistaken when they "regard Chosŏn as a separate jurisdiction and forget the fact that it can become part of our strong empire just like Shikoku or Kyushu."[102] He argued that the laws that separated Koreans from the Japanese needed to change. Koiso's vice governor general Tanaka Takeo stated that failure to recognize political rights of Koreans "violates the principle of Japan-Korea unification."[103]

The outbreak of the Pacific War accelerated changes in the organization of the colonial empire. A closer coordination of the administration of the *naichi* and the *gaichi* became necessary. On September 11, 1942, the cabinet decided to place Korea, Taiwan, and Karafuto under the direct control of the prime minister. The Ministry of Colonial Affairs and the Bureau of Manchurian Affairs were abolished and their functions were transferred to the Ministry of Home Affairs and the newly-created Ministry of Greater East Asian Affairs.[104] In Korea the governor general's political prominence, as recognized in the imperial rescript of 1910, had so far enabled him to spurn successfully attempts by the Japanese government to bring him under the cabinet's control, but the reorganization of colonial affairs ministries augmented pressures on him.[105]

The colonial government resisted the unification of the legal systems of Korea and Japan on the grounds that it would jeopardize colonial administration. The Governor General Minami argued before the Diet in December

[100] Miyata Sesuko, *Chosŏn minjung kwa hwangmin hwa chŏngch'aek* [The Korean People and the Policy to Turn Them into Imperial Subjects], trans. Yi Hyŏng-nang (Seoul: Ilchogak, 1997).

[101] Cited from Yi Sŭng-il, *Chosŏn Ch'ongdokpu pŏpche chŏngch'aek*, 311–312.

[102] Koiso's inauguration speech on June 15, 1942, cited from Yi Sŭng-il, *Chosŏn Ch'ongdokpu pŏpche chŏngch'aek*, 332–333.

[103] Cited from Yi Sŭng-il, *Chosŏn Ch'ongdokpu pŏpche chŏngch'aek*, 339.

[104] Chen, "The Attempt to Integrate the Empire," 266. Concerning the reorganization of the *naichi* and *gaichi* administration, Mizuno Naoki, "Senjiki shokuminchi shihai to 'naigaichi gyōsei itchi gen ka' [The Wartime Colonial Rule and 'the Unification of Administration in *naigaichi*']," *Jinbun kakuhō* 79 (1997): 77–102; Yi Sŭng-il, *Chosŏn Ch'ongdokpu pŏpche chŏngch'aek*, 330, note 170); Yamazaki, *Gaichi tōchi kikō*.

[105] Chen, "The Attempt to Integrate," 271.

1941 that the cabinet's attempt to remove the colonial judiciary from his control would create serious problems in controlling Korea, especially when "a strong coordinated administrative control is necessary for undertaking wartime policy execution."[106] In defense of the concentration of legislative, executive, and judicial powers in his hands, the colonial governor contended that the matters in the colony were so interconnected that it was impossible to separate them: "If judicial power were severed from the governor's power, it would undermine his well-coordinated rule," and the reduction of the governor's power would "result in the decline of the people's trust in the government general in Korea." If the Court Organization Law were implemented in Korea and judicial institutions placed under the Justice Ministry, Minami warned, it would "result in the abandonment of the fundamental spirit of colonial rule and impede the ultimate success of the government general."[107]

As long as the colony remained under the extra-constitutional arrangement of the colonial governor's authority, genuine legal assimilation and the constitutional protection of the colonized people was a distant premise. Matsuoka Shūtarō identified in 1944 three elements necessary for achieving legal assimilation in Korea: first, the abolition, or revision, of the law that granted legislative authority to the governor general; second, the incorporation of the colonial courts into the Japanese court system under Daishinin, removing them from the colonial governor's control; and third, the reorganization of the colonial system to make the government general into an administrative body under the central government.[108] Demands for the submission of colonial courts under Japan's court system shared a significant part of the arguments with the calls for the reduction of the governor general's power, both of which were expected to promote the legal integration of the empire.

For all this, the colonial legal system continued to exist in separation from the *naichi*'s legal system and the colonial governor's *seirei* power remained intact until the end of colonial rule. Japanese scholars and politicians were not able to resolve, before the demise of the Japanese colonial empire, the question of the constitutionality of the colonial governors' legislative power. At least, it is clear that Japanese colonial policy was far from seamlessly coordinated between Tokyo and Seoul. The operation of the colonial state proceeded haltingly. Much of this subtlety is lost in current scholarship of colonial history. Meanwhile, along the bumpy road to the height of the wartime colonial rule, collateral damage seemed unavoidable. The contemplated change of granting suffrage to Koreans was not implemented before 1945.

106 The government general's report at the 79th Imperial Diet (December 1941), Chōsen Sōtokufu Homukoku, ed. *Chōsen Sōtokufu teikoku gikai setsumei shiryō* [Materials of the Government General in Korea for Presentation in the Imperial Diet] (Tokyo: Fuji Shuppan, 1994), vol. 5, 15–16.

107 Ibid.

108 Matsuoka, *Chōsen gyōseihō teiyō*, 15.

The Legacy of the Deviation

In both European and Japanese colonies, the customary law system facilitated colonial management by controlling native customs. Jurisprudence undertook the transformation of customs into customary law by engendering a merger of modern and traditional rules through case law, a kind of common law. But it achieved limited results in European colonies because of the complicated and confused jurisdictional structures in which native justice largely remained outside the European watch. The dual structure of delegating power to native authorities while reserving ultimate control to the Europeans created a chasm between "state law" and "native law." There was a tension between the avowed respect for native custom and the imperatives of colonial domination. The legal policy of most European colonial governments resonated with an evolutionary ideology, tinged with a high moral tone. The reification of "customary law" by government anthropologists was in part responsible for fostering the official line that the natives should be allowed to settle their disputes by local custom. The apparent contradiction between the two conflicting ideals, that is, the respect of custom – the policy of indirect rule purporting to respect traditional institutions – on the one hand and the agenda of the *mission civilisatrice* – the colonial ideology of civilizing native society by improving its law – on the other, plagued the European colonizers.

The Japanese were largely spared this dilemma. The standardization of native customs and their approximation to modern law facilitated legal transformation, first in Japan and subsequently in its overseas territories. Custom was a means of creating a legal system responsive to the needs of modern society. The Japanese colonial customary law was part of a blunt policy of legal centralization pursued by the state. The implementation of Korean law and custom by state judges, who naturally ascertained and interpreted them through Western – Japanese – concepts of legal rights, expedited the transformation of the legal order. In this way, nascent private law in Korea was carefully and effectively directed to conform to Japanese law.

A recent study distinguished between "receptive transplant" and "unreceptive transplant." When a country adapted the imported law or had a population that was familiar with it, the process of transplantation (receptive transplant) was smooth and its legal order functioned relatively well; when the adjustment of foreign legal borrowings to local conditions was lacking, as in legal reception via colonization (unreceptive transplant), the recipient country suffered from problems resulting from the transplantation of an imported legal order.[109] The authors of this study placed Japan in the first group and Korea in the second. Classifying Korea as an "unreceptive transplant" may appear justified initially because Korea received law from Japan through colonization. But it soon becomes clear that Korea's legal reception does not fit the pattern according

[109] Daniel Berkowitz, Katharina Pistor and Jean-François Richard, "The Transplant Effect," *The American Journal of Comparative Law* 51 (2003): 163–203.

to which involuntary reception of law via colonization fares poorly. The reason for this is, at least in part, that Japan brought to its colony a legal system that had already been adjusted to the Japanese local conditions and, more broadly, East Asian legal traditions. Korea received "Japanized" Western law.

The changes brought about by colonial legal reform were many. Adjudication was separated from administrative functions for the first time in Korean history, and the institutional guarantee of judges' status was established. Civil law and procedure were distinguished from criminal law and procedure, and sophisticated jurisprudential activities started. Obviously, Korean people were wary of the colonial courts, mainly staffed by foreign judges conducting court proceedings in a foreign language. But it is too naïve an assertion, and contrary to evidence, that Koreans stayed away from the court because they did not trust the Japanese court. The colonial period witnessed a harshly efficient process of transplantation of legal institutions that led to a thorough transformation of the legal system.

Gauging legality – the extensiveness and effectiveness of colonial legal institutions – is a difficult task, but the ways in which local populations have reacted to legal changes initiated by the imperial power can be an important indicator of legality. Evidence shows that an increasing number of Koreans turned to the courts to resolve their disputes, enticed by the uniformly enforced laws and efficient procedures.[110] Even under a colonial regime, courts functioned as symbols of the law as legal-rational organizations of the state in the Weberian scheme.[111] The colonial politics further contributed to improving judicial administration. In order to prove that colonial legal reform was something that was approved of and trusted by the Korean people, the colonial government paid special attention to building a competent judicial body. They were mindful that even the colonial courts operated under the pressure of public opinion and that they had to seek some degree of public legitimacy. The Japanese government was aware that legal modernization of Korea was one of the few justifications for colonial rule. In this process, judicial professionalism was firmly established. The colonial administrators' fastidious adherence to procedural propriety increased the Korean people's incentive to use the court system and it contributed to the relative success with which modern notions of impartial justice took root in Korea. If legality is something that is determined by the demand for law, it certainly was present in colonial law.

Colonial law destroyed local law and custom everywhere, but there were differences in the intentions and the intensity of colonial legal changes. The Japanese proved to be a more nimble, and thorough, executor of state building in the colonies than their European counterparts. In European colonies,

110 Chōsen Sōtokufu, *Chōsen no shihō seido*.

111 Max Weber defined legal-rational authority as a form of domination which depends for its legitimacy on formal laws of the state or natural law. Max Weber, "The Three Types of Legitimate Rule," in *A Sociological Reader on Complex Organizations*, ed. Amitai Etzioni, 2nd ed. (New York: Holt, Rinehart and Winston, 1969), 6–14.

the native justice systems were widely viewed as unfair and inefficient but the colonial powers shied away from changing them. In Africa, administrators struggled to keep European law and legal traditions out of African courts. The British feared that any reform of native custom could potentially be construed as a challenge to African sensibilities. The privileged place "custom" occupied in the native courts impeded serious reform of the colonial legal order in French West Africa. Advocacy of noninterference with customary law was not always prompted by enlightened consideration, but powerful arguments were made based on moral grounds. In the Netherlands van Vollenhoven and the Leiden School called for the preservation of the Indonesian culture and *adat* law and they succeeded in dissuading the colonial authorities from attempting to change the native legal system.[112] Similar arguments in favor of native culture were voiced in intellectual circles in the French Third Republic.[113]

Japan, too, witnessed the rise of the liberal intellectual tradition. Jurists warned against the wholesale enforcement of Japanese laws in the colonies without consideration of the indigenous legal tradition and practices. But the Japanese scholars' appreciation of indigenous custom was not necessarily at odds with the colonial campaign to overhaul the native legal system in the model of the "modern" Japanese system. In Korea, Ume Kenjirō embodied this model. The concerted efforts for building a new legal order, in which customary law occupied a prominent place, were part of the inexorable goal of building a modern centralized bureaucratic state.

Scholars have long debated the efficacy of colonial institutional modification. Shrouded by the concepts of "custom" and "tradition," native justice in European colonies was left alone to exist beside the European justice system. Customary law as constructed by the Europeans largely remained stagnant and fossilized. Daniel Lev argued that the genuine respect for Indonesian cultures held by Dutch scholars may have "nevertheless helped to imprison them in a cage of elegant policy that rendered them even more vulnerable to outside manipulation."[114] In contrast, the reification of customary law in colonial Korea was an unapologetically integral part of the legal modernization scheme concocted by the Japanese state. The colonial government's controlled grip on customary law seems to have helped palliate a clash between tradition and modernity in Korea.

During the past few decades, there arose a widespread debate over so-called Japanese developmental colonialism. A number of scholars have asked whether dazzling economic success of Korea in the 1960s and on was due to the legacy of Japanese colonialism.[115] A similar question can be posed regarding legal

[112] See Fasseur, "Colonial Dilemma."

[113] See Conklin, "Colonialism and Human Rights."

[114] Lev, *Legal Evolution*, 20.

[115] Scholars see a certain link between colonial changes in Korea and its postcolonial modernization. Bruce Cumings, "The Legacy of Japanese Colonialism in Korea," in *The Japanese Colonial Empire, 1895–1945*, eds. Myers and Peattie, 478–496; Bruce Cumings, *Parallax Visions: Making Sense of American-East Asian Relations at the End of the Century* (Durham, NC: Duke University Press, 1999).

developments. Prasenjit Duara argued that the Japanese pan-Asian rhetoric should be seen as less of a smoke screen than a "self-contradictory ideology of the new imperialism in which domination and exploitation coexisted with development and modernization."[116] To be sure, one cannot assume that the legacy of Japanese "exceptionalism" is the only, or a dominant, factor in Korea's postcolonial developments. For Samuel Huntington, it was "culture" that "had to be a large part of the explanation" of the difference in postcolonial developments between Korea and Ghana.[117] Arguably some of this culture was accreted and bolstered by colonial legal changes. What Africans demanded during the course of anticolonial movement in the 1950s – a unified legal system, integration of customary law and modern law, and a single hierarchy of courts open for all – had already been achieved in Korea during the colonial period.[118]

The colonial modernization process in Korea was, of course, replete with problems. The attempt to build an integrated legal order across ethnic lines was compromised, and its results obscured, by the Japanese pursuit of cultural assimilation. The policy of assimilation of "thought and emotion," a supposedly complete fusion of the Japanese and the natives, rendered the legal unification project inherently suspect to both the contemporaries and later historians. The imperative of ideological assimilation proved much more difficult than mere civilizational assimilation.

The effectiveness of the colonial legal reform diminished as the Japanese teetered over the nature of the colonial empire they were creating. Officially Japanese colonial planners envisioned a full integration of the empire but there was plenty of skepticism about assimilation.[119] The *naichi* extension policy was pursued as a goal but not as practical strategies. A full legal unification and extension of Japanese laws to the colony would require the complete application of the constitution, a prospect for which neither colonial officials nor most politicians in Tokyo were ready. Even many who demanded the unification of judicial systems in the name of judicial independence did so mainly in order to circumvent the control of the judiciary by the governor general. Caught in the middle of conflicting interests, the rights of individual Koreans continued to suffer. Japan's decision to withhold constitutional rights to colonial subjects fundamentally jeopardized its credibility as a missionary of the rule of law and an ardent agent of legal modernization in East Asia.

Here the complex nature of the Japanese colonial legal system is in full display. Japan was serious in its modernizing venture. Little interested in the

[116] Duara, "The New Imperialism."

[117] In the early 1960s the economies of Ghana and South Korea were remarkably similar; thirty years later, noted Huntington, the difference in development between the two countries could not have been more conspicuous. Lawrence E. Harrison and Samuel P. Huntington, eds., *Culture Matters: How Values Shape Human Progress* (New York: Basic Books, 2000), xiii.

[118] T. W. Bennett, "Re-introducing African Customary Law to the South African Legal System," *The American Journal of Comparative Law* 57 (2009): 1–31.

[119] Chen, "Gōtō Shimpei," 54.

notion of cultural or legal relativism, Japan applied its civil law to Korea and facilitated an effective process of legal reception. In this respect, the Japanese deviation was undeviating. Legal changes that took place in the process were thoroughgoing and had lasting effects. The laws and legal system Korea inherited at the time of independence had been crucially shaped by the colonial experience. The fact that the formal legal order established during the colonial period in Korea has remained almost intact after the Japanese were long gone suggests that the colonial legal system calls for careful attention.

Customary law, a seemingly innocuous concept in the colonial legal order, had a critical bearing on both the colonial period and the postcolonial era. The postcolonial civil law system continued to rely on many of the precedents and on the legal reasoning of the colonial courts' decisions in customary law. Chapter 8 discusses the impact of colonial customary law in contemporary Korea.

8

Customary Law in Modern Korea

The myth of customary law looms large in Korean legal history. The Chosŏn High Court constructed customary law through jurisprudential activities and sustained the idea that custom was spontaneous law emanating from Korean tradition and culture. Following Korea's independence in August 1945, major efforts were made to expunge the traces of colonial law. While colonial statutes and ordinances were swept aside, however, colonial precedents in customary law continued to be recognized by postcolonial Korean courts. Many colonial judicial decisions rendered under Articles 10 through 12 of the Chosŏn Civil Ordinance were preserved and observed as "customary law" in postcolonial jurisprudence. Here the major dilemma surrounding customary law is evident: due to the nature of custom, it is intrinsically difficult to distinguish "colonial" custom from "Korean" custom.

In 1985, the Korean Supreme Court published a reference manual for judges titled *Old Custom on Family and Succession.*[1] Its preface stated: "Article 11 of the *Minsaryŏng* [the civil ordinance of 1912] during the colonial period made it a principle to apply our custom instead of Japan's civil code.... The provisions on family and succession in our civil code were drafted according to our custom. For the purpose of accurate interpretation and application of the current civil code, it is necessary to investigate our custom. But the absence of any compendium of custom has caused serious inconvenience."[2] This volume was thus created to be used as a trial reference book. It put together selections from old Korean laws, the *Report on the Investigation of Customs*, the Chosŏn High Court decisions, and scholarly writings. It is apparent that the selection criteria for the materials fit squarely with the colonial definition of "Korean custom." During the colonial period, "custom" referred to virtually anything that was not the colonizer's law. It was seen in Chapter 7 how European colonial

[1] Pŏpwŏn Haengjŏngch'ŏ [Office of Court Administration] ed., *Ch'injok sangsok e kwanhan kugwansŭp* [Old Custom on Family and Succession], Chaep'an charyo [Trial Sources], vol. 29 (1985).

[2] Ibid., 1.

powers' use of the term "custom" obscured the boundaries of law and usages. The problem was more serious in the Japanese colonies like Korea because state law provisions of the Chosŏn Korean codes were clumped together with any Korean usages and practices that the Japanese could put their fingers on, and they were called Korean custom with potential legal force. The conceptual division between law and customs was almost completely overlooked.

The problem continued and exacerbated in postcolonial Korea. Jurists added colonial judicial precedents to this body of Korean customary law and, as a result, the distinction between Korean custom – if it ever existed – and the colonial creation of Korean customary law was obscured.[3] Where does Korean custom end and where does colonial custom start? This is the question that postcolonial Korean jurisprudence and doctrine have grappled with since 1945.

Korea's first civil code after independence was promulgated in 1958 and took effect on January 1, 1960. It recognized customary law as an official source of law. Article 1 provided: "In civil trials, those matters for which there is no written law are governed by customary law, and those matters for which there is no customary law shall be adjudicated by inference from reason." It has been pointed out that in the civil law jurisdictions custom is regularly listed as a major source of law but routinely dismissed as being of slight practical importance.[4] According to John Henry Merryman, custom in civil law countries receives scholarly attention "far out of proportion to its actual importance as law," mainly because of "the need to justify treating as law something that is not created by the legislative power of the state" and also because of the significance it commands as a source of national pride and identity.[5] In Korea, a country of the civilian tradition where all laws are written and judicial precedent is not law, custom not only occupies a prominent place in the civil code but remains at the center of jurisprudential and doctrinal discussion.

The authority of custom as enshrined in the Korean Civil Code represents both a rejection and a continuation of the colonial legal past. The crowning of custom with binding force in the Korean Civil Code was a clear expression of nationalistic legislative will. It is common in postcolonial societies to claim custom as a symbol of national identity. In Korea, native custom was viewed as the embodiment of Korean cultural values and tradition, which transcended the boundaries of the realm of legislative policy. The result was heightened

[3] Most sources included in this volume dated from the colonial years up to the 1930s, prompting the suspicion that the contents were borrowed heavily from a book published by a Japanese scholar, Nagumo Kōichi, *Genkō Chōsen shinzoku sōzoku hōruishū*, published in 1935. See Yi Sang-uk, "Hanguk sangsokpŏp ŭi sŏngmunhwa kwajŏng," 86 (note 650). See also Yang, "Envisioning Feminist Jurisprudence," 38–39.

[4] Mary Ann Glendon, *Comparative Legal Traditions in a Nutshell*, 2nd ed. (St. Paul: West Group, 1999), 129.

[5] John Henry Merryman, *The Civil Law Tradition: An Introduction to the Legal Systems of Western Europe and Latin America* (Stanford: Stanford University Press, 1969), 12 and 23.

attention to indigenous tradition not tainted with colonial influence. The deference to custom as a sort of *volksgeist* of the Korean people is powerfully supported by the language of the constitution. Article 9 of the Korean Constitution declares: "The State shall strive to sustain and develop the cultural heritage and to enhance national culture." Recognition of custom as a source of law was clearly prompted by the desire to preserve the historical continuity of Korean law and to assert the independent legal tradition of Korea.

Ironically, the compelling desires to obliterate the remains of the colonial past that were foisted on Korean law and to liberate the Korean legal system from the vestiges of colonialism seem to have furthered inadvertently the prolongation of colonial law. The concept of custom as law governing private relations originated with the colonial legal order. The colonial notion of custom as "living law" was rarely questioned by Korean courts and was instead powerfully sustained. By declaring custom as a source of law in the civil code, Korea appropriated the colonial framework of customary law and, along with it, the myth of custom as perpetuated by colonial courts.

So far the dominant trend in Korean legal historiography has centered on showing how indigenous Korean law and custom was intentionally suppressed and altered by the colonial judicial authorities for the purpose of assimilation. Yet this thesis of "distortion" of Korean custom fails to distinguish the three different elements that were present under the customary law regime but were nevertheless clearly separate: the practices and usages that existed during the Chosŏn dynasty; the practices that were selectively reworked into legal custom by the colonial jurists; and legal concepts contained in the Japanese Civil Code. The tendency to muddle these elements in post-independence historiography can be ascribed in part to the colonial judges, who had persisted in claiming that they adjudicated according to preexisting Korean customary law and thus blurred the boundaries among these three entities.

This chapter examines the effect of colonial customary law in contemporary Korea. To date, little attention has been paid to the impact of colonial jurisprudence on postcolonial law. There exist two separate questions of "what is custom in Korean law" and "what is Korean custom." Korean jurists have tended to be preoccupied with the latter question, with scant attention to the former; worse, they have often confounded the two. As a result, the meaning of "custom" remains volatile and contested, and the boundaries of "tradition" are fluid and subject to various interpretations. This situation has an unsettling influence on the relationship between custom and statutes.

Recently custom has become the subject of a series of landmark decisions by the Constitutional Court and the Supreme Court. A recurring issue in the debates that took place before the courts and in wider legal circles was whether certain provisions in the Korean Civil Code could be deemed justifiable on the grounds that they were deeply rooted in Korean tradition. Further, there has been an increasing concern with negotiating the legal force of custom so that it does not flaunt legislative supremacy and contravene the values of democracy and liberalism. Both the Constitutional Court and the Supreme Court have tended to distance themselves from automatic reverence to tradition and have taken an increasingly hard look at custom. The stakes are high for protecting individual rights and at the same time preserving traditional cultural heritage. The saga of custom continues as a crucial nexus between national tradition and a modern democratic society in Korea.

Custom and the Korean Civil Code

Much of the colonial legal framework remained in place after Korea obtained independence in 1945. The American military government in occupation of the peninsula abolished a number of colonial laws of a discriminatory and political nature.[6] But it ordered the retention of most of the colonial laws in postcolonial Korea.[7] The Court Organization Law took effect on June 1, 1948, and judicial administration was entrusted to the Supreme Court. The constitution was promulgated the following month. Article 100 of the constitution stated that the laws which were in force under Japanese rule would continue their force unless they conflicted with the constitution: "the current laws continue to have the force of law so long as such laws are not contradictory to this Constitution." The "current laws" referred to most Japanese laws that were effective at the time of the liberation. Thus colonial laws that had governed Korea, including the Chosŏn Civil Ordinance, remained valid laws until they were replaced or abolished by subsequent laws. The Japanese Civil Code continued to be the law in Korea, fully in force, as late as 1960 when the Korean Civil Code took effect.

After independence, custom was celebrated as the embodiment of collective national memory and its recovery and reassertion required full attention. The legislative history of the Korean Civil Code shows that there was no serious opposition to recognizing custom as a source of law.[8] In fact there was a call for revising the language of the draft code so as to grant customary law greater force. Some members of the drafting committee argued that the imperfections of statutes made it imperative to recognize the power of customary law to

[6] The notorious Law on the Maintenance of Public Order and Censorship was abolished; the postcolonial Ordinance of Rehabilitation of Korean Surname voided the Japanese family name system.

[7] Ordinance Number 21 (November 2, 1945), Article 1, Section 1: Retention of Laws: "Until further ordered, and except as previously repealed or abolished, all laws, regulations, orders, notices or other documents issued by any former government of Korea having the force of law on August 9, 1945, will continue in force and effect until repeated by express of the Military Government of Korea." *Mi gunjŏng pŏmnyŏng jip* [Collection of Laws and Regulations of the American Military Government], ed. Naemubu Ch'ian'guk (Seoul, 1956), 23. For judicial administration under the American military rule, see United States Armed Forces in Korea, ed. *History of United States Armed Forces in Korea* (*Chu Han migun sa*) (Seoul: Dolbegae, 1988), 4 vols.

[8] Yang Ch'ang-su, "Minpŏp chŏn ŭi chejŏng kwajŏng e kwanhan yŏngu: Minpŏp an e taehan kukhoe pon hoeŭi ŭi simŭi [A Study of the Codification Process of the Civil Code: Parliamentary Deliberations on the Draft Civil Code]," *Seoul Taehakkyo pŏphak* 33, no. 2 (1992), 153.

abrogate statutes. In this scheme, it was claimed, the more recent customary law should abrogate the earlier statute.[9] But this proposal was not accepted. There were also some doubts about declaring "reason" (*chori* in Korean; *jōri* in Japanese) as a source of law.[10] Eventually it was agreed to adopt the language of the Chinese Civil Code and the Manchu Civil Code. These codes declared both custom and reason as supplementary sources of law, following the framework of Article 3 of Dajōkan Decree Number 103 (1875) in Meiji Japan.[11] Custom, as a subsidiary source, could not supersede a provision in the code which was contrary to the custom.

Despite their widely shared hostility to the colonial past, the drafters of the civil code made little attempt to depart drastically from Japanese law. Formally it was German law, on which Japanese civil law was based, that served as the archetype of Korean law. Reluctant to acknowledge openly the influence of Japanese law and legal science on the creation of the country's new legal order, Korean jurists frequently referred to the prevailing German legal theories that had dominated the Japanese scene for some time. The German code contained no provision regarding the sources of law and instead left the determination to the direction of the courts. The German redactors feared that openly sanctioning the survival of customary law in the new code would defeat the very purpose of unifying the law. No similar concerns existed in Korea where there was no written customary law.

Most scholars have argued that Article 1 of the Korean Civil Code was in the tradition of the famous Article 1 of the Swiss Civil Code.[12] But, as was pointed out in Chapter 3, it is indisputable that the language came from Japanese law. If the Korean redactors were inspired by the Swiss code, the underlying considerations in the two countries for affirming the legal force of custom were rather divergent from each other. In the Swiss Civil Code, custom as a source of law was viewed as necessary because a judge, who was not allowed to refuse to decide a case on the grounds that the statutory text was insufficient, needed to turn to other sources of law.[13] The Swiss Republic recognized custom as a formal source of law as a means to accommodate its history of disunity among different cantons. For Korea with no similar history, the exalted status of custom in its civil code was mainly the result of the urgency and exigency to assert indigenous culture and nationalism. Because the provisions of the new code bore remarkable resemblance to those

[9] Ibid.

[10] Ibid., 152.

[11] See Chapter 3. The civil codes of Korea and Taiwan today share precisely the same language (Article 1) derived from the Meiji law regarding the source of law.

[12] Kim Chŭng-han, *Minpŏp ch'ongch'ik* [General Principles of the Civil Code] (Seoul: Pagyŏngsa, 1980), 51; Chŏng Chong-hyu, "Hanguk minpŏp chŏn ŭi pigyo pŏp chŏk kyebo [A Genealogy of the Korean Civil Code: A Comparative Legal Perspective]," *Minsa pŏphak* 8, no. 3 (1990): 60–104.

[13] Williams, *The Sources of Law in the Swiss Civil Code*.

in the Japanese Civil Code, it might have been perceived as essential to declare "Korean" custom as an express source of law.

The situation seemed analogous to that in Japan in the late nineteenth century. The Japanese Civil Code was drafted in the wake of a fierce resurgence of the virtue of Japanese tradition and custom that were seemingly assailed by Western influence. It was acknowledged that "custom" and "reason" were instruments in helping domesticate the new civil law order so that indigenous popular practices and usages would have a prominent presence. A similar idea was imported to colonial Korea. The concept of custom as law, as defined in prewar Japanese jurisprudence and doctrines, took root during the colonial years. In postcolonial Korea, there was little hesitation in declaring custom as law. In Japan, once the civil code transformed many customs into modern legal provisions, the nationalistic consideration of the importance of custom dwindled. When the civil code was revised in 1947 (enforced in 1948), postwar Japan further shed the elements of obligatory indigenism in customary law. In postcolonial Korea, in contrast, the mounting force of nationalism precipitated the fusing of indigenous culture and customary law.

Apart from Article 1, the key provision in the Korean Civil Code that concerned custom was Article 101, currently Article 106. It provided: "Where there is a custom which is different from any provisions in law that are not concerned with good morals or other social order, if the intent of the parties is not clear, such custom shall prevail." Needless to say, this provision was a recitation of Article 92 of the Japanese Civil Code, with additional clarification that the intent of the parties to follow custom was presumed.[14] Korean scholars have debated whether the term "statutes" in Article 1 includes non-imperative statutes. Most jurists are in agreement that the "statutes" refer to imperative laws only.[15] "Custom" in Article 106 has been seen as custom in fact, not custom in law. The two are distinguished depending on the existence of *opinio necessitatis*, that is, whether citizens had legal conviction that it was law. Lacking *opinio juris*, custom in fact does not override non-imperative statutes; it merely confirms the intent of the parties to supersede the statutes. Article 103, equivalent to Article 90 of the Japanese code, provides that a contract is void if it is contrary to public policy.[16] Following the colonial jurisprudential trend, it was left for the judge to construe the scope of public policy. Article 185 of the Korean Civil Code allowed the creation of property rights by customary law. This provision can be traced back to Article 12 of the Chosŏn Civil Ordinance during colonial years.

[14] See Chapter 3.

[15] Kim Uk-kon, "Kwangsŭppŏp e taehan yŏngu: Tŭkhi ŭri minpŏp ŭi haesŏk ŭl chungsim ŭro [A Study of Customary Law: With Particular Attention to the Interpretation of Our Civil Code]," *Sungjŏn Taehakkyo nonmunjip* 5 (1974): 361–394. For similar discussions on the Japanese Civil Code, see Chapter 3.

[16] Article 103 of the Korean Civil Code provides: "A juristic act of any content which is against good customs and social order is void." Article 90 of the Japanese Civil Code provides: "A juristic act with any purpose which is against public order and good customs is void."

The drafters of the Korean Civil Code were mindful of the prevailing influence of the Japanese Civil Code. Kim Pyŏng-ro (1888–1964), the first chief justice of the Supreme Court from 1948 to 1957 and the figure who arguably played the most prominent role in the writing of the civil code, acknowledged the overwhelming presence of Japanese law in the country's new code. He stated:

> Some might wonder, after reading the draft of the civil code, why there are so many provisions that are exactly the same as, or similar to, those in the Japanese Civil Code. But when we drafted the law, we treated the Japanese code only as a reference, among many different codes of other countries we examined. Japanese law itself was merely a translation of French law or German law. The laws we regarded as the most useful references were the Chinese code and the Manchu code. But these codes were all drafted by Japanese scholars and hence were products of the Japanese people. So here, no matter whether we study German law, French law, Chinese law, or Manchu law, and choose one as the model for our code, it is only natural that many provisions coincide with the Japanese law provisions.[17]

This was rather an accurate appraisal, in a blunt sort of way. The Chinese and the Manchu codes were drafted either by Japanese jurists or under their heavy influence.[18] The significance of Japan's role in introducing Western law to East Asia was far-reaching. It was practically impossible in East Asian countries to write a code independent from the sphere of influence of Japanese law.

The first generation of judges and lawyers in postcolonial Korea, including the drafters of the civil code, were educated and trained during the colonial period. All theoretical and methodological tools came from Japanese legal science. The development of Korean law was led mostly by legal practitioners who had served in the colonial courts. The historical discussion of the relationship between the Korean and the Japanese Civil Codes has generally been accompanied by either criticism of or apology for the drafters of the Korean code for adopting provisions and terminology from the Japanese code. Instead of repeating the tired debate on whether the similarities between the two civil codes should be justified as legitimate borrowing or reviled as colonial vestiges, the following pages examine how modern Korean jurisprudence dealt with the legacy of colonial customary law.

[17] Cited from Yang Ch'ang-su, "Minpŏp an ŭi sŏngnip kwajŏng e kwanhan sogo [A Brief Study on the Process of Drafting Civil Law]," *Seoul Taehakkyo pŏphak* 30, nos. 3 & 4 (1989), 203.

[18] Wagatsuma Sakae and Hozumi Shigeto, professors at the Tokyo Imperial University, participated in the making of the civil code of Manchukuo. See Kokuchi Hikota, "Ilbon t'ongch'i ha ŭi 'Manchuguk' ŭi pŏp [The Law of Manchukuo under Japanese Rule]," trans. Im Sanghyŏk, *Pŏpsahak yŏngu* 27 (2003): 83–112. Hozumi Shigeto was the son of Hozumi Nobushige. The Japanese advisors' role in the Chinese legal reform was extensive. Oda Yorozu, professor of administrative law at the Tokyo Imperial University, compiled *The Administrative Law of the Qing Empire* [Shinkoku Gyoseiho]. For Oda, see Huang, "Enacting the "Incomprehensible China."

FIGURE 8.1. **The Supreme Court of Korea.** The court en banc in May 1956. In the middle is the first Supreme Court Chief Justice Kim Pyŏng-ro (1888–1964). Collection of the Supreme Court Library of Korea. Reprinted with permission.

Colonial Law and Postcolonial Jurisprudence

The Chosŏn Civil Ordinance was officially abolished by the Special Law Concerning the Reorganization of the Old Laws, issued on July 15, 1961 (Law Number 659).[19] Declaring the invalidity of colonial statutory laws was relatively easy; dealing with the continuing legal effect of colonial laws and jurisprudence proved much more difficult. The 1960 civil code provided for the retroactive effect of its provisions but provided that legal acts that had taken place before January 1, 1960, which was the date the civil code came into effect, were not affected by the new law.[20] The civil code specifically pronounced that matters of succession that had begun before January 1, 1960, would continue to be governed by preexisting laws.[21] This arrangement thus

[19] The law took effect on January 20, 1962. See Myŏng Sun-ku, "Ajikto saraitnŭn pŏp, 'Chosŏn Minsaryŏng': Chosŏn Minsaryŏng ŭi sogŭpchŏk pyeji rŭl chean handa [The Law that Is Still Alive, 'Chosŏn Minsaryŏng': Calling for the Retroactive Abolition of Chosŏn Minsaryŏng]," *Chŏsŭtisŭ* 7, no. 2 (2008): 220–236.

[20] Civil Code (February 22, 1958), Supplementary Provision, Article 2: "This law also applies to the matters that preexist its implementation unless there are special provisions otherwise. But it does not change legal effects that took under the old laws."

[21] Civil Code, Supplementary Provision, Article 25, Section 1: "Succession that began before the implementation of this law continues to be governed by the old laws." See Chin Su Yun, "Tradition and Constitution in the Context of the Korean Family Law," *Journal of Korean Law* 5, no. 1 (2005): 194–212.

compelled the postcolonial courts to cope with the continuing effect of colonial laws including customary law.

Departing from Colonial Law

The immediate goal of postcolonial jurists was to blot out colonial remnants from Korean laws. In some cases, the postcolonial courts simply refused to apply provisions of the civil code – the Japanese Civil Code that was the law in force in Korea – declaring that they were "inapplicable" to Korea. Such was a landmark decision rendered by the Korean Supreme Court in 1947 under American occupation.[22] The case involved the issue of the wife's legal capacity to file a suit. As seen in Chapter 5, capacity matters during the colonial period had at first been governed by Korean custom, not by Japan's civil law, but after the revision of the civil ordinance in 1921 they became subject to the Japanese Civil Code.

In the case, the plaintiff filed a suit demanding the transfer of the ownership of a house and the district court found in her favor. The defendant appealed, arguing that the plaintiff was a married woman and that the lower court had failed to take into consideration that she lacked the legal capacity to file a suit. The defendant referred to Japanese Civil Code Articles 12 and 14, among others, that stipulated that the wife, as "a quasi-incompetent person," must "obtain the husband's permission" in performing certain legal acts, including "filing a suit."

The Court dismissed the appellant's arguments. In a brisk and strongly worded opinion, it wrote:

> The restriction of the wife's legal capacity to act under Article 14.1 of the civil code can be viewed as a measure to promote the unity of the spouses, but in fact the main reason was to recognize the superiority of the husband over the wife. We became an independent state on August 15, 1945, and we are in the process of building a country based on democracy. It is our national mission to create our legal, political, economic, and cultural systems on the basis of democratic principles. Every individual is equal.... Article 14 of the civil code that discriminates against women is not suitable for our society's reality, and it is natural to attempt to make appropriate changes of this old system that negates gender equality. This court is obligated to adjudicate in accordance with social advances and to adjust its interpretation of laws as needed. We therefore do not recognize the restriction of the wife's legal capacity provided in the said article.... Articles 14.1 and 12.1.4 of the civil code, and Article 50.2 of the civil procedure required that the wife obtain the husband's permission before filing a suit, but these provisions are inapplicable for the reasons listed above.[23]

[22] Judgment of September 2, 1947, 1947minsang88, reported in *Pŏpchŏng* 2 (October 1947). The text of this case is printed in Chŏng Kwang-hyŏn, *Hanguk kajok pŏp yŏngu*, 272–274. See the analysis in Yang Ch'ang-su, "Urinara ch'oech'o ŭi hŏnpŏp chaep'an nonŭi: Ch'ŏŭi haengwi nŭngnyŏk chehan e kwanhan 1947 nyŏn Taepŏpwŏn p'an'gyŏl e taehayŏ [The First Debate in Korea on Constitutional Adjudication: The 1947 Decision of the Supreme Court of Korea regarding the Restriction on the Wife's Legal Capacity]," *Seoul Taehakkyo pŏphak* 40 (1999): 126–151.

[23] Cited from Yang, "Urinara ch'oech'o ŭi hŏnpŏp chaep'an nonŭi," 127–128.

Note that the Supreme Court refused to apply the provision of Article 14 despite the fact that the civil code was still the governing law of the country. The court treated the case as a question of the intrinsic soundness of law. This case, regarded as the first judicial review case in Korea and often compared to *Marbury vs. Madison*, a landmark decision rendered by the United States Supreme Court in 1803, triggered a fierce debate among scholars. The majority of jurists criticized the court, saying that it had openly disregarded the law and therefore jeopardized legal stability. Some scholars pointed out that the decision amounted to judicial interference with legislative power: "this is a question to be decided not by the court but by the legislature."[24] Besides, they argued, the court could only review the constitutionality of legislation passed after the promulgation of the constitution, but Korea's constitution was not yet in place (it came into effect in 1948). As long as there was no constitution, the court could not exercise judicial review power.

Other jurists acclaimed the court's decision, however. Their opinions were squarely based on the consideration of reason as well as policy implications. According to the supporters, the court must consider reason (*chori*) and supplement positive law with the principles of equity. Legal stability may be sacrificed if the question involves material defects of the statutes or concerns issues of social malfunction. For some scholars, this case involved more than the interpretation of a specific law. They forcefully argued that the court had a duty to abrogate laws that conflicted with the social reality and circumstances in independent Korea. The court could refuse the application of such laws because it was mandated to choose and select laws on the basis of Korea's new situation. Even if the constitution was not yet in place, they claimed, democratic principles, natural law, reasonableness, or consideration of due process could serve as sufficient grounds for judicial review.

Apart from the apparent nationalist sentiment underlying the arguments of the court and of the scholars who supported it, this case clearly bore on the question of whether the court could reject the application of law, and practically abolish law, because of its power to interpret the law on the basis of reason. The court contended that the law in question was automatically unenforceable because it was no longer suitable to the new situation in independent Korea and that reason justified striking it down. What mattered was whether the law was sound and reasonable in existing society, a question to be decided by the court. In the opinion of the justices, the law in question had already lost its validity, therefore the court did not violate the principle of applying the existing law.

This decision can be viewed as an extraordinary judicial feat – the court valiantly tried to mitigate the problems arising from the unfortunate situation that the country, now fully independent, was nonetheless governed by colonial law. It is interesting to note, however, that the arguments of the court and of the scholars in favor of them were strikingly reminiscent of the reasoning of colonial

[24] Ibid., 130.

customary jurisprudence. The Supreme Court cited "democratic principles" as the theoretical foundation for its treatment of Article 14 of the civil code in a way that differed little from the colonial court's invocation of reasonableness. During the colonial period, the assertion that custom must be reasonable allowed the judges to recognize subjectively indigenous usages and practices that seemed compatible to their vision of law. Now the Korean Supreme Court conjured up "reason" to decide whether colonial laws must be avoided. The Supreme Court argued that judicial power had the mission to supplement the deficiencies of law, instead of limiting itself to applying the letter of the law strictly. In this fashion it largely repeated the arguments of its colonial counterpart. The ideal of the judge as a judge-legislator, charged with harmonizing jurisprudence and social reality, survived into the postcolonial period.

The attempt to expunge colonial elements from Korean law was pursued most actively in the area of family law. Family law had demanded serious attention from the colonial judges because Korean family custom, declared as a source of law, was crucially based on Confucian rituals. In implementing custom as a source of law, the colonial judges actively modified or abolished the Confucian practices that departed from the principles in the Japanese Civil Code. Deleting colonial elements in Korean law was thus equated with resuscitating Confucian elements.

As discussed in Chapter 5, the revision of the Chosŏn Civil Ordinance in 1939 allowed non-agnatic adoption. Adoption between persons of different surnames and the adoption of a son-in-law were legalized, in departure from the deeply entrenched tradition in Korean society that had prohibited the adoption of a child with a different family name.[25] An official decree in 1947 abolished the Japanese system of non-agnatic adoption and prohibited the registration of such adoptive relations. What about the adoptions that had already taken place? In March 1949, the Supreme Court of Korea denied the legal effect of the adoption of a son-in-law that had taken place in 1942.[26] This decision thus tossed out colonial precedents and nullified all such adoptive relations completed during the colonial period.

The key legal issue was whether the court had the authority to invalidate the statute (the colonial civil ordinance) that was in force. The constitution of 1948 was silent on who had the power to decide the constitutionality of statutes including the colonial laws. The constitution provided the Constitutional Committee with review power, but this power was limited to the laws enacted by the constitutional assembly.[27] The 1949 decision of the Supreme Court did

[25] The revision took effect on February 11, 1940 (Article 11, Section 2, Subsection 1).

[26] Judgment of March 26, 1949, 1949minsang348, reported in *Pŏpcho hyŏphoe chapchi* 1, no. 3 (June 1959): 95–100 and no. 4 (July 1949): 93–95. The text is printed in Chŏng Kwanghyŏn, *Hanguk kajok pŏp yŏngu*, 276–284. For an analysis of this case, see Yang Ch'ang-su, "Hŏnpŏp chejŏng hu ilchŏng pŏmnyŏng ŭi hyoryŏk [The Effect of Japanese Colonial Law after the Promulgation of the Constitution]," *in Minpŏp sango* (Seoul: Pagyŏngsa, 1998), 43–49.

[27] Constitution of 1948, Article 81, Paragraph 2.

not discuss whether it had the power to review colonial laws, or whether the colonial statute allowing the adoption of a child with a different surname was in violation of the constitution. Instead, the court simply asserted that such an adoption system "had been naturally abolished with the departure of the Japanese" and that "the relationship established on the basis of this system is against public order and good custom. Therefore it is void *ab initio*." In other words, the court asserted that it had the power to decide whether a specific colonial law was valid or invalid depending on its conformity to "public order." There is no mistaking the fact that this language is reminiscent of that of colonial jurisprudence. Subsequent to the decision, the Supreme Court chief justice issued a directive in 1952 to delete from the family registries records of different-surname adoptions.[28]

The Supreme Court's rejection of the colonial adoption system was widely acclaimed in legal circles at the time as a legitimate attempt to delete the unjust colonial laws that had been forcibly imposed on Korean people. The civil code of 1960 allowed adoption of a child with a different surname but the non-agnate child was not allowed to take the new adoptive father's surname. The principle of the immutability of the surname persisted. Throughout the 1970s and 1980s, the Supreme Court repeatedly ruled that the adoption of a child with a different surname that took place under colonial law before 1960 was invalid in accordance with the decision of 1949.[29] It was not until 1994 that the court reversed the 1949 ruling, when it abandoned the position that non-agnate adoptions that took place between 1940 and 1959 were invalid.[30]

The 1994 decision was in line with the legislative changes. In 1989, the civil code was comprehensively revised to reflected important changes in family law. The new code that took effect on January 1, 1991, abolished the provision that prohibited the adoption of the eldest son of the family head (*hoju*) and also abrogated the rule that disallowed the household headship succession by a non-agnatic adopted child. These changes marked a fundamental reform of the adoption system in Korean history, representing a shift from the traditional contractual adoption system grounded on the necessity to continue the family name to a modern declaratory adoption system. The latter system, to take effect with the court approval, was geared to promoting the welfare of the child. The revision of the civil code in 2005, which took effect in January 2008, established the new "real adoption" system to exist in parallel with the extant "general adoption" system, also known as the "incomplete adoption" system.[31] The new system allowed adoption in the fullest sense, without any impediments resulting from the traditional requirements of agnatic relations. The adopted child now enjoys the same legal rights as the birth child and

[28] Yang Ch'ang-su, "Hŏnpŏp chejŏng hu ilchŏng pŏmnyŏng," 45.

[29] Judgment of April 24, 1967, 65ma1163; judgment of March 24, 1970, 69ta1400; judgment of October 23, 1992, 92ta29399.

[30] Judgment of May 24, 1994, 93mŭ119.

[31] Article 908, Section 2.

is able to change his or her surname to the adoptive parents' surname. This change marked a drastic departure from the kinship-based adoption principle that had existed since the Chosŏn dynasty.

Difficult questions abounded in postcolonial jurisprudence. After 1960, when Article 1 of the civil code proclaimed that custom was a source of law, those practices that had been declared by the colonial courts to be Korean custom continued to have legal force, unless the courts specifically denied their legal effects. The Supreme Court's volte-face in 1994 testifies to the complexity of the seemingly clear-cut task of expunging colonial elements from Korean law. The court effectively admitted that it had no power to abolish colonial statutes or deny the effect of legal actions that had taken place under the Japanese colonial law. It was not unreasonable when the Supreme Court reckoned that the customary law precedents established by the colonial Chosŏn High Court needed to be followed for the sake of the stability of legal relations. At the same time, the Supreme Court's position before 1994 clearly reflected the widespread hostility in society to non-agnatic adoption – and other alien practices – that had been imposed on the Korean people. The court had chosen earlier to set aside the existing law on the grounds that it was necessary to protect Korean custom. The fact that it took almost half a century to recognize the effect of the colonial non-agnatic adoptions reveals the profound judicial reluctance to give effect to laws regarded as a colonial legacy.

In many practical aspects, colonial custom became Korean custom. No wonder the postcolonial courts have had to spend so much effort to clarify the meaning of custom in Korean law.

Customary Law and Custom in Fact

The Supreme Court began to consider seriously the issue of custom in the 1980s. During the next twenty-five years or so, the interpretation of custom became the subject of heated jurisprudential and scholarly debate. In 1983, the Supreme Court defined customary law as "existing social norm created through repeated usages in society, which has obtained legal force through society's approval and recognition as legal norm and of which the observance is required."[32] As such, "customary law is a source of law and it has the same legal force as laws and regulations as long as it is not in conflict with laws and regulations." On the other hand, "custom in fact lacks society's approval and recognition that confers on it legal force" and "it is a mere usage without legal force which simply supplements the intent of the parties in a legal act."

The case at hand involved a property dispute. The plaintiff sued the defendant, demanding the removal of a grave and the transfer of the neighboring land. The gravesite, as stipulated by the parties, was under the care of the defendant, the son of the deceased. The defendant requested dismissal of the suit on the grounds of procedural errors. He claimed that custom required that

[32] Judgment of June 14, 1983, 80ta3231.

FIGURE 8.2. **Judicial robe, circa 1960.** A judge in full judicial gear that was used between 1953 and 1965. The robe features the embroidery of a rose of Sharon (Mugunghwa), the national flower of Korea, and the hat has a *t'aegŭk* mark inside the rose of Sharon. The judge, Kim Yoon-Haeng, later a Supreme Court Justice, was the author's father. Personal collection of the author.

only the household head (*hoju*) become the ritual heir as the sole person to exercise the rights and obligations including the maintenance of the gravesite and the performance of ancestor worship ceremony, and that the suit failed to name as defendant the household head on the family registry, who was the surviving spouse. This argument was accepted by the lower courts and the suit was dismissed. The appellant countered that the son was the responsible party under the Regulation of the Simplified Family Ritual Standards (*Kajŏng ŭrye chunch'ik*). The regulation, issued as an executive order in 1973, provided that the surviving spouse or the descendants perform the mourning ceremony and take care of the gravesite and the surrounding land.

The Supreme Court reversed and remanded the case to the appeals court. This decision is important because it was one of the first cases in which the Korean judiciary deliberated on the concept of custom and customary law and tried to clarify the relationship between customary law and legislation. The highest court ruled that the lower courts failed to determine whether the custom claimed by the defendant was customary law or mere custom in fact. In order to do so, the justices said, it would have been necessary for the parties claiming that custom to offer proofs. According to the majority opinion, customary law can be applied by the court without waiting for the parties' proffered evidence but custom in fact must be proved by the parties. It is difficult to decide whether a custom has achieved the status of customary law with the requisite *opinio juris*, the court noted, and therefore the party that relies on custom must prove its nature in cases when the court is unsure whether a certain practice is custom in fact or customary law. Once the existence of custom is proved, stated the court, it would be necessary to determine whether the regulation in question is imperative or non-imperative law.

The justices accepted the plaintiff's argument that, under the Regulation of the Simplified Family Ritual Standards, the son of the deceased had the right to maintain the gravesite and the adjacent land. The provision in the civil code claimed by the defendant was inapplicable, the court ruled, because that provision (Article 996) concerned household headship succession and applied only to the death of the household head, not the death of a family member who was not the household head; the provision could not be construed in such a way that the household head automatically succeeds the rights and obligations regarding the gravesite maintenance regardless of the status of the deceased.

The potentially controversial issue in this case was whether custom could be a source of law when it was in conflict with a provision of legislation, but the court sidestepped the question by focusing on the proof of custom. The court did not determine whether customary law in Article 1 in the civil code referred to imperative law only or it included non-imperative law. The court said "if the lower court determined the said custom to be customary law (it appears so but is not clear), the legal effect of such customary law would be inferior to the statutes and it would have only supplementary force. Therefore allowing the effect of such customary law [to supersede the regulation] would be against the intent of Article 1 of the civil code." Here problems in the reasoning of the court become clear. According to the court, if the party succeeded in proving the *opinio juris* of the said custom, it would become customary law and yet as such it would be defeated by the contrary statute regardless of whether the statute is imperative or non-imperative law. If the party failed to prove the *opinio juris* and the said custom were determined to be a mere custom in fact, however, the court would be willing to consider the legal force of the custom to override the statute, depending on whether it is imperative or non-imperative law. Then the question arises: why would the party want to prove the *opinio juris* when, following the court's logic, custom with *opinio juris* would be granted less legal effect against the statute than custom without *opinio juris*?

Scholars of customary law have argued that it is not sufficient to affirm theoretically that custom is a source of law; on practical grounds it must be clarified whether the party who invokes a custom must prove its existence.[33] Simply remanding the case by declaring that the burden of proof lay on the parties in the case, the court stopped short of discussing the genuine issue of the effect of custom as a source of law. The court did not address the issue that concerning custom, which has its origin in a succession of facts and practices, it is difficult to choose between the rules governing the proof of facts and the rules governing the proof of law. As a practical matter, custom as a source of law comes to have little practical meaning unless the judge takes judicial cognizance. It has been pointed out that placing the burden of proof on the party asserting custom – a burden very difficult to satisfy – was tantamount to a refusal, a priori, to consider the binding force of the custom.[34] In the aforementioned case, the justices' predilection for the enforcement of the regulation, which was a kind of sumptuary law, over any claim of custom was not hard to detect.

The court's decision in the 1983 case left many questions unanswered. It failed to explain adequately the tension between written law and custom. The opinion seemed to reveal deep-rooted ambivalence on the part of the courts. The idea that custom should be enforced in law only if the litigants strictly and successfully proved its legal force can be traced to the school of Exegesis, a school of thought in the nineteenth century that favored legislation. As seen in the previous chapters, the reaction against this legal tenet was the German doctrine which acknowledged that custom constituted in itself a rule of law that the judge must apply. The position of the colonial courts on these contending juristic beliefs was rather clear: colonial jurisprudence consistently held that the judge must take cognizance of custom even if the parties failed to invoke or prove it. While adhering to the supremacy of the Japanese code, the judges did not question the principle that they were obliged to discover and apply Korean custom so it could be adjusted to civil law. This framework provided the colonial courts considerable latitude to mold the content of Korean custom in line with their view of justice and equity. It was inevitable that the postcolonial courts had to struggle with the question of the relative importance of legislation and custom in the modern Korean legal order. Custom as the symbol of national tradition highlighted the importance of customary law but this emphasis on custom needed to be reconciled with the primacy of legislation.

Harkening Back to Colonial Jurisprudence

The Supreme Court revisited the issue of custom in 2003. The case was a complex amalgam of diverse issues: it involved, in addition to the interpretation of

[33] Loussouarn, "The Relative Importance," 252–253.

[34] The court stated that it could of itself find custom in fact without the parties' proof (Judgment of July 13, 1976, 76ta983; judgment of April 12, 1977, 76ta1124). See Sŏ Kwang-min, "Kwansŭp pŏp kwa sasil in kwansŭp [Customary Law and Custom in Fact]," *Kosigye* (August 1991): 112–125.

custom, the question of the legal effect of colonial judicial precedents. The dispute between the parties centered on the custom governing the statute of limitations in the recovery of rights over succession.[35] Because the case involved a succession that had begun before the Korean Civil Code took effect, the trial court decided that colonial customary law was the governing law. As seen in Chapter 6, the Chosŏn High Court declared in 1935 that under Korean custom succession recovery rights expired after a certain delay.[36] In 1937, the court limited the period during which the rightful heir could petition succession recovery to six years from the knowledge of the encroachment of his right.[37] Two years later, the court extended the period to twenty years from the beginning of succession.[38]

The suit was filed in 1998. The parties stipulated as fact that the death took place around 1950, although the family registry recorded the year of death as 1974. Having determined that the colonial precedents were binding on the case, the trial court dismissed the suit on the grounds that it was filed almost forty years after the beginning of succession, well after the statutory period had expired. This finding was in conformity with the Korean Supreme Court's decisions in the 1980s and 1990s which upheld the colonial court decisions that Korean custom required succession recovery rights to expire after the statutory period. This time in 2003, however, the Supreme Court decided that it would not apply the colonial custom because it was not "reasonable."

Here the court introduced the element of the "reasonableness" of custom. The justices did not deny that the Chosŏn High Court's precedents were the governing law to the case. Yet the majority refused to apply the colonial custom at issue because it would lead to an inequitable result. The court stated:

> In order for a certain social practice or custom that has been repeatedly observed to be recognized as a legal norm, it must not contradict the general legal order as provided in the Constitution which is the supreme law, and it must be determined that it warrants justification and reasonableness. Those social customary rules that lack such elements cannot be recognized as customary law even if they have been observed repeatedly in society.

The court thus declared that customary law must be reasonable and just. If the custom in issue in the present case were applied strictly, the true heir would be left without a legal recourse once the statute of limitations had expired. This result would be against the principle that ownership is not affected by the statute of limitations, the majority opinion argued, and it would create an

[35] Judgment of July 24, 2003, 2001ta48781. For the analysis of this case, see Yi Hwa-suk, "Sangsok hoebok ch'ŏnggukwŏn ŭi sihyo e kwanhan kwansŭppŏp ŭi hyoryŏk: Taepŏpwŏn 2003.7.24, sŏngo 2001ta48781 chŏnwŏn habŭich'e p'an'gyŏl [The Effect of Customary Law on the Statute of Limitations regarding the Right to Succession Recovery]," *Kajokpŏp yŏngu* 18, no. 1 (2004): 249–272.

[36] Judgment of July 30, 1935, *Hanketsuroku*, vol. 22, 302.

[37] Judgment of August 27, 1937, *Hanketsuroku*, vol. 24, 317.

[38] Judgment of June 30, 1939, *Hanketsuroku*, vol. 26, 263.

unreasonable situation in which the legitimate heir would be deprived of the opportunity to defend his or her property rights against the pretender. The court concluded that the existing customary law lacked legitimacy under the current constitutional order. The justices declared that "we cannot recognize the legal effect of the said custom as customary law."

So far, the court required as the necessary elements of customary law a usage and *opinio necessitatis*, the belief that the observance of that usage was binding. The Court now added a third requisite element of reasonableness. When custom lacked "social reasonableness" and "justness," the justices argued, it must not be recognized as customary law. Even if it had heretofore been recognized as customary law, it subsequently lost its binding force because it was *no longer* reasonable and just.

Here one notes that the Supreme Court's reliance on "reason" was fundamentally in line with the jurisprudence of the colonial court. In the present case, the justices refused to apply the specific precedents of the colonial court, but that refusal resulted from holding fast to the underlying reasoning of colonial jurisprudence. When the colonial judges approved or quashed Korean custom – that is, when they made and unmade Korean customary law – they implicitly resorted to "reasonableness" and "justness." Conflation of Korean custom with reason not only provided the judges with guidelines and justifications for their decisions when there were no clear predictable rules but also conferred legitimacy on the colonial courts' civil jurisdiction. This was how a number of Korean family and succession matters were brought closer to "modern" civil law through court decisions and precedents. When the postcolonial courts tried to modify the content of customary law to conform to their vision of "justice," they were basically treading the path laid out by their colonial predecessors.

While the postcolonial courts was keen on abolishing colonial statutes and orders, they were relatively wary about rejecting colonial court decisions. In principle, colonial customary law precedents continued to be recognized as law in Korea. After all, the nature of custom was such that customary law obtained legal force through judicial decisions. The instrument of custom during the colonial period had fostered an atmosphere akin to judicial activism in the common law tradition. Likewise, modern Korean jurisprudence was marked by the heightened conception of judicial mission to create a modern private law system. The 2003 case reveals how closely postcolonial courts followed the colonial framework, as they refashioned a specific custom in a way consistent with their modern sense of justice. The decision exhibited a progressive jurisprudential position that legal stability – adherence to custom – must be sacrificed if the question involves the defects of positive law or touches crucially on social dysfunction. Social norms that do not meet these conditions cannot be recognized as customary law, no matter whether they had been long observed in society. The dominant jurisprudential stance in Korea that the court must consider reason in determining the legal validity of custom was inspired by the flexible juridical attitude during the colonial period.

The requirement that custom must be just and reasonable in order to be valid was forcefully reaffirmed two years later. Applying the test of reasonableness, the Supreme Court in 2005 refused to recognize the legal effect of the practice excluding females from the clan membership (*chongjung*).[39] This case had a particular significance because the court ascribed its rejection of the custom to the "changes in our society's legal order." The court acknowledged that the practice in question had been long established as customary law, but declared that it no longer had legal force because it went against the fundamental principles enshrined in the constitution. The majority opinion is worthy of citing in length as the court articulated the evolving notion of constitutional principles in Korean history. It stated:

> Our Constitution, promulgated on July 17, 1948, declared that all citizens are equal before the law and shall not be discriminated against because of their gender in all areas of political, economic and social life. But the principle of gender equality declared in the Constitution was not immediately incorporated into the area of family law that governed the family life relationship.
>
> In the Constitution, comprehensively revised on October 27, 1980, a provision was newly created that marriage and family life shall be established on the basis of individual dignity and gender equality. It is deemed to be the expression of the will of the Constitution that family relationship shall be established and maintained in accordance with the constitutional ideals because the traditional family system dominated by Confucianism is difficult to be seen as grounded on human dignity and gender equality.... The [revised] civil code, which took effect on January 1, 1991, reflects the constitutional philosophy emphasizing the principle of gender equality in family life.

The Court next considered the legal effect of the custom regarding clan membership:

> The legal conviction that the members of our society held in the custom that clan membership is limited to adult males, excluding women, has been significantly shaken and weakened. Above all, our overall legal order, in which the highest law is the Constitution, has changed in the direction of guaranteeing a family life that is based on individual dignity and gender equality, without discrimination between women and men.

The custom of excluding women from clan membership "cannot be deemed justifiable or reasonable as it does not fit with the overall legal order." In accordance with reason, "the descendants who share the family name under the same ancestors shall be deemed to be natural members of the clan when they come of age, regardless of their gender." Therefore, the existing customary law "no longer has legal force."

This ruling thus abrogated existing custom. What is the legal effect of repealing customary law? The court declared that its decision would have no

[39] Judgment of July 21, 2005, 2002ta1178. An English translation of the text of this opinion is at *http://library.scourt.go.kr/jsp/html/decision/2_22.2002Da1178.htm*.

retrospective effect, because otherwise it would unsettle "numerous legal relationships formed on the basis of the past Supreme Court precedents that had been upheld for many years" and it would amount to "a violation of the principle of constitutionalism that protects the legal parties based on legal stability and trust." Therefore it would be reasonable to apply the current decision prospectively only to the legal relationships to be created. But the court was unequivocal in declaring that the task of interpreting customary law in terms of changing circumstances in society belonged to the judge who had the power to determine whether the elements of custom had decayed. This expansive juridical stance of the Supreme Court is highly redolent of the position asserted by the colonial courts. The continuity between colonial and postcolonial jurisprudence in customary law is hard to overlook.

In the 2005 case, the justices grounded the power of the court to make, modify, or abrogate customary law on the fundamental constitutional order. Custom became intertwined with the broader constitutional ramifications of tradition and culture. Soon it was inevitable that the Constitutional Court would get embroiled in the question of customary law.

Custom, Culture, and the Constitution

The Constitutional Court, established in 1988, was endowed with the ultimate authority to review the constitutionality of legislation.[40] The Constitutional Court became mired in unique cultural debates, which a scholar dubbed the "politics of Confucianism" in Korean society.[41] While many Confucian rituals that penetrated Korean society were identified with Korean culture, the same were seen by critics as key obstacles delaying the modernization of Korean society and impeding individual liberties guaranteed in the constitution. The result was a thorough enmeshment of custom, culture, and the constitution. Into this fray entered anti-Japanese nationalism. Shortly after Korea's independence, many colonial laws were invalidated on the grounds that they were incongruent with Article 100 of the constitution. Much of the effort to abolish colonial custom was thus framed in terms of constitutional principles. The result was a veritable "trilemma" in which the elements of indigenism, colonialism, and constitutionalism were entangled.

While the Supreme Court wrestled with the constitutional implications of customary law, what posed more serious problems was the interpretation of statutory law that had been enacted on the basis of traditional customary

[40] For the Korean Constitutional Court and judicial review, see James M. West and Dae-Kyu Yoon, "The Constitutional Court of the Republic of Korea: Transforming the Jurisprudence of the Vortex?" *American Journal of Comparative Law* 40 (1992): 73–119; Kun Yang, "Judicial Review and Social Change in the Korean Democratizing Process," *American Journal of Comparative Law* 41 (1993): 1–8; Thomas Ginsburg, "Rule by Law or Rule of Law? The Constitutional Court of Korea," in *Judicial Review in New Democracies; Constitutional Courts in Asian Cases* (New York: Cambridge University Press, 2003), 206–246.

[41] Chaihark Hahm, "Law, Culture and the Politics of Confucianism," 296.

practices. As seen in preceding pages, the civil code of 1960 included a number of statutes that governed family and succession matters according to Confucian practices. Technically these were statutes enacted by the legislature but they were inseparable from customary law because their legal justification remained that they had been observed in Korean society for a long time with requisite *opinio necessitatis*.

The Korean Constitution provides a division of labor in judicial and constitutional review. Article 107 provides:

> When the constitutionality of a law is at issue in a trial, the court shall request a decision of the Constitutional Court, and shall judge according to the decision thereof. The Supreme Court shall have the power to make a final review of the constitutionality or legality of administrative decrees, regulations or actions, when their constitutionality or legality is at issue in a trial.

The Supreme Court's jurisdiction over custom was grounded on this provision. Now the Constitutional Court became critically involved as many custom-based statutes faced challenges on the grounds of constitutionality.

The 1991 revision of family law abolished a number of legal practices that had been based on traditional patriarchal and patrilineal principles of Confucianism.[42] Conspicuously absent in this reform were the prohibition of marriages between persons of the same surname and place of origin and the system of household headship succession. As seen previously, colonial law had allowed same-surname marriages and imposed the Japanese-style household headship succession. The legality of the colonial laws regarding these two issues proved even more complicated and controversial than the non-agnatic adoption question. After independence, the Korean Civil Code of 1960 restored the prohibition of marriages between the parties of the same surname and clan origin. Interestingly, the civil law did not void the household headship system. The civil code thus seemed inconsistent in the eyes of those who opposed any retention of colonial law. They pointed out that the household headship succession system was preserved in Korean law despite its colonial nature because it conformed to Confucian practices.

Dissension between supporters and opponents of these marriage and succession provisions in the civil code represented a clash of cultures and ideologies pervasive in Korean society. Their resolution required a recourse to the constitutional legal order. It is an understatement that constitutional law has a disproportionate influence on Korean family law.[43]

[42] For a detailed survey of the evolution of modern Korean family law, see Erin Cho, "Caught in Confucius' Shadow: The Struggle for Women's Legal Equality in South Korea," *Columbia Journal of Asian Law* 12 (1998): 125–189.

[43] For analyses of the Constitutional Court decisions on family law issues, see Yun Chin-su, "Chŏnt'ongjŏk kajok chedo wa hŏnpŏp: Ch'oegŭn ŭi hŏnpŏp chaep'anso p'allye rŭl chungsim ŭro [The Traditional Family System and Constitutional Law: With Particular Attention to the Recent Decisions of the Constitutional Court]," *Seoul Taehakkyo pŏphak* 47 (2006): 149–188; Jin-Su Yune, "Tradition and Constitution in the Context of the Korean Family Law," *Journal of Korean Law* 5, no. 1 (2005): 194–212.

Marriage between Persons of the Same Surnames

The Chosŏn dynasty forbade marriages between persons of the same surname and the same place of origin, known as *tongsŏng tongbon* marriages. Such marriage was deemed an anathema to the ideal of a well-ordered society as postulated in the neo-Confucian worldview. The colonial government abolished the prohibition in 1939, but it was resurrected in the 1960 civil code. The main justification in postcolonial Korea for not allowing the marriage of two people, even when there were removed from each other in blood relations beyond any remotest consideration of consanguinity, was the protection of indigenous custom. The law was assailed by its critics as the symbol of degenerate influences from the Confucian past.

The heated debate surrounding this issue illustrates the complex intertwining of the elements of custom, tradition, law, and culture. Those who defended nullifying marriages between spouses with surnames of common geographical origin asserted that the prohibition of such marriages was indigenous to Korean culture and that the requirement of exogamous marriage was vital for the preservation of good morals. Their opponents argued, on the other hand, that the prohibition had originated in China's clan system and hence was not a native Korean practice. For them, the prohibition of such marriages was an outdated relic of Confucian culture that enforced the patriarchal family hierarchy, a system imposed from outside. The proponents of the prohibition countered that even if it was an imported Confucian tradition it had been part of Korean traditional culture for almost six hundred years and was worthy of respect as "our own custom."

The debate whether the prohibition of the *tongsŏng tongbon* marriage was qualified as a genuine Korean custom took a full constitutional turn in the late 1990s when a constitutional challenge to the existing law was brought to the Constitutional Court. Those who demanded the striking down of the law argued that the provision was a violation of Article 10 of the constitution that guaranteed human dignity and the right to pursue happiness. Article 10 reads: "All citizens shall be assured of human dignity and worth and have the right to pursue happiness. It shall be the duty of the State to confirm and guarantee the fundamental and inviolable human rights of individuals." The prohibition of the *tongsŏng tongbon* marriage was, they contended, an unconstitutional restriction of freedom of a family and marital life based on individual autonomy.[44] Undaunted, the opponents of same-surname marriages pointed to Article 9 of the constitution, which read: "The State shall strive to sustain and develop the cultural heritage and to enhance national culture."

[44] The following constitutional provisions were also cited: Article 36, Paragraph 1: "Marriage and family life shall be entered into and sustained on the basis of individual dignity and equality of the sexes, and the State shall do everything in its power to achieve that goal"; Article 37, Paragraph 2: "The freedoms and rights of citizens may be restricted by the Act only when necessary for national security, the maintenance of law and order or for public welfare. Even when such restriction is imposed, no essential aspect of the freedom or right shall be violated."

The pursuit of happiness itself could be allowed, they argued, only within the parameters of this national culture.

In July 1997, the Constitutional Court at last declared unconstitutional the prohibition of marriages between parties with surnames of common geographical origin.[45] The court opinion of this momentous ruling was a veritable survey of the histories of China and Korea, tracing back to the Zhou and Han dynasties in China and the Koryŏ dynasty in Korea, researching the practice of prohibiting marriages among blood relations. The justices eventually concluded that the prohibition was "grounded on Confucianism," not something that derived from the consideration of genetics or eugenics, and that as such it lacked "social appropriateness or reasonableness" in modern times. The court wrote: "Traditional culture that truly must be preserved and protected for progress in accordance with the spirit of Article 9 of the Constitution means traditional ethics or moral precepts that conform to the current diverse social and economic circumstances and continue to maintain their reasonableness today." The court made a point that its decision finding unconstitutional the prohibition of the *tongsŏng tongbon* marriage should not be regarded as "promoting of marriages between the people of the same surnames and ancestral seats or denying the importance of existing reasonable ethical or moral precepts." Notwithstanding such a disclaimer, it was beyond dispute that the court's position was that if a tradition contravenes the dignity of the individual and gender equality it cannot be justified on the grounds of the importance of national culture. The National Assembly passed a bill (Law Number 7427) on March 31, 2005, limiting the prohibition of marriages to those between and under third cousins in blood relations.[46] The new law took effect in 2008.

Household Headship Succession

The Korean Civil Code of 1960 preserved the colonial succession system with little change and securely incorporated the household headship system (*hoju chedo*) into its provisions. The household headship system was one of the most controversial issues in family law that had long polarized Korean society. Just as the legislature was subject to the criticism that it gave selective treatment to colonial laws, so were the Supreme Court and the Constitutional Court subject to the accusation that they interpreted laws dating from the colonial period

[45] Constitutional Court [Hŏnpŏp Chaep'anso], judgment of July 16, 1997, 95hŏnga6 to 95hŏnga13.

[46] The Constitutional Court found the civil code provision prohibiting such marriages "incongruent" with the Constitution. Constitution, Article 113, Section 1, of the constitution requires concurrence of at least six justices for a declaration of unconstitutionality of a statute. Since only five justices found the challenged civil code provision "simply unconstitutional," the provision was instead declared "incongruent" with the constitution. A statute declared incongruent with the constitution remains a valid law but its application is suspended, until the revision by the National Assembly. This is what happened in the *tongsŏng tongbon* marriage case. The Constitutional Court often sets a time limit for the revision of a statute found incongruent; if the legislature fails to act within the time limit, the statute becomes invalid.

unevenly, if not arbitrarily. The Supreme Court had long refused to strike down the household headship system. Opponents of the *hoju* system argued that both the legislators and the justices were willing to preserve the colonial laws because they were deemed to be upholding conservative Confucian culture.[47]

The household headship system, granting a disproportionate amount of economic and social power within the family to the eldest son or grandson, was much reviled in some quarters for its discrimination against women.[48] The *hoju* system began to be seriously challenged in court in the 1990s. In 2005, the Constitutional Court found the household headship system and the requirement that the child take the paternal surname in conflict with the constitution.[49] Just like the 1997 decision that struck down the prohibition of marriages between parties of the same surnames and local origin, the 2005 decision revolved around the question whether the challenged statutes intended to preserve Korean custom and tradition and, more fundamentally, whether constitutionally challenged laws or customary norms could claim protection on the grounds that they were deeply rooted in Korean tradition.[50] Those who defended the household headship system argued that it was based on Korea's indigenous culture and had nothing to do with Japanese colonial influence. For them, it was an important cultural and legal practice germane to Korea's Confucian heritage. Those who opposed the household headship system contended that the Japanese during the colonial period artificially strengthened the authority of the *hoju* by superimposing their own "house" (*ie*) institution and posited the resulting hybrid system as Korean "custom" in which they saw a means to exert tighter ideological control of the colonial citizenry.[51]

The main disagreement was over what exactly constituted true Korean culture, devoid of invidious foreign elements. As if separating genuine Korean

[47] For an analysis of the *hoju* system from postcolonial and postfeminist perspectives, see Hyunah Yang, "Vision of Postcolonial Feminist Jurisprudence in Korea: Seen from the 'Family-Head System' in Family Law," *Journal of Korean Law* 5 (2006): 12–28; Yang Hyŏn-a, "Singminji sigi Hanguk kajokpop ŭl t'onghae pon kabujangje ŭi kukka chedohwa wa 'kwansŭp' munche [The Transformation of the Patriarchal System into a National System and the Question of 'Custom,' Seen from Colonial Korean Family Law]" in *Che 2-gi Han-Il yŏksa kongdong yŏngu pogosŏ* [Report of the Second Joint Research of Korean and Japanese History], ed. Han-Il Yŏksa Kongdong Yŏngu Wiwŏnhoe (Seoul: Han-Il Yŏksa Kongdong Yŏngu Wiwŏnhoe, 2010), vol. 5, 289–315.

[48] See Chapter 6.

[49] Constitutional Court, judgment of February 3, 2005, 2001hŏnga9 to 2001hŏnga15 and 2004hŏnga5 (the household headship system); judgment of December 22, 2005, 2003hŏnga5 and 2003hŏnga6 (the paternal surname requirement). The core articles of the household headship system (Article 778; Article 781, Section 1; and Article 826, Section 3) were found incongruent with Article 36, Paragraph 1 of the Constitution.

[50] Yun Chin-su, "Hŏnpŏp i Kajokpŏp e mich'in yŏnghyang [The Influence of the Constitution on Family Law]," *Seoul Taehakkyo pŏphak* 45 (2004): 233–270; Jin-Su Yune, "Recent Decisions of the Korean Constitutional Court on Family Law," *Journal of Korean Law* 1, (2001): 133–156.

[51] For the view that the Japanese-style *ie* system, forcibly imposed on Korea during the colonial period, vastly increased the eldest son's exclusive inheritance of family status, see Pak Pyŏng-ho, "Ilche ha ŭi kajok chŏngch'aek."

tradition from Confucian tradition was not difficult enough, the apparent need to distinguish indigenous custom from colonial custom posed even more daunting problems. The opponents to the system argued that not all pre-colonial customs originated from the true Korean tradition and that they were merely imported Confucian tradition. For them, the household headship law in the civil code was the result of a curious coalition between the pro-Confucian conservatives and the nationalists who conveniently forsook their anti-Japanese stance in order to preserve the traditional social order. They noted that many otherwise vehemently nationalist legal analysts defended institutions like the *hoju* system that had been imposed by Japan.[52] Whereas Japan abolished the *ie* system in 1948, it was pointed out, the Korean Civil Code of 1960 preserved the *hoju* system. After all, the objectionable tradition can be either of colonial Japanese or dynastic Chinese origin, or both.

The justices in the 2005 case stated that the contents of the traditions and the national culture in the meaning of the Preamble ("We, the people of Korea, proud of a resplendent history and traditions dating from time immemorial") and Article 9 in the constitution must be understood in terms of the history and the times in which they were present. They wrote that "the fact that [practices] existed at a certain point in history does not render them a tradition that deserves constitutional protection." The court admitted that the household headship system was deeply rooted in the traditional family order. However, "even if one acknowledges that the patriarchal family system represents our indigenous family system and that the household headship system has certain relevance, ... the social background that gave rise to and maintained the household headship system no longer exists."

It seems apparent that the justices who formed the majority opinion tried to avoid getting drawn into the controversy regarding the "indigenousness" of the household headship system, that is, whether the system was a genuine Korean family custom or a vestige of the Japanese *ie* system. Their opinion focused instead on the appropriateness of the practice in modern times. But the dissenting opinion contended that it was necessary, and possible, to distinguish the primordial custom from the colonial influence. The dissenting justices acknowledged that the household headship system in the pre-1990 civil code had been closely modeled on the Japanese system. But they argued that the 1990 revision eliminated the Japanese elements from the authority of the household head and that the system in the current civil code "cannot be sweepingly reviled as the remnant of Japanese colonialism." Here one is reminded that any discussion of traditional custom is inexorably swayed by the specter of the colonial past. In both majority and dissenting opinions, obsession with "true Korean custom" seemed to take precedence over legal analysis. The *hoju* system, finally set aside by the Constitutional Court, was abolished in the civil code revised in March 2005, to take effect on January 1, 2008.

[52] Hyunah Yang, "Vision of Postcolonial Feminist Jurisprudence"; Yang Hyŏn-a, "Singminji sigi Hanguk kajop pŏp ŭi kwansŭp munche."

The constitutional cases examined in the preceding pages reveal the extent to which the debate on custom has become politicized in modern Korea. They seemed as if they were veritable scrutiny on the value of the Confucian tradition: is Confucianism part of a national heritage or a reactionary ideology?[53] The power of tradition is a dominant force in Korea, but so is a relentless drive for modernity. The painful memory of the colonial past added variables. The convergence of strong nationalism and Confucian conservatism has long insulated many customs from criticism, granting them almost sacrosanct legitimacy. Practices that were "non-Japanese" were then equated with laudable customs. On the other hand, as seen in the debate over the household head system, the partisan line was often redrawn to bring nationalists and liberals or progressives together as unexpected allies, united against the Confucian conservatives. Few dared to defend the Japanese effort to destroy Korean custom but, in effect, the Japanese-imposed customs were embraced and defended by the conservatives. Opponents to the Confucian practices even argued that legislators and jurists evaded the responsibility of decolonizing law that had falsely been equated with "tradition."

In modern Korea, traditional customs and practices were increasingly attacked by the forces invoking highly individualistic Western principles, such as the right to pursue happiness as guaranteed in Article 10 of the Constitution. Yet, part of the nation equally strongly asserted the importance of tradition, as enunciated in Article 9 of the Constitution that stipulated the state's duty to sustain and develop the cultural heritage and national culture. Legal discussion on the effect of colonial custom was often quickly enveloped with the powerful force of nationalist rhetoric, and the same legal questions often metamorphosed into a debate on the meaning of national identity. In the process, legal issues became subject to polemics and cultural agenda, causing a serious jurisprudential quandary.

Tradition versus Modernity and Jurisprudential Quandary

The recent cases involving custom decided by the Supreme Court and the Constitutional Court represent a willingness – rather, eagerness – of the courts to break free from the overwhelming influence of "tradition" in Korean civil law. Broadly considered together, they reveal a jurisprudential trend to reconfigure the legal arena in which almost anything that could be styled as "custom" tended to claim, as a matter of course, legal protection. The courts have tried to delineate the legal boundaries of custom and coordinate them in the modern legislative order. The civil code was periodically amended to revise outdated provisions of family and succession laws, and the courts often spearheaded such efforts by forcing the legislature to act. The Constitutional Court declared that customary law must be judged according to a new value system in modern Korean society, commensurate with the principles of freedom and equality. The Supreme Court decisions requiring customary law to be "reasonable" pointed in the same direction.

[53] See Chaihark Hahm, "Law, Culture, and the Politics of Confucianism," 254–260.

Still, the dual constitutional dictates of protecting national culture on one hand and promoting liberal democratic concepts and principles on the other have hampered the courts, as even an innocuous civil law dispute tended to be raised to a level requiring constitutional adjudication. Indeed the Constitutional Court, burdened with cultural debate, may have inadvertently contributed to deepening jurisprudential confusion by granting an excessive aura to customary law. The result is a sort of jurisprudential quagmire, with looming uncertainty over the blurred relationship between custom and the written law. This problem was conspicuously exhibited in the capital relocation case.

The Capital Relocation Case

In 2004, the Constitutional Court invoked the novel concept of "customary constitutional law" to strike down a statute.[54] The National Assembly had enacted a law to move the capital away from Seoul, which had been the country's capital for more than six hundred years. The court said that the designation of Seoul as the country's capital had legal force on the constitutional level, even though nowhere in the constitution was Seoul declared as the capital city. This was the first time that a Korean court asserted the legal authority of unwritten constitutional law and abrogated a statute, otherwise valid under the written constitution.

The majority opinion stated:

> Our nation has a written constitution.... However, it is impossible to include all constitutional matters in the written constitution. In addition, because of the nature of the constitution as the fundamental law that seeks brevity full of innate meanings, there is room for recognizing certain matters, although not articulated in the text, to be part of the unwritten constitution or customary constitutional law. In particular, there may be circumstances where certain matters did not call for express provisions in the text because they were self-evident or presupposed, or because they were common constitutional principles at the time of the constitution's writing. To be sure, not all practices or conventions regarding constitutional law matters may be recognized as customary constitutional law. In order to obtain the force as a constitutional legal norm, a custom must satisfy rigorous requirements. Only those customs that satisfy those elements can be regarded as customary constitutional law and be granted the same legal force as the written constitution.[55]

In order to qualify as a customary constitutional law, the court argued, the custom "must have fundamental constitutional significance to such an extent that it may not be regulated by mere statutes but instead must be regulated by the constitution that has superior legal force to statutes." It went on to say: "It is impossible to decide by a common and abstract standard which matters, among general constitutional matters, fall into the category of these fundamental and pivotal constitutional matters. It is necessary to determine each

[54] Constitutional Court, judgment of October 21, 2004, 2004hŏnma554 and 2004hŏnma556. See Marie Seong-Hak Kim, "Customary Constitutional Law," *The Korea Times*, November 11, 2004, 7.

[55] Judgment of October 21, 2004.

individual circumstance by specifically assessing its relevance to the constitutional nucleus, significance, and principles."

Following an extensive survey of the history of Seoul to show that it was the undisputed capital throughout the Chosŏn Dynasty and the colonial period, the court concluded that this historical tradition – custom – that Seoul was the capital of the country achieved the elements necessary to become a customary constitutional law. The identification of Seoul as the capital was the expression of the will of the citizens, the court wrote, which the legislature failed to recognize in enacting the challenged statute. The statute that violated the customary constitutional law must be struck down as unconstitutional, it concluded.

The court's assertion of the existence of unwritten constitutional law alarmed critics who argued that the idea of unwritten constitutional law had no place in nations in the civil law tradition with written constitutions. By declaring that written laws could be abrogated by customary law, the court seemed to create a fundamental uncertainty in the relationship between statutes and custom. Whether custom can repeal legislation is a question that has long been debated among scholars. According to the Constitutional Court, the statute in question deserved abrogation not because of non-usage or *desuetudo* but because of its failure to incorporate the "will of the citizens." The custom that Seoul was the capital had "obtained the approval and informed consensus of the citizens and was firmly established over a long period of time," a fact that the legislature failed to take into account when it enacted the challenged law. The court thus seemed to value the finding of the national consensus in custom more than the decision of the representative body.

The court further declared that the abrogation of customary constitutional law required a process similar to the repeal of written constitutional law provisions. By this the court effectively suggested that abolishing any customary law would likewise require the process of repealing a statutory law. According to the court's reasoning, only the customary law that has a constitutional value would supersede statutes, but that decision is in the hands of the judges, not the National Assembly. Then the question arises: if custom can potentially become a customary constitutional law, can *chori* (reason), another official source of law, obtain a constitutional legal value as well?

The 2004 decision reveals that the positions of the Constitutional Court and the Supreme Court were not always in agreement or harmony. The two highest courts often seemed to send mixed messages. In the previous two or three decades, both the Constitutional Court and the Supreme Court moved in the direction of limiting the scope of customary law by requiring stringent standards for the proof of custom. But the capital relocation ruling by the Constitutional Court seemed to go against that direction. The two courts sometimes treated legislation as a rebuttable guarantee of the rationality of law and other times denied the force of customary law as a legislative alternative.

Indeed, the broad invocation of the constitutional order by both the constitutional and ordinary tribunals in customary law cases seems to have engendered looming uncertainty over the hierarchy of the sources of law and also over the courts' jurisdiction.

Under the constitution, the Constitutional Court has the power to review the constitutionality of statutes ("law") and the Supreme Court has the power to review the constitutionality of non-legislative instruments, in which custom presumably was included. But if custom is declared "customary law" with the potential to trump legislation, as in the case of customary constitutional law, can the Supreme Court's review of custom be construed as an usurpation of the authority of the Constitutional Court?

This question casts doubt over the ordinary courts' power to adjudicate customary law cases. Some scholars have claimed that the Supreme Court's decisions requiring that custom be reasonable and also not be against the overall constitutional legal order went beyond the requirement of "not violating public order" as stipulated in Article 105 of the civil code.[56] Arguments have been made that the Supreme Court's power to recognize (make) and abolish (unmake) customary law on the basis of whether a specific custom conforms to the "general legal order as provided in the constitution as the supreme law" is tantamount to constitutional review, and that the ordinary courts' determination of the validity of proffered customary evidence amounts to the prohibited lawmaking activity. According to this reasoning, the ordinary courts may not abrogate customary law at will once it has been by precedents. The criticism of the Supreme Court's alleged usurpation of constitutional review power in reality represents the view that the ordinary courts' decisions should be subject to constitutional review. But what about the determination of the constitutionality of customary law where the question underlies the result of the trial? The potential complications seem boundless.

Customary law that has been enmeshed with cultural and political implications thus figures now conspicuously in the mounting jurisdictional tension between the Constitutional Court and the Supreme Court. These are the questions that can arise only in the peculiar situation of the Korean legal order in which, first, custom as a legal source tends to be fused with custom as a cultural representation, and secondly, almost any customary law case becomes a potential constitutional case. One cannot but notice that some of the court analyses and their reception in legal circles often resonate with cultural and ideological dissensions simmering in Korean society.

Leaving aside the questions of their jurisprudential soundness or ideological implications, the courts' decisions examined in the previous pages appear strikingly redolent of the colonial court's notion of customary law. Both the Constitutional Court and the Supreme Court seemed to say that the reasonableness of the solution given by the court was what really mattered; this was the principle that had shaped colonial jurisprudence of customary law.

Custom in Korea remains a concept of fundamental ambiguity. As a product of both colonial and postcolonial exigencies, it has become an increasingly contested topic in law. Modern Korean courts' emphasis on custom as a source of law was primarily grounded in their deference to national tradition but it was

[56] Pak Ch'an-ju, "Taepŏpwŏn e ŭihan kwansŭp pŏp ŭi p'yeji [The Abrogation of Customary Law by the Supreme Court]," *Pŏpchŏ* 598 (July 2006): 19–75.

in fact as much a legacy of colonial jurisprudence. Korean colonial customary law was created by the judges with a specific goal of reshaping Korean laws and practices in line with modern legal concepts and principles. Colonial jurisprudence equated custom with reason in order to modify Korean usages and practices and eventually achieve the assimilation of Korean law with Japanese law. Postcolonial courts undertook the mission of blotting out colonial legacy, but modern Korean jurisprudence has largely functioned in the same colonial customary law framework.

The customary law order had granted the colonial courts power that otherwise would have been exercised by the legislature in a sovereign country. The recognition of customary law as a source of law in the Korean Civil Code similarly gave the Korean courts a quasi-legislative instrument. How to use this power pursuant to the nation's constitutional order has presented a serious challenge, especially because custom as broadly conceived has long been a major divisive issue in Korean society, weighed with political and ideological baggage. Grappling with colonial law and reclaiming indigenous custom, all the while promoting a modern democratic order, has consumed much jurisprudential effort. Critical questions still remain regarding how to clarify the relationship between custom and statutes beyond the placid language of Article 1 of the civil code.

It appears that any efforts to resolve jurisprudential confusion should start with the understanding that the notion of customary law was the creation of colonial jurisprudence, and that custom as a spontaneous legal order, based on a sort of tacit popular consent, did not exist in precolonial Korea. Without such an understanding, trying to distinguish indigenous custom from colonial custom and debating over how to juggle the instrument of custom in the nation's constitutional order may largely be a misplaced emphasis, mired in a debate that is more ideological than legal. When one acknowledges that customary law as a coherent legal order was an alien concept in Chosŏn Korea and that modern Korean civil law was the product of legal transplantation, rather than something emanating from the people from time immemorial, one can expect a more accurate understanding of Korean legal past. Only on the basis of that understanding can the courts ensure that the interpretation of custom under Article 1 of the civil code takes place insulated from heady cultural debates and contending social agenda. Only then, the exalted place reserved for custom in the Korean civil law has a veritable chance for justification.

Jurisprudential travail of customary law discussed in this chapter needs to be seen against the backdrop of challenges encountered in historical inquiry. Modern Korean law fully embraces the values of democracy and liberalism and the general principles of gender equality and human rights. The efforts to find the historical continuity of Korean law have prompted historians to search for the elements of contemporary concepts – such as the rule of law or law as a product of popular agreement – in premodern law. However, such an attempt, no matter how gratifying it may be for modern democratic sensibility, risks distorting historical truth. Dispelling the myth of customary law may help understanding Korean legal history more accurately.

Conclusion

The development of civil law in Korea can be explained in terms of a broad pattern of the expansion of law. This book has focused on the role of custom in legal transplantation – both distribution and reception of law. Reference to custom in the process of creating a unified and uniform legal system was a universal occurrence in history, and Korea was no exception. Chosŏn Korea was the epitome of the state law model. Its codes were fundamentally of a penal nature and civil matters were governed by the same code provisions that governed criminal matters. Private law existed as part of the state penal code, not in the form of customary law. It was during the colonial period that the construction of customary law by Japanese colonial judges accelerated the reception of European civil law in Korea. This development featured a long spectrum of legal imperialism. The preceding pages have shown that customary law was an essential part of legal imperialism that operated in both the nation-state and the colonial state setting, from late medieval France to French West Africa to Meiji Japan to colonial Korea.

In the nineteenth century, the expanding force of European law found a remarkably hospitable environment in East Asia. The missionizing character of Western law was facilitated and promoted by Japanese and Chinese legal elites who became willing and eager converts.[1] Once its legal transformation was completed, Japan undertook the role of spreading modernized law to its colonies including Korea. Colonization in East Asia witnessed the creation of a customary law that served as an instrument for the state to acclimate the colonial subjects to a new legal regime that would form the foundation of the colonial state. It seems that the question as to when state formation ended and when imperialism began can be answered only in retrospect. If colonial assimilation policy succeeds and the central authorities achieve legitimacy among the colonial population, one may speak of successful state building; if not, illegitimate colonial aggression.[2]

[1] The diffusing tradition of European law has been attributed to the influence of the Christianity. Whitman, "Western Legal Imperialism," 320.

[2] See Hechter, *Internal Colonialism*, 60–64.

The acculturation of indigenous law was a conventional phenomenon of legal imperialism, but it was more faithfully replicated in Japanese colonies than European colonies because, in part, Japan was less encumbered with legal pluralism. Colonial law, in one way or another, subsumed local law and custom throughout the world. It was commonplace that there was vociferous protest in former colonial states about the continued presence of colonial law. But in most cases colonial law became national law.[3] Imperialism, seeking efficient control of the natives, might have led to important legal developments in the colonies.

Korean scholarship has privileged custom in efforts to prove the disastrous effect of colonialism on the country's legal heritage. Custom supposedly meant the tradition of a primordial Korea that had existed before the coming of the Japanese who wielded Westernized law as a symbol of their supposed superiority. The "myth" of customary law was bolstered in Korean historiography by an effort to safeguard the identify of indigenous legal culture in the dynastic period from the stifling influence of colonial law. The image of beneficent kings respecting customs and making laws on the basis of popular wishes seemed to present a vivid contrast with authoritarian colonial rule. This view, however, is difficult to sustain. It may be enticing for scholars to regard traditional laws and legal principles as having emanated from popular culture or living law. But to argue that East Asia was governed by consensual law, outside the grip of the state penal codes, is distant from historical truth. The legitimate need to be wary of the misrepresentation and misinterpretation of Korean law fomented by the colonial regime does not warrant the infusion of nationalistic instincts into Korean legal tradition.

The preceding chapters have suggested a number of correctives to the dominant interpretations in Korean legal history. Some scholars have attempted to find the antecedents of constitutional norms in Confucian civic virtue. Sophisticated arguments have been set forth concerning the implicit liberal elements in Confucianism and premodern Korean legal culture. If one wanted to find the prototype of constitutionalism and the rule of law in traditional Korea, however, a more pertinent approach would be to point to the state codes. Magistrates were ordered to mete out punishment according to the degrees of gravity of offenses as explicitly and minutely as provided in the law code. The state ensured that the judges did just that, without attempting an arbitrary exercise of power. These characteristics made the justice system in Korea, and elsewhere in East Asia, relatively certain and predictable, the elements that are idealized in modern times in a system of the rule of law. This way of looking at Korean traditional law may prove more profitable than projecting certain liberal and democratic ideals onto the Korean legal past.[4]

[3] Lev, *Legal Evolution*, 28.

[4] There is a danger of "naïve democratism" that "imposes the principles of modern government in the analysis of [traditional] legal systems and ends up adopting the quarrels among the jurists as a historical truth." Jérôme Bourgon, "Coutumes, pratiques et droit en Chine. Quelques remarques sur des termes couramment employés dans des ouvrages récents," *Etudes chinoises* 22 (2003), 273.

It was only natural that strong administrative consolidation in Korean dynasties promoted the development of centralized state law instead of localized customary law. The absence of customary law and civil law in Chosŏn Korea does not mean that its legal system was underdeveloped or incomplete. The portrayal of Korean legal culture as "a-legalistic" and lacking private rights consciousness need not be seen as a challenge to the quality of Korea's legal past. On the contrary, the way most private disputes were resolved outside the stringent code provisions, resorting to solicitous, conciliatory, and flexible approaches emphasizing moral persuasion and social responsibility, can be favorably contrasted with the legalistic, contentious, litigious, and rigid judicial culture in the West. Once one admits that the Korean legal tradition was different from the European legal tradition, one can more lucidly chart the evolution of civil law in modern Korea.

Throughout world history, controlling customs was part of the state's enlarging legislative power. Once codified, customary law was implemented through jurisprudence according to the elite's conception of order and justice. Korean popular practices and usages were collected by the Japanese and colonial jurisprudence turned them into customary law. A custom was named, created, and assigned by the courts to a precise function in the legal order. Colonial judges claimed that they worked within the bounds of traditional Korean custom. They persisted in the fiction of applying preexisting custom, lest they should be accused of meddling with such private matters as family and succession of the colonized people. In reality, however, the colonial judges deviated from native customs as frequently as was deemed necessary, and took an activist role in defining the content of Korean customary law. They were able to do so because a custom was viewed as valid only when it was reasonable. Almost anything – equity, public order, good morals, and so on – could be subsumed under "reason." The judges thus had broad latitude in privileging certain customs and derogating others. Rarely did they feel bound by the popular character of a custom. Legitimation of selected norms and practices became key machinery in reforming colonial society. The fact that government-created customary law was thrust on the Korean population with no tradition of private law explains the relative facility and thoroughness by which indigenous usages were replaced with modern Westernized rules.

In every colonial enterprise, the colonizers needed incentives to engage the colonized people in the newly imposed system. In Korea, the colonial regime placed heavy emphasis on providing the subjects with access to a new and improved legal system. Litigants flocked to the courts, induced by equitable and impartial adjudication. This situation, in turn, provided the judges ample opportunities to reshape customs and reform social norms. The parties framed their cases and arguments so they would be in line with what they expected to be the courts' predisposition in interpreting custom. It was natural that litigants sought to exploit the ambiguities of custom and laws as a legal strategy. In this way they contributed to the formulation of "Korean customary law." A version of customary law emerged, accepted by the colonized people and validated by the colonial state. Whether it was at variance with the practices actually followed in private relations mattered little.

A vibrant law community emerged which served well-defined private interests. The modern legal system created during the colonial period prospered and continued into the postcolonial period precisely because of the benefits it provided to society. The contention that colonial courts were irrelevant to most Koreans contributes little to an accurate understanding of colonial legal history. The paradox in Korea becomes clear: a nation that condemns its colonial experience has chosen to institutionalize its legacy in as complete a replica of the legal system of the colonizer as any country on the globe.

It is beyond dispute that Japanese law and institutions essentially served as an instrument for maintaining colonial domination. One would be hard pressed, though, not to acknowledge that the colonial legal reforms left an indelible mark on the development of Korean law and the justice system. Sweeping dismissal of colonial reforms as a deceptive showcase that was intended to demonstrate Japan's benevolent colonial rule stands in the way of a rounded understanding of Korea's legal past, because it effectively condemns Korean legal history to be dictated by the colonial perspective. Law is certainly part of political policy but law follows its own logic and momentum. Modernization of the colonial judicial system does not negate the reality of Japan's aggression against Korea.

There is an urgent task for historians to revise a colonial legal historiography that saw little development in Korea throughout the dynastic period. Pak Pyŏng-ho was more than justified when he declared that "it is necessary to revisit fundamentally the outcomes of studies during the colonial period and liberate Korean legal historiography from the dogma that views the Korean traditional past as the sum of negativity, corruption, and unlawfulness."[5] Study of colonial customary law in a comparative perspective can constitute a constructive step forward to breaking free from the historical confines of the past. The unresolved problem of distinguishing between colonialism and modernity still looms large, but it is now necessary to go beyond rehashing the theme of the Japanese marring Korean law. One does not need to embrace the discourse of Japan's *mission civilisatrice* or condone the repression and exploitation during the forty years of Japanese rule in order to assess accurately the significance of legal developments during the colonial period.

This book acknowledges that the role of members of Korean society in the formulation and operation of the colonial legal system requires further investigation than has been possible in the preceding pages. A study centered on the policy and actions of the colonial power without sufficient attention to the colonized subjects may be only half complete. It is obvious that an examination of colonial law should ideally discuss ways in which local populations reacted to legal changes initiated by the colonial power. In the Korean case, it would be necessary to find evidence of how individual Koreans perceived

[5] Pak Pyŏng-ho, *Hanguk pŏpchesa ko*, preface.

law and used the courts. Unfortunately, Korean legal elites during the colonial period remain mostly anonymous and their contributions to legal reform before independence are largely unknown. One of the reasons for this lacuna is that participation by Koreans in the operation of the legal system, or any government activities for that matter, during the colonial period risked being seen as collaboration. This tendency to equate serving in the colonial system with supporting colonial domination may explain, at least in part, why scholarship has paid scant attention to Korean legal elites in the service of the colonial government and courts. There is a crucial need to investigate what independent role, if any, Korean elites played in constructing new legal systems and how they carried the momentum to the postcolonial period. This book leaves that issue as a future task.

Legal changes that took place during the colonial period were rapid, thorough, and had lasting effects. The influence of the Japanese legal order on modern Korea is still ubiquitous. Failure to acknowledge fully the significance of legal transplantation that took place during the colonial era risks missing the opportunity to explain the development of Korean law in terms of continuity, instead of highlighting, unwittingly, disjunctions meted by colonialism. Treating law merely as a product of colonial politics is undesirable and studying legal history strictly as a national history is unsatisfactory. Just as the historiographical trend to postulate elements of liberal and democratic ideas in traditional law and custom is problematic, so is the tendency to view legal imperialism invariably as a tool for reinforcing domination. When we move beyond such a limited perspective and acknowledge the extent of the civilizing forces of civil law, we can make better sense of Korean history.

Appendix A

List of Major Colonial Officials

Residents General of Korea

Itō Hirobumi	December 21, 1905	*to*	June 14, 1909
Sone Arasuke	June 14, 1909		May 30, 1910
Terauchi Masatake	May 30, 1910		October 1, 1910

Governors General of Korea

Terauchi Masatake	October 1, 1910	*to*	October 14, 1916
Hasegawa Yoshimichi	October 14, 1916		August 12, 1919
Saitō Matoko	August 12, 1919		December 10, 1927
Ugaki Kazushige (Acting)	April 14, 1927		October 1, 1927
Yamanashi Hanzō	December 10, 1927		August 17, 1929
Saitō Matoko	August 17, 1929		June 17, 1931
Ugaki Kazushige	June 17, 1931		August 5, 1936
Minami Jirō	August 5, 1936		May 29, 1942
Koiso Kuniaki	May 29, 1942		July 22, 1944
Abe Nobuyuki	July 22, 1944		September 28, 1945

Minister of Justice (Residency General)

Kuratomi Yuzaburō	November 1, 1909	*to*	September 30, 1910

Ministers of Justice (Government General)

Kuratomi Yuzaburō	September 30, 1910	*to*	September 20, 1913
Kokubu Sangai	October 23, 1913		August 20, 1919

Directors of Law Department

Kokubu Sangai	August 20, 1919	*to*	December 25, 1919
Yokota Kōrō	December 25, 1919		April 8, 1923
Matsudera Takeo	April 8, 1923		October 30, 1929
Fukuzawa Shinichirō	October 30, 1929		January 30, 1932
Kasai Kentarō	January 30, 1932		October 2, 1934
Masunaga Shōichi	October 2, 1934		November 10, 1937
Yamamoto Gen	November 10, 1937		January 28, 1943
Hayata Fukuzō	January 28, 1943		August 15, 1945

Chief Justices of the High Court

Watanabe Nobu	September 30, 1910	*to*	April 7, 1923
Yokota Gōrō	April 7, 1923		January 30, 1932
Fukasawa Shinichirō	January 30, 1932		September 1, 1934
Ogawa Tei	October 2, 1934		April 17, 1939
Hara Masakane	April 17, 1939		January 28, 1943
Kitō Heiichi	January 28, 1943		August 15, 1945

Chief Prosecutors of the High Court

Kokubu Sangai	September 30, 1910	*to*	September 20, 1920
Nakamura Takezō	September 20, 1920		October 30, 1929
Matsudera Takeo	October 30, 1929		January 30, 1932
Sakai Chōzaburō	January 30, 1932		October 2, 1934
Kasai Kentarō	October 2, 1934		November 2, 1937
Masunaga Masaichi	November 2, 1937		January 28, 1943
Mizuno Shigekatsu	January 28, 1943		August 15, 1945

Appendix B

Selected Law Provisions Cited in the Text

Law Regarding Laws and Regulations to be Enforced in Korea
(Law No. 30, issued March 25, 1911)

Article 1

The governor general of Korea may issue ordinances to regulate matters that require laws in Korea.

Article 2

Ordinances referred to in the preceding article shall receive imperial approval through the prime minister in the cabinet.

Article 3

In case of emergency, the governor general of Korea may immediately issue ordinances referred to in Article 1. Such ordinances shall obtain imperial approval immediately after the issuance; where imperial approval is not obtained, the governor general of Korea shall immediately declare that the said ordinances have no effect thereinafter.

Article 4

The extension of Japanese laws to Korea, in entirety or in part, shall be determined by imperial ordinance.

Article 5

Ordinances referred to in Article 1 may not be in conflict with existing laws in Korea, in particular the laws that were enacted specifically for enforcement in Korea, or imperial ordinance.

Article 6

This law shall take effect from the date of promulgation.

The Chosŏn Ordinance on Civil Matters (Chōsen Minjirei; Chosŏn Minsaryŏng)
(*Seirei* No. 7, issued March 18, 1912)

Article 1

Unless otherwise provided in this ordinance or other laws or regulations, civil matters shall be governed by the following laws.
(1) Civil Code; (2) Law No. 50 of 1902 [regarding the calculation of age]; (3) Law No. 17 of 1904 [regarding the establishment of a pledge on inscribed government bonds]; (4) Law No. 40 of 1899 [regarding liability for accidental fire]; (5) Law No. 51 of 1900 [regarding guardianship for an orphan child in an asylum]; (6) Law No. 13 of 1900 [regarding confirmation of testaments of military or civilian personnel serving for the military]; (7) Law regarding the Enforcement of the Civil Code; (8) Commercial Code; (9) Law No. 17 of 1900 [regarding cases in which signature is required under the Commercial Code]; (10) Law regarding the Enforcement of the Commercial Code; (11) Law No. 32 of 1889 [Bankruptcy Law]; (12) Regulations regarding the Enforcement of the Commercial Code; (13) Code of Civil Procedure; (14) Law for Cooperation according to the Entrustment of Foreign Courts; (15) Law No. 50 of 1899 [regarding foreign nationals' signatures and seals and certificates of lack of funds]; (16) Law for the Division of the Property of a House; (17) Law of Procedure in Actions relating to Personal Status; (18) Law of Procedure in Non-Contentious Cases; (19) Law concerning the Cost of Civil Cases; (20) Law concerning Revenue Stamps for Non-Contentious Commercial Cases; (21) Rules concerning Fees for the Sheriff's Deputy; (22) Deposit Law; (23) Auction Law.

Article 10

Civil matters involving Koreans only are governed by Korean custom, even if a specific custom is different from law, as long as the law is not related to public order.

Article 11

The provisions on capacity, family, and succession in the laws listed in Article 1 do not apply to Koreans. The said matters involving Koreans are decided according to Korean custom.

Article 12

The kinds and effects of real property rights are governed by custom, except for the property rights stipulated in Article 1.

Revision of the Chosŏn Ordinance on Civil Matters
(*Seirei* No. 14, issued November 14, 1921)

Article 11

Unless otherwise provided, matters regarding family and succession matters involving Koreans are decided according to custom and not according to the laws in Article 1. But this limitation shall not apply to parental rights, guardianship, assistantship, or clan association established for the legally incompetent person.

Revision of the Chosŏn Ordinance on Civil Matters

(*Seirei* No. 3, issued December 7, 1922)

Article 11

Unless otherwise provided, matters regarding family and succession matters involving Koreans are decided according to custom and not according to the laws in Article 1. But this limitation shall not apply to minimum ages for marriage, judicial divorce, acknowledgment, parental rights, guardianship, assistantship, clan association, approval of succession, and division of property. The division of a family, closing of a family and reestablishment of a discontinued family, marriage, divorce by agreement, adoption, and dissolution of adoptive relationship by agreement shall not be effective unless it is reported to the magistrate or the head of the township. But adoption by testament takes effect retroactive to the death of the parent.

Revision of the Chosŏn Ordinance on Civil Matters

(*Seirei* No. 19, issued November 10, 1939)

Article 11.1

Unless otherwise provided, matters regarding family and succession matters involving Koreans are decided according to custom and not according to the laws in Article 1. But this shall not apply to house name, minimum ages for marriage, judicial divorce, acknowledgment, judicial dissolution of adoptive relationship, annulment or cancellation of marriage or adoption relation in the case of adoption of a son-in-law, parental rights, guardianship, assistantship, kinship association, acceptance of succession, and division of property. The division of a family, closing of a family and reestablishment of a discontinued family, marriage, divorce by agreement, adoption, and dissolution of adoptive relationship by agreement shall not be effective unless it is reported to the magistrate or the head of the township. But adoption by testament takes effect retroactive to the death of the parent. The name of a house shall be determined by the head of the house (or by the legal representative thereof).

Article 11.2

In adoptive relations among Koreans, the adopted child is not required to have the same family name as the adoptive father. But post mortem adoption is excluded from this provision. Adoption of a son-in-law takes effect upon the application of registration for adoption and marriage. The adopted son-in-law enters the family of the wife. In the case of the dissolution of adoption of a son-in-law, direct heirs of the wife do not leave the house even if the husband leaves the house. Children born after the dissolution enter the house.

The Coordination Law

(Law No. 39, issued April 17, 1918)

Article 1

The "territory" in this law refers to the *naichi*, Chosŏn, Taiwan, and Kantōshū. The *naichi* includes Sakhalin.

Article 2

In civil matters, when a territory decides to apply laws and regulations of other territories, each territory applies those laws and regulations. It is the same when more than one territory decides to apply the laws and regulations of the third territory. Except for cases prescribed in the preceding paragraph, the Law on the General Rules of the Application of Laws shall apply, with the necessary changes, to civil affairs. In this case, laws and regulations applicable in the region to which either party concerned belongs shall be regarded as national laws of the region.

Article 3

A person who enters a family in a region under the law of the region shall withdraw from a family in another region. A person who may not withdraw from a family in a region under the law of the region may not enter a family in another region [the rest of the provision omitted].

Rules for the Conduct of Judicial Affairs

(Law No. 103, issued June 8, 1875)

Article 1

Each court shall judge cases in both civil and criminal matters according to law and without delay. No court shall suspend trial and appeal to a higher court on the grounds that the case is too complicated and open to doubt, except in cases of condemnation to death or forced labor for life.

Article 2

When application is made to challenge a judgment, the judge need not give reason for decision. But the judge must indicate to the dissatisfied party that his right of appeal or re-appeal shall be filed within a prescribed period according to established rules.

Article 3

In civil trials, those matters for which there is no written law are governed by customary law, and those matters for which there is no customary law shall be adjudicated by inference from reason.

Article 4

It is forbidden for the judge to pronounce judgments for the future with the binding power of ordinary established rules.

Article 5

The directives issued by the administrative authorities for concrete cases do not have force as general rules for the courts, except when they concern special declarations and notifications.

Bibliography

Allott, A. N. "What Is to Be Done with African Customary Law? The Experience of Problems and Reforms in Anglophone Africa from 1950." *Journal of African Law* 28 (1984): 56–71.

An, Yong-sik, O Yŏn-suk, O Sŭng-ŭn and Song Hae-gyŏng. "Chosŏn Ch'ongdokpu ha Ilbon in kwallyo yŏngu [A Study of Japanese Officials under the Government General of Korea]." *Tongbang hakchi* 137 (2007): 151–212.

Anan, S. "Mariage extra legem et notion de droit au Japon." *Mélanges Paul Roubier*. Vol. 1, 1–6. Paris: Dalloz and Sirey, 1961.

Asami, Rintatō, *Chōsen hōsei shi kō* [Legal History of Chosŏn]. Tokyo: Ganshodo Shoten, 1922.

"Chōsen hōkei no rekishi teki kenkyū" [A Historical Study of the Legal System in Chosŏn]." *Hōgaku kyōkai zasshi* 39, no. 8 (1921): 26–67.

Asano, Toyomi. *Teikoku Nihon no shokuminchi hōsei* [The Colonial Legal Structure of Imperial Japan]. Nagoya: Nagoya Daigaku Shuppankai, 2008.

"Nihon teikoku no tōchi genri 'naichi enchō shugi' to teikoku hōsei no kōzō teki tenkai [The 'Inland Extension Ideology' as a Principle of Japanese Imperial Rule and the Evolution of the Structure of the Imperial Legal System]." *Shakai kagaku kenkyū* 21 (2001): 207–284. Translated by Ch'oe Sŏk-hwan. "Ilbon cheguk t'ongch'i wŏlli 'naeji yŏnjang chui' wa cheguk pŏpche ŭi kujojŏk chŏngae." *Pŏpsahak yŏngu* 33 (2006): 147–218.

Asano, Toyomi and Matsuda Toshihiko, eds. *Shokuminchi teikoku Nihon no hōteki tenkai* [The Legal Development of the Japanese Colonial Empire]. Tokyo: Shinzansha, 2004.

Shokuminchi teikoku Nihon no hōteki kōzō [The Legal Structure of the Japanese Colonial Empire]. Tokyo: Shinzansha, 2004.

Assier-Andrieu, Louis. "La Dimension juridique d'une anthropologie de la durée." *L'Homme* 30, no. 115 (1990): 121–128.

Baade, Hans W. "Transplants of Laws and of Lawyers." In *Justice in Particular: Festschrift in Honour of Professor P. J. Kozyris*, 21–40. Athens: Ant. N. Sakkoulas Publishers, 2007.

Baker, Edward J. "The Role of Legal Reforms in the Japanese Annexation and Rules of Korea, 1905–1919." In *Studies on Korea in Transition*, edited by David R. McCann, John Middleton and Edward J. Shultz, 17–42. Honolulu: University of Hawaii Center for Korean Studies, 1979.

Ball, John. *Indonesian Legal History 1602–1848*. Sydney: Ouhtershaw Press, 1982.

Barnhart, James. "Violence and the Civilizing Mission: Native Justice in French Colonial Vietnam, 1858–1914." PhD diss., University of Chicago, 1999.

Bart, Jean. *Histoire du droit privé: de la chute de l'Empire romain au XIXe siècle*. Paris: Montchrestien, 1998.

Beaumanoir, Philippe de. *Coutumes de Beauvaisis*. Paris: Alphonse Picard et fils, 1899–1900.

The Coutumes de Beauvaisis of Philippe de Beaumanoir. Translated by F. R. P. Akehurst. Philadelphia: University of Pennsylvania Press, 1992.

Bell, Daniel and Chaibong Hahm. *Confucianism for the Modern World*. Cambridge: Cambridge University Press, 2003.

Bellomo, Manlio. *The Common Legal Past of Europe 1000–1800*. Translated by Lydia G. Cochrane. Washington D.C.: The Catholic University of America Press, 1995.

Benda-Beckmann, Franz von and Keebet von Benda-Beckmann. "The Dynamics of Change and Continuity in Plural Legal Orders." *Journal of Legal Pluralism* 53/54 (2006): 1–44.

Bennett, T.W. "Re-introducing African Customary Law to the South African Legal System." *The American Journal of Comparative Law* 57 (2009): 1–31.

Benton, Lauren A. *Law and Colonial Cultures: Legal Regimes in World History 1400–1900*. Cambridge: Cambridge University Press, 2002.

"Colonial Law and Cultural Difference: Jurisdictional Politics and the Formation of Colonial State." *Comparative Studies in Society and History* 41, no. 3 (1999): 563–588.

Berkowitz, Daniel, Katharina Pistor and Jean-François Richard. "The Transplant Effect." *The American Journal of Comparative Law* 51, no. 1 (2003): 163–203.

Berman, Harold J. "Why the History of Western Law Is Not Written." *University of Illinois Law Review* 1984, no. 3 (1984): 511–520.

Bernhardt, Kathryn and Philip C.C. Huang, eds. *Civil Law in Qing and Republican China*. Stanford: Stanford University Press, 1994.

Betts, Raymond F. *Assimilation and Association in French Colonial Theory 1890–1914*. New York: Columbia University Press, 1961.

Bodde, Derk and Clarence Morris, *Law in Imperial China: Exemplified by 190 Ch'ing Dynasty Cases*. Philadelphia: University of Pennsylvania Press, 1973, 1967.

Bodin, Jean. Les Six livres de la république. [n.p.], 1577.

Boissonade, Gustave. *Projet de code civil de l'Empire du Japon*, 5 vols. Tokyo, 1882–1889.

Les Anciennes coutumes du Japon et le Nouveau Code Civil, à l'occasion d'une double publication de M. John Henry Wigmore. Memoire présenté à l'Institut de France. Tokyo, 1894.

Bourgon, Jérôme. "Ditan de tu'an: shilun Qingdai falü wenhua zhong de 'xiguan' yu 'qiyue' [Figures in the Carpet: "Customs" and "Contracts" in Qing Legal Culture]." In *Ming Qing falü lianzuo zhong de quanli he wenhua*, edited by Qiu Pengsheng and Chen Xiyuan, 215–253. Taipei: Lianjing Chuban Gongsi, 2009.

"Aspects of Chinese Legal Culture – The Articulation of Written Law, State, and Society: A Review." *International Journal of Asian Studies* 4, no. 2 (2007): 241–258 (Part 1).

"Principe de légalité et règle de droit dans la tradition juridique chinoise." In *La Chine et sa démocratie*, edited by Mireille Delmas-Marty and Pierre Etienne Will, 154–174. Paris: Fayard, 2007.

———. "Rights, Freedoms, and Customs in the Making of Chinese Civil Law, 1900–1936." In *Realms of Freedom in Modern China*, edited by William Kirby, 84–102. Stanford: Stanford University Press, 2004.

———. "Coutumes, pratiques et droit en Chine. Quelques remarques sur des termes couramment employés dans des ouvrages récents." *Etudes chinoises* 22 (2003): 243–282.

———. "Uncivil Dialogue: Law and Custom did Not Merge into Civil Law Under the Qing." *Late Imperial China* 23 (2002): 50–90.

———. "Le Droit coutumier comme phénomène d'acculturation bureaucratique au Japon et en Chine." In *La Coutume et la norme en Chine et au Japon*, edited by Jérôme Bourgon, 125–142. Saint-Denis: Presses universitaires de Vincennes, 2001.

———. "La Coutume et le droit en Chine à la fin de l'empire." *Annales HSS* 54 (1999): 1073–1107.

———. "De quelques tendances récentes de la sinologie juridique américaine." *T'oung Pao* 84 (1998): 380–414.

Brooks, Barbara J. "Peopling the Japanese Empire: The Koreans in Manchuria and the Rhetoric of Inclusion." In *Japan's Competing Modernities: Issues in Culture and Democracy 1900–1930*, edited by Sharon A. Minichiello, 25–44. Honolulu: University of Hawaii Press, 1998.

Burns, Peter. *The Leiden Legacy: Concepts of Law in Indonesia*. Leiden: KITLV Press, 2004.

Burroughs, Peter. "The Imperial Gospel according to Frederick Madden." *The Journal of Imperial and Commonwealth History* 30, no. 3 (2002): 110–134.

Capitant, Henri. *Introduction à l'étude du droit civil: notions générales*. Paris: A. Pedone, 1927.

Caprio, Mark E. *Japanese Assimilation Policies in Colonial Korea 1910–1945*. Seattle: University of Washington Press, 2009.

Carbasse, Jean-Marie. "Contribution à l'étude du processus coutumier: la coutume de droit privé jusqu'à la Révolution. *Droits* 3 (1986): 25–37.

Centre de Recherché, Sens, Etique, Société and Association Française de Philosophie du Droit, eds. *Le Pluralisme*. Paris: Dalloz, 2006.

Chanock, Martin. *Law, Custom, and Social Order: The Colonial Experience in Malawi and Zambia*. Cambridge: Cambridge University Press, 1985.

———. "The Law Market: The Legal Encounter in British East and Central Africa." In *European Expansion and Law: The Encounter of Europe and Indigenous Law in 19th- and 20th-century Africa and Asia*, edited by W.J. Mommsen and J.A. de Moor, 279–306. Oxford: Berg, 1992.

Chatterjee, Partha. *The Nation and Its Fragments: Colonial and Postcolonial histories*. Princeton, NJ: Princeton University Press, 1993.

Chen, Edward I-te. "Gōtō Shimpei, Japan's Colonial Administrator in Taiwan: A Critical Reexamination." *American Asian Review* 13 (1995): 29–59.

———. "The Attempt to Integrate the Empire: Legal Perspectives." In *The Japanese Colonial Empire, 1895–1945*, edited by Ramon H. Myers and Mark R. Peattie, 240–274. Princeton, NJ: Princeton University Press, 1984.

———. "Japanese Colonialism in Korea and Formosa: A Comparison of the Systems of Political Control." *Harvard Journal of Asiatic Studies* 30 (1970): 126–158.

Chénon, Emile. *Histoire générale du droit français public et privé des origins à 1815*. Paris: Sirey, 1926.

Chiba, Masaji. *Legal Pluralism: Toward a General Theory through Japanese Legal Culture*. Tokyo: Tokai University Press, 1989.

"Japan." In *Asian legal Systems: Law, Society and Pluralism in East Asia*, edited by Poh-Ling Tan, 82–123. Sydney: Butterworths, 1977.

Cho, Chi-man. *Chosŏn sidae ŭi hyŏngsa pŏp – Tae Myŏng ryul kwa kukchŏn* [Penal Law during the Chosŏn Period – The Great Ming Code and the National Law Code]. Seoul: Kyŏngin Munhwasa, 2009.

"*Kyŏngguk taejŏn Hyŏngjŏn* kwa *Tae Myŏng ryul* – silch'e pŏp kyujŏng ŭl chungsim ŭro [*Kyŏngguk taejŏn Hyŏngjŏn and Tae Myŏng ryul* – Focusing on Substantive Law]." *Pŏpsahak yŏngu* 34 (2006): 5–37.

Cho, Erin. "Caught in Confucius' Shadow: The Struggle for Women's Legal Equality in South Korea." *Columbia Journal of Asian Law* 12 (1998): 125–189.

Cho, Yun-sŏn. *Chosŏn hugi sosong yŏngu* [A Study on Litigation in Late Sixteenth-Century Chosŏn]. Seoul: Kukhak Charyowŏn, 2002.

Ch'oe, Pyŏng-chu. "Minjirei jūichi cho no kanshū to sōson ken oyobi isan no sōzoku ken [Custom in Article 11 of the Civil Ordinance and the Succession Rights of the Eldest Grandson and the Widow]." *Shihō kyōkai zasshi* 17, no. 1 (1938): 7–33.

Ch'oe, Sŏn-hye. *Chosŏn chŏngi chibang sajok kwa kukka* [The Local Literati and the State in Early Chosŏn]. Seoul: Kyŏngin Munhwasa, 2007.

Ch'oe, Wŏn-kyu. "Taehan cheguk kwa Ilche ŭi t'oji kwŏn pŏp chejŏng kwajŏng kwa kŭ chi-hyang [The Establishment and Development of Real Property Law under the Taehan Empire and the Japanese Colonial Period]." *Tongbang hakchi* 94 (1996): 111–168.

Choi, Chongko. "Law and Custom in Korean Society: A Historical and Jurisprudential Approach." *Seoul Taehakkyo pŏphak* 47 (2006): 221–263.

Chŏn, Kyŏng-mok. "Sansong ŭl t'onghae pon Chosŏn hugi sabŏp chedo unyong silt'ae wa kŭ t'ukching" [The Operation and the Characteristics of the Legal System of Late Chosŏn Seen through the Adjudication of the Ownership of Mountains]. *Pŏpsahak yŏngu* 18 (1997): 5–31.

Chŏn, Pong-dŏk. "Ilche ŭi sabŏpkwŏn kangt'al kwajŏng ŭi yŏngu [A Study of the Forcible Takeover of Judicial Power by Imperial Japan]." *Aesan hakpo* 2 (1982): 151–206.

Hanguk kŭndae pŏp sasangsa [A History of Modern Legal Thought in Korea]. Seoul: Pagyŏngsa, 1981.

"Kŭndae sabop chedosa [A History of the Modern Judicial System] (Parts 1–11)." *Taehan Pyŏnhyŏp hoebo* 1–25 (1970–1977).

Chŏn, U-hyŏn. "Ilche kangjom ch'ogi p'allye e nat'anan sang haengwi (kaekchuŏp) sang koridae ŭi yŏksa chŏk p'yŏngka [Historical Assessment of Usury in Commercial Transaction (Loan-Sharking Business) as Seen in Judicial Cases during the Early Japanese Colonial Period. *Pŏpsahak yŏngu* 35 (2007): 109–145.

Chŏng, Chin-yŏng. *Chosŏn sidae hyangch'on sahoesa* [History of Rural Society in the Chosŏn Period]. Seoul: Hangilsa, 1998.

Chŏng, Chong-hyu. "Kwansŭppŏp kwa sasil in kwansŭp [Customary Law and Custom in Fact]." *In Hanguk minpŏp iron ŭi palchŏn: Muam Yi Yŏng-jun paksa whagap kinyŏm nonmunjip*, 3–40. Seoul: Pagyŏngsa, 1999.

"Ume Kenjirō to Kankoku kindai rippō jigyō [Ume Kenjirō's Modern Korean Legislative Activities]." *Hōritsu jihō* 70, no. 7 (1998): 57–61.

"Hanguk minpŏp chŏn ŭi pigyo pŏp chŏk kyebo [A Genealogy of the Korean Civil Code: A Comparative Legal Perspective]." *Minsa pŏphak* 8, no. 3 (1990): 60–104.

"Hanguk minsa sosong pŏp an [A Draft of Korean Civil Procedure]." *Pŏpsahak yŏngu* 10 (1989): 231–336.

Kankoku minpōten no hikakuhō teki kenkyū [A Comparative Legal Study of the Korean Civil Code]. Tokyo: Sobunsha, 1989.

"Hanmal ŭi sŏgupŏp kyesu [The Reception of Western Law in the Late Chosŏn Period]." *Chŏnnam Taehakkyo nonmumchip (Pŏp, haengjŏnghak p'yŏn)* 32 (1987): 97–148.

Chŏng, Kŭng-sik. "Chosŏn sidae ŭi kagye kyesŭngpŏp che [The Family Succession System under the Chosŏn Dynasty]." *Seoul Taehakkyo pŏphak* 51, no.2 (2010): 69–101.

"Singminji ki sangsok kwansŭp pŏp ŭi t'adangsŏng e daehan chae kŏmt'o: kajok in changnam ŭi samang kwa sangsokin ŭi pŏmui [Reexamination of the Legitimacy of Colonial Succession Law]." *Seoul Taehakkyo pŏphak* 50, no. 1 (2009): 287–320.

"Simyuk segi chaesan sangsok ŭi han illye: 1579 nyŏn Kwŏn ji ch'o Chŏng ssi hŏyŏ mun'gi ŭi punsŏk [A Case of Sixteenth-Century Property Succession: Analysis of *hŏyŏ mun'gi* of 1579 by Madam Chong, the Wife of Kwon Ji]." *Seoul Taehakkyo pŏphak* 47, no. 2 (2006): 268–302.

"Simyuk segi iban tu kŏn [Two Cases of *iban* in the Sixteenth Century]." *Seoul Taehakkyo pŏphak* 47, no. 3 (2006): 464–498.

Hanguk kŭndae pŏpchesa go [A Study of Modern Korean Legal History]. Seoul: Pagyŏngsa, 2002.

"Chosŏn sidae ŭi kwŏllyŏk pullip kwa pŏpch'i chuŭi: kŭ siron chŏk koch'al [Separation of Power and Rule of Law under the Chosŏn Dynasty: A Preliminary Examination]." *Seoul Taehakkyo pŏphak* 42, no. 4 (2001): 27–65.

Chŏng, Kŭng-sik, Cho Chi-man, and Kim Tae-hong. *Chosŏn hugi sugyo charyo chipsŏng* [Collection of *sugyo* in Late Chosŏn Dynasty]. 2 vols. Seoul: Hanguk Pŏpche Yŏnguwŏn, 2009–2010.

Chŏng, Kŭng-sik and Chang Ch'ang-min, eds. *Singminji gi sabŏp kwallyŏn charyo: Chosŏn Sabŏp hyŏphoe chapchi ŭi punsŏk* [Materials Related to the Administration of Justice during the Colonial Period: Analysis of the Journal of the Jurist Association]. Seoul: Hanguk Pŏpche Yŏnguwŏn, 2004.

Chŏng, Kŭng-sik and Im Sang-hyŏk, eds. *Simyuk segi sasong pŏpsŏ chipsŏng* [A Compilation of Sixteenth-Century Handbooks for Civil Procedure]. Seoul: Hanguk Pŏpche Yŏnguwŏn, 1999.

Chŏng, Kwang-hyŏn. *Hanguk kajok pŏp yŏngu* [A Study of Korean Family Law]. Seoul: Seoul Taehakkyo Ch'ulp'anbu, 1967.

Chŏng, Tuhi and Edward J. Shultz, eds. *Hanguk sa e issŏsŏ chibang gwa chung'ang, POSCO International Symposium on Korean History*. Seoul: Humanities Research Institute, Sŏgang University Center for Korean Studies, 2003.

Chŏng, Yag-yong. *Admonitions on Governing the People: Manual for All Administrators*. Translated by Byonghyon Choi. Berkeley: University of California Press, 2010.

Yŏkchu Mongmin Simsŏ [Annotated and Translated *Mongmin Simsŏ*, A book for the Heart of the Magistrate]. Edited and translated by Tasan Yŏnguhoe, 6 vols. Seoul: Ch'angjak kwa pip'yongsa, 1978–1985.

Chōsen Kōtō Hōin hanketsuroku [Chosōn High Court Reports]. Seoul: Kōtō Hōin Shokika, 1908–1943.

Chōsen Kōtō Hōin hanrei yōshi ruishū [Summary Reports of the Decisions of the Chosōn High Court]. Seoul: Shihō Kyōkai, 1937.

Chōsen Shinbunsha, ed. *Chōsen tōchi no kaiko to hihan* [Retrospect and Criticisms regarding the Rule of Korea]. Tokyo: Ryūkei Shosha, 1995, 1936.

Chōsen Sōtokufu, ed. *Chōsen no shihō seido* [The Judicial System of Chosōn]. Seoul: Chōsen Sōtokufu Hōmukoku Hōmuka, 1935.

Chōsen Sōtokufu, ed. *Kanshū chōsa hōkokusho* [Report on the Investigation of Customs]. Seoul: Chōsen Sōtokufu, 1910, rev. ed. 1913; Tokyo: Ryukei Shosha, 1995.

Chōsen Sōtokufu Chūsūin, ed. *Chōsen kyūkan seido chōsa jigyō gaiyō* [A Summary of the Campaign to Investigate the Korean Old Customs System]. Seoul: Chōsen Sōtokufu Chūsūin, 1938.

Chōsen Sōtokufu Homukoku, ed. *Chōsen Sōtokufu teikoku gikai setsumei shiryō* [Explanatory Materials for the Imperial Diet by the Government General of Korea]. Tokyo: Fuji Shuppan, 1994.

Chōsen Sōtokufu kanpō [Official Gazette of the Government General of Chosŏn].

Chōsen Sōtokufu Shihōbu Hōmuka. "Chōsenjin aida no rikon soshō [Divorce Litigation among Koreans]." *Chosen ihō* (February 1918): 111–116.

Chosŏn wangjo sillok [The Annals of the Chosŏn Dynasty]. Kuksa P'yŏnch'an Wiwŏnhoe [National Institute of Korean History]. http://sillok.history.go.kr.

Chun, Bong Duck [Chŏn, Pong-dŏk], William Shaw, and Dai-Kwon Choi. *Traditional Korean Legal Attitudes*. Berkeley: Institute of East Asian Studies, University of California Berkeley, Center for Korean Studies, 1980.

Church, William F. *Constitutional Thought in Sixteenth-Century France*. New York: Octagon Books, 1969, 1941.

Clozel, F. J. and Maurice Delafosse, *Haut-Sénégal-Niger (Soudan français)*. Paris: E. Larose, 1912.

Cohen, William B. *Rulers of Empire: The French Colonial Service in Africa*. Stanford: Hoover Institution Press, 1971.

Conklin, Alice L. "Colonialism and Human Rights, A Contradiction in Terms? The Case of France and West Africa, 1895–1914." *The American Historical Review* 103, no. 2 (1998): 419–442.

A Mission to Civilize: The Republican Idea of Empire in France and West Africa, 1895–1930. Stanford: Stanford University Press, 1997.

Conroy, Hilary. *The Japanese Seizure of Korea: 1868–1910: A Study of Realism and Idealism in International Relations*. Philadelphia: University of Pennsylvania Press, 1960.

Cumings, Bruce. *Parallax Visions: Making Sense of American-East Asian Relations at the End of the Century*. Durham, NC: Duke University Press, 1999.

"The Legacy of Japanese Colonialism in Korea." In *The Japanese Colonial Empire, 1895–1945*, edited by Ramon H. Myers and Mark R. Peattie, 478–496. Princeton, NJ: Princeton University Press, 1984.

Damaska, Mirhan R. The Faces of Justice and State Authority: A Comparative Approach to the Legal Process. New Haven: Yale University Press, 1986.

David, René. *French Law, Its Structure, Sources, and Methodology*. Translated by Michael Kindred. Baton Rouge: Louisiana State University Press, 1972.

Dawson, John P. *The Oracles of the Law*. Ann Arbor: University of Michigan Press, 1968.

"Remedies of the French Chancery before 1789." In *Festschrift für Ernst Rabel*, vol. 1: *Rechtsvergleichung und internationales Privatrecht*, edited by H. Dölle, M. Rheinstein and K. Zweigert, 99–140. Tübingen: Mohr, 1954.

"The Codification of the French Customs." *Michigan Law Review* 38 (1940): 765–800.

De Bary, William Theodore. "The Community Compact." In *Asian Values and Human Rights: A Confucian Communitarian Perspective*, 58–89. Cambridge, MA: Harvard University Press, 1998.

De Becker, J. E. *The Principles and Practice of the Civil Code of Japan*. Yokohama: Kelly & Walsh, 1921.

Deherme, George. *L'Afrique occidentale française: action politique, action économique, action sociale*. Paris: Librairie Bloud, 1908.

Detienne, Marcel. *Comparer l'Incomparable*. Paris: Seuil, 2000.

Deuchler, Martina. "Neo-Confucianism in the Early Joseon Dynasty: Some Reflections on the Role of *Ye*." In *Korean Philosophy: Its Tradition and Modern Transformation*, edited by Korean national Commission for UNESCO, 43–53. Elizabeth, NJ: Hollym, 2004.

"The Practice of Confucianism: Ritual and Order in Chosŏn Dynasty Korea." In *Rethinking Confucianism: Past and Present in China, Japan, Korea, and Vietnam*, edited by Benjamin A. Elman, John B. Duncan and Herman Ooms, 293–334. Los Angeles: UCLA Asia Pacific Monograph Series, 2002.

The Confucian Transformation of Korea: A Study of Society and Ideology. Cambridge, MA: Council on East Asian Studies, Harvard University, 1992.

"The Tradition: Women during the Yi Dynasty." In *Virtues in Conflict: Tradition and Korean Women Today*, edited by Sandra Mattielli, 1–47. Seoul: Samhwa Publishing Co. for the Royal Asiatic Society, Korea Branch, 1977.

The Digest of Justinian. Translated and edited by Alan Watson. Philadelphia: University of Pennsylvania Press, 1985.

Direction de l'Administration de la Justice, ed. *La Justice en Indochine, organisation générale, la justice indigène*. Hanoi: Imprimerie d'Extrême-Orient, 1931.

Doak, Kevin M. *A History of Nationalism in Modern Japan: Placing the People*. Boston and Leiden: Brill, 2007.

"What Is a Nation and Who Belongs? National Narratives and the Ethnic Imagination in Twentieth-Century Japan." *American Historical Review* 102, no. 2 (1997): 283–309.

Dong, Wonmo. "Japanese Colonial Policy and Politics in Korea, 1904–1945: A Study in Assimilation." PhD diss., Georgetown University, 1965.

Duara, Prasenjit. "The Limits of Legal Sovereignty: China and India in Recent History." *The Journal of Asian Studies* 68 (2009):122–127.

"The New Imperialism and the Post-Colonial Developmental State: Manchukuo in Comparative Perspective." *Japan Focus*, posted Jan. 30, 2006. http://japanfocus.org/-Prasenjit-Duara/1715.

Dudden, Alexis. *Japan's Colonization of Korea: Discourse and Power*. Honolulu: University of Hawaii Press, 2005.

Duncanson, Dennis J. *Government and Revolution in Vietnam*. Oxford: Oxford University Press, 1968.

Duus, Peter. *The Abacus and the Sword: The Japanese Penetration of Korea, 1895–1910*. Berkeley: University of California Press, 1995.

Ebashi, Takashi. "Shokuminchi ni okeru kenpō no tekiyō: Meiji ritken taisei no hito sokumen [The Application of Constitutional Law in the Colonies: An Aspect of the Meiji Constitutional System]." *Hōgaku shirin* 82 (1985): 3–36.

Eckert, Carter J., Ki-baik Lee, Young Ick Lew, Michael Robinson, and Edward W. Wagner. *Korea Old and New: A History*. Seoul: Ilchokak / Korea Institute, Harvard University, 1990.

Eikemeier, Dieter. "Law, Contract, and Covenant: Aspects of a Korean Mutual Insurance Venture." In *Anthropology of Law in the Netherlands*, edited by Keebet von Benda-Beckmann and Fons Strijbosch, 260–287. Dordrecht: Foris Publications, 1986.

Epp, Robert Charles. "The Challenge from Tradition: Attempts to Compile a Civil Code in Japan, 1866–78." *Monumenta Nipponica* 22, nos. 1 and 2 (1967): 15–48.

"Threat to Tradition: The Reaction to Japan's 1890 Civil Code." PhD diss., Harvard University, 1964.

Ewald, William. "Comparative Jurisprudence (II): The Logic of Legal Transplants." *American Journal of Comparative Law* 43 (1995): 489–510.

Fasseur, C. 1992. "Colonial Dilemma: Van Vollenhoven and the Struggle Between Adat Law and Western Law in Indonesia." In *European Expansion and Law: The Encounter of Europe and Indigenous Law in 19th-and 20th-Century Africa and Asia*, edited by W. J. Mommsen and J.A. de Moore, 237–256. Oxford: Berg, 1992.

Filhol, René. *Le Premier président Christofle de Thou et la réformation des coutumes*. Paris: Librairie du Recueil Sirey, 1937.

Fitzpatrick, Peter. "Is It Simple to Be a Marxist in Legal Anthropology?" *Modern Law Review* 48 (1985): 472–485.

"Traditionalism and Traditional Law." *Journal of African Law* 28 (1984): 20–27.

Fontaine, Laurèline. *Droit et pluralisme: actes du colloque de Caen, les 30 novembre et 1er décembre 2006*. Brussels: Bruylant, 2007.

Foote, Daniel H. ed. *Law in Japan: A Turning Point*. Seattle and London: University of Washington Press, 2008.

Friedman, Lawrence. "Review of *Society and Legal Change* by Alan Watson." *British Journal of Law and Society* 6, no. 1 (1979): 127–129.

Fujita, Tōzō. *Chōsen shinzokuhō sōzokuhō shu to shite Chōsen Kōtō Hōin hanrei o chūshin to shite no kōsatsu* [The Succession Law of Chosŏn, An Examination in Particular on the Basis of the Decisions of the Chōsen Kōtō Hōin]. Seoul: Ōsaka Yagō Shoten, 1933.

Fukaya, Itaru. "Meiji denki no Kumamoto saibansho ni okeru jōri saiban to Furansu minpō [Adjudication by Reason by the Court of Kumamoto in Early Meiji Years and French Civil Law]." *Seinan Gakuin Daigaku hōgaku ronshu* 38 (2006): 59–160.

"Meiji denki no Hiroshima saibansho ni okeru jōri saiban to Furansu minpō [Adjudication by Reason by the Court of Hiroshima in Early Meiji Years and French Civil Law]." *Seinan Gakuin Daigaku hōgaku ronshu* 37 (2004): 1–54.

Fukushima, Masao. "Meiji shonen ni okeru seiō hō no keiju to Nihon no hō oyobi hōgaku [The Reception of Western Law and Japanese Law and Legal Science in the Early Meiji Period]." In *Nihonhō to Ajia, Niida Noboru hakushi tsuitō ronpunshū* [Japanese Law and Asia: In Memory of Dr. Niida Noboru], vol. 3, 161–188. Tokyo: Keisō Shobō, 1970.

"Kyū-minpō ūto kankō no mondai [The Questions of the Old Civil Code and Custom]." *Matsuyama shōdai ronshu* 17, no. 6 (1966): 295–322.

Gann, Lewis H. "Western and Japanese Colonialism: Some Preliminary Comparisons." In *The Japanese Colonial Empire, 1895–1945*, edited by Ramon H. Myers and Mark R. Peattie, 497–525. Princeton, NJ: Princeton University Press, 1984.

Garrigues, E. A. F. "La Cochinchine: du droit applicable aux indigènes et des juridictions le prononçant." In *La Justice en Indochine, organisation générale, la justice indigène*, edited by Direction de l'administration de la justice, 41–81. Hanoi: Imprimerie d'Extrême-Orient, 1931.

Geertz, Clifford. *Local Knowledge: Further Essays in Interpretive Anthropology*. New York: Basic Books, 1983.

Gény, François. *Méthode d'interprétation et sources en droit privé positif*. Paris: Librarie générale de droit & de jurisprudence, 1932.

Ghestin, Jacques. *Traité de droit civil*. Paris: Librairie générale de droit et de jurisprudence, 1977.

Gilissen, John. *La Coutume*, vol. 2. Brussels: De Boeck Université, 1990 (Recueils de la Société Jean Bodin pour l'histoire comparative des institutions, vol. 52).

La Coutume. In *Typologie des sources du Moyen Age occidental*, edited by L. Genicot, vol. 41. Turnhout: Brepols, 1982.

Le Pluralisme juridique: études publiées sous la direction de John Gilissen. Brussels: Editions de l'Université de Bruxelles, 1972.

Ginsburg, Thomas. *Judicial Review in New Democracies: Constitutional Courts in Asian Cases*. New York: Cambridge University Press, 2003.

Girault, Arthur. *Principes de colonisation et de législation coloniale*. Paris: Larose, 1895.

Glendon, Mary Ann. *Comparative Legal Traditions in a Nutshell*, 2nd ed. St. Paul: West Group, 1999.

Glenn, H. Patrick. *Legal Traditions of the World*. Oxford: Oxford University Press, 2000.

"The Grounding of Codification." *University of California Davis Law Review* 31 (1998): 765–782.

"The Capture, Reconstruction and Marginalization of 'Custom'." *American Journal of Comparative Law* 45 (1997): 613–620.

"Are Legal Traditions Incommensurable?" *The American Journal of Comparative Law* 49 (1991): 133–145.

Gluck, Carol. *Japan's Modern Myths: Ideology in the Late Meiji Period*. Princeton, NJ: Princeton University Press, 1985.

Gocking, Roger. "British Justice and the Native Tribunals of the Southern Gold Coast Colony." *Journal of African History* 34 (1993): 93–113.

Gonidec, P. F. *Les Droits africains: évolution et sources*, 2nd ed. Paris: Librairie générale de droit et de jurisprudence, 1976.

Government General of Korea. *Annual Report on Reforms and Progress in Chōsen (Korea)*. Seoul, 1911–1922.

Gragert, Edwin. *Landownership Under Colonial Rule: Korea's Japanese Experience, 1900–1935*. Honolulu: University of Hawaii Press, 1994.

Griffiths, J. "What Is Legal Pluralism?" *Journal of Legal Pluralism and Unofficial Law* 24 (1986): 1–55.

Grimmer-Solem, Erik. "German Social Science, Meiji Conservatism, and the Peculiarities of Japanese History." *Journal of World History* 16 (2005): 187–222.

Grinberg, Martine. *Ecrire les coutumes: les droits seigneuriaux en France, XVIe-XVIIIe siècle*. Paris: Presses universitaires de France, 2006.

Hagiwara, Hikozō. *Nihon tōjika ni okeru Chōsen no hōsei* [The Legal System in Chosŏn under Japanese Rule]. Tokyo: Yūhō Kyōkai, 1969.

Hahm, Chaihark. "Ritual and Constitutionalism: Disputing the Ruler's Legitimacy in a Confucian Polity." *American Journal of Comparative Law* 57, no. 1 (2009): 135–203.

"Negotiating Confucian Civility through Constitutional Discourse." In *The Politics of Affective Relations: East Asia and Beyond*, edited by Chaihark Hahm and Daniel A. Bell, 277–308. Lanham: Lexington Books, 2004.

"Law, Culture and the Politics of Confucianism." *Columbia Journal of Asian Law* 16, no. 2 (2003): 234–301.

"Constitutionalism, Confucian Civil Virtue, and Ritual Propriety." In *Confucianism for the Modern World*, edited by Daniel A. Bell and Hahm Chaibong, 31–53. New York: Cambridge University Press, 2003.

Hahm, Pyong-Choon. *Korean Jurisprudence, Politics and Culture*. Seoul: Yonsei University Press, 1986.

The Korean Political Tradition and Law: Essays in Korean Law and Legal History, 2nd ed. Seoul: Royal Asiatic Society Korea Branch, 1971.

Haley, John Owen. "The Adjudicatory Jurisdiction of Japanese courts in Transnational Litigation." In *Law and Justice in a Multistate World: Essays in Honor of Arthur T. von Mehren*, edited by James A. R. Nafziger and Symeon Symeonides, 705–720. Ardsley, NY: Transnational publishers, 2002.

The Spirit of Japanese Law. Athens: University of Georgia Press, 1998.

Authority without Power: Law and the Japanese Paradox. Oxford: Oxford University Press, 1991.

"The Myth of the Reluctant Litigant and the Role of the Judiciary in Japan." *Journal of Japanese Studies* 4 (1978): 359–390.

Halpérin, Jean-Louis. *Profils des mondialisations du droit*. Paris: Dalloz, 2009.

"The Concept of Law: A Western Transplant?" *Theoretical Inquiries in Law* 10 (2009): 333–354.

Han, Sang-kwŏn. "16–17 segi hyangyak ŭi kujo wa sŏngkyŏk [The Structure and Character of Hyangyak in the Sixteenth and Seventeenth Centuries]." *Chindan hakpo* 58 (1984): 17–68.

Hanguk kŭn hyŏndae sa sinmun charyo [Materials of Korean Modern and Contemporary Newspapers]. Kuksa P'yŏnch'an Wiwŏnhoe [National Institute of Korean History]. http://db.history.go.kr/url.jsp?ID=np.

Hanmal kŭndae pŏmnyŏng charyo chip [A Collection of Modern Laws and Regulations in Late Traditional Korea]. Edited by Song Pyŏng-gi, Pak Yŏng-ok and Pak Han-sŏl. 9 vols. Seoul: Kukhoe Tosŏgwan, 1970–1972.

Hara, Masakane. "Minjirei kaitei shushi [The Key Points of the Revision of the *Minjirei*]." *Chōsen* 82 (December 1921).

Harrison, Lawrence E. and Samuel P. Huntington, eds., *Culture Matters: How Values Shape Human Progress*. New York: Basic Books, 2000.

Haruyama, Meitetsu and Wakabayashi Masahiro. *Nihon shokuminchi shugi no seijiteki tenkai, 1895–1934: sono tōchi taisei to Taiwan no minzoku undō* [The Political Development of Japanese Colonialism, 1895–1934: Its system of Domination and Taiwan's Nationalist Movement]. Tokyo: Ajia Seikei Gakkai, 1980.

Hata, Ikuhiko. *Sen zenki Nihon kanryō sei no seido: seido, soshiki, jinji* [The Wartime Bureaucratic System: System, Organization, and Personnel Management]. Tokyo: Tokyo Daigaku shuppankai, 1981.

Hechter, Michael. *Internal Colonialism: The Celtic Fringe in British National Development*, 2nd ed. London: Transaction Publishers, 1999, 1975.

Henderson, Dan Fenno. *Conciliation and Japanese Law, Tokugawa and Modern*. 2 vols. Seattle: University of Washington Press, 1965.

Heuschert, Dorothea. "Legal Pluralism in the Qing Empire: Manchu Legislation for the Mongols." *The International History Review* 20, no. 2 (1998): 310–324.

Higashikawa, Tokuji. *Hakushi Ume Kenjirō: denki Ume Kenjirō* [Dr. Ume Kenjirō: Biography of Ume Kenjirō]. Tokyo: Ōzorasha, 1997, 1917.

Hirano, Takeshi. "Nihon tōchi ka no Chōsen no hōteki chii [The Legal Status of Choson under Japanese Rule]." *Handai hōgaku* 83 (1972): 33–82.

Hirano Yoshitarō. *Nihon shihon shugi shakai to hōritsu* [Japanese Capitalist Society and Law]. Tokyo: Rironsha, 1955.

Hironaka, Toshio and Eiichi Hoshino. *Minpōten no hyakunen* [The Hundred Years of the Civil Code]. 4 vols. Tokyo: Yūhigaku, 1998.

Hŏ, Tong-hyŏn, ed. *Chosa sich'altan kwangye charyojip* [Sources on the Investigation and Observation Commission]. Seoul: Kukhak Charyowŏn, 2000.

Hobbes, Thomas. *Leviathan*. Edited by Richard Tuck. Cambridge: Cambridge University Press, 1991, 1660.

Hobsbawm, Eric and Terence Ranger, eds. *The Invention of Tradition*. Cambridge: Cambridge University Press, 1983.

Hoeflich, Michael H. "Law, Society and Reception: The Vision of Alan Watson." *Michigan Law Review* 85 (1987): 1083–1094.

Hong, Yang-hŭi. "Chosŏn ch'ongdokpu p'ansa Nomura Chotarō ŭi Chosŏn sahoe insik." *Kajok pŏp yŏngu* 23, no. 1 (2009): 61–86.

"Singminji sigi ch'injok sangsok kwansŭp pŏp chŏngch'aek [The Colonial Legal Policy regarding Family and Succession Custom]." *Chŏngsin munhwa yŏngu* 29, no. 3 (2006): 285–313.

"Singminji sigi ch'injok kwansŭp ŭi ch'angch'ul kwa Ilbon minpŏp [The Creation of Succession Custom during the Colonial Period and the Japanese Civil Code]." *Ch'ŏngsin munhwa yŏngu* 28, no. 3 (2005): 121–145.

Hŏnpŏp Chaep'anso p'allyejip [Decisions of the Constitutional Court], 1989–.

Hooker, M.B. *Legal Pluralism: An Introduction to Colonial and Neo-colonial Laws*. Oxford: Clarendon Press, 1975.

Hōritsu Shinbun. Tokyo: Hōritsu Shinbunsha, 1900–1944.

Hoshino, Eiichi. "Hensan katei kara mita minpō shūi: minpō 92 jō – hōrei 2 jō ron, minpō 97 jō -526 jō -521 jō ron [Gleanings from the Civil Code Seen from Its Compilation: Discussions of Article 92 of the Civil Code and Article 2 of *Hōrei*, and Articles 97, 526, and 521 of the Civil Code]." *Minpō ronshū*, vol. 1, 151–225. Tokyo: Yūhikaku, 1970.

Hoshino, Tōru. *Minpōten ronsō shiryōshu* [Collection of Documents Related to the Civil Code Debate]. Tokyo: Nihon Hyōronsha, 1969.

"San hakushi to minpō seitei [Three Doctors and the Enactment of the Civil Law]." *Hōgaku shirin* 49, no. 1 (1950): 33–55.

Minpō-ten ronsō shi [A History of the Civil Code Debate]. Tokyo: Nihon Hyōronsha, 1944.

Meiji minpō hensan shi kenkyū [A History of the Codification of Meiji Civil Law]. Tokyo: Daiyamondosha, 1943.

Hozumi, Nobushige. *Hōritsu shinka ron* [A Theory of the Evolution of Law]. Vol. 1. Tokyo: Iwanami Shoten, 1924.

The New Japanese Civil Code, as Material for the Study of Comparative Jurisprudence. Tokyo: Maruzen Kabushiki-Kaisha, 1912.

Hozumi, Yatsuka. "Taiwan sōtoku no meirei ken ni taishite [Concerning the Ordinance Power of the Colonial Governor of Taiwan]." *Hōgaku kyokai zasshi* 23, no. 2 (1905). In *Hozumi Yatsuka hakushi ronbunshū*, edited by Hozumi Shigetaka. Tokyo: Yūhikaku, 1943.

Kenpō teiyō [A Summary of Constitutional Law]. Tokyo: Yūhigaku, 1935.

Huang, Cheng-Yi. "Enacting the 'Incomprehensible China': Modern European Jurisprudence and the Japanese Reconstruction of Qing Political Law." *Law & Society Inquiry* 33 (2008): 955–1001.

Huang, Philip C. C. *Code, Custom, and Legal Practice in China*. Stanford: Stanford University Press, 2001.

Civil Justice in China: Representation and Practice in the Qing. Stanford: Stanford University Press, 1996.

Ibbetson, David. "Custom in Medieval law." In *The Nature of Customary Law: Legal, Historical and Philosophical Perspectives*, edited by Amanda Perreau-Saussine and James Bernard Murphy, 151–175. Cambridge: Cambridge University Press, 2007.

Ichikawa, Masaaki, ed. *Kankoku heigō shiryō* [Documents regarding the Annexation of Korea]. Tokyo: Hara Shobō, 1978, 1965.

Ikeda, Masako Kobayashi. "French Legal Advisor in Meiji Japan (1873–1895): Gustave Emile Boissonade de Fontarabie." PhD diss., University of Hawaii, 1996.

Im, Sang-hyŏk. "Sosong kip'i ŭi munhwa chŏnt'ong e taehan chaego wa Hanguk sahoe [A Reconsideration of the Tradition of Anti-Litigation Culture and Korean Society]." *Pŏp kwa sahoe* 24 (2003): 145–160.

"Chosŏn chŏngi minsa sosong kwa sosong iron ŭi chŏngae [Civil Litigation in the Early Chosŏn Dynasty and the Development of Litigation Theories]." PhD diss., Seoul National University, 2000.

Imaizumi, Yoshiko. "Michel Revon: A Forgotten Japanologist and His Study of Shintoïsme" (abstract). http://crjehess.wordpress.com/2010/01/11/michel-revon-a-forgotten-japanologist-and-his-study-of-shintoisme/.

Isambert, François, ed. Recueil général des anciennes lois françaises depuis l'an 420 jusqu'à la révolution de 1789. 29 vols. Paris: Belin-Leprieur, 1829.

Ishida, Minori. "Suisu minpō ichi jō no hōgen ideorogi" [The Ideology of the Source of Law in Article 1 of the Swiss Civil Code] (Part 5). *Hōgaku kyōkai zasshi* 89 (1972): 615–635.

Ishii, Ryosuke. *Japanese Legislation in the Meiji Era*. Translated by William J. Chambliss. Tokyo: Pan-Pacific Press, 1958.

Itani, Zenichi, *Chōsen keizaishi* [An Economic History of Chosŏn]. Tokyo: Daitōkaku, 1928.

Itō, Hirobumi, *Zoku Itō Hirobumi hiroku*. 1930, reprinted edition. Tokyo: Hara Shobō, 1982.

Itō Hirobumi kankei monjo [Papers Related to Itō Hirobumi]. Edited by Itō Hirobumi Kankei Monjo Kenkyūkai. Tokyo: Hanawa Shobo, 1973–1981.

Iwatani, Jūrō. "Wigumoa ate Boasonado shokan 14 tsū no kaidai teki kenkyū: minpōten ronsō to futari no gaikoku hōritsuka hōritsuka [A Bibliograpahical Introduction to the Fourteen Letters Written by Boissonade to Wigmore: The Civil Code Debate and the Two Foreign Jurists]." *Hōgaku kenkyū* (Keio Gijuku Daigaku Hōgaku Kenkyūkai) 73, no. 11 (2000): 154–204.

Jacob, Robert. "La Coutume, les mœurs et le rite. Regards croisés sur les catégories occidentales de la norme non écrite." In *La Coutume et la norme en Chine et au Japon*, edited by Jérôme Bourgon, 145–166. Saint-Denis: Presses universitaires de Vincennes, 2001.

"Les Coutumiers du XIIIe siècle ont-ils connu la coutume?" In *La Coutume au village dans l'Europe médiévale et moderne*, edited by Mireille Mousnier and Jacques Poumarède, 103–119. Toulouse: Presses universitaires du Mirail, 2001.

Japan Weekly Mail. "New Codes and Old Customs of Japan." October 29; November 19, November 26, December 10, and December 17, 1892.

Japanese Court Organization Law [Saibansho Kōzōhō] (1890). http://www.geocities.jp/nakanolib/hou/hm23-6.htm.

Jones, Francis C. *Extraterritoriality in Japan and the Diplomatic Relations Resulting in Its Abolition, 1853–1899*. New York; AMS Press, 1970, 1931.

Kaeyŏk p'an kwansŭp chosa pogosŏ [Revised Translation of the Report on the Investigation of Customs]. Translated by Chŏng Kŭng-sik (translation of Chosen Sotokufu, *Kanshu chosa hokokusho*, 1912]. Seoul: Hanguk Pŏpche Yŏnguwŏn, 2000.

Kahn-Freund, Otto. "On Uses and Misuses of Comparative Law." *Modern Law Review* 37 (1972): 1–27.

Kanayama, Naoki. "Sōchi to shite no hōten to hōgaku: Ume Kenjirō to iu shinwa [The Civil Code and Legal Science as an Apparatus: A Legend Called Ume Kenjirō]." *Hōritsu jihō* 70, no.7 (1998): 6–11.

Kang, Ch'ang-sŏk. *Chosŏn T'onggambu yŏngu* [A Study of the Residency General of Korea]. Seoul: Seoul Kukhak Charyowŏn, 1995.

Kang, Man-gil, ed. *Ilbon kwa sŏgu ŭi singmin t'ongch'i pigyo*. Seoul: Sŏnin, 2004.

Kang, Sin-ung. "Kwansup pŏp sang pŏpjŏng ch'isangkwŏn e kwanhan yŏngu [A Study of Superficies in Customary Law]." *Pŏphak yŏngu* 31 (2008): 97–118.

Kang, Tong-jin. *Nihon no Chōsen shihai seisaku shi kenkyū: senkyū hyaku nijū nen dai o chūshin to shite* [A History of the Japanese Policy to Control Korea: With Particular Attention to the 1920s]. Tokyo: Tokyo Daigaku Shuppankai, 1977.

Karasawa, Yasuhiko, et al. "Kōki teisei Chūoku ni okeru hō, shakai, bunka" [Law, Society, and Culture in Late Imperial China]." *Chūgokushakai to bunka* 13 (1998): 193–281.

Katayama, Naoya. "'*Saikin hanrei hihyō*' wo yomu [Reading *Saikin hanrei hihyō*]." *Hōritsu jihō* 70, no. 7 (1998): 23–28.

Kawakami, Hiroshi. "Saigo Saibansho hanrei minji kankei [Decisions of the Supreme Court of Cases Related to Civil Matters]." *Hōsō jihō* 53, no. 5 (2001): 1351–1387.

Kawasaki, Bunzō. "Chōsen ni okeru Ume hakushi [Dr. Ume in Korea]." *Hōgaku shirin* 49, no.1 (1950): 98–100.

Kawashima, Takeyoshi. "The Concept of Judicial Precedent in Japanese Law." In *Ius Privatum Gentium: Festschrift fur Max Rheinstein zum 70. Geburtstag am 5. Juli 1969*, 85–101. Tübingen: J.C.B. Mohr, 1969.

"Dispute Resolution in Contemporary Japan." In *Law and Japan: The Legal Order in a Changing Society*, edited by Arthur Taylor von Mehren, 41–72. Cambridge, MA: Harvard University Press, 1963.

Kelley, Donald R. "'Second Nature': The Idea of Custom in European Law, Society, and Culture." In *Transmission of Culture in Early Modern Europe*, edited by Anthony Grafton and Ann Blair, 131–172. Philadelphia: University of Pennsylvania Press, 1990.

Kim, C. I. Eugene and Kim Han-Kyo, *Korea and the Politics of Imperialism 1876–1910*. Berkeley: University of California Press, 1967.

Kim, Chae-mun. *Hanguk chŏnt'ong ch'aekwŏn pŏp, kajok pŏp, sosong pŏp* [Obligations, Family Law, and Civil Procedure in Traditional Korea]. Seoul: Tongguk Taehakkyo Ch'ulp'anbu, 2007.

Kim Ch'ang-rok. "Cheryŏng e gwanhan yŏngu [A Study of *cheryŏng*]." *Pŏpsahak yŏngu* 26 (2002): 109–171.

"Singminji p'ijibaegi pŏpche ŭi kich'o [The Foundation of the Legal System under Colonial Rule]." *Pŏpche yŏngu* 8 (1995): 50–78.

"Ilbon chekuk chui ŭi hŏnpŏp sahang kwa singminji Chosŏn [Constitutional Aspects of Japanese Imperialism and Colonial Chosŏn]." *Pŏpsahak yŏngu* 14 (1993): 137–174.

Kim, Chŏng-myŏng, ed. *Nikkan gaikō shiryō shūsei* [The Collection of Documents involving the Diplomatic Relations of Japan-Korea]. Tokyo: Gannando, 1962–1967.

Kim, Chŭng-han. *Minpŏp ch'ongch'ik* [*General Principles of the Civil Code*]. Seoul: Pagyŏngsa, 1980.

Kim, Hong-sik, et al., *Chosŏn t'oji chosa saŏp ŭi yŏngu* [*A Study of the Cadastral Survey in Korea*]. Seoul: Minŭmsa, 1997.

Kim, Il-mi. "Chosŏn hugi chaesan sangsok kwansŭp: Ilche ha ku kwansŭp chosa pogosŏ rŭl chungshim ŭro [Inheritance Practice in the Late Chosŏn Dynasty: With a Focus on the Old Customs Survey Reports]." *Idae sawŏn* 11 (1973): 33–52.

Kim, Kap-ch'ŏn. "Pak Yŏng-ho ŭi kŏnbaeksŏ: Naejŏng kaehyŏk e taehan 1888 nyŏn ŭi sansomun [Pak Yŏng-hyo's Petition: The Memorial of 1888 regarding Internal Reform]." *Hanguk chŏngch'i yŏngu* 2 (June 1990): 245–295.

Kim, Marie Seong-Hak. "Review Article of *Japanese Assimilation Policies in Colonial Korea, 1910–1945*, by Marc Caprio." *The Journal of Japanese Studies* 37, no. 2 (2011): 434–439.

"Law and Reform, Colonial Style: Japanese Legal Policy in Korea." In *Mélanges offerts à Marc Orange et à Alex Guillemoz*, edited by Institut d'Etudes coréennes (Cahiers d'Etudes coréennes, No. 8), 311–321. Paris: Collège de France, 2010.

"Civil Law and Civil War: Michel de L'Hôpital and the Spirit of Legal Reforms in Sixteenth-Century France." *Law and History Review* 28, no. 3 (2010): 791–826.

"Customary Law and Colonial Jurisprudence in Korea." *American Journal of Comparative Law* 57 (2009): 205–247.

"Nihon tōjika ni okeru kankoku no kanshūhō no kōsei [The Construction of Korean Customary Law under Japanese Rule]." *Tōyō bunka kenkyū* 11 (2009): 179–193.

"Comparing the Incomparable: Local Customs and Law in Sixteenth-Century Korea and France." *Journal of Early Modern History* 12, no. 6 (2008): 507–538.

"Ume Kenjirō and the Making of Korean Civil Law, 1906–1910." *Journal of Japanese Studies* 34 (2008): 1–31.

"Higakushi teki sokumen kara mita Ume Kenjirō no hōshisō to chōsen ni okeru minpōten kōsō no igi [Ume Kenjirō's Legal Thought and the Vision of a Korean Civil Code: Some Comparative Reflections]." *Tōyō bunka kenkyū* 10 (2008): 99–136.

"Colonial Courts and Custom: Comparative Reflections on Customary Law and Colonial Modernity in Korea." *International Institute for Asian Studies Newsletter* 17 (2008): 46.

"Law and Custom under the Chosŏn Dynasty and Colonial Korea: A Comparative Perspective." *Journal of Asian Studies* 66 (2007): 1067–1097.

"Custom, Community, and the Crown: Lawyers and the Reordering of French Customary Law." In *Between the Middle Ages and Modernity: Individual and Community in the Early Modern World*, edited by Charles H. Parker and Jerry H. Bentley, 169–186. Lanham: Rowman & Littlefield, 2007.

"Christophe de Thou et la réformation des coutumes: l'esprit de réforme juridique au XVIe siècle." *Tijdschrift voor rechtsgeschiedenis* 72 (2004): 91–102.

"Customary Constitutional Law." *The Korea Times* (November 11, 2004): 7.

"'Gouvernement des Juges' ou 'Juges du Gouvernement'?: The Revolutionary Traditions and Judicial Independence in France." *Korean Journal of International and Comparative Law* 26 (1998): 1–42.

Kim, Min-jŏng. "*Kyŏngguk taejŏn* sangsok ippŏp chuŭi e kwanhan yŏngu: yuŏn sangsok kwa pŏpchŏng sangsok ŭl chungsim ŭro [A Study of Legislative Principles of Succession in *Kyŏngguk taejŏn*: With Particular Attention to Testamentary Succession and Intestate Succession]." Master's thesis, Ewha Womans University, 2006.

Kim, Pyŏng-hwa. *Hanguk sabŏpsa* [A History of the Judiciary in Korea], 3 vols. Seoul: Ilchogak, 1979.

Kim, Sang-su. "Chosŏn Kodŭng Pŏpwŏn p'ansa ka pon Chosŏn ŭi ch'injok sangsok e kwanhan kwansŭp [The Family and Succession Custom of Chosŏn as Observed by a Judge of the Chosŏn Kodŭng Pŏpwŏn]." *Sŏgang pŏphak* 10, no. 1 (2008): 25–46.

"Chosŏn Kodŭng Pŏpwŏn kwa hyŏndae Hanguk pŏp: Chosŏn Kodŭng Pŏpwŏn ŭi saengsŏng ŭl chungsim ŭro [The Chosŏn Kodŭng Pŏpwŏn and Modern Korean Law: With Particular Attention to the Establishment of the Chosŏn Kodŭng Pŏpwŏn]." *Pŏp kwa sahoe* 23 (2002): 91–109.

"Kankoku hō no rekishi: Saigo no Chōsen kōtō hōinshō no koto [Korean Law and History: A Matter of the Last Chief Justice of the Chosŏn Kodŭng Pŏpwŏn]." *Kokusai shōji hōmu* 29, no. 8 (2001): 1020–1021.

Kim, Uk-kon. "Kwansŭppŏp e taehan yŏngu: Tŭkhi ŭri minpŏp ŭi haesŏk ŭl chungsim ŭro [A Study of Customary Law: With Particular Attention to the Interpretation of Our Civil Code]." *Sungjŏn Taehakkyo nonmunjip* 5 (1974): 361–394.

Kim, Un-t'ae. *Ilbon cheguk chui ŭi Hanguk t'ongch'i* [Japanese Imperial Domination of Korea]. Seoul: Pagyŏngsa, 1998.

Kim, Wŏn-t'ae. "Ilche kangjŏm ch'ogi ch'ŏ ŭi t'ŭkyu chaesan e kwanhan kwansŭppŏp: Chosŏn Kodŭng Pŏpwŏn p'angyŏl ŭi punsŏk ŭl chungsim ŭro [Customary Law of the Wife's Special Property in the Early Japanese Colonial Period: Analysis of the Chosŏn Kodŭng Pŏpwŏn Decisions]." *Pŏpsahak yŏngu* 31 (2005): 197–236.

Kim, Yŏng-dal. "Ch'ang ssi kaemyŏng ŭi chedo [The System of Creating and Changing Names]." In *Ch'ang ssi kaemyŏng*, edited by Ch'ŏng Un-Hyŏn, 41–70. Seoul: Hangminsa, 1994.

Kishi, Koichi and Shigetada Nishijima. *Study of the Japanese Occupation of Indonesia*. Ithaca, NY, 1960.

Kitō, Heiichi. *Richō no zaisan sōzokuhō* [Property Succession of the Yi Dynasty]. Seoul: Chōsen Sōtokufu Chūsūin, 1936.

Kiyomiya, Shirō. *Gaichihō josetsu* [Introduction to Overseas Territory Law]. Tokyo: Yūhikaku, 1944.

Kohler, Joseph. "Uber das Recht des Koreaner." *Zeitschrift für vergleichende Rechtswissenschaft* 6 (1886): 400–404.

Kohli, Atul. *State-Directed Development: Political Power and Industrialization in the Global Periphery*. Cambridge: Cambridge University Press, 2004.

Kokubu, Sangai. "Heigō to shihō seido to no kankei [The Relationship between Annexation and the Judicial System]." *Chōsen* (1910) [reprinted in *Shiryō zasshi ni miru kindai Nihon no Chōsen ninshiki: Kankoku heigōki zengo*, edited by Kŭm Pyŏng-dong, vol. 4, 263. Tokyo: Ryokuin shobō, 1999.

"Shihō seido tōitsu ron ni tsuite [On the Theory of the Unification of Judicial Systems]." *Chōsen kōron* 3 & 4 (April 1915) [reprinted in *Shiryō zasshi ni miru kindai Nihon no Chōsen ninshiki: Kankoku heigōki zengo*, edited by Kŭm Pyŏngdong, vol. 5, 478–480. Tokyo: Ryokuin shobō, 1999.

"Sōtoku shisei no shōrai no hōshin ni kansuru iken [Opinion regarding the Future Directions of the Colonial Governor's Administration] (May 1919)." In *Saitō Makoto Monjo*, vol. 13, 129–164. Seoul: Koryŏ Sŏrim, 1999.

"Chōsen shihō seido no kakuritsu [The Establishment of the Judicial System of Chosŏn]." In *Chōsen tōchi no kaiko to hihan*, edited by Chōsen Shinbunsha, 44–47. Tokyo: Ryūkei Shosha, 1995, 1936.

"Kyōtsūhō ni tsuite [On Coordination Law]." *Chōsen ihō* (June 1918): 9–10.

Kokuchi, Hikota. "Ilbon t'ongch'i ha ŭi 'Manchuguk' ŭi pŏp [The Law of Manchukuo under Japanese Rule]." Translated by Im Sang-hyŏk. *Pŏpsahak yŏngu* 27 (2003): 83–112.

Komagome, Takeshi. *Shokuminchi teikoku Nihon no bunka tōgō* [The Cultural Unity of the Japanese Colonial Empire]. Tokyo: Iwanami Shoten, 1996.

Komatsu, Midori. *Chōsen heigō no rimen* [Behind the Scenes of the Annexation of Chosŏn]. Tokyo: Chūgai Shinronsha, 1920.

Korean Court Organization Law (1907). "English Translation of the Korean Law of the Constitution of the Courts of Justice, The Rules for the Operation of the Law of the Constitution of the Courts of Justice, and The Korean Law of Civil and Criminal Procedure, with Supplementary Rules and Orders," 1909. Printed in *Pŏpsahak yŏngu* 22 (2000): 231–274 (Part 1); 23 (2001): 165–204 (Part 2).

Krynen, Jacques. "The Absolute Monarchy and the French Unification of Private Rights." In *Privileges and Rights of Citizenship: Law and the Juridical Construction of Civil Society*, edited by Julius Kirshner and Laurent Layali, 27–55. Berkeley: University of California at Berkeley, The Robbins Religions and Civil Law Collection, 2002.

"Entre science juridique et dirigisme: le glas medièval de la coutume." *Droits et pouvoirs* 7 (2000): 170–187.

Kugyŏk Kodung Pŏpwŏn p'angyŏllok. Seoul: Pŏpwŏn Haengchŏngch'ŏ, 2004–2011.

Kŭm, Pyŏng-dong. *Shiryō zasshi ni miru kindai Nihon no Chōsen ninshiki: Kankoku heigōki zengo* [Modern Japan's Perception of Chosŏn as Seen from Documents and Magazines: Surrounding the Period of the Annexation of Chosŏn]. Tokyo: Ryokuin Shobō, 1999.

Kuratomi Yuzaburō Monjo. The National Diet Library (Japan), Bureau of Constitutional Documents. Vol. 30.

Kwŏn, Chae-mun. "Kwansŭp pŏp sang pŏpchŏng chisangkwŏn ŭi injŏng kunkŏ wa p'ilyosŏng e kwanhan pip'anjŏk koch'al [A Critical Examination of the Foundation and Necessity for Recognizing Superficies in Customary Law]." *Pŏpsahak yŏngu* 37 (2008): 99–127.

Kwŏn, T'ae-ŏk, "Tonghwa chŏngch'aek ron [A Study of Assimilation Policy]." *Yŏksa hakpo* 172 (2001): 335–365.

Kyŏngguk taejŏn [Great Code for Administering the Country]. Seoul: Seoul Taehakkyo Kyujanggak, 1997.

Lambert, Edouard. *La Fonction du droit civil comparé*. Paris: V. Girard & E. Brière. 1903.

Lasser, Mitchel de S.-O.-L'E. *Judicial Deliberations: A Comparative Analysis of Judicial Transparency and Legitimacy*. Oxford: Oxford University Press, 2004.

Lee, Chulwoo [Yi, Ch'ŏl-u]. "Modernity, Legality, and Power in Korea Under Japanese Rule." In *Colonial Modernity in Korea*, edited by Gi-Wook Shin and Michael Robinson, 21–51, Cambridge, MA, and London: Harvard University Asia Center, 1999.

"Talking about Korean Legal Culture: A Critical Review of the Discursive Production of Legal Culture in Korea." *Korea Journal* (Autumn 1998): 45–76.

Lee, Ki-baik. *A New History of Korea*. Translated by Edward W. Wagner and Edward J. Shultz. Seoul: Ilchogak, 1984.

Lee, Peter H. and William Theodore T. de Bary, eds. *Sourcebook of Korean Civilization*, 2 vols. New York: Columbia University Press, 1997–2000.

Leonhard, Rudolf. "The Vocation of America for the Science of Roman Law." *Harvard Law Review* 26 (1913): 389–415

Lev, Daniel S. *Legal Evolution and Political Authority in Indonesia, Selected Essays*. The Hague: Kluwer Law International, 2000.

Lewis, Martin Deming. "One Hundred Million Frenchmen: The 'Assimilation' theory in French Colonial Policy." *Comparative Studies in Society and History* 4 (1962): 129–153.

Lipstein, D. K. "The Doctrine of Precedent in Continental Law with Special Reference to French and German Law." *Journal of Comparative Legislative & International Law* 28 (1946): 34–44.

Loussouarn, Yvon. "The Relative Importance of Legislation, Custom, Doctrine, and Precedent in French Law." *Louisiana Law Review* 18 (1958): 235–270.

Lugard, Frederick D. *The Dual Mandate in British Tropical Africa*, 5th ed., London: Frank Cass & Co. Ltd, 1965, 1922.

Macauley, Melissa Ann. "A World Made Simple: Law and Property in the Ottoman and Qing Empires." *Journal of Early Modern History* 5 (2001): 331–352.

Social Power and Legal Culture: Litigation Masters in Late Imperial China. Stanford: Stanford University Press, 1998.

MacCormack, Geoffrey. *The Spirit of Traditional Chinese Law*. Athens: University of Georgia Press, 1996.

Maki, Kenji. "Meiji hachi nen minji saiban no gensoku [The Principles of Civil Adjudication in Meiji Year 8]." *Hōgaku kenkyū* 17, no. 2 (1927): 349–362.

Mamdani, Mahmood. *Citizen and Subject: Contemporary Africa and the Legacy of Late Colonialism*. Princeton, NJ: Princeton University Press, 1996.

Mann, Kristin and Richard Roberts, eds. *Law in Colonial Africa*. Portsmouth, NH: Heinemann, 1991.

Mass, Jeffrey P. *The Kamakura Bakufu: A Study in Documents*. Stanford: Stanford University Press, 1976.

Matsuoka, Shūtarō. *Chōsen gyōseihō teiyō* [A Summary of the Administrative Law of Chosŏn]. Seoul: Tōto Shoseki Keijō Shiten, 1944.

"Gaichihō [Overseas Territory Law]." In *Gyōseihō* [Administrative Law], vol. 4. Tokyo: Nihon Hyōronsha, 1936–1940.

Mayali, Laurent. "La Coutume dans la doctrine romaniste." In *La Coutume*, edited by J. Gilissen, vol. 2, 11–31 (*Recueils de la Société Jean Bodin pour l'histoire comparative des institutions*, vol. 52). Brussels: De Boeck Université, 1990.

McDermott, Joseph P. "Emperor, Elites, and Commoners: The Community Pact Ritual of the Late Ming." In *State and Court Ritual in China*, edited by Joseph P. McDermott, 299–351. Cambridge: Cambridge University Press, 1999.

Merry, Sally Engle. "Law and Colonialism." *Law and Society Review* 25, no. 4 (1991): 889–922.

Merryman, John Henry. "The French Deviation." *American Journal of Comparative Law* 44 (1996): 109–119.

The Civil Law Tradition: An Introduction to the Legal Systems of Western Europe and Latin America. Palo Alto: Stanford University Press, 1969.

Meunier, Pierre. *Organisation et fonctionnement de la justice indigène en Afrique occidentale française*. Paris: Challamel, 1914.

Meynial, Edouard. "Sur le rôle joué par la doctrine et la jurisprudence dans l'œuvre d'unification du droit en France depuis la rédaction des coutumes jusqu'à la Révolution, en particulier dans la succession aux propres." *Revue générale du droit, de la législation et de la jurisprudence en France et à l'étranger* 27 (1903): 326–351 (Part 1); 446–457 (Part 2).

Mi gunjŏng pŏmnyŏng jip [Collection of Laws and Regulations of the American Military Government]. Edited by Naemubu Ch'ian'guk. Seoul: Naemubu Ch'ian'guk, 1956.

Milsom, S. F. C. *Historical Foundation of the Common Law.* 2nd. ed. London and Boston: Butterworths, 1981.

Minear, Richard H. *Japanese Tradition and Western Law: Emperor, State, and Law in the Thought of Hozumi Yatsuka.* Cambridge, MA: Harvard University Press, 1970.

Minji kanrei ruishū [The Classified Collection of Customs in Civil Matters]. Edited by Tezuka Yutaka. Tokyo: Keio Gijuku Daigaku Hōgaku Kenkyūkai, 1969, 1877.

Minji kanshū kaitō ishū [The Compilation of Replies regarding Civil Customs]. Edited by Chōsen Sōtokufu Chūsūin. Seoul, 1933.

Mitani, Taichirō. *Seiji seido to shite no baishinsei: kindai Nihon no shihōken to seiji* [The Jury System as a Political System: The Judicial Power and Politics of Modern Japan]. Tokyo: Tokyo Daigaku Shuppankai, 2001.

Miyamoto, Gen. "Miyamoto Gen hōmu kyokutzyō enzyu yōshi [Abstract of Law Minister Miyamoto Gen's Speech]." *Shihō kyōkai zasshi* 18, no. 8 (1939).

Miyata, Sesuko, ed. *Singmin t'ongch'i ŭi hŏsang gwa silsang: Chosŏn ch'ongdokpu koui kwalli ŭi yuksŏng chŭngŏn* [The Falsity and the Reality of Colonial Rule: Live-Voice Testimonies of the Elite Officials of the Government General of Korea]. Translated by Chŏng Chae-sŏng. Seoul: Hyean, 2002.

Miyata, Sesuko. *Chosŏn minjung kwa hwangmin hwa chŏngch'aek* [The Korean People and the Policy to Turn Them into Imperial Subjects]. Translated by Yi Hyŏng-nang. Seoul: Ilchogak, 1997.

Mizuno, Naoki. "Chosŏn singminji chibae wa irŭm ŭi 'ch'aihwa': naejiin kwa hondong toegi swiŭn irŭm ŭi kŭmji rŭl chungsim ŭro [Colonial Rule in Korea and the Differentiation of Names: With Particular Attention to the Prohibition of the Names that Could Be Mistaken as the Names of the Japanese People]." *Sahoe wa yŏksa* 59 (2001): 147–174.

ed. *Senjiki shokuminchi tōchi shiryō* [Documents of Wartime Colonial Rule], vol. 3. Tokyo: Kashiwa Shobō, 1998.

"Senjiki shokuminchi shihai to 'naigaichi gyōsei itchi gen ka' [The Wartime Colonial Rule and 'the Unification of Administration in *naigaichi*']." *Jinbun kakuhō* 79 (1997): 77–102.

Mommsen, W. J. and J. A. de Moore eds. *European Expansion and Law: The Encounter of Europe and Indigenous Law in 19th-and 20th-Century Africa and Asia.* Oxford: Berg, 1992.

Moore, Sally Falk. "Treating Law as Knowledge: Telling Colonial Officers What to Say to Africans about Running "Their Own" Native Courts." *Law & Society Review* 26 (1992): 11–46.

Social Facts and Fabrications. "Customary" law on Kilimanjaro, 1880–1980. Cambridge: Cambridge University Press, 1986.

Moriyama, Shigenori. "Hogo seijika ni okeru shihō seido kaikaku no rinen to genjitsu [Ideals and the Reality of Judicial Reforms in Protectorate Korea]." In *Shokuminchi teikoku Nihon no hōteki kōzō*, edited by byAsano Toyomi and Matsuda Toshihiko, 277–317. Tokyo: Shinzansha, 2004.

Nikkan heigō [The Annexation of Japan and Korea]. Tokyo: Yoshikawa Kōbunkan, 1992.

Kindai Nikkan kankeishi kenkyū: Chōsen shokuminchika to kokusai kankei [A History of Modern Japanese-Korean Relations: The Colonization of Korea and International Relations]. Tokyo: Tōkyō Daigaku Shuppankai, 1987.

Mun, Chun-yŏng. "Hanmal ŭi minsa punjaeng kwa singminji sabŏp kwŏllok: kwansŭp e kwanhan chaep'an rye rŭl chungsim ŭro [Civil Disputes and Colonial Judicial Power in Late Chosŏn: Focusing on Litigation concerning Custom]." *Pusan Taehakkyo pŏphak yŏngu* 52, no. 4 (2011): 229–269.

Pŏpwŏn kwa kŏmch'al ŭi t'ansaeng: sapŏp ŭi yŏksa ro ingnŭn Taehanminguk [The Birth of the Courts and the Prosecutor's Office: Judicial History of Korea]. Seoul: Yŏksa wa Pip'yŏngsa, 2010.

"Hanguk ŭi hyŏngsa sabŏp kwa minsa punchaeng hyŏng koso sakŏn: ku Han mal kwa ilche sidae ŭi kyŏnghŏm [Korea's Criminal Justice and Civil Disputes: An Experience in Late Traditional Korea and the Japanese Colonial Period]." *Pusan Taehakkyo pŏphak yŏngu* 48, no. 1 (2007): 1401–1437.

"T'onggambu chaep'anso sŏlch'i e kwanhan charyo: Kuratomi Yuzaburō wa Ume Kenjirō ŭi ŭigyŏnsŏ [Documents regarding the Establishment of the Residency General Courts: The Opinion Papers of Kuratomi Yuzaburō and Ume Kenjirō]." *Pŏpsahak yŏngu* 36 (2007): 331–366.

"Cheguk Ilbon ŭi singminji hyŏng sabŏp chedo ŭi hyŏngsŏng gwa hwaksan – Taeman ŭi sabŏp chedo rŭl dullŏ ssan chŏngch'i ippŏp kwajŏng ŭl chungsim ŭro [The Establishment and Spread of the Colonial Criminal Legal System of Imperial Japan: With Particular Attention to the Political Process of Legislation Surrounding the Taiwanese Judicial System]." *Pŏpsahak yŏngu* 30 (2004): 189–231.

"Hanguk kŏmch'al chedo ŭi yŏksajŏk hyŏngsŏng e kwanhan yŏngu [A History of the Establishment of the Prosecution System in Korea]." PhD diss., Seoul National University, 2004.

Mun, Suk-cha. *Chosŏn sidae chaesan sangsok kwa kajok* [Property Succession and Family in the Chosŏn Period]. Seoul: Kyŏngin Munhwasa, 2004.

Myers, Ramon H. and Mark R. Peattie, eds. *The Japanese Colonial Empire, 1895–1945*. Princeton, NJ: Princeton University Press, 1984.

Myŏng, Sun-ku. "Ajikto saraitnŭn pŏp, 'Chosŏn Minsaryŏng': Chosŏn Minsaryŏng ŭi sogupchŏk pyeji rŭl chean handa [The Law That Is Still Alive, 'Chosŏn Minsaryŏng': Calling for the Retroactive Abolition of Chosŏn Minsaryŏng]." *Chŏsŭtisŭ* 7, no. 2 (2008): 220–236.

Nagai, Kazu. "Tōkanbu no shihō seido kaikaku to so no tenkan o meguru kenkyū [A Study of the Reform of the Judicial System by the Residency General and Its Evolution]." 3 parts (Web Publication Version). http://www.bun.kyoto-u.ac.jp/~knagai/kuratomi/judiciaryreform1.html.

Nagumo, Kōkichi. *Genkō Chōsen shinzoku sōzoku hōruishū* [The Collection of Current Family and Succession Laws of Korea]. Seoul: Ōsakayagō Shoten, 1935.

Naitō, Masanaka. "Kankoku ni okeru Ume Kenjirō no rippō jigyō [Ume Kenjirō's Legislative Activities in Korea]." *Shimadai hōgaku* 25, no.3 (1991): 1–26.

Nakamura, Tetsu. "Ume Kenjirō no senken [Ume Kenjirō's Prescience]." *Hōritsu gaku no yoake to Hōsei Daigaku* [The Dawn of Legal Science and Hōsei University], edited by Hōsei Daigaku Daigakushi Shiryō Linkai. Tokyo: Hōsei Daigaku, 1992.

Nakamura, Tetsuya. "Minpō dai ni hen shinzoku an [The Proposal to Insert Family Law into Book Two of Civil Law]." *Hōritsu jihō* 70, no. 7 (1998): 33–37.

Nam, Andrew C., ed. *Korea under Japanese Colonial Rule*. Kalamazoo: Center for Korean Studies, Western Michigan University, 1973.

Nam, Ki-jŏng, trans. *Ilche ŭi Hanguk sabŏppu ch'imnyak sirhwa* [The Real Story of the Invasion of the Korean Judiciary by Imperial Japan]. Seoul: Yukpŏpsa, 1978 (Korean translation of "Chōsen ni okeru shihō seido kindai ka no sokuseki." In Yūhō Kyokai, ed., *Chōsen kindai shiryō kenkyū*, vol. 6. Tokyo: Kuresu Press, 2001, 1966.

Niida, Noboru and Fukushima Masao, eds. *Nihon hō to Ajia* [Japanese Law and Asia]. Tokyo: Keisō Shobō, 1970.

Nikcevic, Tomica. "Problèmes de réception du droit coutumier dans les codification du droit civil en Servie et au Monténégro du XIXe siècle: Questions théoriques et législative des sources du droit." *Balkan Studies* 24, no. 2 (1983): 531–557.

Noda, Yoshiyuki. "Meiji hachi nen Dajōkan fukoku dai hyaku san go dai san jō no jōri ni tsuite no zatsukan [Reflections on Reason in Article 3 of Dajōkan Decree No. 108 in Meiji Year 8]." *Hōgaku kyōkai hyaku shūnen kinen ronbun shū*, vol. 1, 244–280. Tokyo: Yuhigaku, 1983.

Introduction to Japanese Law. Translated by Anthony H. Angelo. Tokyo: University of Tokyo Press, 1976.

"Meiji hachi nen ni okeru Furansu hō no kenkyū [A Study of French law in Meiji Year 8]." *Nichi Butsu hōgaku* 1 (1961): 3–59.

Nojima, Mikio. "Boasonado to Ume Kenjirō hakushi [Boissonade and Dr. Ume Kenjirō]." *Hōgaku semina* 3, no. 435 (1991): 78–79.

Nomura, Chōtarō. "Chōsen kajoku seido no suii [The Transition of the Family System of Chosŏn]." *Chōsen* 296 (January 1940): 17–37.

Chōsen saishi sōzokuhō ron josetsu [Introduction to Ancestor Ceremony Succession in Chosŏn]. Seoul: Chōsen sōtokufu chūsūin., 1939.

"Chōsen ni okeru shinzoku kanshu no jitsujō to sono hōritsu ue no shuyō mondai [The Reality of Family Succession Custom in Chosŏn and Its Principal Legal Questions]." *Hōritsu jihō* 11, no. 9 (1939).

"Chōsen ni okeru genkō yōshi seido [The Current Adoption System in Chosŏn]." *Shihō kyōkai zasshi* 6, no. 4 (1927): 19–24 [continued through vol. 7, no. 12 (1928): 20–26] (17 Parts).

"Sosen no saishi to genkō no hōritsu [Ancestor Worship Ceremony and Current Law]." *Shihō kyōkai zasshi* 5, no. 4 (1926): 1–24.

Chōsen koseki rei gikai [Interpretation of the Regulation of Chosŏn Household Registration]. Tokyo: Ganshōdō Shoten, 1925.

Nomura, Masao. "Kokubu Sangai." In *Hōsō hūun roku*, vol. 1, 18–30. Tokyo: Asahi Shinbunsha, 1966.

Ocko, Jonathan K. and David Gilmartin. "State, Sovereignty, and the People: A Comparison of the "Rule of Law" in China and India." *The Journal of Asian Studies* 68 (2009): 55–100.

Oda, Hiroshi. *Japanese Law*. 3rd ed. Oxford: Oxford University Press, 2009.

ed. *Basic Japanese Laws*. Oxford: Clarendon Press, 1997.

Ogawahara, Hiroyuki. "Tōkan Itō Hirobumi no kankoku hōtchi kokka kōsō no katei [The Development of Resident General Ito Hirobumi's Ideal of Creating a State of Rule of Law in Korea]." In *Nitchō kankeishi ronshū: Kan Tokusan sensei koki taishoku kinen* [A Collection of Articles on the History of Japan-Korean Relations], edited by Kan Tokusan Sensei Koki Taishok Kinen Ronbunshū Kankō Linkai, 162–87. Tokyo: Shinkansha, 2003.

Oguma, Eiji. *A Genealogy of 'Japanese' Self-images*. Translated by David Askew. Melbourne: Trans Pacific Press, 2002.

'Nihonjin' no kyōkai': Okinawa, Ainu, Taiwan, Chōsen shokuminchi shihai kara fukki undō made [The Boundaries of the Japanese: From the Colonial Domination of Okinawa, Ainu, Taiwan and Korea to the Return Movement]. Tokyo: Shinyōsha, 1998.

Oka, Takashi. "Meiji Minpō to Ume Kenjirō [The Meiji Civil Code and Ume Kenjirō]." *Hōgaku Shirin* 88, no. 4 (1991): 3–47.

Oka, Takashi and Edo Keiko. "Ume Kenjirō chosho oyobi ronpun mokuroku: sono shoji gaku teki kenkyū [The Catalogue of the Books and Articles Written by Ume Kenjirō: A Bibliographical Study]." *Hōgaku shirin* 82, nos. 3 & 4 (1985): 137–214.

Okamatsu, Santarō. *Provisional Report on Investigations of Laws and Customs in the Island of Formosa*. Taipei: Ch'eng Wen Publishing Company, 1971, 1902.

Okamoto, Makiko. "Chōsen Sōtokufu: soshiki to hito [The Government General of Korea: Its Organization and Personnel]." *Tōyō bunka kenkyū* 4 (2002): 141–188.

"Sōtoku seiji to seitō seiji: nidai seitōki no sōtoku jinji to sōtokufu kansei yosan [The Politics of Colonial Governors and the Party Politics: The Personnel of Colonial Governors and the Colonial Government's Operating Budgets during the Two-Party Period]." *Chōsen shi kenkyūkai ronbunshū* 38 (2000): 31–59.

Ōkawa, Sumio. "Gaikoku jin no shiken to Ume Kenjirō [Civil Rights of Foreigners and Ume Kenjirō]." *Ritsumeikan Hōgaku* 253 (1997): 26–48 (Part 1); 255 (1997): 105–40 (Part 2).

"Meiji hachi nen Dajōkan fukoku dai 103 gō saiban jimu kokoroe no seiritsu to Inoue Kaoru [The Proclamation of the Dajōkan Decree, Law No. 103, of Meiji Year 8 regarding the Conduct of Judicial Affairs and Inoue Kaoru]." *Ritsumeikan hōgaku* 205–206 (1989): 506–526 (Part 1); 227 (1993): 1–17 (Part 2); 234 (1994): 174–207 (Part 3).

Ōkubo, Yasuo. "La Querelle sur la premier code civil japonais et l'ajournement de sa mise en vigueur: refus du législateur etranger?" *Revue internationale de droit comparé* (1991): 389–405.

"Gustave Boissonade, père français du droit japonais moderne (1825–1910)," *Revue historique de droit français et étranger* 59 (1981): 29–54.

Nihon kindaihō no chichi Bowasonado. Tokyo: Iwanami Shoten, 1977.

Olivier-Martin, François. *Les Lois du roi*. Paris: Librairie générale de droit et de jurisprudence, 1997, 1988.

"Le Roi de France et les mauvaises coutumes au Moyen Age." *Zeitschrift der Savigny-Stiftung fur Rechtsgeschichte. Germanistische Abtheilung* 58 (1938): 108–137.

La Coutume de Paris, trait d'union entre le droit romain et les législations modernes. Paris: Recueil Sirey, 1925.

Ono, Shusei. "Comparative Law and the Civil Code of Japan." *Hitotsubashi Journal of Law and Politics* 24 (1996): 27–45 (Part 1); 25 (1997): 29–52 (Part 2).

Orlu Nmehielle, Vincent O. *The African Human Rights System: Its Laws, Practices, and Institutions*. The Hague: Kluwer Law International, 2001.

Örücü, Esin. "The Impact of European Law on the Ottoman Empire and Turkey." In *European Expansion and Law: The Encounter of European and Indigenous Law in 19th- and 20th-Century Africa and Asia*, edited by W.J. Mommsen and J.A. de Moor, 39–58. Oxford: Berg, 1992.

Otter, Sandra den. "Rewriting the Utilitarian Market: Colonial Law and Custom in Mid-Nineteenth-Century British India." *The European Legacy* 6, no. 2 (2001): 177–188.

Otto, J. M. and S. Pompe. "The Legal Oriental Connection." In *Leiden Oriental Connections, 1850–1940*, edited by Willem Otterspeer, 230–249. Leiden: Brill, 1989.

Oumé, Kendjiro [Ume, Kenjirō]. *De la transaction en droit romain et dans l'ancien droit français*. Paris: L. Larose et Forcel, 1889.

Oyama, Kenichi. "Kanshuhō riron no denrai [The Introduction of the Theory of Customary Law]." *Kantō Gakuen Daigaku hōgaku kiyō* 1 (1991): 49–166 (Part 1).

Pae, Chae-hong. "Chosŏn hugi sŏŏl hŏt'ong kwa sinbun [The Abrogation of Discriminations against *sŏŏl* and Personal Status in Late Chosŏn]." PhD diss., Kyŏngbuk University, 1994.

Pae, Sang-hun. "Chosŏn hugi punhal sangsok kwanhaeng ŭi chisok e taehan sogo [A Short Study on the Continuing Practices of Partible Succession in Late Chosŏn]." *Hanguk minjok munhwa* 34 (2009): 203–235.

Pak, Ch'an-ju. "Pulmunpŏp ŭi pŏpwŏnsŏng e taehan saeroun ihae [New Understanding of the Establishment of Common Law]." *Pŏpchŏ* 612 (September 2007): 43–81.

"Taepŏpwŏn e ŭihan kwansŭp pŏp ŭi p'yeji [The Abrogation of Customary Law by the Supreme Court]." *Pŏpchŏ* 598 (July 2006): 19–75.

Pak, Pyŏng-ho. "Hanguk pŏphak kyoyuk ŭi kiwŏn: Pŏpkwan yangsŏngso chedo wa Kyŏngsŏng Chedae [The Origin of the Education of Judges in Korea: The Judge Training School System and Kyŏngsŏng Imperial University]." *Kosigye* (April 1995): 86–99.

"Ilche ha ŭi kajok chŏngch'aek kwa kwansŭp pŏp hyŏngsŏng kwajŏng [Family Policy and the Process of Customary Law Formation under Japanese Rule]." *Seoul Taehakkyo pŏphak* 33, no. 2 (1992): 1–17.

Hanguk pŏpchesa ko [A Study of the History of Korean Law]. Seoul: Pŏmmunsa, 1974.

Pak, Ŭn-gyŏng. *Ilche ha Chosŏn in kwallyo yŏngu* [A Study of Korean Officials under Japanese Imperial Rule]. Seoul: Hangminsa, 1999.

Palais, James B. "Chosŏn wangjo ŭi kwallyo chŏk kunju che [The Bureaucratic Monarchical System in the Chosŏn Dynasty]." In *Tongyang samguk ŭi wangkwŏn kwa kwallyo che*, edited by Chosŏn sidae sahak hoe. Seoul: Kukhak Charyowŏn, 1999.

Confucian Statecraft and Korean Institutions: Yu Hyŏngwŏn and the Late Chosŏn Dynasty. Seattle: University of Washington Press, 1996.

Park, Byoung Ho [Pak, Pyŏng-ho]. "Traditional Korean Society and Law." *Korean Journal of Comparative Law* 5 (1977): 1–26.

Park, Pyong-Ho [Pak, Pyŏng-ho]. "Characteristics in Traditional Korean Law." *Korea Journal* (1976): 1–16.

Pascal, Robert A. "The Sources of Civil Order according to the Louisiana Civil Code." *Tulane Law Review* 54 (1980): 916–941.

Pennington, Ken. "Law, Feudal." In *Dictionary of the Middle Ages: Supplement* 1, 320–323. New York: Charles Scribner's Sons-Thompson-Gale, 2004.

Perdue, Peter C. *China Marches West: The Qing Conquest of Central Eurasia*. Cambridge, MA: Belknap Press of Harvard University Press, 2005.

Péri, Nöel. "Review of Michel Revon, *Anthologie de la littérature japonaise des origines au XXe siècle*, Paris, 1910." *Bulletin de l'École française d'Extrême-Orient* 11 (1911): 226–231.

Peterson, Mark. *Korean Adoption and Inheritance. Case Studies in the Creation of a Classic Confucian Society*. Ithaca, NY: East Asian Program, Cornell University, 1996.

Pŏpwŏn Haengjŏngch'ŏ [Office of Court Administration], ed. *Pŏpwŏnsa* [History of Courts]. 2 vols. Seoul: Pŏpwŏn Haengjŏngch'ŏ, 1995.

ed. *Ch'injok sangsok e kwanhan kugwansŭp* [Old Custom on Family and Succession]. Chaep'an charyo [Trial Sources], vol. 29. Seoul: Pŏpwŏn Haengjŏngch'ŏ, 1985.

ed. *Hanguk pŏpkwansa* [History of Judges of Korea]. Seoul: Pŏpwŏn Haengjŏngch'ŏ, 1976.

Pound, Roscoe. *The Formative Era of American Law*. Boston: Little, Brown, 1938.

"The Development of American Law and its Deviation from English Law." *Law Quarterly Review* 67 (1951): 49–66.

Pyle, Kenneth B. "The Technology of Japanese Nationalism: The Local Improvement Movement." *The Journal of Asian Studies* 33 (1973): 51–65.

"Advantages of Followership: German Economics and Japanese Bureaucrats." *The Journal of Japanese Studies* 1 (1974): 127–164.

Ramseyer, J. Mark. "Indentured Prostitution in Imperial Japan: Credible Commitments in the Commercial Sex Industry." *The Journal of Law, Economics, & Organization* 7 (1991): 89–116.

Ranger, Terence. "The Invention of Tradition in Colonial Africa." In *The Invention of Tradition*, edited by Eric Hobsbawm and Terence Ranger, 211–262. Cambridge: Cambridge University Press, 1983.

Rathbone, Richard. "Native Courts, Local Courts, Chieftaincy and the CPP in Ghana in the 1950s." *Journal of African Cultural Studies* 13 (2006): 125–139.

Residency General of Korea. *Annual Report on Reforms and Progress in Korea, 1908–9*. Seoul: H. I. J. M.'s Residency General, 1907–1911.

Reulos, Michel. "L'Importance des praticiens dans l'humanisme juridique." In *Pédagogues et juristes: Congrès du Centre d'Etudes supérieures de la Renaissance de Tours, été 1960*, 119–133. Paris, Librairie Philosophique J. Vrin, 1963.

Reyntjens, Filip. "The Development of the Dual Legal System in Former Belgian Central Africa (Zaire-Rwanda-Burundi)." In *European Expansion and Law: The Encounter of Europe and Indigenous Law in 19th- and 20th-Century Africa and Asia*, edited by Mommsen, W. J. and J.A. de Moore, 111–128. Oxford: Berg, 1992.

Riles, Annelise. "Wignore's Treasure Box: Comparative Law in the Era of Information." *Harvard International Law Journal* 40 (1999): 221–283.

Roberts, Richard. "Representation, Structure and Agency: Divorce in the French Soudan during the Early Twentieth Century." *Journal of African History* 40 (1999): 389–410.

Robinson, David. "Ethnography and Customary Law in Senegal." *Cahier d'Etudes africaines* 32, no. 126 (1992): 221–237.

Röhl, Wilhelm. *History of Law in Japan since 1868*. Leiden: Brill, 2005.

Rowe, William T. *Saving the World: Chen Hongmou and Elite Consciousness in Eighteenth-Century China*. Stanford: Stanford University Press, 2001.

Saada, Emmanuelle. *Les Enfants de la colonie: Les métis de l'Empire français entre sujétion et citoyenneté*. Paris: Editions de la Découverte, 2007.

"Citoyens et sujets de l'empire français: les usages du droit en situation coloniale." *Genèses: Sciences Sociales et Histoire* 53 (2003): 4–24.

Saigo Saibansho Shimu Sōmukoku, ed. *Saibansho hyakunen shi* [The Centennial History of Courts]. Tokyo: Saigo saibansho shimu sōmukoku, 1990.

Saito Makoto monjo, Chōsen Sōtoku jidai kankei shiryō [Saito Makoto Papers, Documents Related to the Government General of Korea]. Seoul: Koryŏ Sŏrim, 1999.

Sakai, Akira. "'Shihō ken no tokuritsu' to Kojima Iken: Ōtsu shiken o tsuishin ni shite [The Independence of Judicial Power and Kojima Iken: With Particular Attention to the Ōtsu Affair." *Kyushu Ryukoku Tanki Daigaku kiyō* 53 (2007): 27–41.

Sakai, Tadao. "Yi Yulgok and the Community Compact." In *The Rise of Neo-Confucianism in Korea*, edited by William Theodore De Bary and JaHyun Kim Haboush, 328–348. New York: Columbia University Press, 1985.

Saleilles, Raymond. "Ecole historique et droit naturel d'après quelques ouvrages récents." *Revue trimestrielle de droit civil* (1902): 80–112.

Sanekata, Masao. *Kyōtsūhō*. Tokyo: Nihon Hyōronsha, 1939.

Sarr, Dominique and Richard Roberts. "The Jurisdiction of Muslim Tribunals in Colonial Senegal, 1857–1932." In *Law in Colonial Africa*, edited by Kristin Mann and Richard Roberts, 131–143. Portsmouth, NH: Heinemann, 1991.

Sasaki, Sōichi. *Nihon kenpō ron* [A Theoretical Study of Japanese Constitutional Law]. Tokyo: Kanesashi Hōryūdō, 1932.

Schiller, A. Arthur. "Conflict of Laws in Indonesia." *The Far Eastern Quarterly* 2, no. 1 (1942): 31–47.

Schmid, Andre. "Colonialism and the 'Korea Problem' in the Historiography of Modern Japan: A Review Article." *The Journal of Asian Studies* 59 (2000): 951–976.

Schuster, Ernest J. "The Swiss Civil Code." *Journal of Comparative Legislation and International Law* 5, no. 4 (1923): 216–226.

Seizelet, Eric. "*Contra legem ou para legem*? La coutume de l'union matrimoniale de fait en croit civil japonais avant 1945." In *La Coutume et la norme en Chine et au Japon*, edited by Jérôme Bourgon, 125–142. Saint-Denis: Presses universitaires de Vincennes., 2001.

"European Law and Tradition in Japan during the Meiji Era, 1868–1912." In *European Expansion and Law: The Encounter of European and Indigenous Law in 18th- and 20th-Century Africa and Asia*, edited by W. J. Mommsen and J.A. de Moor, 59–82. Oxford: Berg, 1992.

"Les Implications politiques de l'introduction du droit francais au Japon." *Revue internationale de droit comparé* (1991): 367–388.

Seoul Taehakkyo Pŏpkwa Taehak Tongch'anghoe, ed. *Seoul Taehakkyo Pŏpkwa Taehak paengnyŏnsa, 1895–1995* [The Centennial History of the Law School of the Seoul National University, 1895–1995]. Seoul, 2004.

Seyssel, Claude de. *The Monarchy of France*. Translated by Donald R. Kelley. New Haven: Yale University Press, 1981.

Shadle, Brett L. "'Changing Traditions to Meet Current Altering Conditions': Customary Law, African Courts and the Rejection of Codification in Kenya, 1930–60." *Journal of African History* 40 (1999): 411–431.

Shaw, William R. *Legal Norms in a Confucian State*. Berkeley: Institute of East Asian Studies, University of California Berkeley, Center for Korean Studies, 1981.

"Social and Intellectual Aspects of Traditional Korean Law, 1392–1910." In Bong Duck Chun, William R. Shaw, and Dai-kwon Choi, *Traditional Korean Legal Attitudes*,15–53. Berkeley: Institute of East Asian Studies, University of California Berkeley, Center for Korean Studies, 1980.

"Traditional Korean Law and Its Relation to China." In *Essays on China's Legal Tradition*, edited by Jerome Alan Cohen, R. Randle Edwards and Fu-mei Chang Chen, 302–326. Princeton: Princeton University Press, 1980.

"Traditional Korean Law: A New Look." *Korea Journal* 13 (September 1973): 40–53.

Shiga, Shūzō. *Shindai Chūgoku no hō to saiban* [Law and Adjudication in Qing China]. Tokyo: Sōbunsha, 1984.

Shihō kyōkai zasshi [The Journal of the Association for Jurists]. Seoul: Chōsen Shihō Kyōkai, 1922–1945.

Shin, Gi-Wook and Michael Robinson, eds. *Colonial Modernity in Korea*. Cambridge, MA, and London: Harvard University Asia Center, 1999.

Shively, Donald H. *Tradition and Modernization in Japanese Culture*. Princeton: Princeton University Press, 1971.

Sim, Chae-u. *Chosŏn hugi kukka kwŏllyŏk kwa pŏmjoe t'ongje*. [State Power and the Control of Crime in Late Chosŏn]. Seoul: T'aehaksa, 2009.

"Chosŏn malgi hyŏngsa pŏp ch'egye wa *Tae Myŏng ryul ŭi* wisang [The Structure of Penal Law and the Significance of *the Great Ming Code* in the Late Chosŏn Dynasty]." *Yŏksa wa hyŏnsil* 65 (2007): 122–153.

Sim, Hŭi-gi. "Ilche kangjŏm ch'ogi singminji kwansŭp pŏp ŭi hyŏngsŏng [The Making of Colonial Customary Law in Early Japanese Rule]." *Pŏpsahak yŏngu* 28 (2003): 5–31.

Hanguk pŏpchesa kangŭi [Lectures on Korean Legal History]. Seoul: Samyŏngsa, 1997.

"18 segi ŭi hyŏngsa sabŏp chedo kaehyŏk [The Reform of the Penal Law System in the Eighteenth Century]." *Hanguk munhwa* 20 (1997): 205–244.

Sin, U-ch'ŏl. "Kŭndae sabŏp chedo sŏngnip sa pigyo yŏngu: Hanguk e issŏsŏ 'sabŏp tongnip' wŏlli ŭi t'aedong suyong kwa chŏn'gae [A Comparative Historical Study of the Establishment of Modern Judicial Systems: The Beginning and Development of the Principle of Judicial Independence in Korea]." *Seoul Taehakkyo pŏphak* 49 (2008): 256–285.

"Kŭndae sabŏp chedo sŏngnip sa pigyo yŏngu: uri pŏpwŏn chojik pŏpche ŭi ch'ogi hyŏngsŏng [A Comparative Historical Study of the Establishment of Modern Judicial Systems: The Early Organization of Our Court Structure]." *Pŏpcho* 612 (September 2007).

Snyder, Francis G. "Colonialism and Legal Form: The Creation of 'Customary Law' in Senegal." *Journal of Legal Pluralism* 19 (1981): 49–90.

Sŏ, Kwang-min. "Kwansŭp pŏp kwa sasil in kwansŭp [Customary Law and Custom in Fact]." *Kosigye* (August 1991): 112–125.

Sŏk, Chin-hyŏng. "Pŏmnyul ŭi p'ilyo [The Necessity of Law]." *Taehan hyŏphoe hoebo* 2 (May 25, 1908): 27–31.

Solus, Henry. *Traité de la condition des indigènes en droit privé; colonies et pays de protectorat (non compris l'Afrique du Nord) et pays sous mandat*. Paris, Recueil Sirey, 1927.

Son, Kyŏng-ch'an. "Minhyŏng sosong kyuch'ik ŭi chejŏng kwa gŭ ŭiŭi [The Establishment of the Civil and Criminal Procedure Regulations and Its Significance]." *Pŏpsahak yŏngu* 30 (2004): 159–187.

"Kaehwa gi kŭndaejŏk minsa sosong pŏpkyu toip e kwanhan yŏngu [A Study of the Reception of Modern Civil Procedural Laws during Late Choson's "Enlightenment" Period]." Master's thesis, Seoul National University, 2002.

Song, Yŏng-min. "T'oji wa kŏnmul ŭl pyŏlgae ui mulgŏn ŭro ch'wigŭup hanŭn mimpŏp t'aedo e kwanhan pŏpsahak chŏk il koch'al [An Examination of the Position of the Civil Code that Treats Land and Building as Separate Things, a Legal and Historical Perspective].” *T'oji pŏphak* 19 (2003): 3–23.

Sourioux, Jean-Louis. “La Pensée juridique de G. Boissonade: aspects de droit civil.” *Revue internationale de droit comparé* (1991): 357–366.

Starck, Boris. *Droit civil: Obligations*, 2nd ed. Paris: Librairies techniques, 1972.

Steenstrup, Carl. *A History of Law in Japan until 1868*. Leidon: Brill, 1991.

Stein, Peter. *Roman Law in European History*. Cambridge: Cambridge University Press, 1999.

“The Civil Law Doctrine of Custom and the Growth of Case Law.” In *Scintillae Iuris: Studi in memoria di Gino Gorla*, 371–381. Milan: Giuffre, 1994.

Stewart, Iain. “‘Customs in Common’: The Old Emperor's Clothes.” *Macquarie Law Journal* 6 (2006): 139–160.

Strauss, Gerald. *Law, Resistance and the State: The Opposition to Roman Law in Reformation Germany*. Princeton: Princeton University Press, 1986.

Sugiyama, Naojirō. “Meiji 8-nen fukoku dai 103 gō saiban jimu kokoroe to shihō hōgen [The Proclamation of Decree Number 103 of Meiji Year 8 regarding the Conduct of Judicial Affairs and the Sources of Private Law].” *Hōgen to kaishaku* [Sources of Law and Interpretations]. Tokyo: Yūhigaku, 1957 [originally published in *Hōgaku kyokai zasshi* 49–50 (1931–1932)].

“La Loi du 8 juin 1875 sur l'administration de la justice et les sources du droit privé.” In *Recueil d'études sur les sources du droit en l'honneur de François Gény*, vol. 2, 446–458. Paris : Librairie du Recueil Sirey.

“L'Evolution générale du droit japonais moderne (1869–1919).” In *Les Transformations du droit dans les principaux pays depuis cinquante ans (1869–1919): Livre du cinquantenaire de la Société de législation comparé*, vol. 2, 219–248. Paris: Librairie Générale de Droit et de Jurisprudence, 1923.

Sukimoto, Takahisa. “20 segi ch'odu Ilbon minpŏp hak esŏ ŭi ‘p'allye’ wa ‘pŏpwŏn’: Suehiro Izutarŏ ŭi sosŏl ŭl chungsim ŭro [‘Precedents’ and ‘Sources of Law’ in Twentieth-Century Japanese Legal Science: With Particular Attention to the Theories of Suehiro Izutarŏ].” *Pŏpsahak yŏngu* 40 (2009): 87–103.

Sŭngjŏngwŏn ilgi [The Daily Records of Royal Secretariat of the Chosŏn Dynasty]. Kuksa P'yŏnch'an Wiwŏnhoe [National Institute of Korean History]. http://sjw.history.go.kr.

Suzuki, Sōgen. “Naichi oyobi Taiwan aida ni okeru horitsurei no kōryoku ni tsuite [On the Effects of Laws and *Ritsurei* between *Naichi* and Taiwan].” *Hōgaku kyōkai zasshi* 23, no. 4 (1905): 355–377 (Part 1); 23, no. 4: 523–534 (Part 2).

Suzuki, Takeo. “Chōsen tōchi no seigaku to zitseki.” In *Nihonjin no kaigai katsudō ni kansuru rekishi-teki chōsa*, edited by Okurasho Kanrikyoki, vol. 3. Tokyo: Okurasho, 1948–1950.

Tabana, Tameo. *Chōsen kyōyaku kyōkashi no kenkyū* [A Study of the History of the Edification of *Hyangyak* in Chosŏn]. Tokyo: Chōhōsha, 1972.

Taehan Pyŏnhosa Hyŏphoe, ed. *Hanguk pyŏnhosa sa* [A History of Attorneys at Law in Korea]. Seoul, 1979.

Taebŏpwŏn minsa p'allyejip [The Supreme Court Reports: Civil Litigation]. Seoul, 1957–.

Tagawa, Kōzō. “Richō no kyōkyu ni tsuite [*Hyangyak* under the Yi Dynasty].” *Chōsen gakuho* 76 (1975): 35–72 (Part 1).

Taiwan Sōtokufu Rinji Taiwan Kyūkan Chōsakai. *Taiwan shihō* [Private Law of Taiwan]. Taihoku: Taiwan Sotokufu Rinji Taiwan Kyūkan Chōsakai, 1910–1911.

Takahashi, Ryūji. "Sōzoku kaihuku seikyūken no jikō [The Effect of Succession Recovery Claim]." *Shihō kyōkai zasshi* 14, no. 11 (1935): 1–32.

Takayanagi, Kenzo. "A Century of Innovation: The Development of Japanese Law, 1869–1961." In *Law in Japan: The Legal Order in a Changing Society*, edited by Arthur von Mehren, 5–40. Cambridge, MA: Harvard University Press, 1963.

"Occidental Legal Ideas in Japan: Their Reception and Influence." *Pacific Affairs* 3, no. 8 (1930): 740–753.

Tamanaha, Brian Z. "Understanding Legal Pluralism: Past to Present, Local to Global." *Sydney Law Review* 30 (2008): 375–411.

"A Non-Essentialist Version of Legal Pluralism," *Journal of Law and Society* 27 (2000): 296–321.

"The Folly of the 'Social Scientific' Concept of Legal Pluralism," *Journal of Law and Society* 20 (1993): 192–217.

Tamanoi, Mariko. "Knowledge, Power, and Racial Classifications: the "Japanese" in Manchuria." *Journal of Asian Studies* 59, no. 2 (2000): 248–276.

Tamura, Akio. "Wakaino kakutei kō [The Effect of the Settlement by Compromise]." *Shimadai hōgaku* 35, no. 4 (1992): 35–81.

"Ima, naze Ume Kenjirō ka: Ume Kenjirō to wakairon [Why Ume Kenjirō Now: Ume Kenjirō and the Theory of Compromise]." *Hōgaku semina* 435 (1991): 76–78.

Tanabe, Kohji. "The Process of Litigation: An Experiment with the Adversary System." In *Law in Japan: The Legal Order in a Changing Society*, edited by Arthur Taylor von Mehren, 85–90. Cambridge, MA: Harvard University Press, 1963.

Tanaka, Ryūichi. *Manchūkoku to Nihon no teikoku shihai* [Manchukuo and Japanese Imperial Rule]. Tokyo: Yūshisha, 2007.

"Teikoku Nihon no shihō rensa [The Linkage in the Administration of Justice in Imperial Japan]." *Chōsen Shi Kenkyūkai ronbunshū* 38 (2000): 61–91.

Taniguchi, Tomohei. "La Loi et la coutume au Japon." In *Etude juridique offertes à Léon Julliot de la Morandière*, 571–582. Paris: Librairie Dalloz, 1964.

Ter Haar, Barend. *Adat Law in Indonesia*. Translated by E. Adamson Hoebel and A. Arthur Schiller. New York: Institute of Pacific Relations, 1948.

Terada, Hiroaki. "The Nature of Social Agreements (*yue*) in the Legal Order of Ming and Qing China." *The International Journal of Asian Studies* 2 (2005): 320–323 (Part 1).

Tete, William Thomas. "The Code, Custom and the Courts: Notes toward a Louisiana Theory of Precedent." *Tulane Law Review* 48 (1973): 1–24.

Tezuka, Yutaka, ed. *Minji kanrei ruishū*. Tokyo: Keio Gijuku Daigaku Hōgaku Kenkyūkai, 1969, 1877.

Thireau, Jean-Louis. *Charles Du Moulin (1500–1566)*. Geneva: Droz, 1980.

To, Myŏn-hoe. "1894–1905 nyŏn gan hyŏngsa chaep'an chedo yŏngu [A Study of the Criminal Adjudication System between 1894 and 1895]." PhD diss., Seoul National University, 1998.

Townsend, Susan C. *Yanaihara Tadao and Japanese Colonial Policy: Redeeming Empire*. Richmond: Curzon, 2000.

"Yanaihara Tadao and the Irish Question: a Comparative Analysis of the Irish and Korean Questions, 1919–36." *Irish Historical Studies* 30 (1996): 195–205.

Tōyō Bunka Kenkyūjō, Gakushuin Daigaku, ed. "Mikōkai shiryō Chōsen Sōtokufu kankeisha rokuon kiroku [New Documents: The Audio Recording of the Personnel of the Chosŏn Government General]." *Tōyō bunka kenkyū* 1–11 (1999–2010).

Troper, Michel. "Fonction juridictionnelle ou pouvoir judiciaire?" *Pouvoirs* 16 (1981): 5–15.

Uchida, Shunichirō. "Meiji minpō no kaishaku to ume hakushi no kaishaku riron riron [The Interpretation of Meiji Civil Law and Dr. Ume's Theories of Interpretation]." *Matsuyama shōdai ronshu* 17, no. 6 (1966): 35–61.

Ume, Kenjirō. *Ume Kenjirō chosaku zenshū shibidan* [The CD Collection of the Complete Works of Ume Kenjirō]. 5 vols. Edited by Oka Takashi. Tokyo: Maruzen, 2000.

Minpō yōgi [Digest of Civil Law]. Vol. 4 (Shinzoku hen). Tokyo: Shiritsu Hōsei Daigaku, Yūhigaku Shobō, 1916, 1899.

"Heigō ato no kankoku hōsei [The Korean Legal System after Annexation]." *Keiji hō hyorin* 2, no. 9 (1910): 52–54.

"Itō kō to rippō jigyō [Prince Itō and Legislative Activities]." *Kokka gakkai zasshi* 24, no. 7 (1910): 32–49 (962–979).

"Kankoku no gappō ron to rippō jigyō [The Theory of Korean Annexation and the Legislation Project]." *Kokusai hō zasshi* 8, no. 9 (1910): 33–35 (739–741).

Saikin hanrei hihyō zoku hen [Commentaries on Recent Court Decisions Supplement]. Tokyo: Hōsei Daigaku, 1909.

"Hōjin ni kansuru Kankoku kanshūhō ippan [Korean Customary Law in General on Corporation]." *Hōgaku kyōkai zasshi* 27 (1909): 714–719 (44–49).

"Futsu doku hōsōkai no hikaku [Comparisons of the French and German Legal Circles]." *Taiyō* 15, no. 5 (1909): 199–203.

"Kankoku no hōritsu seido ni tsuite [On the Korean Legal System]." *Tokyō keizai zasshi* 60, no. 1512 (1909): 7–9 (701–703) (Part 1); 60, no. 1514 (1909): 7–10 (793–796) (Part 2).

"Kankoku kongo no shihō [The Administration of Justice in Korea in the Future]." *Keizai jihō* 42 (October 20, 1909): 13–14 (reprinted in Kŭm Pyŏng-dong, *Shiryō zasshi ni miru kindai Nihon no Chōsen ninshiki: Kankoku heigōki zengo*, vol. 3, 216–217, Tokyo: Ryokuin Shobō, 1999).

"Fudōsan ni kansuru Kankoku kanshuhō ippan [General concepts of the Korean Customary Law of Real Property]." *Hōsō kiji* 18, no. 6 (1908): 7–10.

"Kankoku no chŏndang [Korea's *chŏndang*]." *Hōgaku kyōkai zasshi* 26, no.10 (1908): 780–784.

"Kankoku no hanashi [A Talk on Korea]." *Kokka gakkai zasshi* 21, no. 12 (1907): 1–30 (1437–1466).

Saikin hanrei hihyō [Commentaries on Recent Judicial Decisions]. Tokyo, Hōsei Daigaku, 1906.

Minpō sōsoku [The General Provisions of the Civil Code]. Tokyo: Hōsei Daigaku, 1905.

"Hōritsu no kaishaku [Interpretation of Law]." *Taiyō* 9, no. 2 (1903): 56–62.

"Kajoku sei no shōrai o ronsu [Discussing the future of the Family System]," *Hōgaku shirin* 3 (1902): 9–34.

Minpō kōgi [Lectures on the Civil Code]. Tokyo: Dōbunkan, Meihōdō, 1901.

"Nijū seiki no hōritsu [Law of the Twentieth Century]." *Yomiuri shinbun*, January 5, 1900.

"Gaikoku jin no toji shoyūken [The Land Ownership Right of Foreigners]." *Hōgaku shirin* 4 (1900): 18–37.

Minpō genri [The Principles of Civil Law]. Tokyo: Wafutsu Hōritsu Gakkō, 1899.

"Hōten ni tsuite [On the Code]." *Kokka gakkai zasshi* 8, no. 84 (1894): 77–86 (Part 1); no. 86: 241–251 (Part 2).

"Hōten ni kansuru jukkai [Reflections on the Civil Code]." *Meihō shisō* 17 (1893): 1–24.

"Gaikoku jin no kenri [Rights of Foreigners]." *Hōgaku kyōkai zasshi* 11, no. 1 (1893): 37–39 (Part 1); no. 3: 220–227 (Part 2); no. 9: 746–751 (Part 3, Incomplete).

"Minpō jisshi iken [An Opinion on the Adoption of the Civil Code]." *Meihō shisō* 3 (1892). In *Minpōten ronsō shiryōshu*, edited by Hoshino Tōru, 233–241. Tokyo: Nihon Hyōronsha, 1969.

Ume Kenjirō Hakushi Kenshō Kinenshi Henshū Iinkai, ed. *Waga minpō no chichi Ume Kenjirō hakushi kenshōhi konryū no kiroku* [A Testimonial on the Occasion of the Construction of the Monument of Dr. Ume Kenjirō, Father of Our Civil Code]. Matsue, 1992.

Ume Monjo Kenkyūkai, ed. *Ume Kenjirō monjo mokuroku, Hōsei Daigaku toshokan shozō* [The Catalogue of the Ume Kenjirō Papers, Hōsei University Library Collection]. Tokyo: Hōsei Daigaku Boasonādo Kinen Gendaihō Kenkyūjo, 2000.

Ume, Toku. "Chichi o kataru [Talking about My Father]." In *Kitte ni natta nihon bunkajin* [The Japanese Cultural Elites Who Appeared in Postal Stamps], edited by Takaru Shigeru. Tokyo: Hifumishobo, 1953.

Umekichi, Miyawaki. "Chōsen shihō seido no kaikaku [Reform of the Judicial system in Chosŏn]," *Hōritsu Shinbun*, November 10, 1911.

Umemori, Naoyuki. "Modernization through Colonial Mediations: The Establishment of the Police and Prison System in Meiji Japan," Ph.D. diss., University of Chicago, 2002.

United States Armed Forces in Korea, ed. *History of United States Armed Forces in Korea* [*Chu Han migun sa*], 4 vols. Seoul: Dolbegae, 1988.

Uno, Fumie. "Meiji minpō kisō iin no "ie" to koshuken rikai [The Meiji Civil Code Drafting Committee Members' Understanding of 'Ie' and the Household Headship]," *Hōsei kenkyū* (Kyushu Daigaku Hōsei Gakkai) 74, no. 3 (2007): 523–591.

Vanderlinden, J. "Essai de synthèse." In *Le Pluralisme juridique: études publiées sous la direction de John Gilissen*, edited by John Gilissen, 19–56. Brussels: Editions de l'Université de Bruxelles, 1972.

Wagner, Edward W. *The Literati Purges: Political Conflict in Early Yi Korea*. Cambridge, MA: East Asian Research Center; Distributed by Harvard University Press, 1974.

"Social Stratification in Seventeenth-Century Korea: Some Observations from a 1663 Seoul Census Register." *Occasional Papers on Korea* 1 (April 1974): 36–54.

Waelkens, L. " L'Origine de l'enquête par turbe." *Tijdschrift voor Rechtsgeschiedenis* 53 (1985): 337–346.

Wang, Tay-Sheng. *Legal Reform in Taiwan under Japanese Colonial Rule, 1895–1945: The Reception of Western Law*. Seattle: University of Washington Press, 2000.

Watson, Alan. *Society and Legal Change*, 2nd ed. Philadelphia: Temple University Press, 2001.

The Evolution of Western Private Law. Baltimore and London: The Johns Hopkins University Press, 2000.

ed. *The Digest of Justinian*. 2 vols. Philadelphia: University of Pennsylvania Press, 1998.

Legal Transplants: An Approach to Comparative Law, 2nd ed. Athens, GA: University of Georgia Press, 1993.

"The Evolution of Law: Continued." *Law & History Review* 5 (1987): 537–556.

Sources of Law, Legal Change, and Ambiguity. Philadelphia: University of Pennsylvania Press, 1984.

Weber, Eugen. *Peasants into Frenchmen: The Modernization of Rural France, 1870–1914*. Stanford: Stanford University Press, 1976.

Weber, Max. "The Three Types of Legitimate Rule." In *A Sociological Reader on Complex Organizations*, edited by Amitai Etzioni, 2nd ed., 6–14. New York: Holt, Rinehart and Winston, 1969.

West, James M. and Dae-Kyu Yoon. "The Constitutional Court of the Republic of Korea: Transforming the Jurisprudence of the Vortex." *American Journal of Comparative Law* 40 (1992): 73–119.

Whitman, James Q. "Western Legal Imperialism: Thinking about the Deep Historical Roots," *Theoretical Inquiries in Law* 10 (2009): 305–332.

"Why did the Revolutionary Lawyers Confuse Custom and Reason?" *University of Chicago Law Review* 58 (1991): 1321–1327.

Wigmore, John Henry. *Materials for the Study of Private Law in Old Japan*, 4 vols. Tokyo: Asiatic Society of Japan, 1892.

Wilder, Gary. *The French Imperial Nation-state: Negritude & Colonial Humanism Between the Two World Wars*. Chicago: University of Chicago Press, 2005.

Williams, Ivy. *The Sources of Law in the Swiss Civil Code*. Humphrey Milford: Oxford University Press, 1923.

Wise, Edward M. "The Transplant of Legal Patterns." *American Journal of Comparative Law* 38 (1990): 1–22.

Woodman, Gordon, R. "How State Courts Create Customary Law in Ghana and Nigeria." In *Indigenous Law and the State*, edited by B.W. Morse and G.R. Woodman, 181–220. Dordrecht: Foris, 1988.

Wu, Rwei-ren. "The Formosan Ideology: Oriental Colonialism and the Rise of Taiwanese Nationalism, 1895–1945," PhD diss., University of Chicago, 2003.

Yamabe, Kentarō. *Nikkan heigō shōshi* [A Brief History of the Annexation of Japan and Korea]. Tokyo: Iwanami Shoten, 1966.

Yamada, Saburō. "Kyōtsūhō an ni tsuite [On the Bill of Kyōtsūhō]." *Hōgaku kyōkai zasshi* 36, no. 4 (1918): 66–99 (Part 1); no. 6: 95–122 (Part 2); no. 7: 50–81 (Part 3).

"Shokuminchi hō to naichi hō no kankei ni tsuite [On the Relationship between Colonial Law and *Naichi Law*]." *Hōgaku kyōkai zasshi* 30, no. 8 (1912).

Yamamoto, Yūjō. *Nihon shokumin keizaishi kenkyū* [A Study of Japanese Colonial Economic History]. Nagoya: Nagoya Daigaku Shuppankai, 1992.

"Nihon ni okeru shokuminchi tōchi shisō no tenkai [The Evolution of Colonial Domination Ideology in Japan]." *Ajia keisai* 32 (1991), no. 1: 2–20 (Part 1); no. 2: 34–53 (Part 2).

Yamazaki, Tansho. *Gaichi tōchi kikō no kenkyū* [A Study of the Structure of Governing the Overseas Territories]. Tokyo: Takayama Shoin, 1943.

Yanaihara, Tadao. *Shokumin seisaku kenkyū*. In *Yanaihara Tadao zenshū*. Tokyo, Iwatami Shoten, 1963.

Yang, Ch'ang-su. "Urinara ch'oech'o ŭi hŏnpŏp chaep'an nonŭi: Ch'ŏ ŭi haengwi nŭngnyŏk chehan e kwanhan 1947 nyŏn Taepŏpwŏn p'angyŏl e taehayŏ [The First Debate in Korea on Constitutional Adjudication: The 1947 Decision of the Supreme Court of Korea regarding the Restriction on the Wife's Legal Capacity]." *Seoul Taehakkyo pŏphak* 40 (1999): 126–151.

"Hŏnpŏp chejŏng hu ilchŏng pŏmnyŏng ŭi hyoryŏk [The Effect of Japanese Colonial Law after the Promulgation of the Constitution]." In *Minpŏp san'go*, 43–49. Seoul: Pagyŏngsa, 1998.

"Minpŏp chŏn ŭi chejŏng kwajŏng e kwanhan yŏngu: Minpŏp an e taehan kukhoe pon hoeŭi ŭi simŭi [A Study of the Codification Process of the Civil Code: Parliamentary Deliberations on the Draft Civil Code]." *Seoul Taehakkyo pŏphak* 33, no. 2 (1992): 143–179.

"Minpŏp an ŭi sŏngnip kwajŏng e kwanhan sogo [A Brief Study on the Process of Drafting Civil Law]." *Seoul Taehakkyo pŏphak* 30, nos. 3 & 4 (1989): 186–218.

Yang, Hyŏn-a. "Singminji sigi Hanguk kajok pŏp ŭl t'onghae pon kabujangje ŭi kukka chedohwa wa 'kwansŭp' munche [The Transformation of the Patriarchal System into a National System and the Question of 'Custom', Seen from Colonial Korean Family Law]." In *Che 2-gi Han-Il yŏksa kongdong yŏngu pogosŏ* [Report of the Second Joint Research of Korean and Japanese History], edited by Han-Il Yŏksa Kongdong Yŏngu Wiwŏnhoe, vol. 5, 289–315. Seoul: 2010.

"Singminji sigi Hanguk kajok pŏp ŭi kwansŭp munche (I): sigan ŭisik ŭi silchong ŭl chungsim ŭro [The Question of Custom in Colonial Korean Family Law: With Particular Attention to the Loss of the Concept of Time]." *Sahoe wa yŏksa* 58 (2000): 35–70.

Yang, Hyunah [Yang, Hyŏn-a]. "Vision of Postcolonial Feminist Jurisprudence in Korea: Seen from the 'Family-Head System' in Family Law." *Journal of Korean Law* 5 (2006): 12–28.

"Envisioning Feminist Jurisprudence in Korean Family Law at the Crossroads of Tradition/Modernity," PhD diss., New School for Social Research, 1998.

Yang, Key P. and Gregory Henderson. "An Outline History of Korean Confucianism, Part II: The Schools of Yi Confucianism." *The Journal of Asian Studies* 18 (1959): 259–276.

Yang, Kun. "Judicial Review and Social Change in the Korean Democratizing Process," *American Journal of Comparative Law* 41 (1993): 1–8.

"Law and Society Studies in Korea: Beyond the Hahm Theses." *Law & Society Review* 23 (1989): 891–901.

Yang, Sŭng-du. "Pŏpkwan Yangsŏngso e kwanhan sogo [A Short Study of the Judge Training School]." *Serim Hanguk hak nonch'ong* 1 (1977): 485–506.

Yasuda, Kanta. "Sōzoku kaihuku seikyūken no honsitzu [The Nature of Succession Recovery Claim]." *Shihō kyōkai zasshi* 15, no. 3 (1936): 1–32.

Yasuoka, Akio. "Ōtsu jiken ni kansuru Ume Kenjirō ikensho [The Opinion Paper by Ume Kenjirō regarding the Ōtsu Affair]." *Hōgaku shirin* 94, no. 3 (1996): 141–47.

Yi, Ch'ŏl-u. "T'oji chosa saŏp kwa t'oji soyu pŏpche ŭi pyŏnch'ŏn [The Land Cadastre and the Evolution of the Land Ownership System in Law]." In *Hanguk pŏpsahak Nonch'ong*, 349–370. Seoul: Pagyŏngsa, 1991.

Yi, Chun-hyŏn. "Ilche kangjŏm ch'ogi Chosŏn Kodŭng Pŏpwŏn e ŭihan pudongsan ijung maemae, ijung chŏndang ŭi pŏpchŏk ch'ŏri: *Chosŏn Kodŭng Pŏpwŏn p'angyŏllok* che 1–6 kwŏn ŭi punsŏk" [Judicial Interpretation of Double Sale and Double *Chŏndang* of Real Property by the Chosŏn Kodŭng Pŏpwŏn in the Early Japanese Colonial Period: Analysis of the *Chosŏn Kodŭng Pŏpwŏn Reports*, vols. 1–6]." *Pŏpsahak yŏngu* 28 (2003): 79–108.

Yi, Hwang. *Chŭngbo T'oegye chŏnsŏ* [Expanded Complete Works of T'oegye]. 2 vols. Seoul: Sŏnggyun'gwan Taehakkyŏ Taedong Munhwa Yŏnguwŏn, 1958.

Yi, Hwa-suk. "Sangsok hoebok ch'ŏnggukwŏn ŭi sihyo e kwanhan kwansŭppŏp ŭi hyoryŏk: Taepŏpwŏn 2003.7.24, sŏngo 2001ta48781 chŏnwŏn habŭich'e p'angyŏl [The Effect of Customary Law on the Statute of Limitations regarding the Right to Succession Recovery]." *Kajokpŏp yŏngu* 18, no. 1 (2004): 249–272.

Yi, Hyŏn-chong. "Happyŏng hu chaehan kakkup kŏryuji ch'ŏlp'ye go [A Study on the Abolition of Foreign Settlements in Korea after Annexation]." *Chindan hakpo* 32 (1969): 39–71.

Yi, I. *Yulgok chŏnsŏ* [Complete Works of Yulgok]. Edited by Sŏnggyun'gwan Taehakkyŏ Taedong Munhwa Yŏnguwŏn. Seoul, 1958.

Yi, Pyŏng-su. "Chosŏn Minsaryŏng e kwanhayŏ: Che sibilcho ŭi kwansŭp ŭl chungsim ŭro [A Study of the Chosŏn Civil Ordinance: With Particular Attention to Custom in Article 11]." *Pŏpsahak yŏngu* 4 (1977): 649–676.

Yi, Sang-uk. "Ilche ha chont'ong kajok pŏp ŭi waegok [Distortion of Traditional Family Law Under Japanese Rule]." In *Hanguk pŏpsahak nonch'ong*, 371–399. Seoul: Pagyŏngsa, 1991.

"Ilche ha hoju sangsok kwansŭp pŏp ŭi chŏngnip [The Establishment of the Household Headship System under Japanese Rule]." *Pŏpsahak yŏngu* 9 (1988): 23–61.

"Hanguk sangsok pŏp ŭi sŏngmunhwa kwajŏng [The Process of the Codification of Succession Law in Korea]." PhD diss., Kyŏngbuk National University, 1986.

Yi, Sŏng-mu. "Chosŏn sidae hyangch'on chibae seryŏk ŭi ch'ui [The Development of the Local Powers in Dominance in the Chosŏn Period]." *Chosŏn yangban sahoe yŏngu.* [A Study of *Yangban* in the Chosŏn Dynasty], 198–222. Seoul: Ilchogak, 1995.

Yi, Sŭng-il. *Chosŏn Ch'ongdokpu pŏpche chŏngch'aek: Ilche ŭi singmin t'ongch'i wa Chosŏn minsaryŏng* [A Study on the Legal Policy of the Chosŏn Government General: The Colonial Rule by Imperial Japan and *Chosŏn Minsaryŏng*]. Seoul: Yŏksa Pip'yŏngsa, 2008.

"Chosŏn hojŏngnyŏng chejŏng e kwanhan yŏngu [A Study of the Establishment of the *Chosŏn Hojŏngnyŏng*]." *Pŏpsahak yŏngu* 32 (2005): 37–68.

"Ilche sigi Chosŏn in ŭi Ilbon kungmin hwa yŏngu: hojŏk chedo rŭl chungsim ŭro [A Study on Turning Koreans into Japanese Nationals during the Japanese Imperial Period: With Particular Attention to the Establishment of the Household Registration System]." *Hangukhak nŏnjip* 34 (2000): 67–115.

"Ilche sidae ch'injok kwansŭp ŭi pyŏnhwa wa Chosŏn minsaryŏng e kwanhan yŏngu: Chosŏn minsaryŏng che 11 cho che I ch'a kaejŏngan ŭl chungshim ŭro [A Study on the Changes of Family Law Custom and the Chosŏn Civil General Act Under Japanese Rule: The Second Revision of Art. 11 in Focus]." *Hangukhak nonchip* 33 (1999): 161–197.

Yi, T'ae-jin. "Sarimp'a ŭi hyangyak pogŭp undong [The Sarim Faction's Movement to Spread hyangyak]." In *Hanguk sahoesa yŏngu* [A Social History of Korea], 274–288. Seoul: Chisik Sanŏpsa, 1986.

Yi, Yŏng-mi. *Kankoku shihō seido to Ume Kenjirō* [The Korean Legal System and Ume Kenjirō]. Tokyo: Hōsei Daigaku Shuppankyoku, 2005.

Hanguk sabŏp chedo wa Ume Kenjiro [The Korean Legal System and Ume Kenjirō]. Translated by Kim Hye-jŏng. Seoul: Ilchogak, 2011.

Yokota, Gōrō. "Shihōkan no zōin to yūgū wo nozomu [Desiring the Increase in the Number of Judicial Officials and the Improvement of Their Conditions]." In *Chōsen tōchi no kaiko to hihan* [Reflections and Criticisms on the Governing of Chosŏn], edited by Chōsen Shinbunsha, 237–239. Tokyo: Ryūkei Shosha, 1995, 1936.

Yoshida, Heijirō. "Chōsen ni okeru kanshū to minji hōki to no kankei" [The Relationship between Korean Custom and Civil Law Provisions]. *Shihō kyōkai zasshi* 2, no. 4 (1923): 1–28 (41–68).

Yoshikawa, Ayako. "Ilche sigi ihon sosong kwa Ilbon in p'ansa: 1910 nyŏn dae rŭl chungsim ŭro [Divorce Litigation and Japanese Judges under Japanese Rule: Focusing on the 1910s]." *Pŏpsahak yŏngu* 44 (2011): 171–209.

Yu, Ch'i-hyŏng. *Hŏnpŏp* [Constitutional Law]. Seoul: Asia Munhwasa, 1981, 1908.

Yu, Hong-ryŏl. "Chosŏn hyangyak ŭi sŏngnip [The Establishment of *Hyangyak* in Chosŏn]." *Chindan hakpo* 9 (1938): 86–144 (450–508).

Yūhō Kyokai, ed. *Chōsen ni okeru shihō seido kindai ka no sokuseki* [The Course of the Modernization of the Korean Legal System]. In *Chōsen kindai shiryō kenkyū*, vol. 6. Tokyo: Kuresu Press, 2001, 1966.

Yun, Chin-su. "Chŏnt'ongjŏk kajok chedo wa hŏnpŏp: Ch'oegŭn ŭi hŏnpŏp chaep'anso p'allye rŭl chungsim ŭro [The Traditional Family System and Constitutional Law: With Particular Attention to the Recent Decisions of the Constitutional Court]." *Seoul Taehakkyo pŏphak* 47 (2006): 149–188.

"Hŏnpŏp i Kajokpŏp e mich'in Yŏnghyang [The Influence of the Constitution on Family Law]." *Seoul Taehakkyo Pŏphak* 45 (2004): 233–270.

"Sangsok hoebok ch'ŏnggukwŏn ŭi yŏngu: yŏksa chok mit pigyopŏp chŏk koch'al [A Study of the Rights to Demand Succession Recovery: From Historical and Comparative Legal Perspectives]." *Seoul Taehakkyo pŏphak* 41, no. 1 (2000): 172–208.

Yun, Hyo-jŏng. "Hyŏngpŏp kwa minpŏp ŭi kubyŏl [Distinction between Criminal Law and Civil Law]." *Taehan chaganghoe wŏlbo* 11 (May 25, 1907): 49–52.

Yun, Tae-sŏng. "Ilche ŭi Hanguk kwansŭp chosa saŏp kwa minsa kwansŭp pŏp [The Japanese Campaign for Korean Customs Investigation and Civil Customary Law]." *Ch'angwŏndae nonmunjip* 19, no. 1 (1991): 65–108.

"Ilche ŭi Hanguk kwansŭp chosa saŏp kwa chŏnse kwansŭp pŏp [The Project of the Investigation of Korean Customs under Japanese Rule and the Custom of *Chŏnse*]." In *Hanguk pŏpsahak nonch'ong*, 331–347. Seoul: Pagyŏngsa, 1991.

Yune, Jin-Su [Yun, Chin-su]. "Tradition and Constitution in the Context of the Korean Family Law." *Journal of Korean Law* 5, no. 1 (2005): 194–212.

"Recent Decisions of the Korean Constitutional Court on Family Law." *Journal of Korean Law* 1 (2001): 133–156.

Zenkoku minji kanrei ruishū [The Nationwide Classified Collection of Customs in Civil Matters]. Edited by Hōmushō Shihō Hōsei Chōsabu. Tokyo: Shōji Hōmu Kenkyūkai, 1989, 1880.

Index

For EU product safety concerns, contact us at Calle de José Abascal, 56–1°,
28003 Madrid, Spain or eugpsr@cambridge.org.

www.ingramcontent.com/pod-product-compliance
Lightning Source LLC
LaVergne TN
LVHW011909200926
848484LV00002B/573

* 9 7 8 1 1 0 7 0 0 6 9 7 3 *